SOMETHING ABOUT THE AUTHOR

AUTOBIOGRAPHY SERIES

SOMETHING ABOUT THE AUTHOR

AUTOBIOGRAPHY SERIES

ADELE SARKISSIAN

EDITOR

VOLUME **1**

GALE RESEARCH COMPANY • BOOK TOWER • DETROIT, MICHIGAN 48226

EDITORIAL STAFF

Adele Sarkissian, *Editor*
Lori J. Bell, *Senior Assistant Editor*
Marilyn O'Connell, *Research Coordinator*

Carol Blanchard, *Production Director*
Art Chartow, *Art Director*
Vivian Tannenbaum, *Layout Artist*
Dorothy Kalleberg, *Senior Production Associate*

Laura Bryant, *Internal Production Supervisor*
Louise Gagné, *Production Associate*
Sandy Rock, *Senior Production Assistant*

Alan Dyer, *Indexer*
Donald G. Dillaman, *Index Program Designer*

Frederick G. Ruffner, Jr., *Publisher*
Dedria Bryfonski, *Editorial Director*
Christine Nasso, *Director, Literature Division*
Adele Sarkissian, *Senior Editor, Autobiography Series*

Copyright © 1986 by Gale Research Company

ISBN 0-8103-4450-5
ISSN 0885-6842

Printed in the United States.

Contents

Preface

With this first volume, we are pleased to introduce you to the *Something about the Author Autobiography Series (SAAS)*, a unique collection of autobiographical essays written especially for the series by prominent authors and illustrators of books for children and young adults. This new series takes its place beside other distinguished reference works on young people's literature published by the Gale Research Company: *Children's Literature Review, Children's Book Review Index, Children's Literature Awards and Winners*, the biographical indexes *Children's Authors and Illustrators* and *Writers for Young Adults*, and particularly the highly acclaimed bio-bibliographical series *Something about the Author (SATA)*, to which this *Autobiography Series* is a companion.

You may already be familiar with *SATA*, which has long been recognized as the only comprehensive ongoing reference series that deals with the lives and works of the people who create books for young readers. Now, to complement *SATA*'s wide range of detailed information, *SAAS* presents a "close up" view of some of these fascinating people. In *SAAS* authors and illustrators are invited to write about themselves, especially for you, in the form of an extended essay. This is a new and exciting opportunity—for you, for the author, and for the publisher. A reference work that collects autobiographies of this kind has never existed before, and Gale is pleased to fill this information gap with the *SATA Autobiography Series*.

Purpose

This series is designed to be a place where young readers, as well as adults interested in young people's literature, can meet "in person" the men and women who create the books that children and young adults are reading today. Here you can learn about the people and events that influenced these writers' early lives, how they began their careers, what problems they faced in becoming established in their professions, what prompted them to write or illustrate particular books, what they now find most challenging or rewarding in their lives, and what advice they may have for young people interested in following in their footsteps, among many other subjects. In *SAAS* writers can talk directly to you on their own terms. They are free to choose what they will say to you, and the way they will say it. As a result, each essay highlights the individuality of its writer—that special quality that sets one creative person apart from another.

In *SAAS* young readers, adult students of children's literature, teachers, librarians, and parents can learn more about familiar authors and illustrators and make the first acquaintance of many others. Authors who may never write a full-length autobiography have the opportunity in *SAAS* to let their readers know how they see themselves and their work. Even writers who have already published full-length life stories have the opportunity in *SAAS* to bring their readers "up to date," or perhaps to take a different approach in the essay format. At the very least, these essays can help to satisfy every reader's natural curiosity about the "real" person behind the name on the book jacket. Each of these essays offers a distinctive view of the person who wrote it; taken together, the essays in this series offer a new window on young people's literature.

Even though the *SATA Autobiography Series* has just begun publication, we can look forward to what it will accomplish. The series expects to fill a significant information gap—the primary reason behind every reference book. But we expect *SAAS* to do even more: the original essays in this and future volumes will make *SAAS* a varied and rewarding anthology of contemporary writing for young people.

Scope

Like its parent series, *Something about the Author,* the *SATA Autobiography Series* aims to include writers and artists who produce all the types of books that young people read today. *SAAS* sets out to meet the needs and interests of a broad range of readers from upper elementary school through junior high school and high school. Each volume in the series provides about twenty essays by current writers whose work has special appeal for young readers. We consider it an extraordinary accomplishment that twenty busy writers and artists are able to interrupt their writing, teaching, speaking, traveling, and other schedules to come together in print by a given deadline for any one volume. So it is not always possible to represent every area of young people's literature equally and uniformly in each volume of *SAAS.* Of the twenty writers in Volume 1, for example, about half specialize in fiction and nonfiction for children, and half specialize in writing for young adults. Four of these twenty essayists are also artists who illustrate their own writings as well as the books of other authors. However, these categories do not begin to suggest the variety and vitality of their work. Many of the contributors to this volume have also written fiction and nonfiction for adults as well as work for movies, television, radio, newspapers, and journals.

Format

Writers who contribute to *SAAS* are invited to write a "mini-autobiography" of approximately 10,000 words. We deliberately set no pattern for authors to follow in writing their essays, and we do not limit the essays to particular topics. This leaves the way open for the essayists to speak to you in the manner that is most natural and comfortable for each of them. Writers for *SAAS* are also asked to supply a selection of personal photographs, showing themselves at various ages, as well as important people and special moments in their lives. Our contributors have responded graciously and generously, sharing with us some of their most treasured mementoes, as you will see in this volume. This enticing combination of text and photographs makes *SAAS* the kind of reference book that even browsers will find irresistible.

A bibliography appears at the end of each essay, listing the writer's book-length works in chronological order of publication. Each entry in the bibliography includes the publication information for the book's first printing in the United States and Great Britain. Generally, the bibliography does not include later reprintings, new editions, or foreign translations. Also omitted from this bibliography are articles, reviews, and other contributions to magazines and journals. The bibliographies in this volume were compiled by members of the *SAAS* editorial staff from their research and the lists of writing that were provided by many of the authors. Each of the bibliographies was submitted to the author for review.

SAAS also includes an index that lists all the essayists in this volume as well as the subjects mentioned in the essays: personal names, titles of works, geographical names, etc. Because the index will cumulate in future volumes, the format of the index has been designed to make the cumulating references helpful and easy to use. For every reference that appears *in more than one essay,* the name of the essayist is given before the volume and page number(s). For example, Franklin Delano Roosevelt is mentioned by four writers in Volume 1. The entry in the index allows you to identify the essay writers by name:

Roosevelt, Franklin Delano
  Meltzer **1**: 210, 211
  Uchida **1**: 271
  Wells **1**: 281-82, 286
  Wojciechowska **1**: 317

For references that appear *in only one essay,* the volume and page number(s) are given but the name of the essayist is omitted. For example:

Hughes, Langston **1**: 216, 217, 218

Looking Ahead

While each essay in *SAAS* has its own special character and its individual point of view, these life stories take on a new importance when we see them grouped here in one volume. Together they tell us even more than they tell us as separate essays. Common experiences and common themes in these autobiographies throw a new light on the history that these writers represent.

The Great Depression of the 1930s, for example, touched the life of almost every writer in Volume 1. Doris Gates, then a librarian in California, recalls her first-hand experience in schools for children who had migrated with their families from Texas and Oklahoma, part of the "streaming hordes of penniless people." When a dwindling library budget could no longer support a full staff and regular hours, Gates found herself with a weekly "free day," and she used that time to write her first book. Milton Meltzer was in high school when the stock market collapsed in 1929, setting off the Depression. By the time he graduated, one-quarter of the nation's families had no regular income. He still has a vivid memory of seeing "strung along the Hudson River shore hundreds of shacks made of tin cans, packing crates, cardboard, and old tar paper . . . no bigger than chicken coops." Today Meltzer is well known for his special interest in the underdog. He writes books of history and biography that deal with "human aspiration and struggle, . . .with people who show the will to do something about what troubles them." Robb White also remembers the "stranglehold" that the Depression put on the whole world. "People were homeless, foodless, heatless, starving; and there was no welfare, no food stamps, no Social Security, no aid of any kind to anybody from any government." And yet, White chose just that time to resign his commission in the Navy. In the long jobless period that followed, White "found all the time in the world to become a writer."

Many of the essayists in this volume also speak of their early love for books and reading, not merely the pleasure they experienced but the influence it had on forming them as writers. Joan Aiken has fond memories of the stories that were read to her when she was still too young to read them herself; *Peter Rabbit, Just-So Stories, Pinocchio,* and the *Uncle Remus* stories just start off the list. For Sue Ellen Bridgers, Bible stories and fairy tales were the first thing she recalls from her mother's daily readings. "No present delighted me more," Bridgers writes in her essay, "than a package just so in shape and weight that it could only be a book." Maureen Daly credits her public library as an influence on the life of everyone who lived in her hometown. Daly and her sisters spent hours there, especially on weekends and during the summers. The librarians, she tells us, were their "mentors, the fairy godmothers whose lights shone over all the school and intellectual life of that small town." And Myra Cohn Livingston traces her own love for the rhythm and music of poetry to the stories and poems her mother read and the songs she sang to her young daughter.

These are only hints of what you will find in the essays ahead. We invite you to treat yourself to an exceptional reading experience. Turn the page and see what these writers have to say just to you.

Acknowledgments

We wish to acknowledge our special gratitude to each of the authors in this volume. They all have been most kind and cooperative in contributing not only their talents but their enthusiasm and encouragement to this project.

Authors Forthcoming in *SAAS*

Michael Bond (children's book and short story writer, dramatist, and essayist)—Paddington Bear, an acknowledged part of childhood folklore, is Bond's most popular character. Combining "bearishness and boyishness," Bond has created nearly forty books, while Paddington's antics have been made into more than fifty films. Bond's successes include *Paddington Abroad* and *Paddington Takes to the Air.*

Frank Bonham (novelist, short story and nonfiction writer, and screenwriter)—In books like *Durango Street* and *Mystery of the Fat Cat,* Bonham exemplifies his concern for minority youths and the difficulties they face. His cultural mix of characters speaks directly to less fortunate teenagers in books like *Hey, Big Spender.*

Scott Corbett (novelist)—Well known for his "Trick" series, Corbett blends fantasy and realism to create action-packed books that feature the popular character Kerby Maxwell. Corbett's equally popular mystery novels are fast-paced and humorous and include such titles as *Tree House Island* and *Run for the Money.*

Julia Cunningham (young adult and children's novelist, and editor)—Considered the first existential novel for young adults, *Dorp Dead!* is a controversial book, exemplary of Cunningham's unique approach to young adult literature. Cunningham often uses symbolism and fantasy to shape her fiction, as seen in her award-winning novel *The Treasure Is the Rose.*

Tomie de Paola (picture book writer and illustrator, and novelist)—Recognized as one of the most prolific and popular creators of children's books, de Paola illustrates his works so that children can "read the pictures." Subtle meanings and messages, conveyed by his precise and deliberate use of color, have helped create his award-winning *Strega Nona* and *The Clown of God.*

Lois Duncan (novelist, short story writer, and journalist)—Noted as an exceptional storyteller, Duncan writes mysteries with all the necessary ingredients for good entertainment. Suspense and the supernatural are abundant in such spine-tinglers as *I Know What You Did Last Summer* and *Daughters of Eve.*

Jean Fritz (novelist)—A Chinese-born American author, Fritz writes biographies about the famous and infamous men of the American Revolution. Her light-hearted and humorous approach to history makes for memorable books like *And Then What Happened, Paul Revere?* and *Why Don't You Get a Horse, Sam Adams?*

Lee Kingman (young adult and children's novelist, picture book creator, playwright, and editor)—Kingman has been praised for the accurate portrayal of her characters. Her careful representation of young adults and their parents is seen in books like *The Secret Journey of the Silver Reindeer* and *The Year of the Raccoon.*

Walter Dean Myers (children's and young adult novelist, nonfiction writer, and picture book creator)—The author of *It Ain't All for Nothin'*, Myers received critical attention for his books about black city children and communities. With humor and a deep empathy for his characters, Myers has written the award-winning *Fast Sam, Cool Clyde, and Stuff*.

Richard Peck (adult and young adult novelist)—Distinguished by his realistic young adult fiction, Peck has written such popular novels as *Don't Look and It Won't Hurt You* and *Are You in the House Alone?* Peck's perceptive handling of contemporary subject matter makes him an author widely read by young adults.

Mildred Taylor (young adult novelist)—Winner of the Newbery Medal for *Roll of Thunder, Hear My Cry*, Taylor has been praised for her unsentimental treatment of the black experience. Drawing from her ancestral past, Taylor attempts to refute history's image of blacks in another of her award-winners, *Song of the Trees*.

John Rowe Townsend (novelist, journalist, and children's and young adult book critic)—Praised for the rich characterization of his novels, Townsend creates unforgettable protagonists in books like *The Intruder* and *Good Night, Prof, Dear*. He also focuses a shrewd eye on reality, tempering injustice with humor, hope, and courage as seen in *Good-bye to the Jungle*.

P.L. Travers (novelist, poet, journalist, and critic)—Travers is an Australian-born British writer and the creator of the famous *Mary Poppins*. Using a realistic background to enhance the use of magic, Travers has added many sequels to her first success including *Mary Poppins Comes Back* and *Mary Poppins in the Park*.

Barbara Wersba (novelist, poet, and dramatist)—Characterized as an optimistic fiction writer, Wersba focuses her books on adolescent misfits who rise above their alienation. *The Country of the Heart* and *The Carnival in My Mind* are representative novels that depict her protagonists' struggle for individuality.

Herbert Zim (nonfiction writer, editor, and critic)—Zim's books about science and natural history are a combination of interesting facts and a unique writing style. *Alligators and Crocodiles* and *Monkeys* epitomize Zim's approach—a blend of scientific information with touches of quiet humor.

SOMETHING ABOUT THE AUTHOR

AUTOBIOGRAPHY SERIES

Joan Aiken

1924-

Mermaid Street, Rye, from a painting by A.R. Quinton. Jeake's House is third on left with protruding gable.

A happy childhood is supposed to lead to neurosis in middle age. By which criterion I should be a hundred percent neurotic, for my childhood was, in most ways, extremely happy.

Another maxim from the experts has it that childhood almost entirely shapes one's outlook later; that we can never escape from our early conditioning. Chagall, to his ninety-seventh year, painted the village where he grew up. I go along with this theory. I have total sympathy with Chagall's cows and cottages. I know them too. When I start to lay out a setting for a story—unless it is unmistakably located in Battersea, or Nantucket, or the Pyrenees—I too inevitably begin by thinking of a village—a village of forty houses. That is why a large part of this memoir is concerned with childhood. The adult years are just like anyone else's. Whereas the village—

But I anticipate.

My childhood was divided into two parts, and the first part, until I was five, took place in a town, the medieval town of Rye, Sussex, England. Rye has a population of 4,000 now, probably less in the 1920s, consists of cobbled streets and red-brick houses jostled tightly together on a high little hill rising out of the flat green plain of Romney Marsh. Two miles distant lies the English Channel. Some of Rye's walls and fortified gates still remain. Jeake's House, where I was born, stands halfway up steep, cobbled Mermaid Street, at the top of which Henry James had a house and died in 1918, six years before my birth. Jeake's House, built in 1689 as a granary or storehouse, had belonged to several members of the Jeake family. One Samuel Jeake was an astrologer and mathematician; a huge leather-bound book by him was at one time in the Aiken family possession. I was too young to understand it then, and doubt if I should make much more of it now. One of Jeake's concepts was about particles of infinite smallness called zenzicubes; I can remember my father telling me about that. Then there were even smaller things called zenzizenzizenzizenzizendykes. The book got lost; I think it vanished in World War II. Samuel Jeake also invented a flying machine, and, trying it out, boldly leapt off the high wall of the town. It didn't work, and he crashed into the tidal mud of the river Rother, which partly encircles Rye.

My family had not always lived in Rye; they moved there just before my birth, because there would not have been room for me in the tiny house, Look-Out Cottage, in Winchelsea, two miles away, where they had spent the previous three years. But they had come from America.

My father, the American poet Conrad Aiken, had a family tragedy in his own childhood. His father, my grandfather William Aiken, a doctor from a New England family but practising in Savannah, Georgia, had, in 1901, suffered from a brainstorm and shot first his wife, then himself. Conrad, aged twelve, heard the shots and found the bodies. His sister and two brothers were adopted by relatives. Conrad, the eldest, refused to change his name to Taylor, the condition of adoption, and so grew up parted from his siblings. He had a lonely and unhappy adolescence, haunted by the fear that he might end up as mentally unbalanced as his father, who, towards the end, had suffered from paranoid suspicions and beat Conrad savagely. Nonetheless

Jessie McDonald, age sixteen

Conrad Aiken, 1960

William had been a brilliantly intelligent and original man and, as a child, Conrad had worshipped him.

When he was at Harvard Conrad met my mother, Jessie McDonald, doing her Master's degree at Radcliffe after taking a B.A. at McGill; she was a Canadian from Montreal. She had black hair and green eyes and was, judging from photographs, stunningly pretty; she also had an acute intelligence. More important, from Conrad's viewpoint, she was a peasant: that is, she came of plain sound Scots ancestry on both sides. Her father was a first-generation emigrant from Tain, in Scotland, and ran a successful accountancy firm which he handed on to his two sons. His wife, Jean Cross, was of Scottish and Huguenot descent. Conrad met the family—two brothers, six sisters—during summer visits at Cap-a-l'Aigle on the St. Lawrence. His own parents had been first cousins; he felt that Jessie would supply the solid down-to-earth sense and ballast so notably lacking in his own family. (Other members of it besides his father had suffered from instability; he talks a good deal about the family *petit mal* in his autobiographical book *Ushant.* In fact, even fortified by the prosaic McDonald strain, his own children had precious little chance of growing up well-balanced and sane, he declared in his gloomier moments; I can remember his confidently predicting that *my* offspring would certainly go mad when they grew up.)

At all events, whether their union was based on romantic love or practical common sense, Conrad and Jessie were married in 1912, a year after they met, travelled in Europe for a year, lived for a little in Cambridge, Massachusetts, then moved into Boston, where my elder brother and sister were born in 1913 and 1917 respectively. After a spell at South Yarmouth, on Cape Cod, the family then migrated to England, partly for the benefit of the children's education, partly because, after reading *Tom Brown's Schooldays* as a child, Conrad had always had intensely romantic feelings about the Isle of Albion. Settling in Rye, with all its literary associations, was a natural step. He did not, however, stay very long in Rye at that time. After my birth in 1924 he became ill with a rectal abscess which required several operations. Convalescent from these, he went for a two-month trip to Spain. His travelling companion and long-standing friend, the English writer Martin Armstrong (referred to as Chapman in *Ushant*), was later to play an important part in Aiken family affairs. In 1926, when I was two, Conrad, restless again and desperately worried by shortage of money, returned alone to Boston, hoping to find reviewing or teaching jobs.

So my early recollections of my father, before the age of seven, are minimal. Is there a vague image of him sitting in an armchair in the shadowy drawing room, of my tiptoeing behind to gaze at the back of his head? Perhaps. A family friend, Beatrice Taussig, told of calling at Jeake's House, finding that Jessie was out shopping, Conrad typing in his study, while I yelled my head off in my cot; Beatrice advised Conrad that I needed changing, but he said he didn't know how, so she did it. I don't remember that. Conrad later recalled that when he returned to Jeake's House in 1928 to arrange for a divorce (he had, meanwhile, in Boston, met and fallen bang in love with Clarissa Lorenz), I greeted him with a suspicious scowl, demanding, "Who's that man?"

Much of my childhood was haunted, not unpleasantly, by nostalgia for previous places, previous modes of existence, not necessarily my own. Conrad himself wrote a poem on this theme:

> But alas, alas, being everything you are nothing
>   The history of all my life is in your face;
> And all I can grasp is an earlier, more haunted
>   moment,

And a happier place.

("At a Concert of Music,"
John Deth and Other Poems)

I suppose nostalgia is an infection almost inevitably picked up in the course of such a migratory career as that of our family. During my early years I used to hear John and Jane, my brother and sister, talking wistfully about the joys of South Yarmouth and Winchelsea; then later, Rye, in its turn, became for me imbued with the same haunting charm, the magic of a lost paradise.

Even *before* it was lost, the life in Rye, in Jeake's House, had immense charm. A letter of Conrad's describes the house as it was when he bought it in 1924, vast, tall, "roped with webs, littered with bones and stinking of ghosts," holes in its floors and beetles in its woodwork. My mother, and later, Conrad's second and third wives had a hideous time coping with its inconveniences, cavernous coldness, barbarously steep stairs, precipitous ledges from which children could and did fall, archaic plumbing, antediluvian heating, lack of light, lack of a back door. Just the same it was a house to love. I can instantly, at any time, summon up the individual smell of Jeake's House—a delicious blend of aged black timbers, escaping gas, damp plaster, and mildew; I can remember the exact feel of the brass front-door knob turning gently in one's hand, the shape of the square black banister post, the look of the leaded windows with their small panes (which let in little light and must have been hell to clean). The flight of stairs leading to the third floor was so steep that it had no rail, only a knotted ship's rope; and the flight above *that,* leading to the two little attics where slept my brother John and the maid Alice, was, unabashedly, a ladder like that leading to a yacht's cabin. Conrad's study, a big double room, had a huge, south-facing dormer window that looked out across the marsh to Winchelsea. Between the ages of eight and twelve I spent hours stretched out on the bone-hard couch in that window, reading. From a gully between the two peaked roofs, which could be reached from John's attic window, one could climb on to the roof of the next-door house and, if one had courage, on down the street. John and Jane, and a friend of theirs, Juliet, had a Secret Society called the JJJ Club. Among its conditions of entry was the performance of this and other fearsome roof-climbs. I was too small to belong to the club and admired its proceedings from a distant and humble standpoint.

The activities of my elders were for me imbued with magic. They had a rich fantasy life and lived in a world of imagination, surrounded by invented characters—Robin Hood and all his men, a group called The Playlanders whose leader was called Gold Kingy, not to mention the ghost of Samuel Jeake who was said to haunt the house, quite benevolently . . . Part of this richness came from Conrad, who told them a wonderful serial story called *The Jewel Seed,* in which S. Jeake was the hero, and the villain was a Chinese magician. John wrote it all down, as related, in tiny notebooks. Forty years later I discovered these, cached away in Conrad's house at Brewster on Cape Cod, and typed out the whole saga—but Conrad thought poorly of it when I showed it to him, and said it was best relegated to oblivion. I daresay it is now in the Huntington Library, with the rest of his papers.

As I have said, Conrad played no part in my own early memories, and I imagine that my mother's life at that time was sad enough. She had to cope with existence in a foreign land, on her own, with three children and very little money. Though, apparently, the news of Conrad's various infidelities came as a fearful shock when he broke it to her, she must, by degrees, during his two years' absence, have come to the conclusion that their sixteen-year marriage was at an end, that she had to make a decision about what she would do next. Go back to Canada? She never showed the least inclination to do that. Stay in England? But how? Take a teaching job?

Meanwhile, with characteristic stoicism and reserve, she buried pain and anxiety at the back of her mind and created a cheerful family life: picnics to the beach or to bluebell woods (John and Jane walked; I rode with the food on the back of Jessie's bicycle), birthday and Christmas festivities. The height of the downstairs hall allowed an enormous Christmas tree; John and Jane went out with baskets into the nearest woods and picked enough holly leaves to make an immense rustling chain that wound from top to bottom of the high house.

I remember no conversation from this period, only literature and happenings. The literature was read aloud to me, in the bedroom that I shared with Jane, and it comes back with intensely dramatic emphasis: first *Peter Rabbit* and the *Just-So Stories,* fairly milk-and-honey stuff; then *Pinocchio,* rustling with assassins, evil plots, death, moonlight, and irony; then *Uncle Remus,* told in mysterious dialect, full of lethal intentions, wicked Brer Fox, and ominous characters called Patter-Rollers; then, most dramatic of all, *The Cloister and the Hearth,* in fact read aloud to my elders but soaked up by me with passion. Two scenes were stamped on my mind for all time: the comic one with the ill-intentioned doctor who gets knocked into his own basket of hot coals; and the horrendous siege by brigands including a corpse decorated with luminous paint. For lighter relief came *Peacock Pie*—"Grill me some bones, said the Cobbler"—and the folk tales of Jean de Bosschère—

Joan Aiken, right, with sister Jane in the sitting room at Jeake's House, 1935

one particularly riveting about a forester treed by wolves who climb on one another's backs to get at him; that was the one which upset Freud's patient, the Wolf Man, but all it did to me was increase my passion for the written word. All the scenes from these books take place, for me, in Jeake's House—"Ann, Ann, come quick as you can, There's a fish that talks in the frying-pan!" is in the dark Jeake's House kitchen, and the story of the Butterfly that Stamped out in the little snaily garden.

Notable happenings at that time included my contracting diphtheria picked up while visiting the maid Alice's family in the slummy lower town. (Her family were extremely nice to me; I remember eating pickled cabbage in their kitchen and still have a stool, tossed together from the offcuts of toilet seats, which her father, a carpenter, made for me.) The diphtheria imbued me with a hatred of doctors—no doubt why the scene from *The Cloister and the Hearth* struck such a chord. I was segregated behind disinfected sheets, had to have my own small Christmas tree, and my books were burned when I recovered, but *Peacock Pie* and the *Just-So Stories* were instantly replaced.

At this time I discovered that I could make it rain by emptying a glass of water out of the window. Although much impressed by finding this power in myself I have not found the need to use it much; in fact, never since that time.

The garden of Jeake's House consisted of two little paved courtyards, one about five feet higher in level than the other, approached by a flight of stone steps. I fell down these steps, of course, and my sister Jane fell out of the swing in the lower court and cut her head on the paving stones and needed stitches; I can remember that drama, but not my falling into the river Rother and being rescued by my mother's sister Barbara who dived in fully clothed. Used to swimming in the St. Lawrence, no doubt she found the Rother child's play. I can remember a day when, for some reason, John and Jane took pairs of saucepan lids and, joyfully banging them together like cymbals, went processing round the house; but I can't remember the painful occasion when Conrad returned, in December 1928, to ask Jessie to reconsider the divorce on which she had finally decided. She refused even to talk to him, jumped on her bicycle, and went off to the house of a friend. He took my sister for a walk round the town, then returned miserably to London. Soon after, the divorce went through. Conrad married Clarissa; then, next year, my mother married Conrad's English friend Martin Armstrong and went, with us three children, to live with Martin in his small house Farrs at the other end of Sussex. Conrad was outraged by this and felt that he had been betrayed by both parties. They never met again.

I had heard talk of Farrs before. Martin had often come to visit at Jeake's House—he was actually staying in the house on the night of my birth. My brother John had been to stay with Martin and came back with descriptions of the beautiful aged cottage, close to a line of grassy hills, the South Downs, with a huge garden and fields all around. John was a passionate naturalist and had a collection of pressed wild flowers, sea shells, and snail shells.

I can still recall my original mental image of Farrs—just—and the way in which, as always, this differed from the reality when I finally got there.

The move from Rye really meant the end of childhood for John and Jane, aged sixteen and twelve; for Jane, a painfully premature and abrupt end. Trying to grapple with unhappy and complicated circumstances, my mother acted with uncharacteristic haste and bad

judgment. Farrs was situated in a remote village where there were no educational facilities for my elders, so Jane was despatched to a boarding school recommended by an acquaintance. It was a snobbish place where Jane was laughed at for her American accent and homemade clothes; she was miserably unhappy there and used to cry for days, on and off, before the start of each term. John was sent to London to board with friends of friends and attend University College School, from which in due course he graduated to University College. This was a better choice as he was scientifically minded and later took a first-class degree at U.C., but he was not very happy with the family in whose house he was quartered and missed Rye Grammar School which he had loved. In the school and college holidays John and Jane came to Farrs. Farrs was a tiny house and Martin, born in 1882, had been a bachelor up to the age of forty-seven when he married

Farrs, 1935

Jessie, not at all used to living with children; no doubt she was anxious to keep wear and tear on all parties to a minimum. I missed my siblings sorely when they went and looked forward passionately to their return in the holidays. I can't help wondering if their life would not have been easier if Jessie had remained in Rye and tried to get a teaching job which, with her M.A. degree, should not have been impossible.

Still, her marriage to Martin was a happy one; they remained married until her death, forty years later. "Shine after storm," she said once, comparing it to life with Conrad. They made Farrs into an unquestionably happy home, a solid base for us three Aikens and our half brother, David Armstrong. I think of the house always in sunshine; as one came in the glass-paned front door there would be warmth, a smell of apples and woodsmoke, the contented sound of a house where quiet, busy activities are proceeding, the sound of a typewriter or sewing machine, cooking noises, Scarlatti from the piano, the rustle of a log fire.

I can remember a few moments of my arrival at Farrs. Martin had fetched me from the friends in London who had me to stay during the wedding and honeymoon. It was dark when I arrived and I was put to bed in the room which later became my half brother's. I was impressed by the fact that the bath was low and small enough for me to climb into myself—the bath at Jeake's House had been of Victorian vastness, to match the towering brass gas geyser which sometimes exploded, formidably. Everything in Farrs, I discovered, was of small, manageable size; the stairs had only thirteen steps, ceilings downstairs were low, and upstairs they sloped, so the furniture had to be low-slung.

To my amazement I discovered next day that the street in Sutton, a village of forty houses, was not called a street but a road; there were no pavements (sidewalks, my mother called them), only grass banks with little scuffed paths along the top where children made tracks of their own. Sutton had one shop, which sold everything. Halfway to the shop, four minutes' walk, was a forge, where the blacksmith, Mr. Budd, worked at his roaring bellows or clanged shoes onto the great fringed feet of farm horses. There was one pub in the village, the White Horse, just down the road from our house. Martin went there to drink beer and chat with the village elders. You could walk to the shop and return by a footpath across the fields, for the village swung round in a curve, along the edge of a plateau in a loop of the South Downs. A gate from the fields led into the back of our garden.

This garden was my sudden emancipation from the grown-up world. Half an acre in size, it had been created by an elderly lady, Miss Alice Cohen, from whom, at first, Martin rented the cottage. (Later he bought it from her for £800.) Her standards in gardens were high; Martin had a job keeping up with them. The Farrs garden was a paradise for any child. For a start, there were great expanses of lawn. *Grass!* Accustomed to the unkind paving stones of the Rye garden, I could hardly believe that I was free to walk, crawl, and roll as much as I pleased. Then, there were any number of trees, most of them climbable. The best was a walnut tree, from which hung the swing. You could climb up the rope, and so into the heights of the tree. There were secret places behind lilacs, a summer house that rotated on a circular base, a wild area up at the top of the garden, a wild, steep cliff at the front, leading down to the road, and all kinds of flowers, masses of

them—roses, peonies, lilies, irises, oriental poppies, phlox, anemones, and in spring, masses and masses of daffodils, narcissi, hyacinths, snowdrops . . . There were no flowers, of course, when I first arrived in January, the best month of the year, when everything is starting. For a country child, January is full of promise: drainage runnels by the roads are full of water pouring over white, hollowed chalk beds where one can wade in one's rubber boots; the banks, far higher than my five-year-old head, were neatly trimmed and the hedges clipped, so that one could climb them and explore and see the bones of the landscape.

From this point on, I can remember conversation. With John and Jane away at school, I suppose more remarks were addressed to me.

Martin, though civil and civilised, made it perfectly plain that he was not prepared to be a father to us Aikens; after all, we had a perfectly good father of our own. While my mother was settling in, Martin kindly took me for one or two walks and explained the

Jane, Jessie, Joan, John, and David in the garden at Farrs, 1935

Jessie with son David, and husband Martin Armstrong, 1941

difference between a pub and a club (I knew about clubs, for there had been one next door to Jeake's House). But our conversation was stilted, and remained so for the next fifty years; Martin was not at ease with small children until his own son was born, and by that time his and my relationship had set into its mould; I was rather nervous of him and he, probably rightly, found most of my remarks silly. Still, at meals, in the company of the whole family, he was immensely entertaining, both witty and erudite. Life at Farrs was graceful, in spite of poverty. Martin, like Conrad, depended for his living on what he wrote—novels, short stories, and poetry; my mother had a small income, but this had been invested ill-advisedly by her brothers and she lost most of it in the slump. Her relationship with her brothers had never been good: her father died when she was twelve and the brothers, in their twenties, had been left to deal with most of the family affairs, which probably made them rather bossy. To the end of her life my mother, though gentle, courteous, and accessible to reason in general, had a tendency to bristle into fight if any male tried to lay down the law or get didactic with her. Undoubtedly this was a legacy from her feelings about her brothers.

So at Farrs there was no money to throw about. My mother's depleted income went mostly on educating Jane and John. Conrad paid her a little rent for Jeake's House. I remained at home and she taught me herself until I was twelve, which she was well qualified to do. I learned French, Latin, English, history, arithmetic, geography, a little Spanish and German.

The house had four bedrooms and one bathroom; Martin's study was upstairs; downstairs there was a dining room into which the front door opened, a sitting room, kitchen, pantry, and scullery (in which the cooking was actually done, on a kerosene stove). We had no radio, car, main water, or refrigerator—no electricity at all; water came from a well, pumped by hand; at night we lit oil lamps and candles. One of our daily tasks was refilling all the lamps and the metal tank of the cooker, rubbing down the charred wicks with a twist of newspaper, cleaning the smoke stains off the fragile glass chimneys with more newspaper and a bit of rag. I can still remember the gentle squeaking of the paper against the glass. If you rubbed too hard the glass broke and my mother wrote down "two small lamp chimneys" in the weekly-order book for the shop. The floors downstairs were of brick and icy cold at all times. Our food was sumptuous—fruit and vegetables from the garden grown by Martin; magnificent eggs, cream, and milk from one of the village farms; home-baked bread from the village shop, local meat. Martin was a decided gourmet and my mother a terrific cook. For the first seven years of life at Farrs we had a maid; a local girl would come daily to sweep, dust, scrub, and wash dishes; she was paid about fifty pence a week. The first girl, Lily, came when she was fourteen, having just left the village school. One of the first things she did was to drop a whole trayload of wedding-present Wedgewood china onto the brick floor and smash the lot. She was terribly upset and cried floods, but my mother comforted her.

Lily was fourteen, I was six; she had much more

knowledge of the world than I, because she was the youngest of a family of six. Her mother was a widow. Thinking about it now, I realise what a number of widows there were in the village: Mrs. Standen at the shop; Mrs. Leggatt, who had been Martin's house-keeper and still came up for spring-cleaning; Mrs. Clare, her mother; Mrs. Harwood next door, who sold us eggs and milk, did our heavy laundry, and whose son Frank drove the village taxi; and several others. World War I had taken a heavy toll of the village.

Lily had been to school for seven years and loved reading stories; she lent me *The Golden Key* by George MacDonald, a marvellous tale. I learned to read at once after arrival at Farrs (I expect my mother saw to this); so I was happy to share with Lily the fruits of my reading the Pink, Crimson, and Green Fairy Books, Hans Andersen, and Grimm. For her part, she had been to the movies, and could tell me about them.

Our nearest movie house was a five-mile walk, in a small corrugated-iron shed outside Petworth (where I now live); this was also where our nearest chemist, butcher, draper, ironmonger, fishmonger, and doctor were located. Lily went to the cinema once a week, Saturdays, on her bike. She tried to describe to me what the films were like. "It's like a picture, but it moves, and sometimes you hear the voices too." I sim-ply could not conceive how it worked, and only half believed her; but still she did tell me those amazing stories which I knew she could not have made up. My imagination rose to the challenge time after time, like a horse to an impossible jump, and sank back defeated. But I curled on the striped cushion in the old wicker armchair in the kitchen every teatime, eating fresh crusty bread (often without butter because it was so good on its own), drinking ice-cold well-water, while Lily told me the plots of films she had seen, till they lay embedded in my mind like fossils. Many were war films—*Tell England, The Dawn Patrol, Journey's End*. They were terribly sad. On a lighter note was Tarzan, also Felix the Cat, Charlie Chaplin, and Buster Keaton. The two last I despised, being a little snob. I know better now. We preferred films of heroic action and self-sacrificing friendship. Lily took me for walks in the afternoons; I expect my mother was glad to get us both out of the cottage, whose ancient floors were very thin; one could hear conversation clear through ceil-ings. Going up to the top of the garden among the brussels sprouts was the only way to have any private conference; I can remember various fraught interviews with my mother in that region.

Lily and I used to climb the nearer slopes of the Downs, half a mile away, or pick cowslips and king-cups in the marshy meadow behind Lily's mother's cot-tage (shared with another family), or walk two miles in

hot summer to a shallow pond where one could bathe, after a fashion. On these walks we developed our pri-vate mythology, woven across the framework of the films Lily had seen, the books I had read. I was in love with Kipling; I had read the *Jungle Books* over and over, and knew whole pages of *Stalky* by heart. In our private world Lily was Tarzan and I was Mowgli; we spent a lot of time tree-climbing and swinging on the ropes of wild clematis that hung from beech trees on the Downs. Lily, born in the village, knew all the local names: Sutton 'Ollow, the deep-banked road that climbed to our village, haunted by a ghost who sat on a leaning tree; Crouch Cave, an underground brick vault in a wood, really an old icehouse; The Decoy, another haunted path (by the ghost of a shot game-keeper); The Slipes (possibly an Anglo-Saxon version of slopes?), where we picked young beech sprays to decorate the May Queen's Throne; the Birket, where birches grew; New Barn, several centuries old; the Cuckoo Tree, "where a cuckoo built its nest"; best of all, Burton waterfall, a twenty-foot artificial cascade, underneath which a damp and drippy tunnel ran clean through from one side to the other. Later I used many of these locations in my own books.

The only film I actually saw myself was *The Count of Monte Cristo*. Jane and I and a school friend of hers did the walk there and back, taking a supper picnic and returning after midnight. It was a terrific occasion.

Of course the village had its own festivities: an occasional cartoon or magic-lantern show would take place in the Women's Institute hall; or there would be an evening of song. I can remember a teenage boy, someone's visiting talented nephew, plaintively render-ing "Sing to me, Gipsy," which I found inexpressibly moving, and then we all sang "Flow gently, Sweet Af-ton," as the words were thrown on a screen. In August there was the flower show, when everyone exhibited fruit, vegetables, flower arrangements, cakes, and jam, and the children made wild-flower collections. Once I won a third prize for one of these—two shillings—but my mother would not let me accept the money, for, she said, it should properly go to a village child. I am sure she gave me the two shillings herself, but still her veto filled me with a deep sense of injustice.

The best event of the year, for me, was May Day. This had been revived by the Rector, a morris-dance enthusiast. The festivities opened with a morris pro-cession—the young males of the village, prancing, white-trousered, straw-hatted, cross-gartered, accom-panied by bells, fiddle, and accordion; also by the scoffing comments of their relatives lined along the grassy banks of the village street. Then came the best part, crowning of the May Queen on the grass plot behind the Women's Institute. Of course my personal ambition was to be May Queen myself, but even then I probably knew this was out of the question, since to qualify one must attend the village school. (My mother had quite correctly estimated that I would learn a great deal more from her, without taking into consideration how much this would cut me off from the communal life of the village children. They used to shout "Gin—*ger*!" after me in the street, and I was scared and shy of them.)

The May Queen wore white, and a wreath of primroses and pink campion; while she sat enthroned the schoolchildren did their elaborate dances with ribbons round the white maypole. The music of the maypole dances, the intricate turnings and spiderweb patterns made by the ribbons filled me with supreme ecstacy.

I was writing a lot of poetry at this time in a notebook I had bought for two shillings at the shop on my fifth birthday. From that age I knew I was going to be a writer, like Conrad, like Martin, whose books were to be seen around the house. I knew that writers didn't make much money. Martin used to give me his old royalty reports and typed sheets for drawing paper. I planned to be a novelist and tried to write stories as well as poems, but seldom finished them. An exception was one based on a dream: *Her Husband Was a Demon; or, Eight Tormented Years.* I just managed to get through that one by cramming the action—a fault I have succumbed to ever since.

Lily began writing poetry too, and showed it to Martin, asking how she could get it published. He must know, after all. He found this a trial and complained, also, that whenever he went into the kitchen, there was Lily moonily gazing at herself in the glass instead of getting on with what had to be done; so, shortly after, she left us, which was a shock and great grief to me.

I had planned to tell her about a visit I had paid to some cousins in the north of England who owned a monkey—her dismissal had been tactfully arranged while I was away—and when I encountered her in the street, arranged to meet her next day in Sutton 'Ollow for a long talk. My mother looked doubtful when she learned of this assignation but did not try to deter me from going. I arrived early, waited and waited—but Lily never showed up. At last I went home, dissolved in tears.

"I was afraid that might happen," my mother told me, with her usual mixture of sympathy and realism. Characteristically she had let me go because she thought I might as well learn that people are unreliable. Some years later I heard that Lily had, in fact, suffered from a mild mental breakdown. The mixture of Tarzan and housework had been too indigestible for her, poor girl. But she recovered and married happily.

This episode illustrates a rather drastic side of my mother's apparently mild and gentle nature. Similarly I can remember her, the first time I made pastry, silently watching me as I rolled and re-rolled it. When, later, Martin made some tart comment on its leathery inedibility, my mother said tranquilly, "I thought it would probably turn out very tough if you rolled it so much. But I thought that, once you knew that, you would never make tough pastry again."

My mother had an immense notion of people's right to learn their own lessons, make their own mistakes. Her tact was exquisite; when teaching one some operation which she had done a thousand times, she would say, diffidently, "I *think* you might find it easier if you did it *this* way . . ." When I had a spell as a Little Helpful at the age of ten and, without being requested, filled hot-water-bottles and stuck them in beds, she remarked mildly, "I think you might find a hot-water-bottle makes a more *comfortable* companion if you bend it so as to let out the air before putting in the stopper . . ."

The winters in brick-floored Farrs were arctic. Heat consisted of an iron stove called an Ideal Boiler, which burned anthracite and heated a tank of water; I used to huddle against the tank and wrap my chilblained fingers round the hot pipes. I suffered from excruciating chilblains on fingers and toes every winter until I went to boarding school. There were other coal-burning stoves in the dining room and Martin's study, but they were seldom lit; lack of money I suppose. Towards teatime the sitting room fire, in an open brick hearth, would be laid and lit by Martin. The Persian tabby cat, whose real name was Teglees, but who was addressed by everybody as Pussy, used to spend the mornings crouching on this brick hearth, absorbing the residual warmth from yesterday's fire. I wrote a poem about this habit.

In winter I did lessons with my mother as close to the Ideal Boiler as we could huddle. She used to go out and warm herself by chopping wood. She would come in with a bruised face from flying kindling. On her bike she took corners with such carefree abandon that she often came back with cuts and abrasions. Her nature combined reckless energy with meticulous care and delicacy in such arts as embroidery, knitting, tatting, dressmaking. She was continuously creative and always had some project in hand; she gave lectures, made preserves, sketched, made clothes, worked in the garden (when Martin would let her; he said she was too rash and hasty to be let loose among his more cherished plants); the only thing she didn't do was write books. "I could, if I wanted; there's nothing to it," she asserted. But after her death, my sister and I found the beginning of a novel, written in her thirties, about life in South Yarmouth, which, regretfully, we agreed, would not have succeeded; she had not grasped the mechanics of storytelling. I am sure she would have done so if she had applied herself; but she had other, more pressing concerns. Her criticisms of other people's work were extremely shrewd, and more temperate than those of Martin, who could be witheringly dry.

My stepfather's opinions occupied a very distinct place in my early life; I was conscious all the time of living by a double standard, his and mine. I knew that he thought some of my favourite reading—the poetry of Walter de la Mare, Alfred Noyes, Kipling—sentimental, crude, or vulgar. Martin would sometimes walk through a room where my mother and I were reading aloud, and let fall some light, totally blighting comment:

> " 'And when I crumble, who will remember
>   That lady of the West Country?'
>
> *Crumble!* What an extraordinarily silly word
>   to choose!"

Other, perhaps more deserving targets—Barrie's *Peter Pan, Winnie the Pooh, When We Were Very Young,* a book of John Drinkwater's poems for the young called *All about Me*—also came in for his broadsides. A lot of the books I adored, the Katy books, *Little Women, A Girl of the Limberlost,* he had luckily never opened; full well can I imagine the kind of things he would say about them. I myself lived in a dream world, peopled with characters out of my favourite books; I would never have mentioned it to anybody and was vaguely aware of the huge gulf between it and Martin's realities. Even now in my mind's ear I can hear his voice as I enjoy some best-seller—"Surely this must have been written by an extraordinarily silly young woman?" *Silly* was his most condemnatory adjective and the term *young woman,* as used by him and my mother, had a decidedly pejorative ring.

When I was seven or eight my own father came back into my life again. Like my elder siblings, I began to go and visit him and Clarissa in Jeake's House, for a week or so, two or three times a year. I loved these trips back into the nostalgic past but found it hard getting onto conversational terms with Conrad; we had been parted for too long, all my life really. It was easier when John and Jane were there. But I developed a great romantic devotion to Conrad and used to invent tales of how he and Jessie made up their differences and came together again. Conrad encouraged my poetry writing and gave me books to read—Vachel Lindsay, Fitz-James O'Brien—and books by infant prodigies like Daisy Ashford.

It had been decided that I should go to boarding

school at age twelve, when Jane would be at university. Determined that I should not suffer as she had, Jane looked about and chose a school for me in Oxford where, as she was at Somerville College, she would be able to visit me and see that I was all right. Then Conrad suggested that, so as to mitigate the shock of being plunged into boarding school after hardly having had the chance to meet any other children, I should come to Rye for a summer, live with him and Clarissa, and go to a small day school round the corner. This was agreed and I went.

If Conrad's idea had also been that he and I should get to know one another better, it did not work out; he was on the brink of divorce from Clarissa, they had frequent savage quarrels, and a lot of the time he was not even in Rye. Where was he? I don't know. Meanwhile I was moderately happy at the cranky little school where there were only ten pupils, only one of them my age, a boy called Christopher, the rest much younger. With Christopher I roamed about Rye and flew windup airplanes. Clarissa, despite her rather miserable situation, was very nice to me. In August Conrad went off to America where he met and fell in love with Mary Hoover who became his third wife; in September I went to boarding school in Oxford. My mother had invited the headmistress, Margaret Lee, to stay beforehand, and also came up and spent a couple of nights at Miss Lee's house in Oxford to "settle me in." I am not sure whether her presence on the fringe of school life for those two days helped, or made the agony more severe. I can remember her taking me for a walk down into Christ Church quad and telling me that she had always considered me her special child. Even then I understood this to mean, not that she loved me more than the others—she was always scrupulously fair—but that, since I had had so little attention from Conrad, she was resolved to perform the part of father and mother both. Thinking this over later I concluded that Conrad had neither intended nor been pleased at my birth, which so soon preceded the breakup of their marriage. My rather cursory christening to match the other two—as if we were a batch of factory products—reinforced this view. But when I was in my forties and he in his seventies, Conrad and I became very close.

Back to my initiation at school. Severe the agony certainly was. The contrast between our small, orderly, quiet house, filled with ancient, beautiful objects and civilised practices—and this noisy, bare, crowded, ugly barrack, and its bleak, trampled garden, both filled with girls in uniform, came as an inconceivable shock. Bells clanged, buzzers roared, one was perpetually being hustled, in a clattering throng, up and down steep flights of lino-covered stairs, along dark passages, heaven only knew where. On my arrival at Wychwood School at age twelve I was one of the tallest in my class, but I stopped growing at that point and never increased another centimetre. School uniform, too, was an intolerable constraint. After the freedom and comfort of home clothes—socks, shirts, skirts, shorts, sweaters—suddenly one had to plod about in layers and layers of thick woollen garments: things called combinations, plus two pairs of woollen knickers, plus vest, plus wool blouse, woollen stockings, suspender belt, a cripplingly heavy garment of serge called a gym tunic, all pleats, and over that a school blazer. Still I did stop having chilblains. There was a velour hat for weekday wear, and a felt hat for Sundays; there were Panama hats for summer, lacrosse boots, tennis shoes, netball shoes, indoor shoes, outdoor shoes, dancing shoes, galoshes, and endless sports equipment. All that must have cost my mother a pretty penny; she begged me to be economical at school, and for years I never dared have a bun at breaktime.

Just the change from country to town made my spirit wither inside me. At Farrs nobody questioned one's movements; since the age of six I had roamed for miles, unescorted, all over the grassy landscape. Here we were not allowed outside the school gate. Not that I wanted to go: the roaring Banbury Road, outside, seemed to me hideous, the Oxford parks, where we were taken for walks, two and two, in crocodile, were bare, muddy deserts, utterly unlike the country they were supposed to imitate. Oxford, for the first two years I lived there, confirmed my lifelong hatred of cities. It was a long time before I began to appreciate its beauty.

As for school . . . after a couple of terms I began to realise what it had to offer. I always, always hated and dreaded having to go back at the start of each term; always longed for home, where I now felt no more than a visitor, always pined for its peace, beauty, and civilisation. But school stirred up a strong competitive spirit (inherited straight from my mother, who was a tremendous passer of exams); in no time I was devoting all my energy to getting the highest marks in class, getting parts in school plays, getting poems into the school magazine, being elected Form Representative, and so on. Wychwood was a self-governing school to some degree (not where health, manners, or curriculum were concerned); we held a lot of meetings and did a lot of voting, which has given me a profound dislike of the committee system ever since.

Looking back I can see that Wychwood was, as my sister had judged, a very kindly school. The classes were small, the teaching pretty good, particularly that of English, the staff were intelligent and friendly; but I came there too late. I had had those seven years of living on my own, with adults, in a gracious environment; I could never be reconciled to the world of school. My reports said that I was self-centered, went my own way, was antisocial; as I got higher up the school they began to be critical of my friendships. I had a friend called Evelyn, two years older, two forms higher; she was witty, intelligent, entertaining; I liked her because she reminded me of home. Authority disapproved of this friendship because of the age gap, because we used to break rules and go off to wander about the Oxford colleges, whose beauty we had just noticed. At Wychwood there was a tradition of "pashes," younger girls having raves on older ones, or on the staff; there was nothing of this in my relations with Evelyn, we simply enjoyed each other's conversation and liked walking about Oxford. Our particular enemy was the games mistress (neither of us showed the least aptitude for any form of athletics); later there was a lesbian scandal and that same games mistress left abruptly; it is to be presumed that she had viewed our friendship from her own angle. Evelyn, being older, left two years before I did, and I missed her badly. Then World War II threw the school into disruption; half the staff left, the numbers dwindled, presently the school went bankrupt and had to amalgamate with a bigger school, the Oxford High School. I had just taken the School Certificate examination (what would now be called 0-Levels) in eight subjects and done well, getting five distinctions (over 80%) and three credits (over 60%); but the sudden amalgamation with a larger school completely threw me; I developed a swollen gland in my neck which would not respond to treatment, spent a term in bed, had two operations, and my schoolwork went to pieces. Refusing to attend classes at the larger school, I worked at Wychwood, mostly on my own, tried for Oxford Entrance, failed (shaming my brother and sister who had sailed through and won scholarships), and declared that I wanted to leave school and become a Land Girl. I was now seventeen.

School was glad for me to leave, as I had become a dissident element, but my father, now back in America (Rye, only two miles from the coast, had been declared a restricted area where foreigners were not allowed, even if they owned houses there) wrote expressing his extreme disapproval of such a non-intellectual career. So did Jane, now doing a Master's at Radcliffe. So instead I applied for a job in the British Broadcasting Corporation, having a vague inflated notion that there I might find some interesting niche putting poetry magazines together or becoming a studio manager.

What I really wanted was to marry a rich man who would support me in the country while I wrote books.

The BBC were impressed by my school certificate marks and took me on. But the job they gave me was a letdown. By now it was 1941, the middle of the blitz. Their filing system had been evacuated from London to a mansion in the Thames valley near Reading. Here dwelt thirty women, all ages and classes, sleeping in bunks, filing and indexing the corporation's written matter, scripts and letters, which arrived daily in sacks. My first duties were to open the mail, cycle to the post office four miles distant for more stamps, and (because of the national paper shortage) rule lines on the back of used index cards, so that they could be used again. Life at this hostel (it was called Great Oaks and had been built by the millionaire manufacturer of H. P. Sauce) was almost as rude a shock as the initial arrival at Wychwood. I learned a bit of Spanish and Portuguese, in order to file letters in those languages, but, after nine months, saw that this job would lead nowhere. So I enrolled in a secretarial school and did a course of typing and Pitman shorthand. The course had some fancy touches too: bookkeeping and journalism. None of that, except the typing, has been the least use to me, whereas in the BBC, I had at least learned how to cross-reference. The principal of my secretarial school was a Christian Scientist; when I had appendicitis she sat by my bedside and told me that if I thought hard enough, the condition would go away. I can't have, because it didn't; I had to have the appendix removed.

The secretarial college found me a job in the Ministry of Information. It would have been quite an interesting job, but I found that I would be working as assistant to the mother of one of my school friends. This lady was a very formidable character with a vitriolic tongue; I had seen her in devastating action on excursions from school and did not look forward to working for her; so I politely declined the job and got myself in trouble with my secretarial college, who washed their hands of me despite my 130 wpm shorthand. But a friend was working in the newly formed United Nations Information Office, an offshoot of the Ministry of Information, and she told me of a job going there, in the library. It was extremely well paid, by the standards of those days—£4.10s. a week! A female official at the Labour Exchange, where I had to register myself and my employment, was scandalized that a girl of nineteen should be so lavishly paid. I shared a flat in Earls Court with two friends, and began paid employment, in a bomb-damaged house on the corner of Russell Square. The house got damaged some more during the next three years; the main London blitz was now over, but there were stray raids, and the V-1s and V-2s, which made a lot of noise, interrupted work, and did a fair amount of damage. A V-1 fell in Russell

Square, blowing all the leaves off the trees, breaking the office windows, and messing up my filing system.

Of course I hated living in a city, hated London—yet, looking back, how pleasant it was! The streets were almost bare of traffic. No high-rise buildings had gone up—the trend was the other way; they were toppling down. The blitz spirit was still in being, citizens were friendly to one another. I was working in a group of about fifteen intelligent and interesting people, all nationalities. My two immediate seniors were Irish and Czech. There was a democratic and friendly spirit in the office, and we had a lot of jokes about the United Nations. The Press Officer, Ron Brown, made up a theme song for us:

> For news of the Thirty-five Nations
> *Inter-allied of course,*
> And Russo-Polish relations,
> *Inter-allied of course . . .*

It went to a jingly French tune, "Ca, c'est bien entendu," from one of the French films that used to find their way to London, and we used to sing it when there was particular friction between the Russian and Polish members of our governing committee. For London, then, was the dwelling place of half the exiled governments of Europe, and some were ancien régime while others were nouveau; it could at times be awkward. Two lots of Greeks, two lots of Poles, two lots of French . . .

What about my writing, all this time? Well, I had bought a typewriter from a bookseller, Bob Chris, whose tiny shop off the Charing Cross Road, into which I wandered one day, was the most amazing salon; at different times I met there professor Joad, the philosopher; Dannie Abse, the poet; David Piper, who later became head of the Victoria and Albert Museum; Ruthven Todd; Pamela Hansford Johnson; not to mention my brother John. Half literary London were Bob's friends, if not customers; he seldom seemed to sell a book.

Bob encouraged me to keep writing. I had sold some children's stories to the BBC "Children's Hour," a radio programme, inspired by the example of my stepfather. Martin, a serious adult writer, had been invited to do something for "Children's Hour," and produced a family saga, *Said the Cat to the Dog*, which was immensely successful, repeated over and over, and earned him far more than any of his novels. Impressed by this, I too sent the BBC some stories, a couple of which they took. I had also had a couple of poems accepted, two years before, while still at school, by a prestigious little magazine, *Abinger Chronicle*, run by

E.M. Forster, Sylvia Sprigge, and Max Beerbohm. They printed my poems but never paid me, which gave me the idea that poetry was not a remunerative occupation. However I did keep sending them to the *New Statesman,* who took one but never used it.

While working at U.N.I.O., I fell in love with its Press Officer, the aforementioned Ron Brown, and married him in 1945 at Russell Square registrar's office. He was fourteen years older, had been married

Joan Aiken and Ron Brown, 1945

before and divorced, had had various jobs in journalism, was at Reuter before he came to U.N.I.O. He was handsome, six-foot tall, a Marxist, full of charm and cheer, a tremendous arguer, and could be a trial in an office, as he was convinced that he knew the best way to do everything. To be fair: he often *did* know the best way to do jobs, and his two children have taken after him in this respect. All three are, or were, models of capability around the house or garden; shelves go up,

curtains are made and hung, everything works. But nonetheless, Ron was continually at odds with his superiors, and, soon after we were married he shook the dust of U.N.I.O. off his feet and went, first to *The Times,* then to Associated Press, where he stayed for seven years, engaged in constant bloody battles with the head of his department. Nonetheless he had dozens of good friends and was a lot of fun, one of those husbands who can take care of everything.

"Don't you worry about me," he used to say. "Nothing ever happens to me." He was a very heavy smoker: fifty a day.

Meanwhile I had a miscarriage, quite a bad one, malnutrition from World War II, and was told: no children for at least four years. I was promoted, by a reshuffle at the U.N. office, to Librarian, wrote a number of short stories, not very good ones, and we moved out of London to Lewes in Sussex (midway between Rye and Sutton; Martin and Jessie used to meet there for lunch before they were married). Ron thought country air would do me good. Lewes is quite a large town, bigger than Rye, but country is easily accessible from it. It is a handsome town, too, on a hill with a castle, just across the road from our flat in the High Street, a racecourse, a jail, grassy Downs all round, and the sea only eight miles off down a valley viewed from our windows. It was a fine place to live; our only problem was that we seldom met, as both of us were still working in London, Ron often on night shifts at his news agency, so our life consisted of leaping on and off trains and leaving notes for each other—Feed cat, fish on shelf. The first winter we were there, 1947, was exceptionally severe; trains kept getting derailed or stuck in snowdrifts and taking five hours on circuitous routes to do the trip to London which should have taken one hour and a bit.

I loved Lewes. It started me off writing, and the town formed the scene for a number of my short stories, *The People in the Castle, More Than You Bargained For, Belle of the Ball, The Ghostly Governess,* and a novel, *Foul Matter.*

By now, though still determined to write serious adult novels, I had fallen into the habit of producing quite a few children's stories, mostly fantastic. These are a tremendous pleasure to write—perhaps the most exhilarating among all the forms of fiction that I practise. They must be written in one session, with one idea, mood, voice; the process is fairly close to poetry. As well as these I wrote a nasty satirical story called *The Dreamers,* about a man who boiled up his wife in a pressure cooker, which was accepted by *The New Statesman.* This was very exciting; the first piece of work I had sold to a serious periodical. The *N.S.* didn't print the story for about three years, which taught me some of the patience and resignation so necessary to a writer. When they did print it, a firm of literary agents, Pearn Pollinger and Higham, got in touch with me and offered to take me on. Jean LeRoy handled their serial market; Paul Scott (author of *The Jewel in the Crown*) handled novels.

Ron's hours at the news agency worsened, and the trains to and from Lewes proved inadequate to his needs. So, sadly, after the birth of our son John Sebastian, we moved to the village of Chipstead in Kent, closer to London.

It had always been Ron's ambition to live beside a stream, or river, and in Kent he found a large wild piece of land, part of a park which had been divided, with an indubitable brook at its far end. But would we be allowed to build a house on it? The land was scheduled as Green Belt around London, not for building development. Ron acquired a lawyer who thought he could find a loophole in the local application of this, and managed to battle successfully against the interdiction. Meanwhile, having bought the land, we squatted on it in an old single-decker bus which we converted into a cosy dwelling. It had three rooms, kitchen, nursery, and living room. Water and electricity were laid on, and the loo was in the driver's cab. Ron won his case against the Town and Country Planning Act, and we built our house. Now, if ever I revisit Chipstead, which I do as seldom as possible, I feel drowned in guilt, because our house was the opening end of the wedge. What used to present, in 1950, at

Living in the bus, 1952: from left, Joan, Liz, John, and Ron

least the appearance of a rural community is now a mass of houses, cheek by jowl, intersected by motorways. The inhabitants really had cause to hate us.

I was never happy at Chipstead, though the house we built was pleasant enough. The bit of land, two acres, was too wild for me to manage, and had had its topsoil removed, not once but twice, by the shark who sold it to us; nothing would grow on it but thistles. There was no real country round about; one could not walk for the land all belonged to Government departments guarded by barbed wire. My second child, Elizabeth Delano, was born while we were still in the bus; but the affronted local authorities insisted on my going into hospital for the birth. A bus was not considered hygienic. I wrote an article about our life in it for the magazine *Housewife*.

Now our life began to deteriorate. Ron had really exhausted himself, racing about on his bike, appealing at local courts, interviewing builders, lawyers, architects. His temper worsened, he became morose. We had spent a lot of money and found it hard to keep abreast of bills; all my thoughts were concentrated on how to earn money by writing. I sent stories to women's magazines, but they all came back. I had, however, amassed enough children's stories to offer as a collection. I tried them first on Faber, who refused but made encouraging noises; then I tried Jonathan Cape, who took them. That was my first book, *All You've Ever Wanted*, published in 1953. (I had written a full-length book, *The Kingdom and the Cave*, when I was seventeen, reading it aloud in daily instalments to my younger brother David. It was heavily influenced by John Masefield's *The Midnight Folk*. I typed out one copy and sent it to a literary competition. I assumed it didn't win, as I never heard any more, and never had my copy back. That taught me always to keep a carbon copy.)

Encouraged by the publication of *AYEW*, I thought I would write a children's novel. I had an idea for one, a kind of spoof melodrama. I bought a kitchen table and typed two chapters in a corner of our bedroom as I had no study. I thought I would call the book *Bonnie Green*. I was full of excitement about it.

Now Ron's chest pains and bad temper were found to have a physical cause: tuberculosis. His office gave him six weeks' sick leave, a small amount of severance pay, and the sack. There we were, fairly destitute, with children aged two and six months. My Aunt Grace in Suffolk, my mother's youngest sister, who had married an Englishman, Oswald Sitwell, suggested that I come and housekeep for Oswald while she returned to Canada to superintend the birth of a grandchild. We could rent our house and get some income for it. Ron, who was prescribed six months' bed rest, could take it just as easily in my uncle's roomy Suffolk farmhouse. So that is what we did.

While living in Suffolk I wrote enough stories for another collection. "I bet you can't write a story every day for a week," said Ron, who was enthusiastic and proud of my writing. He lost his bet. Also I fished out *The Kingdom and the Cave* and laboriously revised and retyped it. Cape turned it down, but accepted my second batch of stories, *More Than You Bargained For.*

Winter in Suffolk seemed to do Ron good; he recovered and it was decided that we should move to the West Country, run a guest house, which I could do while writing, and Ron would raise pigs. He had been conducting a long and bitter correspondence with his office, arbitrated by the National Union of Journalists, who managed, in the end, to wring a larger amount of severance pay from A.P. With that, and the proceeds from selling the house in Kent, we had enough to buy a property in Cornwall where the climate was benign and tourists plentiful.

Ron went ahead, stayed with friends of mine, scouted around, and found a dream place. This time it really was a dream place: Milltown, a Georgian farmhouse, white with slate roof, a mill building, barns, pigsties, two orchards full of daffodils, four meadows, a row of cypresses and three ruined cottages—all for so small a sum that it makes me wring my hands when I think of it now. There was a palm tree in the garden, white azaleas that smelt of honey, and not one but three brooks. It would be perfect for the children, secluded in its own deep little valley. We were given a breeding sow by a Hungarian friend, Oswald gave me fifty hens, and I built a yard for them.

Some improvements were necessary before we could run Milltown as a guest house; Ron, throwing off all signs of illness, raced about, organising. We put in an efficient cooker, hot water system, brought down our furniture, and started having guests, which was simple: we advertised in *The New Statesman* and they came flocking. The summer passed in a flash.

Two people we knew had, unexpectedly, moved down to Cornwall when we did. We had not known them long. One was a journalist, Elsie Bourke, who had edited a magazine called *Woman and Home*; the other her elderly friend Muriel Tuck, a retired headmistress. They had been our neighbours in Kent, while Elsie was editing her magazine; then, for some mysterious reason, she threw up her job, went to Australia, came back again, and when we moved west we found them already settled in Cornwall about five miles from us. Elsie was in her forties, Muriel in her sixties. They bought a smallholding, cows, hens, ducks, and were learning, very efficiently, considering their former urban existence, how to tackle this new life. Often they

Ron and Joan with John and Liz, Milltown, 1954

came over to help me with my garden, and, as well as gardening advice, Elsie gave me a lot of practical counsel on writing female fiction. It was no use in the world, she said, my trying to write sentimental women's-magazine stories; I would never bring one off in a million years; I should rather aim at suspense or mystery fiction. With her encouragement I began a prototype gothic called *House of Shadows*. This was before the spate of gothics hit the market in the '50s and '60s; my story had the basic *Jane Eyre* plot: young governess arrives at a mansion to care for little girl who has a Rochester-type father and mad mother. I also, with Elsie's encouragement, wrote some semi-fantastic stories, satirical, inspired by our Cornish neighbours who were upper-crust eccentrics of a particularly picturesque and wild variety. Jean LeRoy, my new agent, sold some of these to the short story magazine *Argosy* which belonged to the same group, Amalgamated Press, who owned Elsie's *Woman and Home*. This turned out to be lucky for me since, after a year in Cornwall, Ron's health deteriorated abruptly. The guest house and pig breeding were now established, nothing challenged him, and he needed a challenge to keep going. A Londoner born, he grew miserably bored with country life, and all his ailments assaulted him at once. He was found to have lung cancer and a condition of muscular dystrophy, probably latent from childhood, aggravated by the huge doses of streptomycin taken for the TB. He went into a London hospital and died in 1955.

I had to leave Cornwall and find some way of supporting myself and the two children aged three and five. Elsie Bourke wrote me a letter of introduction to the director of Amalgamated Press; I went for an interview and was offered a trial period on *Argosy*. They took me on, and I soon settled into a small but congenial office where everybody did a bit of everything. Work was the only consolation in that bad time.

Reading was one of our main tasks. Bales of manuscripts arrived daily, unsolicited ones besides those sent from agents and publishers. We read dozens a day. Jean Malcolm, the formidably efficient Chief Sub, gave me a thorough editorial training, teaching me far more than I'd learned at school about the niceties of grammar, punctuation, spelling, and style. The salary was low, but one could augment it by contributions to the magazine: poems, quizzes, small anthology features, and in my case stories—I sold them about twenty-five while I was on the staff, having worked out the necessary combination of elements—exotic background, touch of sex, twist ending, touch of humour if possible—that would make a story acceptable. I was also set to write an editorial column and allowed to interview contributors to the magazine such as H. E. Bates, Geoffrey Household, Ray Bradbury, Paul Gallico, which gave me new insights into the different ways that writers worked.

I was living in a one-room flat in Wimbledon and my children were living with an ex-sister-in-law who ran a small school in south London for children with parents abroad; I had them at weekends. This was a

miserable situation for all of us and I was resolved to change it as soon as I could scrape up enough money to buy a dwelling—Ron had left me with nothing but debts. So I worked like a beaver, selling stories to *John Bull, Housewife, Vogue,* any magazine that would take fiction other than the woman's sob-type. Jean LeRoy encouraged me to write more and more stories. But I began to feel this was an uneconomic use of time; I wanted to write longer pieces of fiction that would sell for larger sums, and did manage to sell a couple of 30,000-word suspense stories to a monthly, *Everywoman,* which used them serially. These I later expanded into mystery novels, *The Silence of Herondale* and *Died on a Rainy Sunday.*

The work on *Argosy* was of infinite value to me, and I shall always be grateful to the editor-in-chief, D. M. Sutherland, whose shrewd editorial sense taught me a terrific amount about how to improve my work, as well as other people's. One of the more eccentric tasks I was given consisted of writing stories to accompany left-over glossy illustrations bought by our sister magazine *Woman's Journal* from American periodicals such as *Redbook* or *Saturday Evening Post* and then, for one reason or another, not used. One of these illustrations—two people on a beach, a cat, an oil painting—stimulated me to a 30,000-word effort which *W. J.* turned down, but I later enlarged it into my little mys-

White Hart as a pub, about 1930

tery *Night Fall*, which won a Mystery Writers of America Edgar for a teenage mystery in 1971.

After four years on *Argosy* I was offered free accommodation for self and children in Sussex in the beautiful farmhouse of Martin's brother Basil Armstrong, in return for a bit of driving. The children could go to the village school and we'd be together, and I would risk free-lancing. My bosses at Argosy told me I was mad, and gave me the chance of commuting up and down for a three-day week at the same pay I was getting. I began doing this, cramming a week's work into the three days and doing my own writing at home. But the sharing plan with Basil and his wife didn't work out; his health deteriorated, they decided they must move to a smaller house in a town. I had to look, fast, for accommodation for me and the kids, found a house in Petworth unbelievably cheap at £1800—it had been empty for six years and was semi-derelict—borrowed £300 from my mother for the deposit, got a huge mortgage from Barclays Bank, and moved in, with £50 worth of junk furniture from auction sales. That was a happy day: the children rushed about hammering in nails to hang their clothes on, and I for the first time actually had a study, a room to be devoted to nothing but writing. White Hart House, a Tudor ex-pub, was like a rabbit warren inside, with rooms leading out of other rooms, panelled downstairs, sloping ceilings and low doorways above; it was a happy, eccentric dwelling, Jeake's House in miniature, a wonderful house for writing; we stayed in it twenty years and I must have written nearly forty books there. My mother and Martin, still at Farrs, were only five miles off; lacking a father, the children would at least have grandparents close at hand.

One of the first things I did at White Hart was to fish out those two chapters of *Bonnie Green* which I had begun in Chipstead seven years before, and finish the book. It almost wrote itself, I picked up the mood and voice again so speedily.

While in London I had revised, yet again, the book I had written at seventeen, *The Kingdom and the Cave,* and it had been published by Abelard-Schuman. My agents sent them the new one; they accepted it, but were doubtful about it: too frightening, they thought. Would I make it milder, take out some of the wolves? No, I wouldn't. Terrified, wondering if I was mad, I asked David Bolt, who now handled novels at Pearn Pollinger and Higham, to withdraw it and send it somewhere else. He said he would. A year went by. I finally plucked up courage to ask what had happened to my book? Apologetically he confessed that he had forgotten all about it. It was on his office windowsill under a lot of stuff. He would send it to a publisher at once; whom did I suggest? I suggested Cape, who had

published my two collections of stories. Within two weeks I had a lovely letter from Michael Howard at Cape. They saw that the book was meant to be funny; they wanted to publish it. But the title—could I think of something more exciting? So *The Wolves of Willoughby Chase* was retitled. It did moderately well in England, then much better in America, where a wonderful review in *Time* magazine helped sales.

Two years after the move to White Hart I left *Argosy*—though continuing to read and edit for them at home—and worked for a year as a copywriter at J. Walter Thompson's London office. The work there was fun and well paid, but it meant leaving home at 7:30 A.M. and not returning till 8:30 P.M.; I hardly saw the children, and my daughter, aged eight or nine, was showing signs of deprivation. For the second time I decided to leave office work and write full time, and this time I brought it off. The first thing I wrote was a sequel to *The Wolves—Black Hearts in Battersea*. That, too, was wonderful fun to write. I wanted it to be like *The Wolves* only more so—more wolves, a kidnapping, a long-lost heir, underworld nineteenth-century London, a bomb plot, a tragic death—all the ingredients I hadn't managed to cram into the previous book. Instead of taking seven years, it took seven months—I wrote it all in one happy whizz. It and *The Wolves* were set in an imaginary historical period, the reign of James III of England, which I have used intermittently ever since. I did use, however, a lot of real historical detail, and after I had accumulated quite an amount of research material I began writing adult historical fiction of a more serious kind.

After *Black Hearts* I followed a more or less instinctive pattern of alternating juvenile and adult books—with a kind of cementing mix of short stories in between and all around; these ultimately result in short-story collections when enough of a particular kind have accrued to form a book.

My adult books were thrillers at first. Isabelle Taylor, the mystery editor at Doubleday (who had published *Wolves* and *Black Hearts*) wrote asking if I had any adult material; I showed her my *Everywoman* stories, and it was her help and advice that encouraged me to expand them into books.

Jean LeRoy, my first agent, was immensely helpful to me when I was getting started, in persuading me to write short stories and finding markets for them; at that time I had neither the time nor the confidence to produce anything longer, though I did begin a novel which later turned into *The Ribs of Death* (in the U.S. *The Crystal Crow*). Jean, a forceful and dominating character, told me sternly, over and over again, that I had no talent at all for the novel form, that I would never produce one, but that I could write a classic short story and should stick to that genre. *The Wolves of Willoughby* she dismissed as clever pastiche, not likely to lead anywhere. Instinctively I began to rebel against this didactic attitude and to wish for a different mentor. In 1962 I went to the U.S. for the first time, with the children, to visit Conrad, who now had a house on Cape Cod. He paid our fares for a six-week visit. *Wolves* was about to come out there, and we went to New York to meet the Doubleday children's editor, lovely Peggy Lesser. Since Pearn Pollinger and Higham's connecting agency in New York, Harold Ober, had done nothing for me, Conrad had suggested that I should switch to his agents, Brandt and Brandt; so I met Charles Schlessiger at Brandt, and thus began a lifelong friendship. Charles is so enthusiastic, participatory, helpful, untiring, that I can't imagine a writing life without him. No one could possibly ask for a more concerned and caring agent. In England, therefore, I switched to Brandt's connecting agency, A. M. Heath.

On the whole, in my working life as writer, I have not had the intense creative relationship with any editor that some writers achieve. During twenty-five-odd years I have now passed through the hands of numerous editors at my four main publishers, Cape, Gollancz, Doubleday, and Delacorte Press; most of these have been kind, helpful, reasonable; many—Larry Ashmead, George Nicholson, Olga Litowinsky, Carolyn Blakemore—have turned into long-standing friends; but, by and large, they have confined themselves to working on what I produce, and not pointing out further possibilities. Perhaps I am resistant to that. Though I did miss Isabelle and Larry when they left Doubleday. Lately I have had some juvenile books published by Charlotte Zolotow, for Harper, and am

impressed by Charlotte's perceptive and highly creative attitude—not surprising since she is a fine author in her own right. I look forward with excitement to this new relationship.

Meanwhile my children (to whom at first I read books as they were written) grew up and left home. I moved to a house, still in Petworth, with fewer, larger rooms and a larger garden: The Hermitage. It is slightly haunted but I have not seen the ghost. I have written a trilogy of books about it—*The Smile of the Stranger, The Weeping Ash, The Girl from Paris*.

In the mid '70s I married an American, Julius Goldstein, a painter, and now spend a portion of the year in his hometown, Manhattan. This has inevitably affected my writing life, made me more aware of the American literary scene, though not to the point of feeling confident enough, yet, to lay any fictional work in America. Manhattan itself I love—its bookstores, coffee shops, movie houses—in many ways I feel more at home there than in London, which is invested with too many sad associations.

Julius Goldstein, about age thirty

The Hermitage, 1977: Liz (left), John, and Joan

Every writer needs a sounding-board reader. My sister and I perform this function for each other. We read each other's books in manuscript, first draft, and vigorously criticise. I find this an essential stage of the process: comment by a detached critic, assessment by a fresh eye. One may become so involved in writing that obvious faults or needless complications pass unnoticed. Having this built-in sisterly critic is why, I suppose, I have not felt the need for a highly creative editor. Of course when my mother and Martin and Conrad were still alive, first copies of Jane's and my books went automatically to them and we relished their comments. In the case of Martin and Conrad these were often acutely critical—though Conrad could be heart-warmingly enthusiastic too. Our mother was critical, too, shrewdly so, but subjective; she inevitably saw herself as any villainess depicted. But her pride in having two novelist daughters was a great and touching pleasure.

With over sixty books listed on the British Public Lending Right register I feel I have achieved my ambition to be a professional writer. I know that my books

vary. Some I am proud of; some are mere jobs of work, money-earners; a couple now fill me with slight embarrassment. Which do I love best? A pair of books with Spanish settings—*Go Saddle the Sea* and *Bridle the Wind*. Sometimes when you write a book you can feel it take off and lift away from you into unexplored regions—I felt those two did that. With short stories this experience is much more frequent; so, if I am remembered in future times, I think it more likely that it may be for some of those, *Crusader's Toby*, or *The Man Who Pinched God's Letter*, or *More Than You Bargained For*.

More than I bargain for, really.

© Joan Aiken Enterprises Ltd. 1985

BIBLIOGRAPHY

FOR CHILDREN

Fiction:

All You've Ever Wanted, and Other Stories (illustrated from drawings by Pat Marriott). London: J. Cape, 1953.

More Than You Bargained For, and Other Stories (illustrated from drawings by P. Marriott). London: J. Cape, 1955; New York: Abelard, 1957.

The Kingdom and the Cave. (Illustrated by Dick Hart) London: Abelard-Schuman, 1960; (illustrated by Victor Ambrus) Garden City, N.Y.: Doubleday, 1974.

The Wolves of Willoughby Chase (illustrated from drawings by P. Marriott). London: J. Cape, 1962; Garden City, N.Y.: Doubleday, 1963.

Black Hearts in Battersea. (Illustrated by Robin Jacques) Garden City, N.Y.: Doubleday, 1964; (illustrated from drawings by P. Marriott) London: J. Cape, 1965.

Nightbirds on Nantucket. (Illustrated from drawings by P. Marriott) London: J. Cape, 1966; (illustrated by Robin Jacques) Garden City, N.Y.: Doubleday, 1966.

Armitage, Armitage, Fly Away Home (illustrated by Betty Fraser). Garden City, N.Y.: Doubleday, 1968.

A Necklace of Raindrops, and Other Stories (illustrated by Jan Pienkowski). London: J. Cape, 1968; Garden City, N.Y.: Doubleday, 1968.

The Whispering Mountain. London: J. Cape, 1968; (illustrated by Frank Bozzo) Garden City, N.Y.: Doubleday, 1969.

Night Fall. London: Macmillan, 1969; New York: Holt, 1971.

A Small Pinch of Weather, and Other Stories (illustrated by P. Marriott). London: J. Cape, 1969.

Smoke from Cromwell's Time, and Other Stories. Garden City, N.Y.: Doubleday, 1970.

All and More (contains *All You've Ever Wanted, and Other Stories* and *More Than You Bargained For, and Other Stories*). London: J. Cape, 1971.

Joan Aiken, in America, 1972

Barbara Sproul

The Cuckoo Tree. (Illustrated from drawings by P. Marriott) London: J. Cape, 1971; (illustrated by Susan Obrant) Garden City, N.Y.: Doubleday, 1971.

The Kingdom under the Sea, and Other Stories (illustrated by J. Pienkowski). London: J. Cape, 1971.

Green Flash, and Other Tales of Horror, Suspense, and Fantasy. (includes *Belle of the Ball* and *The Dreamers*). New York: Holt, 1971.

A Harp of Fishbones, and Other Stories (illustrated by P. Marriott). London: J. Cape, 1972.

The Escaped Black Mamba (as told in "Jackanory" by Bernard Cribbins; illustrated by Quentin Blake). London: British Broadcasting Corp., 1973; published as *Arabel and the Escaped Black Mamba*, London: Knight, 1984.

Tales of Arabel's Raven (as told in "Jackanory" by Roy Kinnear; illustrated by Q. Blake). London: J. Cape, 1974; published as *Arabel's Raven.* Garden City, N.Y.: Doubleday, 1974.

The Bread Bin (as told in "Jackanory" by B. Cribbins; illustrated by Q. Blake). London: British Broadcasting Corp., 1974.

Midnight Is a Place (illustrated from drawings by P. Marriott). London: J. Cape, 1974; New York: Viking, 1974.

Not What You Expected (includes *The People in the Castle*). Garden City, N. Y.: Doubleday, 1974.

A Bundle of Nerves: Stories of Horror, Suspense, and Fantasy. London: Gollancz, 1976.

Mortimer's Tie (as told in "Jackanory" by B. Cribbins; illustrated by Q. Blake). London: British Broadcasting Corp., 1976.

The Skin Spinners: Poems (illustrated by Ken Rinciari). New York: Viking, 1976.

The Faithless Lollybird, and Other Stories (includes *Crusader's Toby* and *The Man Who Pinched God's Letters;* illustrated by P. Marriott). London: J. Cape, 1977; (illustrated by Eros Keith) Garden City, N.Y.: Doubleday, 1978.

The Far Forests: Tales of Romance, Fantasy, and Suspense. New York: Viking, 1977.

Go Saddle the Sea (illustrated by P. Marriott). Garden City, N.Y.: Doubleday, 1977; London: J. Cape, 1978.

Mice and Mendelson (illustrated by Babette Cole; music by John Sebastian Brown). London: J. Cape, 1978.

Tale of a One-Way Street, and Other Stories (illustrated by J. Pienkowski). London: J. Cape, 1978; Garden City, N.Y.: Doubleday, 1980.

Mortimer and the Sword Excalibur (as told in "Jackanory" by Bernard Cribbins; illustrated by Q. Blake). London: British Broadcasting Corp., 1979.

The Spiral Stair (as told in "Jackanory" by Bernard Cribbins; illustrated by Q. Blake). London: British Broadcasting Corp., 1979.

Arabel and Mortimer (illustrated by Q. Blake). British Broadcasting Corp./J. Cape, 1980; Garden City, N.Y.: Doubleday, 1981.

The Shadow Guests. London: J. Cape, 1980; New York: Delacorte, 1980.

The Stolen Lake (illustrated by P. Marriott). London: J. Cape, 1981; New York: Delacorte, 1981.

Mortimer's Portrait on Glass (as told in "Jackanory"; illustrated by Q. Blake). London: British Broadcasting Corp., 1982.

The Mystery of Mr. Jones's Disappearing Taxi (as told in "Jackanory"; illustrated by Q. Blake). London: British Broadcasting Corp., 1982.

Bridle the Wind (sequel to *Go Saddle the Sea*). London: J. Cape, 1983; New York: Delacorte, 1983.

The Kitchen Warriors (illustrated by Jo Worth). London: British Broadcasting Corp./Knight Books, 1983.

Mortimer's Cross (illustrated by Q. Blake; includes *The Mystery of Mr. Jones's Disappearing Taxi* and *Mortimer's Portrait on Glass*). London: British Broadcasting Corp., 1983; New York: Harper, 1984.

Fog Hounds, Wind Cat, Sea Mice. New York: Macmillan, 1984.

Up the Chimney Down, and Other Stories (illustrated by P. Marriott). London: J. Cape, 1984.

The Last Slice of Rainbow (illustrated by Margaret Walty). London: J. Cape, 1985.

Plays:

Winterthing (illustrated by Arvis Stewart; music by J. S. Brown). New York: Holt, 1972.

Winterthing [and] The Mooncusser's Daughter (music by J. S. Brown). London: J. Cape, 1973.

The Mooncusser's Daughter (illustrated by A. Stewart; music by J. S. Brown). New York: Viking, 1974.

Street (illustrated by A. Stewart; music by J. S. Brown). New York: Viking, 1978.

Moon Mill, first produced at Unicorn Theatre, London, 1982.

FOR ADULTS

Fiction:

The Silence of Herondale. Garden City, N.Y.: Doubleday, 1964; London: Gollancz, 1965.

The Fortune Hunters. Garden City, N.Y.: Doubleday, 1965.

Trouble with Product X. London: Gollancz, 1966; published as *Beware of the Bouquet.* Garden City, N.Y.: Doubleday, 1966.

Hate Begins at Home. London: Gollancz, 1967; published as *Dark Interval.* Garden City, N.Y.: Doubleday, 1967.

The Ribs of Death. London: Gollancz, 1967; published as *The Crystal Crow.* Garden City, N.Y.: Doubleday, 1968.

The Windscreen Weepers. London: Gollancz, 1969.

The Embroidered Sunset. London: Gollancz, 1970; Garden City, N.Y.: Doubleday, 1970.

The Butterfly Picnic. London: Gollancz, 1972; published as *A Cluster of Separate Sparks.* Garden City, N.Y.: Doubleday, 1972.

Died on a Rainy Sunday. London: Gollancz, 1972; New York: Holt, 1972.

Voices in an Empty House. London: Gollancz, 1975; Garden City, N.Y.: Doubleday, 1975.

Castle Barebane. London: Gollancz, 1976; New York: Viking, 1976.

The Five-Minute Marriage. London: Gollancz, 1977; Garden City, N. Y.: Doubleday, 1978.

Last Movement. London: Gollancz, 1977; Garden City, N.Y.: Doubleday, 1977.

The Smile of the Stranger. London: Gollancz, 1978; Garden City, N.Y.: Doubleday, 1978.

A Touch of Chill. London: Gollancz, 1979; New York: Delacorte, 1980.

The Lightning Tree. London: Gollancz, 1980.

The Weeping Ash. London: Gollancz, 1980; Garden City, N.Y.: Doubleday, 1980.

A Whisper in the Night. London: Gollancz, 1982; New York: Delacorte, 1984.

The Young Lady from Paris. London: Gollancz, 1982; published as *The Girl from Paris.* Garden City, N.Y.: Doubleday, 1982.

Foul Matter. London: Gollancz, 1983; Garden City, N.Y.: Doubleday, 1983.

Mansfield Revisited. London: Gollancz, 1984; Garden City, N.Y.: Doubleday, 1985.

Nonfiction:

The Way to Write for Children. London: Elm Tree, 1982; New York: St. Martin's, 1982.

Translator of:

The Angel Inn, by Sophie De Ségur (illustrated by P. Marriott). London: J. Cape, 1976; Owings Mills, Md.: Stemmer House, 1978.

Sound recordings:

The Wolves of Willoughby Chase, Caedmon, 1978.

A Necklace of Raindrops, Caedmon, 1978.

Sue Ellen Bridgers

1942-

I have always loved the One Hundred Thirty-ninth Psalm in which the psalmist sings that his whole life is written in God's book. These words appeal to me, not only because of the implication that I am known to God in a special way, but also because of the image of a book, the actual writing of a history of which my life is a part.

I can't remember a time when I wasn't interested in my connection to other people. "How is this person kin to me?" was one of my favorite questions and one my grandmother Abbott loved to answer. She, too, felt keenly the blood attachments of her family, and drawing from the rich store of her memory, she wove a continuous, dramatic tale of powerful relationships, of connections to the land and the homeplace, of survival. Through her, my heritage was laid out on a map of family memories and there it has remained.

If there is a book with my life written in it, I'm sure that my conscious memories are only tiny, sporadic visions of all the experiences, thoughts, and dreams recorded there. My earliest memory is of my great-grandmother McGlohon. For most of my life I believed I had dreamed of being with her, of seeing her at a distance and then closer and closer until I was looking up at her. This face looking down into mine is crystal clear to me, as if it is a photographic image locked in my brain. Only recently did I discover that this vision of her was not a dream at all but a recurrent happening. Almost every day when I was a baby, my mother carried me down the hall to the room where my great-grandmother was bedridden. I would lie on the bed next to her and she would talk and play with me. I was only eighteen months old when she died.

What is memory that all these years later I am filled with a tearful kind of joy, with such a powerful remnant of love that I am still warmed by it? Memory comes to us floating on smells; it pierces our bustling days with incongruous sounds, makes us pause at a name, an address, a postcard, a photograph, a baby bonnet, a china plate. A melody, a phrase of speech, the walk of someone approaching us on the street, the feel of a certain kind of cloth, makes us remember. Sometimes we can't even discern the stimulus; suddenly we are captured by a memory, locked into another time and, for just a moment, we are someone we used to be.

Bett Abbott Hunsucker with daughters Sandra and Sue Ellen, 1944

I was born afraid of water. I don't think I almost drowned; no one maliciously tossed me off a pier or dropped me into a wave. I was afraid of water in the dishpan, in the bathtub, in an overflowing street gutter. Getting my hair washed was an ordeal that announced my plight to the entire neighborhood. I screamed myself into a frenzy whether a drop of water splashed into my eyes or not. I sat on the sand with my back to the ocean.

I dreaded the swimming pool, hated the dank chlorine smell of the dressing room, the slick footbath we stepped into, the slippery cement, the other children sailing happily over my head as I clung to the side in two feet of greenish water. When I finally learned to swim, it was with a thrashing, anxious motion that exhausted me but by which I eventually reached the other side of the pool without drowning.

I was baptized when I was twelve years old in the baptismal pool behind the pulpit in the Winterville (North Carolina) Missionary Baptist Church. In line with my girlfriends, all of us wearing white dresses, barefooted, prepared to share this experience as we had so many in our childhoods (it was as much a club initiation as anything else), I lay the burden I alone carried (all my friends were good swimmers) in the hands of God and Edward G. Cole, our minister who fished with my father as faithfully as he did everything else. I had seen those tanned fingers dig into a pail of shrimp bait, tie a fly, catch a glistening, flapping trout in mid-air, tighten a winch. I trusted those hands and they didn't fail me. I survived baptism.

I have always loved my sister, but I doubt she can say the same about me. In fact, she has admitted that during our childhood she hated me occasionally but intensely. And no wonder. I came screaming into her life ten days before her second birthday. At first colicky, then a miserable teether, I generated a certain amount of confusion, frustration, and hostility in the small, one-bedroom apartment where she had so recently reigned as queen. I used to bite her but I don't remember what she did to me to precipitate my going for her leg. Surely I didn't bite without cause, knowing that some punishment would follow her screaming charge to Mother.

Mother was not an especially strict disciplinarian. Her spankings "hurt her more than they did us," a probable truth since she had a notoriously weak wrist. Neither Sandra nor I wanted to be first in line since the second victim always received a lighter punishment. One of Mother's frequent disciplinary measures (and one we could hardly object to) was to make us sit in our small rockers until she saw some sign of contrition. Every time she left the room, we moved our chairs around holding them tight to our behinds so we would always be sitting. Our worst punishment was simply her disapproval, a quivering sigh of disappointment that we were less than good.

Every afternoon while we napped, she polished our white hightop shoes and washed the laces. Because of the war, rubber was scarce and there were no rubber pants, no teething rings, few nipples for the sterilized baby bottles. Mother once drove ninety miles to Raleigh to get a teething ring which turned out to be plastic, wearing precious tires in the process. While my sister liked to be fed, washed, and generally cared for, I rebelled. I thought I could do everything for myself and always tried.

In July before I entered first grade, our brother Abbott was born. Sandra and I were hoping for a boy and our Aunt Sue drove us all over town in "Blue Heaven," her 1936 Dodge sedan, going slowly so we could hang out the windows grinning ear to ear and shouting to everyone we passed, "We've got a baby brother!" The whole town smiled back at us, except for Thomas McLawhorn who stuck out his tongue and said with all the vehemence a six-year-old could muster, "I reckon you think you're something now because you've got a brother." His mother had brought home a baby sister a few weeks before.

We lived between two houses. At the turn of the century, Pa—my father's father, Richard Hunsucker—had begun the haphazard building of one of those houses. Pa built the first three rooms before he married. He was a conservative man of German descent who had come to eastern North Carolina to ply his skill as a carriage builder. Hunsucker buggies and surries were popular modes of transportation in the area for many years. Four years after his arrival in

Wayland Hunsucker with son Abbott, 1949

Winterville, he married Rosa Cox, the oldest daughter of the town's founder, "leaning on the arm of his best man," according to the newspaper account. As their family grew, so did the house. Eventually it sprawled across the lawn, a collection of gables and oddly shaped rooms with a porch that zigzagged across the front like a piece of rickrack trim.

Pa died soon after I was born. Ma lived until I was fourteen. We saw her frequently but our formal family visit was on Sunday nights. The grown-ups (there was always one or more of Daddy's six siblings in attendance) visited with Ma in her sitting room while the children were relegated to the parlor accompanied by Alice, our aunt who lived at home with Ma. Alice's task was to keep us entertained while the adults talked. She read to us (we especially liked the Peter Painter stories which appeared in a regional magazine), played Parcheesi, Bible Lotto, or held a Quaker meeting, the only rule of which was complete silence. We acted out our conversation which inevitably resulted in gales of uncontrollable laughter. In desperation, Alice would march us to the kitchen where she made fudge, popped corn, or served the crisp lemony tea cookies she always kept in a tin for Ma's afternoon entertaining. As we got older, we joined the conversation in Ma's room although we were careful to be seen more than heard. At Ma's, we were expected to be "good." Although I remember many happy times there, the "feel" of the house was nonetheless one of strict discipline, of self-control, of judgments passed down with sighs and frowns.

Then there was the Abbott house where my mother had grown up. It was symmetrical, open, deep. If a child stood in the front door in the summertime, she could see the sun at the back, see patches of light in the open doorways along her path, view books, paintings, china and silver, camellias floating in glass bowls, gilded mirrors that reflected each other. But in the winter, when the doors were shut and no light or heat pervaded the hallway until night when the bedroom fires were lit, the hall was like a dungeon, a walk in a horror house where floorboards and shutters creaked, shadows took on monstrous proportions and bloody hands were waiting to pull children into secret passages where they'd never be seen or heard of again.

This was a house for the imagination. In the window seat in the living room I was Jo reading and scribbling as in *Little Women.* On a chaise lounge in the front bedroom I died many deaths. Before a dresser mirror I preached sermons that began with biblical texts and wandered into fairy tales, liberally strewn with bits of poetry and nursery rhymes. On my knees at Grandmother's mahogany and brass tea table, I was an English lady. On cold evenings, with the smell of cedar and

Four generations, 1942: Mother, Bett Abbott Hunsucker; grandmother, Annie McGlohon Abbott; great-grandmother, Elizabeth Kittrell McGlohon holding Sandra. "Mother was expecting me at the time."

winter fruit permeating the warm air of the closed-in back porch and firelight licking the glass pane of Grandmother's stove, I was a pioneer girl. In summer, my sister and I created a world of our own on blankets spread in the pale shade of a weeping willow in the side yard. At night we listened to the frogs that lived near the fish pool, creaking the porch glider between "rib-bits." Here I learned to play "Sally in Her Petticoat" on the piano, listened to Grandmother quote poetry and read Granny Fox stories. (When she became a great-grandmother, it seemed natural that my children call her Granny Annie which was her family name for eighteen years, until she died at the age of ninety-five.) Here I heard the stories of her childhood, of growing up among the McGlohon clan a few miles away at Renston. Here I learned what dying meant, for she could not speak of her dead sisters or her small son without a hard shuddering in her chest that told me she was still bereft and would forever be.

In this house emotions ran high. There was constant company and more work than could ever be done. The emotional demands of her extended family left Grandmother exhausted. Exhaustion made her irritable and demanding. Everybody loved her and she, wearied with protecting her family against the odds of human failure, had little energy to love anyone. The home she created collapsed around her periodically, brought down by her frustration that domestic help was shiftless, that her favorite child had died as the result of a freak accident, that her husband lacked the social aptitude and interests she treasured, that her daughter had missed the family beauty by being black-haired, dark-eyed, a foreign child. She was plagued by terrible headaches and palpitations of the heart. The emotional support she needed she found in her daughter, heaping on her the same expectations and obligations and limitations she felt herself.

Here family life was exposed. Here I was afraid and yet loved. Here I was valued and accepted, but I felt responsibilities too. On Saturdays I set the Sunday table for Grandmother, cherishing each piece of china, each stem of crystal, each dull silver spoon. I pinched off bits of dough from the doughboard to make funny peaked biscuits. I stirred the peach preserves for her to keep them from scorching. I held the casing to the sausage stuffer on hog-killing days. I tried to sew at her pedal machine and made disastrous attempts at embroidery. I delighted in turning the crank handle of the huge victrola, sending whiny recorded hymns into the gloomy hallway.

I took courage approaching her backsteps which were always covered with cats who wouldn't give footspace unless nudged. I didn't like cats. Once when Grandmother was laid up with a broken arm, she sent me out into the backyard to rescue a baby kitten who had been abandoned in a rainstorm. I was terrified at the prospect of touching the limp, mewing little body, but I was more afraid of Grandmother's ire. The kitten died but at least it didn't drown, and I did not disappoint Grandmother.

The house my parents built, and into which we moved when I was six, was beside Grandmother's. Ma's house was perhaps a half-mile away, on the other end of Winterville, an easy walk. One block over from us lived Ma's sister, my great-aunt Dora, in the house their father had built in 1880. Out in the country three miles from Winterville was Renston where Grandmother had grown up. Although the McGlohon homeplace was deserted, the mill and store owned by her parents were still in operation, run by my uncle. We were surrounded by kin.

The lessons of such an upbringing are both difficult and joyful. There were perhaps too many eyes focused on us and yet there was an abundance of concern and well-intentioned affection. We learned to be proud of our heritage; we knew the unyielding, power-ful hold of family; we recognized our dependence on the land, on the weather, on the changing seasons, on daily physical labor. It was the love of land that shaped our lives. Both my grandfathers, in addition to being businessmen, were farmers. Their wives had brought to their marriages large tracts of fertile tobacco and cotton land, packhouses, tenant houses, curing barns, dense woods. Our family's tenacity was itself a product of the earth, for the land was truly priceless then. Its connective powers bonded as much misery as joy, as much history as prospects for the future. It gave us boundaries but also space. This is where I come from, I could always say, holding a dark clump of soil in my hand. And then, opening my fingers, I could watch it fall.

Mother and Daddy's first child, a daughter named Susan Elizabeth, died the day she was born. Sandra Elizabeth was born the next year. Two years later I arrived on my Aunt Sue's birthday, September 20, 1942. Aunt Sue asked if she could name me Sue Ellen and Mother approved. When I was three I became ill, the main symptom being a continuous low-grade fever. Because I already had an enlarged heart and a murmur, my case was diagnosed as rheumatic fever and I led a sort of semi-invalid life for several years. I don't remember this as much of a hardship on me but I'm sure Mother found it difficult to keep me quiet. Rest was the only recommended therapy other than a terrible-tasting liquid, occasional penicillin shots, and treatments in the doctor's office that are best left undescribed.

The pediatrician was in Greenville, eight miles away. Usually Mother drove but sometimes we went on the bus. We always went up to the doctor's office in a freight elevator enclosed in a black metal grid, the door of which unfolded to shut us in, in the most sinister fashion. After being seen by the doctor, we always went to the drugstore and sat on the spinning stools to have a fountain Coke mixed by the waitress and "nabs." If anything appeased my bad disposition more than a trip to the drugstore with its black-and-white tile floor, its heavy medicinal smells mingling with cosmetics and cola syrup, it was getting a new coloring book from a rack in the dime store next door. My favorites were those which purported to depict the daily lives of popular movie stars. Even better than that was going to the movies.

Mother took Sandra and me as often as she could. Those were the days of musicals, when Jane Powell or Doris Day could break into song at any given moment, when Fred Astaire danced everywhere, even on the ceiling (we went home and tried to figure out how), and Judy Garland and Van Johnson fell in love over

Sue Ellen, five years old

and over again. We loved them all. Equally inspiring were the biographical films—*The Great Caruso, With a Song in My Heart, Look for the Silver Lining.* When we were small, we went on Sunday afternoons when the Technicolor movies played. As we grew older, we finagled rides to the Saturday afternoon matinees as well and took in our share of "B" westerns, adventure serials, and gangster films. We even went to the drive-in, all of us piled into Daddy's Chrysler, the staticky speaker attached to the window, trying to stay awake to see Jackie Robinson being cheered around the bases at Ebbets Field. My weekend of movies and church filled me with such dramatic fervor that I wanted to be both a movie star and a missionary.

I remember the strangeness of my first night in our new house. I was in a twin bed rather than sharing with my sister as we always had and although she was in the same room, I felt a separateness. The house felt so big after the cramped space of a one-bedroom apartment occupied by the five of us. The living room looked like a palatial hall, the kitchen big enough to throw a party in (and we did), the paneled den wonderfully cozy.

Soon we had a television and I was immediately addicted to the dramatic shows, all of them live, where

I first saw many stage actors picking up extra work in that exciting new medium. It was acting in the raw, experimental direction, strange plays written more for psychological impact than anything I had ever encountered. Then there was Ed Sullivan bringing New York to me every Sunday night. Before that snowy screen I heard arias for the first time, watched the Dying Swan and the *Pas de deux* from *The Sleeping Beauty,* saw Mary Martin washing that man right out of her hair in a portable shower stall, heard Pearl Bailey sing and talk her jive. With Edward R. Murrow, I went into the living rooms of the famous; from John Cameron Swayze, I heard what was happening in the world. From a news bulletin flashing across the screen, I learned that the Korean War was over and that there was no reason to fearfully watch the sky and race inside at the droning approach of every airplane.

Now television is too much with us; it has become a menace in our lives. But then, in the early fifties, it was a miraculous link to an expanding world.

But there was a world close at hand for me to study as well. In a small town, children see people who affect their lives and yet those people themselves may remain strangers. One such person was Henry, a deaf-mute who also had a debilitating illness that caused him to suffer tremors. Henry rode in a cart pulled by a mule and every day when he passed our house, he would seem to be nodding a greeting to us and struggling to make a lopsided smile. He was, we believed, a madman among us, and we lived in fear that one day he would spring off the cart and take us screaming through the streets while the town looked on, unable or unwilling to save us. I was a teenager before I went close enough to Henry to see that he had only one leg, the other a stump at the knee, and even then I felt not sympathy, but wariness. Even then I did not see a human being when I cast hurried, sideways glances at Henry, for over the years he had come to represent the menace of abnormality. On him I focused my early, unspeakable fears, my first inklings that all was not safe, that there was suffering that could not be soothed. And if my town, even my parents, harbored such sickness, what other horrors lay beyond the boundaries of my narrow world?

Then there was Uncle Mose, a black man who lived in a tiny house on the edge of Daddy's farm. He was an old man even then, doing odd jobs rather than a full day's work. He planted his garden in spring, kept the curing fires going in summer, picked up pecans and raked leaves in the fall, dug potatoes in winter. He would come to our house with something from his garden or with nuts in a soft, ragged paper sack or with cups of vanilla ice cream he'd bought for a nickel apiece at the store, and he'd thrust his gift at Mother and then stand there on the steps and fuss at her, while she stood in the doorway holding the sack, head bent, not really looking at him. Was she ashamed to look? What did the fussing mean?

As a child, I recognized bitterness in his voice, such discontentment at his lot in life, and yet I knew he could speak to her as he did only because he sensed in her a common ground, a core of likeness that went straight to the heart. And she, so free with the black women with whom she cleaned house, made pickles, and rendered lard, lowered her head as if she were taking a deserved tongue-lashing. What strange kinship was between them? Why didn't she talk back, spitting out her own tightly locked frustration at what life had dealt her? I don't know. Perhaps he was just a crazy old man whom the family indulged, but I remember him because together, he and my mother showed me that no race, no condition of living, no degree of ignorance or intelligence, is without its own rage and its own kind of affection.

My parents grew up together. Wayland was two years ahead of Bett in school, a good student, popular with his peers and in the community, industrious and interested in getting ahead in the world. Mother thought she was too big although in all her photographs she is tall, slender, and pretty. She played basketball and starred in the school drama productions. She went to college. Daddy wanted to, but because of the Depression, his father asked him to help out the family financially, so he began farming instead. He always regretted not having a college education.

He and Mother were married in 1937 when he was twenty-four and she was twenty-three. They visited his sister in St. Petersburg, Florida, on their honeymoon and came home to the apartment his father had fashioned out of half of a two-story dwelling he owned. Daddy's brother and his wife eventually moved into the other side of the house. Daddy had been elected mayor of Winterville when he was twenty-one years old and he served the town for thirteen years. During his administration the water and sewer system and the first telephone lines were installed. We had the first residential telephone which was the envy of all our school friends, even though there was no one for us to call. We were more excited when phones were installed in our friends' houses because finally we had someone to talk to.

When I was eleven my father suffered his first debilitating bout with mental depression. The treatment of mental illness was too modern a science for our rural area, and Mother's desperation to find him help led her to a psychiatrist in Raleigh. She drove Daddy to Raleigh twice a week and finally he was hospitalized

there. Periodically over the next fifteen years he was hospitalized, treated with medication and shock treatments until he was able to function, then sent home for a period of time during which he farmed and carried on some semblance of normality before slipping back into a catatonic, depressed state that once again required hospitalization. The effects of his illness on each of us children were individual and private. On the surface, we continued our lives, went to school, had friends over, participated in all the activities of church, school, and community life. It is to Mother's credit that she, frequently ill herself and living under tremendous emotional stress, gave us a supportive environment in which to grow, constantly reminding us of our capabilities, demonstrating every day her unflagging love and commitment to us and her intention that we use our talents both to make our way in the world and in service to the community.

I have always wanted to be a writer. The first sign was, I suppose, that I loved to be read to. Mother bought us books before we had our own resources and they were my most treasured belongings, respected but well used until the pages were soft, the bindings worn, the covers frayed. No present delighted me more than a package just so in shape and weight that it could only be a book.

I wish I could remember the first story I ever heard. I'm sure it was either a Bible story or a fairy tale. Mother read to us daily with good humor and patience because she enjoyed those moments of escape as much as we did. Never mind that our escape route became familiar, even memorized territory. There was such pleasure in knowing the next phrase. There was comfort in the shapes of the letters from which she drew those memorable visual images.

My favorite Bible stories were Old Testament ones—the stories of David, his friendship with Jonathan, how he danced before the Ark, the tragedy of Absalom. Then the story of Abraham, of the brothers Jacob and Esau and the stolen birthright, of Ruth, of Joseph and his brothers—all stories of family and separation. I was both fascinated and terrified by the theme of separation. Those stories defined a child's anxieties and yet they comforted me as well. At least they confirmed my fears rather than ignored them. They also expressed my need for some power beyond human existence.

Of all the secular stories told me, there were two I didn't want to hear and still don't like: *The Three Little Pigs* and Carolyn Bailey's *The Little Rabbit Who Wanted Red Wings*. They are both separation stories but there is no divine hand hovering over them. Mother says she used to start reading *The Three Little Pigs* with bets among family members on how far she'd get before I broke into sobs. It was always about the third line, when the little pigs decided to leave their mother and go out into the big world alone.

I was even more afraid of the little rabbit's tale, so terrified that I was struck dumb with fear at the first words and never cried at all. I would listen breathlessly to the horrible circumstances that surrounded not being recognized by one's own mother. It was too horrendous a fear to ever admit, but for many years I didn't make a wish, trying to avoid the foolish vanity that got the little rabbit into such terrible trouble.

What I did love were the adventures of Winnie the Pooh and his friends, the accompanying Milne volumes of poetry, *A Child's Garden of Verse,* the Uncle Remus stories, a host of children's books from *Poky Little Puppy* to *The Little Engine That Could,* and many more which I learned by heart.

The revelation of my life was probably the moment when, in the first grade, I connected the printed curves and angles in the books at home with the alphabet I was learning to write myself. Now I had the tools! Now I could write a poem! So I did.

I wanted to write as much as I wanted to read, maybe more so. There was a thrill about it that I still can't describe, a sort of letting go that is, at the same time, extremely focused so that in the process actual words appear on the page. I still revel in it. Even now, knowing many of the pitfalls, the difficulties, the struggles of writing, I expect and sometimes receive that burst of spontaneous creative energy I felt as a child. I am always grateful for it.

My early career as a poet was sporadic, even seasonal since most of our creative writing assignments in grammar school were associated with holidays. I covered all the angles of Halloween, Thanksgiving, Christmas, Valentine's Day, Easter, and then went on to Arbor Day, Columbus Day, any celebration I could find. By the time I was in high school I was writing personal poems, my subject matter drawn from real life. Quick and frenetic, born out of that moment of ecstasy when words would spring into my head, I wrote about a bird outside my window, the first snow of the season, the mingled smells of a kitchen on a wintry night, about being in and out of love. I sent several of these poems to a newspaper which published a daily poem and was therefore in constant need. Every one I submitted appeared in print. There was no pay but the sight of a thirteen-year-old's words on the page was heady enough. I was proving myself, at least to myself.

I was also writing short stories. I saved enough money to buy a used typewriter and gave up writing in longhand permanently. During this time I frequently felt as if I were living two lives. At school I was involved in all the typical activities—band, chorus, clubs, cheerleading, piano practice, enjoying a social life; but in my private life, in my room, I was a writer. It is hard to sustain a writer's energy, especially when one has no understanding of it. I didn't know how to tap into it, only felt the necessity of using it when it appeared. I banged the typewriter frantically as my fingers learned how to keep up with my head. I didn't know anything about planning. Wonderful beginnings met defeat on the second page because I hadn't learned about the subconscious thinking that the work required or the conscious period of discovery and thought before any successful writing could be done. I hadn't found my method but, like most people compelled to use their creative energy, I tried everything I could think of: borrowed ideas, themes, even characters; invented plots about which I knew absolutely nothing and then rebelled against the research the idea required. With all these failures, I kept on writing.

All this time, my mother supported me in her quiet, noninterfering way. She never asked to read what I was writing but took it upon herself to tell friends I was busy if they phoned or came by when the typewriter was clicking. Such an attitude from someone whose opinion you treasure is a validation of yourself; it is the beginning of dreams turned into reality.

I remember being in the car with Mother driving when I was twelve or thirteen. I remember the intersection at which we stopped for the light to change. The sensations of that moment—the lights from the service station on the corner, the other cars, the hum of our engine—are still with me. I was talking about the future the way young people do, wanting one minute to be a teacher, the next an engineer. I thought perhaps I would be a nurse. "Oh, Sue Ellen," she said almost sternly, as if to make finally clear what she had always known, "you are going to be a writer." And so I am.

The road took turns I didn't expect. I entered college in the fall of 1960. The trip took twenty minutes on the narrow "tar road" to East Carolina College in Greenville. I knew the campus. It was where Mother had taken me to concerts and plays, where as high school students, my friends and I had cruised to get a look at the college scene. But now it was different. Now it was where I lived. My roommate was my best friend. Elizabeth Carroll and I had known each other all our lives. We were in the same classroom from the first through the eighth grades and then shared most of our high school classes. We had studied together, learned dance steps together, were cheerleaders together, ate, talked, commiserated together. We rode together on the activity bus on band trips and to ball games. She taught me to skate. We shared vacations, church pews, giggling fits, sang alto side by side in the school chorus and the church choir. She was the epitome of a good friend, for in the twenty years we shared, she was never cruel, rarely irritable, and always supportive. When we were eighteen, she was the only person I knew who could and would live with me. What I offered her, I couldn't say unless it was the security of the familiar. She knew me well.

These events colored my college life: John Glenn orbited the earth, John Kennedy visited our campus and subsequently became president, James Meredith was enrolled as the first black student at Ole Miss. We were optimistic, expectant for the future, reveling in being young. (Our music had given us that. The black bebop singers, Paul Anka, Dick Clark, and especially Elvis Presley had made being young a position of power.) And yet we spent a sleepless night during a hurricane, another during the Cuban Missile Crisis.

The first week of college I climbed the worn steps to the third floor of Austin Building and entered without knocking, a small windowless world of literary ostracism. What can compare to a college literary magazine for snobbery, pomposity, ego-tripping, and scorched coffee? It was a community completely foreign to a girl from a small-town high school, but for all its intellectual snobbery, its closed-circuited, heated relationships, it was where I wanted to be. I volunteered as a typist. Intellectuals back then didn't bother to learn to type and so I found myself indispensable, typing correspondence, copy, even drafts of would-be writers' manuscripts. I made no mention of my own ambitions and no one asked.

Meanwhile, I was reading the submitted poems, essays, stories. I was figuring out where I could fit in. I was also discovering that my work, as unpolished as it was, was better than most of theirs. In the winter, I slipped a couple of poems into the submissions box and they appeared in the spring issue. I became the book review editor. The next fall I submitted a short story. The editor read it; the associate editor read it; Ovid Pierce, writer-in-residence who also served as the magazine's advisor, read it. The pronouncement came down as if from on high. It was good. I became the associate editor.

In the fall of my junior year, Mac Hyman came to campus as visiting writer-in-residence. His office, like that of most of the English faculty, was on the third floor of Austin along with the campus radio station and the local literary society. We were all stuck under the eaves with the pigeons and it made for a congenial mix of students and faculty who took phone messages for each other, shared tables at lunch, and socialized in general. Mac who had written *No Time for Sergeants* and was working on another book while teaching American

literature, introduced me to Ben Bridgers, his office-mate who was twenty-three but looked even younger, had curly black hair, blue eyes, and a soft, Southwesternly way of speaking. Ben and I shared many academic interests although his knowledge of contemporary literature went far beyond the Southern genre I was steeped in. I could imagine us in a big, old white house surrounded by books, he writing scholarly essays in one room while I produced poems and fiction in another.

We were married in March 1963, during the break between winter and spring quarters. My professors let me take my exams early. Ben graded the last of his exams on our wedding night, turned in the grades the next morning, and we were off to Washington, D.C., to troop through the National Art Gallery. Books, art, music—we had those things in common. The next year we had a baby as well.

By the time Elizabeth Abbott was born, my life was so strange and complicated I can barely straighten it out even now. At the end of the spring quarter, Ben had resigned from his teaching job at East Carolina, suffering from academic burnout. He wanted and needed a break before tackling a doctoral program. He wasn't even sure he wanted to teach at all. With Mac's encouragement, he joined the Air Force which would provide a living while he mulled over the future. I dropped out of college and went with him to Mississippi for a year. The next year we moved to Rapid City, South Dakota, where Ben was stationed at the SAC base. There, in 1966, Jane Bennett was born. Meanwhile Ben had decided to go to law school and a chance trip to Chapel Hill during a Christmas holiday convinced him that he wanted to attend Carolina. A year-and-a-half later, we were back in North Carolina, with Ben enrolled in law school and me in an apartment across town with two small daughters and a baby on the way. Sean MacKenzie was born in March 1968, and our family was complete.

When Sean was in the first grade, I finally went back to college. We had moved to Sylva, a small town in the mountains of western North Carolina which met our basic requirements: a job for Ben, a college for me, and an Episcopal church for all of us. I graduated from Western Carolina University in 1976, the same year my first novel *Home before Dark* was published. I was finally, after so many years, a college graduate and a professional writer.

With one book to my credit and a recommendation from *Redbook* magazine, I was awarded a fellowship to the Breadloaf Writers' Conference in Vermont that summer. The next summer Ben and I took the children to England for a month, visiting many of the places already familiar from our studies. Elizabeth

Sue Ellen and Ben Bridgers on their wedding day, March 17, 1963

spent her trip with an exchange family in Lincolnshire so we were able to take Ben's teenage sister with us. Returning home, I set about writing a second book, concerned as all writers must be, that the success of the first had been a fluke.

When I was growing up, reading was a way of avoiding housework. Our other deterrents to developing any domestic skills were homework assignments and piano practice. Sandra and I have never been more than mediocre pianists but we became voracious readers. Mother considered reading a serious endeavor and she tried not to interrupt us whether we were reading *Doctor Zhivago* or the *Saturday Evening Post.* She understood that the reader must enter a book and she hesitated to call us out of an invented world into our more mundane one.

Paperback books were affordable then, most of them costing less than a dollar. We discovered writers, exchanged books, read straight through Hemingway, Fitzgerald, Steinbeck, McCullers, Porter, Wolfe, waded into Faulkner.

"Aren't you finished yet?" we would ask although we were never anxious to finish a book ourselves. School assignments introduced us to Thomas Hardy, the Brontë sisters, Jane Austen, George Eliot, Dickens. We read popular novels, too, those by Leon Uris, Allen

Drury, Daphne du Maurier. On Grandmother's shelves we discovered a first edition of *Gone with the Wind,* old copies of women's novels she'd kept, collections of poetry, the works of Sir Walter Scott.

My writing style changed with my reading. While absorbed in the poetic flow of Thomas Wolfe, I flowed a little myself. Escaping into *Tom Jones*'s country, I addressed my reader at every opportunity. When reading Hemingway, my style became spare, sentences chopped, meanings understated. Mother counted five repetitions of the word "fine" in one meager postcard I sent her from the beach.

Sandra and I read in the bathtub, in bed, sprawled on the wicker porch furniture, on the beach. rippling flourishes on an old upright piano as she played "Jesus Is Calling" and "Throw out the Lifeline," songs of tender mercy, of saving embraces, of Jesus lifting us up in gentle arms.

But then the preacher started, casting away our tinny hope, trampling it as he stomped across the rickety platform, pounding the Bible in his hand as if to destroy it. Flinging his arms wide, fingers flapping like a twenties' dancer while he roared out our doom, he exposed our unwashed souls to a God of wrath who wielded a bloody swift sword ready to cut us down if we so much as raised our sinful heads. And then he prayed. Sweat dripped off his nose, ran down his neck into his collar; splotches appeared under his arms, down the seam of his coat. He strained and sobbed and shouted. The way to salvation was made known to me: through this man to Jesus to God. Thus was the straight and narrow path to redemption.

The congregation poured forward to touch him, to reach God through this outstretched hand with its diamond ring, its manicured nails, its soft palm. We lay in the ditch, terrified of exposure, of being the last, the worst sinners, because we had come to spy not to pray, to giggle not to sing. Although watching this spectacle was irresistible, I always felt remorseful afterwards because part of me did believe. Somewhere deep inside, I harbored that black spot the preacher ranted about. I was in need of healing.

I used to put my hand on the radio. Before I saw a faith healer in action and recognized the psychological sham, saw the frenzy of it and knew what a momentary burst of adrenaline could do, I heard these messengers of renewable health on the radio. They were smooth talkers begging for donations for their ministry—"love gifts" they were called—then preaching fire and brimstone and ending with a plea for the listeners to pray with them. Without my particular prayer and my small hand touching the warm surface of the Philco, no healing could take place. I believed it! It was consistent with my belief that I was responsible for the world, that whatever action I took affected the course of all human events. My failure with the last forkful of string beans meant some child in Africa would starve. (What a terrible philosophical approach! Because millions of children heard and discarded that feeble didacticism, we did not believe until it was too late that the Third World was starving.)

In addition to being a believer, I was people-oriented. The natural world didn't interest me nearly as much as the people who inhabited our town, whom I read about, or who came alive in our family stories. I believed in the Easter Bunny, imagining a stand-up rabbit much like the one in the advertisements for *Harvey*. I believed that Jack Frost curled the leaves in fall. No matter that an actual rabbit couldn't possibly carry Easter baskets or that frost appeared with a burst of cold air from the north. For generations, our family had planted seeds in spring, tended corn, beans, cotton, tobacco through the summer, harvested the crops in the fall. I saw no miracle there, only hard work, the labor of humans set against the fickleness of the weather.

I was also gullible. My mother once told me that if I picked up an elephant the day it was born and continued to lift it daily, I would be able to pick up a grown elephant. It made sense to me.

Grandmother told of having seen Santa Claus and

her renditions of this story caused me to hold my breath, seeing in my mind's eye the flickering firelight of the bedroom and a bright red arm with its furry cuff extending across the orange glow to put a china doll in her stocking. In the bed where she lay as quiet as a mouse, she watched the shadow of the figure until it simply vanished. Then she closed her eyes, afraid to believe what she had seen but more afraid to doubt. When she opened her eyes to the gloomy, cold dawn of her room, the fire was ashes, the magical play of light and shadow forever gone, but the doll was there. It was real and she held it gently, carefully, as she would a bird's nest of blue-speckled eggs or a newborn kitten. Her belief in the mystery and magic of what could happen on Christmas Eve made it more true to me than if I had seen Santa myself. I believe in him still.

I have always believed in visions. While I've had no mystical experiences myself, I pay attention to claims of them because in my work I have seen one level of that kind of atunement. Periodically, there occurs in my mind a time of heightened awareness, of sensitivity to everything seen or heard, to every internal sensation, that makes creative energy churn until it boils to the surface, bringing actual words with it—visions made concrete, tangible, formed into these curlicues that represent our thoughts in language. Each of my books was begun because of a visionary moment, a scene that came to me spontaneously with images so potent I couldn't shake free of them.

Home before Dark began with a family whom I visualized in the car with my own family when we were on our way to Winterville for a weekend visit. *All Together Now* began with Hazard Whitaker doing a soft-shoe dance on the front porch, a scene my friend Judy Budd once described to me. The first sentence of *Notes for Another Life* was written on the edge of a pocket calendar because I was driving the car at the time. I heard a girl and her grandmother singing old popular songs, and I knew where they were going and why. I began writing *Sara Will* because I saw Sara coming down the road in the twilight. I recognized her as someone I knew.

After these visionary moments, the hard part begins: months of writing and revising, periods of doubt, moments of rapidly flowing words too intense to sustain, days of mental aridness. But with all that, I know that my writing history sounds too easy. I sent *Home before Dark* to Anne Mollegen Smith at *Redbook* asking for suggestions for placing it. *Redbook* bought the manuscript and Anne suggested I send it to Pat Ross, senior editor and later vice-president in the juvenile department at Alfred A. Knopf. Pat called within a few days to introduce herself and to say that she was enthusiastic about publishing the book. I knew absolutely nothing about young adult fiction, but I was delighted to learn Pat believed the story would find an audience among young people.

Home before Dark appeared in *Redbook* in July 1976 and the hardback edition with Knopf came out in the fall. I received the first copy in New York on my way to Breadloaf. It was beautifully produced and browsing through it, I wasn't embarrassed by it as I'd feared I might be. Instead, I felt quite detached from it. I was a little disappointed with myself because I wanted to get

immunization against the struggles and tragedies of those years. The world came to us via television and although we grieved over the Tonkin Resolution, the murders of civil rights workers in Mississippi, and the burning of Watts, I was too involved with babies and managing a household to be more than a social-gathering activist, always ready to expound the liberal Democratic ideology I was raised on.

In Chapel Hill, with three small children and a law-student husband holding down two part-time jobs on the side, I found myself trapped again, although

The Bridgers Family Portrait. Clockwise: Sue Ellen, Elizabeth, Bennett, Ben, and Sean, 1980. Painting by Shirley Grant.

really excited about this tangible evidence of my success. After all, my name on the title page of a Borzoi book had been one of my lifelong dreams.

I don't think I showed the book to anyone at Breadloaf except Toni Morrison who carefully turned it over in her hands as if testing the feel of it before saying, "A book is a good thing." That was what I needed to hear—not that I was wonderful to have written it or that it was an extraordinary accomplishment, but simply that with it, I had joined the ranks of those with an opportunity for doing a good thing. It is, beyond all else, what we are striving for.

When we moved to Chapel Hill in 1967, I went from one isolated environment to another. The Air Force (and South Dakota) had provided a kind of

most of the time I was too harried to notice. I wasn't doing what I'd intended with my life but I was achieving what seemed necessary at the moment: keeping children safe and clean, putting meals on the table, and being as thrifty as our limited income demanded. I didn't write at all. The typewriter, which I sometimes bumped against while getting the vacuum cleaner out of the closet, seemed like an enemy, a hidden menace that would, I prayed, keep silent as long as it was left undisturbed.

But where was *I* all this time? Hidden in the closet, too, I suppose. I never talked about writing. (I have not changed much in that. Writing still seems something better accomplished than talked about.) Now and then, what seemed like my secret demon raised her head to question what I was doing, chained to either the kitchen sink or the clotheslines. My response was simple and truthful: I loved the people in my care. I had responsibilities to them. There were only so many hours in the day and just having done what seemed essential, I always fell into bed exhausted. There was no time, no place for myself. I hesitate to say that I was a little mad and yet, looking back, I think I was. I was like a prisoner incarcerated in the room. The room was nice and I was busy and productive in it, and yet I knew there were other rooms I couldn't go into. The locked door was maddening, holding tight my doubts about my abilities beyond keeping house. In 1970, I gave the door a tentative push. One of the first stories I wrote was about a young woman who wanted her true self acknowledged by someone, even a stranger, for just a moment. I didn't connect the story with my own life at the time, but I see the connection now.

Ben was supportive of my fluttering attempts at writing professionally but there was little he could do to eliminate or help with the roles I fulfilled in our family. His own taxing lifestyle as student, financial supporter, and parent took all his energy. I'm pleased that the children don't remember the grind of our daily lives during those years. They remember that Daddy was home with them in the evenings from dinnertime until they went to bed. They didn't know that his only studying time was after they were asleep which prevented our having more than occasional private moments and little social life.

I sold my first stories. I wonder if I would have given up had not these small successes come so quickly. It's a question I'll never be able to answer. Wanting desperately to succeed as a writer and believing some minor success was possible, I began searching for ways to make my two lives coexist. Having opened another room, I needed to make sure it fitted with the rest of the house. I began reading the work of women writers with a conscious goal of discovering how they wrote and how they managed their lives. I attended a few feminist meetings in the Chapel Hill area that year but they involved kinds of activism I didn't have time for. Although I supported the goals of these groups, I felt my professional life was too new and needed too much nurturing for me to dissipate my meager store of creative energy on anything but my own work.

However, when we moved to Sylva in 1971, I began to look for other women who were struggling to achieve autonomy. I joined the League of Women Voters and there found a group of young women whose interests in political and social issues came directly from their personal needs for equality, places in the job market, recognition of their value as wives and mothers, but also validation of their decisions to fulfill themselves in other ways. Out of that core of women and

joined by others, we formed a consciousness-raising group which met weekly for several years, forming bonds of support and friendship that time and distance can never obliterate. Three of us—Judy Budd, Sue Hager, and I—went back to college in 1975, and Judy and I graduated together. Veronica Nicholas ran for public office and now serves as a county commissioner. All of us joined the work force.

Although I was involved in the issues crystalized by the feminist movement, I set my second novel *All Together Now* in 1951. One of the main characters, a retarded man named Dwayne Pickens, was based on a person Ben had known in Fort Smith, Arkansas, in the fifties and I wanted to set the story in the same period. *Notes for Another Life* takes place in the present and although I didn't think consciously about dealing with a feminist issue, I know that the choices the mother Karen makes reflect a growing urgency on the part of women to refuse entrapment. *Sara Will,* published in 1985 by Harper and Row, is about a woman who finds her contentment in relationships, but it is a struggle for her. She is working away from isolation into a fuller life and that is also a feminist theme. The chance to be one's authentic self is one of the goals of all worthwhile social movements, but the commitments involved must be personal choices. Those decisions come from the individual heart and mind, not from a platform or agenda.

At forty-two, I am more aware than ever before of my opportunities to make choices. My family heritage

Marching in the Sylva Christmas parade, 1975. Sue Ellen is under the sign Make Policy, Not Coffee.

Sue Ellen (left), with Sue Hager and Judy Budd before graduation from Western Carolina University, 1976

burdened and blessed me with an accumulation of maxims, dictated certain behavior, a life view which it is finally my choice to accept as my own or to reject, like uncomfortable clothing or a shoe that doesn't fit. My cousin Mary Virginia and I shared many experiences growing up in Winterville and on those joyful occasions when we are together now, we frequently compare the steps we've taken since then, each in her own place and time, to find ourselves once again on the same path like the comrades we were as children.

Mary Virginia's great-grandmother and mine were sisters-in-law and frequently, between 1980 and 1982, I spoke at conferences and in classrooms about their fierce commitment to land and family and the courage with which they survived the conditions of their difficult lives at the turn of the century. Their legacy is one their great-granddaughters share, holding close those memories of another time, and yet we want more for ourselves, more visions made reality, more choices, more boundless leaps toward creativity in our individual work. I can only believe that the women of our past would be proud.

My life has been touched by so many people, some of them mentioned here, many of them not. In 1972, Lynn Webster joined our family when she and Abbott were married. I now have a nephew Matthew and two nieces, Megan and Caitlin, who bring joy and excitement to our family gatherings. I have been fortunate that my work has had expert care and nurturing from professionals who saw a place for my characters in the publishing world. Pat Ross, Ed Davis, Suzanne Glazer, and many others at Alfred A. Knopf smoothed the path between Appalachia and New York City. My agent Elaine Markson nudged me through the door of adult fiction. Larry Ashmead at Harper and Row has treated *Sara Will* with the tenderness I think she deserves. At different times, Roger Cooper, Ron Buehl, and Judy Gitenstein at Bantam have been responsible for introducing my work to a paperback audience, resulting in a larger readership than the books would have otherwise had. Doris Bass and Laurel Barnard at Bantam continue to keep me both entertained and on schedule when on the road.

Over the past nine years I've spoken to many teachers and librarians across the country. I am always encouraged by their concern for their students and impressed with the inventiveness and enthusiasm with which they do their work. I have spoken to quite a few students as well, challenging encounters with eager minds that have forced me to think about both the subject matter and method of my work. The mail brings treasures of its own. A girl writes that reading *Notes for Another Life* helped her understand her troubled boyfriend. A sixth grader informs me that *All Together Now* is the first book he's ever read all the way through and now he thinks he'll read another one. An eighty-year-old man writes, in the florid script of another era, a vivid description of a funeral he once attended, the memory evoked by a scene in *Home before Dark.*

Christmas in Winterville, 1984. Front row: from left, Lynn Hunsucker, Bennett, Sean, Elizabeth; back row, Sue Ellen, Abbott holding Matthew, Bett holding Caitlin, Ben holding Megan, Sandra.

And so my world conjures up other worlds, brings into focus the reader's own experience, forms a magical link between writer and reader. As you have read, my personal life is an ordinary one, confined for the most part to small-town living, and yet I have gone many places that only mood and memory can take me and I expect many more such travels. A book, especially a novel, provides a journey into another heart and mind. It urges us to discover and explore. "I shan't be gone long.—You come too," Robert Frost wrote in his poem "The Pasture." Every book is such an invitation. Come and share a life, accept its special reality, be one with it for a little while. After all, we are fellow travelers; and our finest journeys, our most challenging explorations, are those of the spirit.

Sue Ellen and daughter Elizabeth before church service, 1976

BIBLIOGRAPHY

FOR YOUNG ADULTS

Fiction:

Home before Dark. New York: Knopf, 1976.

All Together Now. New York: Knopf, 1979.

Notes for Another Life. New York: Knopf, 1981.

Sara Will. New York: Harper, 1985.

Betsy Byars

1928-

Betsy and Ed at an informal soaring meet in Newcastle, Virginia, September, 1984

In 1968 my husband Ed and I went to our first soaring championship in Marfa, Texas. He was going to compete. I was going to be the crew chief. As crew chief, I was to help put the glider together, fill the wings with water, tow him to the start line, run his wing, then hook up the trailer and follow him around the course and pick him up if he landed away from the airport. The last thing I did before I left home was to buy a spiral notebook because I planned, in my spare time, to start a book.

The closer we got to Marfa, the worse I felt. A crew chief likes to see nice, mowed fields where her pilot can land, short fences, wide gates, and friendly farmers. What I saw was rocky, craggy, cactus-covered land, fences that went on for miles, and no farmers whatsoever.

I said, "Ed, where on earth do you land out here?"

He said, "On the road."

It then turned out that another of my duties was to stop truck traffic while he landed.

That night, unable to sleep in the Paisano Hotel, I wrote the first sentence in my spiral notebook. "The land is hard in southwest Texas."

Every day of the two week contest, I did something wrong, and I am not talking about minor errors. Once I didn't hook the trailer up properly and it fell off the car on a curve. Once I whipped into a gas station, pulled around the pumps, filled the gas tank, and then found out that my thirty-foot trailer was going to knock over the gas tank when I pulled out.

I tried to back up, but that made it worse. I tried to pull forward so that I could back up the other way, and that made it even worse. I ended up locked around those gas tanks so tightly it would take a miracle to get me out.

A miracle happened. Some men came out of a bar across the street, saw the crowd at the gas station and came over to help. They picked up the back of the trailer and moved it over about one inch. I then drove forward one inch. They then picked up the back of the trailer and moved it two inches. That is how I got out of the gas station, literally inch by inch. When I finally drove away, the entire crowd cheered.

My husband had been waiting for me all this time behind a mesa in the broiling sun. He said, "Where have you been?"

I described in detail the incident at the gas station and the angels of mercy who had come from the bar to help me.

He said, "Betsy, why didn't you just unhook the trailer from the car, guide it into the street, drive the car out and hook up again?"

I said, truthfully, that it would never have occurred to me in a million years. And if he hadn't told me, the next time it happened, I would have gone straight to the nearest bar to round up some drunks.

Well, what with one thing and another, when I got home, I still had only one sentence in my spiral notebook. But it was no longer just a sentence. It was the first sentence of my next book, *The Winged Colt of Casa Mia,* set in Marfa, Texas.

Some of the happiest moments in my writing career come when I have the first sentence in a book. I may not know what the plot will be, I may not know all my characters, but I can somehow get a feeling from that first sentence whether it's going to be a book or a few stray paragraphs.

One sentence. All I needed now were about 3,500 more sentences to go with it.

I had no intention of becoming a writer when I was growing up, but I had one thing in common with every other writer I've ever met. I loved books. My earliest memory is of a book.

I am sitting beside my father on the sofa, and he is reading *The Three Bears* to me. Only my father is not reading it correctly. Instead of "Somebody's been eating my porridge," he has the baby bear say, "Somebody's been eating my corn flakes."

This infuriates me. I am hitting my father, trying by brute force to make him read correctly.

It works. He does indeed read it right for a few lines. Then, as soon as I relax, and lose myself in the story, the mama bear says, "Somebody's been sleeping on my Beauty Rest mattress."

More fury. More hits. A great first memory for an author. Already I had respect for the written word.

My father was a hardworking, stern man with, surprisingly, a good sense of humor. He came from the

Guy Cromer and Nan Rugheimer, at a beach near Charleston, South Carolina, during their courtship, about 1924

agricultural part of South Carolina and went to the Citadel, a college on the coast.

While he was a cadet there, he met my mother. My mother was very pretty and lively, and I imagine he fell in love with her instantly. My mother loved acting and music and appeared in amateur shows. She had taken lessons in college in speech and dramatics.

Her interest in speech continued after her marriage and when I was about five, she arranged for me to take a series of preschool lessons in what was then called Expression.

I enjoyed my Expression lessons a lot. I cannot recall any of the poems I memorized, but there was a comic one that allowed me to roll my eyes and make a lot of faces. My mother suffered through my comic recitation for a while, but plainly it was not what she had in mind for me. I had not inherited her dramatic charm, and I soon was diplomatically shifted to piano lessons.

I really had two lives as a child. In one, we lived in the city of Charlotte on 915 Magnolia Avenue, and I did city things. In the other, we lived in the country, close to the cotton mill where my father worked. My father had majored in civil engineering in college, but because times were hard and jobs scarce, he had gone to work in the office of a cotton mill. The community was named after the mill—Hoskins.

At Hoskins we had goats and rabbits, and because I loved animals, I thought life was wonderful. Only later did I realize how hard this move must have been for my pretty mother, how she must have hated the

Betsy Byars' first formal portrait, one year old. "This is the only time I was a cute kid. It was downhill from here on."

train tracks which ran through our front yard, that her closest touch with culture was the rental library in the back of the drugstore.

We were there about three years and one of the highlights was a birthday party my mother gallantly staged for my sister Nancy.

At Hoskins, no one went to a store and bought a birthday present. Everyone just looked around their house until they found something that did not look too bad, and they wrapped it up and came to the party.

My sister got the oddest assortment of gifts that I had ever seen, and I, who loved odd things, was green with envy. One of the things she got was a pair of celluloid cuffs which office workers put on their arms to keep the sleeves of their blouses clean. I loved those celluloid cuffs. My sister could get me to do anything by letting me borrow the celluloid cuffs.

But the most memorable gift was a very tiny one, wrapped in a scrap of notebook paper. I must have been an unimaginative child, because I kept saying, 'Open the little present. Open the little present."

My sister opened it at last and there was a dime.

That gift-wrapped dime stuck in my mind for years. And later, when I was writing *After the Goat Man,*

I decided to pass it on in the school gift exchange to Harold V. Coleman. I hope someday to find a place in one of my books for the celluloid cuffs.

Nancy and I each had one party while we lived at the mill, but my sister got the best presents. I got things like a pair of pink socks that were too little and a china dog with the features washed off.

When I was in fourth grade, we moved back to 915 Magnolia Avenue, which was to be my home until I graduated from college.

Last year, I saw the house for the first time in thirty-five years. There was a For Sale sign out front. I made Ed stop the car and I went up and looked in the window, thinking the house was empty. I looked directly into the face of the woman who was looking out to see who I was. She very kindly invited me in, and I walked through the memory-filled rooms. No other house will ever hold so much of my life.

I was not particularly close to my grandparents, and I cannot remember any of them showing much

Betsy (about four) and her sister Nancy (about six) with their mother. "We wore our hair like this until we were in junior high. I am the one in the tam. Nancy is the one with the new watch."

interest in me. That suited me fine. That left me free to do what I wanted at their houses without getting caught.

I was, however, definitely interested in my Grandaddy Rugheimer's things. He was a dapper man, a tailor, of German descent. He collected rare coins, rare stamps, rare books, and rare tropical fish, all of which we were not allowed to touch. He also had a woodworking shop where he made incredibly beautiful things. We were allowed in there and the floor was always covered with beautiful curls of wood, and we attached them to our heads and pretended we were Shirley Temple.

Grandaddy Rugheimer. "He was dapper even when hiking in the North Carolina mountains."

His rare stamps, books, and coins were kept in a large closet under the stairs. I went in one time to look at some of the books.

The one I remember was a large, gilt-edged book of Bible stories. I only saw the illustrations once, but they are etched into my mind as firmly as they were into the heavy cream paper. They were dark, detailed reflections of the terrible reality of biblical times.

The Jews Descending into the Fiery Furnace, Gabriel Wrestling with the Angel of Death—I can remember those pictures to this day. But the worst was Noah's Ark.

Noah's Ark was no happy scene with the animals clomping into the ark, two by two. The ark was already afloat, in the distance. In the front of the picture was the last mountain top where the remaining desper-

ate people and animals struggled for survival.

I spent a lot of time looking at that picture, worrying about this mother and baby, that little lamb. I'm sure I asked my mother about it later, concealing where I had come across such a picture, but I never got a satisfactory answer.

As a writer, I have a good way of shedding these old childhood concerns—I pass them on to the characters in my books. So it is Harold V. Coleman, in *After the Goat Man,* who gets my Noah's ark concern when he is cast as an extra hippopotamus in a Bible school production, and I can at last put my own concern aside.

My Grandaddy Cromer had a country store which was across the street from his house. I was over there one day at the candy counter, making my daily selection, when he said he was closing the store to go pay his respects to Mr. Joe. Did I want to come along? I did.

We drove out into the country and up to a farmhouse. We got out and went to the door. "We came to pay our respects to Mr. Joe," my grandfather said.

We went inside. Mr. Joe was in a hammered-together board coffin in the living room. We walked over and my grandfather picked me up so I could see over the side. My knee hit the coffin, jarring it, and Mr. Joe's mouth popped open.

It took me a long time to get rid of that concern, but I finally managed it in *The Pinballs.* It felt a lot better when Mr. Mason's knee hit the coffin instead of mine.

When I was in junior high, my father surprised us all by buying a boat. My father had never shown any interest in becoming a seafaring man, and my mother was convinced we would all go down in the Atlantic Ocean. In 1942 we came close.

This was before the age of really good weather forecasting, and so, on a beautiful Saturday, with not a cloud in the sky, we set out on the *Nan-a-Bet* (named for Nancy and me). We planned to pull into coves and behind islands along the South Carolina coast, anchor and spend the nights. My mother wisely remained on shore.

About five the next morning, we awoke and noticed that the boat was beginning to pitch a little. By six it was pitching a lot, and my father made the decision to head back to Charleston before things got really rough.

Things got really rough before we were anywhere near Charleston. My father was frantic. The waves were enormous, and he was not a skilled seaman. This might even have been our maiden weekend voyage.

Nancy and I, however, thought it was wonderful.

The summer of 1942. Betsy and her father in the galley of the Nan-a-Bet. *"During World War II the* Nan-a-Bet *joined the Coast Guard."*

We sat in the cabin, laughing and composing our obituaries.

Finally, in midafternoon, we got a lucky break. We were slammed into shore by an enormous wave. My father tied up the boat and went looking for a phone. Nancy and I stayed with the *Nan-a-Bet*. This was fortunate because almost immediately some cute boys came to see if we needed any help.

All day my mother had been even more desperate than my father—pacing the floor, wringing her hands, crying. Her worst fear had been realized. Her husband and children were at the bottom of the Atlantic. Possibly she even chided herself for not drowning with us. As soon as she got my father's call, she drove to the site, rushed through the weeds and threw her arms around us.

This embarrassed us enormously in front of the cute boys. It was the only bad part of the whole day.

"Oh, Mother!" we said.

In all of my school years—from grade one through high school, not one single teacher ever said to me, "Perhaps you should consider becoming a writer." Anyway, I didn't want to be a writer. Writing seemed boring. You sat in a room all day by yourself and typed. If I was going to be a writer at all, I was going to be a foreign correspondent like Claudette Colbert in *Arise My Love*. I would wear smashing hats, wisecrack with the guys, and have a byline known round the world. My father wanted me to be a mathematician.

I hit high school in 1943, and the important thing—the only important thing—was to look exactly like everybody else. We wore dirty saddle shoes, angora socks, pleated skirts, enormous sweaters (sometimes buttoned up the back) and pearls. If we were fortunate enough to be going with a high school athlete, we wore his sweater. We all had long hair with curved combs in the back so we could continuously comb our hair. We had mirrors taped inside our notebooks so we could check and make absolutely sure we looked exactly like everybody else.

We used lots of makeup, I particularly because my father had given me a twenty-five dollar war bond for not wearing makeup in junior high, and I had to make up for lost time.

We were constantly on the lookout for better beauty products than the dime stores had to offer. My best friend and I discovered one day, when we were shelling walnuts, that the outside rind was leaving a gorgeous stain on our hands. Without a thought we immediately started staining our legs.

We were enormously pleased with the result and promised not to tell any of our other friends how we'd done it, so they couldn't have gorgeous legs too. We went in the house to wash our hands, which were now stained up to the wrist in the same lovely color. We learned at the sink that the lovely color was permanent. Well, not permanent—it did wear off in a week or so, but the impact of the brown legs was definitely lessened by the brown hands.

I spent a good part of my school day arranging to accidentally bump into some boy or other. I would rush out of science, tear up three flights of stairs, say a casual "Hi" to a boy as he came out of English, and then tear back down three flights of stairs, rush into home ec and get marked tardy. I was tardy a lot.

The only actual course I can remember was in math, and certainly not because I excelled. Here's what I remember. When the teacher wrote Pi on the blackboard and we saw the numbers 31416 for the first time, someone said, "That's Cro's phone number!" My nickname was Cro, and I felt like a celebrity. I've had many phone numbers over the years, but that's the only one I remember.

My other memory of the class was fame of the other kind. I was caught cheating.

We were having a test on some formulas, and it just seemed simpler to copy the formulas down on the desk rather than go to all the trouble of memorizing them.

The teacher saw the formulas and called in everyone who sat in that particular seat throughout her daily classes. There were five of us. She then asked us to write the formulas from memory. The other four could. I couldn't.

We were having an assembly program on honesty that Friday, and part of my punishment (the other part was a 0 on the test) was to listen to the lecture seated on the front row beside the math teacher. I didn't mind the 0 at all, but the memory of sitting on the front row by the math teacher still makes me shudder.

"Sister Mathematicians": Betsy (left), a senior in high school, and Nancy, a math major in college

We were never allowed to tell my father any bad news until after he had had his supper. This was my mother's ruling, and I can remember a lot of painful suppers, trying to eat, already filled with the knowledge that I had an item of bad news to break after the meal.

This particular bit of bad news was bad indeed, and I had come home from college for the weekend to break it in person. I was a sophomore, and the bad news was that I was not going to be able to be a mathematician. I was flunking calculus.

When I had gone away to college, I had not put up any real struggle against majoring in math. The only thing I really loved to do was read, but I knew I couldn't get a job doing that. Besides, my sister whose actions I had been copying successfully for nineteen years was a math major, and I, like her, had always been very quick with those problems that start out, "If one farmer can plow ten fields in one-and-a-half days, how many . . ."

Until I hit calculus and came upon sine and cosine and tangent and cotangent and secant and cosecant, I thought there was nothing in the world I could not master if I put my mind to it. This—no matter how hard I tried, and I tried hard—I could not get.

It was a desperate semester for me. My father was paying hard-earned money for me to go to college and he expected me to do well. I had discovered early in life that things were easier all around if I lived up to my father's expectations. Even in high school when I was flitting through the halls, chasing boys, I made sure I never got a grade lower than B.

Now calculus. My father had been disappointed at my midterm calculus grade which had been, to my relief a C⁻. And here's the pathetic, desperate price I had paid for my C⁻.

Dr. Bowen would pass out the tests. I would wait a moment and then go up to his desk. I would say, "Dr. Bowen, would you please start me out on problem one? I've drawn an absolute blank. I know if you do the first line for me, I can finish."

I was the only girl in any of his classes and sort of a novelty. He would, in his enthusiasm for his own problem, work the whole thing.

I would go back to my seat, and I could actually feel the scorn and resentment of the other students as I passed their desks. I couldn't help it. I had to keep up my C⁻ average.

I would try to do the next problem on my own. When I had a couple of meaningless rows of numbers and letters, I would go back to his desk and say, "Is this right? It just doesn't look the way yours did on the board last week."

He'd say, "Now, Miss Cromer, you know that's

Graduation day, June 1950: Betsy with her roommates Barbara Ann Jobe and Fronie Mims. "For some reason that I can't remember, I was class poet laureate. My poem has been lost, but unfortunately I can remember the last line: 'Our tassels turned, we begin a new age.'"

not right. Look at this."

And he'd work the second problem. The only calculus problems I ever got right were the ones he worked for me.

It was the thought of more and more desperate years like this, more and more scorn from my classmates, that sent me into the living room where my father sat in his chair by the radio, smoking a Camel cigarette.

Somehow I broke the bad news. I could not be a mathematician. Even worse, I was switching to English. There was not the terrible explosion that I had feared. To be honest, there usually wasn't.

On my final calculus exam, when Dr. Bowen was working one last problem for me, he asked if I was planning to continue with my math.

"No," I said, "I've decided not to be a mathematician." "Good," he said.

Nineteen forty-nine and fifty were great years. I was a senior at Queens College, just months away from getting out in the adult world where nobody could tell me what to do or what time I had to be in, and I had just met the man I wanted to marry. The sole cloud on the horizon of my life was that he might not ask me.

Ed was tall, good looking, witty, a wonderful dancer. He had a yellow Mercury convertible. Since he was left-handed, he had switched his gearshift over to the left side of the steering wheel, leaving his right arm free to be put around whatever lucky girl was beside him on the front seat. He had already graduated from college and was a man of the world, teaching Engineering at Clemson College. And, as if that weren't enough, he had a Stinson 1931 antique airplane. I was madly in love.

College regulations were very strict at that time at Queens College. We could only date on weekends, and even then we had to sign out and say exactly where we were going and with whom, etc.

One regulation which I obviously had to break was the one that you couldn't fly in an airplane without written permission from your parents. How could I tell a man of the world that I couldn't hop into his Stinson because I didn't have my mother's permission on file in the dean's office?

I remember one of our illegal flights well. We were on our way to Clemson for a football weekend, and we were lost a good bit of the time. The plane had very little in the way of navigational equipment, and the visibility was not good, but we finally got there by reading the names of the towns, which at that time were required to be painted on the top of the most prominent building. I thought it was great. A very cool, relaxed "Oh, that's Gaffney; we'll go this way" kind of navigation.

He proposed in the spring—or sort of proposed. I was sitting in the yellow Mercury convertible on the main street of Rock Hill, the town where his parents lived and he had grown up. He went in a store to speak to a friend. He came back and he said, "If you were going to get engaged, what kind of ring would you want?"

I said, "Oh, I don't know, maybe a diamond one."

He said, "Like this?" He reached into his pocket, took out a box and by a miracle, there it was, the most beautiful sight of my life.

I said, "Yes."

We were married two months later, on June 24. This was exactly three weeks after my college graduation.

It is no longer fashionable to admit this, but I was

Betsy and Ed, June 23, 1950, the day before their wedding

For the next five years I was a young faculty wife at Clemson and married life agreed with me. Two of our daughters were born during those years—Laurie in October of 1951 and Betsy Ann in February of 1953. I was extremely happy.

My only writing consisted of letters and shopping lists.

In 1955 Ed decided to go to graduate school at the University of Illinois. If he was going to remain in teaching—which he intended to do—he would have to have his Ph.D. degree.

We rented our house, stored our furniture, loaned our dogs to Ed's mother, packed everything else in a red trailer and took off. It was a little like going West and I was excited about it.

When we pulled up two days later in front of the barracks where we would be living for the next two-and-a-half years, my excitement faded a little. When we went inside and I saw the barracks furniture, it faded even more.

Well, I told myself, I can fix the place up with posters, and pillows and bright curtains. That took about a week. Now, I thought, I'm as settled as I'm ever going to be. I'm going to start making friends.

As it turned out, every other wife in the barracks complex either worked or was going to school. The last thing any of them wanted was to come to my house to chat. I got lonelier and lonelier. Ed went to work early in the morning and came home late. The kids, after an

very happy to be getting married instead of looking for a job. I had no work ambition. I had always wanted marriage and a family. This was fortunate because my speciality as an English major had been Old English. I could rattle off words like bitraisshe, aungellyke, and fronceles and say the Prologue to *The Canterbury Tales* by heart, but there was not a big demand in the working world for a person who knew what a clow-gelofre was.

We were married on the hottest day of the year. As we were leaving on our honeymoon some of the groomsmen rushed out and locked a cowbell and chain around Ed's neck. This was to make up for the fact that they had not been able to find the Mercury convertible and put dead fish in the hub caps.

When we finally got out of the city, there was the problem of the cowbell. Ed had said, "I think I may be able to slip the chain over my head," but of course he couldn't.

We finally found a garage that was open—it was late Saturday afternoon by this time—and in he went. I waited outside. In the garage, he laid his head on the work bench, a steady-handed mechanic sawed the chain in half, and our married life began.

The Byars family in Urbana, Illinois, 1956: "the barracks where I had two choices—write or lose my mind. I wrote."

initial period of being picked on daily, had gotten over being the new kids and were part of the gang. I alone was at loose ends. The highlight of my day was the arrival of the grocery truck after lunch.

Now up until this point in my life, while I had never done any creative writing, I had always thought that I could write if I wanted to. I thought it couldn't be as hard as people say it is. I thought probably the reason professional writers claim it's so hard is because they don't want any more competition.

I got a typewriter so old I had to press the keys down an inch to make a letter. The *i* stuck, all the circular letters were filled in, the *t*'s were noticably higher than the other letters. I was undaunted.

Years later, when I was writing *The 18th Emergency*, one of the letters started sticking on my electric typewriter, and this was so intolerable to me—I was in the middle of a chapter—that I rushed downtown in my shorts and bought a new Smith Corona.

When my husband came home and saw the old Smith Corona discarded on the floor, he asked what had happened. I explained about the stuck key, and he said, "You've got two other typewriters up in the attic. Why didn't you just get one of those down and use it?"

"I forgot," I said.

Anyway, back at the barracks apartment, I set the old typewriter by my place at the table, and that's where it stayed for two years. I would push it aside when I ate and pull it back when I got through. I wrote constantly.

My target was mainly the magazines. I would look through national magazines, see what they were publishing, write something similar and send it off. Sometimes this very amateurish approach worked.

My first sale was a short article to the *Saturday Evening Post* and I got seventy-five dollars for it. I was elated. I had known all along there was nothing to writing! Seven months passed before I sold a second article.

I was learning what most other writers have learned before me—that writing is a profession in which there is an apprenticeship period, oftentimes a very long one. In that, writing is like baseball or piano playing. You have got to practice if you want to be successful.

In my last year at Illinois—by this time our third daughter, Nan, had been born—I had become aware that I needed some help. I was selling short articles with some regularity, but I had done a mystery novel I couldn't sell and some children's books, and although I was not in despair, I certainly thought I might be able to shorten this endless apprenticeship period if I got some help.

I signed up for a writing course at the university.

I went to class on the first night with the greatest sense of hope and anticipation—not only because I was going to get some valuable professional help, but also because I was going to be in the midst of people who were writing too—living, breathing writers.

I sat there, internally vibrating with excitement. The professor got up. He started the class with this sentence: "All the people in this town who are going to be professional writers are home right now, writing."

So much for my writing class.

We moved back to Clemson, back into our home, and I set up my typewriter in our bedroom on a card table. By this time writing had become an important part of my life. I had not been able to stop in Illinois, no matter how badly things went, because I needed writing to fill my life. Now I didn't need it in that way anymore, but I still couldn't stop. Now the reason was because I loved what I was doing.

I know of writers whose creative drive begins to fade in the face of seemingly endless rejection slips. Starting a new writing project does require enormous energy, and it gets harder and harder to sustain this creative energy when you are being continuously turned down.

In Illinois—out of necessity—I developed a kind of tough, I'll-show-them attitude that I have maintained to this day. Sort of—All right, you don't like that one, wait till you see this one. All right, you turned that down and you'll be sorry. I am now going to do the best book in the entire world.

And the truth was that each time I believed it really was going to be the best book in the world. It never occurred to me that complete and total success was not just one manuscript away.

The thing that was most difficult for me to understand during these years was why I could not get a children's book published. I had started writing them mainly because they looked so easy, but now I was really working on them. It seemed to me that my manuscripts were a hundred times better than any children's books I saw, and yet I couldn't get them published. Probably, I thought, publishers of children's books only publish books of friends and relatives.

I kept writing, and in my spare time I had a fourth child, a son, Guy, born in April of 1958.

In 1962, seven years after I rolled my first sheet of paper into that ancient typewriter, my first children's book was published. It had been turned down by nine publishers, so it was not exactly the book the world was waiting for, but I was absolutely wild with excitement.

I can remember the exact moment I first held the book in my hands. We were living in Morgantown, West Virginia, then. My husband had taken a job at

West Virginia University.

I went to the mailbox. It was snowing. I only had on a sweater. I was shivering. I was always in a great hurry to get the mail.

I opened the box, pulled out the mail, and there was the package.

I knew it was my book. I ripped off the paper there at the end of the driveway and was cold no more. It was a moment of absolute magic.

All the work that I had done on the book—and I had worked hard—faded from memory. All the disappointments, all the frustrations—and there had been lots of both of those too—were gone.

It was as if I had gotten an idea for a book that morning, come to the mailbox, and—presto—here it was. It was completely, absolutely, unforgettably—magic. I was an author at last.

In the same mail with the book came an ad from a clipping service. It said, "We know what they're saying about your book. Don't you want to know too?" I couldn't send my money off fast enough.

As it turned out, I didn't really want to know. The reviews were not good. One publication said that only libraries with unlimited budgets should even consider buying *Clementine,* thereby eliminating every single library in the nation.

So while I was at last an author, according to all the reviews, I still had a long way to go.

I finally sold a manuscript called *The Dancing Camel* to Viking and it didn't do well either. I did a book with Harper and Row—*The Groober*—same thing.

I was not discouraged. I'd show them yet.

About this time I signed up for a course in children's literature at West Virginia University, and this was one of the turning points in my career. For the first time I saw the realistic children's novel. There had not been any of those when I was growing up. It was a Nancy Drew-Bobbsey Twins literary world, and I had been unaware there was any other.

What I had been writing up until this point were children's books about a troupe of pigs who went West to give shows, or an orangutan who enrolled in an all-girls academy—things like that. I had never even considered anything realistic.

Even now I did not jump in the sea of realism all at once. I don't think I could have. I waded in. I wrote a sort of semirealistic book called *Rama, the Gypsy Cat.* This was a book about a pioneer cat, and the character Rama was based on our own cat J.T. This, incidentally, was the only good we ever got out of that particular cat.

The book was published by Viking and, while praise wasn't heaped on it, it was praised. I felt I might be on the right track at last.

I followed *Rama* with a second pioneer novel—*Trouble River.* I had not yet learned to construct an intricate plot and so this, like *Rama,* was a journey book, one of the easiest kinds of books to write. You start your characters out at point A, take them to point B, and let them have some adventures along the way. Hopefully, you will think of the adventures as you progress.

By now I was getting the help I needed from what was to be a series of gifted editors. Annis Duff was the first. Whatever she told me to do, I did. If she said, "Cut," I cut.

If she said, "Add a character," I added. If she said, "This scene needs more work," I worked. If she said, "I'm not sure this will be a publishable book," as she said on the first reading of *Trouble River,* I wept.

And it was mainly through her patient help and keen insight that it turned out to be a publishable book after all.

As a writer, I have always been aware of the enormity of the gap between the brain and a sheet of paper. You write something that you think is hilarious; on paper it isn't funny at all. You write something sad; it's not. You write a story and you know exactly what the finished story should be; and it turns out to be something else.

The first book that turned out the way I had envisioned it was *The Midnight Fox.* (*Trouble River* had been written earlier but it was published after *The Midnight Fox.* As I recall it, we were still trying to make *Trouble River* publishable.)

I look on *The Midnight Fox* as another turning point of my career. It gave me a confidence I had not had before. I knew now that I was going to be able to do some of the things I wanted to do, some of the things I had not had the courage and skill to try. For this reason, and others, it remains my favorite of my books. I was now ready to start *The Summer of the Swans.*

My kids were all in grade school or junior high now, and I wrote during school hours. I never answered the phone while I was writing, so my kids had a secret ring for emergencies. They would dial our number, let the phone ring twice, hang up, and then dial again. Anytime I heard two rings, silence, and more rings, I answered the phone.

One morning the secret ring came. I answered the phone immediately and my daughter said in a broken, tearful voice, "Mom, the principal wants to see you." I said, "What for?" She said, "Just come!"

I turned off my typewriter and went to school. In the principal's office my daughter was sitting on one side of the desk, her best friend on the other. Tears were rolling down every face but the principal's. Between the girls, resting on the principal's blotter, was an enormous drill.

My daughter and her friend had always been in the same room up until this year, and so they had decided it would be a good idea to drill a hole in the wall that separated their rooms so they could pass notes to each other. They had sneaked in during recess, taken the drill from Nan's book satchel and were in the middle of drilling when the teacher came back for her sweater.

At the time, things like this were interruptions in my writing, but later they became my writing. The drill scene was to appear, years later, in *The Cybil War*.

In 1968, I participated in a volunteer program sponsored by West Virginia University. Anybody who was interested—truck drivers, housewives, miners—signed up to help kids who were having learning difficulties in school. I got a third-grade girl and a first-grade boy.

This was a stunning experience for me. Up until this time I had never been around kids who were having real problems in learning. I had not been aware of how much they suffered, not only because they had learning difficulties, but—more importantly—because of the way other kids treated them.

Charlie, the character in *The Summer of the Swans*, was neither of the kids I tutored, but I would never have written the book if I had not known them.

I did a lot of research on the character of Charlie in the Medical Library of W.V.U. I found three case histories of kids who had had brain damage because of high-fevered illnesses when they were babies, and that's where Charlie came from. All the details of his life were from those three case histories. I made nothing up.

I worked hard on the book and I was proud of it. It was published in April of 1970 to a sort of resounding thud. It didn't sell well, it didn't get great reviews; in some papers it didn't get reviewed at all.

I went through a very discouraging period. Maybe, I thought, I am just not going to make it as a first-rate writer. Maybe I never will be good enough. Maybe I should consider doing something else. That fall I enrolled at West Virginia University to get my master's degree in special education.

I had now published seven books, but I had never had one of those long editorial lunches at a swanky New York restaurant that you read about. I had never been in a publisher's office. I had never even met an editor. My contacts with my editors had consisted of long letters and brief phone calls. I did not know a single other writer. Despite having published seven books, I was as green as grass.

I was leaving for class one morning in January when the phone rang. I answered it, and a woman's voice said, "This is Sara Fenwick and I'm Chairman of

The awards ceremony when Byars received her Newbery Medal, June 1971. A replica of the medal is in the background.

the Newbery-Caldecott Committee." My heart rose. "We've been in Los Angeles for the past week going over possible Newbery-Caldecott winners." My heart sank. I realized what she wanted now. She wanted to ask me some questions about writing *The Summer of the Swans,* and I would not be able to answer the questions intelligently and she would go back to the committee and say, "The woman is an idiot."

"And," she continued, "I am so pleased to tell you that your book *The Summer of the Swans* has won the Newbery Medal."

I was stunned. I went blank. I couldn't say a word. She said, "Mrs. Byars, are you there?"

I managed to say, "Yes."

She said, "Mrs. Byars, have you ever heard of the Newbery Medal?"

I said, "Yes."

Obviously, it was not one of my shining hours. At the end of the conversation, she said, "We're having a champagne reception on Thursday and we wish you could be with us."

I uttered my first complete sentence of the conversation. "I wish I could too."

It was midafternoon before my editor called. She said, "What time are you leaving for Los Angeles?"

I said I wasn't planning to go.

She said, "Of course you're going. Get your reservations and call me back."

I got the reservations, rushed downtown and bought two Newbery Award-type outfits. The next morning at seven o'clock I was on my way to Los Angeles. I was a nervous wreck.

When I got out there, it turned out that I had to be hidden for a day-and-a-half to keep people from suspecting I was the new winner. Actually I could have passed freely among all the librarians, not once falling under suspicion. In fact one of the things someone said after the announcement was, "It's so refreshing to have someone win that nobody ever heard of."

The announcement of the Newbery Award literally changed my life overnight. Up until this time I had had a few letters from kids. Now we had to get a bigger mailbox. I got tapes, questionnaires, invitations to speak, invitations to visit schools, requests for interviews. For the first time in my life, I started feeling like an author.

I got my medal in Dallas in June. I was extremely nervous about giving my speech. Just before we went to the awards dinner, Don Freeman, the wonderful author/illustrator, came up to me. He said, "I want to give you my calming stone so you won't be nervous." He gave me a small black stone, very smooth and showed me how to hold it in the palm of my hand and rub my fingers against it.

I gave my Newbery speech with that calming stone in my hand, and it really worked. I don't save a lot of things, but I do still have both my Newbery medal and my calming stone.

When I was in second grade, at Hoskins mill school, there were two boys who terrorized the school—the Fletcher brothers, the absolute bullies of the world. Everyone was afraid of them—the teachers, even the principal. I can't remember anything they actually did, but what they were capable of gave me nightmares.

One of the Fletcher brothers was in my second grade. He was eleven years old. The other was thirteen. He was in my sister's room. Both of them were marking time until they became fourteen and would go to work in the mill. They relieved the boredom of this waiting by creating moments of stark, unrelieved terror at recess and after school.

The Fletcher boys stayed in my mind long after I had forgotten the names of my good friends at the mill, and I decided to do a book about a school bully. I really wanted to call the bully Fletcher, but I thought, well, those brothers are still out there somewhere. I settled on the name Marv Hammerman. I thought that had a good hard ring to it.

I wrote the book, it was published, and one day a few months later the phone rang. A voice said, "Is this Betsy Byars?" I said, "Yes, who is this?" The voice said, "Marv Hammerman." I almost dropped the phone. It turned out he was a sixth-grade teacher who had unwittingly started reading *The 18th Emergency* to his class. He was nice about it. He said his class was delighted to find out there were two terrible Marv Hammermans instead of one.

When I was writing this book, my sympathies were all with Mouse Fawley who was Hammerman's victim. I wanted all the readers to feel sorry for him too. Poor Mouse. Horrible Hammerman. Halfway through the book, it occurred to me what agony it must have been for the Fletcher brothers, both built more like men than boys, to sit in those tiny desks in Hoskins school, and I decided that at the end of the book, I'd pull a switch and let the reader see, just for a moment, what it would be like to be the bully.

It was something that I had not thought of until I was actually into the book, and it's not unusual for insights to come that way. My one regret about that book is that I didn't think to dedicate it to the Fletcher brothers until it was too late.

If we had not moved to West Virginia, I would never have been able to write *The Summer of the Swans, After the Goat Man, The House of Wings,* or *Good-Bye, Chicken Little,* because the ideas for those four books came directly from our daily newspaper.

First, there was a story in the paper about an elderly man who was lost in the mountains around Morgantown. Hundreds of volunteers joined in the search for him. It turned out the old man had gotten bored with the picnic, walked home and gone to bed, but that didn't make the search any less dramatic to me. The story possibilities were great. That was the seed of *The Summer of the Swans.*

Another story—highway I-79 was coming through the area and dozens of people who had been living back in the hills all their lives were being forced to give up their land and move. There was a picture story of one of them—he was known locally as the Goat Man because he kept goats. I had only to look at the picture of him beside his cabin to know that this was wrong and that I wanted to do the book.

Then there was a story in the paper about a huge flying creature which had swooped down at a local farmer as he came from the barn. A follow-up story about a huge flying creature that had crashed into someone's TV antenna. One more story—the huge flying creature had scared some kids riding bikes on a country road. And by now the huge flying creature was known as the Morgantown monster.

The Morgantown monster turned out to be a sandhill crane, lost and injured in migration. Most readers lost interest in the story then, but mine was just beginning. *The House of Wings* was underway.

Finally, a tragic story. A man who had been drinking in a local bar tried to cross the frozen Monongahela river on a dare and went through the thin ice— the opening scene in *Good-Bye, Chicken Little.*

If not for living in West Virginia, I also would not have written *The TV Kid,* or, at any rate, it would have been a different book. The lake house that Lennie broke into was our lake house. Every spring, Ed and I went under the house on our backs in the crawl space to solder the pipes which had burst over the winter. Both of us worried about being bitten by a snake the whole time we were under there. After I published the book, I worried about it even more. Now if I got bitten, it wouldn't even be new material for me to write about.

I started on two master's degrees at West Virginia University, and although I didn't finish either one, my studies were invaluable. Particularly those in library science, because I learned exactly how and where to find what I want in the library.

For example, when I got interested in the news stories about the sandhill crane, I went to the library. What I was looking for was not books on the sandhill crane in the wild, where they make their nests, etc. I wanted to know what it would be like to have a sandhill crane living in the house with you.

I found fascinating stories. I found a story from Florida about two sandhill cranes who would come to a lady's house during fly season. She would let them in and they would eat all the flies off the screens.

I found stacks of old *Audubon* magazines and my interest enlarged as I read. The stories I liked the most were written by men who weren't professional writers, but just men who had a way with injured birds. I was very moved by these stories.

They all started the same way, with the men remembering the exact date someone brought them the injured robin or crow. They remembered what had been wrong, what they had done, and they remembered in detail how the bird had acted in its long convalescence.

I read about a crow who liked to fly over to the dresser, walk past the mirror and admire himself. An owl who caught moths in the bathroom. A canary who would only sit on the frame of an ancestor's portrait.

The end of these stories was the same too. The men remembered the exact day they freed the bird. "It was a windy day, April 3," they would write. "He had

a drink at the sink and he flew over and ate a Wheatie out of my bowl and then he flew to the windowsill. I opened the window and after five minutes he flew to the apple tree. Then he circled the orchard and was gone." And they always added, "I keep watching for him. I would be able to pick him out from a flock of a hundred birds."

By this time, I wanted to do the book about the injured crane, but I also wanted it to be about one of these gentle, patient men who love birds so much they set them free.

Ed and I were on one of our many gliding trips, and I rushed into a grocery store to get something to make him a sandwich before he took off. Making sandwiches is, unfortunately, another of my jobs as crew chief.

I came face to face with two elderly twins. They were probably eighty-five years old; they were dressed exactly alike—their hair was alike, their shoes and their purses. I had never seen anything like it. I followed them around the store for a half an hour. When I got back to the airport, Ed said as usual, "Where have you been?"

I said, "I have just been following the two most interesting people I have ever seen in my life, and as soon as I can, I'm going to put them in a book."

Now I have always been a wonderful eavesdropper and frequently hear bits of conversation that I put word for word in my books. But this was the first time I had ever wanted to put living, breathing people into one.

My opportunity came in *The Pinballs.* I wanted one of the foster kids, Thomas J, to have an odd family

Betsy and Ed in his J-3 Cub, Morgantown, West Virginia, 1974

and what odder family could I give him than eighty-five-year-old twins who were still dressing alike? I then proceeded to figure out for myself what their lives must have been like, what would account for the fact that they were still living together at age eighty-five. When I got through, I felt I was so close to the truth that if the elderly twins ever read *The Pinballs* they would sue me.

A few years later I was back in the same town, and I asked a local person about the twins, if they had always lived together, etc. "Oh no, they got married, moved away, had families, and then when their husbands died, they came home and started dressing alike again." I wish my Benson twins, Thomas and Jefferson, who had been named for their father's favorite president, had been as fortunate.

The Night Swimmers started out to be a mystery. I love mysteries and had always wanted to write one. I thought this was my opportunity.

The three characters, two brothers and a sister, were sneaking out at night to swim in other people's pools. While they were swimming, I planned, they would see something mysterious happening in one of the houses. They would not be able to tell anyone what they had seen because they weren't supposed to be there, and the mystery would develop.

Unfortunately, I could never think of anything mysterious for them to see. The kids were all but getting waterlogged, they had been in the swimming pool in the first chapter for so long. I was worried.

I was writing this book while I was packing to leave West Virginia. Ed and I and our four children had lived in the same house for twenty years and now Ed was changing jobs and we were going back to South Carolina. It was a hard time for me. I was having to throw memories away daily.

Like, one day I came across a small jewelry box tied with ribbon. It rattled. "What's this?" I untied the ribbon. The box contained baby teeth—all the little baby teeth I had taken out from under pillows in my role as tooth fairy. I burst into tears. I said, "Ed, I don't even know which teeth belong to which child." He said, "Betsy, throw those things out." I did, but it wasn't easy.

And one day I found a diary one of my daughters had kept in fifth grade. I would not have read it if I had come across it while she was keeping it, but now she was grown, had a daughter of her own, and I needed a good laugh. I opened it.

The whole diary was how much she hated her sister. On every page was another reason for hating her more. The word *hate* had been written with such force that the letters were still pressed down into the page after all these years.

It made me remember that when my sister and I were growing up, my mother would come into the room which we shared and draw a chalk line down the center of the room to keep us from crossing over and killing each other.

That diary and that memory changed *The Night Swimmers* from a mystery to a book about brothers and sisters who get to the point where they hate each other. They made me realize that not only can brothers and sisters hate each other, but it may be the strongest hate they will ever feel in their lives. Certainly it was the only time in my own life that someone had to draw a chalk line to keep me from murder.

No professional writer that I know ever thinks—Oh, that's good enough. I'm tired of revising. I'll just send it on in. Who cares?

Even if I have rewritten a book seventeen times, if I feel it's not right, I'll write it again.

I had only done seven or eight drafts of *The Cybil War* when I sent it in. At that point, the book was written in the first person. Simon told the story himself.

I sent the manuscript to Viking, it was accepted, I got a contract. I did two or three more drafts. I sat down to read it once more before I sent it in for the last time.

Before I finished the second chapter, on what was supposed to be a quick, last-minute read, I found myself reading slower and slower, and with less and less pleasure. I could not shake the uneasy feeling that it had been a mistake to let Simon tell the story. I should have told it. What I need to do, I thought, is put this book in the third person.

Now, taking a book that is in the first person and changing it to third person is not simply a matter of changing all the *I*'s to *he*'s. Whole paragraphs have to be thrown out, even whole chapters. The things Simon tells, and the way he tells them, were not at all the way I, as narrator, would tell them. And I already had an advance for this book! I had already spent it!

I never hesitated. I was at my typewriter within minutes writing a new chapter one. When I was finally finished, the only thing about the book that remained the same was its title, my all-time favorite—*The Cybil War.*

In the twenty years that I lived in West Virginia, I wrote in a corner of our bedroom. I had a huge L-shaped desk in front of a big window where I could look out over the beautiful West Virginia hills. Sometimes, even when I wasn't writing, I'd sit there.

One of the things that bothered me most about moving was that I wouldn't have that corner and that desk and that view, and I didn't think I would be able to write without them. Also we were moving into a small, modern town house, and there wasn't any corner for my big desk. I didn't tell anybody, but I was absolutely certain I had written my last book.

Two weeks later, in my new town house, I wrote the opening chapter of *The Animal, the Vegetable, and John D. Jones,* the first of my South Carolina books. I was back where I had started, once again on the kitchen table.

I moved to a small desk upstairs with a beautiful view overlooking the lake and a new typewriter that could remember what I'd written and erase it. I started *The 2000-Pound Goldfish* on it. This book was a particular pleasure to write, not just because of the typewriter, but because I loved horror movies so much as a child that everyone said they would ruin my brain.

Then I got a word processor and wrote *The Glory Girl,* my second South Carolina book. Then *The Computer Nut,* my first collaboration—with my son Guy. Then *Cracker Jackson.* I'm now finishing *The Not Just Anybody Family.*

I used to think, when I first started writing, that writers were like wells, and sooner or later we'd use up what had happened to us and our children and our friends and our dogs and cats, and there wouldn't be anything left. We'd go dry and have to quit.

I imagine we would if it weren't for that elusive quality— creativity. I can't define it, but I have found from experience that the more you use it, the better it works.

On April Fools' Day, 1983, I took my first flying lesson. I had been flying with Ed for thirty-five years, but I had never tried it myself. My thought was that flying, like writing, couldn't possibly be as hard as everyone said it was.

Like writing, it turned out to be harder. Months after I had learned how to take off and fly around and navigate, I still couldn't land. The ground was never exactly where I thought it was going to be. I made over a hundred landings before I did a good solid one, and then I made twenty before I did another.

On December 19, 1984, I got my pilot's license, and I am as proud of that as of anything in my writing career.

Uncle C. C. in *Good-Bye, Chicken Little* says, "There's two parts to a man's life. Forget all the junk you've heard about youth, teenage, middle age, old age. There's two parts to a man's life—up and down. Your life goes up like a fly ball and then, like it or not, it starts down. The people who are lucky have a long, long up and a quick down."

At age ninety-seven Uncle C. C. still felt he was on the way up. I, at age fifty-six, feel I am too.

December 17, 1977, daughter Betsy's wedding day: sisters Nan (left) and Laurie flank the bride; her parents and brother Guy are seated.

BIBLIOGRAPHY

FOR CHILDREN

Fiction:

Clementine (illustrated by Charles Wilton). Boston: Houghton, 1962.

The Dancing Camel (illustrated by Harold Berson). New York: Viking, 1965.

Rama, the Gypsy Cat (illustrated by Peggy Bacon). New York: Viking, 1966.

The Groober (illustrated by Betsy Byars). New York: Harper, 1967.

The Midnight Fox (illustrated by Ann Grifalconi). New York: Viking, 1968.

Trouble River (illustrated by Rocco Negri). New York: Viking, 1969.

The Summer of the Swans (illustrated by Ted CoConis). New York: Viking, 1970.

Go and Hush the Baby (illustrated by Emily A. McCully). New York: Viking, 1971.

The House of Wings (illustrated by Daniel Schwartz). New York: Viking, 1972.

The Winged Colt of Casa Mia (illustrated by Richard Cuffari) New York: Viking, 1973.

The 18th Emergency (illustrated by Robert Grossman). New York: Viking, 1973.

After the Goat Man (illustrated by Ronald Himler). New York: Viking, 1974.

The Lace Snail (illustrated by Betsy Byars). New York: Viking, 1975.

The TV Kid (illustrated by Richard Cuffari). New York: Viking, 1976.

The Pinballs. New York: Harper, 1977.

The Cartoonist (illustrated by Richard Cuffari). New York: Viking, 1978; London: Bodley Head, 1978.

Good-Bye, Chicken Little. New York: Harper, 1979.

The Night Swimmers (illustrated by Troy Howell). New York: Delacorte, 1980.

The Cybil War (illustrated by Gail Owens). New York: Viking, 1981.

The Animal, the Vegetable, and John D. Jones (illustrated by Ruth Sanderson). New York: Delacorte, 1982.

The 2000-Pound Goldfish. New York: Harper, 1982.

The Glory Girl. New York: Viking, 1983.

The Computer Nut (computer graphics by son, Guy Byars). New York: Viking, 1984.

Cracker Jackson. New York: Viking, 1985.

Maureen Daly

1921–

I could not write about being a writer if some hope and solution did not lie ahead. Last week, I signed a contract for a new novel to be titled *Acts of Love.* As a free-lancer and a longtime editor, I can both give and take a deadline, so I set my date to complete the new book as midfall of this year, October 15th to be exact.

Right now it is the second week of March and I am alone in a room in the Reef Hotel overlooking the Pacific, the water green, surfed at the shoreline, and deepening into dark blue in the distant sea-lanes where tankers pass. I just came up from the beach and can still smell the sweetness of sun lotions, the damp freshness of the ocean, and the dry, haystack odor of straw tatami mats that everyone sunbathes on, stretched out on the beige sands of Waikiki.

When I made my reservations, I hadn't remembered, but I hit Hawaii right in the middle of spring break. The beaches, hotel lobbies, and dance floors are full of students, all trying to get the most out of tropical sunlight, strangers, and a few days away from classes. Some couples came together, most have known each other only a few days or a few hours. Yet there is a strong feeling of reaching out, of wanting, of looking. Everyone seems good-natured, even gentle, almost on the verge of falling in love.

Last night I went for dinner to the hotel restaurant called The Shore Bird. One side is open to the beach, tiki torches flare along that edge of the terrace. The inside murmur of voices and music is matched by the nearby rise and falling cadences of the sea.

On order, Scotty, my waiter, brought me a portion of raw island fish and a small loaf of bread wrapped in foil. There was a salad bar but self-cheffing was the specialty of the house. I was instructed to cook (and warm) the food myself, the fish five minutes on each side. Scotty pointed out the cook-spot, a huge communal grill at the end of the terrace. Diners, young mostly, crowded around, jostling, laughing, tending their meals over the coals. The air was fragrant with odors of mesquite and dripping juices. Embers from the grill sent out an upward glow that lit the circle of faces, like joyful mystics caught in some ancient island ritual. Suddenly, it was all wrong for me.

I was too alone in that group, not because I was without an escort, not because I hadn't flown in from Washington or Oregon with a group of sorority sisters, and not even because I wasn't wearing a colorful University of Hawaii T-shirt with the bosom slogan: Higher Learning and a Good Tan.

I was alone because I *was* alone. The people I needed were no longer with me and never would be again.

I took my food order back to the table and asked Scotty for a check.

On the balcony of my sixth-floor room, I ate little chunks of the cold bread and looked out over the Pacific, fading now in graying stripes, like a great Rothko painting, holding only last glimmers of light in the foam that touched the sands. Two white pigeons settled on the balcony. There was nothing startling about the birds, the color or number. There were signs everywhere in the hotel, even in the bedroom itself, stating: For Health and Sanitary Reasons, We Request You Do Not Feed the Birds.

For once I broke the rules. What if I were wrong? Who knows for sure what form human souls can take when they need us or just choose to be near? I fed the two white pigeons and they stayed with me long after the last crumb was gone, perched on the narrow black railing, cooing now and then, keeping a precarious balance as night winds rose and fanned out the long, coarse guide feathers of their tails.

There were voices and soft laughter till long after midnight as couples strolled the beach or sat under palm trees, fronds rustling with every breeze. From the end of the rock jetty, I could hear the faint lapping sound as small waves broke on the barrier. Someone stood out there, perhaps two people, but only one cigarette was lit, the tip flaring with sudden brightness now and then, as if someone were smoking in anger or high emotion. At one time, I myself used to smoke.

Everything of the senses seems doubly heightened and emphatic to me now. Each day and night plays through like a double tape, the rhythm and music of my daily life and the insistent, haunting sound track of the past.

Both of them, Bill and Megan, will be in the new book, something of each. There may be more about Megan because her loss is so new, but Bill will be there, big, thoughtful, affecting as he always was. I can hope they know and approve of what I'll be trying to do.

Now I cannot ask the questions. I shall never know the joy of talking to them again except in silent hotel rooms and in the little echoing recesses of my own mind and heart.

I have different reasons now to want to be a writer. But it didn't start out that way. Not at all.

The names of my first two librarians were Miss Kramer and Miss Shepherd. And the head of the library system during all the years of my growing up in Fond du Lac, Wisconsin, was Miss Leila Janes. Those three ladies were the mentors, the fairy godmothers whose lights shone over all the school and intellectual life of that small town. About fifteen thousand people lived there then, highly stratified socially and financially, and yet all one people in that near-rural town, lush and verdant, right on the shores of Lake Winnebago. It seems to me, remembering, that it was that wild and unpredictable lake and the grey stone library, part of the Andrew Carnegie grant, with its iron handrail and broad stone steps, that influenced the life of all of us in Fond du Lac.

The lake, about ten miles wide by fifteen miles or more, had no rills or other inlets. It was fed by summer rains or underground springs that kept its silt bottom shifty and treacherous for swimmers. The lake was subject to rapid changes and never a summer passed without someone being killed in a squall, swept from a sailboat that had set out in sunshine, or drowned somewhere in the deceptive, reedy morass of fishing beds that dotted the shores. The thin wail of an ambulance, rushing to Lake Winnebago, was a standard terror signal of every summer. And sometimes, in winter, the ambulance sounded for an ice fisherman, probably a Norwegian or Finn, not too long away from his native land, angling through a hole cut in the ice, protected by a makeshift shack and even a wood-burning stove. It was fatal to misjudge the thickness of that Wisconsin ice or the treacherous, shifting currents beneath it.

When I first began to read, Fond du Lac, like all the United States and most of the world at that time, was deep in an economic depression. But we had books. On weekly "library day," a van came to public schools to deliver books for selection and exchange. Our library cards were possibly the first items of personal identification most of us ever had. But it was on weekends, and during the long, hot summers, that the library meant most in our lives.

In winter it was kept warm (a true luxury in depression years) with a soft hiss of coal-steam radiators. In summer, the thick stone walls and heavy overhang of trees kept the building cool. And always there was the smell of paper, binding leather, and a lemon scent

The public library in Fond du Lac, Wisconsin, as it looks today. "Why did they cut down the marvellous trees I remember?"

of furniture polish. There were row upon row of stacks, an adult reading room always peopled with old men reading newspapers held firm on spines of bamboo rod. On holidays, we could see the rich boys and girls, home from prep schools in Milwaukee and Green Bay, working with encyclopedias and research books, aloof, confident, each wearing a school blazer with some Latin emblem on the pocket.

For us, in the beginning years, there was the children's room, with smaller tables and chairs, and windowsills so low and broad one could sit on them. Everything there was for *us*, we knew that, even the pervading, mysterious, and valued silences. We spent hours there, leafing through children's magazines or selecting the extra allotment of three books a week allowed on our library cards.

Off a front hallway was a two-stall bathroom with a lithograph of George Washington on a sidewall and a strong, sweet odor of disinfectant, a cross between garden jasmine and pink bubble gum. This bathroom took a special key and it had to be requested at the main desk. Both Miss Shepherd and Miss Kramer were quick and discreet. One need ask quietly, and only once. The key was never refused.

Like the Scandinavians who ice-fished, and the French and Germans who had their own separate Catholic parishes, and the single family of Russians who lived by the old creek and sent painted eggs down the little stream every Easter time, the Daly family—my father, Joseph, and my mother, Margaret Mellon-Kelly, and the three little girls (the fourth, Sheila John, was born in Wisconsin)—were new citizens in the United States. My father, with a wallet full of money, eager for a new life, had come over before us. I believe

Margaret Mellon-Kelly and Joseph Daly on their wedding day in her hometown, Glasgow, Scotland

that's how the explanation went. He sampled New York, Chicago, and then continued to meander west till he came to Wisconsin where the blue lakes and green fields reminded him of Ireland. Then he sent for us.

Later on, I learned that wasn't exactly how the migration had happened.

Joseph Daly actually left his little town of Castlecaufield, County Tyrone, in the north of Ireland after occupying British soldiers laid bales of straw around the base of our white pebble-dash house and warned that it would be lit if Joe Daly was sighted in the village streets after the next St. Patrick's Day. The British military would not tell the day nor the hour the fire would start.

My father was mayor of the village and owned a small bicycle shop and factory. The years of the Irish Civil War were supposedly over, the country had been partitioned, leaving my father and all his family, including his Scottish-born wife and three tiny children, in one of the Five North Counties. Joe Daly had not agreed to submit to British rule. He did not believe in physical violence or taking up arms, but he *did* believe in lending bicycles to "village lads" who needed to transport nighttime messages to anti-English dissidents

still hiding out in the hills. Someone informed on Joe Daly and the British went for the bales of hay and a threatened "burn-out."

The drama was one that has repeated itself often, I believe, in times of civil war and family dissension. It was my mother's only brother, a frequent visitor to our Irish home and a major in His British Majesty's Black Watch Cavalry Division, who had reported on his brother-in-law's anti-British activities.

In his young manhood, my father was not a poor man, so when his wife and daughters left for the United States to join him two years after his departure, they sailed in elegant second-class cabins on the S.S. *Cameronia*, wearing heather tweeds and little leghorn hats with cherries bunched on the ribbon band, landing on the Fourth of July in New York City. For an escort to the new land, we had with us our uncle, my mother's brother, the same ultra-patriot from His Majesty's Black Watch, who had betrayed my father. Blood, of course, is thicker than water, but it also leaves a deeper, darker stain.

We were never told outright of my Uncle Jock's strange perfidy, but the pieces of our Irish past fell into place over the years. Until I was a senior in high school at least, we received weekly copies of an Irish newspaper called the *Dungannon Express*. In the month of March, one edition always arrived with a sheaf of dried shamrocks pressed between the pages. For years and years, we tried to revive them, but no amount of soaking or sunlight could coax life back into those lovely tri-foil green leaves.

Maureen Daly on the lawn of her home in Ireland, one year old. "This picture was on an old roll of film, discovered and developed only in May 1985."

Maureen and her sisters Marguerite and Kathleen with their mother, on their way to America on the S.S. Cameronia. "This picture was also discovered on the 'mystery' roll of film. Certainly not all the luggage was ours."

And from my Grandmama Kelly in Glasgow, Scotland, came monthly packets of magazines with titles such as *The Sacred Heart Messenger* and *Our Lady's Stories for Girls,* with odd clippings about horse shows, golf matches, and concerts in Edinburgh, glimmers of my mother's earlier life.

From this early phase of our family past, there is one incident I never dared ask about and to this day is unexplained to me. I only know that I was young and in the basement of our house in Fond du Lac, looking for a kitten in a dark corner, when I heard loud voices in argument, my father and Uncle Jock. I remember clearly the sound of a single pistol shot. Neither man was hit, I know that; but I do not know who fired the gun. My uncle left our house that night and from then on made his home in Chicago, more than three hundred miles away. We saw him rarely over the years. He prospered somewhat and when he did visit always drove up in a Packard car, wearing pigskin driving gloves and a small black beret. He married late and had no children, but he favored chow dogs, the red variety with characteristic black tongue and full fur ruff. Jock Kelly liked to drive through our small town in his shiny car with a big dog, panting out of each rear window.

After that single act of violence in our house, I never found the bullet I heard and I was never sure which was the exact nick or crack made in the grey cement walls of that little basement. It must have been there. Of one thing I'm sure. I never had to go to a dictionary to look up the meaning of the word "ricochet." I knew what it meant.

My father took out the necessary papers and became an American citizen as soon as the law allowed. As minor children, we automatically became citizens, too, as the law prescribed at that time. My mother was different. Both my parents loved the United States and life without political duress, but Margaret Daly felt a nostalgic and loyal pull to the blue heather and windswept lochs of her first home in Scotland. She did not become a citizen until the outbreak of World War II. But I sometimes think now that it was our "foreignness" that made my family such ardent fans of the new country, so eager and confident about taking advantage of every opportunity it offered. My father frequently ended grace at Sunday dinner with a heartfelt: "And thank God for America, children."

From the very beginning, there were many things to read at home. I remember owning (and sleeping with) a fanciful little volume illustrated in pastels with lots of morning glories and bluebirds, called *Whisk Away on a Sunbeam.* That one was my own. And I shared with my sisters again and again a library book titled *The Hollow Tree and Deep Woods Book,* about talking animals who lived in a tree house in a forest. The Daly house was located at what was then the very edge of Fond du Lac. Just a few blocks away, we were bounded by Lake Winnebago but to the west lay acres and acres of open country of grass and brooks that melded at last into plowed farm fields and the fenced-off cow pasture area of the tiny local airport. The entire open space was ours to roam in and was called simply The Field. We often spent whole days there, playing or picnicking in the high grass, and always bringing with us the household copies of *Burgess' Book of Birds* and *Burgess' Book of Flowers.* As the springs and summers and falls went by, we got to know every species of violet, every stalk of stargrass, and each meadowlark, bobolink, and red-winged blackbird as if we had them tagged and numbered.

In that Great Depression, many people were truly poor and many were also poor who would not admit it. I think we were in the latter group. I can remember one winter when the entire family of four girls went to school dressed exactly alike, in black and green Stuart plaid jackets and skirts, made by my mother out of Uncle Jock's army kilts. My father kept a garden and my mother canned row on row of fruits and vegetables.

We frequently ate spaghetti with a liquid sauce of home-canned tomatoes, vegetable soup made with one meat bone boiled white and clean as a fossil. I can remember many preschool breakfasts of bread and "cocoa," a hot, thin drink made with cocoa and water, no milk, no sugar. And a terrible and too-frequent supper of "jelly roll," some horrible Irish steamed pudding made with flour and suet, rolled up with homemade jelly before steaming. One winter day, we were down to white rice and a quart jar of red cherries from the basement shelves. My mother put the cherries on an outside window sill until they froze into a tasty mush and we ate them spooned over hot rice, our own cherries jubilee.

Strangely, for me at least, deprivation was not always grim. I remember one morning when a neighbor, John DeVoe, came over with a big bowl of fresh, garden-picked strawberries, his only food. I ran to the store with twelve cents for a loaf of white bread. Besides that, the only supply on hand was a pound of thick bacon my father had picked up from a farmer friend. While the bacon was frying, Mr. DeVoe sat at our upright piano and played a brilliant, double-hand rendition of "The World Is Waiting for the Sunrise." My mother opened the windows so the music could flow out into the street. I did not worry then, nor do I remember now, what we did for food the *next* day.

Growing up does not last forever, but my childhood seemed to go on and on, a lifetime of living before I was twelve. I have no recollection of writing anything special in those days, except little letters to my grandmama in Scotland, but reading was always with us. During the lean years, we were the only family on the block who did not cancel its subscription to the town's only daily newspaper, the *Fond du Lac Commonwealth Reporter.* For a Sunday paper, we stopped at a drugstore after Mass to buy for one dime an edition of that excellent newspaper, the *Milwaukee Journal.*

Ours was a small, two-story house with a flight of stairs out front and a large, screened-in porch. (With royalties from my first novel, my parents remodeled the house, converting that porch into part of the living room, putting dormer windows in their bedroom and a second bath on the bedroom floor. I always missed the front porch.)

From the grocery store, my father brought each of us a fruit delivery crate, a sturdy wooden box about two and a half feet high, with a partition in the middle. Set on end, the crates made perfect bookcases. There were four girls and four corners to the porch, with cushions to sit on, and with twice-weekly trips to the library in the summertime, we kept those bookshelves filled. As I remember, "the Daly girls" were allowed to take more than the usual quota of books because we

read fast and returned volumes on time. We selected what we wanted, children's or adult section. There was never advice, or censorship, from the Misses Shepherd, Kramer, or Janes—and never from our parents.

No one kept a family score but my older sister, Marguerite (later Maggie Daly, a well-known columnist for the *Chicago Tribune*) was the fastest, most omnivorous reader. One summer, she received the city prize for the student who read (and handed in written reports on) the greatest number of books. Her total was 113.

Frequently, one sister was drawn by curiosity to read what another sister was reading. Maggie once developed an adolescent compulsion toward books about the Russian Revolution and that much-debated devil-saint, the monk, Gregory Rasputin. The summer Maggie turned seventeen was "the summer of Rasputin" in our household. One had to read her books to talk to Maggie at all that year. Rasputin was as real to us as if he were expected for lunch.

It was that same summer (if Maggie was turning seventeen, then I was ten or eleven) that I felt the first impact of how a single book can affect a life. It was near noontime in August, hot under the low ceiling of my second-floor bedroom. I was lying on top of the bedspread, turning the pages of Sir Walter Scott's *Ivanhoe.* How do they go, those magic and persuasive sentences? At one point, the infamous and villainous Sir Reginald Front-de-Boeuf, meets his death, locked in the flames of his own burning castle . . .

I remember an involuntary paralysis of knowledge swept through me. Words were telling me *more* than the thoughts on the printed page. I experienced a sudden confrontation with reality, then fear and near-panic. From that fictional death, from the power of Scott's prose, I realized for the first time that I too would die someday. I understood the overwhelming certainty of my own mortality. But soon there came a kind of submission, almost a peace. In that acceptance, I grasped the need to find joy in living while one *could* be alive. Sir Walter Scott did that for me.

Even if I never tried to *write* stories in my early school years, I did learn to *listen* to them. My father did not create stories, but he told them. After a long week on the road (he worked for years as a travelling salesman), he would lie on the edge of our bed on Friday nights and treat us to a "story." He liked to recite set pieces, long recitations that had been popular parlor entertainment in Ireland when he was a boy. Our favorite tale was called "The Bashful Man," the funny/sad story of a country lad who goes to a great dinner at a manor house. The young man trips on a rug, sits on the Pekinese, spills his soup—and still wins the heart of his lordship's daughter.

And if he were not too tired, my father would tell us something about Castlecaufield, the people who lived there, how the lanes were laid out, the castle in ruins with the bloody handprint of an Irish patriot still on the stones. And something about the house three of us had been born and lived in (constructed by law to adjoin my grandfather's house; no Irishman in those days could build an independent dwelling) and the great grey stone country estate, overlooking and dominating the town, the house of the absentee English landlord who owned most of the land and flax mills in the area.

My father's memories were vivid and accurate. When I found a way to get back to Castlecaufield with my new family (both Megan and Patrick were born by then), I walked the town and visited that country estate called Park D'Enor (loosely, "Hill of Gold") with the false legend chiseled over the entrance gateway: "Built without Debt to Any Man". . . except the blood and toil of the Irish, my father had told us often, firmly and bitterly.

He was probably right about all that because he was right about other things. In the springtime, there *are* more than two thousand daffodils, nodding and bobbing in golden unison, on the grassy slopes of Park D'Enor.

Years later, when the sad times started (I was twenty-two), I lay beside my father as he was dying, gracefully and without suffering except for the pain of memories and anticipated separations. He said, "Tell me about how the house looks downstairs." I thought he meant our house in Fond du Lac, my mother stirring something in the kitchen, the dog lying near the stairs, Buddy Brockway, the boy next door, come to visit and play his harmonica. I began to describe our house room by room. (Have you read Leo Tolstoy's *Death of Ivan Ilyich?* The longing of the dying to know what is happening in the dear, familiar rooms of the living? I read it later, much later.)

"No, no, Maureen," I remember my father said. "Not this house. It's the wee place in Ireland I'm thinking of."

I told him then of the house he'd been born in, and the house next door he'd built for his Scottish bride. I knew how the rooms were laid out, which pathway was rimmed with pansies, the ditch in front that filled with water in the spring. And even of the two damson plum trees, a surprise among the long row of apples. He had told me everything.

Mentors. What are they and do we all have them? I think so and I hope so. Mentors, to me, are the rare, influential people we meet in life who, suddenly and out of nowhere, become our guides, our

models and, often without words, tell us what to do next. I have had three mentors, people who "just came to me," almost as the nuns used to explain the presence of Guardian Angels. Mentors are not usually family, nor blood kin. Often, they are something closer.

As I remember it, I had Sister Mary Rosita of the Order of St. Agnes for all my four years of English studies at St. Mary's Springs Academy. It was from Sister Rosita that I learned writing is a talent and also a skill that can be practiced and honed. I never heard her use those words but I caught the excitement in her eyes and saw that precise, round face and freckled cheeks reddened with enthusiasm when she read aloud in class. And I began to feel the satisfaction of success when I had a story or essay returned with her pencilled "Good!" somewhere in the margin. In these classes, we used *Scholastic* magazine every week and also shared one copy of the *Saturday Review of Literature* for everyone. (There was a kind of rumor in school, no one dared talk of her outright, that Sister Rosita came from a wealthy family, somewhere in New York, and they

Maureen Daly, age sixteen. A publicity picture taken for Scholastic *magazine when "Sixteen" won their short story prize. "For some reason, I was trying to grow my hair waist-length."*

gave her magazine subscriptions as gifts.)

From her, we came to learn creativity, the power of new words, even something of editors, publishers, book reviewers, critics. At that time, we never considered the word "royalties" because none of us was confident enough to expect to *sell* what we wrote.

It was for Sister Rosita that I joined the staff of the school paper as a sportswriter, covering girls basketball. And I worked with her as editor in my senior year. It was for her I wrote my first story at fifteen, a fragmental piece of work, titled "Fifteen," about a young girl who sees a boy ride by on a bicycle . . . and thinks of him. That is all I remember of the story and do not have a copy. Sister Rosita sent it to *Scholastic* magazine and it won third place in their high school short story contest that year. The prize was to have my name printed in the magazine.

The next year I tried another story, using Sister Rosita's constant advice to our classes: *"Write about what you know. . . ."* I wrote about a boy and a girl who met one night at a small-town skating rink. I do not believe they ever met again. . .

That story was titled "Sixteen" and Sister Rosita mailed it on deadline to *Scholastic* magazine. "Sixteen" won first prize in *Scholastic*'s short story contest that year and was printed first in that magazine, later in *Redbook* and *Mademoiselle* and ultimately in about three hundred anthologies and in at least a dozen foreign languages. The story was also selected to appear in the prestigious *O. Henry Collection of Best Short Stories* as one of the twelve best stories written in the United States that year.

Never a week goes by, still, without someone writing to ask me about "Sixteen" ("Did that boy ever call that girl. . . ?") It was an odd twist of fate, the success of that short story written at our kitchen table in no more than an hour and a half on notebook paper with a pen that scratched. Was I writing with such creative fever to express my own volatile emotions, or just to please Sister Rosita? I shall never know.

I had been considering a career in nursing, but that short story was the beginning of a life of writing for me. As a prize, I was invited to New York to be awarded first prize *on radio*, read the story for broadcast, and be presented with a fifty-dollar check. But there were complications. In the background was the fact I had met a boy I liked a lot. In the foreground were the harsh facts that I was working my way through school cleaning the gym and the auditorium three times a week and helping to serve luncheon in the nuns' dining room except on weekends. St. Mary's Springs was then a private, all-girls school, with hefty tuition fees.

Besides, I had become involved in the senior class play, an ambitious effort titled, I think, *Song of Hungary,* about royalty and Christianity, all backed by a voice-speaking choir. I was cast as the King and had to practice daily to lower my voice tones by reciting my lines against the timber of the piano backstage. Sister Annella, our drama teacher, felt a trip to New York would break into rehearsal schedules, and she was also huffy that I might be showing preference to writing over the theatre as the ultimate art form. I did not go to New York.

Writing that short story, "Sixteen," and winning a prize had been a personal and blissful interlude, a stretching of skills, a playing with words and emotions that was new to me. What happened afterward was tense and awkward, something never forgotten.

When the fifty-dollar prize money arrived from *Scholastic* magazine, my mother signed my name on the check, cashed it, and bought herself a dress costing exactly fifty dollars, a high price at that time, at an exclusive ladies' shop called Minnie Messing's. I remember clearly the dress was a soft silk in a color known as "powder pink," with a matching jacket in heavy lace.

Sister Rosita canvassed the senior class for individual donations to buy me an expensive pen in black and green with my initials "M. D." engraved on a gold band. It was all wrong.

I lost that honorable pen within the month, somewhere along Main Street in Fond du Lac, as I was rushing to meet the current love of my life, Joe Fox. I just hope a doctor found it.

M y second mentor, though I did not realize it till years later, was a combination boyfriend-teacher-lover, a fellow reporter I met my first week with the City News Bureau in Chicago. But I skip ahead in time because I do not want to omit a general assignment reporter for the (then) *Chicago Herald American,* Eddie Sokol, known to friends and through his byline simply as "Dynamite." He was thirty-one, I was twenty-one.

The press room in City Hall had eight free telephones, reams of yellow paper and stubby pencils, a pinochle table, a watercooler and, for me, Dynamite. He was a tough-talking veteran reporter, both loved and feared, loved because he was loyal, good-natured, full of wit, and amusing in a gamin, street-smart way, feared because he knew how to track down a news story and how to get it on the front page. He was also short, nervous, with a distinct cast in one eye, not a crossed-eye but one that was definitely set for a side view, and he smoked big, fragrant cigars.

Eddie Sokol earned the lifelong nickname "Dynamite" when he was a fourteen-year-old copyboy, assigned to an important banquet to honor the great transatlantic pilot and pioneer, Charles Lindbergh. Dynamite's job was to stand in the background, wait for copy from a senior reporter, and rush it back to the city room.

The dinner wore on and the young copyboy, hungry and impetuous, tapped Colonel Lindbergh on the shoulder to ask if he would share his roll and butter. Eddie Sokol got something to eat at once, plus the assignment to do a special feature story on his "friendship with Charles Lindbergh"—and his first byline—"by Dynamite Sokol."

From Dynamite I learned that a reporter, with good manners and perhaps a few up-top introductions, can go anywhere, ask almost any question, and write almost anything he wishes—as long as he, or she, feels what he has learned is important, true, and has kept written notes to prove it. Dynamite had a photographic memory but from him I apprehended the importance of always getting correct names, addresses, and phone numbers, paying close attention to detail, and keeping accurate files and back clippings. And I learned how to turn quiet, to listen and observe when I was already getting the material I wanted to see or hear. So much of journalism is looking and listening.

I was basically shy, convent-trained, and had learned rules of decorum from my mother which pertained mostly to Scottish manners when *she* was a girl. It was Dynamite who helped me to speak out on the job. He convinced me that public files were meant to be open to the public and that public officials must, within reason, remember that they *worked* for the public. "Call 'em on the phone, baby," he told me often. "They got to talk to you, or call you back. You're not a kid anymore. *You're Press.*"

It is never easy to get into the news business, either print or the radio/video mediums. It is a glamor job, in spite of the hard work, a ringside seat at history in the making (or at least the workings of a local city council), and applicants far outnumber the opportunities.

My luck occurred during my senior year in college. I had double-majored in English and Latin, was working for tuition and board, edited the school literary magazine, the *Rosary Eagle,* and managed to write two short fiction pieces a month for the *Chicago Daily News.* My editor was John Lally, a writer himself, much beloved by many young writers of that time and territory. I was paid twenty-five dollars a story, checks which I endorsed and sent home.

At that time, even a twice-monthly writer of short fiction could not get a reporter's job on the prestigious *News.* But fate and a softhearted but savvy news photographer, Eddie Johnson, gave me the introduction I needed to the *Chicago Tribune.*

Eddie Johnson, with an assistant, came to Rosary

Eddie Johnson

A picture taken by Eddie Johnson of the Chicago Tribune *for a St. Patrick's Day spread on "colleens." "The beret was bright green and it got me my first newspaper job."*

College for a kind of demure cheesecake picture spread on "colleens" for St. Patrick's Day. As the only Irish-born colleen on campus, I got a picture all to myself. And Eddie Johnson said to me, "Maybe you'd like to come to work for us someday, Miss Daly."

I did not wait till June graduation but cut classes next afternoon and bussed into the Loop and to the imposing white twin towers of the *Chicago Tribune.* There were then, as there are today, armed guards on every floor but I got permission to surprise Eddie Johnson in his Tower office. Within an hour, I had an appointment with Michael Kennedy, editor of the Sunday magazine, and before the interview was over, I had been hired to do a weekly feature for the magazine, first deadline two weeks away. That assignment grew, after graduation, to a six-day-a-week column called "On the Solid Side," which appeared in the *Tribune* and syndicated papers across the country. Part of the deal was that I should also work as a beat reporter for the City News Bureau on a full-time basis to learn the city and the basic precepts of newspaper reporting. I would draw a paycheck from both organizations (I started at City News for twenty-five dollars per week but the *Tribune* was more generous) and collect whatever royalties accrued from the column syndication.

A week or so after graduation, on a hot, hot day in June, I was taking a streetcar out to a southside police station, Lawndale, I believe, when I sighted a *Tribune* delivery truck with my name and new column banner advertised on its panels.

I mention all this because that's how it happened. And in the years since, when I have interviewed and/ or hired other young writer-reporters, I have been aware of a certain truth: some of the most saleable and hireable commodities in the human marketplace are enthusiasm and animal energy. In my first interview with Mike Kennedy, I do not believe I spoke more than a few sentences. But I had made my desires clear to the *Tribune*. I was *there*.

In Fond du Lac, in my own home, ambition, careers, and even hard work were never discussed. Things were just *done*. There was never a question of skipping assignments or homework. After supper, the table was cleared and study sessions began for four of us. I always had my sister, Kathleen, as someone to imitate. Just two years older than I, she had the characteristic second-child disposition—sweet, sunny and witty. Kay herself was a fine writer and broke ground for me all through high school and college. She too wrote short stories (never commercially published) and worked on both high school and college publications before me. She was the salutatorian (second highest honors) when she was graduated from the Academy and I followed her two years later as valedictorian. Kay, God rest her talented and generous soul, went on to distinction in advertising. As creative vice-president of the cosmetic company, Revlon, Inc., she was—at that time—the highest paid woman executive in the United States, according to a story on her in *Time* magazine.

A curious circumstance occurred in our background which I did not assess until recently. My mother's father, James Kelly of Glasgow and Hunter's Quay, had been an estate manager for a wealthy Scottish thread merchant, Sir Andrew Bain, and the Kelly family had been housed on the vast loch-side estate, living in close imitation of the owner's life, sharing the motorcars, the racing sailboats, the fruits and flowers of the manor greenhouses. One of my mother's deep and endless prides was that the Andrew Bains, who were childless, had asked to adopt her, a beautiful little girl; but her parents refused. Their decision made her feel prized and special all her life.

And from that life, she brought to Wisconsin some of the linens and the silver, the skills and the arts that she had learned from the estate at Hunter's Quay.

Even in the depths of the Great Depression, we had linen tablecloths on Sunday, satin-trimmed eiderdowns on the beds (tattered, as time went by), and a Gorham silver tea service on the dining room sideboard. Why, when we needed money so badly, did we not sell some of these things? The market was glutted with fine possessions, unsaleable at almost any price. Fond du Lac, a small town, did not have enough permanently rich people to help out (that economic recession lasted for years) the "permanently poor."

As little girls, we were "taught" at home, however—how to lay tables correctly, iron shirts and napkins, plant gardens, mend furniture, cut flowers, sweep and scrub floors, and how to think of color and beauty as part of a home. I think my mother, with a dramatic flair, preceded the vaunted Lady Mendl in innovative decoration by painting every wall in the house white, making draperies and huge cushions from bright but cheap fabrics, and polishing bare floors when conventional rugs were worn through to their back-threads. Once, it was springtime with lilacs still in the garden, a neighbor called the local police to report my mother as "immoral" because—with four teenaged daughters in the house—she had taken down the traditional cover-up lace curtains and left the shining windows draped, but in open view of the street. The two young policemen drank tea, with apple scones, and left. We never put the curtains back.

We were taught so much at home, almost effortlessly, just as a part of living, that it left extra time for other learning in school and out there in the big world. There was little cash to "practice with" most of the time, and yet none of the four girls was baffled—or even ill at ease—when it was *her* turn to start collecting paychecks or earning royalties. My parents were strict tutors and we were graduated from "home" long before we graduated from academies or colleges.

For my first two years at Rosary College in River Forest, Illinois, a suburb of Chicago, I paid for my room and board off campus by working as a live-in maid in a private family residence. Duties included all the light housekeeping, most of the laundry and ironing, some shopping, simple cooking, and kitchen clean-up. With children, there was baby-sitting, bath time, and good-night story.

By some perversity of youth and spirit, I loved it. I found a home (my own room, five-dollars-a-week spending money) with the Charles Kinnans in River Forest. They had two tiny children—Lynn and Jere, about four and two—and they were about as comfortable for me to care for as bad puppies, marvelous to play with and lovely to look at when they were finally asleep. The Kinnans themselves were not older than their midthirties and I wonder now how they could have accepted a well-mannered but strong-willed teenager into their lives so readily. On my nights off, I stayed out late. On my nights at home, I studied late. There was always a light shining under my door.

For the first formal dance at college, Mrs. Kinnan offered me a choice of her evening wraps—a black velvet, a fur, and something strange in mauve egret. I picked the last. Joe Fox was home on army leave (we loved each other for a long time) and was with me on "the night of the egret jacket."

College was hard for me, partly because I worked so much outside classes, spent long hours on personal writing, and often did not have enough money to buy the textbooks. (I sent all the money from the *Daily News* stories back to my family.) In freshman American history, using the library and taking class notes, I managed a B⁺ without ever seeing a textbook. That happened in several other classes. I did a kind of personal catch-up for years and years on many of the college courses where I had managed an A or B⁺, barely knowing what the professor was talking about. I bought and read the books later.

I know how customary it is today for young people to hold part-time jobs, even through graduate school, but what a luxury it must be, what a privilege, to be in school as nothing but a student. That was the way we managed to send our children, Megan and Patrick, for their higher education at the University of Southern California. They were both excellent and experimental students, with fine grades, not a bit spoiled by having their own cars and allowances.

Even with small successes behind me, I did not begin to think of myself as a writer until an odd occurrence in my college sophomore biology class. It met at eight in the morning, a wearying hour, since we were all expected to attend seven o'clock Mass *and* fit in a hasty breakfast. An assignment had been given to write an essay on soil erosion. Several days later, the professor asked me to read my paper aloud to the class. To my surprise, my essay was strongly written, full of picturesque facts and valid opinions. By the very fact of being Irish and having grown with such intimacy to love the lands, plants, and waters of Wisconsin, I had, unknowingly, become a vehement and concerned ecologist. It was a small lesson in literary creation. Under maximal conditions of emotion, words almost move out and produce themselves. Passion is a fine trigger to awaken talent.

And a word about other passions. In retrospect, I am sometimes amazed at the freedom our strict parents gave us in our teenage years. In a home where we were treated like hothouse shamrocks, ready to shrivel at first touch, I was allowed to date—Saturday night movies after my stint in the men's department of

the J.C. Penney Company, or evening walks to McKnight's drugstore—at fourteen. All of us, even Sheila when she caught up, were frequent dance guests at the two small country clubs outside town. Those humid Wisconsin nights were so long, so star-filled, full of dancing and laughter; and we had the fun of "dressing up" because my mother knew how to sew and had a distinctive clothes sense. Fabric was cheap—as little as twenty-five cents a yard, but never try to wash it—and could be made into marvelous, swirling formal dresses. No one thought of going completely bra-less in those days but we older three did follow a beauty hint Maggie found in a beauty magazine. We wore our summer formals with only a bosom support of two strips of adhesive tape under each breast. The idea was seductive and there was a certain satisfactory anguish in zipping off those clinging, stinging tapes in the darkness of our bedroom, at home, safe and intact, by two o'clock on a dark summer morning.

I was seventeen (I have a March birthday) in the summer between my college freshman and sophomore year. It was a strangely maturing summer, and I must have set some kind of internal goal because I had a date every single night from the middle of June until the night before I returned to Chicago in early September.

It was also the summer I started my first novel. For several years, we three older girls had worked summers at the Fond du Lac Tent and Awning Company, folding advertising brochures for a mail-out. It was tiring work and we folded so rapidly that often the whalebone ruler we used to crease the circulars became friction-hot, burning to the touch, and had to be cooled in pans of ice water. I did not want to fold advertising that year—not laziness, just restlessness—so I told my parents and sisters one early June evening that I wanted to stay at home and write a book.

I allowed no one to see a word of the manuscript till the book was published but by the morning after my initial announcement, I had an "office." In those days, with the bitter Wisconsin winters, each family had a basement "coal house," just a corner of the cellar boarded off to store coal. My mother had risen early and hosed out our coal house till not a speck of dust was left. My father carried down a small kitchen table and chair, and Sheila potted some garden geraniums and lined them up against the outside of the single, tiny window, since there was no inside sill. (Sheila was always original, inventive. Today she is in advertising, an executive with Chanel, Inc.) My father borrowed an old typewriter from a used-car dealer, also a man from Ireland. There was no electric light in that little cubicle, either, so I worked only in the daytime.

Book jacket picture for the first edition of Seventeenth Summer. *"Obviously I was ready for the big world. I had the pearls and the little black dress."*

By the end of summer, I had four chapters written and a detailed outline for a complete book. With the heavy schedule of college classes and outside work, I did not finish the complete manuscript till the Christmas vacation of my senior year.

When I began the first page of that novel, called *Seventeenth Summer*—a story of a pair of teenagers falling in love, one summer, for the first time, in a small town that had been the world to both of them—I used the simple, almost childish, opening sentence: "I don't know why I'm telling you all this. . . ." I did not realize then that I had inadvertently tuned into the hopes, dreams, and pervasive sexual yearnings of hundreds of thousands of people who had been stirred and then loved, just as I had. I did not anticipate an instant best-seller. (It has just had a March 1985 "celebration reprint" by the original publisher, Dodd, Mead and Company, to mark the one-and-a-half-millionth sale in hard covers. I do not know how many uncounted copies have been sold in paperback through Pocketbooks and Scholastic press.) I had no idea that book would be the cornerstone of my writing career, that it would

never go out of print in hard or soft cover for more than four decades, and that the fan mail from around the world would fill box after box after box. (Yes, I always answer letters sent to me. Is that why I get so many, I wonder?)

The book was submitted to the Dodd, Mead Intercollegiate Novel Contest, which offered as a prize publication and a check for $1,000. I was alone when I received the telegram announcing *Seventeenth Summer* as the top winner. I was dizzy with the excitement of approval, apprehensive at the realization that now my innermost thoughts would go public on a printed page. I phoned Fond du Lac but neither parents nor sisters were at home. Joe Fox was at an army post in Quito, Ecuador, and Sister Rosita was engaged, teaching her classes back at the Academy. My best girlfriends at college, Gini Owen and Mare Walsh, were unreachable, in two-hour seminars. But the college chapel was open.

I slipped into the solace and solitude of a pew in that tiny Gothic church and "told God about the book." I needed to share my joy and gratitude, and the communication worked. Over the years, I've held such conversations often.

World history was changing with stunning rapidity that year, so I record here, with humility and perspective, the events in my own life. Book contracts were signed, the $1,000 check sent home to my parents. Sunday, December 7th, was a quiet, study day in our college rooms until the radio brought news of the disastrous Japanese attack on Pearl Harbor. Joe Fox managed to get a phone call through to ask me, "Are you all right, sugar?" even though I was more than five thousand miles away from the carnage and the embattled, sinking ships just off Hawaii. (I went only yesterday to pay homage at the military shrine at Pearl Harbor and said my prayers again, as I had that very first day, for the more than 1,700 dead, still entombed in the USS *Arizona,* sunken yet still visible beneath the clear and shallow Pacific waters.)

In April, *Seventeenth Summer* was published to rave reviews and big sales, and I began the experience of interviews, public appearances, and autograph parties. After June graduation, I started work with the *Chicago Tribune* and City Press. And I met Bill McGivern.

McGivern was a tall, husky young man, a few years older than I, witty and shy at the same time. He was a high school dropout, employed at loading freight cars in a railroad yard, I learned much later; but he wanted to be a writer, too. He came to an autographing party for *Seventeenth Summer* at Marshall Field's, Chicago's huge downtown department store. Bill bought a book and I signed it. An hour later, he came back, saying he had left the first copy in a taxi and

Bill McGivern, on a street in Philadelphia, "the first day I saw him after his three-and-a-half years of service overseas in World War II. I took the picture."

could he buy another. He did.

Curious the power of words to convey both love and the inner heart. It happened for me when Sergeant William P. McGivern sent me a V-mail note while he was a combatant in the famed Battle of the Bulge, stationed with an antiaircraft crew on an isolated hill above a strategic village in Belgium. He wrote: "On Christmas Eve, we crept down the hill behind the German tank to get to Midnight Mass. An old man closed the church doors and the organist just barely touched the keys with her fingertips to play 'The Star Spangled Banner.' It was so cold there were no echoes. . . I wish you had been there."

Is that a letter of love and declaration? Somehow I thought so. Bill and I were married at Holy Name Cathedral in Chicago, more than four years after I autographed that first book for him.

And he did become a writer. The William P. McGivern byline appeared on twenty-six novels (the

last two were Book-of-the-Month selections), dozens of short stories, prime-time television shows, and a number of movies. Together, we wrote a book about our world travels titled *Mention My Name in Mombasa*, as well as a number of TV shows, including "Kojak," and one of John Wayne's last films, *Brannigan*. At Bill's request, I finished his last book—*A Matter of Honor*—for him. But all that was later, much later.

Immediately after college, I began work for the Chicago City News Bureau, stayed nearly two years, and probably learned more about basic news gathering than if I'd gotten a doctorate in journalism at a university, if such a degree is offered. City News is the backup reporting service used as a news source for all the major newspapers in Chicago. We covered in detail everything from police beats to City Hall. We were expected to be fast, resourceful and, above all, accurate. I believe that Patricia Leeds, later a distinguished Chicago crime reporter, and I were the first women hired by the Bureau. My main boss was a gruff, dedicated newsman, Isaac Gershman (I could never call him by his nickname "Gersh") and next in command was Larry Mulay, the managing editor, soft-spoken, patient and infinitely helpful. Later, Morry Rotman came on the scene as assistant city editor, quick, talented, and a good comrade, now head of one of the world's most successful public relations agencies and a close friend to this day.

It was my duty as a beat reporter to investigate and organize facts on a variety of stories and then call in the information to one of the rewrite men. They were tough, almost like the Hell's Angels of local journalism. They were older men (early thirties, most of them), not only proud to work for the City News Bureau, but determined to make reporters out of "the ladies." My nemesis was a short-tempered bull of a man named Art Kozelka. I can remember my terror and sweaty palms when I phoned in a story and answered his withering, barking questions. ("*Middle initials*, Mr. Kozelka? Of all *fifteen* people injured in the El-train accident?")

To my astonishment (I was reporting from Europe at the time), I learned later that Art Kozelka had left City News to become Gardening Editor of the *Chicago Tribune*. I would have thought his mere presence could wither garlic. Perhaps he did teach me something about being a reporter, but I would have absorbed instruction just as well, I believe, at lower decibels.

Here is a true but strange example of the hold that first reporting job had on my psyche. Because of the nature of the newspaper world, we were required to work many weekends, at least some of us were. In mid-

December, I asked Mr. Gershman if I could have December 25th off to spend with my family. He was courteous but stern, firm. He did not want me to think that just because I was a woman, special preference might be given. . .

I explained that I had not had a day off in the last four months. He was aghast, he checked. By some error, my name had been dropped from the "days off" roster. I was on permanent assignment.

Why had I worked in silence for four months without time off? Was it because I was too stupid to ask questions? Was it because I was a small-town girl, still only twenty-one? No, I believed it was part of the training. I had concluded that overwork was another way the old pros broke in the newcomers at the famed City News Bureau.

Somewhere before my twenty-fourth birthday, I switched cities and jobs and went to Philadelphia as Associate Editor of the *Ladies' Home Journal.* Mary Cookman Bass (now Mrs. Chauncey Newlin), Executive Editor of the magazine, wired me in Chicago for a luncheon meeting. She was a bright, talented woman in her late thirties, experimental, informed, and with an affirmative good-humor. We talked for hours that day. I liked her personality, her politics, her philosophies. I wanted to work with her. She slipped into the slot of new mentor and I had a lifelong friend.

During my tenure with the *Ladies' Home Journal,*

Mary Bass (now Mrs. Chauncey Newlin), "when she was my boss and mentor at Ladies' Home Journal. *When I wanted to learn, I just watched her."*

the editors-in-chief were that renowned couple, Bruce and Beatrice Blackmar Gould. The Goulds agreed, for a husky fee, to reprint *Seventeenth Summer* in the first issue after my joining the staff, splash a banner announcement on the cover of the magazine, with a special introduction and picture of me inside. I had some demands of my own. I asked for a three-year contract, all moving expenses from Chicago to Philadelphia, and a salary that was—for me— a little dizzying even to think about.

The Goulds explained they did not give contracts but I did get the fee for the novel, a cover blurb and inside buildup, the expenses and the salary I had asked for. Something significant about the last item: the salary must have been high. Though I stayed on staff for almost six years, had dozens of bylines, travelled to cover stories in every state in the country and later in Europe—I never got a raise.

I learned many things from Bruce and Beatrice Gould, not always related directly to writing, editing, or journalism. Six months after joining the staff, I asked for a week off to spend Christmas in Wisconsin. My father had died three years before and our family needed unity. Mr. Gould told me then, "You're not really eligible for a vacation, but I'll let you take one. Just be discreet. Don't talk about it. It does you no service in life to make people think you're *too lucky.* . ."

Beatrice Gould had herself been a newswoman and imparted to her staff a feeling for both opportunity and responsibility in journalism. I remember meeting with Mrs. Gould just before flying down to Dallas, Texas, to do the first article in an impressive, yearlong series called "Profile of Youth." We talked of deadlines, length of articles, the usual editor-decisions passed on to a writer. Mrs. Gould gave me no suggestions, no strictures, no advice, but stated simply, "We shall all be interested to see what you find out."

One of the last articles in that series was one I wrote about a young black girl (her policeman father had been killed in a shoot-out) in a ghetto high school in Chicago. I remember the opening line. "Myrdice Thornton lives on Forty-second Street on Chicago's South Side." That article, titled "City Girl," won for me a Freedoms Foundation Award for "humanity in reporting" and later, though other excellent writer-reporters had also worked on the series, I was given sole credit as editor when J.B. Lippincott Company published the series in hardcover under the title, *Profile of Youth.*

There were nearly sixteen million teenagers in the country at that time and, as a magazine, we tried to give at least a partial glimpse of all of them.

The special success of "City Girl" and a later article called "Negro Aristocracy," which I suggested and

Maureen and her sisters in a follow-up story in Life *magazine, ten years after their first one
"when we were young hotshots. In ten years we had nine children between us."*

edited while serving as a consultant to the editors of the *Saturday Evening Post,* came about because of my deep interest and troubled curiosity about the black citizens of the United States. After all, I too had come from "somewhere else." For years, I had immersed myself in reading black history, the study of slavery, conditions before and after Emancipation, but it was not until college that I discovered Richard Wright's scalding account of his boyhood, *Black Boy.* Only then did I learn that in Wright's period, before it, and for some time afterward, most libraries in our South were closed to blacks.

In the *Journal* reference library, I came across an old "educational directory" which listed names and addresses of schools labeled "colored." As a personal project, I began sending out fifty books a month, from fiction to biography, to some black school library. Always I wrote first to the school principal, asking permission to make the gift. I was never refused. After we married, Bill McGivern helped me. It is not easy to bundle-wrap fifty books and get them to the post office every month. We continued the practice till we began to travel and live abroad.

"Negro Aristocracy," based on my outline and many years of notes from black-oriented magazines and newspapers, was completed and bylined by writer Bill Davidson, but it also held a deep personal triumph for me as an editor, because I had made something important, something thought-changing appear in print. On the newsstands across the country, that particular issue of the *Saturday Evening Post* outsold every other issue of the famed magazine up to that date. I cannot accurately remember the figure, but it was in

The office at Daly's farm in Pennsylvania. "I learned to work and care for children at the same time. I don't know who is on the phone, but I do know I am tuning Patrick's guitar with Megan's okay."

the millions. I do not know if that number was ever exceeded.

We had one little daughter, Megan, not quite two years old, when we decided (a giddy but mutual decision) that I would resign my magazine editorship and Bill and I, as a family, would go to Europe to learn, to live, to write. Bill, as a struggling free-lancer, had no job to resign from. We never discussed what we would do if the money ran out.

When I told Mary Bass I was leaving the staff, she hesitated not a moment, and said, "You're doing the right thing. It's what I would do if I were you. . ."

I woke on my thirtieth birthday in a tiny, loftlike suite in the Hotel D'Angleterre at 44 Rue Jacob in Paris. Our luggage was a pair of suitcases and two portable typewriters. Our baby daughter lay sleeping beside me, a favorite teddy bear lying beside her. (Megan celebrated her birthday with a two-candle cake on the famed ocean liner, *Ile de France.* From the beginning, she had her own passport, was a willing and energetic traveller. Ultimately, she learned to speak French, Italian, and then fluent Spanish, but her first encounter with a foreign language was a puzzler to her. Of the French children chattering on shipboard, she said, "They all *talks* but they all *says* nothing.")

And somewhere that morning, out on the streets of Paris, was Bill McGivern, speaking soldiers' French, trying to buy coffee and croissants and a copy of the

Maureen and Bill with Megan and Patrick, photographed by the Irish Tourist Bureau in front of a Dublin hotel. "I do not like to count the countries or homes we lived in because it makes me lonesome for all of them."

In the hat market, Fez, Morocco. "One of our hundreds of travel pictures."

English-language *Paris Herald.*

I had assignments, yes. The *Journal* had asked my sisters and me to do a monthly column, "What Are People Really Like?" I had been given two very special assignments, one in Germany, one in Italy, with Bill to work as my researcher. Certain expenses would be picked up, the articles would be paid for—months later—when they had been shaped, written, and okayed. But that morning in Paris, for the first time since I was fourteen, I was without promise of a regular paycheck. We were both free-lancers now, McGivern and Daly. Could it work out?

We came back to the United States again and again (free-lancers must cultivate both contracts and assignments) but over the years together we had homes in Paris, Rome, Dublin, London, and Málaga-Torremolinos in the south of Spain. We wrote and reported (and did short fiction and novels) from Berlin to Tangiers to the Ivory Coast to Kano, Nigeria. I managed a multitude of interviews from subjects as diverse as Eleanor Roosevelt and Harry S. Truman to Julie An-

drews and artist Andy Warhol. Once I flew to Iceland alone because Bill had been playing winter golf in Ireland, using red golf balls against the snow, and said he was already too cold. I wrote a three-part series on that fascinating country for the *Chicago Tribune.* And I was able to include a profile of an Icelandic youth in my book *Twelve around the World.* For a long time, we kept a forty-acre farm in Pennsylvania (a six-lane highway cut it in half) and when Megan and Patrick reached college age, we had a house in Hollywood with a clear, blue pool and garden walls trellised with yellow jasmine, all within commuting distance of the major movie and TV studios and the urban campuses of the University of Southern California.

Most of the time we were a two-typewriter family. At one point, when Patrick was a small boy and very appealing, I made a creative deviation and wrote a series of children's books that included *Patrick Visits the Farm, Patrick Takes a Trip,* and others. They were surprisingly popular.

I have always stayed shy, almost secretive about writing, keeping most work to myself until it was published, but Bill was outgoing and he loved having an editor in the house. Most days ended with my reading aloud to him what he had written that day.

When Bill, decades after World War II, began his big novel, *Soldiers of '44,* published around the world and hailed by many critics as one of the most significant war books ever written, I worked with him closely. For him, it was an intense, personal experience, reliving "his war" and he wanted to get it right. Many times, in frustration, he would cross out whole paragraphs or whole pages, crumpling the sheets into a wastebasket. Often, while he slept at night, I erased the cross-out marks carefully and sometimes even ironed the wrinkled pages. It worked. Bill got his minor masterpiece. There are many ways to be an editor.

We were always looking for new experiences, as writers, as people, but we were not quite prepared when a certain new experience sought us out. We had planned to drive from our home in Palm Desert, California, to San Diego to join friends at the racetrack. As Bill shaved in the early dawn, he felt a strange little lump on the side of his neck. I remember he said, "If this doesn't go away, I don't think we should stay for the weekend."

We didn't stay for the weekend. Bill had cancer of the throat. With surgery and treatment, he lived nearly three-and-a-half more years, cheerful, grateful, and loving. Health was under control. He never stopped working and had a sheaf of paper and pencil near him every waking moment.

Contracts were signed, an advance taken, a dead-

Maureen and Bill, in their last picture together. "Bill was president of Mystery Writers of America, and at a meeting we were asked to pose with some actual police weapons. We both felt foolish and were."

line set. His new book was to be titled *A Matter of Honor.* A new cancer flared up in the esophagus.

One sad afternoon, Bill asked me if I would finish the book for him, later. He had three chapters completed, some interviews, and a lot of notes. The story had a semi-military background and I knew that a speech by a certain army general was pivotal to the plot. I brought a tape recorder to Bill's bedside and said, "Please tell me exactly what you want the general to say. I'm not sure I can do that alone."

"I've got it all figured out in my mind," he said. "Let me tell you tomorrow."

By the morning, he had died.

That was in mid-November. I clung to those who wanted to cling to me and worked, often through the saddest of tears, to finish Bill's manuscript. November, through a lonely Christmas and a lonelier New Year, into summer and the month of July. *A Matter of Honor* was completed, almost ready to send to Don Fine at Arbor House. I was at my desk, with a jar of sharpened pencils, going over the final typescript when the phone rang. It was Megan from Los Angeles.

I knew she had not been feeling well, tired, a pain in her shoulder. She was busy at living with her excellent husband, Richard Shaw, whom she had met in college, and her two little boys, two and four years old.

Why was she so tired? She had mourned for her father, yes, and perhaps too much. . .

Now Megan had something to tell. She had felt a tiny lump on her clavicle, the bone above the ribs commonly called the breastbone. She had gone with Richard to a hospital for a biopsy. She had cancer. Not like her father's, not related, no explanation except that she had been mourning, saddened, her immunity systems down. That was medical opinion.

Within days, the doctors were able to tell Megan that the cancer was probably in her lungs. Probably. It could be handled. Probably. "An environmental cancer" was what they called it, almost optimistically.

I went to Los Angeles to be near Megan while she had treatment. She had found an apartment for me, furnished it with bright tablecloths, plants, stemmed wine glasses. "Have little parties, Mo," she said. "I won't need you all the time."

She needed us a very short time, in fact—Patrick, her beloved Richard, and me. From the beginning, the radiation was not effective, she became too weak for chemotherapy. Once, as she rested, I asked if she'd like to help check the galley proofs of *Honor* and I heard again those fateful words, "Let me do it tomorrow."

My last moments with that little golden girl from Paris were strangely poignant. She spent her final four

"Our darling Megan on the day she married Richard Shaw, Jr. The day Megan met Richard on the campus of the University of Southern California, Patrick McGivern came home to say, 'Now she's met some-body!'"

days in the hospital, Richard near her always, while I cared for their little boys. I went to see her once. Her illness had progressed so rapidly that she almost avoided pain and had kept her beauty—blue, blue eyes; bright, tousled hair, red with henna; slim, graceful hands with pale, perfect nails.

I stood by her bed while I heard her tell me what she wanted for her little sons—the name of their pediatrician, where their dress-up clothes were kept, the closet that stored the Easter decorations and playmates' homes that she approved of for overnight visits. This little girl, dying, who once had worried only about a teddy bear. . .

I did not want to test her strength by crying myself so I said, "Megan you just rest now. I'll sit here quietly. You know how I am inclined to get excited and natter on."

"Don't say that, please," she said. "You've never bored me, Mo."

She slept and when it came time to leave I touched her hand, feeling the living warmth of her fingers for the last time. It was like saying good-bye to a flower.

Megan died shortly before midnight on the last day of the year, before the clocks of the world could strike twelve. I had lost both my beloved travellers.

I'm back where I was when I was seventeen, alone with a typewriter, but more alone. My new novel will have fictional characters, perhaps, but there will be Megan in my girl character and everything of Bill in my hero. It will be my tribute, my way of holding onto the memory of their voices, their pleasures, their smiles of surprise, my way of keeping us together a little longer.

Is that what you meant, way back then, Sister Rosita, when you said—just tell your story, tell it honestly and put down what you know? Could you not have forewarned me that sometime the sorrows might be too great? That sometime I would know too much for words?

It will hurt to write this book, but it will hurt more not to try. And, after all, it is what I know best, acts of love, the whole process. That's what my life has been about.

BIBLIOGRAPHY

FOR YOUNG ADULTS

Fiction:

Seventeenth Summer. New York: Dodd, 1942.

Sixteen, and Other Stories (illustrated by Kendall Rossi). New York: Dodd, 1961.

Nonfiction:

Smarter and Smoother: A Handbook on How to Be That Way (illustrated by Marguerite Bryan). New York: Dodd, 1944.

Twelve around the World (illustrated by Frank Kramer). New York: Dodd, 1957.

What's Your P. Q. (Personality Quotient)? (illustrated by Ellie Simmons). New York: Dodd, 1952.

Spanish Roundabout. New York: Dodd, 1960.

Moroccan Roundabout. New York: Dodd, 1961.

Editor of:

My Favorite Stories. New York: Dodd, 1948.

My Favorite Mystery Stories. New York: Dodd, 1966.

My Favorite Suspense Stories. New York: Dodd, 1968.

FOR CHILDREN

Fiction:

Patrick Visits the Farm (illustrated by E. Simmons). New York: Dodd, 1959.

A recent picture: "The late James M. Cain, with whom I corresponded, once wrote me, 'I'm glad you're not one of those dish-faced Irish.' I was always proud I was."

Patrick Takes a Trip (illustrated by E. Simmons). New York: Dodd, 1960.

Patrick Visits the Library (illustrated by Paul Lantz). New York: Dodd, 1961.

Patrick Visits the Zoo (illustrated by Sam Savitt). New York: Dodd, 1963.

The Ginger Horse (illustrated by Wesley Dennis). New York: Dodd, 1964.

The Small War of Sergeant Donkey (illustrated by W. Dennis). New York: Dodd, 1966.

Rosie, the Dancing Elephant (illustrated by Lorence Bjorklund). New York: Dodd, 1967.

Nonfiction:

Spain: Wonderland of Contrasts. New York: Dodd, 1965.

FOR ADULTS

Nonfiction:

The Perfect Hostess: Complete Etiquette and Entertainment for the Home. New York: Dodd, 1950.

Mention My Name in Mombasa: The Unscheduled Adventures of an American Family Abroad, as Maureen Daly McGivern, with husband, William P. McGivern (illustrated by F. Kramer). New York: Dodd, 1958.

Editor of:

Profile of Youth. Philadelphia: Lippincott, 1951.

Leonard Everett Fisher

1924–

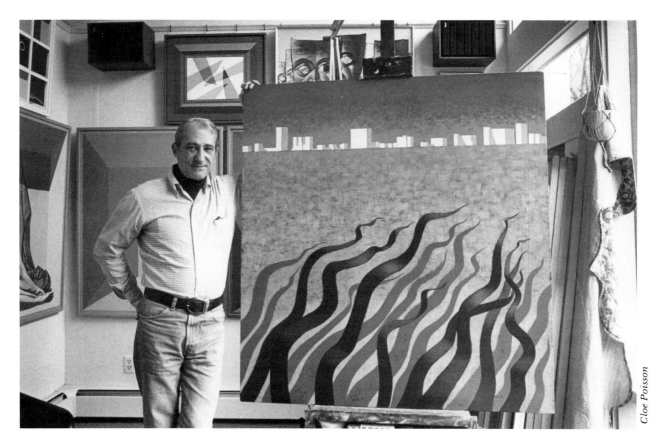

Leonard Everett Fisher in his studio, Westport, Connecticut, 1982. Painting in foreground:
Summerscape, *acrylic, 48"x50."*

It was 1926. I was two years old. Claude Monet had just died in France. The Impressionists were all gone, not that I was aware they had ever existed. I did not know that a more innocent age had slipped beyond my reach.

A Buster Brown hairstyle would mark me for the next few years. It hid gaping wounds behind each ear. Later, the job of giving me a proper haircut to ease my way into first grade went to a dapper barber with a pair of snapping scissors. He, too, had been scarred by mastoiditis and played the heavy as he whispered into each ear how he had been carved up without ether. All the while his scissors kept snapping. I shuddered in that barber's chair every month, listening to his malevolent whispers. I wished he would evaporate. I thought him only too willing to extend my surgery with those snapping scissors. My mother would only smile, discounting the obvious menace.

As I look back through the haze of recollection, that barber represented a hostile world. Snatched by a mastoid operation from death's door while still an infant, I had become the object of family attention and concern. The barber was lucky to get near me. My parents, close relatives, and a Bronx, New York apartment were my shield against the likes of strangers with snapping scissors. And it was in that apartment, made safe and secure by parental enthusiasm for my well-being that at age two I performed a single compulsive act that led to all that I am and ever will be. Perhaps it was not compulsion at all but a predestined beginning. Whatever it was, I would begin to be an artist.

My father kept a small drafting table in the front bedroom of the apartment. The room overlooked a sloping parkland, Mosholu Parkway and DeWitt Clinton High School beyond. Here, Dad pursued his constant, tantalizing dream of becoming an artist. It would never happen. But here he struggled with stiff drawings, fussy watercolors, and frustration. An idle ship designer in a world of closing shipyards, he now worked as a draftsman for New York City's Department of Plant and Structures creating working drawings of jail cells, among other things. Later, he would elevate himself to the Board of Transportation as a civil engineer designing subway stations for the yet unborn Eighth Avenue subway. Eventually, he would find his way back to ships. But not until the Great Depression would lower him into the abyss of unemployment and menial work. At the moment he was planning his great escape through art.

I was much too young to know or even remember his desperation. I saw only pictures, color and the minutiae within them—the expressions of too linear and logical a mind. Dad was a marvelous draftsman and letterer, however. He delighted in the precise turn of a letter and in the measured curve of an arc. And on that bedroom drafting table he tried to free himself of those restraints.

Still, I had an itch to do what Dad was trying to do—make pictures. The moment came. He turned his back on an unfinished work and I was into a bottle of india ink with a sable brush. It was all over in a flash. The picture was permanently altered. Years later, Dad would always insist that I had a "strong and direct approach" whatever it was I scribbled. He never allowed for abstraction—surely not a man of his mental precision—in 1926. His heroes were well defined: Julius Caesar, Michelangelo, Howard Pyle, Admiral Dewey, Theodore Roosevelt, and Benny Leonard, the Lightweight Champion of the World—a play on both our names. Dad's given name was Benjamin.

My early deftness produced immediate results. Instead of being strangled for overpainting my father's picture, I was rewarded. A front hall closet was cleared out. A small dropleaf table and two small chairs were installed inside. I was supplied with paper, pencils, and crayons to challenge my muse—out of harm's way. Liquids were barred. I was not given a bottle of india ink; ergo, no brush either. Paints were a few years down the road. Nevertheless, I was cozily in business, ensconced in my first studio, lit from the ceiling by a naked bulb and about six steps from the kitchen. My father continued his struggles in the bedroom, safely.

Over the next several years I graduated from scribbles to violent scenes of the Civil War, World War I, and Jack Dempsey the heavyweight boxing champion. Once in a while I broke the pattern with linear profiles of my parents or assorted relatives. The choice of subject matter was dictated by impressive events. Jack Dempsey was everyone's hero in the 1920s. My drawings of soldiers and war were seeded by the various parades we always attended, my father's uncompromising patriotism, and the rotogravure section of the Sunday papers which continued to publish gruesome photographs of death and destruction in France, 1914-1918. These crude drawings amused my father's younger brother, Harvey. He had been there.

Uncle Harvey was a bona fide decorated hero. He served in France with Company L, 30th Infantry, 3rd Division—the "Rock of the Marne." I think Uncle Harvey was the rock. The 30th Infantry, comprising a few thousand men, defended Paris with a six-and-a-half-mile line along the Marne River east of Château-Thierry. A German offensive of 24,000 men—three divisions—fell on them one July morning, 1918, in an attempt to capture Paris. The 30th Infantry, outnumbered about eight-to-one, held. The Germans never got to Paris. Not that time, anyway. At the center of this historic battle was Company L. Uncle Harvey was one

Ray Mera and Benjamin M. Fisher, 1922

of a handful of survivors of that brutal combat. He went on to fight elsewhere and was wounded at the Meuse-Argonne. It was all in the papers. He told me everything. I was mesmerized by these accounts and I tried to draw them all. Another uncle was in the Meuse-Argonne, too. The experience left him uncommunicative his entire life. My turn would come, although not quite in the same way. I would serve with the 30th Engineers instead of the 30th Infantry.

Every so often, Dad would look in on me in my closet studio. Mostly, he checked to see if I was using a "how to draw this and that" loose-leaf book he had made for me, containing exercises in basic perspective, simple anatomy, and boats from every angle. He tried to teach me to play chess in there, too. He always won.

My mother would keep an eye on me from the kitchen. Occasionally, she would sit in one of the little studio chairs and read to me from *Mother Goose* or *A Child's Garden of Verses* while I drew battlefield ambulances filled with bleeding heroes. Shortly before I entered first grade my parents purchased *Compton's Picture Encyclopedia.* Each of those twenty-six leather-bound volumes was part of the "read to" repertoire. My father loved all that incidental encyclopedic information without which no one could succeed in this world. So he thought. My mother must have considered her own introduction to first grade. She could not even speak English.

A native of Czarist Russia, six-year-old Mera Shapiro—my mother—arrived in Brooklyn via Ellis Island in October 1906. I related much of that early history in *A Russian Farewell.*

The day after the immigrant Shapiros were settled in their new home on Moore Street in Brooklyn, Mom was taken by an American relative to the local public school for registration. Her account of her Americanization was quick and blunt when asked to describe how it felt to be an alien kid in a Brooklyn elementary school: "When I was registered my name was changed to Ray. That was on a Monday. By the end of the week, Friday, I spoke English."

The impulse that gained a studio for me at the age of two—albeit a spare closet—sprang from my father's psyche. Art had been a part of him since his birth on a desolate Brooklyn farm. His own father, Simon, dreamed the same dreams. He made his living in the waterfront cafes of Riga, Latvia, drawing caricatures of the patrons. Riga was something of an artistic city during the 19th century. It was called the "Paris of the Baltic." The proceeds from these sketching efforts were used to take his wife, my grandmother, Lena Eve, and a couple of small children to America in 1890. Nothing ever came of grandfather Simon's artistic activity beyond one son's artistic yearning and another son who

Fisher at Little Falls, Bronx Park, New York, 1931

was a minor actor. There were other siblings—sons and daughters. None of them showed any artistic interests.

My father was perceptive enough to know that he was chasing a fantasy. He knew enough about art, artists, and skills to realize his delusion. There was something missing in his chemistry and he searched for it in vain. Somehow, he saw himself in me, making a fresh start, and was encouraged. The same thing seemed to be true for my younger brother, Richard. He would, in effect, become one side of my father's brain, a civil engineer and an architect. I would become the other side, an artist. My later interest in writing, a maternal trait, would grow out of my desire to communicate in words those ideas and events that could not be expressed with pictorial imagery.

My career direction was confirmed in second grade—at P.S. 80, 1931. I drew a picture of a pilgrim shooting a turkey. The drawing won a prize in the Wanamaker Art Competition for New York City School Children. I had no idea what it was all about, but the applause and the attention from an important department store—Wanamaker's—made me feel good. Eight years later, in 1939, another drawing of mine won another department store prize. This time it was the R.H. Macy Thanksgiving Day Parade Float Design Competition for New York City School Children. I cannot remember what the drawing was. No matter. By that time I was studying life drawing with Moses Soyer in his Fourteenth Street studio and we were no longer living in the Bronx. Moreover, I was exhibiting for the first time. My pencil drawing of backyards was being shown with other works by high school students at the Brooklyn Museum.

In between all of this I attended art classes at the Heckscher Foundation (1932) on Saturday mornings. My mother waited the three hours for me, in a nearby hallway, I assume. I spent months there trying to paint watercolors of horses. I have no idea why. I recall a well-traveled bridle path near or around Van Cortlandt Park, plenty of mounted police, and the Cavalry on parade. Buried in there is a youthful reason. Those classes were painful. I struggled against my peers whose talents were larger. My indifference today to watercolor and horses is perhaps attributable to that first professional school experience. Many years later, while attending a function at Mount Holyoke College—my wife's alma mater—I met August Heckscher, a trustee of the college. He was amazed to find someone who had attended his grandfather's school pursuing art as a life work.

Saturday afternoons following the art classes were also programmed by my mother. We prowled the American Museum of Natural History, or stalked the galleries of the Metropolitan Museum of Art. Sometimes we attended performances of the Civic Repertory Theater. Visions of Eva LeGallienne as Peter Pan still dance around in my head. My cultural horizons were being broadened. All too often I would have preferred a football or baseball game.

I had a library card, too, well stamped and a year old in 1932. The steady stream of books was always more vital to me than what went on in school. They transported me to places and events far beyond the unimaginative basic school readers. These library books were continuously supplemented by dozens of secondhand books my father would buy in Manhattan for pennies. I could read comfortably beyond my school grade. I seemed to respond to words easily. Paintings were a more mysterious matter. I seemed to know what I was reading in a book. Robert Louis Stevenson's *Treasure Island* with N. C. Wyeth's illustrations haunted me, as did much of what Rudyard Kipling wrote about India. But I was never sure of what I was seeing in a painting. The differences between El Greco and Rubens or Titian and Gainsborough were too abstract and confusing for my youthful, uneducated vision. I did not respond to French impressionism, Italian medieval painting, or any of the more recent movements—cubism, fauvism, dadaism, and more. I was struck by the drama of Rembrandt, the faultless technique of Ingres, the romance of Delacroix and Géricault. I had never been face-to-face with a Michelangelo painting, yet I knew from what I could see in

reproductions that the power was persuasive. By the time I was ten years old I knew what was out there. But that was all. I had no real knowledge of painters or paintings, or of illustrators, for that matter. I read a great deal but my visual responses were all primitive and subjective. Underneath it all there was a surging desire never to be a spectator.

All that transpired in the Bronx during those early years, 1924-1934, might not have happened if my mother had not decided to change the place of my arrival at near-zero hour. Following their marriage in New York in 1922 and a brief honeymoon up the Hudson River on the New York-Albany Nightliner, my parents settled first in Cleveland, Ohio, then in Detroit, Michigan. Dad bounced back and forth between the American Shipbuilding Company and the Ford River Rouge plant, designing lake and river workboats. Apparently Mom had second thoughts about where to give birth. Fourteen days before my appearance, she grabbed a train and headed for the Bronx, for Charlotte Street where her parents, Benjamin and Anna Shapiro, lived. Dad followed a week later. He would not see the inside of another shipyard for ten years; nor would he ever leave New York again to work. I was born there June 24, 1924, my parents' second wedding anniversary.

By 1935, my parents were beginning to climb out of the Depression. My brother was two years old. Dad found work in the Brooklyn Navy Yard's Hull Design Division. And we had moved to the water's edge, Sea Gate.

Sea Gate is a square-mile landsend in Brooklyn. Once the home of the New York Yacht Club and a long gone turn-of-the-century playground for millionaires, it juts into Lower New York Bay east of Staten Island, west of Coney Island. The community's presence by the sea is distinguished by the red beacon of the landlocked Norton's Point Lighthouse. The Point itself, the very spot on which our house sat, and its jetty, separated the tidal flow of the North Atlantic from the quiet waters of Gravesend Bay. Powerful currents swept that rolling sea only to be deflected by the jetty. That jetty, our house, Sea Gate, and the general area served both as background and subject in several of my published works—*The Death of Evening Star, Noonan,* and *Storm at the Jetty,* a picture book, which was culled from an unpublished novel about the jetty.

Sea Gate was not a new experience. We had spent every summer there since I was a baby except for a couple of Depression years. And even then I was sent there to visit relatives for a few weeks. My mother's family had been vacationing in the "Gate" for fifteen summers. I had friends there. I could hardly wait to

The Fisher house, Sea Gate, in New York harbor, Brooklyn

become a year-round resident. What adventure!

In those early days, Sea Gate was a sleepy place at the end of the world, let alone Brooklyn. And we lived at the very tip of that end with our back to the community and our face to the sea. Not unlike Brigadoon, Sea Gate seemed to hibernate in the wintry months and wake up every summer. It was an extraordinary ghetto where a well-defined boundary—an iron fence and the sea—kept out the unacceptable instead of ostracizing the inhabitants. It was an association of homeowners who had a unique deal with the City of New York. Its privacy was assured long ago by a ninety-nine year lease. One needed a pass to enter. No business was permitted to be conducted inside the Gate. There was no movie house. There was no school. We all had to attend school outside the Gate. The practice of medicine, dentistry, law, and the like was forbidden. Those services abounded outside. Doctors did make house calls, however.

There were exceptions. The Sea Gate Garage was one. Another was Johnny Gudice's Fruit and Produce truck. There were a couple of ice cream parlors, too. One was at the rambling Whittier Inn, a hotel—hotels and rooming houses were allowed. The other was at the Riviera, a beachside snack bar by day; an alfresco night club after dark. That was it.

Sea Gate winters were lonely and damp. In the dreary chill of those months, the evenings were long, if not depressing. Movie-going was infrequent and there was no television. Only radio. Besides the usual chores of homework and housework, everyone had something

to do—my father tinkered around in his basement workshop, a place I had absolutely no interest in; my mother tinkered around in her kitchen; I tinkered around with clay, pad, and pencil but not much of anything else. I was floundering in that isolation until there arrived on radio an Art Appreciation program sponsored by New York University. The home listener was provided with a substantial portfolio of masterpiece paintings. These reproductions were large and clear. The radio commentator provided the discussion dealing with one of the prints each week. My art interests began to quicken, not so much for drawing but for art history and analysis. Finally, someone began to lift the veil of mystery about the craft and the background of paintings. Some of these paintings were very familiar. I had seen them at the Metropolitan. Most of the works were less familiar. I had never seen them in the flesh, only in books. Of course, there were those I had never seen in my young life. My thirst was unquenchable now. I wanted to make masterpieces. The sooner, the better.

Toward that end I seemed to race through the New York City Public School System. I was restless and wanted to be done with each day, each week, each month, each year. I had skipped a grade in the Bronx. By 1938, in Brooklyn, I was completing the David A. Boody Junior High School Rapid Advance Program.

As graduation neared, the school staff suggested that I attend the new High School of Music and Art. But my parents objected. They felt such a curriculum would be too weighted in favor of art and that everyone, even an artist, needed a well-balanced education. I registered at Abraham Lincoln High School, a "regular" school that was much closer to home. What neither my parents nor I knew was that Lincoln offered the most intensive art program of any high school in New York City, including the High School of Music and Art. The guiding light of the Lincoln art program was Leon Friend, who also had an influential impact on all art instruction in New York City public education. At Lincoln, he did all he could to whip his art majors, including me, into some kind of shape as graphic designers. Leon Friend was a disciple of the Bauhaus.

Friend had some difficulty with me. I wanted to be a painter. And I wanted to go to college. He discouraged both goals among his potential graphic designers. In fact he once growled at me, "Bauhaus, not Poorhouse." The man was sincerely trying to save me. I did not want to be saved that way. We fought. I refused to take his Graphic Design course. He refused to let me illustrate *Cargoes,* the school literary magazine. Still, I became a member of the elite Art Squad and graduated with a gold medal. Friend was a wonder. Without him I never would have had such early contact with a number of the nation's leading artists who were brought to our classes. Among these were Moses and Raphael Soyer with whom I studied for almost a full year.

In 1938, having just entered Lincoln High, another kindred spirit and I discovered that for fifty cents we could draw from nude models. We knew we needed the experience. We were both fourteen. The class was being offered at a distant school on Saturday mornings. We found the place and a sign:

UNDER 17 NOT ADMITTED

A receptionist asked our ages. "Seventeen," we replied casually. I ran my hand over my face so that she would not notice that I had not yet begun to shave. My companion coughed violently as an excuse to turn his head for the same reason.

"That's what you say," she shot back. She knew. "You got fifty cents?"

"Yup."

"OK. You can go in."

The nude lady took one look at us and quickly put her robe on, complaining that this was no place for "kids." I was glad she did. It gave me a chance to catch my breath and get organized. The instructor, whose name escapes me, convinced her it would be alright. Fifty cents was fifty cents. And we represented a whole dollar. We had to prove ourselves, however, or be tossed out as a couple of fourteen-year-old voyeurs. We did. I attended that class for some weeks and continued to attend other life drawing and life painting classes intermittently over the next ten years: with Moses and Raphael Soyer; with Reginald Marsh at the Art Students' League; Olindo Ricci at Brooklyn College; a brief night class in Sacramento, California, while I waited to be discharged from the army; and with Professor Deane Keller at Yale. The entire figure study experience came to a climax during my third year at Yale when I was privileged to dissect cadavers at the Yale Medical School.

Leon Friend did not summarily pass out of my life when I graduated from Lincoln in January 1941. Grudgingly, he saw to it that I would major in art as a freshman at Brooklyn College. No one majored in anything there until junior year. Friend was going to save me in spite of myself.

Brooklyn College was not an easy passage. I was too young to be in any college, if for no other reason than my social isolation. I had entered in January, age sixteen and a half. That alone was awkward enough on any academic calendar. Also, Europe was at war. By December 1941, Pearl Harbor had come and gone; and so did drawing and painting at Brooklyn College. Enter, Serge Chermayeff, an English architect who helped to introduce a new order to American college art departments: the Bauhaus tradition and Graphic Design. I was disappointed. I felt betrayed. I thought the classes were vacant and humorless. Instead of trying to discover how to probe the human presence and project it with paint, I was now learning how to be a servant of industry in a program designed to produce disposable images for disposable products—learning to create appearances for corporate ideas. That was my perception of the program at the time. Even then, as young as I was, and however much I could not clearly state my own beliefs, I did subscribe to the singularity and independence of art and artists, and to the superiority of content over appearances. To me, painting was and still is a spiritual extension of the human presence. In my mind, art was not to be a marketing tool. I could never be a creative adjunct to commerce. I was interested in humanizing not civilizing.

However, I went along with the new curriculum. I had little choice. The war was coming for me soon enough, anyway. Still, I plotted my escape. On December 1, 1942, I became a U.S. Army Enlisted Reservist and soon thereafter requested active duty. Assigned to the 30th Engineer Topographic Battalion, I joined the war as a would-be mapmaker. A work scholarship obtained that summer at the Art Students' League would have to wait. It still waits. Another scholarship to the Jamesine Franklin School of Art would have to wait. It, too, still waits.

Between the end of January and the beginning of March 1943, I languished first in Camp Upton, Yaphank, New York, while the army ran a security check; then in the Fort Hamilton Post Hospital, Brooklyn. I had come down with the measles. Finally, I reported to Fort Belvoir, Virginia, and the 30th Topographic Engineers. The work that I would eventually do would be so highly classified that all of my training was conducted solely by the 30th Engineers out of view of the rest of the army. It was my art background coupled with nearly two successful years of collegiate study in geology that brought me to the 30th.

The war became a celluloid fantasy on a Norfolk, Virginia, pier in November. While bands played and flags flew and 5,000 of us boarded the *General A. E. Anderson,* including the first contingent of women GIs—WACS—to go overseas, I imagined I was seeing a double-feature movie. It was an unreal scenario. The troops slowly moving ahead of me were, in my imagination, Pathé News segments. It was happening to someone else, not to me. Reels of *Dawn Patrol* and *What Price Glory* ran off on my mental screen.

We sailed Thanksgiving Day. According to Admiral Samuel Eliot Morison, the Navy's historian, it was a memorable voyage. Not only were we the first American troopship to go it alone—without escort—through the worst period of enemy submarine activity in the North Atlantic, it was the *Anderson*'s maiden voyage. "We were the first that ever burst into that not so silent sea," to paraphrase Samuel Taylor Coleridge's line in his *Rime of the Ancient Mariner.* Terrific! We zigged and zagged for ten days—and made it.

But in the dark morning hours before landing at Casablanca, French Morocco, while the ship's murky interior glowed eerily red in its blackout lights, and we were locked deep in a hold without a quick exit, the cacaphonic din of a general quarters alarm jarred us from every sweet dream. "This is no drill! Bong. Bong. Bong." For a few minutes dull hammering sounds echoed around and above us. I never knew what happened. But in the ruby glow of that hold, shoeless and wearing a useless life jacket, I clung to my bunk paralyzed. The movie was over.

Later, on deck I saw the French battleship *Jean Bart* on its side in the harbor, awash like a monstrous dead whale. She had been scuttled months before. Despite that first eye-popping scene my soul was permanently invaded right then and there by wanderlust as the minarets and rooftops of exotic Casablanca shimmering in the morning sun caught my eye.

Traveling in box cars—"40 & 8s" (forty men or eight horses)—through Rabat, Meknes, Fez, Oujda, Tlemcen, Sidi-bel-Abbès, and Oran—shades of *Beau Geste*—we arrived in Affreville, Algeria, ninety miles

October 1944, with the 30th Engineers, traveling from Affreville to Oran, Algeria, on the trip home. Seated at left, Sergeant L.E. Fisher.

south of Algiers, high in the Atlas Mountains. I spent some nine months in this place with Battalion Operations. Here, two- and three-dimensional invasion, tactical, and field maps, and other topographic necessities were produced for United States forces and other military clients. Our group was responsible for the Italian Campaign north of Naples, part of the Normandy invasion, the invasion of Southern France and beyond into Germany. This was my first experience with meeting professional deadlines. And these deadlines were truly deadly. We were mapping predictable battles and battlegrounds that had not yet occurred. I have been a stickler for meeting deadlines ever since.

Before the year was out—in November 1944—I came back to the United States in an emotional homecoming. To all intents and purposes I was out of the war. Three weeks after arriving I was on the *Matsonia* sailing for Hawaii. I remained in the Islands, on Oahu, until the end of the war. There I participated in the mapping of the assault on Iwo Jimà, the invasion of Okinawa, and in what turned out to be the cancelled invasion of Japan.

I was not artistically lazy, either in Africa or Hawaii. There was a mural in Affreville destroyed by local Arabs as we departed. It contained offensive material—a harem. I painted another decoration for a military hospital in Hawaii. The building has been gone for years. The whereabouts of the painting, which was commissioned by the American Red Cross of Hawaii, is unknown. Another painting of mine received a first prize in an army art exhibition during the summer of 1945. I filched the canvas from Boris Karloff's USO show while he was on stage performing. In addition, I was ordered to do a pastel portrait of the Deputy Commander of the Tenth Army, a marine general named Smith. Working on maps midnight to noon, for the most part, I had little time to deal competently with art. The mural was painted in my spare time in our underground complex. I struggled with another canvas above ground on a gun rack in a latrine. An account of some of these shenanigans can be found in an article in *Design* written by Stanley Witmeyer (November 1945 issue).

When the war ended I wrote to Yale seeking admission to the university's art school. I was accepted the following April. Meanwhile, I vacationed on the "Big Island"—Hawaii—and awaited my release from the army.

In February 1946, a month following my service discharge, Abraham Lincoln High School mounted a one-man show of drawings and watercolors I had done during the war, chiefly in Africa. The exhibition, my first solo show, was hung in connection with the awarding of the Lincoln Medal to Mrs. Eleanor Roosevelt. Over the next seven months, I painted two or three

Fisher, a graduate assistant in design theory, Yale University, 1950

dark and heavy-handed canvases; spent more time rediscovering the hometown girls than worrying about painting; and became reacquainted with my brother. Nine years separated us in age. We hardly had a boyhood together.

In July, the Norfolk Art School of Yale University, Norfolk, Connecticut, opened its studios for the first time. I was there painting meaningless pictures with Lewis York, chairman of Yale's painting department; Herbert Gute; and Dean Everett Meeks. I had no idea what I wanted to paint. I had nothing to say. I was lost in that idyllic introduction to the Yale tradition. Those Berkshire foothills seemed more menacing than the formidable Atlas Mountains of North Africa. I could hardly believe the peace, the quiet, the freedom, independence, and solitude.

I spent the next four years in New Haven. In an address before the fiftieth anniversary convention of the Catholic Library Association of America in Cincinnati, Ohio, April 13, 1971, I described the Yale Art School education as I had perceived it:

"Here I was taught a discipline like never before; its history, mechanics and philosophy. Here I learned about optical physics, the chemistry of application, the scheme of drawing, the intent of painting. Here I was exposed to technical and esthetic possibilities I never knew existed. Now I knew what an innocent I really was. . . . Whatever Yale art had been before the war (a school of classic revival) it certainly was different now. . . ."

I may have some trouble with that today. My

Fisher looks on as brother Richard (left) receives his architectural degree, Columbia University, 1964.

perspective has since softened. Times change. We change or perhaps grow differently. Art schools at best represent the composite direction and fallibility of faculty ego. Too many artists use academia to justify their own creative presence and by institutional association give respectability to what otherwise could be insignificant esthetic adventures. Impressionable students are expected to comply. Art faculties, and thus, art schools, have no right to represent finite, uncompromising esthetic values. From the French academic Beaux Arts to the German new order Bauhaus, art schools have traditionally sought to impose their artistic definitions upon unsuspecting students and laypersons alike. The Yale Art School I attended did everything it could to explore the nature of our craft in every direction and to every depth without dragging the student around in an arena of conforming esthetics. Yale may have been out-of-touch with the realities of the new movements that would reshape the entire artistic world, but that was not professionally fatal. It is the student who must recognize or sense or consider how to use the information and skills being offered. Schools do not make artists. Artists make themselves.

Although in hindsight I may take issue with parts of the Yale curriculum to which I was subjected, my art has evolved from that matrix, underwritten by pre-

war and other influences, never radicalized by fast-moving trends or by an esthetic imposed by Yale. Lewis Edwin York, who stood at the center of the painting program of my time, had a deep influence on us all. He was a compelling teacher, the most informed person I ever knew in my life, the pure intellectual. The gifted faculty and student body were a supreme challenge to one's esthetic raison d'être. And all of us, faculty and students alike, in our great desire to achieve something artistic, were wedged in a cultural limbo between the end of the old era and the coming of the new; the art world was on hold in that twilight zone between the war's end and the arrival of the abstract expressionists. It would take me years to shake it all loose. Nevertheless, the Yale experience was memorable. It prepared me for every artistic eventuality. It was up to me to discover those eventualities.

I did manage to keep a quiet professional life going in New York while struggling with the practice of egg tempera painting at Yale. I was a member of "Twenty-Five and Under," a group sponsored by Jacques Seligmann Galleries. Not only were my paintings being seen in Manhattan, but elsewhere in America, arranged by Seligmann. In April 1950, while working on a graduate degree and teaching Design Theory at the art school, I was invited by Lincoln Kir-

Coney Island, *1949, egg tempera on gessoed masonite, 36"x48." In the collection of Joseph Erdelac, Rocky River, Ohio.*

stein to participate in a show, *Symbolic Realism,* at the Edwin C. Hewitt Gallery in Manhattan. I was included with a large allegorical egg tempera, *Coney Island.* Suddenly I was in the company of Andrew Wyeth, Paul Cadmus, Isabel Bishop, and others, who comprised the exhibition. Kirstein wrote, "Art is a cosa mentale, a thing of the mind." Perhaps. In May I received the Pulitzer painting award. By September 1950, my Sea Gate sojourn was ending. My life would take me elsewhere.

Glutted with funds from the William Wirt Winchester Traveling Fellowship (Yale University School of Fine Arts, 1949) and the Joseph Pulitzer Painting Fellowship (Columbia University and the National Academy of Design, 1950), I sailed for Europe aboard the British liner *Mauretania* to finally see all the art I had only known through book and magazine reproductions. As the ship came abreast of Hoffman and Swinburne Islands on the starboard, I could see clearly the lighthouse and "4810" at the seawall on the portside. It was late in the afternoon. The sun setting over Staten Island illuminated the Sea Gate shore. Standing on the seawall were waving relatives and friends. They were holding aloft a white bedsheet and a large American flag both of which fluttered wildly in the breeze.

My first stop was London where I was spellbound by Carlo Crivelli's *Annunciation* at the National Gallery. There were other spellbinders I never dreamed I would ever see—and all these in one room. There were Mantegnas, Bellinis, Verrocchios, DaVincis, Turas, and Sassettas, and more. But it was the Crivelli *Annunciation* that held my interest. A year before, I painted *Coney Island.* There was a direct influential link between what Crivelli had done with egg tempera and one-point perspective and what I did. At the Victoria and Albert Museum I met Jonathan Main, Curator of Painting. I spent the afternoon with him looking at Raphael's tapestry cartoons. I could not have had a better guide.

In Paris at the Louvre, I was struck dumb by two works: Géricault's *Raft of Medusa* and David's *Napoleon Crowning Himself.* It was the scale of them, the size of them that astonished me. In Paris, too, I met Nadia Boulanger, the legendary piano teacher. I was reminded of my own piano teacher, Ruth Benach, an organist in a Brooklyn church. I gave Miss Benach a hard time for three or four years. How I dreaded her student recitals. Neither the piano nor I had much of a future with each other.

I spent a few weeks in Switzerland visiting with friends from home who were studying medicine in Lausanne. My adrenalin overflowed in Italy, everywhere from Milan to Venice to Florence, Pisa, Pistoia, Arezzo, Siena, Perugia, Orvieto, Rome, and on to the tip of the peninsula, across to Sicily and back again. I

spent some time at the American Academy in Rome. I saw every painting I came to see and more. The works that made the most enduring impact on me were Michelangelo's *Sistine Ceiling* and *The Last Judgment.* They claimed my soul. And in a less persistent manner so did all the Botticellis.

I returned home in January 1951 aboard the *Queen Mary,* eager to paint pictures. I painted a few egg temperas and began to realize that this ancient eggyolk-and-water medium on a smooth gessoed surface, which I prepared myself, belonged to a frame of artistic reference from which I had been drifting. While I questioned its validity for me, I continued to comfortably use the medium for nine years, leaving it finally in 1960. Shortly after my return I found myself working for Auriel Bessemer, a commercial muralist. I needed some money. I lasted a week. My trees were not his trees. My rocks, clouds, grass, and pilgrims were not his either. We were working on panels for railroad dining cars. On Friday, as I was being fired, the phone rang. The caller, Lewis Edwin York, invited me to become dean of the Whitney School of Art, a small independent professional school in New Haven. I accepted.

Margery Meskin Fisher, 1983

York, no longer at Yale, was now a member of my faculty.

That October I met Margery Meskin. Margery knew exactly where I was coming from—art. She knew more about Donatello than I thought I knew about Botticelli. Moreover, Margery knew exactly what the world was coming to—the computer. Margery was a systems service representative for IBM and lived on the top floor of a house in Manhattan where Chester A. Arthur took the oath of office as twenty-first President of the United States. Margery reminded me of no one I had ever known, so rare was her outlook, manner, and appearance. Suddenly, nothing seemed as important as spending the rest of my life with her.

In February 1952, I opened in Manhattan with my first New York exhibition. The Edwin C. Hewitt Gallery showed a few drawings and some recent egg temperas. The reviews were encouraging. The *New York Times* approved of my craftsmanship No one bought a thing but the future looked promising. I convinced Margery of that promise. We were married that December in Rockville Centre, New York.

Margery had first to ease her father's fears. He was not sure of the reliability of artists, especially, as he put it, those who paint "gremlins." Margery had to cope with me, too. I was a full menu of unshakeable truths. Margery's mother, Ruth, and her sister Betty were my only allies. Considering the vicissitudes of married life in our time, Margery and I continue to illuminate each other and to be illuminated by our three children.

Following a trip to Bermuda, we settled in a New Haven apartment. Margery represented systems for IBM while I juggled two roles: painting and being an art school dean. The pressure put upon me by the school was enormous. The pressure I put upon myself with regard to painting commitments was also enormous. I was driven to achieve in both areas. The only person who understood what kind of an effort that took in time, concentration, and dedication was Margery. The only person who realized the scope of the effort besides Margery, but who knew the spectre of failure, was my father.

As it turned out, the school began to drown in financial problems. In tandem with that slow demise, my paintings began to look tired and hollow. The art world was beginning to spin too many revolutions per minute. Something was happening on the cultural landscape and to me. A new, aggressive, entrepreneurish esthetic was emerging in New York. I had recurring dreams that all my paintings were under water—Lower New York Bay—held there by Ottoman Turkish rug salesmen with great scimitars. Enough! I needed a new perspective and time.

Conversations with Alex Ross, an illustrator friend, led to Oscar Ogg, designer for the Book-of-the-Month Club. He turned me toward children's books. I went to see Warren Chappell. His advice was so discouraging it hardened my determination to illustrate books.

I left the Whitney Art School in September 1953. Shortly thereafter, Oscar Ogg introduced me to Louise Bonino, children's book editor of Random House. She was nonplussed by my portfolio: some photographs of paintings too large to carry around, and a handful of drawings from the nude. She asked me if I could handle Bourges color separation. "Of course," I replied. I had no idea what she was talking about. I figured I could find out later. I did. Meanwhile, I came away with my first book to illustrate, Geoffrey Household's *The Exploits of Xenophon,* a Random House World Landmark edition.

I asked everyone at Yale about "Bourges color separation." No one knew. I asked Mr. Michaels, the owner of the art supply shop on Chapel Street. He

Book jacket from The Exploits of Xenophon *by Geoffrey Household. Illustrated by Leonard Everett Fisher. (Copyright © 1955 by Geoffrey Household. Illustrations copyright © 1955 by Leonard Everett Fisher. Reprinted by permission of Random House, Inc.)*

knew. "Mike" had never gotten past the eighth grade but he sold the stuff. I spent several sessions with him in the gloomy basement of his shop. There he taught me how to use this acetate material to separate flat colors for printing.

I set three goals with regard to *Xenophon.* The first was researching ancient Greek and Persian military life and matériels, including uniforms. The second goal was to use a graphic technique that had reproduction clarity. The third, to create a series of illustrations in two colors, black and brown, that could evoke a sense of solid form in a spatial setting.

Researching was easy. I knew my way around libraries and museums where books, manuscripts, prime source writings, paintings, statues, and ceramic decorations held the information I needed. Drawing clearly was no problem either. The big problem was creating the illusion of form in the final printing by overlapping two different materials in the artistic process. I knew a great deal about "form drawings"—those black-and-white drawings on toned papers of various colors. Albrecht Dürer's famous *Praying Hands* is a form drawing. I made hundreds of these drawings myself. And I studied hundreds more in the basement of the British Museum. I thought I could bring such drawing to life in this book even though I had to work with a separate color overlay. The outcome fell short of my desire. A true form drawing cannot be effected by some mechanical process aimed at printed reproduction. I should have known that. Nevertheless, it was my way of making a transition from what I knew I wanted to see as a painter to what I did not know how to produce as an illustrator. The effort in all this was monumentally time-consuming: researching, sketching, submitting the sketches for approval or disapproval, creating the finishes, and then nervously awaiting the outcome.

Xenophon finally appeared in September 1955. It was not perfect. I quickly knew I was in a new craft and needed some polishing. A month later, our daughter, Julie, appeared during a violent hurricane. But unlike the imperfections of *Xenophon,* Julie was perfect in every way. I had to give up my studio room to make way for a nursery. I ended up in the building's basement where my kindly landlord had remodeled a studio room for me linked to our apartment by a surplus army field telephone. It was like being in a wartime bunker. I did not get much painting done down there. I spent every spare minute running upstairs to admire our new daughter. After *Xenophon* was published, I became extremely busy illustrating a six-volume reading anthology, *Our Reading Heritage,* for Henry Holt and Company.

My mentor at Holt was Marjorie Wescott Barrows who kept me and several others frantic in creating the great variety of illustrated material for the anthology. Marjorie was the boss. She had a great deal to say about every design, composition, technique and molecule of artistry. But Marjorie Barrows was being pressured by higher authorities including state textbook adoption boards who also had a great deal to say about what the art should look like right down to the last buttonhole. I fought every inch of the way for my self-respect, my art and professionalism, not to mention my independence. It went on like that for a number of years, over hundreds of illustrations. I expected to be replaced every time the phone rang. The product of an artist is the result of long hours of concentration followed by long hours of working with one's hands. It is a product that cannot be duplicated. It is a singular item containing its own unique energies. To have these works rejected—after sixteen-hour days of lonely labor without a paycheck in sight, until the works are revised in ways that demean one's abilities—can be heartbreaking. And it happened. But I persisted. So did Marjorie. She refused to dismiss me even when I once jokingly begged her to do just that.

Instead, she sent me to the New York offices of Science Research Associates (SRA), a Chicago-based company. Lee Deighton, executive vice-president, was looking for artists to work on a new educational concept, the *Multilevel Reading Laboratory* originated by educator Don B. Parker. The first "laboratory," a box, would contain, among other things, 150 reading selections requiring 150 two-color illustrations. Deighton's idea was to commission ten artists to illustrate fifteen selections each. My idea was to do all 150. I convinced Deighton that he would be better off dealing only with me rather than with a group of ten. The depth of my experience at Holt in creating two-color pre-separations, my educational background, literary knowledge, reading skills, and art abilities became the deciding factors. Between 1956 and 1962, I illustrated seven pioneering "Reading Laboratories" involving about 1,000 two-color pre-separated illustrations and countless rough sketches submitted to Chicago for approval—possibly more than 3,000 items in all. About 1,000 of these sketches are, today, in the DeGrummond Collection of the University of Southern Mississippi. Lee Deighton left SRA to become board chairman at Macmillan. The project was continued under the direction of Lee Brown, who later founded Learning Materials, Inc. I was busy here, too.

I cannot say that these illustrations were my "finest hour." It was art by committee. I was not always free to follow my instincts, which in too many cases would have proven better than what we ended up with. Still, for me, it was a challenge to see how often I could break through. The SRA "Reading Laboratories" were not only a foundation course in editorial textbook illustration, they were also a learning experience in how to deal—or how not to deal—with others.

SRA was not the only project that absorbed me in the cellar studio at 20 Lake Place, New Haven. I had obtained my first Holiday House book from Helen Gentry and Vernon Ives—Manley Wade Wellman's *To Unknown Lands.* It was the second "trade" book (non-textbook) of my blossoming career. It was the beginning of a thirty-year relationship between Holiday House and myself that would continue under the egis of Kate and John Briggs. I showed a portfolio of tear sheets to Alice Dickinson at Franklin Watts. I was immediately commissioned to illustrate Richard B. Morris's *First Book of the American Revolution.* That was the start of a twenty-year association that put me on the road illustrating and writing American history for young readers.

American history had a strong presence during my growing years. To my parents, one an immigrant, the other the son of immigrants, the United States was heaven-sent. To all of us it was important to understand American institutions and their origins in order to remain free. Knowledge of American history took precedence over other kinds of information, including art and the bible. "We are the living miracle," my father would intone. Nothing else mattered with respect to continuity. We had not a single European connection. This was indeed the New World.

My interests were wider, nevertheless. I illustrated "Vision" and "Covenant" series for Farrar, Straus and Cudahy—books dealing with Catholic and Jewish histories in America. G. P. Putnam's Sons hired me to illustrate Peter Freuchen's *Whaling Boy.* I met Anico Surany at Alfred Knopf when I illustrated Robert Payne's *The Splendor of Persia.* She and I became good friends and later collaborated on a number of picture books dealing with Latin America, including *The Golden Frog,* a Putnam book. All of these found their way to audiovisual filmstrips.

Soon, other publishers became clients—Little, Brown; Abelard-Schuman; Crown; Vanguard; Appleton, Century and Crofts. It was time to crawl out of the basement.

We moved to Westport in June 1957. Julie cried the entire summer, preferring the cement and din of New Haven to the softer flora and fauna of Westport. I did not sleep the whole summer either. Every snapping twig and chirp in the woods behind us was a lion roaring in my ears. Screaming sirens never kept me awake in New Haven. Crashing tides never kept me awake in Sea Gate. But here, in Westport, silent and green, removed from the commotion of civi-

lization, I heard every marching ant. Margery slept. This is where she belonged.

At last I had an aboveground studio, one of our three bedrooms. Swamped by book illustrating projects, I could now keep a painting in the works as well. But by 1959 I had to give up the bedroom. It was a move in the right direction. We had become five. Susan was born in 1958, James a year later. I was removed to a newly completed studio added on to the house with a library/den. We could never live without books, whether or not I created them. In time we would push out all the walls and remake our home where it stood.

Margery's Dad, Hy, who would rather have

Exterior of Fisher's studio, with a rear view of his house, Westport, Connecticut, 1984

worked a farm than travel back and forth on slow boats to Australia as he did in his youth, had our blessings, horticulturally speaking. His was the greenest thumb of all. An artist of the soil, a planter with an eye and a heart, he created at the base of the large northern window of my studio a bank of lush ferns, a mass some twenty-five-feet long and three-feet deep. He specially transplanted these ferns from Camp Fernwood, Maine, where his two daughters enjoyed many summers. A book collector as well, he taught me a thing or two about rare editions.

As Marge's Dad toiled everywhere with his spade, planting annuals, perennials, trees and shrubs, Marge and I began to think there must be a world beyond children, relatives, friends, Cape Cod retreats, and volunteer work—not to mention just plain work. In October 1962, and without children who we thought needed a rest from us, I dragged Margery all over Italy for

In Fisher's studio, 1964. On the easel: American Lament, *1964, gelatine tempera, 40"x60." In the collection of the Butler Art Institute, Youngstown, Ohio. On the wall:* Jonah, *1964, gelatine tempera, 40"x40." In the collection of Mr. and Mrs. Peter Mack, New York City.*

three weeks, taking the identical routes I had traveled twelve years before. In two instances time seemed to stand still. A waiter I knew in a tiny Chocolateria in the Piazza della Signoria, Florence, was still there flicking his worn whisk broom over the backs of everyone who tipped him properly. Again, two clay pots brimming with geraniums huddled in a corner of an open window that could only be seen from the roof of the Clock Tower in Venice's Piazza San Marco. They were still there. For one fleeting moment I thought I saw the same scene with its clay pots and geraniums huddled in the same corner of a windowsill of a look-alike house on a recent visit we made to Suzhou in the People's Republic of China. Why not? Marco Polo, the Venetian, had been there.

The late 1950s and early 1960s were experimental years both artistically and parentally. For one thing I was a Daddy who worked at home. I was around all the time. I am sure the children were put upon from time to time. But I loved every minute of it. The studio door was always open. They wandered in and out, observing what went on or did not go on. They had free access to every bit of material and equipment in the place. They created their own pictures and never felt compelled to alter any of mine with the quick swish of a sable brush loaded with india ink. Frequently I

would look up from whatever it was I was doing and see the three of them with friends outside, pressing their noses against the window watching me. Their friends were always curious about this species of father who did not take a train to work. My children obliged all young disbelievers with on-the-spot guided tours.

These incidents provided the inspiration for one of two books that Margery wrote and I illustrated: *But Not Our Daddy* (1962). The other was *One and One* (1963), a number book. Both were published by the Dial Press. These two works were very unsophisticated. They were aimed at our own children.

These were the years I began to do scratchboard drawings for books; and I began to paint some transitional works that would slowly lead me out of the vacuum I had been locked in since the early 1950s. The paintings were gelatine temperas which spun off egg temperas and dealt with theo-philosophical concepts, for the most part—prophets and their symbols, etc.

In 1959, Connie Epstein at William Morrow asked me to consider doing one-color illustrations for a distinguished set of books by Gerald W. Johnson, Managing Editor of the Baltimore Sun. The books comprised a trilogy: *America Is Born, America Grows Up, America Moves Forward.* I suggested scratchboard. I liked the drama of scratchboard when the rendering of sharp light picked off the form. It was linear, strong, and direct. I could relate to it through all those form drawings I did and which I had learned to do at Yale. I could see it in my mind as being appropriate in conveying a strong sense of history without being historically imitative. Connie agreed. I just had to take care to make them less precise and methodical than metal engravings. It was my beginning of twenty-five years of soft engraving.

During this same period Dial published my first—and their first—written and illustrated picture book, *Pumpers, Boilers, Hooks and Ladders.* I was not prepared to write a book for young readers. But I did it. I wrote and wrote and wrote. I revised and revised again. It seemed to take forever. By the time the book was published in 1961 the itch to write was firmly in place.

In the year of *But Not Our Daddy,* Franklin Watts asked me to write and illustrate something of my choice. The conversation took place during a seventeen-minute cab ride to a Children's Book Council luncheon. I suggested art—paintings. Watts did not absorb that notion until 1973 when he published my book *The Art Experience: Oil Painting 15th–19th Century.* Instead he countered with a series on colonial American crafts—nineteen titles in all and fourteen years in the publishing process. I spent the first two years, 1962-1964, researching the material. These books became a staple item in virtually every American school. They finally went out of print in the late 1970s and early 1980s. Some of the titles will reappear in the near future, courtesy of David Godine, Publishers.

I enjoyed doing these books. They had more meaning for me than just conveying some colonial American history. More than that I tried to communicate a strong sense of pride in craftsmanship, in working hard to achieve excellence in one-of-a-kind objects. It was something I felt our children knew little about and it was time that they did.

My yen to write some adult material related to art came to fruition in 1984 when Thomas G. Aylesworth, formerly my editor at Doubleday, but now at Bison Books, asked me to write a tome on American painting. That book, *Masterpieces of American Painting,* along with a newer one, *Remington and Russell,* a lesser tome on two painters of the Old West, have become published entities.

Wandering in the realm of my interests, had been the look of letters and alphabetic history. The story of written communication surely belonged within my arena of activity. I never locked onto a strong image around which I could pictorialize this theme until Margery, my wife, now an experienced Westport school librarian proposed an alphabet book with exotic letters large enough for youngsters to use for social

studies projects. Judith Whipple, then editor at Four Winds Press, responded to the concept. In its final form, *Alphabet Art* developed into a series of various alphabets with large scale letters accompanied by an historical account and fully illustrated, both calligraphically and pictorially. *Alphabet Art,* published in 1979, was followed by *Number Art* and the very recent *Symbol Art.*

Some of these works, no doubt had been seeded in part by my return to teaching. It is difficult to know

Book Fair, Department of Commerce, Washington, D.C., 1964

what generates creative impulses beyond suggestion in so many subject areas and what generates the compulsion to communicate it all. I returned to teaching part-time in 1966 at the Paier School of Art in Hamden, Connecticut. I gave it up in 1978 to become the school's academic dean in order to participate in the institution's quest for a State Charter to grant a Bachelor of Fine Art degree. We succeeded in 1982 and I went back to part-time teaching. The school is now the Paier College of Art. My association with the newly chartered college began in 1948 while I was a student at Yale. I was its first contract faculty member, lecturing in Art History.

My need to be connected with the educational process is woven into the tapestry of my creative being. Communication is part of personal expression and creation. Sometimes the creative process is enough. There is no further need to communicate what has been

From Pumpers, Boilers, Hooks and Ladders, *written and illustrated by Leonard Everett Fisher. (Copyright © 1961 by Leonard Everett Fisher. Reprinted by permission of The Dial Press.)*

wrought. Then again, there are times when creation requires communication. Moreover, I like to be around young professional students. I think there is an obligation to see to it that professional generations are not disconnected.

I believe that the information books I write and illustrate are part of that rationale. Books like "Nineteenth-Century America," the seven-volume miniseries (Holiday House, 1979–1983) which describes areas of life in a growing United States, deal with my determi-

Book jacket from But Not Our Daddy *by Margery M. Fisher. Illustrated by Leonard Everett Fisher. (Copyright © 1962 by Margery M. Fisher. Illustrations copyright © 1962 by Leonard Everett Fisher. Reprinted by permission of The Dial Press.)*

From The Potters, *written and illustrated by Leonard Everett Fisher. (Copyright © 1966 by Leonard Everett Fisher. Reprinted by permission of Franklin Watts, Inc.)*

E. Irving Blomstrann

Shadow of a Ribbon, 1970, acrylic, 48"x48." In the collection of the New Britain Museum of American Art, New Britain, Connecticut.

nation not to disconnect. In a culture like ours, wherein today's material gratification seems to deny any historical link, knowledge of the past is often and mistakenly brushed aside as irrelevant to our present and future values, much less the course of our nation. I try to say otherwise.

In any case, creative disconnections were hardly a problem for me in the 1970s. After the death of my father in 1968, I was irrationally victimized by my lawnmower which took its revenge on my right hand. I recovered from that trauma. But in the process I came to realize my own mortality and the mortality of those around me whose lives mean more to me than my right hand. Life and art took on new meaning.

The grayness and low-key quality of the paintings I created during the 1960s disappeared. Gone, too, was the heavy philosophy. Brighter, more colorful, and higher-keyed paintings took their place. The medium was all acrylic. It was as if a veil had been lifted. While the paintings of the 1960s seemed overly concerned with cries in the wilderness and the loneliness of the human presence in an inhospitable world—much of this reflecting events from the murder of John F. Kennedy through Vietnam and my own isolation from the hyped world of painting—the newer works were an attempt to define endless, boundless, infinite space. The paintings were of tapestries and boxes, conveying a less introspective view with more optimistic overtones than previous works. In addition, I began to write books with more lengthy texts: *The Death of Evening Star* and *Noonan* for Doubleday; *Across the Sea from Galway, Letters from Italy,* and *A Russian Farewell* for Four Winds.

Early in that decade I painted the *Stations of the Cross* for St. Patrick's Church, Armonk, New York. These fourteen acrylic panels were the closest I had been to wall decoration since the National Park Service used some of my art for a mural in the Washington

From The Death of Evening Star, *written and illustrated by Leonard Everett Fisher.*
(Copyright © 1972 by Leonard Everett Fisher. Reprinted by permission of
Doubleday & Co., Inc.)

Monument in 1964. Between 1972 and 1978, along with everything else I was doing, I designed a number of United States postage stamps depicting American history and crafts. Eight of these were Bicentennial issues of July 4, 1972, and July 4, 1977. One issue was the 1974 commemorative *The Legend of Sleepy Hollow,* a stamp close to my literary heart.

There were exhibitions and more exhibitions. The largest and most significant of these was the retrospective mounted by the New Britain Museum of American Art in 1973. The exhibition covered twenty-four years of my art.

As the 1970s tumbled along, Julie, Susan, and James began their successful collegiate careers—Julie at Mount Holyoke College, Susan at Brown University, James at Union College. Margery and I spent nine wonderful years enjoying the whole experience with them, including their army of friends. It was an energetic time in our lives. Beyond children, family, publishing commitments, painting projects, and professional school duties, there were serious community activities. I was connected to numerous organizations either as board member, minor officer, president, or all three. These included the Westport-Weston Arts Coun-

cil, the Westport Council on Continuing Education, the Westport Bicentennial Committee, the Silvermine Guild of Artists, The New Haven Paint and Clay Club, and the Yale Art School Alumni Association. There was considerable traveling during this period as well: countless book fairs, lectures, and workshops everywhere in America, trips to Europe, Mexico, and the Caribbean. It all seemed to reach a soaring climax in a five-day stretch in Washington, D.C., when I functioned as a delegate-at-large to the 1979 White House Conference on Library and Information Services. It was a singular honor. But I felt so ineffectual among the 2,000 delegates that I fled the conference a half-day early with the wrong raincoat. I do not know what we accomplished. I do not know why libraries had to be justified to the nation in the first place. In a great and free democracy such as ours, libraries should have unquestioned priorities. They form the backbone of our educational systems. Our freedom is inextricably tied to those educational systems and the free access to information. That information resides in our libraries. And libraries are the repositories of our will to be free, as much as our elected and appointed branches of government.

It is not possible to describe the "free-lance" professional effort that reaches out to a larger world, dividing and subdividing like a living organism, creating with each growing part new interests, new obligations, new responsibilities, more anguish, excitement, and pleasantries, one on top of the other. The invisible thinking and physical activity that ends up in the marketplace—as words, pictures, lectures, speeches, books, paintings, posters, stamps, coins, and whatnot—is staggering. I could not have it any other way. The true witnesses to this are Margery and our children. As no other people can, they bring their bright perceptions and keen understanding to the whole process and the chores upon which that process leans. They make it easier, endurable, and enjoyable. Impacting on all of this, obviously, are our private, personal lives.

Not surprisingly, I reached the 1980s with a different resolve. It felt like a new beginning. I began to shed civic and professional involvements that impinged upon my creativity. There are some exceptions: my seat on the Board of Trustees of the Westport Public Library, for one. I turned away from professional school administration. Now I work my wiles a few hours a week on unsuspecting tyros and have them improve my expressive posture at the same time. Once in a while I try it at Fairfield University. Also, I have become more comfortable at the easel and at the typewriter. The paintings are more fluid. The illustrations, chiefly in the picture book area, are similar to my easel paintings. They are done with a broader, more relaxed brush, reflecting a larger view. The writing seems easier and is at many levels. Margery, patient and trusting, knew all along what had to emerge. After thirty years my wife finally got through to me.

Margery Cuyler, my Holiday House editor, must have tuned in. She made a courageous decision to let

The Fisher children: Julie, Susan, and James, 1984

me do *The Seven Days of Creation* (1981) with an abstract full-color sweep. On the basis of the *Creation,* a fitting piece to signal one's "new beginning," she effected a collaboration between poet Myra Cohn Livingston and me. The happy result was *A Circle of Seasons, Sky Songs, Celebrations,* and the forthcoming *Sea Songs.* These books have a vastly different approach and appearance than all that came before, including those I write as well. They are still not in the expected mold of fairy tales, talking giraffes, teen problems, or what the public at large assumes to be appropriate children's literature or children's pictures. I offer alternatives. I make young people stretch for experience, much as I had to reach and struggle for whatever it was I wanted in my life. I do not reflect, either in my art or my writing, experiences already experienced. And this I do, I trust, without resorting to the occult or worlds of fantasy. My purpose is never entirely factual or the rendering of the obvious although it may appear to be.

I think Deborah Brodie at Viking sensed these things when she and designer Barbara Hennessy visited me and responded to the sharp dimensional realism of the "box" paintings I had done during the 1970s. I had already illustrated and written the fiercely bleak, monochromatic *Storm at the Jetty.* Now we took a great color leap forward and landed with *Boxes! Boxes!* (1984).

The Great Wall, a Macmillan project, is still another work in another dimension, as will be books about the Statue of Liberty and Ellis Island.

The creative essence that consumes me forms the pattern of my artistic leanings—expressions of form, space, form in space, space and movement, survival

Colonial Craftsmen, *U.S. Postal Service Bicentennial postage stamp issue, July 4, 1972. In the collection of the Smithsonian Institution.*

From The Seven Days of Creation, *written and illustrated by Leonard Everett Fisher.*
(Copyright © 1981 by Leonard Everett Fisher. Reprinted by permission of Holiday House.)

Book jacket from Celebrations *by Myra Cohn Livingston. Illustrated by Leonard Everett Fisher. (Copyright © 1985 by Myra Cohn Livingston. Illustrations copyright © 1985 by Leonard Everett Fisher. Reprinted by permission of Holiday House.)*

and continuity. Those are the things that I am all about.

What happens next? More of the same. The looks of these creations—what I have to say pictorially or verbally—might even be a surprise to me. There are ideas and feelings that knocked around inside of me for countless years before they finally emerged. And there are things inside of me hammering to get out that I cannot identify. What seems to have been fundamental to me all of my life is a hunger to express the inexpressible, to make visible the invisible.

BIBLIOGRAPHY

Books written and illustrated:

FOR CHILDREN

A Head Full of Hats. New York: Dial, 1962.

Pumpers, Boilers, Hooks, and Ladders: A Book of Fire Engines. New York: Dial, 1961.

Pushers, Spads, Jennies, and Jets: A Book of Airplanes. New York: Dial, 1961.

The Liberty Book. Garden City, N.Y.: Doubleday, 1975.

Alphabet Art: Thirteen ABCs from Around the World. New York: Four Winds, 1978.

From Storm at the Jetty, *written and illustrated by Leonard Everett Fisher. (Copyright ©*
1981 by Leonard Everett Fisher. Reprinted by permission of The Viking Press.)

Untitled painting, 1984, acrylic, 48"x50."

Margery and Leonard Fisher on the Li River, China, 1984

The Seven Days of Creation (adapted from the Bible). New York: Holiday House, 1981.

Storm at the Jetty. New York: Viking, 1981.

Number Art: Thirteen 1-2-3s from Around the World. New York: Four Winds, 1982.

Star Signs. New York: Holiday House, 1982.

Boxes! Boxes! New York: Viking, 1984.

The Olympians: Great Gods and Goddesses of Ancient Greece. New York: Holiday House, 1984.

Symbol Art: Thirteen Squares, Circles, and Triangles from around the World. New York: Four Winds, 1985.

The Great Wall. New York: Macmillan, 1986.

FOR YOUNG ADULTS

"Colonial Americans" series. New York: F. Watts, 1964-76. *The Glassmakers,* 1964; *The Silversmiths,* 1964; *The Hatters,* 1965; *The Papermakers,* 1965; *The Printers,* 1965; *The Wigmakers,* 1965; *The Cabinetmakers,* 1966; *The Tanners,* 1966; *The Weavers,* 1966; *The Schoolmasters,* 1967; *The Shoemakers,* 1967; *The Doctors,* 1968; *The Peddlers,* 1968; *The Limners,* 1969; *The Potters,* 1969; *The Architects,* 1970; *The Shipbuilders,* 1971; *The Homemakers,* 1973; *The Blacksmiths,* 1976.

Picture Book of Revolutionary War Heroes. Harrisburg, Pa.: Stackpole, 1970.

Two If by Sea. New York: Random House, 1970.

The Death of Evening Star: The Diary of a Young New England Whaler. Garden City, N.Y.: Doubleday, 1972.

The Art Experience: Oil Painting, 15th-19th Centuries. New York: F. Watts, 1973.

The Warlock of Westfall. Garden City, N.Y.: Doubleday, 1974.

Across the Sea from Galway. New York: Four Winds, 1975.

Sweeney's Ghost. Garden City, N.Y.: Doubleday, 1975.

Letters from Italy. New York: Four Winds, 1977.

Noonan: A Novel about Baseball, ESP, and Time Warps. Garden City, N.Y.: Doubleday, 1978.

"Nineteenth-Century America" series. New York: Holiday House, 1979-83. *The Factories,* 1979; *The Railroads,* 1979; *The Hospitals,* 1980; *The Sports,* 1980; *The Newspapers,* 1981; *The Unions,* 1982; *The Schools,* 1983.

A Russian Farewell. New York: Four Winds, 1980.

The Statue of Liberty. New York: Holiday House, 1985.

Ellis Island. New York: Holiday House, 1986.

Books illustrated:

FOR YOUNG PEOPLE

The Exploits of Xenophon, by Geoffrey Household. New York: Random House, 1955.

Carrier Boy, by Florence Walton Taylor. New York: Abelard, 1956.

The First Book of the American Revolution, by Richard B. Morris. New York: F. Watts, 1956.

Good English through Practice, by Marjorie Wescott Barrows. New York: Holt, 1956.

My Eskimos: A Priest in the Arctic, by Roger P. Buliard. New York: Farrar, Straus, 1956.

Our Reading Heritage. New York: Holt. Vol. I: *Ourselves and Others;* Vol. II: *Exploring Life;* Vol. III: *This Is America,* edited by Harold H. Wagenheim, Elizabeth Voris Brattig, and Dolkey, 1956; Vol. IV: *England and the World,* edited by H. H. Wagenheim, Kobler, and Dolkey, 1956; Vol. V: *New Trails,* edited by H. H. Wagenheim, Eleanor L. McGehan, and Margaret Thomas, 1958; Vol. VI: *Wide Horizons,* edited by Wagenheim, E. L. McGehan, and M. Thomas, 1958.

To Unknown Lands, by Manley Wade Wellman. New York: Holiday House, 1956.

America, America, America, edited by Kenneth S. Giniger. New York: F. Watts, 1957.

Father Damien and the Bells, by Arthur and Elizabeth Sheehan. New York: Vision Books, 1957.

The First Book of American History, by Henry Steele Commager. New York: F. Watts, 1957.

The First Book of New England, by Louise Dickinson Rich. New York: F. Watts, 1957.

Mike Fink, by James C. Bowman. Boston, Mass.: Little, Brown, 1957.

Myer Meyers: Silversmith of Old New York, by William Wise. New York: Farrar, Straus, 1957.

The Reading Laboratories, written and edited by Don Parker (eight volumes). Chicago: Science Research Associates, 1957–62.

St. Thomas Aquinas and the Preaching Beggar, by Brendan Larnen and Milton Lomask. New York: Farrar, Straus, 1957.

The Splendor of Persia, by Robert Payne. New York: Knopf, 1957.

Whaling Boy, by Peter Freuchen. New York: Putnam, 1957.

America's Own Mark Twain, by Jeanette Eaton. New York: Morrow, 1958.

The Arabs, by Harry B. Ellis. Cleveland, Ohio: World Publishing, 1958.

Digging into Yesterday, by Estelle Friedman. New York: Putnam, 1958.

Energy and Power, by Robert Irving. New York: Knopf, 1958.

The First Book of the Constitution, by R. B. Morris. New York: F. Watts, 1958.

Here Come the Clowns, by Celeste Edell. New York: Putnam, 1958.

Kateri Tekakwitha, by Evelyn M. Brown. New York: Farrar, Straus, 1958.

Reading Skills, by M. W. Barrows and E. N. Woods. New York: Holt, 1958.

Westward, Westward, Westward, edited by Elizabeth Abell. New York: F. Watts, 1958.

The World of Jo Davidson, by Lois H. Kuhn. New York: Farrar, Straus, 1958.

America Is Born, Gerald W. Johnson. New York: Morrow, 1959.

Boy Joe Goes to Sea, by Edith L. Boyd. Chicago: Rand McNally, 1959.

David's Campaign Buttons, by Catherine Wooley. New York: Morrow, 1959.

The First Book of Indian Wars, by R. B. Morris. New York: F. Watts, 1959.

Paul Bunyan, by Maurice Dolbier. New York: Random House, 1959.

Sound and Ultrasonics, by R. Irving. New York: Knopf, 1959.

This Is the Desert, by Phillip H. Ault. New York: Dodd, 1959.

America Grows Up, by G. W. Johnson. New York: Morrow, 1960.

America Moves Forward, by G. W. Johnson. New York: Morrow, 1960.

Around the World Storybook, by Danny Kaye. New York: Random, 1960.

Declaration of Independence. New York: F. Watts, 1960.

Electromagnetic Waves, by R. Irving. New York: Knopf, 1960.

The First Book of Civil War Land Battles, by Trevor N. Dupuy. New York: F. Watts, 1960.

The Golden Hind, by Edith T. Hurd. New York: Crowell, 1960.

The Horn of Roland, by Eleanor Clark. New York: Random, 1960.

Indy and Mr. Lincoln, by Natalia M. Belting. New York: Holt, 1960.

The Man without a Country, by Edward E. Hale. New York: F. Watts, 1960.

Ten Thousand Desert Swords, by Russell Davis and Brent Ashabranner. Boston: Little, Brown, 1960.

Verity Mullens and the Indian, by N. M. Belting. New York: Holt, 1960.

Cadet Quarterback, by Sidney Offit. New York: St. Martin's, 1961.

The First Book of Civil War Naval Actions, by T. N. Dupuy. New York: F. Watts, 1961.

The First Book of the War of 1812, by R. B. Morris. New York: F. Watts, 1961.

Heroes and Heroines, by David Stone. New York: F. Watts, 1961.

Nikola Tesla: Giant of Electricity, by Helen B. Walters. New York: Crowell, 1961.

The Queen's Most Honorable Pirate, by James Playsted Wood. New York: Harper, 1961.

Steller of the North, by Anne and Myron Sutton. Chicago: Rand McNally, 1961.

William Penn, by Hildegarde Dolson. New York: Random, 1961.

Vasco Nuñez De Balboa, by Emma G. Sterne. New York:

Knopf, 1961.

The World's Most Truthful Man, by Harold Felton. New York: Dodd, 1961.

Before Adam, by Jack London. New York: Macmillan, 1962.

But Not Our Daddy, by Margery M. Fisher. New York: Dial, 1962.

The Golden Child, by Paul Engle. New York: Dutton, 1962.

The Great Archaeologists, by Charles M. Daugherty. New York: Crowell, 1962.

A Horse Named Justin Morgan, by Harold W. Felton. New York: Dodd, 1962.

The Life of Saint Paul, by Harry E. Fosdick. New York: Random, 1962.

The Literature Sampler, edited by Dolores Betler (two volumes). New York: Learning Materials, Inc., 1962, 1964.

Man of the Monitor, by Jean L. Latham. New York: Harper, 1962.

The First Book Edition of A Message to Garcia, by Elbert Hubbart. New York: F. Watts, 1962.

Modern Discoveries in Archaeology, by Robert C. Suggs. New York: Crowell, 1962.

Pilgrim Courage, by Eric B. Smith and Robert Meredith. Boston: Little, Brown, 1962.

The Presidency, by G. W. Johnson. New York: Morrow, 1962.

Sergeant O'Keefe and His Mule, Balaam, by H. W. Felton. New York: Dodd, 1962.

The Supreme Court, by G. W. Johnson. New York: Morrow, 1962.

The Congress, by G. W. Johnson. New York: Morrow, 1963.

The First Book Edition of Paul Revere's Ride, by Henry Wadsworth Longfellow. New York: F. Watts, 1963.

Getting to Know the U.S.A., by Charles Ferguson. New York: Coward-McCann, 1963.

The Gettysburg Address and the Second Inaugural. New York: F. Watts, 1963.

The Golden Frog, by Anico Surany. New York: Putnam, 1963.

One and One, by M. M. Fisher. New York: Dial, 1963.

Patriotism, Patriotism, Patriotism, edited by Helen Hoke. New York: F. Watts, 1963.

The Star Rover, by J. London. New York: Macmillan, 1963.

The Weigher of Souls [and] The Earth Dwellers, by André Maurois; translated by Hamish Miles. New York: Macmillan, 1963.

Alexander the Great, Scientist-King, by R. C. Suggs. New York: Macmillan, 1964.

The Coming of the Pilgrims, by E. B. Smith and R. Meredith (told from Governor Bradford's Firsthand Account). Boston: Little, Brown, 1964.

Communism: An American's View, by G. W. Johnson. New York: Morrow, 1964.

The First Book Edition of Casey at the Bat, by Ernest L. Thayer.

New York: F. Watts, 1964.

The Golden Spur, by Eugenia Miller, New York: Holt, 1964.

John F. Kennedy's Inaugural Address. New York: F. Watts, 1964.

Our Presidents, by Richard Armour. New York: Norton, 1964.

Ride the Cold Wind, by A. Surany. New York: Putnam, 1964.

Riding with Coronado, by E. B. Smith and R. Meredith. Boston: Little, Brown, 1964.

The Archaeology of San Francisco, by R. C. Suggs. New York: Crowell, 1965.

Archimedes, by Martin Gardner. New York: Macmillan, 1965.

The Burning Mountain, by A. Surany. New York: Holiday House, 1965.

The First Book of the White House: Home, Office, Museum, by Lois P. Jones. New York: F. Watts, 1965.

Let's Find Out About John Fitzgerald Kennedy, by Martha and Charles Shapp. New York: F. Watts, 1965.

Rebel Sea Raider, by John Foster. New York: Morrow, 1965.

The Story of Aida, retold by Florence Stevenson (based on the opera by Giuseppe Verde). New York: Putnam, 1965.

The Archaeology of New York, by R. C. Suggs. New York: Crowell, 1966.

The Cabinet, by G. W. Johnson. New York: Morrow, 1966.

Forgotten by Time, by Robert Silverberg. New York: Crowell, 1966.

A Jungle Jumble, by A. Surany. New York: Putnam, 1966.

Kati and Kormos, by A. Surany. New York: Holiday House, 1966.

The Legend of Sleepy Hollow, by Washington Irving. New York: F. Watts, 1966.

The Quest of Columbus: A Detailed and Exact Account of the Discovery of America, adapted and edited by E. B. Smith and R. Meredith. Boston: Little, Brown, 1966.

Rip Van Winkle, by W. Irving. New York: F. Watts, 1966.

The Story of the Thirteen Colonies, by Clifford L. Alderman. New York: Random House, 1966.

The Covered Bridge, by A. Surany. New York: Holiday House, 1967.

The Devil's Disciple, by George Bernard Shaw. New York: F. Watts, 1967.

Franklin D. Roosevelt: Portrait of a Great Man, by G. W. Johnson. New York: Morrow, 1967.

The Great Stone Face and Two Other Stories, by Nathaniel Hawthorne. New York: F. Watts, 1967.

Journey with Jonah, by Madeleine L'Engle. New York: Farrar, Straus, 1967.

Monsieur Jolicoeur's Umbrella, by A. Surany. New York: Putnam, 1967.

The Story of Science in America, by Lyon Sprague De Camp and Catherine C. De Camp. New York: Scribner, 1967.

The First Book of the Founding of the Republic, by R. B. Morris.

New York: F. Watts, 1968.

The Luck of Roaring Camp, by Bret Harte. New York: F. Watts, 1968.

Malachy's Gold, by A. Surany. New York: Holiday House, 1968.

The British Empire: An American View of Its History from 1776 to 1945, by G. W. Johnson. New York: Morrow, 1969.

Exploring the Great River: Early Voyagers on the Mississippi from De Soto to La Salle, adapted and edited by E. B. Smith and R. Meredith. Boston: Little, Brown, 1969.

Lora, Lorita, by A. Surany. New York: Putnam, 1969.

Why the Earth Quakes, by Julian May. New York: Holiday House, 1969.

American Popular Music: The Beginning Years, by Berenice R. Morris. New York: F. Watts, 1970.

Little Calf, by V. B. Scheffer. New York: Scribner, 1970.

The Land Beneath the Sea, by J. May. New York: Holiday House, 1971.

The Wicked City, by Isaac Bashevis Singer, translated with Elizabeth Shub. New York: Farrar, Straus, 1972.

The Journey of the Gray Whales, by Gladys Conklin. New York: Holiday House, 1974.

Juan Diego and the Lady, by Jan Wahl (bilingual edition; Spanish translation by Dolores Jones Garcia). New York: Putnam, 1974.

White Falcon: An Indian Boy in Early America, by Eileen Thompson. Garden City, N.Y.: Doubleday, 1977.

All Times, All Peoples: A World History of Slavery, by Milton Meltzer. New York: Harper, 1980.

A Circle of Seasons, by Myra Cohn Livingston. New York: Holiday House, 1982.

Sky Songs, by M. C. Livingston. New York: Holiday House, 1984.

Celebrations, by M. C. Livingston. New York: Holiday House, 1985.

Earth Songs, by M. C. Livingston. New York: Holiday House, 1986.

Sea Songs, by M. C. Livingston. New York: Holiday House, 1986.

FOR ADULTS

The Year of the Whale, by Victor B. Scheffer. New York: Scribner, 1969.

The Year of the Seal, by V. B. Scheffer. New York: Scribner, 1970.

The Night Country, by Loren C. Eisely. New York: Scribner, 1971.

Some Dreams Are Nightmares, by James E. Gunn. New York: Scribner, 1974.

The Joy of Crafts, by the Blue Mountain Crafts Council. New York: Holt, 1975.

Masterpieces of American Painting. Greenwich, Conn.: Bison/Exeter, 1985.

Remington and Russell. Greenwich, Conn.: Bison, 1985.

Fisher has also created audio-visual filmstrips, book jackets, postage stamps, commemorative medals, coins, posters, stationery, and calendars.

Doris Gates

1901–

Doris Gates, 1983

For most of my life, I have felt three years older than God. To begin with, I didn't start school until I was eight years old. (My mother had ideas about early education.) And though I made it to the fourth grade that first year, I can still remember how uncomfortable those too-small first grade desks were. Then, fed up with formal education by the time I left high school, I refused to go to college. By the time I was twenty-two, however, I realized that if I wanted to reach my goals in life, I had to have a college education.

Entering college at almost twenty-three, I was much more than the actual five years older than my freshman classmates. The difference between eighteen and twenty-three is much more than five years. Time can be relative. Finally, at forty I married for the first time, choosing a man much younger than I. Like most marriages, it had its ups and downs. Our divorce fifteen years later surprised no one, including ourselves.

I really didn't begin to feel young, not properly young, until I turned seventy-one. It was then I decided to buy a horse and to learn to ride English. I had ridden a lot in my teens but had ridden Western. Now I realized that at seventy-one, I would not be able to swing a forty-pound Western saddle onto anything larger than a goat, so Eastern was the way I had to go. More of all that later.

I was born to parents no longer very young on November 26, 1901. Though I've never checked it out, I was always told that it was Thanksgiving Day. At any rate my birthday comes so close to Thanksgiving Day when it doesn't actually fall on the day itself, that in my family the two dates have always been celebrated together. My father, Charles O. Gates, was at this time the leading physician in a small California town called Mountain View, about twelve miles from San Jose, the county seat. Today that small town is part of the throbbing center of what has become known

Charles and Bessie Gates, the author's parents

Down Castro Street, almost to the railroad tracks, was the Weilheimers' store. I loved to go there with my mother. You entered to the good clean smell of cloth and ribbon and shoes and hats. Little boxes running along wires carried the money from my mother's purchases to a small upstairs room where Mr. Weilheimer took the money and sent the box back with a receipt to Mrs. Weilheimer waiting with my mother at the counter.

Another place of interest for me along Castro Street was Kampen's Bakery. In a time when most wives baked their own bread, it is a wonder to me now how the Kampen's stayed in business. Yet they did. I can remember going there on errands for my mother. At the tinkle of a little bell announcing that someone had entered the shop, Mrs. Kampen would emerge from behind a curtain of periwinkle shells which also gave off a gentle tinkle as she parted them.

But the shop of all shops that held fascination for us children (my sister was born sixteen months after me) was Vuscovich's. Mr. Vuscovich was a cobbler. In conjunction with his cobbling he ran a candy shop. Here again a bell tinkled as one entered to be greeted with the combined fragrance of leather and cooked sugar. Mr. Vuscovich was usually seated at his cobbler's bench, his mouth full of nails, a hand vigorously pounding. He seemed to have all the time in the world for us highly undecided buyers. Of course, he didn't rise from his bench immediately. He gave us plenty of time to study the contents of the one glass counter.

as Silicon Valley. A branch of the Bank of America stands on the spot where I was born.

It was a quiet and orderly little town where a small girl could sit on the edge of the sidewalk in front of her house with her feet in the gutter without fear of molestation. Mr. McCoon, our one-man police force (always referred to as "the constable") walked the streets with nothing on earth to do, except occasionally gather in a drunk from off the steps of Manfredi's saloon. The saloon was diagonally across from our house facing Castro Street, the town's main artery. A wide porch ran across the front of it with a long flight of shallow steps reaching up to the floor of the porch. I well remember once watching, with something close to admiration, a drunken cowboy ride his horse to the top of the steps. There he whirled the horse about and went down much faster than he had gone up when Mr. Manfredi emerged from the building, waving his arms and shouting. Mr. Manfredi ran an "orderly house" and was a respected member of the community.

As if to balance the environmental threat of a saloon so near our house, the Methodist Church was just over our back fence.

Bessie Gates and young Doris, 1902

Having done so, we would usually turn to study the wall at right angles to it. Here were located the grab bags. There were three round slots in the wall. Behind these slots were small bags finely striped in blue, green, and red. What they held was secret. But so strong is the gambling instinct in even very young humans, that nine times out of ten, we would decide to squander our whole five-cent piece (an Indian head on it in those days) for one of these little bags. So, surrendering our nickel to patient Mr. Vuscovich, we would put a hand through a slot, feel around for a few seconds, then withdraw the bag of our blind choice. Opening it, we would discover a few pieces of rather stale candy (even we realized it was much better out of the counter) and perhaps a tiny doll, or a small rubber ball good for playing jacks, or a little Japanese paper parasol. I once found in one of my bags a whole set of miniature garden tools: a hoe, a rake, a shovel, and a pitchfork. They were beautifully made and I wish I had them now.

Though we had a very large, completely fenced backyard with a huge oak tree in it along with an arbor completely covered with a Lady Banksia rose, much of my time between my fourth and my eighth year was spent on the sidewalk in front of our house. Here I could see the six-mule teams passing through town pulling a long wagon heaped with tan bark for the tannery just outside of town. They had come from the Santa Cruz mountains some twenty miles away. The two leaders wore bells across their withers and their driver, seated high above the floor of his wagon, would lift a hand threading the many reins to acknowledge the wide-eyed stare of the little girl on the sidewalk.

Sometimes a quick-stepping pony pulling a basket cart would come into view with a small horse galloping beside it, a pig-tailed girl on his back. These were the White sisters: Eleanor and her governess in the basket cart and Helen White on Freddie. My heart sang at the sight of them. Because they never failed to stop while Helen flung herself off Freddie and leading him up to the curb, would hoist me into the saddle for a ride up and down the side street. To this day, I can see Freddie clearly. His saddle pad was a dark blue with a white star in all four corners of it. What a wonderful child Helen White must have been to understand so fully what it meant to this little five-year-old to have a ride on Freddie! Exactly seventy-eight years later, I find myself regularly riding a gelding named Fred, and all the thrill of those early rides in Mountain View come flooding back to me along with grateful memories of a kindly ten-year-old named Helen White.

These early years of my childhood were quiet, happy, and secure. A much-loved cousin named Claire

Doris (with white bow) and her sister, 1906

assisted my mother in the house. My father was busy in his office or making house calls, sometimes until late in the night.

The tranquillity of these days was rudely shattered early on the morning of April 18, 1906.

I was awakened by the severe shaking of my bed. I couldn't imagine how this was happening since there was no one shaking it. My sister was in her small bed beside mine. Frightened, I cried out, waking her. Moments later my father was in the room and had grabbed up both of us. I demanded to know what was happening and he informed me that it was an earthquake.

It is hard to explain an earthquake. There is a weird rumbling and a rolling and shaking which makes it all but impossible to stand. I am speaking of a very severe earthquake, as this one was. A few years later, on our prune ranch I saw a team of horses plowing in the orchard brought to their knees during another earthquake. In 1906 we were more fortunate than a lot of people, for our house was not seriously damaged.

There was much broken crockery, furniture had been hurled about the rooms, and the chimney and hearth were in ruins. Strangely, it had not stopped the clock!

But then came the real tragedy. As a result of the earthquake, San Francisco was burning. Our parents took my sister and me out onto the front porch a night or two later and pointed to the angrily red western sky and said, "That's San Francisco burning."

Before long, streams of refugees came straggling through the town. My father's office was smack on the corner in front and at one side of our house, and to those who needed it, he offered first aid. He told me years later that many of these unfortunates seemed to be in a daze. Some were pushing what they had managed to salvage from their doomed homes in baby carriages. Others pushed wheelbarrows heaped with their belongings. I have no vivid memories of these wanderers, so I presume that our mother kept her daughters confined to the house and fenced yard during this time.

But what I do vividly recall is my sister tossing all my picture books down the hole in the dining room where a hearth had been and into the cellar. I, of course, assumed they were lost forever and a terrible row ensued which terminated only when our cousin Claire went down to the cellar and retrieved them.

It was great fun watching my mother and Claire cooking over a campfire in the backyard as the stove was out of use until the chimney could be rebuilt. Since every chimney in the town was down, this took a little while.

When I was half-past seven, we moved to the prune ranch. My paternal grandfather had developed it and when he and my grandmother were gone, it fell to the combined ownership of my father and his brother. For health reasons, my father wanted to leave the practice of medicine for a while and bought out my uncle's interest in the ranch and we moved into the high-roofed old house my grandfather had built at 234 South Lincoln Avenue, some three miles outside of San Jose. That fall I entered Willow Glen Elementary School and in November turned eight years old.

This move would have significance for me many years later when I decided to try my hand at writing books for children.

My childhood, even for those times, was unusually happy. Besides the big old house with five bedrooms, there was a big red barn with a hayloft which would figure largely in my growing up. There were three stalls, two of them occupied by the heavy-boned work horses that pulled the plow, the disk, the harrow, and the flat-bed truck. The empty stall immediately caught my attention; I longed for a saddle horse to put in it, a horse like Freddie.

Doris and her sister on the ranch, 1909

My father considered me too young for a horse, so he bought me a burro, a little gray burro, named Jinny. For the next several years, Jinny and I were constant companions; I even rode her to school now and then where she relished the peanut butter and jelly sandwiches the children offered her. She figures largely in my first published book, *Sarah's Idea.*

Though my mother was not a social woman in the sense of belonging to clubs or a bridge group and certainly was no party-giver, she was very hospitable and guests were always coming and going on the ranch. Our birthdays were always celebrated within the family, but neither my sister nor I ever had a birthday party during all the years of our childhood. My mother had few friends outside the family. The closest non-relatives were the Ehrhorns, and there was quite a lot of visiting between the six Ehrhorn children and the Gates family. This was to bear fruit later when I came to write my most famous book, *Blue Willow.*

Animals played a big part in my childhood. Besides Jinny, there were several dogs, mostly Irish setters. In addition to the two work horses there was a cow, many rabbits, and a flock of handsome Plymouth Rock chickens. Much of all this is recorded in a book which is really the biography of my childhood on the ranch. It is called *The Elderberry Bush.* Though long out of print, it can still be found on the shelves of some public libraries that haven't cleared all their shelf space for Walt Disney productions and their ilk.

We were a family of readers. Though I didn't learn to read until I was eight years old, my mother read to me. From the very beginning, she read to me. But I remember best, of course, those books she read to me as I grew older. Every evening, beside the lamp which I still have on my desk, she read such things as *The Princess and the Goblin, The Story of King Arthur, Lives of the Hunted, Little Women,* and *Black Beauty.* And I was reading to myself. One book which made a heavy impression on me was Zane Grey's *Riders of the Purple Sage.* (It will be seen from this that I was allowed free range of my parents' bookshelves.) Perhaps this particular book should have been forbidden me, for I really lived it. I went around in a kind of daydream while reading it. Of course I was Jim Lassiter, the two-gun hero of that book. Jinny became a coal-black horse, the swiftest on the range. Together we stalked the prune orchard hunting Mormons. I didn't know what they were, but it was plain Lassiter had no use for them, so neither did I. This left no scar on my psyche. I am proud to say that one of my most valued friends and riding companions is a Mormon, and I have enjoyed the cordial reception of Salt Lake City teachers when, over the years, I have gone there to lecture. At the age of nine, the word "Mormon" was merely that—a word designating some necessary villains in a very exciting book. Then one day I finished the book and emerged from the daydream to receive an almost mortal shock. I would never be Lassiter! I had been born a girl! There was no hope for me. I shall never forget that bitter day. As usual when I had a problem too difficult to cope with easily, I climbed up into the hayloft. There, huddled on the highest bale of hay up under the dusty eaves with the black eye of a nesting pigeon warily watching me, I wrestled with the greatest frustration I had ever known. Happily for me, there had been lesser frustrations along the way, so eventually I was able to conquer this one. I descended from the hayloft at last, having found a modicum of comfort. If I couldn't be Lassiter, perhaps with luck I could grow up and marry him. But this seemed a drab substitute for a girl who wanted to be a boy.

To this day I lean toward the superstition that men are somehow superior to women. Speaking generally, that is. Which illustrates, I think, the dangers of the wrong kind of reading for children. For better or for worse, *Riders of the Purple Sage* and that afternoon's struggle with frustration produced a sequel to *Sarah's Idea.* I called it *Trouble for Jerry.*

My mother was a rare kind of person for her day: a woman with a bachelor of arts degree. She graduated from Milton College in Wisconsin with a degree in the classics. She could read Homer in the original Greek. I have some of her college textbooks in my study. She deeply loved Greek mythology, and as soon as she thought I was ready to enjoy them, she began reading

these stories to me. I was immediately captivated by them and could rattle off the names of the family of gods on high Olympus as easily as you could name today's twelve most popular rock stars. When many years later my eyes took in my first Greek landfall from the deck of a cruise ship, I felt satisfaction in knowing that I had done my homework. Out of those early readings came my desire to share these stories with boys and girls when I became a children's librarian and a storyteller. Subsequent to that experience, I wrote a series of books for young readers on Greek mythology. The series is now in paperback and has proved to be popular. I even receive fan letters from boys and girls who have enjoyed one or all of these six books.

A love of nature was strong in both my parents, and they early developed a sense of wonder in me. Animals, flowers, grass in springtime, the stars at night, the music of a running stream, the sound of wind in tall trees—they made these things magical for me.

This sense of the wonder of the world climaxed for me one memorable night when our whole family gathered in the backyard of the ranch to contemplate Halley's comet blazing across the western sky above the barn. I was then going on nine.

"It won't come again for seventy-six years," Claire informed me.

It seemed a very long time into the future, but as I studied that streak of fire, I never doubted but that I would see it again. Now here I am at eighty-three confidently looking forward to seeing it again in 1986.

All of this, with the exception of Halley's comet, has been reflected in the books I have written for children.

Some time during the year I turned fourteen, my father sold the ranch and we moved into San Jose and settled in a house within easy walking distance of the city's one and only high school.

The next four years were painful ones. Adolescence is difficult for most parents and their children. It was especially difficult for me. In those days, children had little say about what they wanted to do or how they felt. I knew I was loved; I knew I was secure. My father would never be penniless nor would my parents ever separate. But I also knew I was a somewhat weird-looking creature. I was far from pretty and unlike these more sensible times, if you weren't pretty there could be almost no hope of your ever being popular. My mother made no effort to assist me socially and I was inordinately shy. It would have been inconceivable to both my parents that I should have a boyfriend. There were, of course, dances and games and proms then as there are now in high schools. But all that was a closed

Doris Gates, 1920

book to me. I had no friends and my teachers liked me, a kiss of death in those days as it is now. Of course I had very good grades. I had plenty of time for study! But as I look back on it, strangely there were very few times when I felt depressed by my "loner" status. I always had the feeling deep inside me that I was going to do something, sometime, worthwhile. For a time I entertained the idea of becoming a singer. I had a quite unusually good mezzo-soprano; I even started singing lessons following my graduation from high school. But that petered out.

For a year following graduation, I spent a large part of my time on horseback. We had moved to Los Gatos and my father had opened an office there. Los Gatos is situated at the beginning of the road over the Santa Cruz mountains to the coast. The road the mule teams had taken on their way to the tannery. Much of the town climbs the surrounding hills and among these hills and along the road to Santa Cruz beside Los

Gatos creek, Louise Spreckels and I went riding almost every day. Usually I was mounted on a big, black seventeen-hands gelding named Dandy, one of the Spreckels' horses.

The next few years were uncertain and unsatisfactory. I refused to have anything to do with further schooling and largely drifted, working for a while in the local library and then in a grocery store. My father, disenchanted with Los Gatos, decided to open an office in Fresno where he had purchased land. It was to be my home for most of the next twenty years and by far the most significant move in all my long life.

About this time I began to realize that if I were ever to decide on a goal in life with hope of attaining it, I would have to go to college.

So in the fall of 1924 I registered as a freshman at Fresno State College, now Fresno State University. Two years later I entered the library school of the Los Angeles Public Library, later to become the School of Library Science at the University of Southern California. I chose children's library work as my elective in the general course and had my first storytelling experiences in a settlement house not far from the library.

On finishing my course, I accepted the position of assistant in the children's department of the Fresno

Doris Gates on Dandy, 1921

County Free Library as it was then known. Little did I dream then that one day the fine, big children's room in the new library would be called "The Doris Gates Room"! My immediate superior and head of the children's department was a well-trained and very capable children's librarian, Evelyn T. Ross. Our county librarian, heading up the second largest county library system in the country at the time, was a really remarkable woman, Sarah E. McCardle. In every successful life there are a few people to whom one owes a very large measure of his success. Miss McCardle was one of those people in my own life.

After assisting in the children's department for a year, I took a leave of absence (most willingly granted by Miss McCardle) and went to Cleveland where I entered the senior course in children's library work at Western Reserve University now Case Western Reserve University. While I was gone, Miss Ross decided to accept a position in the Los Angeles library system and Miss McCardle wrote to me offering me her job, the directorship of the children's department where I had served as an assistant. In accepting her offer, I opened the door to a modest amount of fame and a not inconsiderable amount of fortune.

So it was that in the summer of 1930, with the Great Depression already firmly established and the tragedy of the Dust Bowl beginning to be felt, I took over the directorship of the children's department of the Fresno County Free Library. The Depression deepened; unemployment grew. To appreciate this desperate situation it is necessary to remember that in those days there was no unemployment compensation, no welfare, no food stamps, no Social Security, and no Medicare or Medicaid. If you were out of money and out of a job you had to depend on the dubious charity of your better-off relatives or friends.

Caught in this hopeless economic situation, out of the Dust Bowl and into the San Joaquin Valley came streaming hordes of penniless people. Hardworking, deserving men, women, and children blown off their farms in northern Texas and Oklahoma, mostly, and now seeking help in the inland valleys of California. They came in their pitiful jalopies heaped with what they could salvage of their household possessions. Though many were proud and humiliated by the circumstances in which they found themselves, a large number of them were unschooled and unfitted for anything but the most rudimentary farm work, and such work was not to be found. Several thousand of them settled on uncultivated land lying west of the city of Fresno. They were bitterly resented by the established residents of these rural communities especially since they sent their children to the local schools where they very quickly crowded the classrooms to the bursting

Doris Gates, 1930

point, rendering any real teaching an impossibility.

So migrant schools were built. That is to say, schools for migrant children. These were fairly crude but adequate structures, unpainted and with a bare minimum of teachers and books. Out in front, though, was an unpainted flagpole where every day Old Glory flapped when there was a breeze or hung disconsolate in the valley fog. At the close of each day, the flag was ceremoniously lowered, folded, and put carefully away. I visited these schools as often as I could, telling stories to the children and bringing them discarded books from our branch children's rooms.

I remember reaching one such school just at the close of the school day when they were lowering the flag. I followed the boy who was taking it into the school building and when he spread it out on a trestle table to fold it, I moved over to help him. He quickly stopped me; I wasn't doing it right. I had never been taught how to fold the flag!

But with that innate courtesy so many of these children had, he felt it necessary to explain the situation.

"You see," he said, "it's the American flag and it

stands for something."

Besides visiting schools in Fresno and other towns around the county, with increasing frequency I was invited to speak at parent-teacher meetings. Miss McCardle was generous in allowing me these activities. It was good publicity for the library. Finally, radio station KMJ asked me to present a story hour once a week. Again, Miss McCardle was heartily supportive. The "hour" ran for thirty minutes and was a great success.

The Depression continued to worsen. Municipal and county budgets had to be cut as taxes had to be lowered. My own salary was cut from $150 a month to $135. It was agreed by the board of supervisors that in the light of such cuts, we shouldn't be expected to work as many days as formerly. Instead of six and a half days a week, we would work five and a half. But the gentlemen of the board refused to give us an extended weekend. "They'll all just spend their money out of town," was the general feeling among them. So we in the library were given Wednesday off. That is, the library was closed all day Wednesday and Wednesday evening.

What to do with this extra day? Contrary to what the supervisors were thinking, shopping was out of consideration, since we had no money to spend. And Fresno in those days offered few leisure distractions.

I was determined not to lose this day.

For some time I had been considering the possibility of trying to write. As the head of the children's department of the library, I was constantly reading children's books as they were published. I was already a storyteller. It began to dawn on me that I might have something to say to children.

I would use this given Wednesday to try to say it!

Thereafter, every Wednesday morning punctually at nine o'clock, exactly as if I were going to my desk at the library, I would sit down at my portable typewriter and write. At noon I would stop for an hour and eat some lunch. At one, I would be back at my work again. I quit at five.

The book I wrote that year has never been published. Someone has said that you write your first million words for the waste basket. Certainly I wrote my first fifty thousand for the waste basket. But the work I did that year on those Wednesdays taught me how to write.

The next book I attempted, working now during evenings and on weekends, was the story of a little girl on a prune ranch who wanted a burro. There was a lot in it about the prune industry; the story of Sarah and her deep desire was really the sugar-coating on the factual pill.

I sent if off to May Massee, at that time the editor of the junior division of the Viking Press. Back came a letter from Miss Massee along with the manuscript. The most exciting letter I had ever received up to that time.

"This is almost good enough to be a book," she wrote. "But I am more interested in Sarah than I am the prunes."

So I took another year out of my leisure time and rewrote the book, entitled it *Sarah's Best Idea,* and sent it off again to Miss Massee. She accepted it, though she changed the title. My first published book came out as *Sarah's Idea.* The year was 1938.

In 1940 *Blue Willow* was published. This is still my best-known book. It was the first sociological novel for young readers, was widely reviewed (not always favorably), and eventually became runner-up for the Newbery Medal, the important annual award given for the "most distinguished" contribution to children's literature for the preceding year. Armstrong Sperry's *Call It Courage* was the winning book.

Blue Willow is the outgrowth of those years I spent in the Fresno County Public Library, visiting migrant schools and observing the fortitude and the patience with which those unlucky people faced their miserable lives. I knew there was a story here and a lesson to be drawn from it for more fortunate young people if only I could get it down.

Blue Willow is the story of Janey Larkin, aged ten, the daughter and stepdaughter of migrant parents. The story opens with them settled, more or less, in a shack on the west side of Fresno County. In planning the novel I knew that this child would want above everything else, a permanent home. But I also realized it wouldn't be enough merely to state this as a fact, or even to have her state it. The longing must be pervasive to everything taking place in the story. In other words, I needed a symbol for that longing. What should it be? Since the family was travelling in an old jalopy without benefit of a trailer, the precious thing would have to be something that didn't take up much space in a car already crowded with what they could save from the debacle of their fortunes. It couldn't be a doll; Janey was too old for dolls. It might be a picture if it weren't too large. But glass within a picture frame breaks easily.

Suddenly I had it! In the days when I was a child and visiting our close friends, the Ehrhorns, in Mountain View, I remembered that their dinner china was the blue willow pattern. I remembered the large dining room with colored glass in the sun-filled windows. I could see again the long, extended table with Uncle Ad at one end, carving the roast, and Aunt Lily at the other, serving up the vegetables. I, as guest of honor, sat at Uncle Ad's right hand. Besides us seven children, there was always a sprinkling of uncles and aunts. So as he passed the plates to me to send on their way to Aunt Lily, as plate after plate went past my nose, each garnished with a succulent slab of rare roast beef, I, hungry as a young wolf, thought there could be nothing so lovely in this world as a blue willow plate with or without roast beef on it. So now, all these many years later, I knew what Janey's treasure would be. A blue willow plate! It should symbolize for her all her longings and her hopes. Thus a hungry little girl's musings crystalized creatively for her in her middle age. I was thirty-nine the year *Blue Willow* was published.

That same year I was invited to join the faculty of San Jose State College (now San Jose State University). The college was then largely a training school for teachers and librarians. I was part of the library faculty, teaching children's literature and storytelling. As a part-time assistant in the college library I was in close touch with the teacher training program.

When, a few years later, Ginn and Company was about to engage in publishing a series of textbooks for the teaching of reading in elementary schools and was looking about for the right person to take on the responsibility for selecting the content of those books (subject always to the approval of an editorial committee) they decided on me. I had already established myself nationally as a speaker to large meetings of teachers and children's librarians and had established a reputation as an expert in the field of children's literature. For the next several years I was busily engaged in the selection of material for the fourth-, fifth-, and sixth-grade readers of the Ginn Basic Reading series, known as the GBR.

I still found time occasionally to write a novel for young people, all published by the Viking Press. Probably the most important and best known of these later books was *Little Vic.*

From the time I first met Helen White's horse, Freddie, I had loved horses. As already mentioned, in my late teens I did a lot of riding. But during the years of my professional activities there was no time for horses. My life's pattern just couldn't include them. But I never lost my love of them. Somewhere along in the late 1940s, I became enamoured of a great thoroughbred, Citation. He was a son of the all-time great thoroughbred, Man o' War. I had long since left San Jose State and was living in southern California when Citation came to the Santa Anita racetrack. I had been entertaining the idea of writing a horse story with Citation as its hero. Now with the great horse so close at hand, the idea became a compelling urge.

It took a little doing to get a pass to the Calumet stables where Citation had his stall. But I persevered

and at last got a pass. I used to drive out to the racetrack early, early in the morning to watch Citation work out.

My first morning there is still vivid to me. As workout time approached, I took my stand just outside the stable door. An exercise boy was at my elbow. Eagerly I awaited the appearance of Citation. In minutes a beautiful horse emerged from the barn.

"That's Citation," I exclaimed excitedly.

"Naw," said the boy at my elbow, chewing gum vigorously. "That ain't Citation." There was almost contempt in his voice.

Another horse approached. "Is that Citation?" I asked.

"Naw," said the boy, still chewing. "Listen, lady, when Citation comes out, you'll know it."

I was silent after that as one horse after another walked past me. Then a horse approached like none of the others. It wasn't that he was so different in build or color. He had presence; he projected great power. And he walked like a very king of horses.

"That's Citation," I announced.

"Yeah," said the boy, nodding and chewing. "That's Citation."

I began writing my book. I had already entitled it *Little Vic.* It went smoothly and I was enjoying the writing of it, for again I was living, if only vicariously, in a world of horses.

Three or four chapters had accumulated when one day a very strange thing happened. As I sat typing, satisfied with the way the book was going, suddenly I saw a boy standing at the end of my desk. He was in his late teens or early twenties, not very large, and he was black. I stopped typing to stare in utter amazement. I saw him as clearly as I see this piece of paper on which I am at present typing. Then he spoke. "My name is Pony Rivers," he said, "and I want to be in your book."

Now, of course, there was no boy there. My unconscious or subconscious or whatever you want to call it, that sixth sense which all creative people possess in varying degrees, had put him there. Deep down inside me all the while I had been at work on this book was another story quite different from the one I had embarked on. Wisely, I think, I always listen to my subconscious. My hunches, you might say. And I listened this day. I tore up all I had written and started over again. This time the book was not about a horse, but about a boy who happened to be black and about his faith and love for a great racehorse, the focus of all his longings and ambitions.

The book, *Little Vic,* was instantly popular, got fine reviews, and in 1954 received the William Allen White Award, the gift of the children of Kansas. I am

Doris Gates, 1961

very proud of the handsome medal which is safely ensconced in a closed case in the entrance hall of my house.

In 1951 I was living in Carmel, California, in a beautiful old house on the edge of the sea. Across the road which the house faced, was a wide sandy beach stretching white and clean to the water. Across the water, reaching out from the mainland, rose the wooded heights of Point Lobos. The place had had a series of careless tenants and the garden, except for the monitoring cypresses, was in bad shape. There was a fish pond that had been dry for years. I decided to remedy the situation.

First, I went to work on the fish pond. I removed from it all the beer cans and other refuse, filled it with water, and got some water plants to put in it. I was proud of the results. Now it was ready for fish.

There was a pet shop in the village where I bought five goldfish, paying sixty-five cents a piece for them, a goodly sum in those days. Happily I slipped them into the pond and watched as they glided in among the plants I had provided for their enjoyment and well being.

Next morning, in my bathrobe and slippers, I hurried out to the fish pond to see how my fish had fared during the night. Four of them were swimming about as I had expected them to be. But where was number five? Nowhere in sight, certainly. When he continued absent, I found a stick and began carefully poking among the water plants. No number five emerged. *Something had got that goldfish during the night.* Next morning, there were only three. And that afternoon I went to a hardware store in the village and bought enough chicken wire to cover the pool.

It was while I was at work covering the pool that I heard a voice. "It won't do a bit of good," it said.

Astonished, I looked up to see between the stakes of the fence running along the front of the property, a large, thin, and mangy-looking cat. And while I sat back on my heels watching him, he picked up a paw and slowly wiped his nose with it. One of the most insolent gestures I had ever witnessed.

The mystery seemed solved, for it was perfectly plain to me that here before me, the westering sun illuminating his scarred ears, was the reason for the disappearance of my two goldfish.

Well, the long and the short of it is that the cat and I made a bargain. I began feeding him and he became a lazy, contented, fat cat, no longer wanting to wet his paws fishing.

Out of all this came *The Cat and Mrs. Cary* a favorite with me among the books I have written.

For the next ten years I was principally occupied with travelling about the United States giving talks to teachers and librarians on various aspects of children's literature and the importance of books in children's lives. I also spent long periods of time in my textbook publisher's offices in Boston as new editions of the reading series were in preparation.

Then a period of comparative leisure started my thinking in a new direction. Years before, as a storyteller, I had tried to pass on to children my enthusiasm for Greek mythology. I tried telling some of the stories and met with instant success. Encouraged, I arranged to tell a cycle of Greek stories in one of the junior high schools of Fresno. I had long noticed that in collections of Greek myths the stories were presented to young readers like beads on a string. Except that they all concerned the Greek pantheon, they were totally unrelated to one another. But I was convinced that they should be presented like links in a chain. Around every god was a constellation of tales relating to him or her. This is the way I would present my cycle. I did, and my listeners loved it.

So now, years later, I began planning a series of

books about the Greek gods based on this "chain link" principle.

But first I had to go to Greece. I had a storyteller's knowledge rather than a scholar's knowledge of the myths. I thought it was essential that I should see the landscape in which they developed.

My first trip to Greece was in 1971; my second in 1972. And in 1983 I made my third trip. The first two books of the series were published in 1972. They are *Lord of the Sky: Zeus* and *The Warrior Goddess: Athena*. The other four books in the series in the order in which they were published are as follows:

> *The Golden God: Apollo*
> *Two Queens of Heaven: Demeter and Aphrodite*
> *Mightiest of Mortals: Heracles*
> *A Fair Wind for Troy*

The last named concerns the incidents leading up to the start of the Trojan War. All today are in paperback.

Then, quite suddenly, my life changed markedly. In 1973 I bought my first horse.

Unlike Jane Austen's "Mrs. Bates," at seventy-one I was far from being "past everything but tea and quadrille." Now and for the first time in my life I had the money and the leisure for a horse. It takes both.

It had been at least forty years since I had sat a horse, a fact in itself to discourage any prudent septua-genarian from wanting to get back in the saddle. And to add folly to hubris I now intended to ride English.

The first horse I bought was a little round-bellied bay gelding named Choco. He looked a lot like Freddie. The friend who brought him up to me from Santa Barbara proved to be a tower of reassurance and knowledge. It was she who helped me select my tack and urged me to keep Choco at her place for a week while I tried him out. Even with our sanguine expectations we were forced to consider the possibility that this might not work out. Every day I would drive out to Carol's and she would have Choco tied up and ready for me. All went well that first week and I joyously sent off a check in payment of my first horse. That was the very day Choco showed his true mettle. His specialty was to whirl around suddenly and without warning. We would be going along quietly, I admiring the trees and their shadows, the sky and the clouds resting on the crest of the hills, when, all at once, I would be sitting in a cloud of dust and facing in the opposite direction. Why I wasn't thrown off in these sudden whirls I shall never know. Unless, as in riding a bicycle, certain fundamentals never leave one, and I had been a good rider once. But the day Choco whirled with me three times in a two-hour ride, I decided I had had enough. I sold him.

Gates on her Morgan gelding, Aranaway Ethan, 1975

Gates with Merry Jo (left) and six-month-old Willie, 1979

My next horse was a beautiful chestnut Saddlebred. No one seemed to know what his name was, so I called him Little Vic.

He, too, proved to be a mistake. Sixteen hands high, with a mouth of iron and the hide of a rhino, he was stubborn as a mule. Remember, all this time I'm riding English. Of course I knew nothing whatsoever about it, having always ridden Western. It didn't take Little Vic long to find this out. He also had a specialty. It took the form of bringing me back to the barn when he thought it was time to go home. In short, he was barn sour. I could kick him, hammer him with my crop, and yell my head off; nothing I did made any difference. He was very nice about it all, never bolted or bucked or did anything ungentlemanly. He just very quietly and determinedly went home. After being delivered back to the barn a few times in this ignominious fashion, I decided Little Vic was just too much for me. I would get another horse, still keeping Little Vic. He was so beautiful!

They say the third time is always a charm and so it proved to be for me. I learned about a Morgan gelding for sale up the Carmel Valley. I went to see this Morgan, fell instantly in love, and subsequently bought him. But that wasn't all the luck. His owner turned out to be not only a first-class horseman, but a fine instructor of horsemanship and he took me on as a pupil. In no time at all he had me posting, cantering, turning, and doing everything just right.

The happiest years of my life had begun.

With two horses, I now needn't ride alone anymore. For that first year of the Morgan, Aranaway Ethan, it was often Dale, his previous owner who rode with me. Little Vic knew better than to try any of his tricks on Dale!

Some time later, Dale told me about Oakhills Merry Jo. She was a grand-champion Morgan. I thought it might be fun to have a mare and eventually some foals. So I gave Little Vic to a young girl who lived not far from the Red Barn where I had for some time been keeping my horses. She rode him joyously for several years and he never took a wrong step with her. There's something to that myth of the unicorn, I believe. Young girls can often get intractable horses to perform in ways that not even professional trainers can accomplish.

Merry Jo gave me two foals. The first one, a colt, I named Blue Willow. The second, a filly, I named Sensible Kate, another one of my book titles. Both were a joy to have and to try to train. I remember the day I led Willie, as we called him, *away from his mother*. Sensible Kate was the most beautiful foal I have ever seen and she is proving her quality today in the show ring. Willie is now owned by a man who keeps him at the Red Barn. He has turned out to be a good and willing little Morgan.

Out of all this horse experience have come my last two books: *A Morgan for Melinda*, in 1980, and *A Filly for*

Melinda in 1984. The name Melinda is the name of the young daughter of the man who sold me Aranaway Ethan and made me, if not the best jump-seat rider in the world, at least a creditable one. Good enough, at least, to enjoy every moment in the saddle.

Melinda's trials and triumphs in learning to ride as described in *A Morgan for Melinda* were the ones I experienced when first I bought Ethan. And the pleasures she knew with her foal, Little Missy, in the second book, were the same as I had with my two babies.

In preparing to write this memoir I had first to consider how I was going to approach it, since I could see no way of compressing all the events of eighty-three busy years into approximately ten thousand words. I have chosen to focus on those incidents and episodes which bore directly on my writing. Therefore I have mentioned no foreign travel except the trips to Greece. Nor have I enlarged upon the friendships which have colored and enriched my life. Though a "loner" in my youth, I can hardly be described as one now.

For the past twenty-one years I have been living in the beautiful house built for me on a cliff overlooking the Pacific Ocean, five miles south of the town of Carmel. White water breaks against the rocks below my windows and claws its way up the sides of the headlands pointing out to sea. In the cove just north of the house, I can often catch sight of sea otters diving and feeding or just floating on their backs up and down with the swell. My only housemates are a big bronze-colored Doberman named Brodie and an ageing white whippet named Fancy. The latter figures briefly in my last two books.

Though I am sure no young person reading this will believe it, my old age has been the happiest time of my life. It has been a period of fulfillment and deep satisfactions for me. It's had its downs. In 1977 a coronary came close to ending things for me, and I have had the pain of seeing many of my books going out of print. But I made a good recovery from the coronary; I continue to write and to receive letters from readers.

Most of the letter writers have questions: How did you start writing books? Where do you get your ideas? How long does it take to write a book? How do you get to become a writer?

I hope this essay has answered all or most of these questions. As regards the last one, I would advise anyone wanting to become a writer first to be a reader. I do not personally know of any writer who wasn't first a reader. I don't believe anyone can teach you to be a writer. But I do believe that through reading you can absorb a good deal of knowledge as to how a book is structured and certainly you will enlarge your vocabulary. Words are the tools we writers work with.

Finally, you must just start in and learn by doing. While I don't believe that anyone can teach you to write, a class in writing can be helpful because it will force you to write. Learning your craft and developing a style will not be easy. It will take time. And perseverance. A very talented person, without the will to work to improve that talent, will not know success. Choose a subject you know about and then try to make it all come alive on the page.

Doris Gates and her dog Argus, 1983

Above all, believe in something bigger than yourself and never lose a sense of the wonder and the worth of living.

Good luck!

BIBLIOGRAPHY

FOR CHILDREN

Fiction:

Sarah's Idea (illustrated by Marjorie Torrey). New York: Viking, 1938.

Blue Willow (illustrated by Paul Lantz). New York: Viking, 1940.

Sensible Kate (illustrated by M. Torrey). New York: Viking, 1943.

Trouble for Jerry (sequel to *Sarah's Idea*; illustrated by M. Torrey). New York: Viking, 1944.

North Fork. New York: Viking, 1945.

My Brother Mike. New York: Viking, 1948.

River Ranch (illustrated by Jacob Landau). New York: Viking, 1949.

Little Vic (illustrated by Kate Seredy). New York: Viking, 1951.

The Cat and Mrs. Cary (illustrated by Peggy Bacon). New York: Viking, 1962.

The Elderberry Bush (illustrated by Lilian Obligado). New York: Viking, 1967.

Lord of the Sky: Zeus (illustrated by Robert Handville). New York: Viking, 1972.

The Warrior Goddess: Athena (illustrated by Don Bolognese). New York: Viking, 1972.

The Golden God: Apollo (illustrated by Constantinos CoConis). New York: Viking, 1973.

Two Queens of Heaven: Aphrodite and Demeter (illustrated by Trina S. Hyman). New York: Viking, 1974.

Mightiest of Mortals: Heracles (illustrated by Richard Cuffari). New York: Viking, 1975.

A Fair Wind for Troy (illustrated by Charles Mikolaycak). New York: Viking, 1976.

A Morgan for Melinda. New York: Viking, 1980.

A Filly for Melinda. New York: Viking, 1984.

Textbooks:

Becky and the Bandit. Boston: Ginn, 1952.

Roads to Everywhere, with David Russell and Constance McCullough. Boston: Ginn, 1961.

Trails to Treasure, with D. Russell and C. McCullough. Boston: Ginn, 1961.

Wings to Adventure, with D. Russell and Mabel Snedaker). Boston: Ginn, 1961.

Along Story Trails, with D. Russell and others. Boston: Ginn, 1962.

Down Story Roads, with D. Russell and others. Boston: Ginn, 1962.

On Story Wings, with D. Russell and others. Boston: Ginn, 1962.

Nonny Hogrogian

1932-

Nonny Hogrogian, 1985

William Stafford

I was born at 2854 Kingsbridge Terrace in The Bronx, New York, to Rachel and Mugerdich Hogrogian on the seventh day of May in 1932.

I was born into a family of six, including my Uncle Bobby who was just preparing to be married. I am told, though I remember none of it, that he would toss me in the air and catch me, singing "Hey, Nonny, Nonny and a Ha-Cha-Cha." I must have loved it for he did it often enough that Nonny was the only name I answered to.

When Uncle Bobby left I became the sixth member of the family—my grandparents, Roupen Hrahad and Ehleezah, being the heads, then my parents, and my sister Gloria Zabel.

My first memory was of being in a carriage on the stone porch of our house. I remember the stones and being very high up (we were living two stories up from the street). The sky was very blue with soft white, fluffy clouds that floated by. The air was cool and crisp and I wanted to be moved in to the warmth and comfort of my home and family. I cried and screamed. But my mother was determined that I would have my sleep alone in the fresh air. She came out, tucked me in, and purred some words to me . . . and left me alone again.

My grandparents were born in Ersingah, Armenia (now and at that time a part of Turkey), long before the massacres; but there were always troubled times for them. Ehleezah was the daughter of a wealthy silk merchant and Roupen Hrahad was the youngest son of a long line of tillers of the soft black earth on which babies were laid in olden times. Their name was Hoghgrogh-ian (with a couple of more *h*'s) which means earth-carriers. One day when they were digging the soil they came upon a buried treasure which belonged to a fifth-century Armenian king. They kept the treasure a secret for a long time because they were afraid of the Turkish officials, but as time went on, their affluence became more and more apparent. They bought a mansion with quarters for all the sons and their families. But aside from the tapestries on their walls and the few gold circlets the women wore, they lived a simple life. My grandfather was a quiet man, a reader and a dreamer. He had a small shop in the Armenian sector of the city where he did very little business but had a lot of free time for reading.

Ehleezah was a fifteen-year-old with a strong passion for life and a very sharp tongue.

Their families arranged the union.

A horse-drawn carriage took the young bride and groom along the Euphrates River to her new home. They had a difficult marriage from the beginning.

By the time I knew them, they were sharing the same house and family but not much else. And the air held the tension of their non-compatibility. We jokingly called it "divorce, Armenian style."

My father came to America when he was thirteen, along with the two youngest children and my grandmother. The oldest son had come earlier to help his father earn enough money to bring the whole family to America. The wealth was all left behind to the plunder

129

Wedding portrait of Rachel and Mugerdich Hogrogian

Talent, if that is what you call it, ran strong in my family. My father, a photoengraver by trade, was an artist in his heart. He was short and handsome, shy and serious, and what he cared about was God, family and work, painting and gardening. I am not sure of his order of importance except that he put his responsibility for being a good householder first before anything. That included family, work, home, and garden. As for his connection with God, I didn't clearly understand it as a child. He didn't go to church every Sunday as my grandfather did, but whenever there were some quiet moments in his day he would pick up the Bible and read it, always keeping it private. As for his painting and artwork, it took up a small corner of our living room and in the evening after work and on weekends he would stand before his easel and paint.

Mugerdich Hogrogian, in front of the house where Nonny was born

of the Turks, the only remnants being my grandmother's silk underwear.

On my mother's side the influences and circumstances were not so different. She was born on the island of Cyprus during her family's emigration from their troubled Armenia. She was a baby when she arrived in this country and was caught in the difficulties of growing up in two cultures. She wasn't allowed to attend the local high school because it was coeducational, but her mother secretly agreed to send her to a business school so that she could at least learn some secretarial skills. By the time my mother was seventeen her family and my father's had arranged a match, and when she was eighteen they were married.

For the most part our home was warm and our life was full. My father was the only one of his family to keep a job during the Depression, and that, coupled with the fact that we lived with my grandparents, made our home the hub of the whole family on my father's side. At least once a week there would be a big family gathering at our dining room table with places set even at the corners. We children would eat in the kitchen but after the meal we would run into the dining room and climb on someone's lap and listen to Nasreddin Hodja stories and finally to my Uncle Onnig as he sang the songs of the old country.

Nonny, right, and sister Gloria, at a camp in the Catskill Mountains

My mother, it seemed to me, could do almost anything with her hands and do it well. She sewed for all the women in the family and during the Depression, when money was so scarce, she helped the family income by crocheting silk evening purses at home. She called it piecework.

Once a week she and my dad would go to a sketch class together. I thought that her drawings were beautiful, but you couldn't convince her of that. She also was—and still is—a great cook, although she didn't show it when I was little because she took her place in the kitchen as my grandmother's helper. She washed the dishes and helped to form the dough and chopped the onions and never complained that she wanted a more creative job. But when her opportunities came she made the best apple pies I've ever eaten, along with many other incredible main dishes and desserts. Preparing food with simplicity and interest has always been her way and the results of her labors—superb!

The pattern of my life was set very early. My fascination with artwork and fine handwork goes back as far as I can remember. Love of work itself was strong in

the family and whenever there were spare moments some one would start a new project. And so, with these influences, when I was about three or four years old, I began to putter with my father's paints and brushes.

My grandfather, who had a large basement room that was his study and sleeping quarters, had many, many books. One wall of his room was filled with them. The books were mostly in Armenian but there was one shelf (or maybe two) which I could reach that had books in English—*Evangeline, Joan of Arc, King Arthur,* Andersen's Fairy Tales and Grimm's, some poetry—all beautifully illustrated. He never said they were *our* books. But *he* couldn't read them. They were simply there and we were welcome to go there anytime to read them. He never needed to tell us to treat them with respect. It was like a library in his room and all the books were so well cared for. Papa would sit at his desk reading his Armenian journals and I would sit in the big chair by the bookcase going through the illustrated books and dreaming about the possibility of making such beautiful pictures.

There was a time, between the discovery that I could use my hands to paint or draw and the point when artwork became a serious part of my life,

Nonny at the Art Students' League, New York, about 1970

Vasgen Houssian

131

that I remember very little about. But I do recall a few incidents connected with artwork. I was shy and retiring and embarrassed to be in any situation outside my immediate family life, which kept me comfortable and (I thought) secure. I knew that I had a gift that everyone didn't have, and I used it for the attention that I didn't know how to get in any other way. Once when I was ill and in bed, someone brought me a gift of some Walt Disney comic books. I read through them and was pretty quickly bored until I began to notice exaggerations of line that were used to create certain expressions on the animals' faces. I became fascinated. Eyebrows tilting down into the center of the face made the character look angry, and tilting up in the center, made him look innocent or wondering. I borrowed my mother's little purse-mirror and began to make faces in it. It was true! I knew then that I could also draw these expressions on paper. I began to imitate Walt Disney characters until I excelled at drawing them. The word quickly got around my classroom at school that I could draw a mean Donald Duck or Mickey Mouse. It became my entry ticket to life on this planet and I used it—to please the teachers, to attract "friends," to have adults exclaim over me, and for my own amusement when I was alone. And in its own way, it worked.

There were a few incidents in grammar school that left strong impressions on me. One incident brought into perspective something about my artistic ability. We were drawing Thanksgiving pictures. It was clear to me that I could draw a pumpkin. I knew pumpkins . . . the stem end . . . those beautiful rounded ribs that grew up and out and around from the center. I could even draw the pilgrims or facsimiles in pilgrim's clothing; but when it came to the turkey, I was stuck. I knew I couldn't draw one because I hadn't seen a live one and the pictures were unclear to me. I could draw a cartoon based on a picture of a turkey but I had no sense of what a real turkey was. Years later, my husband wrote this poem after we had shared our life on a piece of land with "Penelope and Franklyn Turkey."

Turkeys

Say it: the tom is all ego and male.
Puffs one second, unpuffs the next.
And what is the cause of his puffing,
and why did he cease?
A cat will leap from a butterfly
shadow sometimes, but he will do so
with humor, enjoying his own fright
in a game he plays for himself.
But for the tom it is not even
butterfly shadows.
It is simply, one moment all feathers

and fight, the next minute
nothing—Mr. Nonentity himself.

It's a hell of a life. Consider it!
The fluff and feathers serve no purpose,
and signal his own fear—though he
pretends to be scaring others off—
and his face (that turns blue from fear)
and that silly, flappy foreskin on his face.
Really!—is that what ego is all about?

But then there is the hen, all squawk
and whining sex. Everything, just everything,
is a complaint. Come here, go away (she says
to Tom), get me more, get me less. Why can't
you see what I want? You never can, you
never will. Oh, never mind . . . it's too late,
and doesn't matter anyhow.

Oh God, the point is clear, why You
have put turkeys here.

Although I could not formulate it, the point was clear to me as a child . . . that I must know something in order to depict it (as David knows turkeys). Knowing must come from "seeing," which brings an understanding between myself and the thing drawn.

Other than one or two more such incidents that clarified for me something important about artwork, I don't remember working at it with intention . . . until that time between my twelfth and thirteenth year when I was forced to think about my future. And that meant which high school I would attend. It was natural that I would dream about going to Music and Art High School in New York. It was *the* school for future artists. And everyone assumed that I would be an artist, including me. So I applied. The times were difficult for my family. My grandfather and grandmother had both just died and within two months of each other. The rest of us were trying to pick up the pieces of our lives and find the inevitable new directions that would be true for each of us.

There were tests to pass before a student was accepted at Music and Art High School. We were to be judged by an examination on the basis of portfolios of our past work. I had no idea how to go about putting together a portfolio, but I thought a variety of my work would show what I could do. I picked out about six or eight of my best drawings and my father bought a manila envelope for me to carry them in.

The day came. I was the only child from my school who tried out for Music and Art. I took a trolley car, a bus, and a subway to get there. It was the first time away from my neighborhood that I was completely alone. It felt very strange but somehow right that I was alone in this endeavor. When I arrived at the high school everyone looked as if they belonged except me. Every child I saw had a big black, shiny portfolio filled with drawings. They seemed to have prepared for this for a long time. I wished I could hide myself but my wish to go to the school was stronger, so I stayed in the line and opened my skimpy little envelope and showed my few doodles. The woman hardly looked at them and condescendingly moved me on.

I was confident that the test would make up for my lack of a proper portfolio. I knew I could draw.

The tester (as she was called) came to the front of the room. The atmosphere was tense. I was perspiring for the first time in my young life.

She talked about the true test of talent. She said there was one sure proof of a person's talent: whether or not a person could do a good contour drawing. "You will know for yourself," she said, "when you have completed this test whether or not you should pursue this work."

I didn't know what a contour drawing was and that scared me, but it infuriated me that she could say it would decide my future. She gave the rules. She said no previous training was necessary, or even relevant. Either we were able to do a contour drawing, or not. We were to draw the model with one fluid line, without taking our hand from the page or our eyes from the model. Anyone who did would be disqualified.

The tension in the room mounted and my wet hand clutched my pencil tighter. The paper was flimsy. My dad had always given me good paper to draw on. The model came up to pose. I had never drawn from a live model before. The tester said our drawing should fill the page. How could I be sure I was filling the page without looking at the paper? My rigid hand began to move on the page. I sneaked a peak. I had drawn the ugliest little squiggle. The shock of my ugly drawing cleared my head a little and I realized that it happened because her tight rules had filled me with fear. I would simply turn the paper over and begin from a freer place in myself. I knew I could do it. My mistake was in asking permission to start again. She smiled condescendingly and said the proof was on the page. There was no second chance. I began to cry from rage and frustration. She gave me some water to calm me and I went home, but my future was decided that day. The seeds of my talent were sown before I was born but the fertilizer they needed to push out of their shells was given to me in the judgment of the examiners that day. (I went on and trained myself to excel at contour drawing.)

During my high school years my parents sent me to study painting and charcoal drawing with my Aunt Angele who was our official family artist. Aunt Angele was born in Constantinople and studied at the Sor-

bonne; she wore colorful French berets with a contrasting scarf around her neck. Several times a week she would spend her whole day at the Metropolitan Museum copying the paintings of the "old masters." Her copies were exquisite. The walls of her apartment were covered with them and some originals as well. Mainly, she encouraged me and pointed out certain things I didn't see or avoided seeing, always making it seem more possible to stretch myself, and my skill. I worked with Aunt Angele every Saturday morning for about two years. Then one day I heard there were Saturday art classes for young people at Pratt Institute in Brooklyn. I took an illustrating class there with a young woman who was training to be a teacher.

I jumped at any chance to hone my skill. In high school I spent my study periods hand-lettering cards for one of my teachers and I worked on scratchboard illustrations for my high school magazine. One hot summer my family drove out to California and after seeing one cotton field too many, I slouched in the back seat of the car with my feet up on the back of the front seat, and I began to draw. I spent at least five days of the journey crossing America drawing my feet and I've always enjoyed drawing feet since then.

During my high school years I also hand-painted greeting cards. There was a woman (a friend of one of my art teachers) who hand-printed greeting cards for one of the more elegant stores on Fifth Avenue. I painted them for her in dry-brush technique for a nickel a card. It hardly paid since I took pains to make each one as beautiful as I possibly could, and the deadlines came up too quickly. Sometimes my family would even help paint in the little red bows while I concentrated on dry-brushing the fluffy little poodles. It was a short-lived experience but good training.

When it came time to go to college, my family assumed that I would attend Hunter College since all the girls in the family had gone there. But I applied to The Cooper Union. I don't know where I found the nerve but the day of the examination I woke up with a pounding headache. It didn't stop me. I took my place in the large auditorium where there were two or three empty seats between each applicant and each applicant's seat contained the examination booklet. We were told to turn the first page after the bell sounded. I turned it. The instructions told me to complete the incomplete drawing on the page. It seemed ugly to me. How could I possibly complete it? I realized that they not only wanted me to complete it but to tack on some personality—pizazz—call it what you will. My headache became worse. I realized that I neither would nor could do what they wanted. I closed the booklet and put down my pencil and walked out into the fresh air. I did attend Hunter like all the women in my family and it was no worse nor better than Walton High School. I was an art major with an art history minor and I filled my programs with as many art classes as I could fit in. And when I graduated I didn't fit into a slick art school mold but had had many, many hours of artwork behind me and a smattering of many different techniques. I was ready to go out and find my way in the world.

I had found a few jobs after I graduated from Hunter but they were all horrid. I was either fired after a few days or I quit before they had the chance to fire me. I didn't know what I wanted to do but I knew I needed to do artwork and I was beginning to notice that my college portfolio was not knocking the employers dead. I supposed I could stay home and spend six months working on a new one but I felt the time had come to earn some money.

Was I really as untalented as the interviews made me feel? Everytime I had a bad one I would want to throw out my portfolio, crawl into bed, and stay there. But I knew I couldn't stay there forever. The only thing that egged me on was that my mom was always nudging me to study the secretarial skills because there was security in secretarial work. That simply made me want a job that required my own skills even more.

I finally began checking the employment agencies. There was one that was known for having jobs for people interested in publishing. They had one job available for a "girl Friday" in the advertising department of William Morrow. Could I type, the woman asked. Yes, I lied. I had taken one class in college (at my mother's insistence), which I failed. What was my speed, she wanted to know. "Oh, I'm not very fast, but I can type well enough for a girl Friday." "Well, I suppose it won't do any harm to send you down there," she replied. "I'll call Mr. Baker and see if you can have an interview this afternoon." He said "yes" if I came right away and so I grabbed the first cab I could hail.

I felt at home with Ross W. Baker III (better known as Jerry). He asked me a few questions, about my schooling and my typing skills. I told him I was slow but accurate. He looked through my portfolio and I could tell he liked my work. Maybe he has no taste, I thought, since he was almost the first person since college who responded in a positive way. He asked me questions about technique and I relaxed and chatted with him. Then he told me he wanted to give me a short typing test. Even that didn't throw me. I just laughed and told him I couldn't type fast enough to be tested. I had to face it anyway. I hunted and pecked a few letters on his old machine and my heart began to sink. "It's no use," I said. "I can't type well enough."

"I can see that," he answered. "Well, let me take another look at your portfolio."

The interview was soon over and although he said he would call me, I had lost all hope.

Two weeks went by and one day Jerry Baker *did* call me. I could hardly believe it. He asked if I had found a job yet and said he'd like to see my portfolio again, and he couldn't seem to remember—had I taken a typing test? I reminded him that I was too slow for a typing test.

"Well, why don't you just come in and let me take another look at your portfolio and maybe you can type a few short sentences."

I wasn't about to argue with that. I was beginning to think that Jerry Baker was a little weird, but I was also beginning to feel that there might be a place for me in this world and that it could be at William Morrow and Company.

At my second interview we went through the usual amenities; he checked out my portfolio again and had me struggle with the typewriter again. Then he excused himself and took my portfolio with him.

About fifteen minutes later he came back and told me he wanted me to meet the president of the company. He looked nervous and it was catchy. I wanted the job very much. He led me through the old office building and we descended the circular metal staircase to the floor below and Thayer Hobson's office. Jerry introduced us and then disappeared. Thayer Hobson was an elegant, blustery old codger, seated at the biggest, most beautiful desk I ever saw. When I commented on it, he grinned and told me his first wife (the Jewess, he called her) had it made for him. I knew he was testing me so I responded and asked if she was Laura Z. Hobson. I knew, of course, that it must be.

He told me he heard I couldn't type but he really didn't seem to care. He spoke about how one was spoon-fed in college—but that working was more like graduate studies. One had to figure out things for oneself. I wondered if he knew how much I would have to figure out, like all the things I lied about being able to do—like paste-ups and layouts. I would simply figure it out.

I loved Thayer Hobson and I loved those offices. I practically floated back to Jerry's office. He was standing at his window aiming a paper airplane at the street below. He jumped when he saw me. After asking how things went, he excused himself again. I waited in silence, but I was singing inside. I knew already that the job was mine.

I began work at Morrow the Monday after my interview. I arrived at a quarter to nine, a shade anxious. Richard, the assistant advertising manager, was there to let me in. It turned out that he had worked there for twenty-five years in the same job, placing ads in newspapers and guiding new people (including Jerry Baker, when he began to work there) through their early difficulties. Richard helped me through many disasters during my first months at Morrow.

Betty was the copy chief of the department. She was a mannish, short-tempered woman who shared Richard's office when she was around. She came in late, took long lunch hours, and left early. But when she worked, her typewriter flew and she expected those who worked for her to work with the same clarity and speed.

There were also two secretaries (also named Betty)—one old and crotchety and the other a young Belgian-Jew who had been hidden away by some nuns during the war. She was more Catholic than Jewish although she was always bringing in samples of her mother's wonderful gefilte fish.

The elder secretary Betty did a bit of typing for Jerry but she spent most of her time going through newspapers from all over the country, clipping reviews of Morrow books.

There was one additional job in the department: a copywriter. It was the only job in the department that turned over while I was there. But whichever copywriter happened to be there at the time, that person became my friend. They came from schools like Radcliffe, Smith, and Reed—and I learned from them about books and music and politics and even art. As Thayer Hobson had told me, my education was just beginning.

My own small corner of that department was wonderful. My job consisted of working with book-jacket artists, choosing type, getting the artwork approved—starting with Jerry and then each of six salesmen and finally Thayer Hobson. I always argued with the salesmen because they would want the lettering bigger and brighter on every jacket. But I even enjoyed my anger at them.

I did jacket mechanicals and small ads; and whenever they wanted to save money on a book, I would offer to do the jacket art myself. I'd stay after hours and sneak into the jacket files and examine how other artists did their work. I studied the different methods until I understood how type and color separations worked best for me.

There weren't many great writers at Morrow then but there were some good ones. And they always had at least one book on the *New York Times* best-seller list.

Earle Stanley Gardner was Thayer Hobson's first author and "Uncle Earle," as we called him, came to visit a couple of times a year with big boxes of candied fruit from sunny California.

I loved that job until the day I left. I worked as hard as I could for myself and for the company. Almost everything I know about type and design I learned from struggling with them at Morrow. It was a time of awakening for me and I never missed an opportunity. Every person that I met there was unlike anyone I had met before. Everything in my life seemed alive and open and new. I worked at Morrow for three years, which is the longest I ever stayed at any job. I realized finally that my time there was over, and I left to try to do my own artwork. But I left a bit of my heart there, too.

Nonny and husband, David Kherdian, in Armenia, 1971

From One Fine Day, *written and illustrated by Nonny Hogrogian. (Copyright © 1971 by Nonny Hogrogian. Reprinted by permission of Macmillan, Inc.)*

I was twenty-four years old and entering a more difficult time in my life. I had been working at woodcutting at about the time I left Morrow. I added all of my woodcuts to my portfolio, removed a few old pieces, and went to see Estelle Mandel, an artist's agent whom I had worked with at Morrow. I heard that she took a forty-percent commission from her clients but that she was one of the best agents. Estelle wasn't impressed. "Do line drawings," she said. "That's what art directors are buying now."

"But I don't do line drawings. I'm doing woodcuts now. Maybe there is an art director somewhere who will like them."

"I wish it were true, Nonny, but they are just not commercial enough. You go home and do about fifty line drawings and then come back and see me."

My life was entering a new phase and whatever I tried seemed not to work.

One evening while I was visiting my sister, she mentioned something about the Haystack Mountain School of Crafts in Maine. In fact, she said, there was a young Armenian-American designer that she knew who would be teaching there that summer. She thought I might be able to get a scholarship.

Well, to make a long story short, I got the only scholarship I have ever gotten, and not because my work was thought to be so great, but because Ruben Eshkhanian, the young Armenian-American designer, worked for Jack Larsen, the textile king, who was on the board of directors of the school and my sister bought a lot of fabrics from Larsen as part of her job. I didn't care how it happened. I needed the opportunity, and I took it.

Sixteen of us scholarship students arrived two days before the paying guests—in time to clean out the cabins, and to get acquainted with each other, our studios, the rules, and the summer chores.

Maine was different from New York, right down to the bugs. By my second day there, I was covered with welts. My first job was to clean out the bureaus and put bed linens in each room. The bureaus were filled with toilet paper nests of mice! Ugh! Didn't these people know that I was a city girl? After cleaning out about five drawers I began to notice the baby mice in detail. They were actually cute. Walt Disney wasn't making it all up. They really looked like his drawings—big ears and all.

Our quarters were primitive and there was a shortage of water. We were not allowed to do our own laundry or even to bathe more than once a week. I couldn't believe it. There was a woman who worked for the school who washed our clothes in the brook for a small fee, but we were warned not to expect them to

Book jacket from The Animal *by David Kherdian. Illustrated by Nonny Hogrogian. (Copyright © 1984 by David Kherdian. Illustrations copyright © 1984 by Nonny Hogrogian. Reprinted by permission of Alfred A. Knopf, Inc.)*

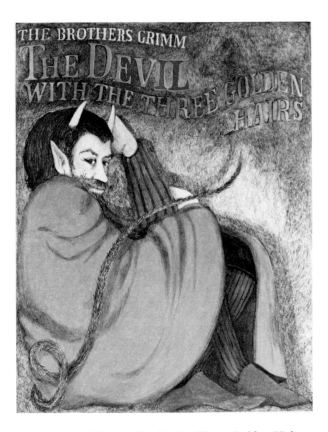

Cover from The Devil with the Three Golden Hairs, *retold from the Brothers Grimm and illustrated by Nonny Hogrogian. (Copyright © 1983 by Nonny Hogrogian. Reprinted by permission of Alfred A. Knopf, Inc.)*

stay bright with the hard water of Haystack Mountain.

It was a good, difficult summer for me but I began as a misfit and remained one all summer long.

There were sixty people in all, including the scholarship students, the paying guests, and the director, Fran Merritt, and his wife, Priscilla. The scholarship students were supposed to shine as guides and examples to the paying guests. One of my duties was to wait on the table where I ate plus the one next to mine. I was never the picture of grace, but if I looked anything like I felt as I juggled huge trays of food through the dining room, I must have been quite a sight.

I only worked at two woodcuts the whole summer long. I went to the first Friday night seminar and realized that I had no connection with what the rest of the people were saying about art, so I never attended another of their seminars. I realize in writing this that I never really understood what my relation to artwork was, but I knew somewhere inside that it was what it was, and that I had a responsibility to work with it as best I could. My work at Haystack was disliked. The acceptable form there was more experimental—more "creative"—more modern—more abstract. The unspoken consensus of opinion was that it was a mistake for me to be there but they would have to suffer it. I real-

Nonny working in the print shop at Two Rivers Press

ized this after my first woodcut which I tried to do in a modern Japanese technique (taught by my woodcutting instructor, Hodaka Yoshida). The method had no life in it for me. My work seemed dead even to me. I burned the woodblocks.

I spent the rest of the summer playing hooky from the print shop. I wove a small rug, I tried to throw some clay, I played at woodcarving but, most of all, I experienced what it was to be nearly alone with sixty other people.

It was in a way a wonderful summer. Even the wasps began to accept me. I went for a walk one day with a young man named Peter, also a misfit. Suddenly Peter flung me across the road, grabbed an old tree limb, and seemed to be fighting with the dead leaves on the ground. But the leaves were moving and I realized that Peter had saved me from stepping on an eight-foot golden adder. Of course, I fell in love with him but our relationship was like being in the army together. We knew that when we walked away from Haystack it would all be behind us.

The last week of the summer Peter spent the evenings sitting on a tall stool in the print shop as I cut my first real woodblock of the summer (of Peter, of course). Peter said it was good, I knew it was good, and no one else commented. But I knew that for that summer I had kept the skill protected inside me, just where it belonged.

You've heard a bit now about my first twenty-four years. The next thirty years included my good fortune in illustrating and my marriage to David Kherdian (a

late and special marriage), and more. But my life as an illustrator is what I have tried to concentrate on here. I tried to retire from illustrating many times in my life, the first time—almost before I started—when I thought of changing my major so I could become an occupational therapist. The second time was a couple of months before I received the Caldecott Award in 1966. The award turned everything around and I forgot about going back to school for my Master's.

I have just gone through another bout of trying to retire and now I am beginning to get interested in what exactly is going on here. I see, for one thing, that I only make a pretense of not caring enough about my work. In fact, I identify completely with my work and if anyone dares to "slight" it, I am very quick to shut down the doors, to bar my work from the offenders. Beyond that, I am always dissatisfied with my work, always left with the feeling that I must try harder the next time, that I never seem capable enough to paint something as beautifully as it deserves to be painted. If I can just see that my work is simply what it is—that other people's opinions are simply their opinions. . . .

All of it in the end is part of my life, and is only interesting if I can learn something in the process of living it. Right now I am looking forward to the next book that I will illustrate.

BIBLIOGRAPHY

FOR CHILDREN

Books written and illustrated:

One Fine Day. New York: Macmillan, 1971.

Apples. New York: Macmillan, 1972.

Billy Goat and His Well-Fed Friends. New York: Harper, 1972.

The Hermit and Harry and Me. Boston: Little, Brown, 1972.

Rooster Brother. New York: Macmillan, 1974.

Handmade Secret Hiding Places. Woodstock, N.Y.: Overlook Press, 1975.

The Contest, adapted from an Armenian folk tale. New York: Greenwillow, 1976.

Carrot Cake. New York: Greenwillow, 1977.

The Pearl: Hymn of the Robe of Glory. Aurora, Ore.: Two Rivers, 1979.

Cinderella, retold from a story by Jacob and Wilhelm Grimm. New York: Greenwillow, 1981.

The Devil with the Three Golden Hairs, retold from a story by the Grimm Brothers. New York: Knopf, 1983.

The Glass Mountain, retold from a story by the Grimm Brothers. New York: Knopf, 1985.

Noah and the Ark, retold from the Bible. New York: Knopf, 1986.

Dave Kangas

Nonny, David, and Sossi the cat, Aurora, Oregon, 1984

Books illustrated:

King of the Kerry Fair, by Nicolete Meredith. New York: Crowell, 1960.

Down Come the Leaves, by Henrietta Bancroft. New York: Crowell, 1961.

Gaelic Ghosts, by Sorche Nic Leodhas, pseudonym of Leclaire G. Alger. New York: Holt, 1963; published as *Gaelic Ghosts: Tales of the Supernatural from Scotland.* London: Bodley Head, 1966 (includes *Ghosts Go Haunting*).

Always Room for One More, by Sorche Nic Leodhas. New York: Holt, 1965.

Arbor Day, by Aileen L. Fisher. New York: Crowell, 1965.

Ghosts Go Haunting, by Sorche Nic Leodhas. New York: Holt, 1965.

Hand in Hand We'll Go: Ten Poems, by Robert Burns. New York: Crowell, 1965.

The Kitchen Knight, by Barbara Schiller. New York: Holt, 1965.

Once There Was and Was Not, Armenian tales retold by Virginia A. Tashjian. Boston: Little, Brown, 1966.

Poems, by William Shakespeare. New York: Crowell, 1966.

The White Palace, by Mary O'Neill. New York: Crowell, 1966.

Bears Are Sleeping, by Julie Whitney. New York: Scribner, 1967.

The Day Everybody Cried, by Beatrice Schenk De Regniers. New York: Viking, 1967.

The Fearsome Inn, by Isaac Bashevis Singer; translated by Elizabeth Shub. New York: Scribner, 1967.

The Renowned History of Little Red Riding Hood. New York: Crowell, 1967.

The Story of Prince Ivan, the Firebird, and the Gray Wolf, translated from the Russian by Thomas P. Whitney. New York: Scribner, 1968.

The Thirteen Days of Yule. New York: Crowell, 1968.

The Three Sparrows and Other Nursery Rhymes, by Christian Morgenstern; translated by Max Knight. New York: Scribner, 1968.

In School: Learning in Four Languages, by Esther Hautzig. New York: Macmillan, 1969.

Sir Ribbeck of Ribbeck of Havelland, by Theodor Fontane; translated from the German by E. Shub. New York: Macmillan, 1969.

The Time-Ago Tales of Jahdu, by Virginia Hamilton. New York: Macmillan, 1969.

Deirdre, by James Stephens. New York: Macmillan, 1970.

Favorite Fairy Tales Told in Greece, retold by Virginia Haviland. Boston: Little, Brown, 1970.

Vasilisa the Beautiful, translated from the Russian by T. P. Whitney. New York: Macmillan, 1970.

About Wise Men and Simpletons: Twelve Tales from Grimm, by Jacob Ludwig Karl Grimm; translated by E. Shub. New York: Macmillan, 1971.

The Armenian Cookbook, by Rachel Hogrogian. New York: Atheneum, 1971.

Paz, by Cheli Durán Ryan. New York: Macmillan, 1971.

Three Apples Fell from Heaven, retold by V.A. Tashjian. Boston: Little, Brown, 1971.

Looking Over Hills, by David Kherdian. Aurora, Ore.: Giligia, 1972.

One I Love, Two I Love, and Other Loving Mother Goose Rhymes. New York: Dutton, 1972.

Visions of America: By the Poets of Our Time, compiled by D. Kherdian. New York: Macmillan, 1973.

Poems Here and Now, edited by D. Kherdian. New York: Greenwillow, 1976.

The Dog Writes on the Window with His Nose, and Other Poems, collected by D. Kherdian. New York: Four Winds, 1977.

Country Cat, City Cat, by D. Kherdian. New York: Four Winds, 1978.

I Am Eyes, Ni Macho, by Leila Ward. New York: Greenwillow, 1978.

Pigs Never See the Stars, translated by D. Kherdian. Aurora, Ore.: Two Rivers, 1982.

Peacock from Heaven, by Count Bobrinskoy. Aurora, Ore.: Two Rivers, 1983.

Right Now, by D. Kherdian. New York: Knopf, 1983.

The Animal, by D. Kherdian. New York: Knopf, 1984.

Root River Run, by D. Kherdian. Minneapolis, Minn.: Carolrhoda, 1984.

M.E. Kerr

1927–

"M.E. Kerr"

I grew up always wanting to be a writer.

My father was a mayonnaise manufacturer, with a strange habit, for a mayonnaise manufacturer, of reading everything from the Harvard Classics, to all of Dickens, Emerson, Poe, Thoreau, Kipling, and John O'Hara, Sinclair Lewis, John Steinbeck, all the Book-of-the-Month Club selections, plus magazines like *Time, Life, Look,* and *Fortune,* and all the New York City newspapers, along with the local Auburn, New York *Citizen Advertiser.* I would like to say that it was his love of reading that made me want to be a writer . . . and that certainly contributed.

So did English teachers who encouraged me, and librarians who had to pull me out of the stacks at closing time. And there were my favorite writers like Thomas Wolfe, Sherwood Anderson, the Brontës, and our hometown hero, Samuel Hopkins Adams. (I'd pedal past his big house on Owasco Lake, just to see where a real writer lived!) But in my heart, I know who was responsible for this ambition of mine to become a writer: it was my lifelong abettor, still going strong today, my eighty-eight-year-old mother.

One of the most vivid memories of my childhood is of my mother making a phone call. First, she'd tell me to go out and play. I'd pretend to do that, letting the back door slam, hiding right around the corner of the living room, in the hall. She'd have her pack of Kools and the ashtray on the desk, as she gave the number of one of her girlfriends to the operator . . . My Mother would begin nearly every conversation the same way: "Wait till you hear this!"

Even today, when I'm finished with a book and sifting through ideas for a new one, I ask myself: Is the idea a "wait till you hear this?"

Saturday nights in summer, my mother'd get out her Chevrolet coupe, and we'd go downtown and park for awhile in various places, beginning outside the one theater in town, the Auburn Palace. My mother would take out her knitting. We'd watch who went into the movies, while my mother did a running commentary. "Don't tell me Lois Gilbert's daughter is still going out with Chippy Palmer? That'll be over as soon as she goes to college and Chippy goes into the plumbing business with his father. Chippy ought to use his common sense and not waste his time and hard-earned money on someone from South Street . . . There's Polly Otter by herself again. Carl's probably down at Boysen's Bar . . . Loretta Hislop in the same old dress, year after year after year. That's what happens when you marry a man who gambles."

We would stay there until everyone had gotten into the first show, and then we'd slip down to the front of Boysen's Bar, just as it was beginning to get dark.

"I'm right," my mother'd say. "There's Carl Otter's white Buick. He's in there . . . Don't tell me the Leonards are *eating* in there! Well, there they are in the window. Of all places to eat dinner, with that stale smell of beer and Carl Otter getting crocked at the bar! I guess it's those dinner specials. Len Leonard has to watch every cent since his accident. Poor Len owes all over town, tells everyone 'The check's in the mail.' The check's in the mail like I'm from Paris, France . . . Oh!Oh! There's Eleanor budd on her way in."

On and on.

Always, before we went home, a swing by the Women's Union, where many single women had apartments, up into the parking lot to see if there were any familiar cars, a good way to tell who was seeing who in the Women's Union . . . My mother knew the color, make, and year of everyone's car, and so did all her girlfriends.

Then we'd go up Genesee Street at a crawl, my mother still talking. "The Henrys are eating in their dining room for a change. They must have company. . . . If I thought it would help, I'd get up on a ladder and paint the trim on the Stewarts' house myself, but nobody's going to get Harry Stewart to care about his house, his lawn, his shrubbery, or anything but bridge!"

Then home . . . and a lesson from my mother on the importance of fiction. Fiction, I learned early on, spins off grandly from fact. Our trip downtown would be related over the phone, beginning, "Wait till you hear this! Carl Otter sent poor little Polly off to see *Brother Rat* so he could have a night on the town, that dear little woman with her face down to her shoes, standing in line by herself while he treats Ellie Budd to old-fashioneds down at Boysen's."

Long before the character in one of Salinger's short stories ever peeked into someone else's bathroom cabinet to inspect its contents, I'd learned from my mother that that was the first thing you did once the bathroom door was closed in other people's homes.

"What are you looking for?" I'd ask.

She'd say, "Shhhh! Run the water!"

I learned that the first thing you look for is prescription medicine, then all the ointments and liquids that tell you what ailments are being treated in the house you're visiting.

My mother taught me all a writer'd need to know about socio/economic/ethnic differences, too.

The Reyersons are very R-I-C-H, she'd say, and if she didn't spell it out, she whispered it: *rich*.

In our little upstate New York town, in the thirties, there were very few Jews, and my mother was never sure "Jew" was all right to say, so she'd instruct me not to go around town calling people "Jews," since my father was in business in that town. I was to say "a person of the Jewish persuasion."

She taught me to cut out all the labels from my coats and jackets, anything I might remove in Second Presbyterian Church on a Sunday morning, so that no one knew that we often bought out-of-town.

My mother'd come from a poor immigrant German family twenty-six miles from Auburn, where she'd been raised in a convent. She'd taken a step up in her marriage, a fact she was always defensive about in Auburn, always proud of in her hometown, Syracuse; and the labels she'd cut out were sewn back in for visits there.

She took an unusual interest in the boys who came to call on me when I was in my early teens. She

Marijane Meaker, a Girl Scout, age ten

warned me that if I married a Catholic, there'd be one baby right after the other; that if I married an Italian I wouldn't be allowed to wash the salad bowl, they just wiped it dry; and that any boy whose father was bald, would be bald himself one day.

When I was around fifteen, I was dating the son of the local undertaker, and my mother said I'd better not marry him, or I'd end up doing all the cosmetic work on the corpses. Don't say I didn't warn you, she'd tell me, it's a family business—*everyone* in an undertaker's family has something to do in a funeral home.

Our small town housed Auburn prison, where executions still took place when I was a child. The identity of the man who pulled the switch was a secret. Eight or nine men would march into the prison on the night of an execution, one of them the actual executioner.

My mother and her girlfriends would be parked outside Auburn prison to watch who went in on one of those nights. When everyone came back to our house after, for cookies and tea, the guessing game would begin. I'd be upstairs, hanging on the banister, listening wide-eyed while they went down the list. Was it Russ from the tobacco store? Kenny Thompson's father? Melanie Rossi's father?—listening to my mother insist, "Never! Not Mike Rossi! Mike wouldn't harm a fly!" Etcetera.

When I was around five or six, there was a high-school teacher who rented a small house on our street. She had the wonderful last name of St. Amour. She was a mysterious lady who smoked with a long cigarette holder, played piano, and on summer nights could be heard singing songs like "Ah, Sweet Mystery of Life." She was quite beautiful, in her thirties, never married so far as my mother could figure out. No one knew where she'd come from, and she didn't pal around with the other teachers at school.

At the same time, our mayor was a widower, a dashing fellow who drove around in a black Packard convertible, with the initials PKT-1 on the license plates.

He began seeing Mademoiselle St. Amour, as my mother always referred to her, though she only taught French, was not really from France. The mayor never parked outside of the house, but drove all the way down the driveway and parked behind the house.

"Marijane," my mother'd say, "go down through the fields and see if Mayor Tallent's car is at Mademoiselle St. Amour's."

"Why?"

"Just do it! Be sure the license plate reads PKT-1. You don't know a Packard from a Chevrolet!"

A few years later, I got the idea to form a spy club, rounding up several other kids to go out on "missions," to go look in people's windows and report back to my clubhouse what we'd seen, and to list all the cars in the driveways with their license plates.

We were found out when two of us, on a mission over at the Goldmans', tripped over ash cans, the noise alerting the Goldmans that there were intruders in the bushes.

"How'd she ever get that idea?" my mother asked my father. "It's this war talk, talk of German spies loose."

One summer before the war, the family drove across the country to California to visit my mother's sister, Agnes. Aunt Agnes, my mother, and I would go on all the bus tours past movie stars' homes, my mother taking notes so she could write it up in my baby book . . . We'd go up to Pops Willow Beach, where Agnes said anyone who was anybody went.

"There's Kent Taylor!" my mother whispered, though this famous movie star was all the way down the beach. "Go get his autograph, Marijane!"

"I don't want his autograph!"

"Just do it!" my mother said. "Tell him your name is Ida, and you'd like him to write something for Ida."

Aunt Agnes (an apple never falls far from the tree) said, "Honey, tell him you have a sister named Agnes. Tell him to write something for Agnes."

Second only to gossip about citizens of Auburn, New York, was gossip about Hollywood stars.

Every Wednesday afternoon I waited in suspense for my mother to return from Mr. Billy's Beauty Salon.

Mr. Billy also played the organ at Second Presbyterian Church, and he played piano for Laura Bryan's dance classes. He wore a toupée and spats and an Adolphe Menjou mustache, and although he almost never left Auburn, where he looked after his invalid mother, it was never doubted by my mother, her girlfriends, or me that he knew all the Hollywood gossip.

My mother, with her hair newly set, still smelling of lilac Permafix, would recite to me all the latest news: that Jack Benny was in love with Ann Sheridan, breaking Mary Benny's heart; that Joan Crawford's entire face and body were covered with freckles the size of lima beans; and that Gary Cooper and Marlene Dietrich fell in love filming *Morocco.*

I can still remember sitting in the darkened Palace theater, on one of those occasions when we weren't parked outside watching people go in, unwrapping a Baby Ruth bar in the middle of *Sweethearts,* starring Jeanette MacDonald and Nelson Eddy, my mother leaning down to whisper to me, "Mr. Billy says they hate each other! In real life, they don't even speak!"

Soon, a world war was raging. Downstairs in our basement a map of the world was tacked to the wall. My kid brother, fourteen years younger than me, and my father tracked the war with thumbtacks, everything from the battle in North Africa, to the taking of the islands in the Pacific, the invasion of Sicily, the Netherlands, New Guinea, the bombing of Berlin, the evacuation of Cassino—all of it, and my older brother by then was flying off a carrier in Torpedo 9, famous in the Battle of Midway.

But upstairs, in front of a Monopoly board, my mother and I sat listening to the "Lux Radio Theater" or "Grand Central Station," while my mother said things like: "You've landed on my hotels—wait! I think she's going to find out that this Uncle Alan of hers is her real father—hush!" turning up the volume on the Stromberg-Carlson. Or: "Hold it! Don't roll!" her ear bent in the radio's direction. "Oh, no! She's not going to marry *him*! Him? With a prison record?"

Even after I went off to Stuart Hall, in Staunton, Virginia, I was never totally, never even partially invulnerable to what my mother had to say.

Letters from my father would arrive, carefully typed in thin envelopes, filled with consent and advice.

> *"Yes, your mother and I will allow you to go to Richmond for the weekend . . . Marijane, if you persist with this wish to be a writer then, yes, apply to a Journalism school, so you can at least earn your living until you're married. You won't earn a dime writing stories of your own invention! Writers like that starve! . . . And please, don't apply to The University of Missouri Journalism School, or you'll*

The Meaker family portrait, 1944: standing, Ellis, Jr., Marijane (age sixteen), Ellis, Sr.; seated, Charles and Ida.

marry someone from St. Louis, and that's the last we'll see of you on holidays, since wives go home with their husbands . . . So investigate Syracuse University near us, where there's a fine school."

But it was the fat envelope with the unruly handwriting I saved to open in my room, by myself, sitting atop the Bates bedspread, eager to take it all in, words running together, misspelled, no punctuation except for exclamation points.

Well Marijane the McIntees house blew up from the furnace all their things out on the lawn for everyone to see and I mean everything! But Robert Annan in a marines uniform said say hi to you in church and did you like school his pimples gone very sharp as youd say. But Buddy Smith came home a lootenant on leave and Mildred Spring dropped him just like that war or no war for some sailor no one knows the family of in Penn Yann she'll regret it all her life and next door Margie Waterhouse dating a sailor who claims to be from Maine but who knows if thats true.

Recently, I visited my mother, just outside Auburn, in a place called Presbyterian Manor, where she lives now with eight other old women and one old man. There's a view of Skaneateles Lake, where we'd go summers past to hear band concerts in the park, and she's right next to Krebs' Restaurant. On the days the family'd go there for dinner in the thirties and forties, my mother would always warn in the morning: "Don't eat anything all day! You know the size of their portions! Only Gertie Lord can eat everything they put down in front of you at Krebs." (Gertie Lord was Auburn's fat lady.)

Most of my mother's girlfriends are gone now. But she still reads every word of the *Auburn Citizen,* and in two minutes can tell me what happened to any of my schoolmates of forty and fifty years ago, how many children and grandchildren they have, who's divorced and who recently advertised for a maid, or put the house up for sale.

She sat with her television on, telling me how badly she felt that young Alan Thicke's show was cancelled on top of the fact his wife, the soap star, was divorcing him, and they have these two nice boys. But no one, she told me flatly, can compete with "Johnny." "Johnny," she insisted, bounced right back no matter what happened in his marriages, and then she leaned forward and said, "Shhhh! Do you hear that?"

"What?"

She turned down the volume with her remote control paddle.

"Did you hear that, Marijane? That's Eunice Tutton outside the door, seeing if we're in here. As soon as we leave, she'll be in this room, in a second, to look in my closet."

"Why?"

"*Why?* She counts my dresses. She's always trying to find out if I've got more dresses than she has."

She struggled to her feet, balancing herself on her cane, as we prepared to go for a walk. "Well, let her, poor old Eunice. She's ninety-two. That's all she's got to think about: how many dresses I have."

We walked outside into a beautiful autumn afternoon. "I can tell you right now, Marijane," she said, "when no one's listening, that I didn't like your book *Me Me Me Me Me* at all!"

That was my latest book then, my teenage autobiography, with generous mention of the family.

"I don't know why you want to tell everyone's business," she continued. "I try to go back and figure out why you never liked things like knitting, with all the knitting *I* did, or where this writing idea ever came from in the first place . . . Look across the street now, Marijane. See that bent-over old man? (Don't let him see you looking, or he'll see me and start over here!)

That's Dave Daw. Remember when you went to high school with Cathy, and he ran off with Gloria Alexander? Years ago! Gloria never brought Dave any happiness, with her hair falling out, chasing off to scalp specialists. God's punishment! . . . Anyway," my mother continued, "you were always up in your room writing those stories. It was all those books your father had everywhere in the house . . . You're your father's daughter, all right."

At the University of Missouri, where I went despite my father's warning that if I did go there, I'd end up marrying someone from Missouri, I switched my major from Journalism to English . . . partly because I failed Economics, which one had to pass to get into J-School, and partly because I realized I didn't want anything to do with writing fact. I wanted to make up my own facts. I wanted to do creative writing.

It was the end of World War II, and Columbia, Missouri, was a real college town, filled with kids right off the farm, or coming from little towns like Bolivar and Poplar Bluff, plus an abundance of young men straight out of the service. Girls who'd never been any farther than St. Louis or Kansas City were matched on blind dates with fellows who'd fought in Okinawa, or already seen London and Paris, as sorority/fraternity life commenced. My very first week there I went with some classmates to a popular hangout called The Shack, and learned the game of Chug-a-Lug, which was a beer drinking contest, in which you drained your full glass in one breath, while everyone sang "Here's to Marijane, she's true blue, she's a drinker through and through!"

Although it was very much a party campus in those postwar years, it was still the end of the 1940s, and there were rules: a time to be in at night, no men above the first floor in a sorority house, no alcoholic beverages . . . and in our sorority, Alpha Delta Pi, dating men who were not in fraternities was frowned on. They were called "independents"; they were unwelcome (though tolerated) at major sorority functions.

I found someone to date (and fall in love with) who gave my father far more to worry about than the boy from St. Louis or Kansas City whom he'd envisioned. George was from Hungary originally, a Jew who'd barely managed to escape the Nazis in his teens by being smuggled into Venezuela.

By the time he arrived on the Missouri campus, he was an ardent Communist. He was the furthest thing from a Joe College type there was. He didn't drink, or smoke, or go out for sports, or go down to any of the campus hangouts to sing and play after classes, and he didn't own a pair of jeans or a tie . . . and he was more interested in reading Karl Marx and Lenin than

Thomas Wolfe or Sinclair Lewis. He was SERIOUS.

George would show up at the Alpha Delta Pi sorority house in his dark pants and turtleneck sweater, with a briefcase filled with Communist propaganda, and spend any rare free time he had lecturing me on the class struggle and dialectical materialism. He wasn't around a lot because he was working his way through college as a counterman and also as a Spanish teacher at Stephens College . . . but he was there often enough to irritate my sorority sisters, and to delight me.

Under his spell, I joined the Communist party, and voted for Henry Wallace for President of the United States, the only one in Cayuga County, New York, to do so.

I stayed on for summer sessions, too, because of George, and although he'd politicized me, he hadn't cured me of my wish to be a writer.

I wrote story after story, sending them off to New York-based magazines, accumulating so many rejection slips that I attended a sorority masquerade party as a rejection slip, wearing a black slip with rejections from all the magazines pinned to it.

Because George was so busy, I made many friends to spend my spare time with, most of them would-be writers, few of them sorority/fraternity people.

One of them was a young man named Ernest Leogrande, who ultimately became a writer for the New York *Daily News.* Ernie was my closest confidant, until his death in 1985, and from the time I first met him on the train to St. Louis, en route to the university for my freshman year, he stayed in my life, moving to New York City when I did, never living too far from where I lived . . . In nearly every book I wrote, there was a character called Ernie Leogrande. He was my good luck charm, and by the time I was M.E. Kerr, writing for teenagers, he was my adviser on contemporary music, since he covered all the rock concerts for the *News.*

Afternoons in Columbia, Ernie and I and other "writers" sat in coffee shops talking about F. Scott Fitzgerald, and Hemingway, and the "new" writer Carson McCullers, and dreamed of going to New York City, and getting published.

Evenings, by phone, or in the university library, George and I talked about getting married and going to Venezuela, or back to Hungary. "If you marry me," George promised, "you'll have something consequential to write about: a *real* life, not this playpen here in the United States."

I was definitely torn.

No one was more typically American than I was, coming from small-town life, probably more privileged than most girls, worrying as I grew up about little

Meaker with Ernest Leogrande, East Hampton, New York, 1982

more than how to get a bigger allowance so I could buy more clothes or the latest Glen Miller records.

If George had helped to raise my consciousness about the *real* world, he hadn't been able to totally convince me that all the things American I loved—our literature, our music, our holidays and customs—were all little more than a Capitalist/Wall Street plot against the working people. I couldn't imagine moving away from everything and everyone I loved . . . But I couldn't imagine letting him go, either.

To this day, I believe it was my mother who solved my problem, though she sort of denies it. ("I don't know what you're talking about," she says, with a thin little smile.) Somehow, George came to the attention of "the authorities" shortly after my mother and my father came to Columbia for a visit. At the time, my mother's only comment about George was, "He's going to land you in Russia if he has his way, and he's shorter than you are!"

She may or may not have written a letter to the FBI, but the FBI visited George a few weeks later, filled with questions about his affiliations, and his future plans. Around that same time, there were many witch-hunts going on in the country, rumors of faculty members in large universities being Communists.

George would laugh about it, saying they always looked in the wrong places: investigated political science teachers, when the real party members were in the agriculture school, for example.

It was also around this time that Whittaker Chambers was accusing Alger Hiss of having been a Communist when he worked for the State Department in the thirties. Also, Communist party members were being arrested for advocating the overthrow of the government.

The pressure was very much on George. He felt he had to leave the country immediately. There was no money to take me with him, even if I had gotten up the courage to go.

In my book *Me Me Me Me Me*, I describe his leaving, as well as his letter to me many years later when, disillusioned by what he found in Hungary, he'd escaped with his wife and children . . . I also describe in that book, our last meeting, in 1968 in my New York City apartment, when he came one night for dinner, catching me up on his new life as a journalist in Caracas.

In 1949, I arrived in New York City, with several sorority sisters, bent on a career as a writer.

In those days, New York City was still a place where you could take a subway at night and not fear getting mugged. You could also find a two-bedroom apartment for $150 a month, if you wanted to live in Washington Heights, where the four of us found ours.

My roommates all got good jobs in advertising/ publishing, because they knew shorthand. In those days, a good job, for a female, was a job as a secretary, at about fifty dollars a week.

I had never been able to master shorthand, though I had studied it at my father's insistence . . . My first job was at Dutton Publishing Company, as something like an assistant to the file clerk, at thirty-two dollars a week.

I can still remember the woman who trained me saying, "When you answer the phone, tell whoever's calling your name, Marijane Meaker," as though I might not know my own name.

My job had no real title. I worked in the art department, in the bull pen, carrying my lunch every day in a paper sack, after a long subway ride with two station changes; it took me an hour to get down to lower New York from Washington Heights in hose, heels, hat, and gloves.

I remember once passing an editor's office, where a sort of scruffy character was seated talking to the editor about "Truman." I thought, "That guy knows President Truman?" because he was saying things about seeing Truman, talking with Truman . . . It was one of Dutton's authors, Gore Vidal, speaking of Truman Capote. Vidal was younger then, not successful yet, wearing an old camel's hair coat, and hair longer than most men wore it in those days.

I wasn't worth the thirty-two dollars Dutton paid me to file letters and answer phones and carry things from one floor to another. My own work came first with me. I was always sitting there scratching out short stories and poems. I think the only time I looked up was when an author came into the area to discuss the artwork on his/her cover. I was in awe of all the authors. I remember one young, tough fellow who never liked his covers, who always gave the art director a hard time. He was Mickey Spillane, not too well known yet.

Life away from the office, up in Washington Heights, was busy on weekends with boyfriends who chipped in fifty cents apiece for Sunday pot roast dinners.

Friday and Saturday nights we'd go to places like the Old Garden, on West Twenty-ninth Street, the Jumbo Shop on West Eighth Street, or Albert French Restaurant on University Place, where you could have dinner for $2.50. If we couldn't afford that, we'd eat dinner in, and go out later to drink beer at Joe King's

Rathskeller (draught beer was ten cents a glass) or listen to jazz at Nick's in Greenwich Village, or hang out at Arthur's in the Village, where occasionally actors and writers from the Circle in the Square theater would come in for drinks. I remember seeing Tennessee Williams there one night, and Geraldine Page, and Marlon Brando, and a TV star called Wally Cox.

Although we lived in Washington Heights, we always seemed to head to the Village on weekends, or someplace "downtown" where we thought "the action" was.

Always, there was talk of writing . . . One of my roommates worked on a confession magazine, and for awhile I churned out confessions, selling several at $250 apiece, but not considering them real sales, because they were made-to-order stories about unfortunate females who didn't know that the men they married were dope addicts or bigamists or second cousins.

Another roommate had a boyfriend who wanted to write westerns, and she would make pots of coffee for him weekend nights while he borrowed my typewriter. I'd come home and find a sheet of paper in my Smith-Corona with a beginning story: "Mungo was back in town, and so was the smell of gunfire." Exhausted from his stint at my typewriter, David would be asleep on our couch, and as the rest of us came in from our dates, we would have heated discussions about whether or not we'd let him sleep there. How would it look to our neighbors, a man overnight in our apartment?

Dutton soon found me out, and fired me for not doing my work, and I went from Dutton to a series of flunkie jobs, everything from a proofreader on *The Review of Gastroenterology*, to a clerk at Compton Advertising Agency, to a reader at Fawcett Publications.

Not knowing shorthand was my great curse, and my great blessing. I was inept. Time and time again I was asked to turn in my key to the Ladies' Room, and report to the front office for my final paycheck.

All the while I was going from job to job, I was writing stories and sending them out. When I couldn't find a literary agent to represent me, I took the money from a sale to a confession magazine, and had stationery printed up: Marijane Meaker, Literary Agent . . . I began sending stories out under pseudonyms, with Marijane Meaker raving about her new discoveries, to various editors.

On April 20, 1951, a letter came in the mail from the *Ladies' Home Journal*, to Marijane Meaker, Literary Agent, saying they were going to buy Laura Winston's story "Devotedly, Patrick Henry Casebolt."

The $750 from that sale launched me on my writing career.

I never worked at a full-time job again.

Bruce Gould, then the editor of *Ladies' Home Jour-*

Ted Kavanaugh

Meaker (left) on the "Mary Margaret McBride Show," ABC Radio, 1951

nal, liked the story so much, he came to interview me in New York City about a position opening up on the magazine, as a columnist for young people. It meant I would have to go to Philadelphia to live. I declined, but I also admitted that I was both Laura Winston and Marijane Meaker. Gould decided to plug that issue of the magazine with this story of a young writer posing as her own agent. He managed to get me on several radio shows, including one conducted by the then-famous Mary Margaret McBride.

That publicity came to the attention of an editor named Dick Carroll. He was launching a new original paperback series called Gold Medal Books, published by Fawcett Publications. He'd heard me say on the radio that I'd once worked for Fawcett in some menial capacity.

"How about trying a novel for our new line?" he asked me. "How about a book on boarding school life?" (My story for the *Ladies' Home Journal* was set in a boarding school.)

"How about one on sorority life?" I suggested.

"Give me a few chapters and an outline," said Dick, "and if you do well, maybe I can get you an advance."

I went to work on it, and in a few months sent him the result.

He called me for lunch, and as we taxied to the restaurant we went under the ramp near Grand Central Station, and in that dark tunnel he told me, "We're taking your story. I'm advancing you $2000," and then we emerged into the sunlight of Park Avenue. I was now under contract for my first novel, a paperback original which came to be called, not by my title *Sorority Girl,* but by one Dick thought up, *Spring Fire,* an idea he'd gotten from *The Fires of Spring,* a fast-selling novel by James Michener.

Spring Fire was an instant paperback success, selling 1,463,917 copies in 1952, more than *The Damned* by John D. MacDonald or *My Cousin Rachel* by Daphne du Maurier, both published that same year in the U.S.

Long out of print now, *Spring Fire* enabled me to become a full-time free-lance novelist, enjoy a trip to Europe, and get my first apartment, sans roommates, on East Ninety-fourth Street, off Fifth Avenue, where I would live for eight years.

The apartment building at 23 East Ninety-fourth was very small, only two apartments per floor, five floors altogether.

About a year after I moved in, a new tenant moved across the hall.

He rang my bell one day to tell me that he worked at the Frick Museum, and was not home during the day to receive deliveries. Would I accept a small drum for him?

A drum? I hated the whole idea—that just across the way there'd be some drummer. He'd neglected to point out that it was a drum of china and crystal, sent from his home in Omaha, Nebraska.

He was a man a few years older than me, tall, sandy-haired, an art historian who'd graduated recently from Princeton.

Thus began a very close friendship, that still remains today, with Tom Baird. We began spending most of our free time together, and I always think that one day he looked over my shoulder as I was working at the typewriter, and told himself "*I* can do that." Because Thomas Baird soon became an author, as well as an art historian, beginning with a short story called "Remember, Remember," which I sold for him (I was still a half-hearted literary agent) . . . the first story I ever sold for a legitimate client. In 1962, his first novel, *Triumphal Entry,* was published. Today he has eleven novels to his credit, two of them young adult novels.

I think of my New York years (1949–1973) as the best of times!

I began taking courses at The New School, in everything from writing to adolescent psychology, and there I made another friend, who would open up new worlds to me. She was a professor there named Martha Wolfenstein, married then to Nathan Leites of the famous Rand Corporation, which I always thought of as "the think tank," there were so many brilliant minds employed there. Through Martha and Nathan, I met New York's psychoanalysts (Martha was a child analyst), and many sociologists, political scientists, and anthropologists (including Margaret Mead) I'd have never had the opportunity to even glimpse as a mere beginning writer.

And I read all of Freud, under Martha's formidable influence, and began subscribing to *The International Journal of Psychoanalysis, The Psychoanalytic Study of the Child,* plus reading everything by Reik, Stekel, Kubie, Mahler, Fromm, Ernest Jones, on and on and on.

It was the fifties, a time when many young people in New York City were undergoing lengthy psychoanalyses. I always think my friendship with Martha spared me that process (and expense). I got it by osmosis.

Certainly this friendship and its resultant interest in what makes people tick, enhanced my writing, for I had moved into suspense novels, whydunits instead of whodunits, writing as Vin Packer. This move was mo-

Tom Baird, East Hampton, New York, 1984

tivated solely because I'd heard that the *New York Times* mystery and suspense columnist, Anthony Boucher, would review paperbacks as well as hardcovers.

As Vin Packer, I wrote twenty novels of suspense, all paperback originals, encouraged by Boucher's good reviews of my work. I particularly liked to fictionalize famous contemporary murder cases like the "Wolf Whistle" Mississippi murder of the young black boy Emmett Till, and the Fraeden-Wepman matricide. A good many of my stories were told from the point of view of a teenager, again probably Martha's influence, since many of her patients were young adults . . . and she often discussed their problems with me, without ever identifying anyone under her care.

The fact that I wrote many novels about teenagers would come up in conversation years later, when I became friends with a writer named Louise Fitzhugh.

Louise was an artist turned writer, who had done a very successful book called *Harriet the Spy.* It was published by Harper and Row as a "young adult" book. I had never heard of such a category.

"You'd be a good young adult writer," Louise would tell me, "since you're always writing about kids."

"But not from their viewpoint," I'd answer, and I'd dismiss her suggestions that I should try to write for this field.

I went on to hardcover, eventually, as Marijane Meaker, writing first a nonfiction study of famous suicides for Doubleday, called *Sudden Endings.*

I suppose it was natural to move from homicide to

suicide, since suicide is often described as self-directed homicide.

My book on the subject studied the lives of everyone from Arshile Gorky, to Ernest Hemingway, to James Forrestal, Robert Young, the railroad magnate, Virginia Woolf, Joseph Goebbels, Hart Crane, etcetera, and I learned two important facts while I was researching the material. The first fact was that while I could locate a famous person in every field from business to art, I could not find a famous sports figure or a famous musician who had ever committed suicide (this was before our rock stars came along). The second fact I learned was that since I was not an authority of any kind, only a reporter, I was not allowed by my editor to comment on the first fact, or speculate about it. I was told I had "no editorial excuse" to make anything of this discovery.

I found this most dismaying, and I also found an abundance of errors I had made when the galleys were returned to me. I was not a very careful researcher. I seemed to hate facts.

I quickly decided I would stick with fiction. There I could invent and speculate. I went on to do the obligatory family novel that I guess every young writer must get out of his/her system.

It was a terrible bomb called *Hometown,* and the only attention it got was in upstate New York, where my aunt was busy getting it out of the local library, and various other relatives were decrying its publication.

It was described by *Publishers Weekly* as "a long, boring novel, all the more surprising because it comes from the facile pen of Vin Packer." I was beginning to believe that my real name was a jinx, though ultimately I went on to publish a successful novel called *Shockproof Sydney Skate* as a Marijane Meaker. It became a Literary Guild alternate, and a selection of the Book Find Club, and the paperback money was exceptional, enough eventually to buy me the house I live in today, in East Hampton, New York.

Again, my friend Louise Fitzhugh was nudging me about writing a novel for young adults. Again, she reminded me that my protagonist, Sydney Skate, was a teenager.

Louise, by that time, was interested in writing mystery and suspense. She thought that maybe if we traded typewriters, a young adult book would emerge for me, and my typewriter would produce for her a crime story.

We laughed about it. I took a look at some of these young adult novels and decided I could never write one . . . *until* I picked up one called *The Pigman* by Paul Zindel.

Right around that same time, I'd just finished participating in an experiment, whereby writers went into high schools, taking over English classes for one day a month, trying to get kids interested in writing.

I'd been assigned to some classes at Central Commercial High School, in New York City, on Forty-second Street. These kids worked half a day and went to school half a day. They were wild, unruly, wonderful kids who didn't give a fig for reading, but who responded to writing assignments with great vigor and originality.

The star of one of my classes was a very fat black girl nicknamed "Tiny."

She wrote really grotesque stories, about things like a woman going swimming and accidentally swallowing strange eggs in the water, and giving birth to red snakes.

I always "published" Tiny's stories in the little mimeographed magazines we ran off for the kids. One day her mother appeared, complaining that Tiny's stories were hideous and that I was encouraging her to write "weird."

While we discussed this, I learned that Tiny's mother was an ardent do-gooder who worked with her small church helping drug addicts. Tiny would come home from school to an empty apartment, fix herself something to eat, watch TV, and wait for her mom to come home from her churchwork. Then they'd eat dinner, her mom would go back to her good works, and Tiny would eat and watch TV.

Tiny was getting to be enormous. She was also glued to the TV all the while she was alone.

In other words, while Tiny's mom was putting out the fire in the house across the street, her own house was on fire.

I was thinking a lot about this.

A book was coming to me.

I had just read Zindel's books.

That was the birth of my first book for young adults. Tiny translated into "Dinky," and since I knew that this story could be told about any family, black or white, rich or poor, I decided to stick close to home. I'd just moved to Brooklyn Heights, which abounded with lawyers because the courts were right nearby. I set my story there, and made Dinky's mother a middle-class lawyer's wife who was involved in rehabilitating dope addicts.

The result was *Dinky Hocker Shoots Smack.*

Since I love pseudonyms, I decided to call myself M.E. Kerr, a play on my last name, Meaker.

Since I had done well with the paperback sale of *Shockproof Sydney Skate,* I thought of this book for young adults as a little sideline, an indulgence. I only received $2000 from Harper and Row for it. I didn't expect to make much more on the paperback sale.

To my astonishment, this "sideline" made money. The paperback sale was enormous. It was optioned for the movies (many times) and ultimately made into an afternoon special. It is still going strong today.

I decided to take a second look at this new, to me, young adult category. I was in my forties, by then, and not very interested any longer in murder and crime. The passion I had brought to that interest was waning, as I became more mellow, more liable to see the light in the dark, or the light *and* the dark. As I looked back on my life, things seemed funnier to me than they used to. *I* seemed funnier to me than I used to, and so did a lot of what I'd "suffered."

Miraculously, as I sat down to make notes for possible future stories, things that happened to me long ago came back clear as a bell, and ringing, and making me smile and shake my head as I realized I had stories in me about *me*—no longer disguised as a homicidal maniac, or a twisted criminal bent on a scam, but as the small-town kid I'd been, so typically American and middle class and yes, vulnerable, but not as tragic and complicated as I used to imagine.

So I had a new identity for myself in middle age: M.E. Kerr.

I also moved to a new place, East Hampton, on Long Island, New York, which would eventually become Seaview, New York, in many of my novels. My old hometown, Auburn, would appear from time to time as Cayuta, New York.

I've never married nor had children, and I've lately thought this has been a great asset. If I'd had children, I'm sure I would have been tempted to keep them tied to something in an upstairs room, so no harm would come to them. I think the youngster in me remains vivid because I've never raised any children to compete with her, or compare with her, and I have not had to pace the floor nights worrying where they are or with whom, and what has happened to the family car.

Again, these experiences come to me through osmosis. When I first moved to East Hampton, a sweet seventeen-year-old kid next door to me was going through his first love affair with a very rich girl who spent summers in our community. His family disapproved of this girl; his dad was a policeman, and Kippy was brought up strictly. He was working as a soda jerk the summer he met this rather sophisticated young lady. He had a new bicycle; she had a new Porsche.

Kippy would come over to my house, agonizing about what to wear, what fork to pick up on the table when he was invited to her house for lunch. She had a butler. She lived by the ocean. She was a year older than Kippy. She'd gone to high school in European boarding schools.

That same summer, I was reading a book by Howard Blum called *Wanted! The Search for Nazis in America.*

That book, and what Kippy was going through, became all mixed together, until finally I sat down to write a novel called *Gentlehands.*

Gentlehands was about a boy in Kippy's situation, who looked up a grandfather the family was estranged from, in order to impress this girl. The erudite, opera-loving grandfather proved to be a Nazi war criminal the Immigration Service was investigating.

Of any book I've ever written, *Gentlehands* was the easiest. It poured from my typewriter as though a tape was inside with the whole story put down on it.

Another time, I'd gone to a local high school football game. At halftime I'd watched a pretty blond girl run up to the pom-pom cheerleaders, greeting them as though she hadn't seen them in a long time. She was carrying something in her arms, in a blanket. Behind her, a tall black guy was waiting for her, not joining in the reunion.

When this blond girl unfolded the blanket, there was a tiny black baby gurgling up at everyone.

I was standing beside my dentist's wife, and I said something about supposing that was inevitable in a community where there were blacks and whites going to school together: intermarriage.

She said, "Ah, but that's not the real story. The real story is the anger black girls here have because white girls date 'their men.'" She said many of the black boys were sports heroes, and the white girls went out with them, but white boys didn't in turn date black girls.

This incident, on an ordinary autumn afternoon, was the background for a book called *Love Is a Missing Person.* It was the story of a girl whose sister fell in love with a black boy, and ran off with him at the end of the novel. Not a lot of local teachers and parents were thrilled about this Kerr, but it has elicited many letters from kids familiar with the problem of interracial dating.

Sometimes my ideas come from the past, and I update them. That was true of my book about boarding school life called *Is That You, Miss Blue?* Nearly everything that happened in that story, happened to me when I was attending Stuart Hall. A present-day Stuart Hall student wrote to tell me she liked the book, ". . . but boarding schools just aren't that strict anymore." I think it was a valid criticism.

I had always hesitated writing a book for kids set in the forties, when I was growing up. I remembered how I hated reading "historical" novels, when I was a kid. Still, the years during World War II haunt me, and I am filled with stories about what happened to teenage girls back then. There have been so many, many stories about what went on in the lives of young men . . . so few about "us."

Finally, I decided to tackle the problem by attempting a novel that would begin in the forties and end in the eighties. I didn't want to write a long three-generational type thing, so I came up with a new approach, for me. I wrote three short stories about the same characters: one set in the forties, told from the first person; one set in the sixties, told from the third person; the last, a letter in the second person, written by a boy to his dad, set in the eighties.

The three stories, read together, are a novel.

I called this *I STAY NEAR YOU*—one story in three.

the likes of Paul McCartney, Mick Jagger, Lauren Bacall and Alan Alda, but the rest of the year we are a sleepy little place without an industry or very much going on. And I missed the easy access to other writers, the chance to meet casually with someone who wasn't a weekend house guest, to talk about the latest books, and what's going on in the publishing world.

I decided to form a writers' workshop, by putting an ad in the paper to see what interest there was out there. I would lead this workshop. It would be a non-profit undertaking, benefiting the Springs Scholarship Fund—"Springs" being the section of East Hampton where I live. I arranged for us to meet at a place called Ashawagh Hall, a community center near me.

The response was quick and most enthusiastic. We had to turn some people away, we had so many signed

A meeting of the Ashawagh Hall Writers' Workshop, 1984

One great advantage in writing for kids is keeping up with the times. I've developed a very enthusiastic interest in today's music. I listen faithfully to the top ten, and I follow all the groups from pop to rock to heavy metal. I'm an MTV watcher, mesmerized by all the groups from Police, Duran Duran, Wham!, Van Halen, and Aztec Camera, to Twisted Sister, Kiss, and Motley Crue. Some of the videos I love, and some I really hate, but all of them teach me about kids today. It's a whole new world for me, one I probably wouldn't have investigated if I wasn't a Y.A. writer.

When I first moved to East Hampton, I missed New York City a lot. Three months of the year our little village jumps with tourists and summer people,

up. Thus, The Ashawagh Hall Writers' Workshop was born. We meet once a week for two hours, fall and spring sessions running for twelve weeks at a time. Our group age ranges from the early twenties to the seventies, twenty members in all, everyone from the minister at the Amagansett Presbyterian Church, to the bartender from a hotel in Sag Harbor, to a famous artist's wife, a beautiful young girl who only writes horror stories, and local teachers, a real estate salesperson, a retired editor, etcetera.

We're going into our third year.

Probably none of us would have ever met each other socially, but all of us are focused on each other's work, as well as what's current, and what's being published in the various genres from suspense to literary. We have our own literary agency, though no one has to pay a ten or fifteen percent fee . . . and each semester we try to take in one or two new members.

I have few interests that aren't related to writing.

I read like a fat person eats. I read everything from magazines like *Time, The Rolling Stone, Interview, New York Magazine, Redbook, Fortune, Business Week, Vanity Fair, Woman's Day,* and *Ms.* to the best-sellers—Anne Tyler (a particular favorite), Raymond Carver, Elmore Leonard, Eudora Welty, Robert Cormier, Alice Munro, Bobbie Ann Mason, Alice Walker, Joyce Carol Oates, Barbara Pym—on and on and on. And I reread wonderful Carson McCullers. I love poetry, too—Yeats and Auden and Kastner and Rilke and Wakoski and Leo Connellan.

I watch a good deal of television, talk shows and news programs like Ted Koppel's. I'm a movie fan . . . I guess I'm just a media freak.

Long ago, despite my WASP training, I learned that motion isn't work, that sitting at the typewriter when you have no clear idea of what you want to write, is wasted time. When I'm "stuck" between novels, I mostly read, walk by the ocean, and complain that I can't work to other writers who complain back that they are finding what they're working on too hard, impossible, or not worth it.

The hardest book I ever wrote was one called *Little Little,* about teenage dwarfs. I don't know why it was so difficult, except I couldn't seem to get much humor into it, and what was there often seemed too dark . . . Another thing was that I was afraid to tell *anyone* I was writing a book for young adults about dwarfs. I was afraid of the reaction, and of being discouraged by it. So I kept it to myself as I started the story over and over again, worked on it up to about fifty pages, then abandoned it. It seemed unworkable after several years of trying.

One day I decided to write an essay about it for the Long Island section of the *New York Times.* It would be about the one story I wanted to write but couldn't.

In the middle of this essay, I stopped, and started the book again, and this time finished it.

Maybe it is my favorite book, not because I think it's better than the rest, but because it was such a struggle. Maybe a parent, who's finally raised a particularly difficult child, feels this same affection and pride when that kid turns out okay.

I love writing, and I particularly love writing for young adults. I know other young adult writers who claim that their books are just slotted into that category, and claim there's no difference between an adult novel and a young adult one . . . I beg to disagree. When I write for young adults I know they're still

wrestling with very important problems like winning and losing, not feeling accepted or accepting, prejudice, love—all the things adults ultimately get hardened to, and forgetful of. I know my audience hasn't yet made up their minds about everything, that they're still vulnerable and open to suggestion and able to change their minds . . . Give me that kind of an audience any day!

BIBLIOGRAPHY

FOR YOUNG ADULTS

Fiction, as M.E. Kerr:

Dinky Hocker Shoots Smack. New York: Harper, 1972.

If I Love You, Am I Trapped Forever? New York: Harper, 1973.

The Son of Someone Famous. New York: Harper, 1974.

Is That You, Miss Blue? New York: Harper, 1975.

Love Is a Missing Person. New York: Harper, 1975.

I'll Love You When You're More Like Me. New York: Harper, 1977.

Gentlehands. New York: Harper, 1978.

Little Little. New York: Harper, 1981.

What I Really Think of You. New York: Harper, 1982.

Him She Loves? New York: Harper, 1984.

I Stay Near You. New York: Harper, 1985.

Night Kites. New York: Harper, 1986.

Nonfiction, as M.E. Kerr:

Me, Me, Me, Me, Me: Not a Novel (autobiography). New York: Harper, 1983.

FOR ADULTS

Fiction:

Hometown, as M.J. Meaker. Garden City, N.Y.: Doubleday, 1967.

Game of Survival, as Marijane Meaker. New York: New American Library, 1968.

Shockproof Sydney Skate, as Marijane Meaker. Boston: Little, Brown, 1972.

Fiction, as Vin Packer:

Dark Intruder. New York: Gold Medal Books, 1952.

Spring Fire. New York: Gold Medal Books, 1952.

Look Back to Love. New York: Gold Medal Books, 1953.

Come Destroy Me. New York: Gold Medal Books, 1954.

Whisper His Sin. New York: Gold Medal Books, 1954.

The Thrill Kids. New York: Gold Medal Books, 1955.

Dark Don't Catch Me. New York: Gold Medal Books, 1956.

The Young and the Violent. New York: Gold Medal Books, 1956.

Three-Day Terror. New York: Gold Medal Books, 1957.

The Evil Friendship. New York: Gold Medal Books, 1958.

5:45 to Suburbia. New York: Gold Medal Books, 1958.

The Twisted Ones. New York: Gold Medal Books, 1959.

The Damnation of Adam Blessing. New York: Gold Medal Books, 1961.

The Girl on the Best-Seller List. New York: Gold Medal Books, 1961.

Something in the Shadows. New York: Gold Medal Books, 1961.

Intimate Victims. New York: Gold Medal Books, 1962.

Alone at Night. New York: Gold Medal Books, 1963.

The Hare in March. New York: New American Library, 1967.

Don't Rely on Gemini. New York: Delacorte, 1969.

Nonfiction:

Sudden Endings, as M.J. Meaker. Garden City, N.Y.: Doubleday, 1964.

Nonfiction, as Ann Aldrich:

We Walk Alone. New York: Gold Medal Books, 1955.

We Too Must Love. New York: Gold Medal Books, 1958.

Carol, in a Thousand Cities. New York: Gold Medal Books, 1960.

We Two Won't Last. New York: Gold Medal Books, 1963.

Take a Lesbian to Lunch. New York: MacFadden-Bartell, 1972.

Norma Klein

1938-

Norma Klein, 1984

I was born on May 13, 1938, in New York City. Except for summer vacations and one year of college (I went to Cornell for my freshman year) I've never lived anywhere but New York. I love the city, love cities in general and New York in particular. For me as a writer it's been an ideal place to live because after writing in the morning (I never write beyond noon or one o'clock), I can go out and have lunch with friends or see old movies, two of my favorite leisure-time activities. I like the fact that there are so many continuing close connections for me in New York; friends going back to my childhood, my parents, my brother. Many of my friends know each other but have no contact except when they meet at my apart-

ment for a dinner party, so I see the city as a backdrop for intense, intimate relationships which are unconnected; there's no group or network of people, just individuals. To me New York is not only an exciting city with all of its museums and opera and art galleries, it's also my hometown. I can look at any street and know what it looked like five years ago, ten, twenty. I have a sense of familiarity here which is precious to me; I feel I could never really be happy anywhere else.

I've also enjoyed raising a family in New York. My daughters are now teenagers, but I see how being city kids has given them the same sense of freedom and independence it gave to me and my brother. From the age of ten they've taken buses to their music lessons or to friends' houses. On weekends, when my husband and I go to our country house in Rockland (which is only about half an hour from the city), Jen and Katie often stay in our city apartment since for them the city holds more attractions—movies, parties, variations of the attractions it holds for me. I should add that, like many people who've grown up in New York, I've never learned to drive. I wish I could, but by now (I'm forty-six) I've accepted it as a phobia. I think I'm a daydreamer and might just drive off a cliff while plotting the last scene of a novel.

I emphasize the background in which I grew up because it's also the background of most of my books. When I started writing novels for young people in the early seventies, many people told me my work would appeal mainly to the kinds of kids in the books—kids who, like me, had gone to private schools, came from an upper middle-class background, were bright and fairly sophisticated. I've discovered this isn't true, that more of my readers grew up in small towns in Arkansas or Montana. Perhaps the way one *didn't* grow up always seems more exotic. When I was a teenager, one of my favorite series of books was the Betsy Tacy and Tib novels by Maud Hart Lovelace, about three little girls growing up in turn of the century Minnesota. The details of small town life that Lovelace described were as wonderfully exotic to me as the New York City background of my books may seem to my readers.

The only other background I know at all well or have ever used fictionally is the small town in which my husband grew up: Aurora, a village of 300 people in upstate New York. Aurora is a town situated on a huge forty-mile lake, Cayuga. You could drive through Aurora and almost not know you had passed through a town, it's so small. There are several churches, a hardware store, the local inn, a small IGA grocery store and several huge white houses with porches fore and aft. I set *The Swap* in Aurora: the teenage characters in that book were more like the kids my husband grew up with, who didn't necessarily go on to college, who grew up on farms. I don't feel I know teenagers like this intimately, but I enjoy writing about a different kind of background occasionally. Aurora is also a college town; it contains a small women's college, Wells, where my in-laws taught German for forty some years. I used the academic setting in my second adult novel, *Coming to Life.*

My parents were Jewish, but not religious. They had a cultural affinity with Judaism, but were atheists who had rebelled against the kind of formal religious training they had to undergo when young. They would make jokes about not wanting to go to Israel because they didn't want to be around that many Jews, but they also got angry if anyone made an anti-Semitic remark. I've inherited my parents' attitude in regard to religion—I feel all religions are basically sexist, cause divisions between people, set up rigid and inhuman

Norma's parents, Sadie and Emanuel Klein, in their thirties

Else and Otto Fleissner

systems of behavior. But, like my parents, I feel an identification with Jewish culture which I see as irreverent, intense, outspoken—telling it like it is. It seems significant to me that Judy Blume and myself are the only two writers for young people who've written openly about sexuality; we're both Jewish. Jews are outsiders in America and I think that gives us a special detachment when we look at America and its mores.

It was almost inevitable that I marry a non-Jew. For me, as for many American Jews, there is a fascination with gentile life: its formality, its politeness, its emphasis on "doing the right thing." My husband is preppy looking, like most of the men I've ever liked: tall, thin, sandy haired, good at sports. He went to classically Wasp schools: Deerfield, Yale. He wears tweedy jackets and camel hair sweaters. He has the small nose I always wanted. He jogs, he loves nature. All these differences have intrigued me for twenty-five years and, I imagine, will continue to in the years to come. But in other ways my husband's background is not that different from my own. His parents were both born in Germany, met in America in the 1920s and lived the rest of their adult lives in Aurora. Thus, he grew up with parents who spoke with funny accents and never knew what the "American" thing to do was. His parents, like mine, were not religious. His mother was raised as a Lutheran, but never went to church. His father was raised as a Catholic but was also a nonbeliever. When we got married, I remember Otto, my father-in-law, asking us what we intended to do about religion in regard to any children we might have.

When we said "Nothing," the topic was dropped and never raised again. Yet, when I asked my children recently if they thought of themselves as Jewish, they said, "Not especially," and I was hurt. I wanted them to, without having given them any reason to regard themselves as such.

My father, Emanuel Klein, was born in Poland in 1904. When he was five his family moved to America. His parents had an arranged marriage. My grandfather Jacob was a Talmudic scholar, a quiet man whom I remember reading the Yiddish newspaper, but not talking much. While he was alive, we celebrated a seder, but after his death this last remaining connection to formal Jewish ceremonies was dropped. I was never taken to a synagogue; we always had a Christmas tree and celebrated Christmas. My grandmother, Yetta, was a lively, dynamic woman who rebelled against Judaism and encouraged my father, as a boy, to join her. When my grandfather was away, she and my father would eat bacon and pork and other forbidden foods, getting a kick out of disobeying the rules. Perhaps because her marriage was not a love match, she adored my father. She had been deprived of a formal education because of her sex and was determined that her children (my father had a sister four years older than himself) should get one. She trained herself as a masseuse and used to spend winters in Florida, giving massages to wealthy women. She would take my father along as a tutor to the spoiled, not very bright sons of these wealthy women; the two of them were a "team." As a result of her love and encouragement, my father not only went to college (Cornell), but to medical school. He also retained throughout his life, the feeling of self-confidence and being able to conquer the world that is bestowed on many children who are the favorite of their parent of the opposite sex.

My father died seven years ago, in 1977. It's only recently, in a novel I just completed, that I've been able to write about any of the negative feelings I had about him. During his lifetime we were intensely, claustrophobically close. It was partly because of my relationship with him that I never left New York, that I transferred from Cornell to Barnard after a year away from home. I was my father's favorite, and he made this favoritism open in the family, causing extreme jealousy and ill-feeling on the part of my brother Victor and my mother. The fact that my father was a Freudian psychoanalyst and should have known better is one of the many reasons I now view the psychiatric establishment with some mixed feelings. I was born after my parents had been married for eight years. My mother told me much later that my father didn't want children at all because of the state of the world at that

Emanuel Klein with Norma

time. My brother was born very close to me, sixteen months later.

In the home in which I grew up, my father was like a god to me. I remember a story he told me about how, when I was very little, he began ordering me to bed. When he raised his voice and yelled, "Go to bed!" there was a great crack of thunder and a flash of lightning. I ran to bed, terrified. He said, "I was afraid you would think I caused the thunder and lightning; I was afraid you would think I was God." I *did* think my father was God. This wasn't conscious, but I still remember the feeling I had when I was told my father had died. I was standing in the kitchen of a summer house we had rented in Aurora. My father had collapsed without warning and simply lost consciousness. He was seventy-four and had been a chain-smoker all his life, was overweight, and had had open-heart surgery several years earlier. Still, I expected not only that he would live forever, but that the world would somehow come to a halt when he died. It didn't, but my own world did. Several months after his death I had a breakdown and was unable to function for about a year.

What was captivating about my father was his warmth, his zaniness, his outspokenness. Perhaps because he heard so many stories of human misery and knew what people were really like, when their defenses were down, he had a certain cynicism about people. He loved "putting one over." When we went to the ballet or opera, he always bought standing-room seats, though he could have afforded better, just for the fun of bribing the usher and sneaking into the orchestra. Whenever he was stopped for speeding, he would offer the policeman a pack of cigarettes with a ten-dollar bill tucked into the front of it; he never got a ticket. When I asked him, "Daddy, what if you meet an honest policeman and he's insulted?" he said, "Don't worry. There *are* no honest policemen." When my daughter was applying to private school, he tried to bribe her way in by donating erotic etchings to the headmaster's secretary! I think my father not only enjoyed seeing vindications of his theory that every man (and woman) had their price, but he also enjoyed the fun of manipulating people. He had a jocular, bantering way of talking, a little like Groucho Marx. If we were in a restaurant, he would ask the waitress, "My dear woman, could you possibly do me the kindness of giving me some extra cream? If you do, I will be eternally and forever grateful." I feel I spent my childhood murmuring, "Daddy, don't," but getting a secret thrill out of my father's carryings-on.

My father thought I could do anything. No matter what field I would have gone into, he assumed I would rise to the top. I think that conviction has given me an inner self-confidence which has stood me in good stead in a field like writing which is so erratic and where one is constantly meeting failure. I've never had a writing block. I'm almost ashamed to admit that most of the time when I'm involved in the actual act of writing, I think: "God, this is almost frighteningly

Norma Klein in high school

good!" My downers come when the world doesn't necessarily agree with this inner conviction. I considered becoming a psychiatrist, like my father. I'm interested in people and I think it's a profession I would have enjoyed. But I'm very glad I didn't. It was an attempt at independence from my father that made me choose writing. Writing was something he admired, but couldn't do himself. It wasn't only that he couldn't have written novels; he had trouble writing anything. For years he tried to write a book on creativity and psychoanalysis, but never got beyond reams of notes. When I was at camp, I never got letters from him, just postcards written in a big childlike scrawl. I remember when I was given the assignment to write *Sunshine,* a novel about a young woman who died of cancer, my father came up to our apartment to give me suggestions on how to write the book. Because he was a doctor, he felt he could give me helpful tips. I remember the sense of exultation I had when I realized none of his "tips" would be of any use, that I knew how to write the novel on my own, and did.

But this independence from my father was partial and I was never really able to rebel against him in his lifetime. His adoration of me was such an erotic thrill. There was no physical aspect to it, but it had all the overtones of a mistress relationship. He would buy me fur coats, jewelry; we would have intimate dinners where he would murmur, "Your mother would kill me if she knew about this!" All through the early years of my marriage, my father gave my husband and me sporadic sums of money so that I could afford household help and continue writing, even after the children were born. The money was never in a trust fund. It always came in wads of bills which he would stuff into my pocket as I was boarding a bus. He said there were no strings; it took me years to see that there were. I think when I got married, I entered into a state of bigamy. Instead of one man with whom I had a close, intimate, talking-on-the-phone-every-day relationship, I had two. I didn't divorce my father in order to marry my husband. And in some ways I feel that until I was forty, when my father died, I had a weird kind of balance in my personal life between a man like my father who was passionate, kooky, and impulsive, and a man like my husband who is calm, thoughtful, and reliable. One motivation in my having children was that one day my father said how much pleasure it would give him if I did. When my first daughter, Jennifer, was born in 1967, my father tried to repeat with her the relationship he'd had with me. When she was five, he would take her to Madison Avenue art galleries, where she would point to a painting on the wall and say, "That's by Miro," or Picasso, or whoever; my father would beam with pride.

Sadie Klein at her college graduation, 1983

My mother, Sadie Frankel, came from a very different version of a poor Jewish family than my father's. His was, I think, more typical. He grew up on the lower East side; though there was little money, there was a reverence for learning and education. My mother's family was large—she was the youngest of seven, four brothers and two sisters—and uneducated. There were unwed mothers, retarded brothers who slept on the sofa for forty years, sisters who ran off in their seventh month of pregnancy to marry gamblers who left them soon afterward, suicides. My mother got little encouragement or support; she was beaten by her brothers, neglected. She had to leave school at the high school level in order to get a job. None of her brothers or sisters rose much beyond the lower middle class; they worked in bakeries or ran small pharmacies in the suburbs. My mother was shy and intense, never held a job for long during the period I was growing up, seemed to me melancholy and sensitive, like the photo of Virginia Woolf which hung in her sewing room. Ironically, since my father's death, she has bloomed. At seventy-seven she finally, after years of attending classes, got her college degree! She now travels, has many friends, and has a cheerfulness and zest for life which I saw less often when I was growing up. Time has softened and improved our relationship.

I've been asked why I write so often about divorce since I've never been divorced myself, and since my parents were never divorced. I think it's that I grew up in a home where there was so much open tension be-

tween my parents. I was frequently called upon to be the mediator. I see this theme repeated in many of my books, like *Taking Sides* or *Angel Face:* the closeness of a teenager with the parent of the opposite sex. Much of my mental energy in childhood was spent trying to figure out who was right, whether I had perhaps caused this dissention between my parents by simply being born.

My brother Victor and I grew up in a competitive, yet close relationship. We were not only close in age, but always went to the same schools: Dalton from nursery school to high school, Elizabeth Irwin for high school. Like most first children, I was the parent-pleaser and the teacher-pleaser. I loved school, enjoyed studying and always got good grades. My brother was more rebellious, less attentive. I remember a teacher saying to me once, "If I shook both of you up in a bag, I'd get two average students." Perhaps in a more typical American family, my father would have preferred my brother because he was a boy or would have taken pleasure in going out and playing baseball with him. But my father wasn't especially interested in sports, and the doting admiration I had for him was perhaps easier to handle than the more mixed feelings that emanated from my brother. My brother, after trying various professions, became a social worker. This summer, at the age of forty-five, he married for the first time.

There is a dichotomy in my life that I'm increasingly aware of and now accept, but which still

Victor Klein, Norma's brother

bothers me. In my views I am an ardent feminist. I see the world men have created as essentially cruel and unfair. I feel men as a group use their physical aggression to abuse women physically and their verbal aggression to increase the sense of inadequacy most women already have about themselves. These feelings aren't just abstractions to me. Hardly a day goes by that I don't see examples of them that curdle my blood and can, if I dwell on them, cause me to sink into a deep and overwhelming depression. Yet, throughout my life I have had very intimate, warm relationships with individual men: my father, my brother, my husband, men friends. Indeed, I have never spent a day of my adult life without a man on whom I leaned for support and encouragement. I've had men editors who have helped me tremendously in my writing. I would like to be more independent in this regard; I would like to think I could enjoy living alone, coping on my own, but deep down I hope I won't have to, because the humdrum routine of day-to-day living with a man has been such a source of pleasure for me.

When I met my husband, Erwin, I was twenty-one, just starting my senior year at Barnard from which I graduated in 1960. Erwin had graduated Yale in 1957 and spent two years as a Rhodes scholar in England; he was just beginning his doctoral work in biochemistry at Columbia. Although we were different in background, we were similar in many ways. We were both intellectual, had always done well at school, were physically attractive, but felt ill at ease and shy

Norma and Erwin, 1962

with the opposite sex. My husband had never had a close relationship with a girl; it was first love for both of us. When I asked him, in connection with writing this autobiography, what he would write if *he* had to write one, he said, "I would write, 'I was alone until I looked across the room and saw a beautiful pair of dark eyes staring back at me.'" I, in my more impulsive manner, would have gone to bed with my husband a few weeks after meeting him; I'd lost my virginity the summer before in a brief romance with a would-be English professor who was thirteen years older than I was. My husband was more cautious. We finally became lovers in February 1960, the year I graduated college. We then lived together until 1963 when we got married by a Unitarian minister in a small church in New Haven. Living together was unusual for that era, but my parents, who knew of the arrangement, were also unusual in their liberal views. I think, however, that both sides of the family were equally pleased and relieved when we finally got married.

Since relatively few couples stay married over twenty years today, one is conscious of being peculiar if one does, but in fact almost all of my friends' marriages have also endured. I think one factor that has provided balance in my marriage is that, although my husband and I are very different in character, we share the same views on politics, art, children—the same general values. Because I am intense and volatile in my emotions, I need someone thoughtful, reflective, held back. Our

Erwin Fleissner, Norma's husband

marriage has gone through different stages. We didn't have children until 1967 when Erwin was thirty and I was twenty-eight, so we had quite a few years of living together as friends, trying to get established in our professions. I don't think we saw ourselves as coming together primarily in order to have a family. In fact, I think we could have been happy without children, though we are both unequivocally glad we had them. I knew from the beginning that writing was important to me, that it was central to my life. One of the first things I did when we started dating was to show Erwin one of my short stories. He knew he was marrying a writer, not just a housewife-mother, with a mild desire to write "on the side."

Because my mother seemed so ambivalent about being a mother, I grew up not expecting to have children, but assuming I *would* have a career. I thought the two were incompatible. There have been so few women writers who have done both, so few husbands who have really supported their wives in intellectual careers. I think I was realistic in assuming this might not be possible, and that, if I had to choose, I would choose writing. We waited longer than most couples we knew to have our first child, but the advantage to this was that when she was born, she was thoroughly and totally wanted. I had always wanted daughters. I'm still not sure I could have been a good mother to a son, unless he had been quiet and somewhat unassertive. Jen, our first daughter, was like a mail-order baby for a woman writer. She was fat, jolly, verbal, calm, fascinated by the world, responsive. I don't think she cried once in the first four years of her life, but she seemed to find everything around her a source of interest and curios-

Daughters Katie and Jen, 1984

ity. When I put Jen as a baby in my first adult novel, *Give Me One Good Reason,* someone wrote me saying I had made things too easy for my heroine by giving her such an ideal baby.

Katie was born three-and-a-half years later. She is now fourteen, a blithe spirit, intense, artistic. Jen is eighteen—warm, generous, already a published poet. Both girls have considered writing as a profession, though Jen, about to enter college, is thinking of medicine, possibly pediatrics. Jen and Katie have always shared a room and seem to me unusually close in a way I never was with my brother. Perhaps it's easier for siblings of the same sex to share experiences and thoughts. I think I could have enjoyed being the parent of an only child since I like intense one-to-one relationships. But I'm glad we became a famiy of four. For both Erwin and me, who tend to be absorbed in our work, having children has brought us down to earth. Being parents has been an important and life-enhancing experience.

My family has always been crucial to me—originally my parents, then my husband and children. But among the most important things in my life—right up there in terms of emotional support and devotion and warmth—are my women friends. If they live in New York, I see them often. If they don't, we speak on the phone or write. For me, friendship is like marriage. It's something that lasts for life; it's based on love; it's people who will be there for you forever and for whom you will be there. I have some friends I could live with easily, others with whom I mainly communicate by letters. (One friend in California and I have exchanged thousands of letters, almost one a week for ten years.) My friends have seen me through tough times. What I used to try in vain to get from psychiatrists, I feel my friends give me free— objective advice, sharing, laughter. I was amazed when one of the "discoveries" of the women's movement was, "Women can be friends." Is there a woman alive for whom this was not always true? I have to add that in recent years I've added some men friends to my group of confidantes, but I think this kind of relationship is trickier in our society, where men and women are raised to regard each other as potential lovers or mates, or as enemies. I have envied many people throughout my life for their looks, money, or writing ability. But I've never believed that it's possible for anyone to have better friends than mine.

Until the time I was twenty, I was as interested in art as in writing. Perhaps my interest in art preceded my interest in writing because my nursery school reports tell of how, at three or four, I would spend all morning painting. I was very shy and, from my earliest days, retreating into a fantasy world where I had total control was a source of wonderful excitement. One reason that I ended up choosing writing over painting was that there was little interest in art at Barnard. You were allowed to study art history, but studio art wasn't even offered in the curriculum. I feel now I would have been happier at a more artistically inclined college, like Sarah Lawrence or Bennington, where I could have painted as a part of the curriculum. You could, however, take writing courses at Barnard, which I did. By the time I graduated, I had already met professional writers such as George P. Elliott and Robert Pack, who encouraged me in my work. I had begun sending my work out to magazines. It's a lot easier to get started as a writer than as a painter. All you need to do is put your stories in an envelope and mail it with postage to an editor. To enter the art field, as I understand it, you have to go around to galleries in person, and wait there while the gallery owner leafs through your slides. That kind of direct reaction would have been much harder for me than receiving a form letter while I was alone.

I still miss painting. There are things you can say visually that you can't say verbally. Color and form are so much more important. Painting seems to me freer, less intellectual. For years I simply gave up painting because I felt if I hadn't chosen it as a profession, I wasn't "allowed" to do it. Then, in the early eighties, I hit on the idea of spending every Sunday morning making collages. I take a sheet of heavy white paper and paste shapes cut out from magazines on it, connecting these shapes with black india ink drawings, which I apply with a fine sable brush. I usually do about ten a morning. At the end of the year I've accumulated several hundred collages, and make them into collage calendars which I give to friends. Then I start over in the New Year. I love these Sunday morning sessions; they give me the feeling of peace and well-being many people get from going to church. I work in a small room in our country house, which is quiet and looks out on a wide green lawn.

Throughout school, I had teachers who encouraged me in my writing. The first who was important to me was my seventh- and eighth-grade English teacher, Hortense Eugenie Tyroler. (Someone once said that sounded like the name of a shoe, not a person.) She was an elegant middle-aged woman who wore wide-brimmed, black velvet hats, had been divorced and had a special air of mystery to me because she was a writer, a ghost-writer. I wasn't sure what a ghost-writer was, but I imagined it was something wonderfully complex, possibly having to do with haunted mansions on rocky coasts. I remember how disappointed I was when Miss T., as we called her, informed me that she wrote

simply to supplement her small income as a teacher; she was then working on a book for a doctor entitled "Diseases of the Scalp"!

The teacher who probably had the greatest influence on my desire to become a writer was my high school English teacher, Ed Stillman. He had a wonderful and invigorating love of literature, an excitement about it. Also, which I think was good training, he made us do a great deal of creative writing, a "theme" as they were called, every week or two, all year. These were short pieces, but they could be about almost anything. Prior to high school my creative writing efforts had been fantastical works about talking animals. In high school I shifted to what I think is my forte: low-key descriptions of fairly everyday events: a fight with my brother, a school dance, a conflict with a friend.

In college I became a Russian major. I had two reasons for this, only one of which strikes me as even halfway intelligent in retrospect. The good reason was that I loved Russian literature, particularly the stories of Anton Chekhov. The less good reason was that everyone seemed to be majoring in English. I wanted to be more "original." But throughout those four years I took many creative writing courses. The teachers I had in college were all professional writers. I think this was helpful because it showed me that writing was something one could actually pursue as a profession. I also learned that none of these writers, although they were frequently published and respected in their fields, could earn a living as a writer.

My intention, when I graduated college in 1960, was to combine writing with college teaching. I began working on a doctorate in Slavic languages with that end in view. But in the three years I was in graduate school, from 1960 to 1963, I found I couldn't combine studying intensively and writing creatively. I have a writer friend now who is a chef on the side. She says it's much easier for writers to earn their living at something totally different from writing. Perhaps that was part of the problem. I was spending much of my time writing, but it was dull, tedious, scholarly stuff. Most of the teachers were bored and indifferent. By that time I realized that I should have chosen Comparative Literature, where the emphasis would have been on books, not linguistics. Instead, I was bogged down in trying to master Old Church Slavonic, Czech, German. I've never had an aptitude for languages. The upshot was that when I got married in 1963 I decided, in what now seems to me a very unliberated way, that Erwin could support me and that I'd do what was most important to me: write fiction.

In college I had begun publishing short stories. My first acceptance came when I was nineteen. It was

Norma with Isabelle, one of her basset hounds, 1964

a short story, "Ceremony of Innocence," based on Lewis Carroll, the author of *Alice in Wonderland,* a bachelor and mathematics professor who used to photograph preteen girls in his spare time. The magazine that published it, the *Grecourt Review,* was a small literary quarterly. Of the sixty short stories I ultimately published, all but a handful appeared in similar magazines. Pay was either ten free copies or twenty to thirty dollars. Basically I spent my years from twenty-five to thirty being married and writing short stories. I don't consider the time I spent on stories wasted. In fact, I feel stories are a natural and good way for a young writer to begin. It's much easier to put together a connected piece of prose that lasts ten to fifteen pages than two hundred or three hundred. But by the time my first daughter, Jennifer, was born in 1967, when I was almost twenty-nine, I had begun to realize some of the disadvantages of being a short-story writer in contemporary America. Stories are ephemeral. They appear in one issue of a magazine and then vanish. The magazines in which I was publishing had tiny audiences; I never met a person who had read any of my stories. My average income, although I was working as hard as I do now, was about $500 a year. Also, ironically, very few publishers will even consider publishing a collection of short stories unless the author is working on a novel. Short-story collections, with the exception of those by writers who have appeared in *The New Yorker,* rarely make money. I had received letters from editors over the years, asking if I would consider writing a novel. Thinking of Chekhov, who had lived to the age

of forty-four, written six hundred short stories and, to my mind, said more in those stories than any novelist, I always replied vehemently, "I will never write a novel." Resolutions are made to be broken. One morning I woke up and said to myself, "Tomorrow you are starting a novel. It will be three hundred pages long. You will type ten pages a day, fifty pages a week. You have one day to think up a plot."

I can hardly recommend such a drastic method to beginning writers and yet it turned into a pattern that has helped me ever since. Like everyone who is his own boss, I quickly discovered that you can be a real Simon Legree to yourself. Essentially you divide yourself into two halves. While one half is whimpering and pleading, "I don't feel well, I didn't sleep well, this is a lousy plot," the other half just says, "I don't want to hear any of that garbage. Just get in there and do your ten pages and we'll talk about it when you're done."

My methods of writing were essentially established with that first book. I compose on an electric typewriter. I've always preferred being able to re-read my work in typed rather than handwritten form. I used to feel overly mechanized because I didn't write by hand. How times have changed! Now I'm one of the few writers who doesn't have a word processor! Yet, though I may ultimately break down and buy one, an electric typewriter still seems to me one of the great inventions of the modern world. It is easy, reliable, and one of the few machines of which I am not totally terrified.

Since that first book, I've tried typing five pages a day and, at other times, fifteen. Five, for me, is simply too few. I usually just get going by about page four, and to stop right at that point would be foolish. Fifteen I am capable of, but find too emotionally exhausting. For me, ten pages is a morning's work, two or three hours. I always prefer having the afternoon free to do something totally unlike writing—taking a walk, seeing a movie, having lunch with a friend. At the end of each day I usually re-read what I've written in the morning and pencil-in corrections. But essentially this is all the revising I do unless an editor makes suggestions when I hand in the manuscript. For me writing is an emotional process. While I am doing it, I lose track of time. I feel as though I am wherever my characters are, feeling what they are feeling. I follow them, letting them lead me where they choose to go. When I begin a book, I know the essential plot. Usually I've written the first and last scenes as well as several others in my head. I don't put much down on paper, only a page of perfunctory notes which to me are a kind of condensed sign language—"He leaves for California . . . They fight in the rain." I generally know before I begin how long the book will be. A book in which the main character is eleven or twelve is usually 100–125 pages. A teenage novel is 200; an adult novel, 300–500.

Although my schedule changes, I now usually write a teenage novel in October which happens to be my favorite month. I then take a break till January. The winter months seem ideal to me for writing a long book so I do an adult novel then, roughly January through March. Then I take off again till late June when my children are in camp. I hate the heat, and only feel up to a short novel in the summer, so it's then that I write a book for younger children. I used to retype my own manuscripts, but I realized that this was purely mechanical work. I wasn't making any changes as I went along so now I either give the manuscript to Jen, whom I pay $1.50 a page, or to a professional typist. I don't use the blocks of time between books to do anything very exotic or exciting. Erwin is a molecular biologist who does cancer research at Sloane-Kettering; he is tied to an eleven-month-a-year schedule. I do paperwork, answer fan mail, tidy the house, give talks to librarians. But for me, having these breaks is crucial. I feel really wrung out when I finish a book and definitely need time to regear. Often it's during those quiet, in-between periods, that I start playing around in my head with the idea for a new book.

I wrote my first novel, *Pratfalls*, in 1970 when I was pregnant with Katie. Keeping to my method, I gave myself overnight to think of a plot. Please don't ask me how or why I thought of writing about an intellectual Jewish girl from California who was separated from her black astronomer husband and who had always nurtured a desire to become a professional clown. I have no idea, though I'm still very fond of the book. I typed my three hundred pages and gave the novel to my agent. I had thought many editors were sitting there eagerly awaiting my first novel. Ten rejections later I was a bit daunted. For one, although *I* thought I'd written a funny book, no one else seemed to think so. Finally, Dan Wickenden, a lovely editor at Harcourt Brace, whom I will remember forever though he never became *my* editor, said how much he had liked *Pratfalls*, except for the first one hundred pages which he thought were slow and pointless, "as though the author didn't know exactly where she was going." Truer words were never spoken! What I did then was something I would never advise any writer to do. I simply hacked off the first one hundred pages and had my agent send the much-abbreviated manuscript back to Dan Wickenden. "Goodness," he wrote, "this now moves along like a hook-and-ladder truck on the way to a four-alarm fire." But he added, regretfully, that he still felt something was missing.

After that, everyone who saw *Pratfalls* loved it.

One editor accepted it, only to have it rejected by her boss. Finally, another editor accepted it—this was all within six months. My first editor was Harvey Ginsberg who was then at G. P. Putnam's. I think I made a mistake with Harvey and with *Pratfalls*. He thought the book was a little short which indeed it was, under two hundred pages. Yet I was afraid to even show him the one hundred pages I'd hacked off. The result was that, ultimately, ironically, the novel was included as a novella in a short-story collection called "Love and Other Euphemisms," published in 1972. I think *Pratfalls* should have been published on its own as a novel. It really had no connection to the other stories in the collection. Thus, by writing a novel, I achieved what had been my earlier goal: to get a short-story collection published. Things usually happen that way: upside down. One tries to learn and accept it.

During this same era, Jen was nursery school age. After I read her dozens of picture books, an old idea revived in my head. Everyone had always said I'd be good at illustrating children's books. Why not give that a try? I wrote a bunch of picture book texts accompanied by my own illustrations. I approached a children's book agent with them. "Forget it," she told me. "Your illustrations aren't professional enough and what editors are really looking for is realistic contemporary novels about eight-to-twelve-year-olds." At first I was stymied. My own children were six months, and four. Unlike many children's book writers, I am not blessed with total recall of everything that has happened to me since fourth grade. What to do? I went to the library and took out a few recent novels for this age group. Oddly, I didn't read any of the books my own were later compared to, *Harriet the Spy* or Judy Blume's early books. What I read, however, encouraged me in one sense. They didn't seem very good. "Okay," I thought, "I'll give it a try. And maybe if I can get one of these in print, they'll let me illustrate my own picture books." In the spring of 1971, I sat down and wrote—in two weeks—*Mom, the Wolf Man and Me*. I approached it differently than I had my adult novel. I wrote it in the first person because most of the novels I read for that age group were written that way. All my short stories had been in the third person, and I found my first venture into the first person a real liberation. To many writers the first person is an autobiographical form. Not for me. I've never written anything strictly autobiographical, but I love the colloquial, relaxed, "talking" form of the first person. Kids, I've found, love it too. It seems to make them feel as though the main character was talking directly to them. I also found the shorter length, one hundred pages, easy because it wasn't that different from a short story.

I am sometimes asked which I prefer—writing for

children or writing for adults. The one form I doubt I'll return to is the picture book. I never did convince anyone to let me do my own illustrations and I feel that picture books are essentially an illustrator's medium. Often the pictures accompanying my picture-book texts were at odds with what I was trying to say. In many cases I never met the illustrator and had no say about what kind of illustrations were used. I found this frustrating. Of the two types of children's books I've done most, those in which the main character is eleven or twelve and those in which the main character is seventeen and in the last year of high school, I prefer the latter. For one thing, the type of controversial material I enjoy dealing with isn't considered as controversial in books for teens. These books, like my recent *Beginner's Love* or *It's O.K. If You Don't Love Me,* can be published for adults, thus avoiding the wrath of the children's book establishment which still, alas, seems to be extremely conservative. But in paperback, where most of my readership lies, they can be read by teenagers. I should add parenthetically that I don't really care who reads my books or at what age. Almost all of my fan mail is from ten- to fourteen-year-old girls. I gather that this is the most ardent group of readers. Of these the more advanced readers will often read my adult books as well. Fine. To me the only sin a book can commit is to be boring. When I was eleven, I read "ahead"—Dickens, Somerset Maugham. I didn't always understand what I was reading, but I always found reading an exciting thing to do, and still do. I couldn't care less if a six-year-old, my own or anyone else's, wants to try reading *Lady Chatterley's Lover.* In fact, I wish there was *more* cross-reading. I wish more adults outside the children's book field were willing to read young adult books. We live in an age where everything must be packaged and marketed. It infuriates me that my work is always seen as potentially for teenagers, even if my main character is an eighty-year-old man.

I like writing about the last year of high school because it seems to me such an important, exciting, and troubled time of life, so close to adulthood, yet often seeming so far away. At eighteen I was not very different than I am now. I had experienced very little, but my character, thoughts, and feelings were virtually the same. If anything, when I write for teenagers I can express many of the doubts and confusions I still feel at forty-six but should, supposedly, have gotten over by now. When I write for adults I sometimes feel I have to pretend that I *am* an adult, that I now know how the world fits together and why. If anything, adulthood often seems to me a downward path to wisdom, things losing their edges the longer one stares at them. It's true that life for a teenager today is different than it

was when I was that age, but it doesn't seem to me very different. From what I see when I visit schools, sex stereotypes are, alas, alive and well throughout America. I think girls have greater freedom now than they did when I was growing up, but I think they still go forth into a world where the cards are often viciously and disastrously stacked against them. I admire and like to write about teenage girls who have the courage and wit and perseverance to sally forth into such a world. I wish them the best, but at the same time I want to describe, as truthfully as I can, what it is to live in a world where the double standard still flourishes in almost every profession, to say nothing of sexually and socially. Perhaps all this is just a roundabout way of saying I am a feminist, as, I like to assume, is every sensitive and thinking human being alive on this planet.

In the past five years I've written several novels in which a boy was the main character: *Robbie and the Leap Year Blues,* in which Robbie, who is eleven, lives part time with his mother and part time with his father; *Beginner's Love,* a last-year-of-high-school novel in which Joel, a virgin, has his first affair with Leda; and *Angel Face,* about fifteen-year-old Jason whose parents are getting divorced, who smokes pot a lot, is doing badly in school, and is having trouble with his girlfriend. Just as I wish there were more good novels about modern, intelligent young women, I wish there were more good novels about teenage boys, particularly about what boys feel about girls, their families, school, the future. I have read dozens of novels about how a teenage girl feels upon getting pregnant, for instance, but none about how a teenage boy feels upon learning he has gotten his girlfriend pregnant. We still want, despite all evidence to the contrary, to perpetuate the idea that boys don't feel. Feelings are supposedly for girls. Boys "do things." Yet I think any of us who have fathers, brothers, sons, men friends, know how absurd this is. Boys feel just as deeply as girls, even if they sometimes have trouble articulating their feelings. I think novels could be a way of indicating to boys that it's all right to have romantic as well as sexual feelings for both the opposite sex and one's own. I intend to write more of these books, even if they'll only be read by girls.

One reason I find it congenial to write for teenagers is that novels about them are usually shorter. I feel I can handle two hundred pages, but get nervous when I sail out into the seas of a four or five hundred-page project. But in all other ways—use of language, seriousness of approach—I don't regard my novels about teenagers as any different from my novels about adults. They are no easier to do; I don't "knock them off," saving my best self for my adult work, as some members of the adult literary establishment sometimes condescendingly assume. I want to continue writing for adults because the passage of time interests me as a theme. Teenagers, I think, live more in the present; their life's history is short, and the future seems endless. At my age, I find myself looking both backwards and forwards. I like writing about what time does to people—in both good ways and bad. My most recent adult novel, *Lovers*, spans twenty years in the lives of its three main characters. They are different people at the end than they were at the beginning, and I enjoyed developing these changes, showing how they came about, some by design, others by chance.

In writing adult novels, just as in writing teenage ones, I'm not trying to help people escape from their boring, mundane lives. Most commercial fiction seems to me essentially escapist. Men find themselves trapped in tedious jobs and so want to read about James Bondish heroes, seducing gorgeous blondes and fighting off packs of fearsome enemies. Women are spaced out unloading clothes from the dryer so they want to imagine themselves dressed in Edwardian gowns, pursued by lords in satin dress coats. I myself have a peculiar addiction: real life fascinates me. I like to read, as well as write about the particular, the mundane, the everyday. I don't really care to write about people who are wealthy or beautiful or amazingly gifted. When I write about adult women, I want to write neither about a

feckless housewife stewing in the suburbs, nor a mindlessly aggressive businesswoman whose sole aim is to be a vice-president of a multimillion-dollar corporation. I want to write about women who have satisfying careers, children they love, and husbands, lovers or men friends whose presence in their lives is both satisfying and important. And, although I want to write about and from the point of view of men as well, I hope I'll live long enough to see the demise of the concept that a book in which the main character is a woman is a "woman's book," and a book in which the main character is a man is for everyone. A pox on such stereotypes!

"Should I be a writer?" kids write to me. "What advice do you have for someone who wants to be a writer?" I always repeat what a teacher, who was a writer, said to me in college. "If there's anything else you can possibly do, do it." Most people have a very idealized and distorted idea of what it means to be a writer. They imagine writers as rich, glamorous people who go to cocktail parties, make witty conversation, fly to exotic places on their vacations. First of all, the average published writer in America earns $5000 a year. Maybe that's more than a migrant worker earns picking peaches, but I doubt it. What it means to be a writer is this: you will spend most of your adult life alone in a little room hunched over a typewriter. If

The family: Erwin, Katie, Jen, and Norma, 1984

that sounds like a thrilling and wonderful way to spend your life, I say do it. Writers have to be able to not only tolerate solitude, they have to love it. They also have to realize that they will not be paid more for doing better work: most of the writers in America who earn the most money write garbage. Most excellent writers don't earn enough to pay the rent. A writer never has security. You can publish ten novels and then have your next ten rejected. You can, as an alarming number of American writers have done, simply lose your talent. Or you can run out of steam, start writing according to a formula, dry up. At that point, as I know from once having looked for a job, your options are, to put it mildly, limited. To have on your resumé, "I wrote twenty novels," is roughly equivalent to having robbed twenty banks. Maybe you'll sneak off during lunch hours to write poetry! You're an artist, a dangerous character.

And yet, were I given the choice again, even knowing what I know now, I'd still become a writer. Some of the happiest moments of my life have been spent writing. I've been happy doing other things, but for me there's been nothing quite as exciting and wonderful. As a writer you lead a thousand lives. In real life most writers are shy, introverted people who have anxiety attacks crossing the street against the light. But in our books we murder people off, we defeat our enemies, we change the world. For a male or female Walter Mitty, that's terrific. I myself never learned to drive a car, but I have in my head a novel about a woman who's building an airplane in her backyard and will take several people up for a test flight. As a writer, you can become a person of any age or either sex whenever you want. You can make it rain or snow. When I think back on my life, it often seems to me I've had all kinds of the most amazing adventures, and it's with a start that I realize none of those things ever really happened—except in my head. But maybe that's enough. At any rate, I know it's the only kind of life that ultimately made sense to me. I hope my writing will go on as long as I do.

BIBLIOGRAPHY

FOR YOUNG ADULTS

Fiction:

Mom, the Wolf Man and Me. New York: Pantheon, 1972.

It's Not What You Expect. New York: Pantheon, 1973.

Confessions of an Only Child (illustrated by Richard Cuffari). New York: Pantheon, 1973.

Taking Sides. New York: Pantheon, 1974.

What's It All About. New York: Dial, 1975.

Hiding. New York: Four Winds, 1976.

Tomboy (sequel to *Confessions of an Only Child*). New York: Four Winds, 1978.

French Postcards (a novelization based on a screenplay of the same name). New York: Fawcett, 1979; London: Coronet, 1980.

Breaking Up. New York: Pantheon, 1980.

A Honey of a Chimp. New York: Pantheon, 1980.

Robbie and the Leap Year Blues. New York: Dial, 1981.

The Queen of the What Ifs. New York: Fawcett, 1982.

Bizou. New York: Viking, 1983.

Baryshnikov's Nutcracker (adaptation of the *Nutcracker* ballet; photographs by Ken Regan, Christopher Little, and Martha Swope). New York: Putnam, 1983.

Angel Face. New York: Viking, 1984.

Snapshots. New York: Dial, 1984.

FOR CHILDREN

Picture books:

Girls Can Be Anything (illustrated by Roy Doty). New York: Dutton, 1973.

Dinosaur's Housewarming Party (illustrated by James Marshall). New York: Crown, 1974.

If I Had My Way (illustrated by Ray Cruz). New York: Pantheon, 1974.

Naomi in the Middle (illustrated by Leigh Grant). New York: Dial, 1974.

A Train for Jane (verse; illustrated by Miriam Schottland). Old Westbury, N.Y.: Feminist Press, 1974.

Blue Trees, Red Sky (illustrated by Pat Grant Porter). New York: Pantheon, 1975.

Visiting Pamela (illustrated by Kay Chorao). New York: Dial, 1979.

FOR ADULTS

Fiction:

Love and Other Euphemisms (short stories). New York: Putnam, 1972.

Give Me One Good Reason. New York: Putnam, 1973.

Coming to Life. New York: Simon and Schuster, 1974.

Sunshine (a novelization based on the television production written by Carol Sobieski). New York: Holt, 1975; London: Everest, 1976.

The Sunshine Years (a sequel to *Sunshine*). New York: Dell, 1975.

Girls Turn Wives. New York: Simon and Schuster, 1976.

It's OK If You Don't Love Me. New York: Dial, 1977.

Sunshine Christmas (a second sequel to *Sunshine*). New York: Dell, 1977.

Love Is One of the Choices. New York: Dial, 1978; London:

Futura, 1981.

Domestic Arrangements. New York: M. Evans, 1981; London: Futura, 1982.

Wives and Other Women. New York: St. Martin's/Marek, 1982; London: Macdonald, 1983.

Sextet in A Minor (short stories). New York: St. Martin's/Marek, 1983.

Beginner's Love. Buffalo, N.Y.: Hillside Press, 1983.

The Swap. New York: St. Martin's/Marek, 1983.

Lovers. New York: Viking, 1984.

Myra Cohn Livingston

1926–

Myra Cohn Livingston, with Taran, named after the character in Lloyd Alexander's Prydain Chronicles, *1978*

Writers work in drafts. That's not to say they work in windy rooms; it means they write something once (the first draft), then rewrite it (the second draft), and so on. The first draft of this autobiography was written when I was in seventh grade. I read it recently and saw it was too short (two pages) and not quite complete or accurate enough. "I am going to be a dress designer," it began. "I will marry a French horn player and we'll have a child."

The truth is that I've never designed a dress in my life. (If I sew on a button, my family applauds!) My husband Richard, a certified public accountant, knows *nothing* about playing a horn. And we have *three* children. So much for predicting the future! I am certain that the element of chance and accident is an important part of everyone's life. I could not have predicted that the opportunities and events of my life would lead me to become a musician, secretary, book reviewer, poet, teacher, and lecturer.

In the same box with the first draft of my autobi-

*Mayer Louis "Bud" Cohn, Myra's father,
in his World War I uniform, 1917*

*Gertrude Marks, Myra's mother, in her
engagement picture, 1923*

ography are countless papers, plays, stories, and poems I wrote during my school years, among other snippets of memorabilia. Scattered about are ticket stubs, my Hollywood Canteen card and arm band, sheets of popular music, bits of original counterpoint—all reminders of things I've learned. But they are also symbols of the Three Great Lies I have told. I've never written of them before because I was certainly raised to tell the truth. Still and all, my life would have been different had I not told those lies. They may even have helped me learn two of the most important precepts by which I've lived.

So on to music, writing, precepts, lies, and all of the events which prompted them!

When I was very young my father would spin out his dreams at the dinner table. Someday, he told us enthusiastically, scientists will split the atom. . . . man will go to the moon. . . . people will discover a way to go so far into space that the events of history on earth will be viewed again. Nothing is ever lost, he believed. "We will be able to see Hannibal cross the Alps and the Battle of Bunker Hill being fought." The day that the atom was split, and the day of the first moon landing he was overjoyed. It remains to be seen if his third dream will ever come true.

Father told us about his own boyhood. At eleven he built a laboratory in his parents' home in Omaha, Nebraska, where he discovered for himself the principle of neon light and built his own wireless station, communicating with people many miles away. At sixteen, as a student at the Northwestern Military Naval Academy, he designed and built, with the help of the Cadillac Company, the first turret-control car in the country, touring the West with an exhibit to show the possibilities of the armored car in war. At seventeen he enlisted in World War I and fought with the Twelfth Balloon Company of the American Air Force in France. He survived the Battle of Verdun.

But my father's abiding passion was cars. As a boy, he would sit with a friend on a curbstone with his eyes closed, guessing by the sound of the motor what make of car was passing. He learned to drive before he was twelve. Later in life he collected and restored vintage and classic cars. The BBC made a feature film about father, praising the man who started many car clubs which held Concours d'Elegance to raise money for charities. For many years he took part in the London-to-Brighton race. He died in London just a few nights after the 1977 race. At the age of eighty-one he was down on the ground in a garage inspecting his car to make sure that it was in perfect condition.

When I visit his grave, I always notice a parade of busy ants hurrying around his tombstone. Somehow they typify my father, always involved, always moving, always curious and interested. Never an unused moment.

From both my parents I inherited the Puritan ethic, a love for work and a dislike for idleness. Father would devour books on history and science; Mother is sensitive to nature, the color of the sky, the smell of the air, the beauty of flowers. She is a perfectionist who makes many demands on herself and always taught my sister Hannah and me to do our best in whatever we undertook.

Mother read to me when I was young. At the age of three I developed rheumatic fever and she nursed me for three months. There was no television then and despite the rigors of the Depression she saved enough to buy me beautiful books. There was *Spin Top, Spin, When the Root Children Wake Up,* a German book *Tanderedarei,* the verse of A.A. Milne, Hans Christian Andersen's tales, and *Bookhouse.* She would sing to me and recite from memory Edward Lear's "The Owl and the Pussy Cat" so often that it became the first poem I

The Cohns' fiftieth wedding anniversary: Myra left, her parents, and sister Hannah, 1974

memorized. My two books about Lear, *How Pleasant to Know Mr. Lear!* and *A Learical Lexicon,* may have grown out of my love for that poem.

Like most women of her generation, Mother has always devoted herself to her family and home, although she has worked for charities. She has long been a member of the California Association of Adoption Agencies and the California Children's Lobby, concerning herself with child care, adoption, and child abuse. She has collected paintings and beautiful furniture. From her mother she learned to recognize the beauty of fine design, of fabrics, of the many elements of taste and quality. Father felt this same passion for cars. I feel it for books.

It is amazing how both of my parents—my father born in Keokuk, Iowa, my mother in Chicago—developed over the years, how they survived the Depression, moved to California, and became part of a bigger world than they knew as children. Both of them believed, as do my husband and I, that each generation should improve upon the generation before. My father never went to college. My mother could attend the University of Chicago for only one year. Yet they made it possible for my sister and me to go East to college, knowing that an important part of our education would be to meet other kinds of people than those we knew at home. The provincialism of their lives, they believed, was not good enough for us!

In my first book, *Whispers, and Other Poems,* I wrote about my childhood, and I wrote more about my par-

The Cohns, in period costume, riding in a 1905 Reo, 1959

ents, aunts and uncles, and grandparents in *Worlds I Know, and Other Poems.* So many of these relatives are now gone that somehow I need, through writing, to preserve my memory of them.

I remember only three of my grandparents. My grandfather Cohn died when I was a year old. Nanny, my father's mother, had been around the world many times. Sometimes she visited in Omaha and stayed with my father's sister, Aunt Blanche. But she loved California and moved to Los Angeles. We visited her when I was ten years old and I was awed by the trunks of clothes she kept, her souvenirs of travel. At eighty-nine she announced that she was "going home to die" and moved back to Omaha. Within a few months she was gone. In a poem in *Worlds I Know,* I write about her:

> Nanny rode on a camel
> in Egypt
> and sailed on a boat
> up the Nile,
> But the picture of her
> on a camel
> doesn't show she has much
> of a smile . . .

My mother's parents, Grandmother and Grandfather Marks, lived in Council Bluffs, Iowa—just across the river from Omaha. Twice a week, on Thursdays and Sundays, we would go to visit them. Once a year on the river bank a circus came to town and I could hardly wait for the merry-go-round rides. In *Whispers and Other Poems,* I chronicled that event:

Myra, riding in the car with her mother

> The merry-go-round
> whirls round and round
> in a giant circle on the ground . . .

I still vividly remember how Mother would put my baby sister in a large white basket on the back seat of the car. (There were no infant seats, no safety rules then.) Omaha was the hub of the Union Pacific Railroad and often, as we entered Council Bluffs, we would have to stop while the trains sped by. I would count the cars, sometimes as few as ten or twelve, sometimes as many as eighty or ninety, until the caboose came in sight. The wig-wag signals would go up and we could continue our ride. Mother would sing "My Blue Heaven" or songs she had learned in school. I remember loving the music for the words.

> Once more, dear home,
> I with rapture behold thee . . .

which, I later learned, was the "Pilgrims' Chorus" from Wagner's *Tannhauser.* She would also sing Tennyson's

> Sweet and low,
> Sweet and low,
> Wind of the Western Sea . . .

We would go to Council Bluffs in the afternoon and return by night. The nights were enchanting, with the lonesome train whistle echoing through cold winter or steamy summer darkness and the clackety-clack of the train wheels—sounds that I miss even to this day. For I now live where it is quiet. An occasional car will go by, the owls will hoot and the coyotes howl and make their kills. But there is something about a train whistle in the night . . .

Does the remembrance of songs and sounds like those have anything to do with a love for poetry, its rhythms and music? I do not know. Yet I am quite certain that a mother who sings and reads to her children must foster in them a love for language and rhythm and sound. Reading aloud—hearing the music—nothing can replace it. If we want to write poetry, the rhythms must be heard. If we want only to listen, the music of the poet will catch us up in what T.S. Eliot has described as "music heard so deeply / That it is not heard at all, but you are the music / While the music lasts." That is as near to what poetry means to me as I can put into words.

Grandmother and Grandfather Marks raised six children, my mother the eldest. And after that there were eleven grandchildren who came for dinner or lunch or cookies and treats. My aunt and uncle and two cousins who lived in Kansas came to visit every summer. I could hardly wait to see my cousin Joan

Myra, foreground, about 1931, "with friends whom I've written about in Worlds I Know*"*

who was just a year younger. The minute they arrived, we began to write a play and make crepe paper costumes for the "show" we would put on for the grown-ups. Grandmother would find a sheet for a curtain and we would string it up over the front stairwell. Each play, as I remember, had a king and a queen. Joan insisted on being the queen and her sister Ruth and my sister Hannah would take the other parts. I remember my costume was always a cape made of purple crepe paper, with a border of white paper speckled with ink spots to resemble ermine. We always began our plays with a verse, like the one I still remember:

> This poem leads you far away
> On dainty fairy wings,
> Across the sea, across the isles,
> To see enchanted things.

Hardly great poetry, but we thought it was splendid!

At Grandmother's we would run through the hose on hot summer afternoons. Once a week we were allowed to walk down North Second Street, a steep hill, and buy a package of Kool-Aid for a nickel. Grandmother had a real ice box and the ice man delivered blocks of ice several times a week. Grandmother grew grapes and sometimes the kitchen would be filled with the smell of grapes, their juice oozing from bags and dripping into pans. There was a spigot from which rain water could be pumped and Grandfather would sing:

> O little playmate,
> Come out and play with me,
> And bring your dollies three.
> Climb up my apple tree.
> Shout down the rain barrel.

> Slide down my cellar door
> And we'll be jolly friends
> Forevermore.

I was delighted recently to see that Virginia Hamilton remembers the same song in her book, *Willie Bea and the Time the Martians Landed.*

Grandfather was often a mystery to me. He knew Indians, traded in cattle, and had a store somewhere in Missouri. I remember him at the head of the table, a napkin tucked into his collar, making deep wells in our mashed potatoes for an ample ladling of gravy. He sat in the downstairs hall in a chair which no one else ever used. Sometimes he'd take me on his knee and sing a song in Chinese which he learned on a trip to China. (I know now that he had never been there!) Oftentimes he would just sit in the chair, brooding and dozing. The most wonderful time was when he brought me a large lined writing tablet with the picture of an Indian chief on a red cover, and a new pencil. For me, clean paper and a pencil are magical. (I will probably never write on a word processor.) I can still smell that paper and the shavings from the pencil!

Council Bluffs has many memories for me, recorded in many of my books of poetry and especially in *Worlds I Know;* the Lincoln Memorial, the cemetery at the top of North Second Street, the railroad crossing, and most of all, the house on Fletcher Avenue with a bookcase in the upstairs hall where I found and read *Pollyanna, Emily of the New Moon, Mrs. Wiggs of the Cabbage Patch,* and *Daddy-Long-Legs.* One of my mother's sisters, Aunt Ruth, a victim of infantile paralysis, could never leave her bed. Once she had been able to sit in a

Myra, with her maternal grandmother, aunts, and uncle, 1936

wheelchair and get out for a ride. Now she was crippled, her arms and legs and even her smile crooked. I would spend hours in her room. There was a round oak table by her bed and she taught me to play Old Maid, Rummy, and Steal Casino. Bonnie the dog stayed with her most of the time. On stormy days he would hide under her bed. Aunt Ruth died when I was about ten and Bonnie died of grief a few days later. After that it was difficult for me to spend the night at Grandmother's because the wheelchair frightened me.

But there was also Aunt Flora who delighted me with her astounding use of the English language. She was not "surprised"—she was "flabbergasted." She wished me "voluminous felicitations on my natal day" instead of a dull "happy birthday." She kept a chart just for me on which she'd paste gold, silver, and blue stars. I wish I could remember what I did to merit the stars! My Aunt Evelyn lived there too until she married and moved to Chicago. When we visited her there I fell in love with Chicago, her apartment on East Delaware, the elevator, and Marshall Field's. A trip to Chicago was one of the most wonderful things that could happen.

> She lives in Chicago.
> I want to go there
> and visit Aunt Evelyn
> On East Delaware . . .

Myra and Hannah with their dollhouse, 1937

In Omaha there were many great-aunts and uncles. My own Aunt Blanche and Uncle Harry and my cousins Frances and Harriet lived in a big house on Happy Hollow Boulevard. Although they were older than I, they took me on toboggan rides and let me play up in the attic with the huge dollhouse which Uncle Harry had built. It had a real roof and electric lights. That dollhouse has gone through four generations of my family; it was even shipped to California for my daughter Jennie to play with when she was a child. I wrote a poem about the doll with real hair who lived in the house. I still have her.

It must be difficult for young people today to imagine what life was like then without television, when newsboys ran through neighborhoods shouting "Extra, extra, read all about it." I remember especially the news of the Lindbergh kidnapping for I was afraid someone would kidnap me. The Lindberghs were very rich, my parents explained; but that did no good. I thought myself rich—I had good food, a good home, and almost everything I wanted.

Almost everything but not quite—for I had a great obsession. And that obsession led me to my First Great Lie—and perhaps even sparked my later life as a writer. It is difficult to know which was stronger—my need to express myself in words or my dream of owning a Shirley Temple doll. Although my mother did not allow me to see movies every Saturday like all of my other friends on the block (she thought it was better I stay in the fresh air and play), I was allowed to see every Shirley Temple movie that came to Omaha. The pictures were shown at the Orpheum Theatre and just before Christmas—I think I was eight years old at the time—the theatre held a contest. The child who wrote the best letter as to why she wished to have a Shirley Temple doll would win a doll, a *big* one. I wanted that doll more than anything in the world.

I guess it was partly spite. My sister Hannah, born when I was seven, had received a small Shirley Temple doll the Christmas when she was barely six months old. I asked my mother if I could have it. "No," she told me, "it belongs to your sister. It was a gift to her." One day in secret I took the doll from a shelf and played with it. I let Shirley play with my other dolls. And the more I thought about it, the more I thought my mother was wrong and cruel. And so I hid the doll under my parents' bed. A few days later it was discovered and I was severely scolded. "You must *never* take anything that does not belong to you!"

But I made up my mind I would win my *own* doll, much bigger than my sister's. So I wrote a letter explaining that I was a poor orphan with no one to love me and no one whom I could love. Only the Shirley Temple doll would make me happy. On the day the

Myra, age nine, and Hannah reading a book

winners were announced, I was hot and cold all over, barely able to contain myself. I did win—*second* prize, two tickets to see the next Shirley Temple movie. But overriding both my disappointment and my joy was the knowledge that I had told a lie. Still—I had apparently written a good letter and I was inspired to continue writing!

Many writers speak about their unhappy childhoods as though one *must* be unhappy in order to write. I don't think that is true. Childhood in Omaha was a happy one for me. We lived on Fifty-third Street on a block where there were about twenty children. In the summer we would make mudpies, put on plays, swing into the apple tree, play games each night in the empty lot after supper. My next door neighbor, Shirley Ann, and I would run pulleys from her bedroom to mine and send each other notes. My friend Marjorie, who lived three houses away, and I would walk to school together and moan and groan about her older brother who was a pain! Laura and Adelyn lived across the street and told us about their parochial school and their communions. Barbara complained about her silly older brother and sister, and we marveled at the antics of the one boy our age, John, who conceived a plan to build an underground house and whispered tales about sex. We walked to school and back twice a day for there were no sack lunches or cafeterias. We joined the Brownies and the Girl Scouts. In the winter we sledded and in the spring we played jacks and marbles and roller-skated and rode bicycles. In the fall we made bonfires and burned the leaves. And the very things that made me unhappy—for I was not happy all of the time—turned out to be good things after all.

The first unhappy thing was my glasses. My second-grade teacher discovered that I could not read the problems on the chalkboard (we called them blackboards then). The next thing I knew I was wearing glasses. Of course everyone teased me and called me Four-Eyes; for years I dreamed that one day my eyesight would become normal. I hated glasses and when I grew old enough to notice boys, I didn't wear them. Being half-blind didn't help me, of course. I'd pass people I knew at school and not even recognize them. But I am also convinced that being myopic enabled me to see in a way that people with normal vision can't. It was much easier for me to deal in metaphor—to see a bush as an animal, to look at lights and see great brilliant globes shimmering at night. Sometimes I even feel sorry for people with good eyesight; they see only the reality, and not the dream!

Another thing that made me unhappy, at first, was my short upper lip, my crooked teeth, and my bad overbite. The orthodontist assured Mother he could straighten my teeth and correct the overbite, but the short upper lip would improve only if I learned to play a brass instrument. My mind danced with the thought of playing my father's trombone, stored in the downstairs closet. But Mr. Otte, the band director at Wash-

Myra "with the hated glasses," 1938

Myra playing her French horn, about 1937

ington School, had different ideas. He pointed out my arms were not long enough to play the trombone. The tuba was too big for me. And he didn't need any more trumpet players. What I should play was the E-flat alto or mellophone. So I became one of two girls in a band of twenty members and learned the meaning of the word *practice.*

Shortly after that we left Omaha. Those were the days of the Depression. The farmers and everyone else in Nebraska were having lean times, and my father's business (a store where he sold automobile parts) was failing. I remember lying in bed at night listening to my parents talk in whispers and serious tones. Father wanted to move to California. Mother did not want to leave her family and friends. In the end Father won, the house was sold, and we left in the green Packard. It was then that I began to write in my journal every day. One entry after another reads "The crops are bad." I must have heard my father say this so many times that they became my own words. And as we travelled westward, I echoed my parents again, "Look at the green, look at this new country." California was, for my father and his father before him, a promised land!

Being uprooted just after sixth grade was a shock to me! In spite of my parents' enthusiasm for all that California offered, I found entering a new community difficult. The cliques of seventh graders at John Burroughs Junior High School shunned anyone who invaded their territory. I always enjoyed being alone at times, but I was also gregarious enough to want some friends. I did find Barbara, Pat, and Marjorie; we ate lunch together and visited each others' homes. I became involved in the Safety Patrol, Scouting, journal-

ism, and making marionettes. But it was music that saved me, for John Burroughs had more than a band. It had an orchestra and it had Rosa B. Perry. It was she who decided that a mellophone wouldn't do. I had to have a French horn to be a proper member of *her* orchestra.

Rosa B. Perry was a formidable woman. Short in stature (about 4½ feet) she was exactly as wide. I can still see her pudgy arms and hand waving the baton above the music stand that almost hid her face! Andre Previn, a world famous conductor today, was another member of that orchestra. He had come as a refugee from Germany. Seated at an organ that had to be pumped, he was so short that he could hardly see over the top of the organ. But hearing her voice encouraged us. And if I did not know how to find a horn teacher, Rosa B. Perry did.

So I found myself one day at the home of Sinclair Lott, a tall, handsome young man who looked like a Greek god. Not only did he play the horn but he also played football at UCLA. (Later he became principal horn of the Los Angeles Philharmonic.) Once a week I went for a lesson and practiced very hard during the other six days in order to gain his approval. It wasn't easy. I was still wearing those miserable braces, and striving for the perfect embouchure made my lips bleed. The lessons cost $1 a week, a great deal of money for my parents then. But worst of all, Mr. Lott was my first real crush. I was just beginning to notice the opposite sex and he was a great deal to notice! One day, because my Girl Scout troop needed a bugler, he was kind enough to offer to take me to a music store in Hollywood and pick out a bugle. So we set out in his black convertible. Those were the days when running boards on cars had become unfashionable. He had removed the running board from his car, so that when I stepped out of the passenger seat, hoping the entire world would see me on Hollywood Boulevard with this handsome man, I quite naturally fell right on my face!

Eventually, my hard work and Mr. Lott's good teaching were confirmed. I played second horn with the All-City Orchestra, a local group of young musicians. Later I won a nationwide competition and played first horn in the National Junior High School Orchestra made up of the best young musicians in the country. When Mr. Lott was drafted into the armed services, I went on to study with my second teacher, Odolindo Perissi, who was also a horn player in the Los Angeles Philharmonic.

Just after I had started with him, I tried out for the California Junior Symphony. It had been organized by violinist Peter Meremblum, a Russian refugee who made his living by working in the movie studios. I was accepted for the Pioneer Orchestra, a group of younger players. An older group, the Big Orchestra, had been making a movie with Jascha Heifetz, *They Shall Have Music.* Unfortunately, by the time I was promoted to the Big Orchestra six months later, the movie was just being finished. But I can look at the film on television even today and recognize all the people I knew then, including Dolly Loehr, a child-pianist who later became the movie star Diana Lynn.

The orchestra was such a success in that film that Warner Brothers decided to make a short documentary about the group. That became my first movie job. The rules were strict: we had to join the Musicians' Union, we had to have a health clearance and permission to leave school and study on the set. I shall never forget the thrill—I was fifteen—of being led into the make-up room where a uniformed person applied pancake make-up and lipstick, made up my eyebrows, and told me I resembled Merle Oberon. There was also the wonder of sitting under bright lights, of learning to watch not only the conductor but the movie director and cameramen.

After that documentary I also worked in other films when young musicians were needed. One that I see on television occasionally is *A Song of Russia* with Robert Taylor. We lived then in Coldwater Canyon and I used to see Taylor leave his home on his motorcycle when I drove to MGM in my beige bomber, an old Chevrolet that my father bought me.

W orld War II was on and the patriotic thing for all of us to do was to help in some small way— make a stick of butter last a family for a week, use as little gas as possible, and for me, as a member of the Musicians' Union, to work at the Hollywood Canteen. But the rules specifically stated that one had to be sixteen to work at the Canteen.

Thinking it over, knowing how I could personally cheer up all the young servicemen who flocked to the Canteen on Sunset Boulevard each night, I decided that if I lied about my age by only one year, it would be for the Good of the Country. With a straight face I filled out the form: born in 1925. And there it is on the card today—my Second Great Lie! Twice a week I would drive to the Canteen before dark, serve food and dance with the young men, but when the Canteen closed my mother (to my utter horror) would appear in her car and follow me discreetly home. But I had the pleasure of seeing all the great movie stars of the day who entertained there. I shall never forget Jimmy Durante tearing a piano to pieces in his hilarious act!

At Fairfax High School I was the literary editor on the newspaper. I never liked writing essays and would always turn a report into a play or a novella or poetry. (In my box of keepsakes is a ninety-six-page play on minstrels, a play on Christmas in Sweden, a novella about a California Indian girl.) To this day, although I write many of them, essays are a torture for me. I always seem to need an editor to put the commas in the right places. For me, being a writer means loving expression in words, but not worrying too much about the details. That isn't good. I *should* have paid more attention to grammar in school.

Between my sophomore and junior years in high school I attended summer school at Mills College in Oakland to study counterpoint with Darius Milhaud, the renowned French composer, and sculpture with Antonio Sotomayor. We had a glorious summer living in the French house, wearing berets and tramping off to San Francisco in the evenings to pretend we were in Montmatre. Madame Milhaud taught dramatics and her students put on plays. Monsieur Milhaud wrote the music for whatever combination of instruments happened to be there. As a horn player I shared the stage with a flautist, a pianist, and a drum player. I wish I had a copy of the small pieces he dashed off for us to play. (There were no xerox machines then.)

Living in the French house meant I was allowed to speak only French outside my room. That presented problems at the dinner table, a family style affair where we had to ask for food to be passed. Milhaud watched me suffer (I was a Latin student) and would whisper to me the proper words which I haltingly repeated. Milhaud was ridden with arthritis; each movement he made must have been painful. To me he was a god.

One morning I took my assignment, a series of counterpoint exercises, to class. He sat at an upright piano and we would place our music there for him to play. He played through all I had written.

"Miss Cohn," he said, turning his head with great pain to look at me. "Do you know that we must know the rules before we break them?"

If I have remembered nothing else in my life, it was that principle and I have lived by it. Learn first that there *are* rules, and then learn patiently when to leave them behind.

That same summer I heard about Sarah Lawrence College. A Mills student told me about its unique approach to education and urged me to read the book written by its president, Constance Warren. From the moment I picked up the book I knew Sarah Lawrence was for me. Fortunately I was accepted and left for college in the fall of 1945 with a suitcase of new clothes, my French horn, and my mother to settle me in. I made it a rule, there and then, not to accompany whatever children I might have to college, and have stuck to my vow!

Sarah Lawrence was a new world! The young women there amazed me with their knowledge. They knew names like e.e. cummings, T.S. Eliot, Freud, and Jung. My high school education had been painfully lacking in any connection with the intellectual world. I had read *Ivanhoe* but certainly not Huxley or Proust. I was hungry for knowledge and fortunately, because it was war time, not distracted by social life. The men who were around were mostly what we called 4-F's and not particularly attractive.

I was lonesome at first, for I knew no one in New York except some distant, older cousins who would invite me to White Plains for dinner. But it was a thrill to be near New York; Bronxville was a half hour from the city and I plunged into what it had to offer. There was the Metropolitan Opera on Monday nights, the Ethical Cultural Society where I attended a class on Tuesdays, Columbia University classes on Thursdays, and on Friday I would go in for the Philharmonic concerts, often see a play or movie, sit in Times Square and drink endless cups of coffee, and catch the last train back to Bronxville. I filled my journals with overheard conversations. I did write two stories at college. The first was published in the college literary magazine, the second I sent to *The New Yorker*. I received a handwritten reply. "This is not quite right for us," it read, "but let us see the next one you write."

I never wrote another story because, by sheer accident, the second assignment I received in my freshman writing class was to use examples of alliteration, onomatopoeia, and repetition. For some reason, I wrote seven verses and turned them in to the instructor, Katherine Liddell. We met once a week in her office, a small closet in one of the dormitories. She greeted me that particular week with the usual reek of her Sano cigarettes and a smile on her face. "These," she said, pointing to my typed verses, "would be wonderful for children. You must send them to *Story Parade* magazine."

Verses for *children?* My face fell. I wanted to write love poetry, stories, plays! I wanted to make great music on the horn! "No," I told her, "I don't want to write for children. I don't know anything about *Story Parade* or how to submit verses. No, but thank you."

But Miss Liddell was not to be crossed. Obedient (and somewhat intimidated), I consented. *Story Parade,* published by Simon and Schuster, was then the outstanding magazine for children. Well-known authors wrote for it. She told me exactly what I *must* do: type the poems, enclose a letter of submission and a self-addressed stamped envelope. I thought she was looney, but I also feared she would drop me from the class. So I sent the poems and a week later the self-addressed envelope was in my mailbox. "Ha," I said to myself,

"it is just the same batch of poems I sent, just as thick. Miss Liddell is wrong." I carried the envelope back to my room and threw it into a desk drawer. Two weeks later she asked if I had received an answer. "Yes," I said. "They sent the poems back."

"What did they say about them?" she asked.

I answered her truthfully. "I don't know."

"But they must have said something. Did you receive a rejection slip?"

"I don't know."

Miss Liddell lost her temper. I returned to my room, opened the envelope and discovered that indeed they had accepted three of my poems for publication. "Whispers," my first poem, was published in *Story Parade* the next fall.

I often wonder what might have happened to me if not for that chance opportunity. I went away to college loving music, yet doubtful that I wanted to be a musician. At that time women were not generally accepted as brass players. There was only one woman French-horn player of whom I had read, Ellen Stone with the Chicago Symphony Orchestra. And many musicians, I had discovered, were tunnel-visioned. All my musician-friends wanted to talk about was music. My other friends could speak about plays and books, about philosophy. I had loved my days with Mrs. Perry, with the All-City Orchestra and especially with the California Symphony where I had the opportunity to play under the many great conductors who visited our rehearsals: Leopold Stokowski, John Barbarolli, Bruno Walter, Artur Rodzinski. Yet a nagging voice had told me that there was something else for me in life.

In addition, there was no orchestra at Sarah Lawrence. To make music I had to join the chorus, a wonderful group with the famous composer William Schumann as director, and later Norman dello Joio. It is difficult to play the horn without an orchestra and it requires hours of playing each day to keep up one's lip. Had there been an opportunity to play with others at Sarah Lawrence, I might have stayed with music. But the acceptance of those three poems turned me to writing. I began to write other verses about my childhood. And before the year was out I had what I thought would be a wonderful book, *Whispers and Other Poems*.

But there were many things I had to learn. Poetry is not the most popular of literary forms; publishers usually publish it for prestige, rather than for profit. And during the war years relatively few books were published; paper was at a premium. But I didn't know that then, so when Alfred Harcourt, the publisher, came to speak at the college, I asked him about my book. He told me to write to the children's book editor, Margaret K. McElderry. Her answer was prompt and kind. "Keep on writing and publishing in magazines," she advised me, and wished me luck!

So I returned to writing poems about love and studying at Sarah Lawrence with Robert Fitzgerald, the fine poet and Greek scholar, and poet Horace Gregory, and Hortense Flexner who had published one story for children. I learned all that I could about the basics of poetry—scansion, rhythms, feet, figures of speech, and forms. Mr. Gregory made me write heroic couplets for an entire year. Mr. Fitzgerald told me never to start a poem with "O" (a rule I broke later in life) and Hortense Flexner inscribed one of her books to me—"To Myra Cohn, in whose writing I believe."

My writing flourished in a number of ways. I became involved with the literary magazine, helped organize a poetry hour to which we invited famous poets, including e.e. cummings from whom I received a letter beautifully spaced in the middle of a large sheet of paper. I helped write shows that a group called "Hits & Misses" put on for the college. Once, when I was literary editor of the newspaper, I won a contest that offered an autographed copy of *Kingsblood Royal* by Sinclair Lewis for the five best reviews written by college students. But when the Master Brewers Association of America sent a copy of a book about beer and offered a $200-prize for the best review published in a college newspaper, I sought out a few of the male students who had entered Sarah Lawrence after the war. They liked beer. I didn't. But they all laughed.

So I read the book, wrote a review, and had it published. And lo and behold, I won. Two hundred dollars was a fortune in those days. My winnings went into what I loved most—combing small bookstores and acquiring a library. My father was furious at me one summer when I sent home all my books in a trunk! I could not travel without my books, and in those days they were all hardbound—and heavy!

The same year that Milhaud had told me about breaking rules, I learned the second great lesson of my life from Mrs. Chaudet, my piano teacher. She had given me the first movement of Beethoven's "Moonlight Sonata" to learn. I had started out bravely and practiced, but after about 200 bars it was apparent I had not done my homework. "I'm sorry," I told her, "but I just haven't had the time to practice."

"You will never *have* the time," she said to me kindly. "You have to *make* it."

So then and there I learned to *make* time for whatever I wanted to do; even during the years when I was busy raising children and keeping house, I found that I had to *make* time to do my writing.

My parents had always made it quite clear that they would give me a college education; but when I was through, I had to earn my own living. For months

after graduation I knocked on doors in Los Angeles in vain. Then some small jobs came my way: reviews for a local magazine; book reviews for a newspaper (where Scott O'Dell was the editor of the books section; later he wrote *Island of the Blue Dolphins*); and eventually a job with *Campus Magazine* as a rat catcher, secretary, paste-up person, and writer of occasional articles. But like many young people just out of college I was looking for something better—something to bring excitement into my life.

Then came the Third Great Lie. Through friends of my parents I heard of a job as personal secretary to Dinah Shore who was at the height of her popularity as a singer. I arranged an interview and went to see her and her husband, George Montgomery, for the job meant working at their home in the valley, just over the hill from where I lived. Yes, I told them, yes I could type and write letters, I had a good telephone voice, I could manage the household help and the dinner parties and answer the fan mail and talk to the lawyers and business managers. Yes, I could work from nine to five or even later if necessary and yes, a salary of $100 a week would be fine. (Fine—it was a fortune then!)

"And you take shorthand?" Dinah asked me.

"Of course," I said quickly, hoping that my lie would not show all over my face.

"Then you can begin next week," she said.

Of course I rushed to a bookstore, bought a Gregg Shorthand Manual and enrolled in a night class at the local high school. For six weeks I studied, even while I was working at the job. By the time I confessed my lie, no one cared. I had learned shorthand.

Those were days of great fun and lavish parties. Dinah was a hard worker. George made occasional films but his heart was in designing and making furniture. I was busy continually, taking dictation, answering fan mail, learning how to tell half-truths to the reigning gossip columnists, Louella Parsons and Hedda Hopper. I went to Chicago with Dinah when she was appearing in person in a theater and there met a young man who was one-third of the Will Mastin Trio, Sammy Davis, Jr.

I worked for Dinah and George for almost two years and left when I became engaged to Richard Livingston. Dick and I had met in Dallas at a wedding when I was eighteen, but lost touch. We met again in October of 1951 when my Dallas cousin invited me to visit for a week. On the night I arrived Dick took me to a football game. (He wasn't going to spend his money on a visiting cousin and take her to dinner too!) Dick was impressed that I paid so much attention to the game he loves. He didn't know that I could hardly see well enough to follow the play of the ball! A week later

William V. Figge

Richard and Myra Livingston on their wedding day,
April 14, 1952

Myra and Jascha Heifetz playing ping-pong at his
beach house in Malibu, 1967

he proposed.

Because Dick is a CPA we couldn't get married until after March 15, the deadline for income taxes then. So I left my job with Dinah to get ready for the wedding and the move to Dallas. But chance intervened again. A friend of my mother's knew that Jascha Heifetz was looking for a secretary. Would I be interested? It could only be for a few months, I explained, but what could be more exciting than working for the great violinist?

The story of that interview has been told by both Jascha and me many times. I was shown into the living room of his home and when he walked in, I stood up to meet him. "How do you do," he said to me. "How do you spell Mendelssohn?"

"M-e-n-d-e-l-s-s-o-h-n," I answered.

"Miss Cohn," he said, "you are hired."

Those too were exciting days; Mr. H. (as I called him for many years) was in the process of giving many of his precious musical manuscripts to the Library of Congress. One of our first tasks was to wrap them carefully and pack them in boxes. I winced when he cut the string with a knife, when he knotted and pulled the tape around the cartons. Such hands, I thought, should not do these things. But over the years I have watched him repair things with hammers, screwdrivers, and all

manner of tools. His hands were made for more than playing the violin. I was told that he laughed when someone suggested he insure his hands with Lloyds of London.

The job with Mr. H. was quite different from the job with Dinah. I worked in an anteroom to his studio where I could hear him practice every day, both violin and piano. I learned that even a world famous violinist must never stop playing scales. I took dictation, wrote letters, and played with his son Jay. When April came, I regretted leaving this fascinating work. But he has remained a friend, and I helped out again for a few years when we moved to California. Many weekends Dick and I spent at his house in Malibu, learning to love the ocean and the simple life that he, who has known kings and queens, most enjoyed. (I dedicated *The Malibu and Other Poems* to him.) I honor Jascha as one of the greatest violinists of all time and I honor him for his teaching and his integrity in music. It has been a privilege to know him and to have him in our home for dinner and ping pong (his favorite game) over the years. He has been a good friend.

Dick and I had our honeymoon in Mexico and returned to a third-floor walk-up apartment in Dallas. "Please find an apartment," I told him over the phone, "with a view." For I had learned as early as our move to California that a room without a view is anathema to me; each place where I have lived had to look out over something beautiful. From the window where I sit now in the Santa Monica Mountains I can see hills and trees and beyond that a ten-mile view to

Heifetz, with Myra at his left, 1974

Ray Huff Studios

Publication picture for Livingston's first book
Whispers, *1958*

the Pacific Ocean which glimmers on smogless days.

> O, I am mad with the maddest of men
> Who lean from their windows now and again
>
> To catch a breath of October air
> When all that remains is a trace somewhere
>
> Of a wind gone to stench and a fume of gas
> Floating over the cars that pass
>
> On the crowded streets dressed in yellow fog,
> The gray of buildings lost in smog;
>
> And I turn myself from the window view
> And I weep for blue, I weep for blue.

We spent twelve years in Dallas. The first year there was very difficult for me because I had never before lived in such a community with a surfeit of parties and social life. I enjoyed that very much but I needed something else. The second year I found a job in an antiquarian bookstore. When the owner, Sawnie Aldredge, heard about my book, he suggested I take the manuscript to Siddie Joe Johnson, head of children's work at the Dallas Public Library. "Send it to Margaret McElderry," she told me. But even when I explained that I had sent it to her when I was a college freshman, Miss J. said "Try again." I did, and *Whispers and Other Poems* was accepted.

I learned that all things have their time; and one can write something whose time has not yet come. I also learned something about the importance of patience.

Three of the most exciting events of my life were the births of our children, Josh, Jonas, and Jennie.

They all found their way into my books. I wrote *Wide Awake and Other Poems* for Josh whose interest in trucks and bugs and plumbers is in those poems. *I'm Hiding* was a game I had played as a child and I found Josh playing it too. *I'm Not Me* was dedicated to Jonas who was always telling me not to call him by his name. "I'm a fireman," he would insist. "I'm an Indian." And I remembered how, as a child, I would also wish to be someone else. I wrote *See What I Found* after I watched Josh and Jonas playing one Christmas with a battery-operated ship for which they had begged, only to discover that once broken, it was useless. A set of blocks or an old box could be a boat, or anything . . . or everything. All it took was imagination.

When Siddie Joe Johnson asked me to speak to a group of teachers in the early '60s I discovered that I needed to learn a great deal more about poetry that children enjoy. A new career began for me accidentally when she asked me to teach a creative writing class at the Dallas Public Library's new branch. From that day in 1962 to now, I have been involved not only with teaching about poetry but working with children from kindergarten through high school. I have also written dozens of articles on this subject and have conducted

Josh, left, and Jonas Livingston, with their parents, Dallas, Texas, 1958

workshops and lectured throughout the country. I also teach in the Writers Program and Education Department for UCLA Extension—classes in the background of poetry for children, teaching creative writing in the classroom, and creativity. From 1966 to 1984 I was Poet-in-Residence for the Beverly Hills Unified School District.

We had wonderful times and wonderful friends in Dallas. Our boys grew up learning to catch catfish in Turtle Creek, to ride their bicycles to piano lessons, and live a sort of idyllic life. But in 1963, three events prompted us to leave Dallas and move to California. One was the appearance of Adlai Stevenson at a Dallas Council on World Affairs meeting when he was hit over the head and heckled by the audience. Another was the treatment afforded Blacks (they were called "colored" then) which we felt was unjust. And the third was the world-rocking assassination of John Kennedy. Dick and I had gone to the Trade Center for a luncheon in Kennedy's honor. We heard the ambulances speeding to the hospital, and we drove home in silence. "We're leaving Dallas," Dick said to me. "This is no place for us to bring up our children."

The days that followed Kennedy's assassination were terrifying. Lee Oswald had asked a lawyer, one of our neighbors, to defend him; suddenly our block was surrounded with cars parading up the street and through the back alley. Threatening phone calls were made to the lawyer, his wife, and children. People car-

ried guns. I remembered those days in *No Way of Knowing: Dallas Poems*.

> When Kennedy
> Come to our town
> He come with dreams
> Got shot right down . . .

We left Dallas, but not before a friend had erected a monument to Kennedy and I had chosen the words from a poem by William Blake. Those events left a mark on us forever.

Life began anew in California. It was a struggle for Dick to leave his practice and begin again, but with initial help from our parents and lots of imagination we survived! We bought a home in the mountains with room enough for all of us to be together but to have our privacy. After a bit I began to work as a teacher and continued my writing. Mae Durham Roger, a professor at the University of California, Berkeley, held summer symposiums on children's literature and during one of these asked me to read some of my favorite poems one evening to an assembled group. The next day she suggested that I might put some of these into an anthology, and this became *A Tune Beyond Us*, the first of fourteen anthologies I have edited.

Josh and Jonas, with their sister Jen, 1967

Since 1958 and the publication of *Whispers* I have published forty-two books thirty-nine of which are poetry. I have written one allegory, *Come Away,* and a new book which sums up many years of my experience with children and creative writing, *The Child as Poet: Myth or Reality?* which is for parents, teachers, and educators. It took me three years of constant work, and I drew upon boxes and boxes of articles and information I had saved for many years. But I have much more to do; there are always ten books waiting to be written.

Of course there is much more to tell. Josh graduated from Massachusetts Institute of Technology and worked for a number of years in public broadcasting, his great love classical music. He won an award for his program on the 80th Birthday Salute to Jascha Heifetz. Jonas, who attended Reed College and graduated from Sarah Lawrence, is a writer for Warner Brothers Records and knows people like Prince and Madonna. Jennie graduated from Yale two years ago and won the Sudler Prize for her photography, drawing, and painting. She is finishing up the last of two fellowships she has already won. I can only wonder what part accident or chance will play in their lives, what opportunities and events await them.

I am not really a traveler but in 1976 Dick and I went to England where I was inspired to write *A Lollygag of Limericks,* verses based on the names of places I found there. In 1979 we spent a month in France and it was there I found the magnificent forests that inspired me to write *Monkey Puzzle and Other Poems.* These days I spend a lot of time working but I also spend time with my book collection—poetry, Victorian illustrators, the work of James Joyce, W.B. Yeats, and other books I love.

Theodore Roethke has a line in one of his poems, "I learn by going where I have to go." These are words I repeat to myself often, remembering as far back as I can how I've thought of myself. I have always had a need to fit into the world around me; yet, for the most part, I prefer being alone. Somehow I've always felt different, as though I were on the outside of things looking in, always an observer who needs to put all that I feel or see into a poem, to somehow sort out its meaning, to look at it for myself, to view it afresh. I miss a great deal that others see, things that are important to many, and yet I am aware of responses other people fail to express. Perhaps this is what being a poet or a writer means.

I have kept a journal since I was ten years old; all of the feelings and observations I have go into that journal. Some eventually come out as poems, others are snatches of conversations or ideas that I may use someday. These journals are more than a record of my life however; they represent ideas that one day I will

The author at her desk, 1981

make the time to sort out and use.

I know there will never be time enough for me in life. My father always said he would die with twenty-five things undone and I know that will be true of me too. I would like to study astronomy. I'd like more time for bookbinding. I want to plant a rock garden. I want to plant and grow more gingko trees. I'd like to write a play. I want to visit Italy with Dick. But being a writer is almost a full-time job—the thoughts do not leave me alone. As soon as one book is finished there are others to plan. There is my family and my teaching and my home, which I love.

I've been very fortunate for I've had a career since I was very young and I've known many wonderful people who have given me the support to pursue the career, especially my parents, Dick, and my children. I am just a lucky woman who can only wish for all others the courage to tell a few Great Lies, to relentlessly pursue the dreams of their imaginations, and to always count the joys rather than the sorrows.

I believe that I was born into the right age, when women can have a career as well as a husband, family, and home. But in my next life I plan to be an opera star with beautiful flowing red hair and a glorious singing voice. More dreams, more music. But that comes later.

BIBLIOGRAPHY

FOR CHILDREN

Poetry:

Whispers, and Other Poems (illustrated by Jacqueline Chwast). New York: Harcourt, 1958.

Wide Awake, and Other Poems (illustrated by J. Chwast). New York: Harcourt, 1959.

I'm Hiding (illustrated by Erik Blegvad). New York: Harcourt, 1961.

I Talk to Elephants! (photographs by Isabel Gordon). New York: Harcourt, 1962.

See What I Found (illustrated by E. Blegvad). New York: Harcourt, 1962.

I'm Not Me (illustrated by E. Blegvad). New York: Harcourt, 1963.

Happy Birthday! (illustrated by E. Blegvad). New York: Harcourt, 1964.

The Moon and a Star, and Other Poems (illustrated by Judith Shahn). New York: Harcourt, 1965.

I'm Waiting (illustrated by E. Blegvad). New York: Harcourt, 1966.

Old Mrs. Twindlytart, and Other Rhymes (illustrated by Enrico Arno). New York: Harcourt, 1967.

A Crazy Flight, and Other Poems (illustrated by James J. Spanfeller). New York: Harcourt, 1969.

The Malibu, and Other Poems (illustrated by J.J. Spanfeller). New York: Atheneum, 1972.

The Way Things Are, and Other Poems (illustrated by Jenni Oliver). New York: Atheneum, 1974.

4-Way Stop, and Other Poems (illustrated by J.J. Spanfeller). New York: Atheneum, 1976.

A Lollygag of Limericks (illustrated by Joseph Low). New York: Atheneum, 1978.

O Sliver of Liver: Together with Other Triolets, Cinquains, Haiku, Verses, and a Dash of Poems (illustrated by Iris Van Rynbach). New York: Atheneum, 1979.

No Way of Knowing: Dallas Poems. New York: Atheneum, 1980.

A Circle of Seasons (illustrated by Leonard Everett Fisher). New York: Holiday House, 1982.

Monkey Puzzle, and Other Poems (illustrated by Antonio Frasconi). New York: Atheneum, 1984.

Sky Songs (illustrated by L.E. Fisher). New York: Holiday House, 1984.

A Song I Sang to You: A Selection of Poems (illustrated by Margot Tomes). New York: Harcourt, 1984.

Celebrations (illustrated by L.E. Fisher). New York: Holiday House, 1985.

Worlds I Know, and Other Poems (illustrated by Tim Arnold). New York: Atheneum, 1985.

Fiction:

Come Away (illustrated by Irene Haas). New York: Atheneum, 1974.

Editor of:

A Tune beyond Us: A Collection of Poetry (illustrated by J.J. Spanfeller). New York: Harcourt, 1968.

Speak Roughly to Your Little Boy: A Collection of Parodies and Burlesques (illustrated by J. Low). New York: Harcourt, 1971.

Listen, Children, Listen: An Anthology of Poems for the Very Young (illustrated by Trina S. Hyman). New York: Harcourt, 1972.

The Poems of Lewis Carroll (illustrations by John Tenniel and others, from the original editions). New York: Crowell, 1973.

What a Wonderful Bird the Frog Are: An Assortment of Humorous Poetry and Verse. New York: Harcourt, 1973.

One Little Room, an Everywhere: Poems of Love (woodcuts by A. Frasconi). New York: Atheneum, 1975.

O Frabjous Day: Poetry for Holidays and Special Occasions. New York: Atheneum, 1977.

Callooh! Callay! Holiday Poems for Young Readers (illustrated by Janet Stevens). New York: Atheneum, 1978.

Poems of Christmas. New York: Atheneum, 1980.

How Pleasant to Know Mr. Lear! (selections from Edward Lear). New York: Holiday House, 1982.

Why Am I Grown So Cold?: Poems of the Unknowable. New York: Atheneum, 1982.

Christmas Poems (illustrated by Trina Schart Hyman). New York: Holiday House, 1984.

The Scott, Foresman Anthology of Children's Literature, with Zena Sutherland. Glenview, Ill.: Scott, Foresman, 1984.

Easter Poems (illustrated by John Wallner). New York: Holiday House, 1985.

A Learical Lexicon (illustrated by Joseph Low). New York: Atheneum, 1985.

Thanksgiving Poems (illustrated by Stephen Gammell). New York: Holiday House, 1985.

FOR ADULTS

Nonfiction:

When You Are Alone/It Keeps You Capone: An Approach to Creative Writing with Children. New York: Atheneum, 1973.

The Child as Poet: Myth or Reality? Boston: Horn Book, 1984.

Norma Fox Mazer

1931-

To start, when writing about oneself, "I was born, dada dada da..." strikes me as dull. Of course I was born. Does it matter where? (New York City.) Or when? (1931.) These are only facts, and facts most often tell us far less than we like to think they do. Besides, I have not been much interested in my birthday since I was about twenty.

My mother has never been convinced of this. I remember, as a child, hearing my father, year after year, tell us to forget his birthday, he didn't care about it, he didn't care for celebrations and parties. And year after year, my mother assured my sisters and me that Daddy didn't mean it, that he really loved to get presents and have a fuss made over him. (Of course she's the one who loves birthdays, adores to get presents and have a fuss made over her.) I used to wonder—did Daddy mean it, or was Mom right? Now I know. I am like him. I dislike the fuss of birthdays—not for other people, just for myself—and he did, too.

I will start, though, with where my parents were born because that does matter. I am first-generation American on both sides. My parents came to this country with their parents at a very young age. And, growing up, I was always aware of that.

My father's family came from the Ukraine. Jewish boys, some as young as twelve, were always at risk to be conscripted into the Czar's army. To be taken for twenty-five years was not uncommon. Often, these boys and men, too, would disappear into Russia, never to be seen by their families again. My grandfather, Israel Gamaliel Fox, so the story goes, fled the Czar's agents. He was young, he was newly married, he was of a mild and temperate disposition; I hope he was in love with my grandmother. (I don't know how their marriage came about, whether arranged or a true love match.) In every way, conscription into the army was a horrendous fate.

But think how brave people of that generation must have been—brave or desperate. To leave your family, your homeland, your town or city, the streets you knew so well, the language and people and customs you'd grown up with and took for granted—imagine leaving all that and trading it in for nothing but uncertainty.

And how did my paternal grandmother, Anna Ravinsky, the young bride, feel about the move? Did

Norma Fox Mazer, 1971

she welcome it? Was she sad? Resigned? Rebellious? No answers. The past is darkness; bits of light shine through here and there, tiny pinpoints radiating from the fragments of stories that are all that is left of so many lives.

One of my cousins told me a story she had heard about my father's mother: on a train, the young Anna opened a window, took off her wig (which all devout married women were required to wear) and threw it out the window. That took spirit and courage. So I see a young woman saying good-by with gratitude to the restrictions of the past.

My grandparents, when they left the Ukraine, went to England, to London. They lived there eight

185

Paternal grandparents, Anna and Israel Fox, 1933

years. Israel worked as a bookbinder, a good trade; they lived well. Israel and Anna learned to speak English there. (For the rest of her life, Anna spoke with an English accent.) Three children were born there—Rose, Michael, and Hymie.

Anna, no doubt, had her hands full with the children, the language, the strange country. Once, my father, an infant, went into convulsions, his eyes rolled up into his head, he went into a coma. The doctor came. "Nothing to be done. The child is as good as dead." He left.

Did the doctor care about these immigrant Jews with their strange speech and odd ways? My grandmother walked up and down with the baby in her arms. Her baby dead? She heated a pan of water, put the baby in it, and moved him back and forth. She kept this up, moving him in the warm water. He became conscious again. She wrapped him in blankets and kept him close to her. She walked around with him in her arms for days. He recovered. Then an Official Someone arrived at the house. "Where's the dead baby?" Reasonably, my grandmother said, "There is no dead baby." She showed the Official Someone the very live baby.

In the way of officials everywhere, he refused to believe her. The doctor had filed a report. The report said there was a dead baby. Therefore, there was a

dead baby and she was ordered to produce said dead baby forthwith.

No dead baby, my grandmother said. The official went away with the promise that he would return shortly. The dead baby must be produced. My grandmother went to the doctor with little Michael in her arms. The doctor refused to see her. He didn't want to see a dead baby. She went home. The official came again. I imagine he raised his voice, trying to get through to this stupid foreigner. Maybe he screamed. "Dead baby! Dead baby!" Again Anna insisted, "Look, here is the baby. He's fine now. No dead baby."

The official delivered himself of more threats and more warnings. In desperation, Anna went back to the doctor and forced her way into his office. "Look! Here is the baby! A living baby!" At last the doctor conceded; perhaps out of sheer weariness, the matter was settled. But years later, telling her youngest daughter, my aunt Bobbi, this story, my grandmother would sigh repeatedly with the pain of the memory.

So my father, Michael, was born in London. A strange and wonderful place, it always seemed to me, for the Jewish son of Ukrainian-Jewish parents to be born. Somehow, growing up myself in a small town in the foothills of the Adirondack Mountains, growing up in a town *Look* magazine called Hometown U.S.A., I didn't quite believe in the reality of English Jews. Russian Jews, yes. Polish Jews, yes. Even German Jews. I knew those people. But English Jews? Yet there was my father, an English Jew by birth. And, indeed, in my eyes, it lent him an added enchantment, and often enough in the family we would joke, "Oh, that's his English nature," when speaking of my father's extreme reticence, his modesty, his reserve.

My father said his mother rarely spoke of her family. "She was ashamed." It seems that her father—and this is all I know of my Ravinsky great-grandfather—had disappeared when she was a child, leaving her mother with two little children to bring up alone. And where had her father disappeared to? Was it possible the Czar got him for the army? Probably not. Shame suggests that great-grandfather ran off with another woman.

His daughter, my grandmother, was a proud woman. It was said of Anna that if someone came into her house whom she didn't like, she wouldn't even serve that person a cup of tea—something unheard of in a Jewish home. But this was never spoken of in the family as inhospitality; rather, it was seen as pride, a surge of strength that wouldn't allow Anna to demean herself to pretend friendship when what she felt was scorn or disapproval. She was a righteous woman with principles. I see that that goes along with shame for the father who disappeared, not a hangdog shame, but shame that she shared the blood of a man with such a weak character. And her son Michael, my father, also had a strong character; he also had principles, he believed in things like loyalty and family and working hard.

Why did Israel and Anna leave London with their three children? Why make another move? They had settled, they were making a good living. What drove them on another journey, another break with the past? Loneliness, it seems. They both had family in the United States: Anna's only sibling, her brother Harry, and Israel's two sisters and his brother. So they came here and never again were they as prosperous as they'd been in London. My grandfather worked at first in the garment trade. Then he had a succession of little grocery stores. He was doing well enough with one of these little mom-and-pop stores, but gave it up to enter into partnership with a man who promised big things. Israel was, they tell me, a sweet and trusting man. His partner deceived him. My grandfather lost everything. Once again he had to start over. I never heard that he was bitter.

The Fox family (they may originally have been the Ochs family, renamed by immigration officials) came here when my father was about three years old; that would have been 1901. A picture from a year or so later: Israel and Anna with their three children. My grandfather dominates the picture. He sits on a cushioned chair with wooden claw feet, his right arm around the oldest son, Michael, my father. Grandfather wears a three-piece suit, the vest has a double row of buttons, and a watch chain is draped across the bottom of the vest. He wears a bow tie, a starched white shirt, his shoes are shined. He has a dapper mustache, turned up at the ends, and wavy hair.

Michael, then about four, stares as solemnly into the camera as everyone else. His left hand rests on his father's leg. He is dressed all in white, except for black stockings and black high-top shoes. He has beautiful curls which, I know from family legend, were white blond. (One of his nicknames as a child was Whitey.) The baby, Hymie, is in a full white dress, sitting on the table, held from behind by his mother. The mother's hair is rolled up on top of her head, she wears a long dark skirt and a white blouse with frills at the cuffs.

The father's eyes are heavily lidded, but the mother's eyes and the eyes of the children are all open, looking directly at us. Rose, the oldest child, is standing on the other side of the table, her hair in long ringlets, her hand resting on a basket of flowers.

What are these people thinking? What goes through the head of the little boy Michael as he stands

with his hand resting so confidently on his father's thigh? Are they thinking at all? Or are they merely tense, waiting for the camera click that will release them back into life and speech and realness again?

I recognize none of these people in the picture. As often as I have studied this picture of my father as a boy, I cannot see the man he became. Nor can I see the man I knew as my father in *his* father. Nor do I recognize in that slim woman holding the baby, the grandmother I saw only rarely. My most vivid memory of her: a tiny stout woman all in black, pressed shyly into a corner as I rushed unheedingly past her. I was thirteen. I do not know if I even spoke to her. And this admission hurts me more than I can say.

After I grew up, I often asked my father, "What was your mother like?"

"Oh, very nice." Details filtered out slowly. The rag around her head on Friday night after all the cleaning and preparation for shabbis. Shabbis? The Sabbath? But my father was an atheist, a nonbeliever in the mysteries, and so, I thought, were his parents. But no, every Friday, his mother performed the ceremonial cleaning of the house in preparation for the holy day of rest. And he remembered going to Shul with his father, he remembered his father putting on the prayer shawl. And then suddenly his father stopped going. My father never knew why.

My father was thought to be the family's bad boy; he spoke of himself that way. "I gave my father a lot of trouble . . . I was always in trouble . . ." And I knew that he thought of Hymie, his younger brother, as the good son. Hymie didn't give his parents trouble. He didn't throw cats off roofs (Mike did), or leap out of the dark stairwell to frighten his father (Mike did), or play hookey from school and then finally drop out altogether in the eighth grade (Mike did).

But this same bad boy, this tough kid who rode a motorcycle, who always had a chip on his shoulder and who said of himself, "I was always ready for a fight," this same Mike lived at home on and off until he was twenty-eight and married my mother. He washed the floors for his mother, he sent her money whenever he left home to work someplace else, and he spent time teaching his fifteen-year-old sister to drive.

When Hymie was sixteen, he died. I think that deeply affected my father, perhaps froze his image of himself as the unsatisfactory son. And who knows—I don't, since, typically, my father was all reticence on the subject—how much guilt was mixed with his grief, how much self reproach for not having loved his brother more and better? (This theme appeared in my novel *When We First Met*. After her sister dies, Jenny is filled with remorse for the bickering and fighting that characterized their relationship and thinks that now

*Michael Fox with daughter Norma, two months old,
New York City*

they will never have a chance to know each other and become friends.)

My father again—he was always a difficult person, moody, tense. And shy! My mother says that when they were first married if people came to visit he would sit in the room and never say a word. "I would sweat buckets," he told me. "I was shy and aggressive at the same time."

He did become easier on himself, easier to be with as he got older, but he never fully lost that shyness. For instance, it was like pulling teeth to make conversation with Dad on the phone. Well, one ordinarily didn't make small talk with him, anyway. He was interested in politics, the world around him, facts, hard solid things he could bite into, remember, absorb, mull over.

I remember him sitting close to our radio at home, his head bent, absorbed, twisting the dial to catch the foreign-language stations, although English and Yiddish were the only languages he knew.

He was a route man: bread routes, milk routes, a dry-cleaning route. He did some factory work, too, but always preferred the outdoors, loved driving, moving swiftly at his own pace, meeting the customers on his route. He was a good route man; he built business for anyone he worked for. Maybe with a case of milk bottles in his hand, or a big basket of loaves of bread, or hangers full of dry-cleaned clothes, he wasn't so shy. He talked to his customers and they liked him. When he opened up, when he relaxed, there was a charm that people responded to. And then, too, he was a very handsome man, and most of the customers on the routes were women. It's always nice to have a handsome man deliver your milk or bread.

Years later—this was when I was grown—when he could no longer drive because of poor vision, he worked as a dishwasher. I felt humiliated for him—this man who had read *War and Peace* five times—but he needed a job. He never complained about being a dishwasher, but in his way made friends with everyone in the kitchen and at the same time kept himself aloof from them. And even with bad eyesight, he went on reading and poring over maps.

Even when he was legally blind, he never gave up reading entirely. Somewhat reluctantly, he began to listen to books on records, because he couldn't live without the written word. But he also used a magnifying glass and every day when his eyes were "clear" he would laboriously read a page, two pages, three pages in whatever book he was reading—or most likely, re-reading—because by that time the new books didn't draw him.

We were a family of readers. There were always books in our house, shelves of them in the living room and more in the hall. Here I am, thirteen, walking to school with my sister, reading a book and falling behind. Reading and walking with my sister who walks fast, with long-legged strides. She's inches taller, she's older, prettier, smarter, better in every way. "Wait up," I yell. She walks on. I run to catch up. She pulls ahead. "Waaaaait!"

She looks briefly over her shoulder. "Then stop reading," she commands. Why should I? She doesn't stop walking. I run, catch her for a moment, then she's ahead of me again. I hate her passionately and think of

Norma with her father, 1975

many interesting ways for her to die. Maybe that lumber truck rolling through our town from the Adirondacks will roll over her. Oh, my deeeear sister. . . . I'll sob at the funeral, everyone will feel sorry for me, losing my beloved older sister in such a tragic accident. . . . "Wait for me," I scream—and *thunk thunk thunk,* I run after her, books jouncing in my arms.

She never did wait for me.

I never did stop reading. None of us did.

My mother worked in department stores, a sales clerk. I used to visit her sometimes after school, look at the cashmere sweaters piled softly in the don't-touch glass cases—that was as close as I'd ever get to cashmere. At various times Mom sold sweaters, baby clothes, women's dresses. At the end of the day, she'd come home and cook supper—vegetable soups from scratch, nothing out of a can, baked potatoes I could mash with beets or peas, and always on Friday nights, chicken. (I got the neckbone, considered it a terrific privilege until I heard the mournful chorus, "I alwaaaays get the neck of the chicken.") After supper my mother would say, "Norma, do you want to dry the dishes?"

"No."

"Why are you so uncooperative?"

"If you want me to dry the dishes, order me."

"I want you to do it of your own free will."

Then I'd stomp off to the bathroom, lock the door, read a book. The dishes were waiting for me when I got out. I dried them, but not of my own free will.

After that, my mother would get in bed with a book and a pile of magazines. My father would be in the living room in "his" chair with a book, and we three girls would be scattered around the house with our books.

I wonder which of my ancestors were writers. I'm sure that some of them must have been, but there's no way I'll ever know. When the six million Jews of Europe were exterminated by Hitler and the Germans in World War II, the past of those of us living was also obliterated. But I'm ready to believe that there might have been writers on both sides of my family. Mickey Ross (an anglicization of Ravinsky), a first cousin to my father, is a writer, one of the two men who created (among other shows) "All in the Family." My cousin, Vivian Pollock, whose mother is one of my father's sisters, just published a book on Emily Dickinson. And on my mother's side, there's her brother, my uncle Alex, a fabled storyteller in the family, my childhood hero because he was a newspaper reporter, a real writer.

My mother was born in a small town in Poland to Udell Rothenberg Gorelick. Udell and her sister lost their mother when they were small girls. They were left in the care of their father, Alexander, who was slim and good looking, with a long red beard. (Two of my uncles and one of my aunts on that side are redheads.) About the time my grandmother was seventeen or eighteen, she found a job in a bakery. She had bright blue eyes, high cheekbones, dark hair. She was poor, but energetic, hardworking, and bright. The baker had a son who was also good looking, young, and intelligent. There the resemblance between the two young people stopped. The girl, Udell, had native intelligence, but little schooling. The boy, Aaron, was not only a reader, but desperately in love with books. Any chance he got, and a lot that he shouldn't have gotten, he was off in a corner reading, bread-baking the furthest thing from his mind. His father, watching the pretty young girl take hold in the bakery, decided to make a match. He didn't care that she was poor, that his son outstripped her in learning; he saw in her a woman who would be good for his impractical son. He wasted no time. He took his son aside. "Aaron. That is the girl for you."

Indeed she was. The family story has it that Aaron was already in love with pretty Udell. And she? Her feelings about him? This is never quite as clear. In any event, they married. And lived happily ever after? Debatable on several counts. To begin with, Poland was not then, nor ever was, a happy place for Jews. But the young couple established themselves; they had five children—four boys, then a little girl, who would be my mother. About their life in Poland I know very little.

The next time I hear about them, Aaron is in the United States with the second oldest boy, and Udell is hiding in a cellar in Poland with the other three sons and the baby girl. The cellar is their Christian neighbors'. These good (in the deepest sense of the word) neighbors have, as further protection, nailed a cross on the front door of the temporarily abandoned Gorelick home.

The family is in the cellar. Outside there are soldiers, Cossacks, Jew-hunters. Outside there are shots, screams, the pounding of feet on pavement. And then there's a particular shot, a particular bullet among the hundreds that were fired that will always be remembered in our family. One of the Gorelick boys, Max—how old is he, about nine? ten?—is hit in the throat.

I've always imagined him restless, as nine-year-olds are, curious about the noise, perhaps just wanting to see the soldiers, and then, when his mother is distracted, running to the cellar window, standing on tiptoe, looking out . . . And then the bullet. Maybe not even intended for him, maybe just a stray bullet.

My mother, the baby then, doesn't remember all

this. The family—maybe Max, maybe his mother or the other brothers—talked about it when she was growing up. Yes, I can imagine how often they must have thought about that moment: the bullet, the little boy falling to the floor—or not falling to the floor, maybe turning with a bewildered and guilty smile, not yet realizing what had happened to him. Growing up, I heard this story, only I didn't think of it as a "story"—it was too real, became too much a part of the life of my mind. I could *see* that dark, damp cellar; the boy, Max, up on tiptoes to look out the dim little window; I could hear the horses hoofs on the cobblestones and the coarse shouts of the soldiers.

Sometime after this, the Gorelick family came to the United States. Max was never strong and he died at eighteen. My mother remembers him: thin, red-headed and, she says in Yiddish, *oysegedart*. Explaining, "You know, like a squeezed-out lemon." He was always that way, she says, but I wonder, because his brothers and sisters—my familiar aunts and uncles—are anything but *oysegedart*. They are, one and all, a strong, quarrelsome, opinionated, sassy lot.

The Gorelicks left Poland. They went to New York City, then to Burlington, Vermont, and from there to Glens Falls, New York. Along the way their name went through a few changes: Gorelick—to Garlic—to Garlen. (And my mother's name, Zlatchy, became its American equivalent, Charlotte; became a nickname, Slats; became a name of her own choosing, Jenny; and the final metamorphosis—Jean.)

In Burlington, from relatives of people who lived in Glens Falls, Aaron and Udell heard about a bakery for sale in Glens Falls. Off they went.

The bakery was located across from the circus grounds and close by the red-light district, altogether a rough area. One night a man tried to chloroform my grandmother. She screamed and Aaron came running. But after that, she wouldn't live there, so they moved again to an old house at 61½ Broad Street. A poor neighborhood, but respectable. The Jewish community raised money for the family to build a bakery. An oven builder came from New York to construct the brick ovens.

Family story: Aaron would make the loaves, put them on the long wooden paddle, slip them into the high brick oven, slam the door, lie down with a sigh of relief on one of the wooden dough troughs and open his book. And while he read, the bread burned. So the family got along, but not ever prosperously. And my grandmother, fulfilling the promise my great-grandfather had seen in her, the promise of a practical, energetic woman who would save his son from himself, rushed around borrowing money "from schmerl to pay berl," in order to keep the family afloat.

My grandfather was not meant to be a baker. In another life he might have been a researcher, a classics professor, a teacher of languages. He read and spoke German, Yiddish, Polish, Russian, and Hebrew. One of my uncles, the namesake of that red-bearded Alexander, says of him, "He was a fine man, a proud man, an unusual man. He was a small man, not strong physically, but every day of his life he had to do hard physical labor."

My mother worked in the bakery, too, getting up at 4:00 A.M. to wrap bread. She left school when she was sixteen and went to work. One summer, working in a camp as a waitress, she made friends with a lively young woman named Bobbi Fox. Bobbi introduced Jean to her brother Mike. They met in New York City. They went to the theatre several times. A week after he met her he asked her to marry him. It was late, they were outside her sister's apartment, and she was dying to pee. Nice girls didn't say things like that. To get away from him, she said, Yes!—although she was engaged to someone else at the time.

They were married. My sister was born, then I was born, both of us in New York City. My father drove a milk truck for Sheffield Farms. Then there was a strike and my father (that shy man!) was pinpointed

Michael and Jean Fox, 1946

as one of the leaders. He didn't think of himself as a leader. He just got mad once and stood up and said what he had to say. What he had to say was heartfelt, rousing, and made sense to the other men. It was influential in getting the strike vote. But later on, he was blacklisted. Which meant no job would open for him, and this was 1935, the middle of the Depression. So my uncle, my mother's brother, asked him to come upstate to drive a bread truck for the bakery, which had passed to him.

For me, growing up in Glens Falls meant, as much as anything, my uncle Charlie's fresh bread every day: dark pumpernickel, Jewish rye bread, crusty rolls, the holiday Challahs, braided and shiny. When we first came to Glens Falls, we lived in one-half of the by-then restored house at 61½ Broad Street. There's a picture of my baby sister tucked into one of the big wooden baskets that my father packed with loaves of bread as he made the rounds on his route. The bread truck was horse driven, as was the milk truck my father had driven. Sparrows picked at the horse balls in the street. Later, the horses went and the truck was mechanized.

After we moved from Broad Street, I'd often walk the mile or so to the bakery to get rolls or bread. The best times were bitter-cold winter nights when I'd walk home slowly and slowly eat a hot roll, the soft inside first, the crusty outside last. We Foxes scorned "store bought" white bread, that soft mushy stuff. One day I went home after school with a friend. Her kitchen was dark and musty. I sat on the edge of my chair and hastily, my face hot, swallowed a folded-over piece of white bread spread with jam. White bread! How good it was. The taste of sin and all the things that were bad for me.

There were three of us girls. I was the middle sister. My older sister, Adele (named for our grandmother, Udell), was beautiful, smart, and admired throughout the family. My younger sister, Linda, was a cutie pie with freckles, blonde braids, and a swift, sassy mouth. My uncle called her dynamite. And there I was, caught between these two sisters, one wonderful, one (when she wasn't in trouble) adorable.

Well, I did some things, too. I taught myself to read and my first-grade teacher, Miss Dooty, loved me. Never again did a teacher love me as much. I put Miss Dooty in a short story I wrote, called "Why Was Elena Crying?"

The principal of my first elementary school, Broad Street School, was Miss Dwyer. She had been my mother's principal, too. And the kids still sang in secret the same song my mother sang as a schoolgirl. "God made nails, God made wire, had some left over and made Miss Dwyer!" Once she called me to her

office, perhaps to tell me I was to be skipped half a grade. I tiptoed across the vast space that separated her desk from the door. She spoke to me. As if she were God or the sun, I didn't dare look into her eyes, lest I be blinded.

Broad Street was where I became acquainted with Crazy Charlie and Crazy Art and Cigarbutt Annie. Crazy Charlie had bottle-thick glasses, wore shabby brown coats and stained baggy trousers, and spent his time diligently peeling twigs that he held as close as possible to his eyes. He was always smiling and I remember, as a little girl, being more frightened of crossing the street than I was of him. But Crazy Art scared me. There were whispers floating around about him, whispers that I could never quite grab hold of but that told me in some odd, wordless way, Stay out of his way! Cigarbutt Annie, a short humpbacked woman with enormous thick lips, who muttered and talked constantly to herself, patrolled the gutters of Glens Falls for cigar butts.

Strangely, while the town easily tolerated their eccentrics and crazies, they segregated out all the chil-

Norma, five years old

dren who were "different." No mainstreaming in those days. The retarded, the hearing-impaired, the physically handicapped—all were lumped together and sent to special classes. I particularly remember one girl whose younger brother was in my class. Sylvia was probably brighter than half the kids I went to school with, but she'd had polio as a child. As a result, she limped and wore a metal and leather brace on one leg. Because of this, she was in the special classes. These kids even entered the school through a separate door.

All that seemed, then, to have nothing to do with me, but I've always been fascinated by eccentrics. I wrote about a couple of them in *Mrs. Fish, Ape, and Me, the Dump Queen* and in a short story called "Amelia Earhart, Where Are You When I Need You?"

I mostly loved school and in second grade, I began to love boys, as well. I was receiving notes in my desk from an especially handsome boy named Joseph. Then we moved away from Broad Street to Ridge Street. I went to another school. No more Joseph. A couple years later, though, Joseph reappeared in my life. I was eleven and very susceptible. I fell in love with him all over again. He seemed to love me, too. He gave me a gift, a tiny china elephant. My first love gift. A week later he demanded its return. "I," he said, with heartless logic, "don't like you anymore."

The year we lived on Ridge Street, when I was eight, I learned to ride a two-wheeler, changed my name (briefly, because I kept forgetting I'd changed it) to the more glamorous Diane, made up triplet brothers in the Navy to impress my new girlfriend, and was caught stealing.

Norma (right), with sisters Adele and Linda, about 1941

Our landlords owned a mom-and-pop candy store in the front of the building we lived in. Under the influence of a blond girl named Joan, I stole a candy bar. I was not a very good thief. My mother found out almost at once. I hadn't even had the good sense to eat my loot. My mother insisted not only that I return the candy bar, but that I confess my crime to the owners. Ashamed, trembling, frightened, furious, I did. And then I had to promise both my mother and Mrs. C. in the candy store that I'd never steal again. I didn't. I don't know about Joan, though. Stealing was probably a hobby for her. She was the first person I remember being aware of as rich. Probably her parents were actually not rich so much as just a whole lot better off than mine, but I was awed because (1) they owned their house, (2) had an attached garage, (3) a screened sunporch, and (4) a stone fireplace in the living room.

After Ridge Street we moved to another apartment on First Street. There was a crab apple tree I climbed in the spring. Rhubarb grew wild alongside the garage and in summer I ate the red stems raw, puckering my lips. I played marbles, hide-and-seek, was called a tomboy. Now and then I got pennies for the candy store. Winter meant galoshes which left black marks on the back of your legs, and King of the Hill of snow, and nostrils fragile as glass from twenty degrees below zero. I ice-skated behind my school and at Crandall Pond at the edge of the city, but my ankles always collapsed and I walked home with feet so cold they felt like blocks of wood.

Our school gave free music lessons. I took the violin and drew screeches from the strings that made my family either laugh or cover their ears. For several weeks in sixth grade, I toted home a bass fiddle far larger than I. In junior high came clarinet lessons. I liked the clarinet. My teacher went into the army, promising that his successor would look up the pupils with promise. No one ever looked me up. I was quite disconsolate over this and never took another music lesson.

The First Street house had wooden steps going up to our second-floor apartment—the same wooden steps Bitsy Kallman climbs in the story "Dear Bill, Remember Me?" In our apartment there was a door which opened onto a long enclosed flight of stairs which, in turn, led to a shed on the ground floor. In this shed there was a trapdoor. Open the trapdoor and another flight of stairs led down into the cellar where there was a coal furnace. Winter mornings my father went down there before work and shoveled coal into the furnace. I'd go with him sometimes, watch him shovel up the coal from the tall pyramid that the coal-man left when he delivered through a little cellar window, watch the flames lick up, then settle down blue. Winter mornings we woke up to a cold house, the windows covered with frost flowers.

Our landlord and landlady lived on the first floor of that stucco house with their St. Bernard and their youngest son, Bobby. These people seemed immensely old to me, she had white hair and glasses, a kindly woman. Her husband I don't remember at all, but the St. Bernard I remember vividly for the time he took my kitten in his teeth and shook it to death, while I sat on the steps and screamed in misery and helplessness.

(Another moment: a girlfriend and I are playing near those same wooden steps. I have forgotten the game, although I made it up, but not her words. "Norma Fox! What an imagination!" And perhaps it was precisely then that I realized that my imagination had some other function than to torment me with witches in doorknobs and lurking figures in the shadows of the stairs.)

Bobby, too, I remember vividly: a grinning boy with thick glasses, rumored to be a science genius, something awry in his eyes and his grin, something awry in the way he hunched his shoulders and peered around at you, grinning and sly. He must have been seventeen, eighteen, something like that, and was kept, I think, like a slightly dangerous pet in his parents' house.

Our shed was a twin to Bobby's shed. It was possible to peek through the boards into the other shed where Bobby did his experiments, the mad boy-genius scientist. Once or twice when I was peeking, Bobby had rushed toward the wall, muttering, spit at the corners of his mouth. The thudding of my heart as I backed away only added to the delicious horror of my spying. One day, though, Bobby moved deliberately. Perhaps that's why I remained glued to my peekhole as he raised a syringe of chemicals and squirted them directly into my eye.

The next thing I remember, I'm upstairs in my house, my mother and Bobby's mother both bending over me. Then the doctor is there. "A fraction of an inch closer and she'd have lost her sight."

(Some years later a girlfriend and I are playing a game, the game of blind. I am the blind one. She is leading me. Along comes our English teacher. "Hello, girls," she chirps. My eyes fly open in embarrassment. Our teacher has a fresh, high complexion, a please-love-me smile. She passes us, and Nancy and I fall over each other, hysterical with laughter. We look after our teacher, she's tall and primly dressed in a pink suit. She seems old to us, though she's just out of college. She's our sophomore English teacher. That means we were fourteen or fifteen and playing this game. Writing this, I'm surprised that I'm that old. But growing up is surprising and strange. One is often older at ten and youn-

Norma, age twelve, at Seven Keys in the Adirondack Mountains

ger at fifteen than wisdom would have it.)

"A fraction of an inch closer and she'd have lost her sight." I remember how my eye hurt, how it stung, how frightened I was. How the doctor's words reverberated. But what I remember most is that I didn't cry. That was a conscious decision, a choice I'd never made before. I was a famous crybaby. In the family they called me the faucet. They said, "You only have to look at Norma cross-eyed and she cries." I cried if the boys teased me. I cried if someone hit me. I cried if my father threatened to hit me. I cried if I was scared. Or sad. Or happy. But that day, I didn't cry.

I did a story about crying, about a faucet girl, "Why Was Elena Crying?" That question is about the older sister (wonderful, beautiful, admirable), who never cries until the night before her wedding. The question is asked by her younger sister, who always cries.

One of my uncles ran a summer camp for adults in the Adirondacks, all bright hot days and cool starry nights, a clear, clean lake and pine forests. That was in the days before people went flying off to Europe or the Bahamas or Japan for their vacations. I spent quite a few summers in Seven Keys, working at various jobs: in the office as a gofer, cleaning guest rooms, in the laundry, putting sheets through the mangle, and (the plum job) as a waitress—the low point being when I slid a mess of scrambled eggs onto a guest's lap instead of his plate.

Perhaps my sense of myself lurking around the edges of adult society comes from there, from the summers I spent working in the camp, working and looking at people, watching, listening, making up stories about those people, making up stories about myself, living in a dream, the dream of "Someday I'll show them . . ." and "When I . . ." and "They'll all pay attention to me when . . ."

It was around this time, too, that I was newly defined in the family: I was now the Cold One, the Selfish One. (My younger sister had metamorphosed from the Cute One to the Brat, the Bad One. My older sister remained responsible, beautiful, and bright: the Good One.)

My being called cold and selfish had a certain dreary justification. In my teens, I was more and more in my own world, at once shiveringly aware of everything going on around me and keeping it all away with an invisible wall. So many things hurt. (That wall showed up in *Saturday, the Twelfth of October*, when Zan at first can't handle the shock of finding herself trapped with Stone Age cave dwellers.) I saw myself as clumsy, shy, awkward, stiff; but to others, so I heard years later, I appeared cool, poised, and self-contained.

The sense of myself as different became something I lived with, almost unnoticed, yet I was never free of its effects. I felt an outsider, someone poised on this earth, but not solidly planted. I even felt an outsider in the small Jewish community in Glens Falls: we Foxes weren't religious, we were radicals politically, and we didn't mix a whole lot (except for my mother).

Were I to be asked to use one word to describe myself then and for years afterward, it would be—eyes. There's a picture of me around thirteen, sitting in a high-backed leather chair, looking out of the corner of my eyes, looking around, watching, a little frightened smile on my face. Along about then, it struck me, a bone-aching truth, that grown-ups—adults, these powerful mysterious people—were all play-acting; they weren't, in fact, any older, any more grown-up than I was.

It was harder to watch kids my own age. All those "in" girls, the sorority girls, the prom-queen types with their long, smooth, tawny legs and strings of pearls and cashmere sweaters, those magic girls whose boyfriends were always presidents of the senior class or played football for Glens Falls High. I never went to a pep rally in my life. My legs were impossibly short and

solid. I blushed when a boy I liked spoke to me or even passed me in the hall, not a sweet, pale blush, but a bright red, fiery blush that covered my neck and face.

(One of the first stories I published was about a girl who couldn't bring herself to speak to a boy she liked. She watched and suffered while a beautiful girl carried on gaily with him. The story was an early effort and, mercifully, it's disappeared into the Great Wastebasket in the Sky, without which most writers might be shamed out of existence.)

Once, in senior high, I was visiting a friend whose family lived year round in Lake George, about fifteen miles north of Glens Falls. Jane drove to school, one of the first girls I remember having her own car. That weekend we went out for a ride in her family's motorboat. A boy was with us, a delicious boy who was president of the senior class and the student council and anything else you could think of. His girlfriend was, of course, the most beautiful girl in school. She had been the junior prom queen, she was the tallest girl in school and had thick black hair and a creamy complexion sprinkled with freckles. They were seriously in love and everyone knew that nothing, no one, could come between them.

Despite all this, it was impossible not to be a little in love with Dick. My girlfriend steered the boat. The wind blew through my hair. I leaned back on my hands and smiled winningly at Dick. He leaned toward me. Ohmygod. Was it happening? At this very moment was he falling out of love with the glorious Madelein and falling in love with me? He smiled and leaned

Norma, Glens Falls, New York, 1946

closer, looking into my face. I nearly fainted. "Geeze," he said in tones of awe, "you have really big front teeth."

In grade school I had confided to my diary that I wanted "adventures" or, failing that, to be a nurse. By the time I went into junior high, there was something else: a longing, a need to write, so palpable it seemed it must always have been with me. I hooked up right away with the school newspaper and for the next six years the newspaper was the focus of my school existence.

What did I learn as a writer for the school newspaper? On reflection, not much. To begin a story with the five W's: who, what, when, where, and why. I can't remember anything else. It didn't matter. I was around print, I was a reporter. I wrote feature stories and sports stories and editorials and headlines. I stayed late in school and "put the paper to bed," and when the issue came out I sniffed the good clean ink smell and knew I was as close to heaven as I was going to be allowed to get.

But I wanted to write more than newspaper articles. There was a longing in me, vague, inchoate, but real, almost an ache. Once I wrote about a storm. An A plus from my English teacher. Another time I wrote about an old man seen on the street. Again A plus. My English teachers sighed contentedly over my compositions. I helped out my friends with their essays and themes and wondered why it was so difficult for them to do what was so easy for me. But nobody told me anything about writing. No hints, no encouragement, no advice, no direction. There just wasn't anybody around to do that sort of thing.

Actually, rather later on, there was one person, one of my older sister's boyfriends, who was also a would-be writer. Mark told me to write down descriptions of what I saw and to compare one thing to another. I thus put down a few paragraphs about trees dotting the hills like dotted swiss curtains or lightning splitting the sky like yellow forks, or some such. And I remember, too, writing on a piece of paper *The Secret of the Boarding School—A Novel of Girlhood*, by Norma Fox. Then the excitement of writing the first paragraph. A girl arrives at a mysterious boarding school. Yes? And who is she? And why is she there? And what happens? I didn't know, and I didn't know how to find out, and I didn't know that it was absurd for me to write about boarding schools.

Meanwhile other things were going on. Boys, boys, boys. I had crushes, one after the other. I was crushed under the weight of my feelings. If I saw the boy in the hall—and I certainly tried very hard to do so—I would blush and hurry past, hardly looking at him. Boys were distant, strange creatures. I had no

brothers. My near cousins were girls. My father himself was a distant creature, meant to be placated and adored. A friend undertook to let one of these adored ones know he was in this favored state and who it was that adored him. Then she brought back the Adored One's message: Tell Norma Fox she's a bird. This scene shows up in slightly altered form in the short story "Mimi the Fish." I suspect it's going to show up again somewhere, if it hasn't already.

The year I was fifteen I met a friend of my newly married older sister. He was twenty-one, tall, curly haired, a veteran of the air force. I came home and reported to my best friend that I'd met an incredibly handsome guy, name of Harry Mazer, too bad he was so—ughhh—*old*. Two years later, in the fall of my seventeenth year, I met him again. He was still six years older than I, but by one of the lovely miracles of nature, not *that* old anymore. By then, even though I still was wounded with the memory of "tell her she's a bird" and "geeze, what big teeth!" three or four other young men had fallen in love with me. My confidence had risen a little. I decided that I would let Harry Mazer fall in love with me, also.

Unfortunately for my plans, he thought I was too young. I had to work some to make him notice me. I did. He did. We fell in love. Out of love. In love. I went off to college, Antioch; fell out of love. Then in love again. We quarreled and made up, and quarreled and made up. We decided to get married. An uncle, aghast at the thought of his baby eighteen-year-old niece getting married said, "For god's sake, live with the guy, don't marry him!" But that was 1950 and I was deeply insulted by such advice and wondered if I could ever forgive my uncle.

We were married. We talked about books and writing and literature. We also talked about politics, unions, injustice, the atom bomb, the cold war. We were radicals and ready to reform (re form) the world, if not in ninety days, then in five years. Five years—good god, it was a lifetime! If we couldn't straighten out the world in five years, then things were really in a bad way.

In between all this talk, we refinished furniture, laid tiles in our tiny kitchen, went to movies and plays, worked at boring jobs, and tried to learn to cook. Neither of us knew how, but he knew more than I did. My mother was an excellent cook and I'd never been asked to cook, nor had I much wanted to. Our joke—true enough—was that I didn't know how to boil water for a cup of tea. Still, somehow, it seemed that cooking was really my job. Everyone knew that "girls" cooked and cleaned, while "men" only helped. I wished the first year of being married would hurry up—it dragged on

Harry Mazer with daughters Susan, Gina, and Anne, about 1969

endlessly. I was tired of being a bride: I didn't like bride jokes, I wanted to get on with my life, I wanted to be an old married lady.

Eventually, in the way of these things, I got my wish. If not yet old (my conception of old having radically altered in my twenties), I was well married and had three children: Anne, then about five, Joey, two, and Susan, the baby. I went around with a little pad stuck in my jeans pocket, taking down the clever things my kids said. They were all fascinatingly different. Anne was a talker, had been at it since she was seven months old. Joey was independent; we used to joke that he started running away from home when he was two years old. Susan had been born with energy streaming out of her. Early on, she'd lie in her crib, shrieking long operatic baby arias from the sheer joy of being alive.

I was Mommy; I had almost forgotten Norma. One day, looking around at the houseful of kids and listening to the never ending cries of Mommy! Mom! Mama!, it occurred to me that the day I'd been both putting off and waiting for—the day when I was all grown up—had arrived without my noticing. Indeed, it must have been here for quite a while. And that famous question "What are you going to do when you grow up?" had not gone away. What *was* I going to do when I grew up? I'd gone on fooling around with writing, beginning stories, jotting down ideas and nifty little perceptions. But that wasn't being a writer. That was being "someday when I am a real writer . . ."

Along about this time, things were happening to

Harry, too. Some of the same stuff—wondering why, now that he was a grown-up, he was doing work he didn't like, not making his old dreams come true. We talked. Our best talks always came with long walks around the old section of Syracuse where we were then living. It was the First Ward, the first settled part of Syracuse: the oldest church in the city was down the block from us, on a further corner there was an octagonal limestone house, around the corner a house made of round cobblestones. In spring as we walked, we picked mushrooms that grew through the cracks in the sidewalks. And in winter we'd stop at a small Italian bakery that made round loaves of crusty bread in the same kind of ovens my grandfather and then my uncle used to bake their Jewish rye bread.

So we walked and talked. We both knew what I wanted—to be a writer. But then something surprising happened. Harry began to talk about his longing to be a writer, a dream he'd harbored—or hidden—since he was in his teens. And I hadn't known anything of it. I thought we talked about everything. Maybe I vaguely knew he was interested in writing. There were all those notebooks he kept, yet he had never actually said the words: I want to be a writer.

Now that he'd said it, I think he looked at me in amazement when I didn't fall over laughing at the idea. But why would I laugh? As far as I could tell, my own longing to become a writer was no less arrogant than his.

But if arrogant, I was also practical. Since we both wanted to become writers, wasn't it about time we did something real about it? I thought that what I needed—what we both needed—was to develop the habit of writing. Not to write only when we could squeeze in a few minutes here or there. Not to write only when "inspiration" struck. But to write something every day.

It was winter when we began, deep cold February, days when the morning air was almost blue. That day I had bundled the kids up till they could hardly move, put the baby for her nap in the carriage on the porch and hustled the other two little ones out. They were not happy about this. They turned around and banged on the door, whining and calling, "Mommmy! Mommmy! Let us in." Poor little waifs. Their voices trembled with reproach. It was cold out there. I was inside in the nice warm house while they suffered.

Behind the door I trembled, too, wondering if the neighbors were watching and listening. What would they think of me? Cruel mother!

I remember sitting down and opening my green notebook to its first fresh page. I tried to fashion the events of the morning into a little story. It was clumsy, it was crude, but I sat there and finished it.

Every night, after supper, after the kids had been bathed and read to and had been brought the requisite number of glasses of water, and after we had found each child's particular stuffed animal or blanket necessary for good sleep—every night after Harry had spent a day working in a factory and I had spent a day taking care of the kids, we sat down across from each other at the old oak table in the dining room with our notebooks and pens.

Gina, Joe, and Susie, 1965

We stuck to our schedule, an hour a day at the end of the day, for about three years. Little as it was, it made a difference. I was writing, finishing what I began, learning about rewriting. The notebooks didn't last long; typewriters took their place. Writing and kids filled our lives. During the day I could think about the story I was working on. At the end of the day we'd take a walk, talk about the kids and writing. We read other writers and tried to analyze what they did, how they achieved their effects. I wonder now how we found time to write between the kids and talking. Half our talk was dreaming still. Would we ever make it? Were we any good? Wouldn't it be wonderful if we could write for a living? Was it even possible? Maybe . . . since there were two of us . . .

I sold a few things—we both did. I sold a few little quizzes and anecdotes, a story here and there. One publication sent me a check for $1.50. Not exactly the big time. Still, every acceptance made the dream of a life as a free-lance writer that tiny bit more real.

Then I was pregnant again—despite the scorn of a friend who told me I evidently didn't care about overpopulating the world. Yes, I did! Only I so much wanted another baby. I was restless during that pregnancy, I didn't sleep well and often found myself in the middle of the night, wandering forlornly around the house, wondering what to do all by myself. Maybe I should put in some time writing? Weird hour, but since I was awake . . .

I suggested to Harry that he might want to get up with me in the middle of the night and write, too. Just think, I said, how tired you are at night after working all day. How hard it is to sit there and put the words down on paper. Now think how good you feel in the morning, how much energy you have then.

We began to get up at 3:30 A.M. and write for the two or three hours before the official day began. We did this for almost a year. The dark winter mornings were the hardest times.

And then something unexpected happened. A few years before, there had been an accident. I had been driving with my mother and a couple of my kids when another car ran a stop sign and slammed into us on the driver's side. My kids and my mother were okay. I came out with an enormous bruise on my left hip and a whiplash that affected me off and on for the next fifteen years. That was the bad news. The good news was that, now, there was a settlement—twenty-five hundred dollars. It seemed like a fortune to us. With care, day-old bread, and thrift-shop clothes, we could live on that for six months.

Gina, our fourth child, was two months old. We had four children under the age of ten and twenty-five hundred dollars. Harry left his job in the factory and we became free-lance writers. It was mildly terrifying. I had some days when I sat in front of the typewriter and shook because I couldn't think of what to write next.

We decided we would write for the women's romance and confession market. It was a steady, reliable market that needed plenty of stories and the bulk of the stories, despite lurid titles, were stories of relationships: men and women, parents and children, brothers and sisters. Someone—the narrator or the chief character—made a mistake, did something wrong, "sinned." Every action had a reaction, a consequence. The world of these stories was strict and moral. Being human, a character would surely do wrong, but never go unpunished, unrepentant or, finally, unenlightened.

The stories were all published without a byline. They were all written in the first person and the readers were meant to think that the events of the stories had been lived by the "people" who wrote them. Eventually there were issues of magazines in which as many as three or four stories had been written by Harry and/or me. One story might be in the voice of a sixteen-year-old girl, another in the voice of a thirty-five-year-old woman, and still another "by" a nineteen-year-old boy.

The stories were typically about five thousand words long and paid by the word—two to five cents per word. To earn enough for our family, week in and week out, for years, each of us wrote a story. Coming up with ideas and writing at that pace meant long hours and no days off. Early on, we got the habit of writing seven days a week. But it also meant doing what I wanted to do and learning while I was doing it. Writing story after story forced me to learn how a story is constructed, how to hold a reader's attention, how to write dialogue and narration, how to do simple, yet previously baffling things like transitions.

We tried other kinds of writing: short stories, screenplays, a first attempt at a novel for children. We were both anxious to break out of romance writing, but not at all tired of living the life of free-lance writers. Although my housekeeping had gone steadily downhill since I went to work side by side with Harry to earn our living, my spirits had gone steadily uphill. But I was still dreaming about the future. If only I had the time to write a novel . . . One little problem: to write a novel, I needed time away from the pulp fiction. To get that time, I needed money. To get money, I had to write the pulp fiction. For some years, it was our own version of Catch-22.

Then in 1970 I scraped together the time to write *I, Trissy.* I had fun writing that book. I used a variety of literary techniques to tell the story of a girl who was quite stubbornly unhappy about her parents' separation. Trissy, volatile, spirited, and outspoken, seemed to me entirely unlike myself. (But now, I think perhaps Trissy is not so much the me I never was, as the me I had actually once been and forgotten about. As a little kid, I hear, I was fearless, curious, a bit of a daredevil. At barely three years old I strapped on roller skates and whizzed down a long, very steep hill. I was on the go, ran into things, fell over steps—my mother called me Miss Trip and Fall—always had bruised knees. Once I climbed up onto the broad marble windowsill of a butcher shop to investigate and caught myself on a meat hook right below the eye.)

In December of 1970 I sent the manuscript of *I, Trissy* off to my agent and prepared myself for a long wait, a long series of submissions and rejections. I expected to wait at least one year, possibly two years. But Delacorte Press accepted the manuscript less than a month later. And about a month after that, they also accepted Harry's first book, *Guy Lenny.* Both books were published in the fall of 1971.

Out in Arizona, a reviewer found *I, Trissy* "funny and heartbreaking," and in Kansas another reviewer said it was "the soul of childhood." But some people were quite sincerely upset by Trissy. A reviewer in Texas found it to be a "disgusting story." Another thought Trissy was "severely disturbed" because she destroyed a chocolate cake her father's girlfriend had baked for him. My Trissy "severely disturbed"? A book I wrote "disgusting"? That hurt. But to write for yourself is one thing, to publish, another. Publishing means putting yourself out there on the shooting range. You've made that choice and you've either got to live with it and go on writing, or give up publishing.

Two years after *I, Trissy* came *A Figure of Speech.* This was quite a different book from *I, Trissy,* much more of a real novel—longer, more serious, more sustained. I remember meeting a member of the National Book Award Committee some time after *A Figure of Speech* had received a National Book Award nomination and hearing him say to me, ". . . and you just came out of nowhere." I laughed. My "nowhere" had been the ten years I'd spent writing full time and learning the craft.

I went on writing pulp fiction to earn money, squeezing in time here and there to write my books. For a long time I had been fascinated by the lives of tribal peoples. I had read and reread Colin Turnbull's *The Gentle People* about the pygmies of the Ituri Forest, and Laurens van der Post on the Bushmen of the Kalihari. And always, as I read, the thought behind my eyes was, What if I could live with these people? What would life be like for me?

Then, by chance, I saw a film on public TV about

the discovery of a group of Stone-Age people, the Tasaday, on the Philippine island of Mindanao. The Tasaday lived in caves, quiet, gentle, gathering their food; one generation after another had gone on without change for ten thousand years.

Watching the Tasaday, I almost jumped out of my skin with excitement. That night I couldn't sleep and began to imagine a story about a girl, an ordinary girl from this world of ours, somehow finding herself among Stone-Age people. It would be utterly different from my first two books, a time-travel book, aspects of science fiction and fantasy, a book as far from "reality" as the Stone-Age people were from our twentieth century.

It was not an easy book to write. I researched, mostly by reading the reports of anthropologists who had lived with tribal peoples. I wrote and rewrote. The manuscript was rejected and I had the first anxiety attack of my life, sitting up in bed at night, gasping for air, wondering if I could carry off this story. I've written ten books since then but none as difficult as *Saturday, the Twelfth of October*. It's unlike any of my books and it's one of my favorites.

After *Saturday*, I wanted very much to write some short stories and hoped Delacorte would publish them as a collection. Some of these stories had been waiting around for at least fifteen years for me to write them, but when I mentioned this project to my editor, his first reaction was negative. "Kids," he said, "don't read short stories. Short stories are shelf-sitters. Everyone knows this." But, thinking about it, he went on to say, "Well, maybe now's the time for a change. Why don't you go ahead and write them."

The short stories I wrote became the book *Dear Bill, Remember Me?* It was a New York Times Notable Book, a School Library Journal Notable Book, an American Library Association Best Book for Young Adults. It won a Christopher Medal and a Lewis Carroll Shelf Award.

But better than all that is a battered, coverless paperback copy of *Dear Bill* that I keep on my desk. A fourteen-year-old girl I met one day in a school wrote in it, "Dear Mrs. Mazer, We liked your book so much over 52 people read this book. Amy Sue Lewis and Friends."

And something else about that book: during the months I spent working on the stories, I somehow lost the secret fear that I was only masquerading as a writer. For the first time, I began to believe fearlessly in the endless vitality of that mysterious source from which my imagination is constantly replenished. Writers have different names for it. Some call it dipping into the well. Some speak of being guided by another hand, or simply putting down what a voice tells them

to. I've heard my husband refer to it as though it were a buried coil of rope on which he pulls, bringing out one surprise after another, and no one more surprised by the surprises than he.

By the time *Dear Bill* was published, I had been free-lancing for thirteen years. These years had made enormous differences in our family. Our "baby" was now thirteen years old. Anne and Joe were both young adults and mostly living elsewhere. We were, on a daily basis, a two child family.

We all loved the country. It was an annual rite of spring for us to mosey along back roads looking longingly at isolated farmhouses and vacant fields. After years of dreaming, we bought an old farmhouse for a weekend place. No windows, no plumbing, no heating, no electricity. Even the outhouse had fallen in on itself and was useless. We loved it. It took every cent we had to buy it, but we wanted it too much to care.

The farm appeased the ache inside me for the quiet and space of the country. For a year Harry and I and our two youngest daughters spent most of our weekends with crowbars and hammers, tearing out the insides of the farmhouse, putting in windows, and repairing the old porch. We made a rough camp, brought in a wood-burning stove, hung a wooden swing on the front porch, and read by lantern light at night.

We dug a pit for an outhouse. Anne brought up one of her boyfriends for an extra pair of hands, but as

At the farm: from left, Jean Fox, her daughter Norma and granddaughter Anne, 1970

Norma and her daughter, Gina, 1978

far as any of us can remember, all he did was lean against the old collapsed outhouse and look thoughtful. We borrowed a flatbed truck from my sister's husband and traveled twenty miles to bring back an outhouse. A three-seater, complete with door and windows. It took five of us to load it on the truck. The road was rutty from spring mud. Halfway back, Gina looked out the window. "Mom, the outhouse is falling off the truck."

We stopped and the four of us shoved it back on. Back at the farmhouse, we had to get the monster off the truck and over the hole we'd dug. I believe one of my nephews stopped by to help with that.

This farmhouse was the model for the house Jenny Pennoyer and Grandpa go to in *A Figure of Speech.* Some of the stories Grandpa tells about his visits to his grandparents on the farm in his youth were stories told me by the previous owner. His grandparents had been turkey farmers and I named the hill in the book Turkey Hill Farm.

One weekend Gina brought one of her friends up to visit. Amy didn't like our farm. She didn't like the kerosene lanterns or the cots we slept on or that we didn't have running water. She especially didn't like our outhouse. She said her camp was much better and

that was where she wanted to go. Right away.

Amy said it was easy to find her camp. You drive up to the border, go through Canadian customs, take the road that goes to the right, drive until you see the big stone that's painted yellow like an egg, make a right turn, then look for the tree with the funny branches . . . Somehow we found Amy's camp. Her directions were okay. And Amy was right about her camp, too. Her camp was much better than ours. Running water, electricity, a real toilet. In fact, it wasn't much of a camp, more like a house. We didn't fall in love with Amy's camp, but we did fall in love with Canada. The lakes bordered with pine forests reminded me of the Adirondack Mountains and unexpectedly a wave of passionate longing and nostalgia took hold of me.

We started looking for Canadian lake property that we could afford. Actually we couldn't afford anything. Within the past couple of years we had moved to another house and bought the farm, both of which had stretched our always shaky finances to the limit. Nevertheless, we found and fell in love with seventeen acres of Canadian scrub and woods on a rocky cliff one hundred feet above a tiny lake. Getting down to the water meant slipping, sliding, and scrambling down the rocky slope. Hardly prime lake frontage. We didn't care. We gave the agent ten dollars, all the money we had with us that day, as earnest money, put our farm up for sale, and remortgaged our house.

To get to the land, we drove two miles through fields and woods. The road ended about a quarter mile away from the spot between two enormous white pines where we wanted to put our camp. We hauled in everything on our backs and in our arms, from tents to boats to a picnic table. We hacked out a path down the slope to the water and talked about building log-and-stone steps. We were besotted with joy. So much land. So much space and quiet. The water, clean and cool as velvet, reminded me of childhood in the Adirondacks. We cooked outdoors, in April with frozen fingers, slept outside, too, until the no-see-ums in May and the mosquitoes in July drove us into the tents.

After a couple years of tenting, we built a little bunkhouse for our daughters. About the size of a rug, eight by twelve. I'd never built anything, never handled tools. I learned something about tools and a whole lot about feeling "dumb" and insufficient.

That summer the mice were everywhere, running under our picnic table like chipmunks, nesting in sneakers and my ancient Smith Corona. We wanted to mouseproof the building and headed for the nearest dump to pick up some scrap metal. There we found not only old tin roofing and Coca Cola signs to nail to the underside of our building, but a dump that was astonishingly neat, orderly, and fly-free. When I drafted *Mrs. Fish, Ape, and Me, the Dump Queen* a few summers later, that dump became the prototype of the dump Ape cared for.

Memories of other books are all tied up with summers at camp. A lot of the feeling about living in the weather that I got into *Saturday, the Twelfth of October* came from camp. Harry and I worked on a revision of *The Solid Gold Kid* together at camp, passing the sheets of manuscript and then galleys back and forth across the picnic table. It was there I drafted *When We First Met*, a further story about Jenny Pennoyer, and it was there I wrote a fair number of the stories for my second short-story collection, *Summer Girls, Love Boys*.

Almost since the publication of *Dear Bill, Remember Me?* I'd kept a folder of short-story ideas, sometimes no more than an odd phrase that appealed to me like "my crazy aunt." This turned out to be the germ of a story about an eccentric aunt and her too-sensible niece, "Amelia Earhart, Where Are You When I Need You?"

I rewrite a great deal on the novels—some have been completely rewritten five or six times—but I tend to get the short stories right much faster. "Dear Bill, Remember Me?," the title story of the first collection, which has been reprinted numerous times, was hardly touched after the draft. I often "hear" the first line of a story and then the rest follows. I remember writing "Down Here on Greene Street" and "Avie Loves Ric Forever" that way. On the other hand, "Summer Girls, Love Boys," the title story, went through about six drafts over a period of as many years, and "Carmella, Adelina, and Florry" was a story I tried to write in various ways for over twenty years.

I wrote more books: *Up in Seth's Room, Someone to Love, Downtown, Taking Terri Mueller*. Each one, in its own way, took me over. I lived in the world I was creating; it became real to me. Sometimes I'm asked about "writer's block." I don't have it and I don't fear it. Those years of writing pulp fiction taught me that there are always more words. And writing my novels taught me that there are things inside me waiting to come out that I hardly know are there.

I write every day when I'm home. I go down to my office as early as possible—sometimes, if I can't sleep, at that old 3:30 A.M. time. I love the morning. I write between four and six hours a day. Over the years I've gone from that green notebook to a manual typewriter to an electric typewriter to a word processor. I usually work from eight months to a year on a book. Most of that time is spent rewriting. A draft—a first writing—takes no more than a couple of months. I enjoy it for a little while and then come to a point where all I want is to get it finished. What I really like is the rewriting, when I can tinker around and get everything just right.

When *Taking Terri Mueller* won an Edgar from the

Norma and Harry, in Canada, 1982

Mystery Writers Association of America, I was both delighted and astonished. I had not written it as a mystery. Of course there is a mystery in it—Terri's present life with her father and her past—but there's a kind of mystery in every book: I write and my readers read to find out the answers to questions, secrets, problems, to be drawn into the deepest mystery of all—someone else's life.

I get a fair number of letters from readers. Sometimes they strike a deep note. A child wrote me recently about *Mrs. Fish, Ape, and Me, the Dump Queen.* "I hope," she wrote, "you now your book discribes my life!" My book couldn't possibly have described her life, not in a literal sense, since that life didn't exist until I imagined it and put it down on paper. But that child knew what she was talking about. She meant the life she lived in her mind and emotions and imagination.

Sometimes I wonder at myself, an adult sitting here at my desk, making up stories, creating little worlds. But I can't imagine living without writing. I can't imagine any other way I want to live. I have a Steig cartoon pasted in front of one of my notebooks. It shows an ape, decked out in trousers and a shirt, sitting on a wooden bench in front of a simple wooden table. There's an inkpot on the table, a partially peeled banana. The ape has a pen in her hand and, with an expression of utmost gravity and slightly wry perplexity, she's writing away on a sheet of paper. Probably because she's a writing ape and doesn't know how to do anything else. I scribbled my name across the front of her shirt.

BIBLIOGRAPHY

FOR YOUNG ADULTS

Fiction:

I, Trissy. New York: Delacorte, 1971.

A Figure of Speech. New York: Delacorte, 1973.

Saturday, the Twelfth of October. New York: Delacorte, 1975.

Dear Bill, Remember Me? and Other Stories (includes *Mimi the Fish*). New York: Delacorte, 1976.

The Solid Gold Kid, with husband, Harry Mazer. New York: Delacorte, 1977.

Up in Seth's Room. New York: Delacorte, 1979.

Mrs. Fish, Ape, and Me, the Dump Queen. New York: Dutton, 1980.

Taking Terri Mueller. New York: Avon, 1981.

Summer Girls, Love Boys, and Other Short Stories (includes *Amelia Earhart, Where Are You When I Need You?*; *Avie Loves Ric Forever*; *Carmella, Adelina, and Florry*; *Down Here on Greene Street*; and *Why Was Elena Crying?*). New York: Delacorte, 1982.

When We First Met. New York: Four Winds, 1982.

Someone to Love. New York: Delacorte, 1983.

Downtown. New York: Morrow, 1984.

Supergirl. New York: Warner Books, 1984.

Milton Meltzer

1915-

I was born on May 8, 1915, in Worcester, Massachusetts. Woodrow Wilson was serving his first term as President. The Woolworth Building, the tallest in the world at that time, had just gone up and Grand Central Terminal had recently opened. Henry Ford had started the first assembly line to produce his Tin Lizzies. The first transcontinental telephone call was made that year by the same two men who had made the original phone connection back in 1876. Then they had been in the next room to each other. Now one was in New York and the other in San Francisco.

The day before my birth, a German submarine had sunk the steamship *Lusitania,* drowning many Americans. The anger roused by those deaths helped push America into the first World War. And from that time to now, I've lived through four major American wars and a lot of minor ones.

I'm sure war was one of the reasons I was born in America rather than in Europe. Poverty and discrimination were the other reasons. My parents both came from Austro-Hungary. They were among the four million Jews who left Eastern Europe between 1880 and 1924. Over three million of them came to the United States.

Tens of thousands of Jews were killed in the pogroms of that era. Millions of others were victims of a "cold" pogrom. By that I mean the growing body of restrictive laws directed against the Jews. In Czarist Russia ninety percent of the Jews were penned-up in a huge ghetto called the Pale of Settlement. They were humiliated and hounded by hundreds of restrictions. A terrible burden for them was the military draft for a term of twenty-five years or more.

Quotas barred all but a few Russian Jews from the schools and universities. Jews had little choice not only about where to live but how they could make a living. The vast majority starved in the villages or in the city slums.

My mother and father were raised just across the Russian border, in the Austro-Hungarian provinces of Galicia and Bukovina. There the Jews were not quite as badly off. They too knew poverty, although their political and civil disabilities were not so harsh. Samuel Richter, my grandfather on my mother's side, decided America was the place to raise his children, not Gali-

cia. (Galicia had been a part of Poland until that kingdom vanished, its pieces taken over by three other countries. Galicia in 1772 became part of Austria.) So he got up from the village of Skoryk and left. Imagine the courage it took for a young father to make that decision. To quit the place you grew up in, to leave your wife and children behind, to cross strange land for a distant seaport, then to take steerage passage across the frightening Atlantic and, at the other end of a harsh voyage, drop like some anonymous atom into the vast chaos of New York. Where would you find a place to sleep? What could you do to make a living? How would you make yourself understood in a language you didn't know?

Benjamin and Mary Meltzer

It was 1895 when my grandfather came to New York. He went back to Skoryk in 1897. I don't know why. Lonely? Unable to earn and save enough in New York to bring the others over? Two years later he tried again. And the next year, 1900, his daughter Mary, my mother, followed him. She was fourteen then, the oldest of her many sisters and brothers, a capable girl with enormous energy and will. Together she and my grandfather in 1905 managed to bring over her mother Rachel and the rest of the big family.

My father, Benjamin Meltzer, born in 1879, came from a farm family in the village of Havrilesht in the Austro-Hungarian province of Bukovina. The Jews of Bukovina—the land of the beech trees—had settled there long ago, the first of them probably arriving together with the legions of Imperial Rome. The family name was originally spelled "Melzer"; when or why the "t" was added I don't know. The family kept an inn for some time but then gave it up to farm a small number of acres. They lived in a two-room house, with a cellar and attic, and a barn for the livestock. The house was wooden, with a straw roof. They lived on what they raised, and on the sale of cattle and poultry. My father, I learned from his sister many years later, was an expert farmhand and so strong he could lift a hundred-kilo load of grain as though it were a feather. Their village held about twenty Jewish families and some four hundred Ukrainian peasants. The two groups lived much the same lives, except for religious differences. Anti-Semitism lay underneath, but was restrained somewhat under the Austrian rule. My father's education was limited to the compulsory public elementary school, where everything was taught in Ukrainian, the local tongue.

My father was the eldest of five brothers and two sisters. But the first to emigrate was his brother Max. He left for America to avoid military service. Then, at eighteen, my father followed, reaching New York in 1897. Later his brother Joseph and Vitya, one of his sisters, came too. But his mother Leah and father Michael did not come. Probably because my grandmother was very pious and feared an America where many Jews lost their religious faith. Later, when she was ready to go, it was too late. Restrictive immigration quotas made it impossible. My grandfather Michael, at fifty-three, was killed by Russian soldiers when they invaded the region in the first World War. His death came in 1915, the year of my birth. Leah died in Bukovina in 1947, at the age of ninety-four. After he left home my father never saw them again.

Mary and Ben met in New York. She worked in the garment industry, he in a bedspring factory. I think he was a boarder in my grandparents' flat in the Bronx. They married and had their first child, my

brother Allan, in 1911. Then they heard that a better living might be made in Worcester. A cousin living in Boston told them that window-cleaners—a trade that required almost no training—were in short supply there. So my family moved to Worcester. With them came my uncle Joe (my father's brother) and my aunt Gussie (my mother's sister). The two families settled on the east side of town—the immigrant and working-class district—and Ben and Joe began cleaning windows. It was a business partnership with no workers but themselves. For some reason I never could determine, the two brothers fell out, ended their partnership, and stopped speaking. Their wives maintained their sisterly closeness, and their children too (three sons on our side and three on theirs) remained friendly.

My father made a modest living, though the manual labor was harsh and unrewarding in any other way. He washed the windows of factories, stores, restaurants, offices, and homes. His day usually began around two in the morning, and often did not end until late afternoon. He rose early to go downtown to the city center where he cleaned windows before the places opened up for business. Afternoons he went to private homes on the West Side, where the well-to-do could afford to have their windows done. No matter how cold or raw the weather my father was on the job, dipping his hands all day long in icy water. I remember how rough and blackened his hands were, ridged and cracked by that brutal exposure and by the many glass cuts he suffered.

My mother ran the household—cooking, baking, cleaning, washing, sewing, shopping, worrying. She was a super-organized woman. Everything in its place, neat and clean; everything done to a plan and always on time. Her meals were always tasty and nourishing, and she often made the clothes her children wore, as well as her own. I loved to sport her handsome sweaters and mackinaws.

The three-decker house I was born in was at 2 Chapin Street, one block long, atop a steep hill. Right across the street was the grammar school I'd go to, Union Hill School. And taking up many acres on the hill was Worcester Academy, an old prep school drawing upper-class boys from all across the country. My father cleaned its windows. The place seemed so patrician to me that I hardly dared venture through the gates. The students lived in a remote dreamworld I identified with the Frank Merriwell stories I used to devour.

When I was about three we moved to the foot of Union Hill, to 52 Vale Street, another three-decker. This time we had the top floor, with a piazza, as we called it, out front where you could read or nap or sun yourself. It's the time of my youth I remember best. I didn't leave there until I went off to college in 1932.

Our neighborhood held all the ingredients of the mythical melting pot. There were Italians, Poles, Swedes, Lithuanians, Irish, Armenians, and Jews like us from Eastern Europe. Many of the parents were recent immigrants. The kids were almost all first-generation, born in America. We played on the streets together; less often we entered one another's homes; and rarely if ever did we intermarry.

My younger brother, Marshall, was born when I was five. That was the year I began climbing the steep slope to go to Union Hill school. It was a three-story reddish stone building, and looked as though it had squatted there forever. My brother Allan, going on nine then, took me the first day, and long after enjoyed telling how I cried piteously when he left me with my teacher. The crying must have stopped quickly, for I took to school as though born to learn. I liked everything about it—learning to read, to write, to figure, to find out where Worcester sat on the map of the world, to play the part of Chief Massasoit when he greeted the first white settlers.

Meltzer in grammar school, early 1920s

There were few teachers I didn't like. All of them were women. Many of them came from the best women's colleges in New England. None of them were married. (I don't think it was allowed then.) The principal was a plump majestic woman named Miss Draper; we thought it hugely funny to refer to her secretly as "Old Dropperdrawers."

After school we played games on the street—Prisoner's Base, Ringelevio, King of the Mountain. In the long Massachusetts winters we took out our Flexible Flyers to coast down Union Hill, belly-whopping alone or two sitting up. The street would be closed to traffic to protect us. But once in a while there was delicious danger. I remember a truck suddenly appearing out of a side street and my sled zipping under it and on down to the end where I offered myself to the other kids as a hero. (Back then, by the way, horses still drew the wagons that delivered ice and milk and coal.)

Just back of Vale Street was a vast open area called Cheney's Field. It was a bit marshy, and in the winter if it rained and then a freeze set in, the whole field was sheeted ice. Glorious for skating. In good weather we played football or baseball there. I was feeble at either sport. My game turned out to be tennis. I learned it on the dirt courts of Vernon Hill playground. None of us had money for lessons. We learned by playing, and picked up bad habits that persisted for a long time. Though I find I can overcome some of them even now, at this age, when I still play regularly.

Summers some of us would hitch rides to Lake Quinsigamond. It was several miles long and magnificently straight for the intercollegiate crew races and the Olympic sculling trials we loved to watch. The city set aside Lake Park for a public beach and playground. We swam out to the raft and spent hours throwing one

Meltzer (left), with his brother, Allan

another off and jumping in on top.

After elementary school I went to the Grafton Street Junior High, brand-new then. I was twelve when I began junior high. It was 1927, the year Charles Lindbergh flew the Atlantic solo, in his little one-engine plane, *The Spirit of St. Louis.* I still remember the wild excitement when we heard he had made it. Airplanes were so rare then that whenever a plane droned overhead we'd run into the street and scream "Aeroplane! Aeroplane!", pointing to it in the sky. Lindy was our national hero overnight. He rose even higher in public worship than Babe Ruth or Jack Dempsey.

Grafton Junior High was a sprawling brick building with so many rooms and corridors it intimidated me after the coziness of Union Hill. But here I met boys and girls from other neighborhoods and discovered I could fall in love with almost any girl. In grade school I was mad for a girl named Gertrude and used to follow her home, at a safe distance, and wait patiently outside for hours in the hope of glimpsing her again. By the time I was ten we were going to Saturday afternoon parties in the girls' homes, chiefly to play kissing games. At junior high I was less shy, and developed crushes, first on a Polish girl, then an Italian girl, a Swedish girl, and a Russian girl. I felt like the ambassador to all nations.

We learned what was going on in the world from the newspapers and the radio. The radio at first was a tiny crystal set. I'd poke the wiry whisker around to touch the crystal at whatever point it would produce words or music. Later we got a Silver-Marshall radio, built into a glossy wood cabinet. It was almost the sole entertainment my father had. He loved the comedians—Jack Benny, Lou Holtz, Ed Wynn—and never missed their weekly shows. I can't forget the hearty laughter they brought from a man who rarely talked. I don't recall having a single conversation with him. He was gone most of the day and when he was at home, he ate, read the paper, listened to the radio, and went to bed early so that he could get up in the middle of the night to start work again.

Once in a while my Uncle Joe, who had a car (we didn't), took us with his family to swim, or for a picnic somewhere. My father never came along. Because he didn't like such excursions? Or because he wouldn't accept anything from the brother he didn't speak to? Once my Uncle Joe drove us to New York. It took endless hours because the Boston Post Road was so primitive and tires blew out each way. In my grandparents' crowded Bronx flat we kids slept on the floor, explored the neighborhood, and got to know the many aunts and uncles we rarely saw. My Uncle Harry took me to Yankee Stadium to see a big league game, and put me in a box seat right behind the Yankee dugout. I don't remember the game at all; I do recall that Walter Winchell, the gossip columnist everyone listened to on the radio or read in the papers, sat near us. I couldn't wait to get back to Worcester to tell my gang.

It was around this time that I began to work. We three sons were all expected to pitch in and help. I had a newspaper route for a while, and signed up enough new customers to win a beautiful red scooter. A little later, I got a job in a wholesale grocery. After school and on Saturdays I worked in the warehouse, moving packing cases and cartons around with a hand truck. It was hard and dull work, with no one to talk to. The pay was fifteen cents an hour. I gave the pay envelope to my mother each week and she let me have a bit of it for spending money.

A much better job was one I had in summertime. I helped deliver milk on a neighborhood route. I got up hours before dawn, dressed and slipped downstairs to the street where the driver waited for me. When he stopped the truck I'd balance on the tailboard, lean into the truck, grab a metal rack, fill it with bottles and jump down, taking the customers on one side of the street while he'd take the other side. One bottle on the first floor for the widow Polasewicz, up the stairs and five bottles for the big Murphy family, another flight for two milks and the cream that Mrs. Gould had to have. Then clattering down the steps, picking up the empties on the way, back into the truck, stow the empties on one side, and load another rack for the next three-decker.

Here and there we'd stop at grocery stores to drop off cases of milk in their doorways. Best part of the night was around 4:00 A.M., when we'd both feel hungry and we'd swipe a fresh-baked loaf from the basket the bakery truck would leave at the grocery, and tear off big mouthfuls, washing down the delicious crusts of warm bread with swigs of cold milk.

With the small change I was allowed to keep I used to buy the nickel or dime paperbacks of that day—Nick Carter, Frank Merriwell, Horatio Alger, Deadwood Dick. If you managed to acquire a modest stock you could barter them for other titles your friends owned. I read a marvelous amount of trash and loved it. Then there was the more sober stuff you ran across by chance. One neighbor had an encyclopedia I would browse through when my parents dragged me along on visits to their friends. Another had a stout medical book with illustrations of the human anatomy. These I studied with great care, astonished, and disturbed too, at the differences between male and female. My father bought on Sundays a newspaper with a fat rotogravure supplement. Its illustrated features were a window onto a world remote from Vale Street and Union Hill. Its vivid stories of the opening of King Tut's tomb or the flight of Admiral Byrd over the North Pole enriched the news that trickled in over our crystal set.

But the first reading I can remember enjoying was "Gasoline Alley," a comic strip that began appearing in our local paper when I must have just learned to read. The newspaper was the only thing to read in our house. My folks had no time or money for books. They spoke immigrant English which improved with time. Somehow they never turned on to books, although they delighted to see their children take up reading.

Then I found out about the public library, a jumble of old red brick downtown. Saturdays became a double delight. I began them at the library, yanking books off shelves at random, sampling everything. I lugged them long blocks down to the movie theater we called The Dump, where I'd see the latest Charlie Chaplin, Tarzan, and Pearl White while I ate a hot dog and gulped down chocolate milk. And home at last to hole up in the bedroom and read myself into a daze.

What I liked most were adventure stories that took me out of my skin. And biographies. I was always trying on a new hero for size—explorer, reporter, detective. Reading had much to do with shaping my picture of the world as I grew up. Perhaps as much as the real world itself. Thoreau says in *Walden,* "How many a man has dated a new era in his life from the reading of a book!" I remember some books, read in youth, which gave me the sense of awakening Thoreau speaks of. There was *Leaves of Grass, Spoon River Anthology* and the short stories of Sherwood Anderson, *Of Human Bondage, The Way of All Flesh, An American Tragedy,* Sandburg's *Lincoln,* the autobiographies of Clarence Darrow and Lincoln Steffens. I stumbled across them or someone told me to try them. I spent no time analyzing them. It was enough that they spoke directly to me. Here were words that I could use to shape my own experience.

I think now I got more out of my independent reading than out of my studies in school. When I look back at the schools I went to they seem like some kind of mildly totalitarian society. Benevolent, yes, but nonetheless lacking in all democracy. The principal ordered the teachers around and they ordered the pupils around. The only responsibility we were given was to come to class, to come on time, and to do our assignments. Almost no one back then protested. With exceptions—my brother Allan among them. He couldn't stand the discipline of school and was expelled from two or three of them. (At fifteen he ran away from home, but returned a year later.) The rest of us ex-

pected to be treated as obedient children, and it is no wonder that we were.

I have another major gripe against the schools of my day. They were hell-bent on Americanizing us. A great many of the students were first-generation Americans like me. Yet implicit in the way we were taught was the belief that we should drop whatever made us different, forget where our parents came from, what they brought with them, their own feelings and experience, their own beliefs and values. Our job was to become one hundred percent Americans. That was the only way to make it here, we understood. So while I diligently studied the history of ancient Greece and Rome (and enjoyed it!), I learned nothing about the Eastern Europe where my roots lay. I identified far more with England; that was the literature and the history we studied. Anglo-Saxon culture was everything; where we came from was nothing.

My parents fell in readily with this. Allowed only a few years of schooling in the old country, they were in a grand rush to become Americans. They did not want to be ridiculed as greenhorns, and since Yiddish was the badge of foreignness, they spoke so little of it at home that I learned scarcely a word of it. Nor did they tell me anything about their own early lives. Perhaps because they wanted to forget the world they had left behind. Or because they knew I had no interest in their culture. I didn't realize until much later how much meaning their early life would have for me. When at last I had the sense to want to know about it, it was too late. They were gone.

Whatever being Jewish meant to my mother and father they took for granted. (They were not observant; rarely, if ever, went to the synagogue.) It was passed on unself-consciously to their sons. They did not talk about it. Still, their behavior—the way they moved, walked, laughed, cried, talked—their attitudes, the way our family functioned, imprinted upon us something of the social history they brought with them.

I learned what it was to be a Jew mostly in the negative sense: the insults voiced, the jobs denied, the neighborhoods restricted, the club doors closed, the colleges on quotas. And our history as Jews—anniversaries of catastrophes, expulsions, wholesale murder. No wonder an alarm bell rang when I heard the word "Jew" in an unexpected setting. It might be the sound of the word slashing into my ear while playing basketball in the YMCA gym or swimming in its pool. Or the sight of those three letters on the page of a book I was reading. When we studied Walter Scott's *Ivanhoe* in school I was captivated by the marvelous story he told. But jolted by his many references to Jews as usurers, liars, hypocrites, as covetous, contemptible, inhuman. Most readers remember his sympathetic portrayal of

Rebecca, and forget the rest.

Dickens's *Oliver Twist* was another novel that absorbed me for its portrait of the dark places of London. But the shadow of Fagin, that "villainous-looking, repulsive, greasy, shrivelled old Jew," fell over everything in the story. And then there was Shakespeare's *The Merchant of Venice,* a play read in my high school English class. We played the parts and discussed the story. My teacher made us feel how superb the poetry was, but she said nothing of Shylock as Jew, or how the medieval mind could breed such abuse of and contempt for a whole people.

Not till the 1970s did I do any systematic reading in the history of the Jews. It came about when an editor asked me to write a children's book about the Jews in America. I took it on because I knew so little, and realized at last that I needed to learn so much. Writing a book was the best way to do that. The uncovering of a vast collective memory was so exciting I went on to write several more books about aspects of Jewish life and history.

I don't remember how it happened, but when I reached my last year in junior high I was elected class president. It meant a brief moment of glory at graduation. I was awed to share the platform with our principal, a huge white-haired old man who often reminded us that he had been a drummer boy in the Civil War. (That war ended only fifty years before I was born.)

I moved on to Classical High School. Most of my classmates went instead to commercial or technical or vocational high schools. Classical was the college prep school. We had no money, and college seemed a very dim prospect for me, especially in a time when only a tiny fraction of all young people got a higher education. Most of them were middle or upper class. America had almost no free city colleges and the state universities usually stressed agricultural studies. Still, I simply took for granted that somehow I *would* go to college. I knew my parents expected it, probably because my marks were so good and I liked to read and study. None of our family on either side had ever gone to college. My older brother went to work after being expelled from high school.

I started at Classical in September of 1929. The next month the stock market collapsed and the Great Depression began. Our family did not go broke. We started broke. We owned no stocks and didn't know what they were. All we owned were our clothes and furniture. The shock spread rapidly from Wall Street to the poorest unskilled worker. By the end of my first year at Classical seven million were out of work. By the time I graduated the number was fifteen million.

Meltzer at high school graduation, 1932

As factories cut down production and stores were boarded up, there were few windows for my father to clean. He was home more and more for lack of work. Extra jobs were hard to find. But I managed to help out with a Saturday job in a cheap shoe store on Front Street. Twelve hours for two dollars. My mother was a good manager and we never went hungry. Food was cheaper then and the Depression drove prices even lower. Eggs were nineteen cents a dozen, bread a nickel a loaf, beef eleven cents a pound.

Fathers in our neighborhood were out of work for months, for years. And there was no relief but private charity. Breadlines. Soup kitchens. President Hoover could only urge people to tighten their belts. By my last year in high school, one-fourth of the nation's families had no regular income.

The windows in the high school grew so filthy you could hardly see the girls passing by on the sidewalk. First the school board had cut down on maintenance, then they stopped buying books and supplies, and soon there was a rumor there wouldn't be money for teachers' pay.

At Classical the men and women who taught us were pretty good. Again, many of them were the product of first-class colleges. Their methods were traditional; nothing experimental. But if you cared to, you could learn a great deal in a systematic way. The best teacher by far was Anna Shaughnessy, a graduate of Radcliffe College. She was Irish Catholic, young, tall, very thin, wore glasses, had a reserved manner but somehow gave out warmth. And she was brilliant. No student ever forgot her. She made you think, she encouraged you to read. Conversation with her helped you to develop ideas and to talk more intelligently. She was my teacher for only two years but those years meant a great deal in the rest of my life. English was her subject. She challenged everyone to do better, knowing how little use we made of our capacities. And most of us responded. In my day we couldn't get enough of her in the classroom. So some of us asked if she'd meet with us each week outside school and let us discuss with her some book we'd all read. She agreed, and we haughtily dubbed ourselves The Club.

It was now that I began to take writing more seriously, doing pieces for the school paper and the literary magazine. Miss Shaughnessy's criticism was always to the point and moved me to try to do better. I joined the debating club too, and began to feel more at ease in the school. When I entered Classical, I was pretty dismayed by how different most of the students were from me. They had Anglo-Saxon names, they dressed elegantly, they spoke a precise English, they played different games, they went to country club dances. I felt alien to all that and wondered what their homelife was like. I soon found they were no brighter or dumber than the rest of us. But they had "class." They took good living for granted. I envied them, and feared them a little, too.

When I fell in love with one of them I couldn't believe she returned my affection. Her name was Dorothy—a tall, slim, dark-haired girl, with huge amber eyes, quiet in manner but intense in feeling. We discovered in class that we shared many of the same interests. She joined The Club too, and we began seeing each other outside school. She lived on the "right" side of town, and came from a Protestant middle-class family. I could never ask her to my home. But she invited me to hers. It was a private home, full of books and records and magazines and with pictures on the walls. I was scared of meeting her parents but they were very welcoming. Dorothy took me to her church on a Sunday afternoon now and then. Not to services, but to young people's socials. Even so, I felt strange sitting there. We would often walk in Elm Park, a beautiful landscape on her side of town, with old trees and a winding stream. We talked, talked, talked, about everything and anything. No one at home ever did that, nor did any of my neighborhood friends.

I never mentioned her to my parents. Perhaps because I still felt bitter about the time a few years before

when I dated an Irish girl from our neighborhood. My mother heard about it from a local gossip while I was shopping with her in the corner grocery. She turned and in front of everyone slapped me hard.

Dorothy and I often went to the Worcester Art Museum. There I saw my first Impressionist paintings. Going into that gallery was like discovering what eyes are for. These artists painted the most joyous pictures, filled with light and color. It was like I had been born with dark glasses, and suddenly someone tore them off and let me see the whole shining world. When I looked at a Van Gogh painting of a man working in the fields, I wondered how he would have painted my father.

Another door to the arts opened for me when we went to the annual music festival to hear Serge Koussevitzky conduct the Boston Symphony. It was the first time I'd heard a symphony orchestra play, and the ecstatic feeling Mozart's *Eine Kleine Nachtmusik* gave me is still with me. I started to listen to classical music on the radio, and to read about composers and the forms they worked in.

At school the senior year came on. The local papers carried stories of worse unemployment and hunger. One student's father, a businessman gone broke, shot himself. A young actress who had gone off to Broadway full of hope and ambition came back to Worcester. She had failed to find even a walk-on role in a starving theatre. She sat at home a few weeks, then took the trolley out to Lake Quinsigamond, chopped a hole in the ice, and drowned herself. The owner of Thornby's, a downtown restaurant, disappeared, leaving a note for his wife, saying his debts had piled so high he could not go on. In school the talk was about the senior dance, the basketball games, electioneering for office. I made the yearbook board and was elected class prophet.

I didn't know what to do about college. For years I had thought I'd like to be a teacher. Miss Shaughnessy told me that Columbia University was launching an experimental college to train teachers in a different way. They were looking for candidates and promising some scholarships. She thought I'd like New York and that kind of school. I applied, was interviewed in Worcester, and accepted with a full scholarship and a job in the college dining room in exchange for all my meals. My father said he'd try to send me five dollars a week.

Dorothy decided to go to Antioch College. I never saw her again after graduation. Many years later I heard she had gone to England, married there, and died in World War II.

Before starting at New College I spent the summer in New York. I lived with family and earned money doing unskilled work in an uncle's garment factory.

Riding down to work each morning I saw strung along the Hudson River shore hundreds of shacks made of tin cans, packing crates, cardboard, and old tar paper. They were no bigger than chicken coops, these rent-free homes, and their tenants named them Hoovervilles in honor of the president.

I hated the garment job. The big workroom was hot, crowded, noisy, the pace feverish, and the seething ocean of people on the streets almost drowned me. I saw how frantically my uncle tried to keep the business from going under. Up in the Bronx where I stayed, nights were lonely. We worked Saturdays too and on Sunday I was too tired and blue to explore the city. But September of 1932 finally came. I moved into John Jay Hall on the campus, and started a different life.

We were a very small school, our classes and offices tucked into the buildings of Teachers College, the graduate school. Most of the staff were young, and eager to try something new. The few hundred students were largely New Yorkers, impossibly sophisticated, I thought. We were allowed to take courses almost anywhere in the university. I took full advantage of that and sat in the classes of such great people as Franz Boas, Ruth Benedict, and John Dewey. Our own teachers were open to friendships with students who interested them.

One of my teachers was Charles Obermeyer, a small, dark, wiry, intense man from South Africa, fluent in many languages and a marvelous talker. His lectures on literature sparkled with references from an encyclopedic knowledge. We all listened eagerly, afraid to miss the revelations and insights that came so fast. He was an influence upon me almost as great as Miss Shaughnessy.

Soon after school began, Roosevelt was elected President. While FDR and the country waited for the inauguration, Adolf Hitler took power in Germany. I remember a cold January night at a professor's apartment when we students hung over his shortwave radio, unable to believe the hysteria vomiting from Hitler's throat and the roar of his audience's response.

As Roosevelt took office the country dropped into the bottommost pit of the Depression. The whole banking system collapsed overnight. Millions more lost everything they had, and worst of all, their pride and self-respect. We were up against forces we could not identify, could not fight.

FDR promised "action and action now," and a "New Deal." He moved so swiftly and powerfully that it was possible to hope again. You could feel the excitement on the Columbia campus. Our university was among the many from which the president drew advisors to plan the major measures the Congress passed in his first hundred days. Dozens of our best brains moved into New Deal agencies.

I didn't follow every move the president made. I was on my own for the first time in my seventeen years, and that was troublesome enough. Everyone in my class was a stranger to me, and I did not make friends easily. Then there was New York itself, a monstrous city to a boy from a New England town.

But it didn't take me long to learn what joys it had to offer, even when you had no money. I often went to the theatre, waiting for the first act intermission, then sneaking from the lobby into an empty seat to see the rest of the play for nothing. That way I saw Dublin's Abbey players do most of Sean O'Casey and London's D'Oyly Carte do almost all of Gilbert and Sullivan. At a musical revue I first heard "Brother, Can You Spare a Dime," the song I borrowed thirty-seven years later as the title for my book on the Depression. I did pay to see Fred Astaire dance on the stage (balcony seats were fifty-five cents) in the last Broadway show he did before going off to Hollywood. His witty feet, his grace and delicacy could make me feel as debonair as a duke.

At college I roomed with Bernard Werthman, a man ten years older, who had given up a concert pianist's career because he wanted to teach music to children. He took this child's musical education in hand and brought me to hear many great soloists, such as Josef Hoffman and Walter Gieseking. We went to art galleries and museums together where I soaked up something of what he had learned from years spent in Europe. Through him I met many older friends who helped break down some of my provincial fears and uncertainties.

Part of the New College program called for students to spend a year working in industry or on a farm. I went back to Worcester for my sophomore year, living again at home, this time on View Street, where my family had recently moved. Somehow I found a miserable job in a factory, painting women's shoes with a spray gun.

Evenings I read voraciously, keeping careful notes to show my instructors. I meant to get credit not only for the year's industrial experience but for teaching myself in new fields. My file shows I read close to a book a day.

Busy as I was I had time to be lonely. My high school friends were now scattered. Then I met a girl who lived nearby and was commuting to a college in Boston. She was a year older. We shared many interests, including tennis. Soon we were spending all our spare hours together. Saturdays we might drive to Boston in her car to go to the theater. She herself acted in college plays. By the year's end we were in love.

In the fall of 1934 I returned to school which was now swept by feverish discussions. Many of my professors were either deeply committed to the New Deal or radical critics of its shortcomings. And so I became more sensitive to what was going on in the larger world. The New Deal was in trouble because it had not brought about economic recovery. So far it had failed to improve the lot of workers, tenant farmers, old people, or small business. FDR had provided federal funds for public works projects and for direct work relief, like the Civilian Conservation Corps and the National Youth Administration. Many of us students picked up useful money by doing NYA jobs part time. In addition I worked Saturdays in a Fifth Avenue department store, selling women's shoes.

My social life focused entirely on my girl. Every few weeks she took the bus into New York to visit me, and I'd go home every once in a while to see her. We decided to get married in the spring of 1935. My parents were strongly opposed; they liked her but knew we were too young and had no means of supporting ourselves. Nor could they help us. But marry we did, in a brief City Hall ceremony in Worcester. It was three days after I turned twenty.

She came to New York and we found a small apartment. She was a college graduate now, and got a secretarial job in a publishing house. That was how we managed to live while I had a year to go for my degree.

The marriage was the mistake my folks predicted. Neither of us knew much about life, about marriage, or even about ourselves. I think we must have come together out of loneliness. We soon drifted apart, and after a while were divorced. Now it's something in my life that seems to have happened to somebody else.

As I began my last year in college, private employment was still hard to find. Eight million people still had no jobs. Nearly three million young people, sixteen to twenty-four, were on relief. The surface aspects of the Depression had almost disappeared. No apple-sellers on the street, breadlines gone, Hoovervilles vanished. But I knew many young people who had finished college and failed to find work. They had gone home to live or were drifting about the country.

The failure of the government to find basic solutions troubled us. In the big industries—steel, auto, coal, rubber—workers were carrying on dramatic sit-in strikes for the right to organize and bargain. I went to see Clifford Odets's radical plays and read many of the new novels about working class life. Paul Green's *Johnny Johnson* and Irwin Shaw's *Bury the Dead* were plays that intensified the pacifist mood on the campus. Many of us joined the radical student movement.

I remember a union on campus struggling to organize the service and maintenance workers at Columbia. I was doing student-teaching then at the Horace Mann School on campus, and I urged the girls to join the picket line outside, where I marched every lunch hour and handed out leaflets. When the headmaster heard what I'd said in class he suggested perhaps I was better fitted to organize labor than to teach children.

Maybe he's right, I thought. Though I reminded him New College and John Dewey stood for uniting thought with action. I did like the small teaching experience I'd had, combining social history with literature. But I had just seen something I wrote published in a minor magazine. One of my professors, without telling me, had sent an editor an essay I wrote comparing plays that dealt with the Sacco-Vanzetti case. He liked it enough to publish it. Seeing my name in print made me think writing would be better than teaching. (Though as it turned out the two seem inseparable in my work.)

That was the beginning of what became a lifelong calling—writing. It was a craft I learned slowly, and by a dozen different uses of it I made a living. But it would take perhaps half a lifetime before I found the best and happiest use for it.

I began to feel there was no point to going on with my studies. The papers said a third of the previous year's graduating classes had been unable to find any work at all. Another third had gotten jobs for which they had no interest, talent, or training. So what was the sense of a degree?

I had no desire to enter business or pile up property. It seemed impossible anyhow. And everything I read and saw strengthened the belief that there must be something better to live for than to get rich. The unending years of depression had led many people to lose faith in an economic system that helped a minority to enjoy luxuries while millions went hungry. Especially among the people I admired most—writers and artists and intellectuals—was this disillusionment evident.

Many of us supported what FDR tried to do to make life a little less harsh for the underdog, but believed it was no more than patchwork on a system that needed radical reconstruction. But how, in what form, by what means? Some joined organizations of young socialists or communists or found hope in Technocracy or Share the Wealth or other utopian schemes that flared briefly in those desperate years. Some of us turned to the right, seeing in America's little fuehrers their savior. Just as blind were those of us on the left who saw in Stalin a savior. Whether on the extreme political right or left, human lives were being sacrificed to abstract ideas. With terrifying ease, believers in some great cause lose their moral bearings and take unto themselves the right to destroy the lives of others.

Toward the end of my senior year I dropped out of college. (My mother never forgave me for that. No matter what else I achieved in the years that followed, she always lamented, "But you didn't get your degree!") My father, fifty-seven, died of cancer that year. I had sat beside his sickbed, unable to say anything to him, and at his funeral I couldn't cry. But as the years go by I think about him more and more, and wonder about the unspoken thoughts and feelings that never passed between us.

My mother came back to New York to live, along with my younger brother. I found a furnished room on the West Side that rented for three dollars a week. Stepping through the frontdoor of the old brownstone was like entering a public urinal. At the top of five flights of stairs was my room, so narrow I could almost touch the walls with outstretched arms. There was an iron cot, no sheets, a frayed army blanket, a rickety wardrobe that leaned menacingly over me, and a small window through whose smeary glass I could barely see the brick walls of the tenement opposite.

I applied for help at the city's relief bureau. I can't recall how many days I waited before an investigator came. It felt terribly long because I was so nervous. But at last I qualified, and the relief began coming. The city paid my rent, and every other Friday gave me $5.50. That was what I lived on. Dinner was a cheese sandwich and a cup of coffee. Price: twenty cents. When rain or snow began squishing up through the holes in my shoes, I couldn't afford to have them repaired. Neighbors showed me how to take the pulpy separators out of egg cartons and stuff them into my shoes for protection. A few months later my luck changed. The Federal Theatre Project gave me a job.

I reported for work at a decaying Greek temple on Eighth Avenue near Forty-fourth Street, once the home of a bank that had gone bust. Now it was the headquarters of the project for theatre people sponsored by the Works Projects Administration (WPA). I got the job because, when I applied for home relief, I listed myself as an unemployed writer. A bold claim to make on the basis of college pieces and some writing for obscure magazines. I had to put something down, and I did want badly to become a professional writer. My brother Allan had had some experience as a publicity writer in New York, had gone on relief before me, and had been given a Federal Theatre job in the press department. He showed me the ropes and talked his chief into hiring me. Allan was very good at his work, and his boss must have figured I would be too.

I fitted into a small niche of the big department, joining a few men who wrote stories explaining the project to teachers and students. Many Federal Theatre productions were performed in the schools, and pupils often came in organized groups to attend the performances in our theatres.

My pay was $23.86 a week. It was the salary everybody got who came from the relief rolls. We were ninety percent of the workers on all the projects—Music, Writers, Theatre, and Art. The pay sounds very small now, but it was enough to support me, and those who had families, too. And as steady pay every week of the year, it was more than most actors earned in the commercial theatre. It was job security they had never before enjoyed.

I spent over three years in that job, the first decent one I ever had. And one that did more good than most jobs people find themselves in because they have to make a living somehow. The New Deal not only provided work for thousands of unemployed people in the arts, it also satisfied the hunger of America's millions for plays, books, music, art. It was a revolutionary idea, to decide that concertos, poems, novels, sculpture, paintings were not just luxuries for the rich to enjoy, but a vital part of popular education and culture. I was glad to be part of that great enterprise, and I look back proudly on those years. Long after, I worked that personal experience into a book I wrote called *Violins and Shovels: The WPA Arts Projects.*

The press, heavily conservative in the Thirties, attacked the WPA concept of work relief. It targeted the arts projects, ridiculing and misrepresenting what we did. Periodically Congress would demand cuts in the WPA budget, and we would be showered with orders for dismissals. Only a few months after I started, I was one of many who got pink dismissal slips.

We hit the pavement at once, joined by a small army of pickets mustered by our union, the Workers Alliance. For two weeks we kept it up, demanding our jobs back, parading, shouting, chanting, singing, waving placards with our slogans. The cut was rescinded and we went back to our desks. That happened to us again and again; it made life very precarious. But I hung on for years, learning that militant struggle could make a difference. It taught me what unions were all about and gave me the itch to study labor history.

In the Thirties I was one of many who joined the anti-war movement that swept the college campuses. We marched in "No More War" parades and thousands of us signed the Oxford Pledge of absolute refusal to serve in the armed forces. The churches too condemned resorting to war as a sin. But our pacifism met a severe test with the Civil War in Spain that began in 1936. It seemed a just war when the Spanish democracy tried to defend itself against a fascist uprising aided by Hitler and Mussolini. Thousands of Americans—among them a childhood friend from Worcester—volunteered to fight in the International Brigades. Al thought if democracy could be saved in Spain, it would end Hitler's chances to start another world war. But he was killed his first day of battle. In April of 1939 the fascists won in Spain. I thought it was now inevitable that I'd be in uniform soon.

In June 1939 Congress abolished the Federal Theatre. The Civil War in Spain ended about the same time. For the three years it had gone on it had gripped the hearts of most of the people I knew. Over three thousand had volunteered for the Abraham Lincoln Brigade, fighting for Spanish democracy against Franco's troops. Franco's victory marked the end of an era. Without a job, and certain that Hitler would start a world war soon, I did not feel like hunting for work. I decided to join two friends and see the USA. I had a little money salted away, and borrowed some more. One man took his father's car, which we packed with a gas stove, pots and pans, canned goods, sleeping bags, a small tent, and many road maps.

I learned to drive along the way and was soon sharing the wheel with Les and Gil. We made our own meals and slept out of doors. For two months we drove across the country, zigzagging to see all we could, reached the Northwest, and headed down the West Coast for Mexico.

We had visited auto plants and airplane factories, logging camps and lumber mills, iron mines and fisheries, ranches and canneries and the huge fruit and vegetable farms of California. There we went into the federal camps put up for Okie migrant workers whom Steinbeck had just depicted in his novel, *Grapes of Wrath.* (Forty years later I would write about the migrants in my biography, *Dorothea Lange: A Photographer's Life.*)

We were driving through the plains of Texas when at 8:00 A.M. on September 1 we heard a calm voice on the radio announce that Hitler's armies had invaded Poland. The news stunned us. Not that we did not believe war would come. But not now, not this day, not this year!

We debated whether to go on. We had planned to stay a month or so in Mexico and then travel slowly up through the deep South. But the war news wrecked our plans. We entered Mexico, stayed a week or two, and drove home to see what would happen next. Along the way I had written several enormously detailed letters to friends, trying to capture the immediacy of the experience. I had never been anywhere before, so this was a marvelous time for me. I had hoped, upon my return, to mine those letters for some articles. But the war pushed everything else offstage. No one would be interested in what I had seen and learned. The war

changed everything.

My own life changed wonderfully as soon as I got back. Through a blind date arranged by mutual friends I met Hildy, my wife-to-be. She was going to City College at night and working as a clothes model during the day. A year younger than I, she had come up from Philadelphia to try living in New York, acting in small theatre groups, modelling, and working for a college degree all at the same time. She was beautiful, gentle, compassionate, and, like me, felt society had to be remade into something more humane and just. We were soon in love; and after my divorce came through, we married in June 1941.

Hildy continued to work and take courses while I did various odd jobs in journalism, writing or editing, always for low pay. In August of 1942 I was drafted. I was twenty-seven, and much older than most of the GIs. They called me "Pop." I was placed in the Army Air Force and sent to school to become a control-tower operator. For three-and-a-half years I worked in towers at domestic airfields where fighter or bomber pilots

Meltzer and Hildy, at the time of their marriage, 1941

Corporal Meltzer in the Army Air Force, about 1943

were being trained for combat. I was never sent overseas. Most of the time I was in Arkansas or Alabama. At least I saw a lot of the South, spending many off-duty passes wandering around the countryside and the small towns and taking photographs. I was stationed at Craig Field in Selma, Alabama quite a while. It seemed a town still asleep in the nineteenth century. Some twenty years later, when worldwide attention focused on the Selma-to-Montgomery March for Black Freedom of 1965, I couldn't believe this was the same town I had known.

I volunteered to write for service newspapers and gave lectures on democracy and fascism and why we were in this war. One of the best—and sometimes most painful—parts of those years was the chance to get to know all kinds of young men from all over the U.S. If you stay in New York too long you can begin to think everyone else is like you.

When the war ended I had a wife, a baby—Jane—and no job. My brother Allan helped find me work at the CBS radio network in New York. They were doing a weekly dramatic documentary illuminating the many different problems of the GIs who returned from the war. My job was to interview them,

their families and friends, therapists, counselors, social agencies, and work out a story each week, centering on a veteran who typified a problem. Then a dramatic writer took over and did the action and dialogue. Finally they let me write a script myself, and it was thrilling to sit in the studio and watch the actors broadcast it live to the whole country. The program was sponsored by the U.S. Veterans Administration, and did much to help men and women returning to civilian life in that difficult time.

As my first year ended I heard a job was open on the public relations staff of a committee planning the candidacy of Henry A. Wallace for President on an independent ticket in 1948. (Wallace had been FDR's Vice President and was now Truman's Secretary of Commerce.) I applied and got the post. It was more money than at CBS, and promised to teach me a great deal about something new. The work proved hard—very long hours every day of the week—but it was rewarding.

My job was to write news releases and the copy for leaflets and posters and brochures, draft background memoranda on issues, handle the reporters at press conferences—the usual political PR chores. I worked with many people who had rich experience in government affairs and learned a lot about politics from the inside.

I doubt that any of us, including Mr. Wallace, expected him to win, but we thought our new Progressive Party would get a sizeable vote and incline the country toward a more liberal domestic program and a less belligerent foreign policy. Our hopes were crushed when Wallace got little more than a million votes. That was the year Harry Truman surprised everyone but himself by beating Tom Dewey.

The campaign over, I looked for work. For the next two years I went back to odd jobs in journalism. I teamed with another writer to do magazine pieces, I wrote a column for a labor paper, I produced a daily radio program for a national union during a six-month-long strike (which we lost). It was a precarious living, but we managed somehow to get along. Hildy went back to work modelling when our Janie entered nursery school. Free-lance work could be fun because of the variety it offered, but its uncertainty made me nervous.

Then a permanent job popped up. A new public relations agency was started by a clever man who saw that the rapidly growing pharmaceutical industry needed the skills he could muster. It was an age of discovery. All sorts of new antibiotics and hormones and other drugs were being developed in the laboratories and they made good stories to tell a public intensely interested in its own health.

The Meltzers vacationing on Cape Cod with their daughter Jane, summer, 1951

Although I said I knew nothing about science or medicine, the boss told me that knowing how to write was more important. I could learn the facts on the job. And that's what happened. He paid me well and threw in a generous expense account. Hildy and I felt secure enough to have another child—Amy.

There were only a few accounts in the shop and a few employees when I started, but several of the biggest firms were soon on our list and the staff grew rapidly. I had never dealt with big business before, and was a little scared of encounters with corporate executives. But I found they were human and approachable. I was assigned to the Pfizer account. I plunged into learning all I could about its business history, its research goals and methods, its marketing needs. I was a quick study, as the actors put it, and soon could handle the business well at both ends—with the company brass and the media I had to reach with the story.

Early on I made a big coup that entrenched me solidly with both the account and my boss. I mustered vivid details and worked out the story line for the discovery of antibiotics and convinced the veteran *New Yorker* writer, Berton Rouché, that it was a good bet for him. He followed up with his own research and the magazine ran a very long article that delighted the Pfizer people and the readers. Later the piece was anthologized several times.

I found I enjoyed the give and take with the executives in the business offices and the scientists in the labs. I came up with fresh ideas and managed to get the media people to make use of many of them. As our staff and my responsibilities grew I discovered I had a knack for administration too. Perhaps compulsively well-organized, I was able to get others to work coherently and well together.

After some four or five years with the agency, Pfizer asked me to join them to help create an internal public relations department. I took up the offer, and we built a large staff to carry on a more extensive program. Working inside now, I saw much more clearly how a corporation operates. With a bigger budget, we could do the things I especially liked—make science films, plan international scientific meetings, publish educational books and brochures. The more directly commercial aspects had to be taken care of, too, and this I liked less. The eternal conflict between profit and use, between real needs and induced needs, was abundantly clear. And the jockeying for power and position found in almost any institution, whether for profit or not, was just as plain and painful.

I stayed on for five years, able to save something out of a good salary. Then I left because I wanted a job that would permit me greater control of my own time. This, because I wanted to write books. Earlier, while at the agency, I became aware that I was nearing the age of forty. I had become a suburban commuter, living in a house in northern Westchester. Life was easier for us than ever before. But I wasn't satisfied. Forty was the mid-life mark. I probably had fewer years than that ahead of me. What had I done with my time? I called myself a writer, but would anything I'd written endure? Would anyone want to go back and read that dead-and-gone journalism? All this time I had never tried my hand at fiction or poetry. Not even as a schoolboy. Nonfiction was my natural medium. So I decided to try to write a book, a book about something important, a book that might make a difference in how its readers understood the world. I never stopped to think it might be a rotten book!

While I was casting about for a subject, I began to see it would not be easy to hold a job, help with the housework and the kids, and write a book, too. My wife was very understanding. "I'll let you out of the dishes," she said, "if you'll work on a book." (Later, she turned this around and told everybody the only reason I wrote books was to get out of doing dishes.)

I found my subject—a history of black people in America, to be told with a big and solid text combined with a thousand illustrations. When I began to read and make notes, I knew only a little about black history, and the enormous magnitude of the research task became clear only as I made some headway. My job took me all over the country and I was able to combine business trips with research into pictorial material on black life. It was never a chore. It was a stretching of the mind, a deepening of my sympathies, a disciplining of my organizing powers.

Still, after blocking out the entire book, assembling a great many pictures, and working with a book designer to prepare about thirty layouts to show how it might look, I felt shaky about going on alone. I wasn't black, nor had I ever attempted so big a piece of work. So I looked for a collaborator, and was incredibly lucky to find Langston Hughes willing to share the work with me. It meant the beginning of a friendship that lasted until his death fifteen years later. I owe much to him for his professional example, his encouraging sympathy, his understanding of the world blacks and whites live in together—if so differently.

Despite Langston's position in American literature, we had great trouble finding a publisher. More than a dozen turned us down because they thought the book would find too small an audience. Then one day, in a chance encounter at a dinner table, I told the stranger next to me about the book, and he said instantly, "We'll publish it!" This without seeing any part of it. He was Robert Simon, a partner in Crown publishers. We finished the book and Crown issued it in the fall of 1956. (I was forty-one.) It came out just as the tremendous struggle for civil rights was mounting and proved to be exactly what everyone concerned needed and wanted. The book is still in print thirty years later, and has gone through five revised and updated editions.

The success of that first book launched me on a double career. For the next dozen years I would hold full-time jobs while I wrote books in the early morning hours before going off to an office, and in the evening and on weekends. I know it was rather hard on my family. It meant less time spent with them. But they liked what I wrote, and thought it worthwhile. I had only warm encouragement from them all.

The first book appeared while I was working at

Langston Hughes and Meltzer during a lecture trip to Worcester, Massachusetts, 1956

The Meltzers, "delighting in their return to New York City after escaping suburbia," 1960

Pfizer. I gave a copy to the company president; he was pleased with it and proud someone on his staff had done it. He never suggested I should be giving twenty-four hours a day to the company. He was a self-made man and liked to see others try to make something of themselves. He generously had me take long trips to Europe to inspect overseas operations and then let me stay on for vacations with my wife.

Still, I wanted to give even more time to writing books. In 1960 two close friends who managed a medical publications firm understood my desire and took me on. I edited a pediatrics paper for them, and so long as I did it well and on schedule I was free to use my time any way I wished. That same year our family moved back to New York City, finding an apartment on the West Side that we have lived in ever since. It made research for my books much easier, for now I was close to many superb specialized libraries. More importantly, the move made it possible for my wife to return to college, completing work for both her bachelor's and master's degrees. She worked at City College for many years, then left to conduct assertiveness training workshops.

In the next eight years I was able to publish thirteen books. The first several continued to be for adults—including a big book on Mark Twain and two on Thoreau. Then I turned to writing for young readers as well. I did biographies of several figures in the abolitionist movement and in the fight for women's rights. And others on aspects of black history, including the three-volume *In Their Own Words*, another book

about blacks between the two world wars, and again with Langston Hughes, our *Black Magic: A Pictorial History of the Negro in American Entertainment.* Sadly, when we had finished it and were waiting for the proofs, Langston took sick, and entered the hospital. Two weeks later he died there. It was a terrible blow; he was only sixty-five. During his last year he agreed to let me write his biography for young people. He looked it over and gave me some criticism just before his death. But I couldn't work on it again for some time. Then I picked it up and finished it. When it came out in 1968 it was nominated for the National Book Award.

That year I decided to go it on my own and quit my job. My income from my books was equal to my salary as an editor. I talked with my wife and we agreed we should be able to live on what I might earn from books alone. At the time, the federal government was putting large sums into subsidies for schools and libraries. It meant a steep rise in the sale of children's books and in the income of writers for young people.

Publishers felt optimistic and looked for new ideas. I made proposals for three series of books which were accepted. My role was to come up with the ideas for specific titles within each series, to find the right authors, and to edit their manuscripts. For Crowell I edited some twenty-five feminist biographies called "Women of America," for Doubleday the Zenith black culture series, and for Scholastic, the Firebird history series. I enjoyed the chance to work with experienced authors and to help launch new ones. Each series, I

A winter holiday in Puerto Rico with daughters Amy and Jane, 1961

think, added something original to children's book publishing.

Out of my own work have come frequent opportunities to write scripts for radio, television, and documentary films, their subjects usually drawn from my books. And quite regularly I take part in seminars or give lectures at schools and colleges and for professional groups of teachers and librarians. Many times I talk directly with the readers themselves, from grade school through college, either about the subject matter of my books or about writing itself.

I mistakenly thought the prosperity of the Sixties would go on indefinitely. I didn't realize that our growing involvement in the war in Vietnam was changing this picture at that very moment. Within a few years income shrank considerably as many writers like me saw their work taken out of print because school and library budgets had been savagely slashed. A Columbia University survey shows that the median annual income of American authors is still under five thousand dollars. It is terribly hard for writers to survive; most have to work at other jobs.

In those first years I wrote books without any great self-consciousness about the subjects I chose. Then one day a reviewer described me as a writer known for his interest in the underdog. A pattern had become obvious. It was not a choice deliberately made. But that is how it has gone, books about human aspiration and struggle—the black American's struggle to organize for freedom and equality; the worker's struggle to organize and improve his living standards; the struggle of the hungry and dispossessed in the Great Depression for bread and a job; the struggle of various racial or ethnic groups—Native Americans, Black Americans, Jewish Americans, Hispanic Americans, Asian Americans—to live and grow and work in secu-

rity and freedom.

As for my biographies, they deal with the lives of people who appeal to me for many different reasons. But what links them all is the fact that each one has fought for unpopular causes—Samuel Gridley Howe, Margaret Sanger, Langston Hughes, Lydia Maria Child, Henry David Thoreau, Mark Twain, Thaddeus Stevens, Dorothea Lange, Betty Friedan, Mary McLeod Bethune . . .

All these people share one quality: they never say there is nothing they can do about an injustice or a wrong they encounter. They are not victims of apathy, that state people get themselves into when they believe there's no way to change things. My subjects choose action. They show the will to do something about what troubles them. Action takes commitment, the commitment of dedicated, optimistic individuals. Our American past is full of examples of people like these who tried to shape their own lives. Of people who sometimes understood that they could not manage their own life without seeking to change society, without trying to reshape the world they lived in.

I try to make my readers understand that history isn't only what happens to us. History is also what we *make* happen. Each of us. All of us. And history isn't only the kings and presidents and generals and superstars. If we search the records deep and wide enough we find ample evidence of what the anonymous, the obscure ones have done—and continue to do—to shape history, to make America realize its promise.

Meltzer with author Jane Langton during a children's literature seminar, Exeter College, England, 1973

Meltzer (right) with Robert Cormier at a meeting of the National Council of Teachers of English, New York, 1977

I try to be useful in the same way wherever and whenever I can. I've joined unions, campaigned for political candidates and helped build political parties, voted, petitioned, paraded, lobbied my representatives. All my writing comes out of my convictions. I've never had to write anything I didn't believe in. As a professional author, I've been active in the Authors Guild for nearly thirty years and have served on its national council since 1972.

I feel lucky that I have been able to write for readers of all ages, from the very young to the old. Sometimes the one feeds into the other. Many years after I did my juvenile biography of Lydia Maria Child I received a four-year grant from the National Historical Publications and Records Commission (sponsors of the Presidential papers) to head a team of scholars gathering and editing the letters of Mrs. Child. With it went an adjunct professorship in the W.E.B. DuBois Department of Afro-American studies at the University of Massachusetts, Amherst.

The 2,600 letters we uncovered were published in a microfiche edition in 1980, and two years later the University of Massachusetts Press issued our selected and annotated edition of her letters. In the 1970s I spent three years working on a scholarly adult biography of Dorothea Lange, the great photographer of the 1930s. Recently I wrote a short life of Lange for very young readers.

As I finish this essay, a new book is appearing—one that has come out of my intense hope that we can find a way to avoid nuclear war—*Ain't Gonna Study War No More*, the story of the peace-seekers in American history. And now I go to work on a book for young adults about poverty in today's America—fifty years after I experienced what that was like when I was growing up in the Thirties.

BIBLIOGRAPHY

FOR YOUNG PEOPLE

Nonfiction:

In Their Own Words: A History of the American Negro. New York: Crowell, 1964-67. Vol. I: 1619-1865; Vol. II: 1865-1916; Vol. III: 1916-1966.

A Light in the Dark: The Life of Samuel Gridley Howe. New York: Crowell, 1964.

Tongue of Flame: The Life of Lydia Maria Child. New York: Crowell, 1965.

Time of Trial, Time of Hope: The Negro in America, 1919-1941, with August Meier (illustrated by Moneta Barnett). Garden City, N.Y.: Doubleday, 1966.

Black Magic: A Pictorial History of the Negro in American Entertainment, with Langston Hughes. Englewood Cliffs, N.J.: Prentice-Hall, 1967.

On a country road in Hillsdale, New York, 1980s

Janet Fletcher

Bread—and Roses: The Struggle of American Labor, 1865-1915. New York: Knopf, 1967.

Thaddeus Stevens and the Fight for Negro Rights. New York: Crowell, 1967.

Langston Hughes: A Biography. New York: Crowell, 1968.

Brother, Can You Spare a Dime? The Great Depression, 1929-1933. New York: Knopf, 1969.

Margaret Sanger: Pioneer of Birth Control, with Lawrence Lader. New York: Crowell, 1969.

Freedom Comes to Mississippi: The Story of Reconstruction. Chicago, Ill.: Follett, 1970.

Slavery. New York: Cowles. Vol. I: *Slavery: From the Rise of Western Civilization to the Renaissance,* 1971; Vol. II: *Slavery: From the Rise of Western Civilization to Today,* 1972.

To Change the World: A Picture History of Reconstruction. New York: Scholastic Book Services, 1971.

Hunted Like a Wolf: The Story of the Seminole War. New York: Farrar, Straus, 1972.

The Right to Remain Silent. New York: Harcourt, 1972.

Bound for the Rio Grande: The Mexican Struggle, 1845-1850. New York: Knopf, 1974.

The Eye of Conscience: Photographers and Social Change, with Bernard Cole. Chicago, Ill.: Follett, 1974.

Remember the Days: A Short History of the Jewish American (illustrated by Harvey Dinnerstein). Garden City, N.Y.: Doubleday, 1974.

World of Our Fathers: The Jews of Eastern Europe. New York: Farrar, Straus, 1974.

Never to Forget: The Jews of the Holocaust. New York: Harper, 1976.

Taking Root: Jewish Immigrants in America. New York: Farrar, Straus, 1976.

Violins and Shovels: The WPA Arts Projects. New York: Delacorte, 1976.

The Human Rights Book. New York: Farrar, Straus, 1979.

All Times, All Peoples: A World History of Slavery (illustrated by Leonard Everett Fisher). New York: Harper, 1980.

The Chinese Americans. New York: Crowell, 1980.

The Hispanic Americans (illustrated with photographs by Morrie Camhi and Catherine Noren). New York: Crowell, 1982.

The Jewish Americans: A History in Their Own Words, 1650-1950. New York: Crowell, 1982.

The Truth about the Ku Klux Klan. New York: F. Watts, 1982.

The Terrorists. New York: Harper, 1983.

The Black Americans: A History in Their Own Words. New York: Crowell, 1984.

A Book about Names (illustrated by Mischa Richter). New York: Crowell, 1984.

Ain't Gonna Study War No More: The Story of America's Peaceseekers. New York: Harper, 1985.

Betty Friedan: A Voice for Women's Rights. New York: Viking, 1985.

Dorothea Lange: Life Through the Camera. New York: Viking, 1985.

Mark Twain: A Writer's Life. New York: F. Watts, 1985.

A Picture Album of American Jews. Philadelphia, Pa.: Jewish Publication Society, 1985.

Fiction:

Underground Man. Scarsdale, N.Y.: Bradbury, 1972.

FOR ADULTS

Nonfiction:

A Pictorial History of the Negroes in America, with Langston Hughes. New York: Crown, 1956; fifth revised edition, with C. Eric Lincoln, published as *A Pictorial History of Black Americans,* 1983.

Mark Twain Himself. New York: Crowell, 1960.

Dorothea Lange: A Photographer's Life. New York: Farrar, Straus, 1978.

Editor of:

Milestones to American Liberty: The Foundations of the Republic.

New York: Crowell, 1961.

A Thoreau Profile, with Walter Harding. New York: Crowell, 1962.

Thoreau: People, Principles, and Politics. New York: Hill and Wang, 1963.

The Collected Correspondence of Lydia Maria Child, 1817–1880: Guide and Index to the Microfiche Edition, with Patricia Holland and Francine Krasno. Millwood, N.Y.: Kraus Microform, 1980.

Lydia Maria Child: Selected Letters, 1817–1880, with Patricia Holland. Amherst, Mass.: University of Massachusetts Press, 1982.

Series editor for "Women of America," Crowell, 1962–, "Zenith Books," Doubleday, 1963–73, and "Fireside Books," Scholastic, 1968–72.

Film documentaries:

American Family: The Merlins. Anti-Defamation League.

The Bread and Roses Strike: Lawrence, 1912. District 1199 Cultural Center.

The Camera of My Family. Anti-Defamation League.

Five. Seagram-Distillers, Silvermine Films, 1971.

History of the American Negro. McGraw Hill Films.

Evaline Ness

1911-

Evaline, six years old, with her mother

As an artist I was an instant success, winning kudos in kindergarten at the age of four. My teacher gave me a grey cardboard sheep and pieces of white wool and told me where to paste the wool. I did it obediently and neatly. The kudos came from my mother when I took the art object home. She said in her soft Virginia accent, "Now! That's right nice!"

In 1915 five was the usual age for kindergarten in Pontiac, Michigan, but my mother must have been eager to get me out of the house as soon as possible. Whatever she told the Board of Education must have convinced them to change the strict age regulations.

I don't blame my mother for pushing her "baby" out of the house. She had four children—my brother, age fourteen; my two sisters, ages twelve and nine; then me, born late and an unwelcome surprise.

My mother was tired. Too many children. Too much cleaning, cooking, washing, ironing for six people. Too little money.

She was also tired of her husband, my father. Once he had been a dashing, young roving photographer from Sweden who rode a white horse into the village of Roanoke, Virginia, where my mother taught school and lived with her parents. He kindled her romantic spirit with his foreign accent and his exotic-looking photographic gear. It was love at first sight; they eloped in spite of the protests and warnings from her parents.

After five years of "roving," and having added three children to their lives, the lovers came North, lured by the high wages the Ford Motor Company offered in Detroit.

In Pontiac, twenty-five miles outside Detroit, they found a small, dingy house to live in. There were no "darkies" to help my mother keep house. That Southern luxury was a thing of the past.

My father put aside his photography and put on overalls. Every morning my mother packed his lunch pail. In the morning darkness he rode with other workers on the Interurban streetcar that ran from Pontiac to Detroit. In the evening darkness he rode home—every day except Sunday. Sunday he retreated from his family and slept in his bed. Never my mother's bed.

My father's and mother's romance was over and never revived.

In grade school I started my career as a book illustrator in earnest. My sister Josephine, who was five years older than I, had already started her own career as a writer. In lined note-books she wrote shocking stories of heroines locked in castle towers or tortured in murky, damp "holds" in the lower depths of the castle. The heroines were always princesses with names like Dulcie, Consuela, or Esmé (we pronounced it *Ess*-mie). The stories were full of mystery, with secret instructions to make doors open with the code word: Sesame (pronounced *See*-same by us. Numerous knights on white horses—as well as princes, dukes, lords and evil underground kings—came to rescue the captive princesses.

The miniature palace Ness made "because I was annoyed by my father for not being a king—thus not making me a princess."

I illustrated this heady material with pictures that I tore from magazines and pasted, neatly of course, on the pages that Josephine left blank in her notebook.

Kudos from Josephine. I was a success.

In high school, I spent two weeks copying a full-masted pirate's ship from the cover of a Sears Roebuck catalogue. I used pastels, ink lines, smudges from fingers on cheap paper. The result was a perfect copy.

I showed it to the art director of the high school yearbook with the hopes of getting on the art staff. But I was turned down.

No kudos. No success.

I forgot all about pictures neatly pasted or perfectly copied when I met my True Love! It happened in the Pontiac Public Library where I worked after graduating from high school. He was an Adonis. He was also an English teacher and the sports coach at a parochial high school in Pontiac. His dream was to become a doctor.

Since I had no dream of my own, his dream became mine. *Any* dream suited me if only I could be a part of his life!

We started our idyllic life of being together by separating immediately. He went back to Iowa, where his parents lived, to work as a warden in the state prison there and save enough money for his first year of medical school at Northwestern University in Chicago. I went to Chautauqua, New York, for the summer to study library science. I never did become a librarian.

I met Rosalie, instead.

Rosalie was a talented pianist from Muncie, Indiana. She played concertos with the Chautauqua Symphony Orchestra. She also had tuberculosis and smoked numerous cigarettes secretly. In an antique carved ivory box she stashed the butts, gloating over them like King Midas with his gold.

Even though Rosalie and I were the same age, she had "worldly ways" that I admired. She spent more afternoons visiting the famous opera singer, Charles Kullman, in his "practice shack" than she did in her own. I was appointed her Lookout—*look out for mother; if you see her coming, yell BEETHOVEN.*

One day I asked Rosalie what they talked about. She said, "What makes you think we talk?"

When the summer was over, Rosalie wanted to go away to college instead of returning home. But Rosalie's mother would not allow it. Finally, Rosalie told her mother she would attend Ball State Teachers College in Muncie *only* and *if* I went with her.

Rosalie's mother, who lived in a hazy, ethereal world of her own (she wrote poetry), invited me to live with them. I had no intention whatsoever of becoming a teacher, but I accepted. Why not? I had nothing else to look forward to but an endless, bleak year before I could see my Love again.

In college I resumed my fledgling art career briefly. In English 1 the professor gave us a choice of writing a paper or illustrating King Arthur's Court. I illustrated . . . in full color. My series of paintings were hung on the wall for a whole week!

Meantime, hundreds of love missiles soared through the air between Indiana and Iowa. Then the long-awaited day finally arrived; the star-crossed lovers clasped each other in Chicago. And soon unclasped.

For him, it was classes and study all day, all week.

Ness, at eighteen

Every night and every weekend he worked at the hospital for his room, meals, and tuition.

I went to the Chicago Art Institute five days a week and worked after school in the Burnham Architectural Library there. I made thirteen dollars a month—exactly what I paid in rent for my tiny, top-floor room in a mansion-converted-into rooming house. Noons, I bussed dishes in a cafeteria in exchange for my food. Weekends, I modeled for artists to earn tuition money.

And still I thought love was glorious. . . .

But art school was *not* glorious. It was confusing. I tried to draw and paint what was placed in front of me, still life or figure. But my drawings and paintings were muddled. I could not understand the meaning of *composition.* The word "values" remained a mystery even after the instructor explained it (or did he explain it?). Art history seemed to have nothing to do with my world as it was then or ever had been. And the tuition that came due every three months was so high that I missed more classes than I attended.

No kudos. Never.

After two years, having only a smattering of anatomical terminology, I quit and found a job for fifteen dollars a *week*! Now, *that* was glorious. My job was in Mrs. Parson's Fashion Studio where artists drew fashions for Carson Pirie Scott, a large department store in Chicago. I posed for the artists and in between I carried the finished drawings and merchandise to the store.

I had my own drawing board crowded into a small room with three other young "apprentices" as we were called—Bonnie, Meggie, and Eddy. Bonnie was a Barnard graduate and engaged to Westy, the son of Dr. West of toothbrush fame. Meggie hailed from California and soon left to marry a millionaire, age sixty. Eddy was humorless and fat and drew nothing but ferocious fanged animals. Only Eddy and I had to run errands through rain, sleet, slush, and boiling sun. Bonnie and Meggie only posed. We all, except Eddy, worked on fashion samples with high hopes of becoming one of Mrs. Parson's artists.

I went to the studio on Saturdays and Sundays when nobody was there and worked double-time. I loved drawing figures dressed in fashionable clothes, using ads from the *New York Times* as my models. I was no longer confused. I was ambitious.

One lovely September morn, Mrs. Parsons stormed into the apprentice room and frantically snatched several samples from Bonnie, Meggie and me, muttering something that sounded like "There's no pleasing the old witch! We'll see *new* and *different*! We'll see *original*!" And out she stormed.

The "old witch" was Miss Samel, head of the Advertising Department at Carson Pirie Scott. She always wore a hat, even at her desk. She was rude. She was loud. Not once, in all the many times that I had brought drawings to her for an OK, had she ever glanced at me or made a sign that I might be part of the human race. For her I had a better name than "witch."

Now she was giving Mrs. Parsons a pain in the head. Again and again Miss Samel turned down full-page layouts created by the studio artists for a back-to-college fall promotion.

It was the end of the day when Mrs. Parsons returned to the apprentice room. She carried in her hand one large sheet of drawing paper. In the center of the sheet was a large gray circle. Surrounding the circle were ten or twelve small figures in action—mine!

Mrs. Parsons laid the sheet on my drawing board and looked sternly into my eyes. "Evaline," she said slowly, "tomorrow you are going to repeat this drawing *line for line.* The only difference will be Carson Pirie Scott clothes on the figures."

I stared at Mrs. Parsons as if she were insane.

She smiled and hugged me. "I told the old witch it was the work of a New York artist who happened to be visiting me."

The next day was sublime. No errand running. No modeling. Just angry, jealous Bonnie posing for me while I drew my first full-page fashion ad for the *Chicago Tribune.*

The following day was even more sublime. I was an errand girl again but with a heavenly difference. I put the finished drawing on Miss Samel's desk and stood quietly while she called in her assistants. They all said, "Great! Great!" Miss Samel sniffed. "Whaddya mean, 'great.' It's superb."

Without looking up, she waved her hand disdainfully, signaling me to leave the room.

I left, all right. On air.

Kudos incognito.

Mrs. Parsons moved me out of the apprentice room into a room of my own. My salary was doubled: $30 per week—$120 a month! I was given children's fashions to draw for Marshall Field's basement (another large department store in Chicago). Now and then I drew women standing in front of their sinks or stoves in Sears Roebuck Catalogues. Sometimes the women put away linens in their linen closets. Sometimes they washed the baby in its bathinette.

I was really an artist at last. Or I thought I was.

And my Love had "arrived" too. He had graduated from medical school and served his two-year internship. He had become a real doctor and was given his first post: a small mining town in North Dakota. At last we would be married and start our magic life together.

Magic life? I thought of my mother—washing, ironing, cleaning that one bathroom for six people . . . cooking . . . having children. I had come a long way from that. I was paralyzed with horror. I knew I couldn't do it. I wanted to be an artist more than anything else . . . more than I loved my Love.

I ran away.

I ran away with Mac the Scotsman and married him. Mac was a commercial artist who had his studio in the same building as Mrs. Parsons'. She called him a genius because he was self-taught. Also, he was color-blind and painted electrifyingly beautiful illustrations for magazine ads. Through his color-blind eyes all colors were gray, so he depended completely on varying depths and shades of gray—in other words: *values.* (At last, my art school "values" mystery was explained to me.) Consequently, Mac's arrangement of colors always worked. There were fascinating dissonances but never discords. His art taught me that values in a superior composition are far more important than color.

Mac was not an Adonis but we had more laughter and wonderful silly play than I had ever had with my

Vacationing with Mac in Canada, 1935

True Love. So I played with Mac and silently mourned for my Love lost. The only trouble was— Mac should have been my brother . . . not my husband.

One perfect day in June, I was on a train headed for Canada to visit friends who owned an island there. On the train I met my second True Love. His name was Eliot Ness. At that time, his dramatic "untouchable" tussle with Al Capone was behind him. He had been appointed Safety Director of Cleveland by Mayor Burton (who later became a Supreme Court Judge). His job was to "clean up" Cleveland, at that time a bloody playground for gangster mobs.

Eliot and I talked a lot . . . looked at each other at the same time a lot . . . laughed a lot and kissed a lot when I got off the train. He was married. So was I. I thought that I would never see him again. I was wrong. Eliot had many talents but his "detective" skill was the one I liked best. Two years later he "tracked" me down in New York City.

Mac and I had been living there for a year. I was the one who wanted New York. I had always felt that it was *my* city, and I recognized it the minute I put my feet on its pavements. But New York didn't recognize *me*.

Mac had no trouble getting work from the ad agencies there. I did. Unfortunately, with my scant fashion drawing (derivative of New York artists' styles) and my lack of art training, I couldn't compete with the dynamic talent that pervaded New York.

I went back to modeling for artists. Day by day, my low spirits slumped lower. I bickered with Mac. I refused to laugh. I was tired of playing. I was tired of living. And I was twenty-five years old.

I left Mac and moved into a murky room with the bathroom down the hall. I modeled all week and slept all day Sundays—shades of my father's dark Swedish despondency . . . or maybe I was just feeling sorry for myself.

One Sunday the telephone rang. Eliot! Would I have dinner with him? Yes! Would I meet him at the Sherry-Netherland Hotel? Yes! Would I hop on one leg all the way there? Yes! (Or did he say that. . . .?)

When I saw him in the hotel lobby, he stood still and opened his arms wide. I walked into them and smothered my face against his chest. It was the most comforting feeling that I could remember.

Eliot told me that his marriage was untangled. I told Eliot I was in the process of untangling mine. "Why don't you move to Cleveland," he said, "where I can see you, touch you, talk to you in the process?"

"I will," I said. And I did.

One year later, my divorce from Mac was granted. Eliot and I were married and stayed married for twelve years.

Cleveland wasn't New York but my life was exciting, busy, and full of love. Eliot was called the "fair-haired boy" of Cleveland for his scourge of public enemies: a corrupt police force, night club syndicates, labor racketeers. He was in the limelight constantly, and I along with him. I loved it because I felt like a star. But I hated it, too. It meant my having to make speeches to women's groups, appear before book clubs, hand out medals to Girl Scouts when they had jamborees—all those things that a public figure's wife is expected to do. I was no good at it.

In our house across the street from Lake Erie, I tried to paint in the glass-enclosed room on the roof. I was no good at that, either. I floundered, all sense of direction lost. I despaired of ever becoming an artist.

When World War II gripped the United States, Eliot and I moved to Washington, D.C. His job in the Federal Security Agency was to battle venereal disease on the nation's army bases. We traveled for months living in dreary hotels in towns near army bases where

Ness, Florida, 1941

Eliot conferred with the mayors. He tried to win their cooperation in breaking up the concentrated red-light districts in their cities.

Between trips, we returned to crowded Washington and another hotel (if we were lucky). While Eliot was at his office, I sat on a park bench, sometimes for as long as five hours, waiting for a hotel room to become available. I would have said "War is Hell!" if General Sherman hadn't already said it. I longed for a home. I longed for something to *do*—something more than simply, eternally waiting for a husband to return from *his* activities. I felt useless.

My longing came to an end when we found an honest-to-goodness apartment. A miracle home! In the dark entrance hall, a vase of cut laurel leaves actually bloomed in the spring.

My first activity was to join the AWVS (American Women's Volunteer Services). I paid for a snappy navy blue uniform with brass buttons and a hat to match. I volunteered our car and gas rations and drove admirals, generals and lesser brass here and there, waited for them, and drove them back again.

When Eliot realized that most of those trips were

Eliot Ness, Florida, 1941

to cocktail parties, he said, "Enough!" "But what shall I do!" I wailed. "Go to art school," said Eliot. "If Renoir could paint through *two* wars, you are allowed to paint through *one*."

Some comparison—Renoir and me . . . me and Renoir.

In the Corcoran Gallery of Art in Washington, I found an art school tucked between the exhibition rooms. As I climbed the steps to my first class, I couldn't have guessed what lay ahead: that day the walls of Jericho came down . . . the Red Sea parted . . . manna fell from Heaven! All because I met the right teacher at the right time. His name was Richard Lahey, a fiery Irishman whose red hair had turned white. His classes had been depleted by the war, and Lahey was bored with the transient elderly ladies who had always painted pretty flowers in pretty vases—and always would. The only male in the class was an untalented young man who had a hunchback.

Something in my first figure drawing sparked this dedicated teacher. He took me in tow and never set me free for the two years that I studied with him. Everything he told me to do, I did, because everything he said made sense to me. I learned to draw every bone and muscle in the human body. Then I went on to the bones and muscles of horses, cats, dogs, elephants, and all of Noah's Ark. I learned the meaning of composition and balance. My painting flourished because he urged me to experiment. With his sensitive perception, he led me to express feelings that I never knew I had.

There were five other teachers on the faculty who no doubt inspired their students too, but I know now that it was sheer lottery luck that I checked Lahey's name on those entrance forms.

At the end of the first year, I won the school's top prize in painting. At the end of the second year, the prestigious Bi-Ennial Show accepted one of my paintings for exhibition. There I hung . . . surrounded by the famous painters of the United States of America! The day the show opened, I went up to my painting and whispered, "Kudos, eh?"

My passion for painting replaced everything else in my life. I found everything dull except working in front of my easel or looking at paintings in the Corcoran Gallery or the National Museum or the Frick Collection. And Eliot found me dull. He said I was no longer the woman he married. He was right. I wasn't—and what's more, I never wanted to be that woman again.

The End . . . end of World War II . . . end of Eliot and me together.

Eliot returned to Cleveland. I went to New York and this time that preposterous, outrageous, fantastic, mercurial city recognized me.

Although I continued to paint large canvases, there was an illustrator in me that liked making pictures from the printed word. (Josephine and the hapless-princess-in-the-tower syndrome.) Also, I needed the money.

I was moved deeply by a book of Thomas Wolfe's and decided to illustrate it. The title was *Look Homeward, Angel.* I made about fifteen paintings small enough to fit in an artist's portfolio and took them to ad agencies. I was told I was "too free" for commercial art. They suggested that I "tighten up"—trace and copy photographs which was the popular technique for illustration at that time.

A new magazine with a new point of view appeared on the market about that time. It was called *Seventeen.* When I showed them my paintings, they said, "Hallelujah! You're just what we're looking for!" And they gave me a story to illustrate.

That did it. After my illustration appeared in *Seventeen* my telephone started ringing with offer after offer from other magazines. Smaller advertising agencies, with a self-styled "forward look," gave me freedom to

Ness, New York, 1948

interpret from ABC to XYZ: airports, blankets, and candy to xerox, yachts, and zippers.

The Art Director of Saks Fifth Avenue called too. He said he wanted fashion drawings done in my style—a breakaway from the "old hat stuff," as he put it.

I lived in that land of Bliss for about three years . . . drawing, painting, raking in lots and lots of money until one morning I woke up and screamed silently— LET ME OUT OF THIS.

I put some clothes and a sketch-pad in a bag and got on a slow boat to Bangkok, Siam (now called Thailand). I planned to live there and let the Mysterious East pour its mystique over the hustle-bustle New Yorker I had become—and had come to dislike.

In Bangkok I had a friend named Payung. She was half French and half Siamese, married to a Siamese doctor. She graciously introduced me to her British and French ex-patriot friends who lived in Bangkok with their families. I can't remember what they all did for a living but I can remember that every night was a social night either at the country club or in one of their homes. A party in Bangkok, no matter where it was, had the same ritual. The first act of hospitality was to pass around to all the guests a bottle of Citronella. No, no. Not to drink. To rub on one's face, legs, and arms to keep mosquitoes at bay. There was neither air-conditioning nor screens on the windows then. The mixture of Citronella and the women's cologne made a doubtful aroma. We all smelled alike.

Not very mysterious.

I would have been happy with a nice, simple apartment, but the only housing available to me in Bangkok in 1949 was a large house, complete with the kitchen—a hundred yards away. That meant I had to be surrounded by at least three servants: one to cook my food, a "runner" to bring it to me, and another to clean my house and wash and iron. And if I wanted a midnight snack? No. All leftover food was either eaten there by the servants or taken home with them.

I had seen pictures of beautiful, long-haired Siamese women in flowing trousers but I discovered they no longer existed in Bangkok. Women had cut their straight black hair short and frizzed it with permanents. They went to work in offices clad in white blouses and navy blue skirts. The men wore white shirts and navy blue pants.

The closest I came to finding my dream of historical romance was seeing the Golden Temples of the Buddhas or a priest in a diaphanous saffron robe walking in the street. I was disappointed. I also realized that I had nothing within myself to relate to the Eastern world.

So I went West . . . to Italy. I found a marble apartment in Rome. It had windows that opened on the Tiber River and an art school (Accademia di Belle Arte) just around the corner. Rome suited me. I felt at home sitting in the ruins of the Colosseum, feeding the enormous cats that roamed there. I enjoyed the huge painting studio at the art school. The instructor came once a week to critique our work. Our conversations were short since he spoke no English and I, no Italian. He would look at my paintings and say *bella* (beautiful). I would say *prego* (thank you).

Ness on apartment terrace, Rome, Italy, 1953

*In New York after her return from Rome, 1957.
The tapestry behind Ness is her recreation of
the Borghese Gardens.*

aches attached.

About the time when my bank account assured me that I was no longer a poor little match girl, the Children's Book Editor at Houghton Mifflin asked me to illustrate a book. I was reluctant to accept. The money offered was considerably lower than anything I had been used to. In the book business, an author or artist is offered an "advance" (a partial payment) which is taken out of the "royalties" (a share in the proceeds from the sales of the book). But how did I, or anybody, know if the book would sell? I was used to lavish cash-in-the-hand when a job was finished. However, if a book did sell well, money would continue to flow *after* . . . something like "free" money. What to do? Sometimes I am brilliant. I decided to read the book before I made money decisions. The book was *The Bridge* by Charlton Ogburn, Jr. I loved it! I would have illustrated it for nothing.

That was thirty years ago when I first entered the serene atmosphere of book publishing, so unlike the frantic hot-air environment of advertising production. I never went back to the "rat-race" again.

To date, I have illustrated fifty-seven books and written sixteen of them. One book, *Sam, Bangs and Moonshine*, received the Caldecott Medal for "the most distinguished American picture book for children." It has been translated into six languages.

Kudos from around the world!

Italian kudos are as nice as American ones.

After three happy years in Rome, my money was gone. Sadly, I packed up my paintings and left. Instead of returning to New York, I went to California, where the terrain and climate reminded me of Italy— low warm valleys by the sea, snowy mountains aloft.

San Francisco art directors greeted me warmly because they knew my work. They paid modest prices for my Italian paintings which they bought for themselves. But they offered me no commercial work in spite of my frequent reminders that I was in need. They always expressed surprise when I telephoned: "What? You still here? Thought you'd gone back to New York by now." It took me a whole year to translate that into: "Why the hell don't you go back to New York? We don't want you here."

Like many other people, I came to recognize that the outward friendliness on the Western seaboard masks an underlying insularity.

I went back to New York where I belonged.

Nice old art directors, and some nice new ones, all said *we missed you*, and to prove it they piled my drawing board sky high with commissions—and the head-

Evaline and Arni in their apartment, Philadelphia, 1964

From Sam, Bangs, and Moonshine, *written and illustrated by Evaline Ness. Copyright ©
1966 by Evaline Ness. Reprinted by permission of Holt, Rinehart & Winston.*

I have never had children. It seems amazing that I already knew when I was young that I could not follow my way in the abstract world of art and rear a human being at the same time. Both would have suffered.

I have now been married for twenty-six years to my True True Love, Arnold A. Bayard, a successful mechanical engineer, now retired. Arni also knew what he wanted when he was very young.

From the time he was five, Arni wanted to design and manufacture heavy machinery—huge cranes for the United States Navy, intricate window-washing gear for tall glass buildings, atomic energy valves, elevators for anything that must go up and then come down. That's what he wanted to do, and he did it.

Today, Arni is my greatest and best art critic—with, of course, kudos for me.

BIBLIOGRAPHY

FOR CHILDREN

Books written and illustrated:

A Gift for Sula Sula. New York: Scribner, 1963.

Josefina February. New York: Scribner, 1963.

Exactly Alike. New York: Scribner, 1964.

Pavo and the Princess. New York: Scribner, 1964.

A Double Discovery. New York: Scribner, 1965.

Sam, Bangs, and Moonshine. New York: Holt, 1966.

Long, Broad, and Quickeye, adapted from Andrew Lang's version of the Bohemian fairy tale. New York: Scribner, 1969.

The Girl and the Goatherd; or, This and That and Thus and So. New York: Dutton, 1970.

Do You Have the Time, Lydia? New York: Dutton, 1971.

Yeck Eck. New York: Dutton, 1974.

Amelia Mixed the Mustard, and Other Poems, edited by Evaline Ness. New York: Scribner, 1975.

Isobel was a girl of six, almost seven, who didn't have a doll to push around in her doll carriage. But wait! Don't feel sorry for Isobel. Instead, she had a real live lion cub.

Her mother and father, who were lion trainers in a circus, gave it to her.

Isobel named her lion cub Fierce. He was soft and snuggly. She didn't push him around in anything, because whatever she'd put him into, he'd jump out of.

From Fierce the Lion, *written and illustrated by Evaline Ness. Copyright © 1980 by Evaline Ness. Reprinted by permission of Holiday House.*

Marcella's Guardian Angel. New York: Holiday House, 1979.

Fierce the Lion. New York: Holiday House, 1980.

Books illustrated:

The Story of Ophelia, by Mary J. Gibbons. Garden City, N.Y.: Doubleday, 1954.

The Bridge, by Charlton Ogburn. Boston: Houghton, 1957.

The Sherwood Ring, by Elizabeth Pope. Boston: Houghton, 1958.

Lonely Maria, by Elizabeth Coatsworth. New York: Pantheon, 1960.

Ondine, by Maurice Osborne, Jr. Boston: Houghton, 1960.

Across from Indian Shore, by Barbara Robinson. New York: Lothrop, 1962.

Listen—The Birds, by Mary B. Miller. Boston: Houghton, 1962.

Macaroon, by Julia Cunningham. New York: Pantheon, 1962.

Thistle and Thyme: Tales and Legends from Scotland, by Sorche Nic Leodhas. New York: Holt, 1962.

Where Did Josie Go? by Helen E. Buckley. New York: Lothrop, 1962.

All in the Morning Early, by Sorche Nic Leodhas. New York: Holt, 1963.

Funny Town, by Eve Merriam. New York: Crowell-Collier, 1963.

The Princess and the Lion, by E. Coatsworth. New York: Pantheon, 1963.

Some Cheese for Charles, by H.E. Buckley. New York: Lothrop, 1963.

Candle Tales, by J. Cunningham. New York: Pantheon, 1964.

Josie and the Snow, by H.E. Buckley. New York: Lothrop, 1964.

A Pocketful of Cricket, by Rebecca Caudill. New York: Holt, 1964.

Coll and His White Pig, by Lloyd Alexander. New York: Holt, 1965.

Favorite Fairy Tales Told in Italy, by Virginia Haviland. Boston: Little, Brown, 1965.

Ness, New York, 1978

Tom Tit Tot: An English Folk Tale, by V. Haviland. New York: Scribner, 1965.

Pierino and the Bell, by Sylvia Cassedy. Garden City, N.Y.: Doubleday, 1966.

Josie's Buttercup, by H.E. Buckley. New York: Lothrop, 1967.

Mr. Miacca: An English Folk Tale. New York: Holt, 1967.

The Truthful Harp, by L. Alexander. New York: Holt, 1967.

Kellyburn Braes, by S.N. Leodhas. New York: Holt, 1968.

Joey and the Birthday Present, by Maxine Kumin and Anne Sexton. New York: McGraw, 1969.

A Scottish Songbook, by Sorche Nic Leodhas. New York: Holt, 1969.

Some of the Days of Everett Anderson, by Lucille Clifton. New York: Holt, 1970.

Everett Anderson's Christmas Coming, by L. Clifton. New York: Holt, 1971.

Old Mother Hubbard and Her Dog, by Sarah Catherine Martin. New York: Holt, 1972.

Don't You Remember? by L. Clifton. New York: Dutton, 1973.

The Woman of the Wood, by Algernon D. Black. New York: Holt, 1973.

The Steamroller, by Margaret Wise Brown. New York: Walker, 1974.

Colonial Paper House: To Cut Out and Color, designed by Evaline Ness. New York: Scribner, 1975.

A Wizard's Tears, by M. Kumin and A. Sexton. New York: McGraw, 1975.

The Lives of My Cat Alfred, by Nathan Zimelman. New York: Dutton, 1976.

Paper Palace: To Cut Out and Color, designed by E. Ness. New York: Scribner, 1976.

The Warmint, by Walter de la Mare. New York: Scribner, 1976.

Four Rooms from the Metropolitan Museum: To Cut Out and Color, designed by E. Ness. New York: Scribner, 1977.

The Devil's Bridge, retold by Charles Scribner, Jr. New York: McGraw, 1978.

Victorian Paper House: To Cut Out and Color, designed by E. Ness. New York: Scribner, 1978.

What Color Is Caesar? by M. Kumin. New York: McGraw, 1978.

Shaker Paper House: To Cut Out and Color, designed by E. Ness. New York: Scribner, 1979.

The Hand-Me-Down Doll, by Steven Kroll. New York: Holiday House, 1983.

Robert Newton Peck

1928-

SOUP'S BEST PAL

Peck with Soup, named for the author's boyhood friend

It began with a woman. Everything worthwhile does. Her name was Miss Kelly, and she taught first, second, third, fourth, fifth, and sixth in a tumble-down, one-room, dirt-road school in rural Vermont.

She believed in scholarship, manners, and soap.

But more, she believed in *me*. In all of us, telling us that in America you don't have to be what you're born. Haven Peck, my father, killed hogs for a living. Hard work, but he was a harder man. Like all hard men, he was kind, quiet, and gentle. I wanted to be like Papa, yet I wasn't sure I'd grow up only to kill hogs.

"Robert," said Miss Kelly, "perhaps you'll surprise us all, and amount to something."

It was years later when somebody pointed to a large building and said, "That's a library."

I didn't believe it, because in Miss Kelly's little one-room school, we all knew what a library was. Not a building. It was a *board!* A three-foot-long shelf in the corner, a plank, upon which sat our few precious worn-out books. According to custom, we washed our hands before touching them.

So there we sat in her school, soldier straight, learning about people like Mark Twain and Calvin Coolidge, and Ty Cobb and Charles Lindbergh and Booker T. Washington.

We were the sons and daughters of illiterate farmers, millworkers, and lumberjacks. Some of the folks, in town, called us uproaders. And we called *them* downhillers. But I knew they could do what I had me an itch to do.

They could *read.*

Sometimes, at home, a learned scholar would stop by, and he was always asked, following supper, to read to our family. There was only one book in our mountain home. It was black and large, yet we never referred to it as our Bible. It was known only as The Book.

Then, after I'd fetched it, the clerk of the local feed store in town (if he happened to be our guest) would read to us. Mama's usual favorite was Isaiah, especially the part about swords into plowshares and spears into pruning hooks.

We listened.

The grown-up people nodded their heads, as if absorbing and agreeing with whatever verses were being read. As an interesting aside here, you might be surprised to learn that a neighbor of ours named his two sons Chapter and Verse.

At school, our teacher Miss Kelly read to us by the hour. She gave us *Tom Sawyer* and *The Wind in the Willows* and *Ivanhoe,* in an effort to lead us from the bondage of ignorance and poverty.

She earned her thirteen dollars a week.

I was the youngest of seven children, yet the first to attend any school. Papa and Mama had opposed my going. Yet when I finally introduced Papa to Miss Kelly, initially he said nothing. But he took off his hat.

"Thank you," Miss Kelly told my father, "for giving me Robert. I shall try to be deserving of your trust."

"We hope he's got manners," Papa told her with a straight face. "And whatever he breaks, we'll pay for."

Miss Kelly smiled.

At school, I met Soup.

He was a year and four months older than I was, and became my best pal. When a boy has a best friend, he's the richest kid on Earth. His real and righteous name was Luther Wesley Vinson, and he grew up too, to become a minister.

It's only honest to admit here, as an aside, that when I was in college I seriously considered becoming a minister . . . in order to become the first Protestant Pope. However, upon viewing my character (or lack of it) I decided I was unworthy. Were I a preacher, my worry would be that my flock might harken to some of my eccentricities and be like me. But today, were I a minister, I would fight pro-left organizations such as the National Council (and World Council) of Churches.

During much of my so-called *mature* life, I've protected my soul and my wallet by avoiding doctors, lawyers, and the clergy. Yet three of my closest and dearest cronies all became ministers . . . Hank Gooch, Fred Rogers, and Soup Vinson.

The Vinsons lived uproad from the Pecks. And most times, Soup and I were nothing but trouble, to everyone in our path.

He started it, and I usual caught the blame, and often Miss Kelly's ruler. She didn't have to fill out a form, or assemble witnesses, in order to whack a kid. Those were the sensible days in education. One ruler was worth a dozen rules.

Somehow, both Soup and I came to realize, as our behinds were smarting, that Miss Kelly was our ticket out of a sewer, or a manure pile. She was a small and resolute candle, flickering in darkness, proud to be a teacher, prouder still of all we learned.

"Teachers and farmers," Miss Kelly once informed us, "are alike. But I'm luckier, because a farmer has to go to his garden. My garden comes to me."

We were the young, the green, the growing. Buds of life, opening to her warmth, her sunshine, and her strength. She called us "her flowerbed of pansy faces." We were hers, we knew, and she was ours. In her shoddy clothes, she stood ramrod straight, instilling in us all the sterling, character-building Vermont virtues and values.

She liked *me* the best.

Every kid thought the same. Now you know why Miss Kelly deserved to bear that most noble of titles:

Teacher

As a first grader, I viewed our Miss Kelly as being very tall. As years flew by, she magically grew shorter. When, at age nineteen, I came home from Europe and World War II, she was almost tiny. She rushed up to me, hugged me with her thin little arms, and said, "Praise God."

Everyone in the county called her Miss Kelly.

Lots of people bowed to her as she passed, holding her head up high, a patrician among peasants, a beacon in their darkened world. One of the toughest brawlers in town, a man named Buck Dillard, a lumberjack, always brought her a dressed capon for Christmas.

He had never attended school. Yet local rumor held that Miss Kelly had, one evening, taught Buck Dillard to write his name. He sported a big, mean wood-hook scar across his face and had a slightly crippled hand which had been crushed beneath a log. Some folks claimed there was little good in him. Others claimed none.

Buck weighed close to three hundred pounds, and for some strange reason, nobody kidded him much. Not even when he silently sobbed at Miss Kelly's funeral.

She died at age ninety-seven. For me, this was difficult to believe, because when we were her pupils, Soup and I both suspected that Miss Kelly was at least 144. I am most thankful that she lived to share in my success as a writer. I've dedicated more than one book to her, and she became almost as proud of me as I will ever be of her.

Dedications, in the front of a book, offer readers an insight into what an author believes and holds dear. *Clunie,* my short novel about a retarded child, bears a dedication which reads as follows:

"This book is dedicated to kids who will never read it, hoping that the kids who can will care."

Writing is not showing off with big words. Nor is teaching. The dearest rabbi who ever lived, a Nazarene carpenter, preached of little things in common terms . . . loaves and fishes, a camel passing through the eye of a needle, a mustard seed.

Tangibles. Stuff, not abstracts.

My latest novel, *Jo Silver,* is dedicated to a remarkable woman, elderly only in years and winters, whom I met on a Montana mountain, a lady this author shall ever remember. Her name is Sally Old Coyote.

Dedications are gestures of thanks.

Soup is dedicated "to the Reverend Luther Wesley Vinson, a shepherd of his flock, from his first sheep."

Other pals warrant a salute.

Banjo pays tribute to a college buddy, who was

Peck with Thunderbolt

my best man when I married Dorrie, my favorite librarian. "I dedicate this book to a great guy who will always be my pal . . . and I'll always be his . . . Fred Rogers." Yes, you're right, TV's famous Mister Rogers.

Fred and I don't see eye-to-eye on anything. You name it, we differ on it. Yet we've always been able to disagree without becoming disagreeable. Pals forever.

That is America.

We are God's garden of variety, in color, race, and creed. How dismal life must be to live in a country where there's only one political party, one origin, or one faith.

In the summer of 1984, in Los Angeles, we Americans all held a party for the entire world, the Olympic Games. (Russia didn't come. No matter, as Communists never enjoy anything and seldom grin.) What I liked best was watching two athletes hug each other, one white and one black, or one from Japan and one from Brazil, and a Frenchman hugged a German!

It was a blend of music, fun, excellence. People smiled, and praised one another, a party of human brotherhood and sisterhood.

In my opinion, now that we've seen what works and what doesn't, we ought to dissolve the United Nations, and instead, hold the Olympic Games every year or two. We'd replace talk with action, mediocrity with excellence; and best of all, replace hatred with friendship. Sure, I was rooting for our USA kids. But when that courageous Belglian boy rolled over the finish line in his wheelchair, the *world* cheered.

Oh, I love our USA. I'm the corniest flag-waving patriot ever to skip along the pike. If you can't find scores of things, and folks, to admire in these United States, then perhaps loving is beyond your reach and grasp.

For example, take Early Pardee.

His real name was Earl. He was illiterate, as so many wise and poetic mountain people are.

Early Pardee and I were hunting, one cold day in Vermont, resting, our backs against spruce trees and sitting in snow. Two red foxes were dragging a dead snowshoe hare across a white meadow. It was too doggone beautiful to raise a gun and cut down.

Early spat out a brown stream of Red Man, and spoke. "Ya know, Rob . . . them snowshoes be the bread of winter."

It was truly, what Early Pardee said, because all of life is predatory. Roots of a tree clutch at earth the way the talons of a hawk stretch for an unwary rabbit. Even a carrot is a predator, one orange talon, stabbing into the earth to seek that which is not yet its own.

Unfortunately, we now smother in a world of law, much of which (civil law and canon law) is enacted by senile males, in churches, courts, and legislatures. Di-

Peck with Great Island Karl, his 2,600-pound Charolais bull.

vine Law is all that really counts, law ordained by God and practiced by Nature.

Today, trouble is, we're all up to our vulnerable wallets in *lawyers*. We citizens want less law, and more referenda. Lawyers dominate Congress, lobbies, government bureaus, state legislatures, city and town councils, and our courts. I hold even less respect for judges. In short, lawyers should practice the law, but should not be allowed to determine which laws are enacted, many of which benefit themselves.

No lawyer should run for office. We ought to board-up all law schools for at least twenty years. Laboratory experiments should use lawyers instead of white mice, as lawyers multiply more rapidly, and are less lovable.

We citizens are always warned: "You can't take the law into your own hands." Poppycock! This is exactly where law belongs, in *our* hands, not in the hands of lawyers and judges.

Now then, on to more pleasing matters.

Earth, our beautiful planet today has only one problem.

Excess human population.

This dreaded disease, human pregnancy, is the mother lode which spawns disease, poverty, litter, crime, animal annihilation, and war. Not to mention traffic, or din.

Because of this mire of people, which I dub *peoplution,* our animals are dying. Whale, panther, moose, bluebird, even our American eagle is endangered.

Human life is no more sacred than *all* of life. Morality, therefore, is acreage per head, for all of Earth's bio life.

As I write these words, there is mass starvation in Africa, and today's newspapers abound with heart-wrenching photographs of emaciated children.

Nature's corrections are always massive, occurring without pity. Horrible, yet because of this starvation, many other forms of life will survive in Africa, and future generations may hopefully prosper. Perhaps it is part of some unknown Divine Order which a mortal mind cannot, or will not, comprehend.

Religion and sociology save no life. Only our Earth's *biology* has that honor.

God's will cannot be fairly translated into human words. To humanize God is demeaning. Prayer should not offer God direction, only gratitude, for a brutal-beautiful natural balance created to work so well. "In the beginning, God created." *We* did not. Ergo, we best not criticize Divine Order, its drought, or its rain.

I wish not to improve the world. Instead, to give thanks I'm allowed to be part of it, a very insignificant part.

Even though I work as a writer, and speaker, it's a pity that *language* was invented. It's fouled religion. God's purpose should not be etched into words, and Moses erred in herding us, like sheep, down that dreadful wordy path.

My own Bible is often read.

I thankfully accept God's rain and rainbow, God's leaf and tree. But if you tell me God spoke in *words,* I'm changing my pew. Blue Goose, a red Huron warrior, once said that he had never seen God; yet whenever he looked at a sundown sky, he knew that God sees Blue Goose.

God and sunsets are best absorbed by silent unspoken feelings of gratefulness, not described by the paltry and petty words of prophets or authors or priests or preachers, or nuns, or nitwits like me.

The future of our planet Earth depends on women, not warriors. The soil we walk upon is not neuter. Earth is female. Pour seed into her and she bears fruit. The atmosphere which surrounds Earth, however, is male. The wind carries pollen, seed, and spore. Sometimes by a bee or a bird.

Advice to Women: For a sweetheart, choose a physically strong man. He will be secure in his manhood to be tender, gentle, delicate. Only the unproven sissy will bully you. Manhood, like trees, is rooted in soil. If you are a woman, beware of a man who does not yet own *land.*

You know who taught me a few things?

Ed Nocker.

I met Ed away out in the middle of nowhere, in our Florida Everglades. He was dumping a mixture of acorns and corn mash onto the ground. I asked him why. Answer, to capture some wild hogs. "All I do," Ed said, "is git 'em lazy enough to depend on me. Soon as that happens, they're my slaves."

What he told me, I thought, applies to citizens and government. So I told Ed I'd someday write about him. Thus I have, but I won't send him this article. Ed can't read.

But he sure can cook possum.

When I met Ed, his mule, Esme, had just died. Only mule he'd ever owned who would lift up a hoof to shake hands. He showed me the harness he'd made for her, then a mound of fresh amber sand he'd dug for her, under which she lay buried.

That, my friends, is the core of research for a writer, or for anyone curious to learn.

Research is a dirt road!

It is *getting off pavement* to find the Ed Nockers of America, rural sachems of distant domains, unwashed, unread, yet rarely unwise. Don't go to talk. Go to listen. Meet enough Eds, and you'll be EDucated.

Speaking of the Florida outback, land, and hardy folk (human or mule), I just finished a novel about a Florida cattle ranch, and a determined and scrawny little widow trying to raise calves and children. Ed Nocker would respect Violet Beecher and maybe so will you. *Spanish Hoof* is a book I'm proud to author.

There's music in it too.

Not surprising, as so many of my books feature a simple song or two which I've composed. I play self-taught ragtime piano, by ear, sometimes by fingers. To get raised as an uproader country boy means you've been treated to a spate of toe-tapping tunes.

We had us a near and dear neighbor, Miss Haddie, who'd sit barefoot on a half-broke, front-stoop rocking chair, and plunk a banjo which she'd fashioned by her own two hands. Miss Haddie (can't recall her final name) could almost make her banjo go out and bring in the mail. Or so it sounded to Soup and me, her fan club.

Music enters a child's *soul,* not his mind. It enters through an ear, not an eye. Even today, a sheet of music looks to me about as easy to savvy as a page in the Tokyo phonebook.

Some of the most spiritual and rewarding mo-

ments of my fun-packed life occurred when I sang *lead* in three barbershop quartets. A lead singer has to snarl out the most authoritative part, and he's also usual the best looking. *Names* of barbershop quartets are always fun. We were the Humbugs, the Deep Throats, and the Broadjumpers.

We were beer, cigars, outrageous macho jokes, and best of all, *buddies.* Dave, Pete, Don . . . I miss y'all more than remembering can abide, or a heart can hold.

Rob Peck is a sentimental slob.

Soon, I intend to attempt a book about many of the people who have so enriched my life. Not celebrities, just common folk. Peasants, like me. Lumberjacks, farmers, hermits, ladies like Miss Haddie and Sally Old Coyote, men like Buck Dillard and Ed Nocker and Early Pardee. Their wit and wisdom ought to get *shared* as well as remembered.

A man keeps only what he gives away.

Whoa!

Hold it right there. My book won't be free. I'll sweat to write it and you'll sweat to buy it. America's fount is human sweat. Government cannot create wealth. Our fortunes are created by selling goods and services to each other. The brighter a person is, the more he wants to stand independent, and shun federal aid.

Pick any nonprofit governmental institution and you've got a pigsty mess. God sure did a nifty thing creating *greed.*

Too abrasive a word? Okay, then aspiration.

That's when the son of a pig butcher worked toward becoming an author. And if Miss Kelly said it was okay, it's *okay.* America, in the long run, must reward brains, guts, and ambition . . . rather than sloth or stupidity.

Complainers and gripers rarely amount to squat. They're usual too occupied with wailing about people who are busily handling the chores.

Speaking of chores, *work* is a solid thing to believe in. Vermonters usual do. Granite folk on granite land. Much like their statues in village squares, they are the granite sentries of liberty, standing free.

Sure, I remember the guys I played on teams with, and drank beer with, and sang with . . . but I don't guess I remember them any more fondly than the men I *worked* alongside. Farmers, lumberjacks, old woodhooks at a paper mill, men I helped slaughter hogs, and fellow soldiers when I was a seventeen-year-old private overseas in the U. S. Army.

These special people, so many of them unschooled, sit upon an honored throne in my heart.

In later years, I worked as an advertising execu-

Soup and his friend, Rob Peck

tive in New York City, with people whose hands were always clean. Yet sometimes, their mouths, deeds, and souls were so filthy. They frittered away their hours in bars and fancy restaurants, and frittered their money on an analyst's couch. Why? Because they somehow suspected that what they did for a living served no rightful purpose. Their work built nothing. Fed no one.

Ask yourself this. Who got chosen by the carpenter of Nazareth to be His closest friends? Were they the richly-robed Pharisees and Sadducees? Not hardly. His friends were Galilean fishermen, men who sweated, and no doubt smelled of fish heads and salt from the sea.

Work!

That dirty four-letter word. Yet where would any of us be without it? Begging our government for support, I dare suppose. My happiest mornings are when I jump out of bed at six o'clock, knowing I have a lot to do. And I'm so grateful God has given me the back to start it (that's the tough part) and the will and fortitude to get it completed. Never quit when you're tired. Only when you're *done.*

Advice to kids: As you're growing up, find a type of *work* you enjoy. Any wimp can enjoy play, or TV.

Also, here's an extra bonus thought, one I discovered by personal experience: People who do hard *physical* work talk more sense to me than people who rarely soil their hands.

This is why, in this author's opinion, education better get up off its duff and move outdoors. Kids are being raised today who couldn't even kill a chicken, pluck it, gut it, or cook it. From their limited scope of living, they probable conclude that survival is ordering up a coke and fries at Burger World.

If you eat meat, you ought to be able to butcher it yourself, instead of tripping blissfully through life thinking that a hamburger is made by duPont out of soybeans.

Perhaps what is really being butchered is education. How long has it been since *you* have actually touched a cow? Go touch her. She's as warm and sweet as her milk.

People in America today are possibly becoming teachers at too young an age, too often fresh-hatched out of a college egg. From one cloister to another. Now then, I'm not quite sure how this would work, but perhaps the noble title of *teacher* should only be bestowed upon a citizen who has ventured off a campus and into the real outside world, and has actually accomplished something. Maybe a teacher should be no younger than thirty, or forty.

Little saddens me more than my suspecting that educational institutions judge teachers on the criterion of what *degree* they hold.

For kids, education should perhaps consider balancing all of its conceptual thought with tangible training, so that a youngster doesn't graduate from college able to manipulate a telephone, a pencil, a keyboard . . . and little else.

Some teachers, the lesser ones, gripe about some self-concocted disorder known as Burn Out. These teachers should be allowed to work in the chipper room in a paper mill, where the noise is literally deafening, for an eight-hour shift. I did. Then, when your relief man reports drunk, you work another eight hours. This might convince a teacher or two that a classroom ain't so doggone awful.

What I'm saying is not that I dislike teachers. No way. I'd just like to remind a few complainers that all jobs have a negative and a positive side. The goose that'll lay a golden egg will also drop a lot of other stuff.

Laugh Department: I speak to groups of teachers rather often. Generally, they're a super bunch and love to laugh. The biggest round of applause I ever received was after I'd confessed that I had attended only one PTA meeting at a school, where my kids went, and *one* was quite enough. The ovation came when I said, "I'm convinced that teachers and parents should never meet."

A most jovial, bright, and friendly fellow was this junior-high principal I met near Chicago. After speaking at his school, the two of us escaped to a local pub for refreshment. He had recently returned from a na-

tional convention in Austin, a meeting of principals and superintendents. The most popular session had been called *Career Change.*

I asked him why so many upper-echelon educators wanted *out.* His answer startled me. "Politics," he said. "In my opinion, public education is becoming swamped with too many political causes, and not enough learning or fun."

His daughter, age of ten, was in elementary school. She came home with a list of new words. One of them was *feminist.* She spelled it for him. But then the young principal asked his daughter what it meant. Her reply? "Lesbian." This was not, he said, a definition supplied by her teacher, but rather a consensus of student conclusion.

Thus, we all might conclude that more of today's education could embrace a few studies which are tangible as opposed to conceptual and abstract.

Today's child is eager, almost salivating, to *drive* the family car. But have we adults ever manifested the courage, or foresight, to insist that the child understands even the most rudimentary concepts of an engine? Worse yet, do any of us so-called adults know?

Can we put a worm on a hook? Or remove a hooked catfish and prepare it as a meal? In other words, we should be fully-vested as people, not helpless, incomplete, *over-texted* weaklings, wondering when Mom (or Swift & Company) is going to spoon-feed us.

Peck, mending a saddle

Are we men? Or do we merely wear trousers?

I hope you long-suffering folks who are reading this gig won't mind if I continue to ramble a mite, sort of like an old Vermont cowpath, going nowhere. But, come to think of it, cowpaths *do* go to worthy places; to a barn for the welcome hands of milking, to the shade of a meadow elm, or to a cool brook. So I'll ramble, talking to you over the back fence, as if you're Rob Peck's next-door neighbor.

Here goes:

1. Two people recently robbed me. One, a mugger,

tal is how much you *save.* Always save half, and you'll be rich beyond measure. The man who told me so was Mr. Carliotta, born in Greece, who came to America as a penniless boy, spoke no English, and prospered in full measure. He drove a big black Cadillac and respected America more than a few of us who were hatched here.

People who have to *have* so many things, early in life, often wind up with *having nothing.* They feel that they have to buy a stereo, flashy clothes, jewelry, fancy cars, and eat in expensive restaurants. Some complain that their salaries are too meager,

Jo Voigt

Robert Newton Peck with Conan

stuck a gun in my ribs and took my money. The other robber, a college prof I never met, applied for a federal grant, and took *your* money as well as mine. Of the two, I respect the mugger more. At least he tackled his own dirty work.

2. Cost-of-living adjustments do accomplish one thing. They continually increase everyone's cost of living.

3. The amount you earn has little to do with your eventually becoming wealthy. Study the difference between income and capital. It's pig simple. Capi-

yet if their salaries doubled or tripled, they would continue to squander instead of save. Regardless of their income level, nothing would be left. All spent.

Poor people load their supermarket carts with junk food and carbonated beverages. Most of it is outrageously expensive.

What I would do, were I poor, is go to the meat department and buy a large left-over bone. Sometimes they'll give it to you, for free, because they're discarded as scraps. Then buy big sacks of potatoes, carrots, onions, rice, turnips, and barley . . . and prepare a nutritious *stew,* in one pot.

It sure would beat Fritos.

4. Never buy anything, including religion, from someone who telephones you. Whenever one of these pesky people call, politely ask him, or her, to hang on because there's someone knocking at your door. Five minutes later, hang up the phone.

5. In my hands I hold two objects: an acorn, and my Bible. Were I *forced* to choose only one, to cherish forever, I would keep the acorn, as it is entirely of God's making.

6. Men are smarter than women. Because no man would consider buying a shirt that buttons up the back.

7. If you wish to have friends, *be a friend* to someone. Learn where his soft spot is. (We all have them, areas in our mind where we can be easily hurt.) So don't stomp on somebody else's. Tiptoe graciously around it, and never let him know that you are aware he has a vulnerable underbelly which is undefended against a barbed tongue.

8. Justly so, people who try so hard to get *something for nothing* end up with far less than the rest of us who pay a merchant for its worth and value.

9. Education is not a social service. In truth, it is a commodity, like pork jowls. Health is also a personal concern. It is not a governmental problem that legions of us prefer our forks to exercise, smoke to fresh air, and booze over orange juice.

10. We need new prisons. They should be enclosed, colorful factories (not gray dungeons) where criminals learn a craft, produce products other than license plates, and earn a wage. A modern prison could, on cheap labor, support itself without a penny of public funds.

11. One tiny birth-control pill, properly used, accomplishes more to preserve our beautiful planet than ten social workers or twenty environmentalists.

12. Socialism is merely shared poverty. The disease of socialism could have been cured, like a ham, had only the unfortunate victim (the socialist) been raised on a farm.

13. Authors, old buildings, and retired hookers have one thing in common. If they manage to stand up long enough, they become quaint.

14. Taxation is theft.

We all realize, however, that our city, state, and national governments can't operate without it. I'm willing to pay reasonable taxes, yet I believe we could dispense with the Internal Revenue Service. Instead of taxing income, which is largely impossible, *tax sales.* Every product or service purchased should be federally and locally taxed, at very low rates.

Best of all, this sales tax arrangement would not only eliminate the expense of running the IRS, it would do away with the horrors of filling out those idiotic tax forms every April.

We also need a Constitutional Amendment that requires our federal government to *balance the budget!*

15. Most of my wisdom (what little I have) was given to me by a mother, a father, an aunt and a grandmother . . . none of whom could read or write. Yet I am so grateful to all of my teachers who taught me their crafts and artistry.

16. I like movies in which cop cars crash.

17. A child's first musical instrument should be a ukelele, because it so simply embraces the prime blending of melody, harmony, and rhythm.

18. Judges should not be former lawyers. A judge should be a citizen; like you, me, and the jury. If the systems in your body became as fouled-up as our judicial system, think how sick you'd be.

19. I respect teachers, so much so that I intensely distrust their unions who prey upon teachers and rob them of their money. Worse yet, when a teachers union hops into bed with a political party, education gets a slap in the face.

20. The teachers who are characters in my books are always strict, sensitive, and caring.

21. The dumber people are, the louder they play a radio. This explains the origin of dumb's double meaning.

22. Every school needs a hero. But first, learn how a hero *acts.* He makes other kids feel big. The bigger they all feel, the higher they hold him, and the louder they cheer.

23. I'm sick of seeing blue jeans. Denim bores me almost as much as a Meryl Streep movie. Why, in any one school, are some teachers dressed so neatly and others dressed as slobs?

24. For some reason, even though I'm a jingo patriot, I just can't abide The *Star Spangled Banner.* "Rockets red glare and bombs bursting in air" isn't what our Republic is all about. Besides, at ballgames, hardly anyone sings it, and worse, we all stand there thoroughly bored, until it's over. Musically speaking, its range isn't within the capabilities of

Peck with the horse he named for Ronald Reagan

our limited voices, unless we're operatic sopranos.

I vote for *America the Beautiful.*

25. The high point of my life would be for me to visit a high school and meet a principal who is *not* a former football coach.

26. There is only one ironclad rule in today's public school. All other rules may be broken. One cannot. *Never alter the lunch schedule!*

27. If you're a blacksmith who is working on a stallion, always heft up a *front* hoof first, for safety. When you meet a stranger, shake his hand, before you're tempted to stomp on his toes.

28. Most automobile damage could have been avoided had the drivers employed a modicum of courtesy. After a two-car crash, it is usually the driver yelling the louder who is at fault. Brakes are poor substitutes for brains.

29. Farmers are the hardest-working people I know. Also the healthiest and happiest. Maybe there's a connection.

30. Ethnic jokes will always be told. It is natural and normal to snicker at the other fellow, especially if he's different, or hails from somewhere else. Up in

Montana, every joke I heard began as follows: "Seems like there's these two guys from Idaho." And faces were already smiling.

31. Cowards always kick a dead lion. Politically speaking, Richard Nixon is a dead lion, but the cowards are still kicking. I pity them, and I'd guess old Mr. Nixon pities them too.

32. Winners always smile, whether they win or lose. Losers grumble, make up excuses, frown, cuss. They throw golf putters, tennis racquets, and tantrums. But your opponent won't remember the score. He *will* remember whether or not you were a lady or a gentleman.

33. Not long ago, upon hearing of his death, I wept. And then sat at my piano and played all of the *'S Wonderful* songs he had written . . . *Lady Be Good* and *Embraceable You* and *My Love Is Here to Stay.* Wherever you are, Ira Gershwin, I pray there's a piano, and angels to sing you the kind of delightful music you gave to us.

34. As I write these words, a cat is sleeping with her head resting on the toe of my boot. I wish my foot were bare, to appreciate her comfort.

35. Many of today's schools are too big. Middle schools and high schools should be smaller, just for one neighborhood, so that the ridiculous cost of busing could go toward improving the salaries and quality of teachers and the manners of students.

36. Teachers, please *hug* your kids. Some of them have never been lovingly touched. Only slapped. Miss Kelly hugged Soup and me. So hug even the pupil who is defiant. Why? It is the rule-breaker who will someday explore the stars.

37. She hugged *me* the most.

38. Never let humility encumber you. Arrogance is a lot more fun. *Humble* is useful, however, as it's the name of my oil company.

39. Women, please learn that men are interested only in one thing. But, after you feed us, our interests may be augmented into other areas.

40. Compared to the work of so many talented authors, my novels aren't really so doggone great. Yet secretly, I truly believe that I am the best teacher of creative writing in the entire galaxy. If you don't believe it, read *Secrets of Successful Fiction* and also *Fiction Is Folks.* But please, when talking to students, do *not* refer to them as *text* books, a term which makes my book about as appealing as eating a mattress. They are *fun* books, filled with the meat and potatoes of my craft, not written by a prof, but by a pro. Humor is my chief teaching tool. I've learned far more wisdom from clowns

than I have from funeral directors.

41. Every hunting dog should own a man.

42. I own a dog who owns me. He's getting old, lame, and blind. Soon I must take him, a shovel and my gun, into the woods for our last trip together. He will not die indoors with a vet or a needle. I promise you he will feel no pain. I will feel it all. It will be our final outing, as friends.

43. Manhood is doing what has to be done.

44. One of the biggest thrills of my life happened in Missouri, in 1982, when I won the Mark Twain Award. The little bronze bust of Mark Twain that they gave me is here, in my den, and stands only seven inches high. Rob Peck stood seven feet that evening and he's been growing ever since.

45. If you possess courage and will, it will amaze you how much you'll accomplish on a day when you feel absolutely rotten.

46. Ain't it just peachy that the fools of the world hold their own annual festival. It's called New Year's Eve. And if *you* climb into your car on 31 December, and venture out on a highway, you'll be the biggest fool of all, especially in some flimsy Japanese car.

47. If your aim is to bore people, tell them about everything and everyone you hate. To charm your friends, tell them what you like.

48. My idea of a crashing bore is a guy who was born in Texas, served in the Marines, and then went to Notre Dame.

49. My favorite conversational ploy at a stand-up cocktail party is to corner a liberal and torture it.

50. I smoke cigarettes. Too many. But all of you non-smokers will be amused to know that I once bought a suit with three pairs of pants, and burned a hole in the jacket. Have you ever tried to wear out three pairs of green pants?

Franklin Grant

Peck on his five hundred-acre ranch in Florida

Where is America going? West, and South. Places like Boston, New York, and Philadelphia (and their Ivy League colleges) represent our rich heritage of yesterday. But today, what I call Cowboy America is now holding the reins of command. The Northeastern Establishment doesn't know Roy Acuff from Roy Clark . . . but folks who do, control elections.

Folks who do, cheer the United States and *not* the United Nations. They holler "U-S-A!" and *not* "U-N."

Cowboy America is positive, prosperous, and pleasant. More than a difference of geography, I see it as a difference of attitude. I live in Florida. Driving a car, one time, I entered a northeastern state, and no-

ticed an official roadside sign which "welcomed" me to its border. It read "Conviction Means Loss of License." In contrast, as a motorist enters a particular southern state, the sign reads "Drive Friendly."

In short, Harvard's nasal wail of doom (so many Ivy League men talk slightly pained, as though their Fruit-of-the-Looms are a size too tight) is becoming unheard in most of our country.

It's rather a pity that the headquarters for all three broadcasting networks (ABC, CBS, NBC) are all in New York City, and continually pumping out NYC philosophies across the plains where most of us people live. That, however, will also change. Say what you will about the rural electronic evangelists, at least they're offering a balance for the see-saw.

No, I'm not, in any way whatsoever, a member of The Moral Majority.

Yet I must observe that much of what is broadcast, music-recorded, and filmed these days could use a bath. As obscenity comes, also comes censorship. I'd prefer a powder-blue-suited electronic evangelist for a neighbor rather than a foul-mouthed, hip-grinding, pot-smoking, herpes-carrying, gender-questionable electronic guitarist.

To conclude this tirade, I guess my personal preferences for America can be best typified by hearing old Gene Autry singing "Back in the Saddle Again."

And that is Cowboy America.

Well, that's it. It's all I have to prattle and here's hoping it's enough. I can hear you screaming. "Too much!"

Whatever you do, don't let innocent children read any of this glop. We can't allow them to grow up into another warped and twisted Robert Newton Peck. Heaven forbid! Yet I must confess to you that Rob Peck has led one heck of a great life. It's been a ball. And a brawl. The rich and famous are often attacked.

Mediocrity resents talent. And believe me, I resent all those talented people.

My richest talent is making a kid smile. And getting him to read and to write. So invite me to your school, or to your teacher/librarian convention. Call (305) 788-3456.

Sometimes I write close to 100 letters a week, to kids all over America and the world. If you write to me, send all letters flat and please include a *school address,* so I can write one letter back to you. My address is:

> Robert Newton Peck
> 500 Sweetwater Club Circle
> Longwood, FL 32779

My first hurdle, whenever I lecture (do a gig) at a college or university, is to open up minds. Not the minds of students, because theirs are already open. I try, and often fail, to open the minds of the *faculty.* They resent me, because I represent success in the off-campus world. Colleges persist in evaluating someone by what degree he holds, or what title. At lunch, bank presidents never ask me. On a campus, there are so many *doctors* I feel like I'm watching television's *General Hospital.*

Life is fun. It's a hoot and a holler. If you can't revel in America and enjoy all the wonderful Americans you meet, you wouldn't be happy in Heaven or even in Florida.

I doubt I'll go to Heaven, that is, if I have a choice. So many of my closest buddies will probable go somewhere further south, where there's a red piano, a red poker table, and a red pool table with corner pockets that are eight inches wide. And I'll be there, filling inside straights with bourbon, and making old Hades a Heaven for the ladies.

Looking back, I sure ain't missed much, so I probable won't be missed.

Don't panic.

I'm not going just yet, because I have more books to write, more horses to tame, and a lot more songs to sing. Every day ought to represent the whole of a person's life. A full day.

My three morning rules are these: Up at 6:00, breakfast at 6:15, and at 6:30 . . . back to bed. But come to think about it, my life has been mostly work. I was a mite too busy for hopes, prayers, or dreams. So here's my personal motto.

"Wish not for apples. Grow strong trees."

BIBLIOGRAPHY

FOR CHILDREN

Fiction:

A Day No Pigs Would Die. New York: Knopf, 1972.

Millie's Boy. New York: Knopf, 1973.

Soup (illustrated by Charles Gehm). New York: Knopf, 1974.

Bee Tree and Other Stuff (illustrated by Laura Lydecker). New York: Walker, 1975.

Fawn. Boston: Little, Brown, 1975.

Soup and Me (illustrated by Charles Lilly). New York: Knopf, 1975.

Wild Cat (illustrated by Hal Frenck). New York: Holiday House, 1975.

Hamilton (illustrated by L. Lydecker). Boston: Little, Brown, 1976.

Hang for Treason. Garden City, N.Y.: Doubleday, 1976.

King of Kazoo (words and lyrics by Robert Newton Peck; illustrated by William Bryan Park). New York: Knopf, 1976.

Rabbits and Redcoats (illustrated by L. Lydecker). New York: Walker, 1976.

The King's Iron. Boston: Little, Brown, 1977.

Last Sunday (illustrated by Ben Stahl). Garden City, N.Y.: Doubleday, 1977.

Patooie (illustrated by Ted Lewin). New York: Knopf, 1977.

Trig (illustrated by Pamela Johnson). Boston: Little, Brown, 1977.

Eagle Fur. New York: Knopf, 1978.

Soup for President (illustrated by T. Lewin). New York: Knopf, 1978.

Trig Sees Red (illustrated by Pamela Johnson). Boston: Little, Brown, 1978.

Basket Case. Garden City, N.Y.: Doubleday, 1979.

Clunie. New York: Knopf, 1979.

Hub (illustrated by Ted Lewin). New York: Knopf, 1979.

Mr. Little (illustrated by Ben Stahl). Garden City, N.Y.: Doubleday, 1979.

Soup's Drum (illustrated by Charles Robinson). New York: Knopf, 1980.

Trig Goes Ape (illustrated by Pamela Johnson). Boston: Little, Brown, 1980.

Kirk's Law. Garden City, N.Y.: Doubleday, 1981.

Justice Lion. Boston: Little, Brown, 1981.

Soup on Wheels (illustrated by Charles Robinson). New York: Knopf, 1981.

Banjo (illustrated by Andrew Glass). New York: Knopf, 1982.

Trig or Treat (illustrated by Pamela Johnson). Boston: Little, Brown, 1982.

Dukes. Englewood, Fla.: Pineapple Press, 1983.

Seminole Seed. Englewood, Fla.: Pineapple Press, 1983.

Soup in the Saddle (illustrated by Charles Robinson). New York: Knopf, 1983.

Soup's Goat (illustrated by Charles Robinson). New York: Knopf, 1984.

Spanish Hoof. New York: Knopf, 1985.

Jo Silver. Englewood, Fla.: Pineapple Press, 1985.

Soup on Ice. New York: Knopf, 1985.

Nonfiction:

Path of Hunters: Animal Struggle in a Meadow (illustrated by Betty Fraser). New York: Knopf, 1973.

My Vermont. Longwood, Fla.: Peck Press, 1985.

FOR ADULTS

Nonfiction:

Secrets of Successful Fiction. Cincinnati: Writer's Digest, 1980.

Fiction Is Folks. Cincinnati: Writer's Digest, 1983.

Yuri Suhl

1908-

Yuri Suhl, 1983

Even before I had opened my eyes for the first time to the world my parents were already concerned about my future disposition. Because I was born on the ninth day of the Hebrew month of Ab, a day of mourning and fasting in Jewish history, when the Romans destroyed both the Temple and Jerusalem in 70 A.D., they feared that I might forever be wrapped in gloom. As a preventive against such a possibility they added to my first name, Uri (Light), the middle name Menachem, for consolation. I don't know whether my parents' precautions did the trick but something seems to have worked, for I am generally known as a man with a sense of humor, a hearty laugh, and a cheerful disposition.

I was born on July 30, 1908, to Shaye and Miriam Fiksel Suhl in the small Galician town Podhajce, which was then part of the Austro-Hungarian empire ruled by King Franz Josef.

In the summer of 1914, when I was barely six years old, World War I broke out and that part of the southern Ukraine was the first to be occupied by the Russians, an occupation that lasted two years.

I have no fond memories of that period. What stands out most vividly in my mind even now is a night of terror when the Cossacks went on a spree of robbing and looting Jewish homes. My parents and grandparents, with whom we then lived, barricaded themselves behind a heap of furniture they had piled up against the door. When the Cossacks approached, shouting commands to open up and pounding on the door, we held our breath in terrified silence until they left.

Another memory sharply etched in my mind is an early morning when the Russians routed the Jews from their beds and marched them to the outskirts of town to dig trenches. I was walking beside my mother who was still in her nightgown. I also retain a vivid image of my father being slapped in the face by a Cossack.

Aside from these memories I remember little else about my childhood. I have only the haziest recollections of my mother. I remember her lighting the Sabbath candles, and I remember taking a trip with her to Vienna for her health. All else is a blank.

I cannot recall the presence of a single children's toy in my home, or a birthday party for me, or a special event planned for the enjoyment of my younger brother Berel and myself. In the insulated, poverty-stricken life of the East European *shtetl* such extravagances were alien to parents. What they themselves had not experienced as children they could not give to their own children.

My father was an enlightened orthodox Jew with a scholarly bent, a Talmudist with a touch of worldliness who trimmed his beard and wore his caftan short. He taught himself German well enough to do a little private tutoring and to read some of the German classics, but he spent most of his time in the House of Study poring over the Talmud, an occupation that engendered much respect in the eyes of the Jewish community. Parents of a marriageable daughter considered it an honor to have such a young man as their son-in-law and offered him an attractive dowry that included a long-time period of room and board to enable him to pursue his studies unencumbered by financial worries. That was how my father married my mother.

As it happened, his in-laws could not live up to their promise of room and board, and my father had to strike out on his own. He became an agent for several companies, such as Singer Sewing Machine and Atlas Insurance, but none of these jobs lasted. My father simply was not suited for any business enterprise.

In 1916 the combined Austrian and German armies liberated Galicia from the Russians and gave the Jewish populations the opportunity to flee that war-torn area. Together with other families from Podhajce we were sent by freight train to Bazin, a Hungarian village which, after the war, became part of Slovakia. There we were housed in a condemned school building and assisted by the local Jewish community. Hungarian Jews did not speak Yiddish and because my father could converse in German, he became the refugees' spokesman. During our two years there both my mother and paternal grandmother died. My mother was only thirty-five and I was only ten. I expressed my

Miriam Fiksel Suhl

Shaye Suhl, 1923

grief and sorrow at her loss by fervently saying *Kaddish* (the prayer for the dead) every day for a whole year.

In 1918 when the war ended and the refugees were sent home, we could not go back to Podhajce because the Poles and the Ukrainians were still fighting over the possession of Galicia. We were sent instead to Oswiecim, a town in upper Silesia which belonged to Poland. In 1939, when the Germans occupied Poland they renamed it Auschwitz. The town was only six kilometers away from the notorious Auschwitz death camp which became the symbol of Hitler's "Final Solution."

What I remember most distinctly about our four years in Oswiecim was that hunger was a perennial dweller in our house. The round loaf of black bread was kept under lock and father doled it out to me and my brother at mealtime. There were times when that slice of bread constituted the entire meal. Tante Bertha, my father's only sister, was the breadwinner. She would set out in the morning for the countryside with a rucksack of drygoods and return at dusk with a rucksack of potatoes and other vegetables. Father, as usual, was in the House of Study poring over the Talmud and accruing respectability. It did help some. Out of respect for him the grocer would extend our credit.

Sabbath was always a day to look forward to. Somehow Tante Bertha would manage to put a more festive meal on the table. There was *hallah* instead of black bread, a piece of gefilte fish instead of herring, and thin egg noodles swimming in chicken broth instead of potato soup.

The Sabbath had yet another virtue. It was the only day of the week when there was no *cheder* and I could play my favorite game of soccer with my *cheder* mates, but that was not an unalloyed pleasure. Father did not approve of a Jewish boy kicking a ball on the Sabbath. On the living room wall hung a cat-o'-nine-tails to remind me that father meant business. Furthermore, my flaming cheeks after a game were a tell-tale sign of my transgression. I tried to overcome this by rubbing on a pinch of white flour but it was useless. We didn't even have a regular ball. We stuffed an old sock with rags so tight it could even bounce a little.

One Sabbath afternoon as we were playing on

Rose and Abraham Suhl, Yuri's aunt and uncle

some out-of-the-way lot we were approached by a bunch of Polish boys who challenged us to a game. We dared not say no and accepted the challenge. We won, but the Polish boys would not forgive us our triumph. One of them took out his penknife and stabbed me on my left cheek.

It was a deep gash, and I was bleeding profusely. I ran to the doctor, who was a Pole. Since I had no money at all, he refused to treat me and sent me away.

The neighbors put their heads together and came up with an old wives' remedy for bleeding wounds— cobwebs. There was no dearth of this nostrum in the corners of our ceiling. The cobwebs may have arrested the bleeding but did nothing for the swelling that kept me housebound for days. It was during that time that the culprit appeared with one of his pals to show off his handiwork. No one in my house dared to do anything to him for fear of retaliation.

My father was the oldest of four brothers, two of whom had earlier emigrated to America and settled in Texas. Abraham, the youngest, and Bertha, the only sister, followed them in 1921, and two years later they sent for us. My father had, in the meantime, acquired a new wife, Laura, a woman much younger than himself, the daughter of a Hungarian Jewish family he used to visit during our stay in Bazin. After we returned to Poland, my father corresponded with Laura's father. When he learned that we were going to America, he offered Laura in marriage to my father who was flattered by the offer, quickly accepted and rushed off to Hungary to claim his young bride.

Our boat to America left from Antwerp, Belgium. At the immigrants' health inspection prior to our departure, my younger brother Berel was barred from the

Antwerp, Belgium, 1923, en route to America: Yuri, age fifteen, with brother Bernie (Berel), age eleven

trip because of a mobile speck on his shirt. In other words, his voyage to America was "loused" up. My poor frightened little brother had to remain behind. My father left him in the care of some fellow immigrants who brought him over on the next boat, while the three of us continued on our journey. We arrived at Ellis Island on October 22, 1923.

We settled in Williamsburg, Brooklyn. My process of Americanization began with my name. Some of my relatives called me Isadore; some shortened it to Izzy, while my close family continued to call me Uri as they had done in Poland. One fancy cousin from the Bronx thought I should be called Ira. Eventually it evolved into Irving and so it has remained to this day in all my dealings with the government. When I started writing in English, I chose my original name Uri as my pen name only I spelled it Y-u-r-i, not realizing then that this was a popular Russian name. I still have to explain from time to time that I am not Russian, but with that I can live.

When we arrived in this country in 1923, I was fifteen, but I looked much younger. Years of hunger had stunted my growth. My catching up began with my very first meal in America. The basketful of white rolls on the table disappeared very fast. I could eat a dozen at one sitting and be hungry again two hours later. White rolls were one of America's wonders.

Another of its wonders were the children, who, compared to me, looked like giants. As I watched with fascination their unrestrained playfulness after school, the ease with which they rode their bicycles and played their various ballgames, I felt that a vital part of my childhood had passed me by unlived. Like other children who had their movie or sports idols, mine was Benny Leonard, the lightweight boxing champion. When I saw him on the inside cover of a Dixie ice-cream cup or on a life-size wall poster, his white trunks monogrammed B. L., his black hair sleeked down and parted in the middle, his gloved fists poised to strike or ward off a blow, he cut the image of a man I someday wanted to be.

It was not until much later that I began to perceive the true psychological meaning of this so unlikely-for-me choice of a role model. But at the moment, it appeared to me as a most natural pursuit. I began reading *The Ring* and immersed myself in the world of pugilism with an uncommon zeal and passion. I followed the fortunes of contemporary prize fighters—who KO'd whom and in what round, their heights and weights, the measurements of their biceps and calves, their individual styles in the ring, and the legends that sprung up about them. The one about Benny Leonard appealed to me most: Woe to the fighter who dared muss up Benny's sleeked-down hair

in the ring. He was as good as finished.

I followed religiously Bernarr Macfadden's physical fitness page in the *New York Evening Graphic*, and on the butcher-boy job I then had, performed my duties with special gusto. Sawing beef bones, scrubbing meat blocks, and delivering orders on a bicycle became part of my muscle-building exercises. I even went so far as to buy myself a punching bag for a daily workout at home.

In my fantasies I went much further. I went all the way to Oswiecim. I had left it as a timid, fragile, fearful boy and in my dreams I returned as a fighter of reputation with a true Benny Leonard punch. I came not to punish but to warn: Woe, to the gentile boy who would dare lay a hand on me, or on any of my *cheder* mates.

With this cathartic culmination of a psychological healing process that the subconscious had devised for me, the curtain fell on the Benny Leonard scenario. One day I put aside *The Ring* never to open it again, disposed of the punching bag, and switched from muscle-building to building my English vocabulary with an ever greater fervor.

I always carried with me a small pad and pencil for jotting down new words I came across. Store signs, billboards, posters on walls, even snatches of overheard conversation, they were all potential texts for the enrichment of my vocabulary. And when I discovered a new word in a book I read, I copied it down together with the sentence I found it in, to have an example of its proper use.

For my Talmudist father, the transition from the Old Country to the New was a bewildering and alienating experience. It was difficult for him to reconcile his spiritual values with the pervasive materialistic spirit of America. In the European *shtetl* a man of learning was respected even more than was a man of material possessions. Here it was not learning but earning that was respected, an art in which my father was woefully deficient.

More and more my father reverted to his past, unable to adjust to a life of "hurry up," where time is money and money the measure of success. He carved out for himself an Old World niche where he could maintain a certain dignity and self-respect he had thrived on in the *shtetl* despite his material deprivations. He became a *shokhet*, a ritual slaughterer of chickens and in his later years he served as sexton in a small synagogue, where he earned little but had ample time for studying the Talmud.

There was also his disastrous marriage to cope with. Laura was young, attractive, high-strung, and highly neurotic. My father was infatuated with his young wife though there was not a thimbleful of reciprocity on her part. She hankered for high life in America, and what he couldn't provide, she sought from others. She would disappear for weeks and months at a time and when she returned, sick and abandoned by those she had been with, my father would nurse her back to health. Out of frustration she was often mean to me and my brother.

Whatever the demons that drove her to an early grave, she was still in her twenties when she died. Shortly before her death I came to her bedside at a Brooklyn hospital. She was genuinely glad to see me. I was then working as a butcher boy and going to night high school. She inquired eagerly about my studies and was genuinely pleased with my progress. I felt as though we were getting to know each other, for the first time. This is how I wish to remember her.

Years later, when Macmillan accepted my first autobiographical novel, *One Foot in America,* the editor assigned to work with me once asked which part of the book was based on actual experience and which was invented. I played coy for a moment, saying that I don't as a rule divulge the secrets of the trade. "But surely," he said, "that chapter about your kind stepmother must be a true story." I had to disappoint him. That particular one happened to be pure fiction.

I read somewhere that the writing of fiction is a journey of self-discovery. I would add that in certain instances it is also a journey of self-healing. I did not set out deliberately to invent for myself the kind of loving and considerate stepmother that would be the dream of every stepson, but that's what evolved. What I so desperately needed and wanted but did not attain in reality I achieved in fantasy with a kind of cathartic result that is akin to healing.

I look back upon my three years at Eastern District Evening High School as the highlight of my adolescence. My day began at 6:00 A.M. when I did my homework on the BMT subway during the hour-long ride to my butcher-boy job in Bay Ridge, Brooklyn. Later in the morning when I was out on the bicycle delivering orders, I would compose in my head the writing assignment for my English class that evening. Between deliveries I memorized each sentence and by the end of the day I knew the whole composition by heart and wrote it down from memory. It was thrilling to hear my English teacher validate the usage of my newly-acquired words in the context of my composition.

Of the poets we studied in Auslander's *Winged Horse Anthology,* Frost, Longfellow and Poe appealed to me most, particularly Longfellow. When I read his "Psalm of Life" I felt as though it spoke to me directly. Often, when I was alone at home I would get up on a chair and recite it from memory. I would jump off the chair feeling exalted and renewed with an unshakeable determination to pursue, to achieve, and to leave "footprints on the sands of time."

One evening a student editor came to the English class to solicit material for the school publication, the *Firefly.* Several days later I submitted the following poem:

For Life Is So

The farmer plows and tills the soil
And others feed upon his toil.
The gardener plants with care a tree
Whose fruit his eyes may never see.
The hunter hunts throughout the day
And may not live to taste his prey.
Yet farmers plow, and gardeners grow
And hunters still let loose their bow.
For life is so.

Shortly thereafter the teacher who acted as advisor to the student editorial board sent for me. "We like your poem and want to print it," he told me, "but I know how long you've been in this country so I must ask you a question and want you to be honest with me. Did you write the poem yourself or did you plagiarize it?"

The word plagiarize was not yet in my vocabulary, but I knew what was bothering him. "I took it from my own head," was my spontaneous reply. He smiled and said, "I believe you."

That same teacher proposed that I become the *Firefly's* poetry editor. I told him I didn't think I was qualified for such an assignment, but he insisted that I would do all right. My sole criterion then for judging a publishable poem was that it rhyme. Mine did. And so did most of the poems in the *Winged Horse Anthology.* I shudder to think what I would have done if a budding Walt Whitman had submitted a poem to the *Firefly.*

The publication of my first poem served as a strong incentive for me to continue writing and I became a steady contributor of both poems and stories to the *Firefly.*

One day a student came up to me after classes, introduced himself as Judd Teller, told me that he read my things in the *Firefly* and asked me if I had ever considered writing in Yiddish. This question startled me. Yiddish was my mother tongue, the language I spoke in the Old Country and with my father and other immigrants who didn't speak English. Now, after only four years in this country I was writing poems in English and dreaming about going to college to advance myself; why should I suddenly want to write in Yiddish? Would that enable me to "leave footprints on the sands of time?" I told Judd that the thought had never occurred to me. He then revealed to me that he was writing in Yiddish and was being published in the *Jewish Morning Journal,* an orthodox Yiddish daily that my father read.

He gave me one of his published pieces to read, a vignette of a Zionist Youth outing to the Catskills, which I liked very much; and he invited me to his home on the lower East Side of Manhattan to get better acquainted. When he learned that my upbringing had been a strictly religious one and that I had no knowledge whatsoever of Yiddish literature, he lent me the novel *Noch Alemen* (*When All Was Said and Done*) by the master of Yiddish prose, David Bergelson. Though the story had little plot it held my interest throughout by the sheer beauty of the language. I didn't know that Yiddish could be so rich in nuance and imagery. It was like discovering my mother tongue anew.

As soon as I finished reading the book, I was overcome by a desire to write a story in Yiddish. I didn't have far to go for my theme. Across the hall from us there lived a recluse, a short, shriveled pretzel vendor whose two rooms were filled with every conceivable piece of junk he could find in the street. He lived by himself and stayed up late into the night, counting and recounting the pennies he had earned from the sale of his pretzels.

I wrote the story while still under the impact of the Bergelson novel and gave it to my young mentor, Judd Teller, who submitted it to his editor. Several weeks later it appeared in the Sunday supplement of the *Jewish Morning Journal.* On that Sunday I paused at every newsstand in the neighborhood for the sheer pleasure of watching customers buying that paper, but nothing was more gratifying than the look of pride on my father's face when he discovered his son's story published in his favorite paper.

Still riding high on the excitement generated by the publication of my first Yiddish story, I wrote in quick succession two Yiddish poems, both of which were also printed in the same paper. Then came a hiatus in accidental reading and writing and a need for conscious learning and direction.

I began making weekly trips to a public library on East Broadway in Manhattan and came home from each trip with six volumes of Yiddish poetry I had picked off the shelves at random, not knowing the qualitative difference between one book and another. In time I brought home fewer books and kept them longer. One day I returned all except one, and that one I kept renewing for as long as the librarian would allow.

The book was *In New York* by Moishe Leib Halperin (1886–1932). I responded to his poems with the spontaneous thrill of discovery. I wasn't yet able then to perceive the deeper resonances of Halperin's creations, but I knew I had come upon a poet worthy of emulation.

I was nineteen when I cast about for a more substantial occupation than plucking chickens and delivering orders on a bicycle. An immigrant acquaintance of mine, an upholsterer, suggested that I learn the upholstery trade. I found a job with a beginner's pay of three dollars a week.

When I reported to work the next morning the boss said to me, "Go down and pick yourself a pair of horses and we'll set you up."

I hesitated. I didn't see any horses around and didn't know what horses had to do with upholstery. Was I being tricked into some kind of initiation rite beginners are sometimes subjected to? "C'mon," he urged, "get the horses." I went down to the lower floor that was filled with naked frames and bales of excelsior, but there wasn't a horse in sight.

In the meantime the boss got impatient and came down to see what happened to me. "I can't find any horses," I told him. "Here they are, staring you in the face," he said, pointing to two wooden structures, narrow on top and wide at the bottom, leaning against the wall. "Don't you know a pair of horses when you see them?"

"I thought you sent me for real horses," I said embarrassedly.

"We have a regular cowboy with us," he announced to the whole shop when I returned with the two structures. "He was looking for real horses."

Amidst a roar of laughter a nickname was born. Henceforth I was known in the shop as "Cowboy." Years later when Macmillan brought out my second autobiographical novel it was called *Cowboy on a Wooden Horse.*

I looked upon learning the upholstery trade as a stopgap measure prior to going to college, but when I graduated from Eastern District Evening High School in 1928, my prospects for entering college as a full-time day student were rather dim. My poor marks in math disqualified me from being accepted in a tuition-free city college and my poor financial state made it impossible for me to apply to a private college. The best I could do that first year after night high school was to take more evening courses, this time in the Brooklyn Center of City College. At the end of the spring semester I found a job as a waiter in a summer resort near Peekskill, New York, where I also doubled as entertainer though I had never been one. My tip money that summer was sufficient to pay for a year's tuition at New York University on a full-time day schedule.

The dream was launched. In the eyes of my father, my relatives, the *landsleit* (townsmen from the old country), I had achieved the coveted status of a "college boy." It meant liberation from the vicissitudes of the shop, the precariousness of slack and busy seasons; it meant respectability. When asked what I would be when I graduated, I said a teacher. It seemed the easiest answer to give and it met with unanimous approval. Where else but in America could this happen.

But the next year was 1929, the year that ushered in the Great Depression of the thirties, and I began to have difficulty meeting my tuition payments. One day I was called into the dean's office and told that I was the kind of dedicated student New York University was proud of and that my scholastic record was excellent. The rest was agony to listen to. I was advised to go out and find myself a job and solve my financial problem; and was assured that the doors would always be open to me for NYU's evening program.

I left the dean's office dumbfounded and devastated. On my way from Washington Square to Fourteenth Street where I took the subway home, I stopped at a nearby automat for a cup of coffee and chose a table by the window, facing Fourteenth Street.

As I was sipping my coffee perfunctorily, my mind was back on Washington Square playing out a repeat of my visit to the dean's office down to the last painful detail, when my attention suddenly shifted to a large canvas sign flapping in the breeze on a building directly across from me. In large black letters it announced: JEWISH WORKERS UNIVERSITY.

The exterior of this university, a drab looking three-story building, wedged in between two others of similar appearance, was certainly a far cry from the one I had just been invited to leave. But that only whetted my curiosity about its basic interior, what it had to offer.

The first thing that caught my eye was the famous portrait of a bushy-bearded man—Karl Marx. So I already had an inkling of this institution's orientation. The rest of the pertinent data was supplied to me by the short, squinting secretary who told me that this was a night school for workers, offering a two-year program. Most students came just for the education, others to make themselves eligible for teaching Yiddish in the afternoon schools. The University provided the teaching job. Tuition was fifty dollars a semester, but payment could be deferred until you could afford it. He said I would be credited for my year at NYU and would need only one more year to graduate. He was ready to register me right then and there. I said I would need a few days to think it over.

I left with mixed feelings but in a much better mood than when I had walked out of the dean's office

Suhl, left, with Yiddish poets Aaron Kurtz and Martin Birnbaum

an hour ago. A university in hand was better than none. Several days later I returned with two of my friends who had graduated from Eastern District Evening High School together with me and we all registered at the JWU.

It was 1931 and I found myself in the swelling ranks of the unemployed which meant that my day often began with a tense three-word greeting tacked on a factory door: No Help Wanted. So, in partnership with a fellow student I became my own entrepreneur. We rose at dawn, bought two bushels of fruit at the wholesale fruit market on Fulton Street, rented a pushcart with a scale for half a day and I shattered the quiet of the Williamsburg Streets by chanting in Hebrew, in my best cantorial voice, a phrase from a holiday prayer. Instantly windows were flung open, startled housewives stuck their heads out and business was brisk. By eleven in the morning the partnership was dissolved and we each went home with some money in our pockets and a bag of fruit for the house. The rest of the day I would spend in the reading room of the New York Public Library on Forty-second Street, preparing for my classes in the evening where I gradually gained a better understanding of the social and economic forces that could lead to such staggering mass unemployment affecting millions of people. I also learned something about the interrelatedness of art and literature to society.

I began writing poems under the influence of these studies. After publishing several in the left wing daily *Morgen Freiheit,* I was referred to as the "young proletarian poet" and was invited to join the writers organization Proletpen (Proletarian Poets, Essayists, and Novelists).

At twenty-four I was the youngest of the group. I was well received, particularly by the poets Aaron Kurtz and Martin Birnbaum with whom I quickly became close friends. It was a warm and enduring friendship that continues with Martin to this day. Aaron died in 1964.

Soon after meeting Martin, and with his help and encouragement, I moved to Manhattan, into the rooming house on East Eighteenth Street where he then lived. My room was claustrophobically small; the furnishings—Salvation Army; the cheap print on the wall (a shepherd tending his flock)—vintage Woolworth. Its most redeeming feature was the rent—three dollars a week. An added benefit was its view of the turret clock on the Con-Edison building on Fourteenth Street. You could always count on it for the correct time.

The thirties were turbulent times. At home there were widespread demonstrations and hunger marches often tinged with violence. Abroad, menacing clouds of fascism were darkening the skies over Europe. There was the Spanish Civil War, Hitler's rehearsal ground for his imminent global conflagration. I responded to such events not only as a concerned citizen, but also as a creative writer. Often the morning paper's headline became the subject of the poem I worked on late into the night. At such times I wrote with the conviction that through my poems I was participating in the building of a new and just world, free from hunger and oppression. It was an uplifting feeling.

I graduated from the Jewish Workers University in the spring of 1932 and in the fall of that year I was assigned to a teaching job in Bay Ridge, Brooklyn, where classes were held three times a week from 4:00 to 7:00 P.M. The school consisted of one room, a storefront off the sidewalk on a main thoroughfare.

The pupils, ranging in age from five to twelve, were children of Yiddish-speaking workingclass immigrant parents who were eager for their children to learn some Yiddish and Jewish history. The parents were responsible for the teacher's salary and upkeep of the school; but this was the height of the Depression and they couldn't always meet their obligations. A Yiddish teacher was expected to subsist on part-salary and part-idealism, occasionally supplemented with a meal at the home of one of the pupils.

My first collection of Yiddish poems, *Dos Licht oif Mein Gass (The Light on My Street)* was published in 1935, the year that Roosevelt initiated the Works Progress Administration (WPA). It was followed by a number of projects in the arts, of which the Federal Writers Project was one. After a stint of ditch-digging on the WPA, I was assigned to the Jewish Division of the Federal Writers Project.

My economic situation was now greatly improved. The $22.50 a week from the Federal Writers Project enabled me to abandon my depressing three-dollar-a-week room and move into a cheerful six-dollar-a-week room at the Hotel Broadway Central in downtown Manhattan. I could also digress more frequently from the predictable automat fare and top a meal at a decent restaurant with a splendid show uptown produced by the Federal Theatre Project at twenty-five cents admission. And there was the added gratification of earning your keep with your pen as Uncle Sam's writer-in-residence.

In addition to my Yiddish poetry, I also wrote in Yiddish the book and lyrics of several musical works, all commissioned by the Jewish Music Alliance. The first was a choral pantomime called *Benjamin der Dritter (Benjamin the Third)*. It was based on an allegorical novel by the classic Yiddish writer Mendele Mokher Sforim about the adventures of a Jewish Don Quixote. The music was composed by Max Helfman; the dancing was choreographed by Benjamin Zamech. It was performed at Carnegie Hall in 1938 with a chorus of three hundred voices off-stage and sixty dancers on stage.

In connection with the Tercentenary of the American Jewish community (1654–1954), I wrote *Di Ballade fun Asser Levey (The Ballad of Asser Levy)* with music by Paul Held. Asser Levy was one of the first twenty-three Jews to land in New Amsterdam in September 1654 after fleeing the Portuguese Inquisition in Recife, Brazil. Peter Stuyvesant, governor of the Dutch colony, tried to keep the Jews from acquiring the same rights as other colonists had. Asser Levy fought against him and won the right to guard the colony under arms and the right to citizenship. The ballad was performed in Town Hall, New York, in 1954.

The cantata, *Gedenk, Mein Folk! (Remember, My People!)*, with music by Maurice Rauch, was about the famed ghetto historian and archivist Emmanuel Ringelblum. It was sung by the Jewish People's Philharmonic Chorus in a performance in Town Hall, New York, in 1963 on the occasion of the twentieth anniversary of the Warsaw Ghetto Uprising.

Although I had been writing solely in Yiddish for nearly fifteen years, I had an urge in 1942 to write a story in English on a theme related to the war. I called it "Farewell to Jack." It was a story of contrasts. At a farewell party for his son about to be inducted into the U.S. Army, an immigrant father harkens back to that night in a Russian *shtetl* thirty years ago when he had escaped to America to avoid being drafted into the Czar's anti-Semitic army. Now he feels that for the haven he found here, he can pay back Uncle Sam with his biggest treasure, his only son.

The story was accepted by *Story* magazine. Prior to publication I received a request for a brief biographic note to accompany the story. In my inexperienced hands the note grew into three typewritten pages. My attempts at condensing it did not satisfy me, so I sent it off uncut.

The story appeared in the July-August 1942 issue with the biographic note almost intact. The editors told me that they, too, found it difficult to cut because they liked it as I wrote it. They also said that they thought it could be the basis of a novel and suggested that I should give it a try.

I took their suggestion seriously and began the novel. When I got to page twenty-seven, Uncle Sam pointed his famous finger at me and to everyone's surprise, including my own, I found myself two weeks later at the Fort Dix induction center in New Jersey. From there I was shipped for my basic training to Camp Stewart, an anti-aircraft camp in Georgia.

I can't say that I was a model soldier. I started off my first day in basic training on the wrong foot, or to be more exact, on the wrong feet. The drill sergeant, Sgt. Tonetti, was a man with an uncanny ear for the slightest misstep. Amidst the thumping cadence of two hundred pairs of marching feet, he was able to detect that one pair was out-of-step. "Get in step, Suhl," he called out in his hoarse voice. From that moment on "Get in step, Suhl!" became a familiar cry on the drill field.

I didn't do much better in target practice. At first I had the euphoric illusion that I was hitting the bull's-eye with every shot until it was pointed out to me that I had been shooting at the wrong target.

I never performed well under stress and I don't know of anything more stressful than going over the obstacle course, an absolute must for the completion of basic training. With live bullets whizzing overhead to simulate actual battle conditions, I was too confused to follow directions.

It was consoling, however, to know that I wasn't the only one who failed the test; I did pass it the next time around. But I also had my shining moments. Once when the entire company went out on a nine-mile forced hike, wearing gas masks and weighed down with heavy equipment, I made it all the way, while men much younger than me kept dropping out from exhaustion. That day I was the talk of the shower stalls, if not the entire company. In the journal I kept infrequently, I summarized the event in one sentence, "Today I wrote a poem with my feet."

There was a fellow in my barracks, bigger and taller than me, who often returned from the PX at bedtime tanked up with beer and railing against the Jews to his captive audience. "The Jews," he would say, "ran this country long enough. It's time for the Americans to take over," and on and on he went in this vein. What angered me even more than what he said was *where* he said it. He was spouting Hitlerisms in the U.S. Army that was currently engaged in a bloody war against Hitler.

One night I couldn't take it anymore. Without giving any thought to the difference in our sizes, I shouted, "If you don't shut your trap, I'll shut it for you."

"You and who else?" he snarled, leaping off his bunk and making for me with his fists in swinging position.

Suddenly I remembered something I had read in *The Ring* in my pugilistic period about the clinch—the exhausted boxer sometimes embraces his opponent and holds him tight until the referee separates them. That's what I did, and while I held my opponent tight, I said to him, "I'm not your size. I don't want to fight you with fists. I want to fight you with words."

"Words," he snickered contemptuously, disengaging himself from me, and slunk back to his bunk.

For as long as we were in the same barracks, I never heard him utter another anti-Semitic remark.

Tonetti was known as a tough sergeant, perhaps the toughest in the company. I was surprised, therefore, when he came to me with a most unlikely request. He had heard that I was a poet and wanted me to write a poem for his girlfriend. As if to show me that he was no stranger to poetry, he produced a clipping of an Edgar Guest poem that he carried around with him in his wallet. I said I would try. By lunchtime I had the first two stanzas rhymingly secure in my head. Toward the end of the day I called him aside and read to him the finished four-stanza poem. His response was, "Gee, that hits the spot. Makes me want to go over the hill." The payoff came a week later when the response of his girlfriend arrived. "Gee, the poem you sent me is swell. It's grand. Thank Private Suhl a million."

Soon there was a steady pilgrimage of men to my bunk, pleading for poems for their mothers, their sweethearts, their sisters, even their fathers for Father's Day. Some of them offered me money. Overnight "get-in-step-Suhl" became a celebrity, the poet laureate of his barracks. From that day on Tonetti never raised his voice to me and he saw to it that others didn't either.

As part of my training I was assigned to a 40-mm anti-aircraft gun that required a fifteen-man gun crew to operate it. Because of my deficiencies in mathematical and mechanical skills I was relegated to the position of ammunition and water carrier. I wasn't happy with my job. I felt I could serve the army better by doing something more in consonance with my professional abilities. Therefore, I responded eagerly to an item in *Yank Magazine* announcing that the army had initiated a special course in Japanese to alleviate the severe shortage of Japanese-speaking personnel needed as translators and interrogators in the Pacific theatre of war. Those interested were told to see their camp librarian.

It turned out that the librarian knew nothing about the matter, but promised to query Washington. Ten days later she had the information for me. To qualify for the course one had to be a Phi Beta Kappa college graduate. Since I had not graduated from college, it was back to the ammo box for me.

Two weeks later I received a call to report to the library. I hoped that it meant that Washington had changed its mind about allowing me to take the course after all. I was wrong. What happened next was a typical army snafu. Instead of getting permission to learn Japanese, to my amazement the librarian asked me to teach it.

It seemed that several hundred Japanese language guides, which no one in camp had requested, had suddenly arrived in the library. Each booklet contained about three hundred essential Japanese words and phrases in English translation for the use of American GI's in Japan. The Japanese words were spelled phonetically. The shipment included a recording of the first two lessons as an aid to the instructor. Since the colonel was too embarrassed to return the shipment to Washington, he asked the librarian to find an instructor and, naturally, she chose me. I was so stunned by the proposal that before I could come to my senses to say "No," I said "Yes."

I was relieved of all after-training duties, such as KP and guard duty and was given the use of a small but pleasant room in the Red Cross building and a record player to prepare myself for the course. I played the first two lessons until I heard them in my sleep. A week later I informed the librarian I was ready. The next day a notice appeared on all the bulletin boards in camp announcing the time and place of classes in Japanese open to all military personnel on the post.

On the way to the Red Cross building to give my first class, I beheld an uncommon sight in that segregated army of 1942. The neatly trimmed lawn in front of the entrance was packed with soldiers—Black and white. The two groups were facing each other across the narrow path that divided the lawn while several white soldiers were guarding the entrance, and the air was charged with tension. Presently a jeepful of MP's arrived, followed by the colonel himself. After a hasty consultation between the colonel and the MP officer,

Suhl in U.S. Army uniform, Camp Sutton, North Carolina, about 1943

the doors were opened to all. For that one day history was made in Camp Stewart. On the neutral grounds of the Red Cross building the army was temporarily desegregated.

By the time the next class came around, the "error" had been corrected. Black attendance was down to a token few and then dwindled away altogether.

At times, when I surveyed my class, I had a strange feeling of unreality as I saw officers of the rank of captain and major earnestly taking instruction from me, a private. Sometimes after class a major would offer me a ride to the movies in his chauffeured limousine and I never denied myself the pleasure. Once a captain came up to me at the end of a class and told me that he had just returned from the Pacific and that he had taken a course in Japanese. "You're doing very well, soldier," he added. From then on I was teaching other languages in the same style. If I could teach Japanese, I could teach any language.

After completing my basic training for combat duty, I was reclassified to limited service on medical grounds and given the choice of working either on the camp paper or in the camp library. I chose the latter.

Not very long afterwards I was transferred to Camp Sutton, an engineering camp in North Carolina. There, too, I worked in the camp library. The librarian, a young woman who was fond of horseback riding and dating officers and was away from the library much of the time, arranged that I move into the library altogether to keep it running.

One day one of her suitors presented her with a puppy, a black Belgian shepherd. She called her Midnight, soon shortened to Nighty, and entrusted her to my care. While the librarian was busy tending to her social calendar, I had much time to read and reflect and raise Nighty.

Sometime during that year of 1943 I was transferred to the newly established Education and Information Department that was set up in a small, white, one-story building which I moved into. Not long afterwards Nighty discovered my whereabouts and moved in with me.

My duties at E & I were various and challenging. I wrote radio skits, taught languages in the same format that I had taught Japanese at Camp Stewart, showed 16-mm army films to the troops and edited a daily news bulletin. As an extra-curricular project that I took upon myself, I wrote *Something to Think About,* a pamphlet on morale which the camp published and distributed widely.

I did not fare so well with the second pamphlet that I wrote called *Letter to a Negro Soldier.* (In those days the accepted name for a Black person was Negro.) It was occasioned by a racial incident that had occurred in camp and that had erupted into a shooting confrontation. It was serious enough for the War Department to send a Black major to Sutton to investigate and to cool tempers.

It was during those tense days that the idea for *Letter to a Negro Soldier* occurred to me. The E & I lieutenant, remembering the positive response to my first pamphlet, encouraged me, but when it came to putting down words on paper, I did so with great reservation. I wondered if it was proper for me, a white soldier, to inject myself into such a sensitive and explosive situation.

I had already done several pages when the Black major walked into the office. With much trepidation I showed them to him. To my surprise, he told me that I was on the right track and urged me to continue, adding that he would postpone his return to Washington if I could finish it soon.

The major's response to my several pages gave me a surge of renewed energy that sustained me till late into the night to complete the *Letter.* The major was pleased with the finished piece.

To save time we by-passed the printer and put it out in mimeographed form. The entire staff got busy cranking out the pages, collating and stapling them. The cover consisted of a simple sketch of a Black soldier and a white soldier, drawn by our Chinese staff artist. The lieutenant grabbed the first finished copies and took them to the camp commander.

Shortly thereafter the telephone rang. It was the lieutenant calling from headquarters. "Stop mimeographing *Letter to a Negro Soldier.* Destroy all finished copies. Colonel's orders." Not even the major could rescue the pamphlet once the colonel had given his orders.

Not long after this incident, in December 1944, I was honorably discharged from the army on the grounds that I was "below minimum physical standards for induction." It seemed ironic to me that the army had come to this conclusion after I had already served two years. But this time I was not as disappointed as I had been two years earlier, when, after four months of basic training for combat, I saw my outfit shipped overseas while I was reclassified to limited service and left behind.

The war was winding down. The E & I office was getting ready to close shop. Some of the staff were transferred elsewhere, others, like myself, were discharged. My only concern was Nighty. I had become very attached to her, but my next destination was the Separation Center at Fort Dix, New Jersey, and I could not possibly take a dog along with me. My lieutenant knew how I felt about Nighty and promised to ship her home to me if I missed her.

I began my civilian life with little more than the $200 mustering-out-pay and the army uniform I was allowed to wear for the first two weeks after my discharge. I rented a six-dollar-a-week room in the Claremont Hotel, a rundown, dilapidated place on Claremont Avenue across the street from Grant's Tomb and International House.

I dug up the first twenty-seven pages of the novel I wrote prior to my induction and took them to the literary agency, Brandt and Brandt, someone had told me about. Bernice Baumgarten, of the fiction department, asked me to leave them with her and promised to give me a report in ten days. When she called ten days later, it was to tell me that she liked what she had read thus far and urged me to continue.

In the meantime, I had written to the lieutenant that I missed Nighty and one cold afternoon American Express delivered her in a huge crate. I found a temporary home for her with an elderly woman in the Bronx until I could wear down the hotel owner's resistance to letting her stay with me in the hotel. Because she was big and black, people were often afraid of her, but the truth was that she was a gentle, affectionate dog. She not only wouldn't bite anyone, she wouldn't even bark at anyone. Her one obsession was chasing motorcycles.

On my limited $20 a week budget—the weekly sum I was entitled to for the first year after discharge—I couldn't possibly take on the support of another dependant, so I offered the editor of the Yiddish children's magazine *Yungvarg (Youth)* the story of Nighty's wartime exploits in monthly installments on the stipulation that the royalties cover the expense of Nighty's upkeep. The offer was accepted and that marked my beginning as a writer of children's stories.

With shrewdness aforethought I began bringing Nighty to the hotel for one-day visits. Little by little her affectionate nature won over the owner until eventually he relented and allowed her to move in with me.

Park, a young woman sitting in the lobby leaned over to pat Nighty as she was passing by. As sometimes happens among animal lovers, a pat easily leads to a chat. It happened that morning, only it led to much more than a chat.

I found out that the young woman's name was Isabelle Shugars, that she came from Baltimore by way of Pittsburgh where she had just completed a degree in library science. She had recently started working as a children's librarian in the New York Public Library and had just moved into one of the few apartments in the Claremont with her roommate.

It was obvious that she was fond of animals, especially Nighty. It was not long after that first meeting in the lobby that she began taking care of her whenever I had to go off on a speaking engagement or a poetry reading. As the dog became more and more welcome

Suhl with William Saroyan at a writers' conference, Berlin, German Democratic Republic, 1965

Yuri and Isabelle with Nighty, 1950

I rented a second-hand typewriter and settled down to work on the novel. Before I started typing I read a page or two from William Saroyan's first book of stories, *My Name Is Aram.* The apparent simplicity of his style had a reassuring effect on me. By the time I reached the end of a page I was already itching to write. I called this daily ritual "tuning up the instrument."

Twenty years later I had the opportunity to tell Saroyan in person of the role his stories played in the writing of my first novel. That was in the spring of 1965 when the Writers Union of the German Democratic Republic invited a number of American writers, including Saroyan and myself, to attend their twentieth anniversary celebration of Hitler's downfall.

One day in October 1945 as I was returning to the hotel with Nighty after her morning romp in Riverside

in her apartment, so, too, the master. I soon became the man who came to claim his dog and stayed for dinner.

Eventually, when the relationship culminated in our marriage, we began referring to Nighty as our *shvartzer shadchen* (black matchmaker).

Early in 1948 the Yiddish Poets Club of America, of which I was a member, received a communication from the Cultural Committee of the Jewish community of Lower Silesia (formerly part of Germany, now a part of Poland) inviting a poet to come to them as their guest for five months. Most of Poland's Yiddish poets and writers had perished in the Holocaust. The Jewish community of Lower Silesia was nearing the third anniversary of its existence and wanted to see its new life and achievements reflected in some form of creative work. This would be the mission of the invited poet.

I was the fortunate one to be chosen. I arrived in Poland in time to attend the historic event of the unveiling of the Warsaw Ghetto monument. A thirty-foot-high sculpture of bronze and granite, created by the Polish-born Jewish sculptor Nathan Rappoport and erected on the very spot where the Warsaw Ghetto uprising began on April 18–19, 1943, it is a towering symbol of martyrdom and human courage. It was unveiled in the presence of the entire Polish government and Jewish delegations from all over the world.

Toward the end of April, I arrived in Wroclaw (formerly Breslau), the capital of Lower Silesia. My hosts put me up at the Hotel Monopol which became my base for the duration of my stay. I was told that during the war Hitler delivered one of his harangues from the hotel's balcony to a crowd of 50,000 Germans, promising them that if one Jew remained alive anywhere in Europe at the end of the war, he would make him a minister. Now in 1948 Hitler was dead and 50,000 Jews were living in Lower Silesia.

My hosts had prepared a schedule for me that encompassed a visit to every Jewish community in Lower Silesia. Armed with my three volumes of poems, and a dozen children's stories I had written after the Nighty series, I set out with a companion appointed by the cultural committee, on what was to be the most memorable journey of my life.

In every hamlet, village, or town on our itinerary the entire Jewish population turned out for the reading. Only yesterday, it seemed, these men and women had emerged from the ghettos, the camps, the hiding places, the forests—everyone of them a miracle of survival. Now they were feverishly engaged in rebuilding their shattered lives, savoring each new day as an affirmation of their freedom, a celebration of life itself. Listening to Yiddish poetry was a vital part of that celebration. There were times when I was kept on the platform until my voice gave out.

One bright June day our itinerary took us to a small, picturesque village called, Pietroleshu (a literal translation from the German, Peterswald). My companion pointed out a large structure in a courtyard where a thousand Jewish women from Poland and other parts of Europe had been imprisoned during the war. They had been used as slave labor in a nearby German plant that produced high-precision war materials, such as watches that timed the explosions of bombs. At great risk to their lives they frequently produced defective watches.

I saw a young woman strolling past that courtyard, pushing a baby carriage, and wondered if three years earlier she had been one of the women prisoners.

A one-story building we passed on the same street was the village's Jewish cultural club that also served as a Yiddish children's school in daytime. And the short, stocky man driving by in a horse-drawn cart loaded with fresh produce was a Jewish farmer, who only three years ago knew nothing about farming.

Throughout the journey I was always aware that the welter of impressions I was absorbing daily would comprise the substance of what I would eventually have to write at the end of my Silesian visit. With each stop on our itinerary that future task grew ever more enormous.

My mind had been searching for some central core, some symbolic entity around which this wealth of impressions and the thoughts they generated would coalesce into a unifying whole, and it seemed to me that I found them in this village. I knew because the first stirrings of a poem I was to write later began shaping themselves into words within the first hour of my arrival. I told my companion that I would like to prolong my stay here and he arranged that I remain in Pietroleshu for two weeks.

I was the guest of a Jewish children's home, named after the famed Polish-Jewish pedagogue and children's writer, Janusz Korczak, who perished in Treblinka together with the children of his orphanage in the Warsaw Ghetto.

I occupied my pleasant, sunny room on a day of the week when rooms and bedding were being thoroughly aired and I noticed, to my horror, that a large swastika was stamped on the reverse side of my mattress. I ran down to the director's office to report my

*Yuri with Marysha at the Children's Home,
Pietroleshu, Poland, 1948*

shocking discovery.

Smiling, the director informed me that mine was not the only swastika-stamped mattress in the house. Until three years ago, she explained, this had been a Hitler Youth Home. Now Jewish children whom the Germans had orphaned slept on their mattresses.

I understood the poetic justice of the situation. Still, in deference to a guest, they managed to find a swastika-free mattress for me.

The children, ranging in age from six to sixteen, were all survivors who had outlived their deported parents. Some survived with the aid of kind-hearted strangers, others by their own daring ingenuity or sheer luck.

At the request of the staff I began reading my Yiddish stories to the children after supper in the home's spacious reception room. A vivacious little girl of about nine or ten, named Marysha, attached herself to me and followed me around. She had a touch of wildness about her and I was told why.

During the war her parents, to avoid falling into the hands of the Germans, made a hiding place in the woods for themselves and their infant daughter. Every day at dusk they would venture out to the countryside to scrounge for food.

One day they went out and never returned. The fate they had sought so hard to escape had apparently caught up with them. After a while little Marysha who possessed neither speech nor the ability to stand erect, propelled only by her instinct for self-preservation, crawled out into the woods on all fours and began to nourish herself with anything that the earth provided within her grasp.

In time her skin shriveled like an old woman's and the sounds she emitted bore no human resemblance. By the time she was discovered she had evolved into some wild creature that was part-human and part-animal.

After prolonged medical treatment she was brought to this home where, with continuing care and attention, she made a remarkable recovery. I recently learned she now lives in Israel, is happily married, and has children of her own.

My stay in Pietroleshu was a fruitful interlude, both restful and creative. I was able to continue my journey with renewed vigor.

Before I had left on the tour through Lower Silesia a committee of schoolteachers read the children's stories I had brought with me and selected the seven most suitable for their situation to be published in book form.

It so happened that the American painter and cartoonist William Gropper was then visiting Poland. My hosts proposed to him that he illustrate the stories.

Cover of Der Alter fun Lompaduni *(Yiddish children's stories) by Yuri Suhl. Illustrated by William Gropper. Published in Poland, 1948.*

He readily agreed and even assisted with some of the technical problems of production.

There were many such problems, the foremost of which was the lack of Yiddish linotypes. They had all been destroyed during the war and replacements were still unavailable. They did, however, have some excellent Yiddish printers who had survived the war, an old printing press and unbounded determination to publish in Yiddish. They fell back on a centuries-old method—carving letters of the Yiddish alphabet out of wood and handsetting each letter individually. It was a long, slow process, yet they managed to publish a biweekly newspaper and an occasional book. It took them two months to produce my fifty-page collection of children's stories called *Der Alter fun Lompaduni* (*The Old Man of Lompaduni*). Producing it had been a labor of love. At Gropper's suggestion they used various colors for the text as well as the illustrations. The result was a very original and attractive soft-cover book.

In August 1948 I was reunited with Isabelle when she came to Poland on her vacation to attend an international conference of working youth in Warsaw. At the conclusion of the conference she joined me in Wroclaw for two weeks. During that time we both attended the Cultural World Congress for Peace, the first such gathering held in Poland after the war.

Among the delegates were Martin Andersen Nexo of Denmark, Ilya Ehrenburg of the Soviet Union, Julian Huxley and the Dean of Canterbury from England, Pablo Picasso sitting as an exile with the Spanish delegation, Mme. Irene Joliot-Curie of France, Otto Nathan of the United States representing Albert Einstein, and many other leading figures from all over the world.

By the time my five-month stay in Poland had come to a close I had completed the first three of a cycle of eleven poems that would constitute the fulfillment of my commitment. The other eight were still more in my head than on paper. I explained this to my hosts and promised to send the rest of the poems as soon as they were finished. My hosts were very understanding.

The concluding highlight of my visit came when I was invited to read the three poems in the Wroclaw Opera House before an audience of 3,000 that had gathered to celebrate the third anniversary of the existence of the Jewish community of Lower Silesia.

After I left Poland I did not go directly home, but I continued traveling abroad, sometimes with Gropper, sometimes alone, to Czechoslovakia, Switzerland, Italy, and France. We returned together on the Queen Mary which suffered the indignity of getting stuck in the mud for almost a week. We finally arrived in New York in early January 1949.

For a long time after my return from Poland I continued to thrive emotionally on the stored-up impressions of my Lower Silesian experience. In the summer of 1949 Isabelle and I were invited by friends to their summer home in Mountaindale, New York, a small resort in the Catskills, where I combined vacation with working on the remaining eight poems to complete my commitment.

In September 1949 Isabelle left the New York Public Library to accept the position of school librarian in an independent progressive high school in Greenwich Village, a change that was satisfying to her both professionally and personally. From then on we were able to travel together during her frequent school holidays.

In that year I also began a special program set up for professional writers under the GI Bill which entitled me to a stipend. The program was under the aegis of New York University. I was assigned an editor with whom I had to have bi-weekly sessions on a work-in-progress. Later I was also required to take some courses

at NYU. I remained with the program until 1952.

From the moment I signed a contract with a publisher for my first novel, I knew at last my true profession—to be a full-time writer. It has not always been an easy decision to live with because royalty payments are often small and far between and one does have to pay rent. To supplement my earnings I would from time to time take on a part-time job outside my profession. That was how I came to be for one season (1949-50) the business manager of the Jewish Theater Ensemble, a group of Yiddish actors and actresses who descended from the famed Artef Players. They were nonprofessionals who were workers during the day and actors in the evening. My official duty was to fill the house with theater parties and individual sales of tickets. As it turned out I also had an unofficial duty—to hold in rein a temperamental director and to hold the hands of the actors whose feelings he had ruffled. It was an exhausting job, but an interesting experience.

The 1950s were a decade crowded with events both sad and joyous. In March 1950 my father died. At the time of his death he was living with his fourth wife in Trenton, New Jersey. After the death of Laura, his second wife, he had another brief and unhappy marriage that ended in divorce. His last wife was a simple, kind woman who revered him and took good care of him in his latter ailing years. I felt deep grief at his death. Our relationship had become strained when I struck out on my own in ways that were alien to him. As we both grew older, we both mellowed and understood each other better. In his last years there was a warm bond between us.

After almost five years of a steady but sometimes

Yuri and Isabelle Suhl, 1951

stormy relationship, Isabelle and I finally got married on June 24, 1950. We didn't go on a honeymoon, but we did have a whole summer together to do as we pleased before Isabelle had to return to her school job in September.

In October 1950 Macmillan published my first novel, *One Foot in America.* On the day of publication I did what many new authors do on that occasion. I went looking for it in the bookstores. In Brentano's on Fifth Avenue I made the mistake of asking a clerk to help me find it. When he quickly produced a copy, there was nothing for me to do but buy it.

On June 24, 1951, our first wedding anniversary, we received an unexpected gift. The *New York Sunday Compass* published the first installment of their serialization of *One Foot in America.*

Late in 1951 I became actively involved in the clemency campaign for Ethel and Julius Rosenberg. Like many others in this country and abroad I was disturbed by the cruel and excessive death penalty imposed on two young parents with two small children. When the National Committee to Secure Justice in the Rosenberg Case was formed, I volunteered to speak publicly on the case whenever necessary. As the clemency campaign gained momentum in late 1952 and into 1953, I was frequently away from home. I flew to Detroit, Chicago, Denver, Houston, Los Angeles, and other cities around the country. The White House was flooded with appeals for clemency from millions of people in this country and abroad, including such notables as Albert Einstein, the President of France, and the Pope. The lawyers kept making legal moves in the courts hoping to change the verdict or to win a stay of execution, but in the end all efforts failed. On Friday, June 19, 1953, on the eve of the Sabbath, the Rosenbergs were executed. On Sunday, June 21st 50,000 people turned out for their funeral.

I learned that when the president of the Macmillan Company, my publisher, read the news story the next day and discovered that I was a speaker at the Rosenbergs' funeral, he was very disturbed and sent for my file.

This bit of news gave me some anxious moments. Although my second novel was already in galleys, there was no guarantee that it would be published. I had good reason to harbor some doubts, because Macmillan had added a new condition to my second contract that gave the company the right to postpone or suspend publication of the work under contract if "in the opinion of the Company, conditions existing by reason of the present national crisis make impossible normal publishing programs." In those days "national crisis" was a euphemism for the anti-communist hyste-

ria generated by the Korean War and the witch-hunting tactics of Senator Joseph McCarthy, both of which had started in 1950 and by 1953 had swept the country.

The president of Macmillan apparently found nothing reprehensible in my file. *Cowboy on a Wooden Horse* was published on schedule to favorable reviews and was kept in print for the next ten years.

Several months after the execution of the Rosenbergs I was appointed one of the five trustees of the Rosenberg Children's Trust Fund. Although they are now grown men with children of their own, I am still in touch with them.

In the summer of 1952 Isabelle and I went to Mexico. I was still a bilingual writer then, writing poetry in Yiddish and prose in English. While there I gave a number of poetry readings in Mexico City. This led to the formation of a book committee that sponsored the publication of my last collection of poems, *A Vort fun Trayst (A Word of Consolation).* I should point out here that with rare exceptions there are no commercial Yiddish publishers. It is the readers themselves who fill that void in the form of book committees. They sell

Suhl with Diego Rivera holding a copy of Suhl's novel, One Foot in America, *in the garden of Rivera's home, Coyoacán, Mexico, 1952*

copies in advance through subscriptions, host a celebration when the book appears, and actively continue to promote its sale after publication. Thus, publishing by committee has become an old and honored tradition in the world of Yiddish letters.

Thanks to the Mexican book committee, I was introduced to Diego Rivera, who promised to make a drawing for the book's cover. I quickly made a summary in English, which Rivera both read and spoke, of the main themes of my poems—the Holocaust, the new life of the Jewish survivors of the Holocaust in Lower Silesia, discrimination against Black people in the United States, and a few others on miscellaneous themes. The only poem that I translated line-by-line was one I wrote in Mexico dealing with the plight of a homeless Mexican woman, entitled "Tzu a Mexicaner Froy" ("To a Mexican Woman"), and which I dedicated to Diego Rivera.

Getting the promised drawing from him was easier said than done. He was a very busy artist, working concurrently on portraits in his studio and on several murals in various parts of the city. We spent much of our time in Mexico City pursuing the elusive drawing.

When I finally held it in my hand, I was very disappointed. I felt that his portrayal of the Black man and the Jew in the drawing was stereotyped, and I decided not to use it.

As might be expected the book committee reacted with shock and outrage at my decision. It was incomprehensible that I could reject a drawing by the maestro, who to them was beyond reproach.

I was torn. I had been honored by Rivera's willingness to do the cover drawing for my book and I wished I could use it. That was why I took time to consult friends and Mexican artists, soliciting their reaction to the drawing. Many agreed with my view of it. I even went so far as to visit Rivera in his home in Coyoacán to express my reservations about his depiction of the Black man, whereupon he lauched into a lecture about his view on the subject. His main point was that if Black people felt insulted by his drawing it was because white people in the United States had made Black people feel ashamed of the way they looked. He felt they did look the way he drew them and that they should be proud of it. I was not convinced by his arguments. I knew that many Black and white Americans at that time would find the portrayal offensive. Sadly and reluctantly I decided to stick with my original decision. The book was published with a plain cover.

I had considered doing a third autobiographical novel, taking the story into the Depression years of the thirties, but I had, in the meantime, accepted a grant from the Emma Lazarus Federation of Jewish Women's Clubs for a biography of the Polish-born nineteenth-century women's rights advocate and abolitionist, Ernestine Rose, as part of the American Jewish community's commemoration of the tercentenary of the arrival of the first twenty-three Jews in New Amsterdam in 1654.

When I started my research on Ernestine Rose, I found the first sixteen years of her life in Poland so fascinating that the novelist in me saw the possibilities of a historical novel on this remarkable woman. On the basis of this I wrote the first sixty pages of the novel and both the Federation and my publisher were interested. But as I went on with the research into her adult life, I discovered to my sorrow that there were no papers or documents in existence about her personal life. If I were to continue with the novel, I would have to invent a personal life for her. I felt that would not be fair to Mrs. Rose, so I reluctantly abandoned the idea of the novel and began instead to write a biography of her. It took five years of concentrated research, ably assisted by my librarian wife to complete the project. We both got so involved with Ernestine that we jokingly referred to her as the other woman in our life. Under the title *Ernestine L. Rose and the Battle for Human Rights,* the book was published by Reynal in 1959. Some years later I wrote a teenage version of the biography entitled, *Eloquent Crusader: Ernestine Rose,* which was published by Julian Messner in 1970.

My interest in a third novel for an autobiographical trilogy had waned. I turned instead to a subject that had its origin in my first trip to Poland in 1948—the Holocaust. In August 1959, Isabelle and I set out for a year abroad; she on a sabbatical from the private school where she was a librarian, I on a research trip for a documentary anthology on Jewish resistance in Nazi Europe.

Six months of that year we spent in Poland where I did my research at the Jewish Historical Institute of Warsaw, a leading Holocaust documentation center. During that time we made side trips to Czechoslovakia and to East Germany. In Leipzig I met for the first time a cousin of mine, a survivor of the Theresienstadt concentration camp, who had lived since childhood in Germany.

The rest of our itinerary took us to Rumania, Bulgaria, Greece, Israel, Italy, France, and England.

The anthology was five years in the making and was turned down by thirteen publishers on the ground that there would not be a market for it. Crown Publishers took it and brought it out in 1967 under the title *They Fought Back: The Story of the Jewish Resistance in Nazi Europe.* Six weeks after publication it went into a second printing. Now, eighteen years later and after various

*The Suhls celebrating their tenth wedding anniversary, Villa d'Este, Tivoli, Italy,
June 24, 1960*

editions, both here and abroad, the book is still solidly in print. So much for that perennial euphemism—the market.

In 1968 I had an experience of writing under ideal conditions that writers dream about. For a month I was a fellow at the MacDowell Colony in Peterboro, New Hampshire. I had a studio in the woods where I could work without interruption all day. Occasionally I would share with a gray fox some of the lunch that was brought to my door. In the evenings I had the company of fellow writers and artists. Above all, I was freed from all responsibilities except the work-in-progress.

During the decade of the 1970s I wrote exclusively for children. Between 1970 and 1980 I had nine books published. I had always liked to tell stories. Thirty years earlier I had been hired as a storyteller in a children's camp and I made up tales to tell them at the weekly campfires. In the postwar years I wrote the Yiddish stories for children mentioned earlier, but it was not until 1970 that, inspired by a Jewish folk tale, I wrote my first children's story in English, *Simon Boom Gives a Wedding.* It was published in 1972 as a picture book, illustrated by Margot Zemach, and was an instant success. It won a number of awards and citations, including the 1972 Lewis Carroll Shelf Award. The

School Library Journal called it "one of the wittiest books this year." This success prompted me to write two more "Boom" picture books—*The Man Who Made Everyone Late* (1974), illustrated by Lawrence Di Fiori, and *Simon Boom Gets a Letter* (1976), illustrated by Fernando Krahn.

My two other illustrated books are for older readers. *The Merrymaker,* illustrated by Thomas di Grazia and published in 1975, is a tale set in the Old Country about a man who makes up rhymes at weddings. The *Purim Goat,* illustrated by Kaethe Zemach and published in 1980, is a story also set in an Eastern European village at the turn of the century, about a poor boy who saves the life of his pet goat in an unusual way.

During this decade I also wrote two young adult novels on Holocaust themes. The first one was *Uncle Misha's Partisans,* published in 1973. It evolved from a true story, in my documentary anthology *They Fought Back,* about a twelve-year-old boy who joined the Jewish partisans after his family was killed by the Nazis. In 1974 it won the National Jewish Book Award of the Jewish Book Council for a juvenile book. The second novel, *On the Other Side of the Gate,* published in 1975, which grew out of my research on the Holocaust, tells the story of how a young couple living in a ghetto during World War II managed to save the life of their infant child.

I had two nonfiction books published during these years—*Eloquent Crusader: Ernestine Rose* (1970) mentioned earlier and *An Album of the Jews in America,* a pictorial history of the Jews in the United States. It was published in 1972.

In 1971–72 I taught a course at the New School for Social Research, New York City, on the Holocaust and Jewish Resistance to Nazism. Among the students there were some children of survivors who took the course in order to find out what their parent were emotionally unable to tell them about their own Holocaust experiences.

In 1979 I lost two members of my family. First my brother Bernie died suddenly. He was a warmhearted, generous man, who had worked hard all his life, married, and raised two sons. We had never had any interests in common and saw each other infrequently, but that had never kept us from loving each other as brothers. A few months later my beloved

Tante Bertha died.

In 1961, the year after we returned from the year abroad, we rented a small cottage for the summer on Martha's Vineyard, an island off the coast of Cape Cod. We continued renting it for the next six summers and, in May 1967, we were able to buy it. We enlarged and winterized it and since then have spent not only every summer there but also made frequent visits during all the other seasons as well. Now that my wife has retired from her school library position, we stay there six-to-eight months of the year. We are once more enlarging it, this time with the hope of living there year round in the very near future.

It was on the Vineyard, sometime in my middle fifties, that I made the happy discovery that I could also express my creativity in a medium other than writing. There on the island's sprawling beaches I became interested in driftwood as a potential art object. I was fascinated by the suggestive forms of these sea-soaked, sunblanched, and wind-swept pieces of wood, shaped by the elements, by their velvet-smooth texture and

Alfred Eisenstaedt

Suhl, with driftwood sculpture on the deck of his house on Martha's Vineyard, Massachusetts. Photograph by Alfred Eisenstaedt, 1975.

seemingly endless versatility.

To date I have had nine one-man shows of driftwood sculptures and assemblages in addition to having exhibited in a number of group shows. Something that was initially perceived as a hobby has grown into an avocation.

I'm sometimes asked if this dichotomy of creative expressions doesn't interfere with my writing. The answer is no. On the contrary I find it beneficial. It often liberates me from the mounting frustration of staring at a blank page when the right words refuse to come. I simply rise, walk into my shop and lose myself in the tactile and visual world of driftwood. An hour later I return to the mental world relaxed and refreshed, and the blank page usually fills up more readily.

When the basic component common to all arts—invention—is present, two distinct forms of creative expression can coexist side by side, to their mutual benefit.

I have not had any books published since 1980. From time to time I return to one or the other of two unfinished novels with a fresh burst of energy and determination to once and for all bring it to completion, only to be diverted by some more urgent project. I'm not unique. There's hardly a writer alive who doesn't have a few such skeletons rattling in his literary closet. It's important to remember that when they rattle, there is still hope.

In the meantime the next item on my agenda is the completion of a new children's story and getting ready for the tenth exhibit of my driftwood sculpture on Martha's Vineyard in August 1985.

BIBLIOGRAPHY

FOR CHILDREN

Fiction:

Der Alter fun Lompaduni un andere meises ("The Old Man of Lompaduni and Other Stories"; illustrated by William Gropper). Wroclaw, Poland: Niedershlesie, 1948.

Simon Boom Gives a Wedding (illustrated by Margot Zemach). New York: Four Winds, 1972.

Uncle Misha's Partisans (for young adults). New York: Four Winds, 1973; London: Hamish Hamilton, 1975; Hamlyn, 1977.

The Man Who made Everyone Late (illustrated by Lawrence di Fiori). New York: Four Winds, 1974.

The Merrymaker (illustrated by Thomas di Grazia). New York: Four Winds, 1975.

On the Other Side of the Gate. New York: F. Watts, 1975; Avon, 1976.

Simon Boom Gets a Letter (illustrated by Fernando Krahn). New York: Four Winds, 1976.

The Purim Goat (illustrated by Kaethe Zemach). New York: Four Winds, 1980.

Nonfiction:

Eloquent Crusader: Ernestine Rose. New York: Messner, 1970.

An Album of Jews in America. New York: F. Watts, 1972.

FOR ADULTS

Fiction:

One Foot in America. New York: Macmillan, 1950; Paperback Library, 1968.

Cowboy on a Wooden Horse. New York: Macmillan, 1953; published as *You Should Only Be Happy.* New York: Paperback Library, 1969.

Nonfiction:

Ernestine L. Rose and the Battle for Human Rights. New York: Reynal, 1959.

They Fought Back: The Story of the Jewish Resistance in Nazi Europe. New York: Crown: 1967; London: Macgibbon & Kee, 1968; New York; Paperback Library, 1968; Schocken Books, 1975.

Poetry:

Dos Licht oif Mein Gass ("The Light on My Street"; illustrated by L. Bunin). New York: Signal, 1935.

Dem Tog Antkegen ("Toward the Day"). New York: Signal, 1938.

Yisroel Partisan ("Israel the Partisan"). New York: Signal, 1942.

A Vort fun Trayst ("A Word of Consolation"). Mexico, D.F.: YKUF of Mexico, 1952.

Yoshiko Uchida

1921-

Yoshiko Uchida, about three, and sister Keiko

"Mama, be sure to bring me my umbrella if it rains," I would say. "I will, Yo Chan, don't worry," Mama would answer. "Now be careful crossing the street."

Every morning my mother and I repeated this little ritual before I trudged off to Longfellow Elementary School in Berkeley, California. The sun could be shining in a clear blue sky and the rainy season long gone, but I always had to have this reassurance from my mother before I left home.

I don't think it was really the rain that concerned me. It was just that I had to know my mother was always there for me if I needed her. I know part of my insecurity came from being four years younger than my only sister, Keiko, who could do everything better than I, and who could make me do just about anything by threatening, "All right for you, if you don't!" But there was something else that added to my timidity. I was an American of Japanese descent and, although we had several close white American family friends, I lived in a society that in general made me feel different and not as good as my white peers.

I grew up asking such questions as, "Will you rent us a house? Will the neighbors object? Can Japanese swim in your pool?" When I went to a beauty parlor for my first professional haircut, I called first to ask, "Do you cut Japanese hair?" There was also the time when a stranger on the street shouted to me, "Go back where you came from!"

All I longed for in those early years was to be like everyone else and to be viewed as an American. I was born in Alameda, California, and grew up in Berkeley. And yet, when people saw me, they usually saw only my Japanese face.

When I was ten, my parents took my sister and me to a small village in Connecticut to visit my mother's white American pen pal. We were probably the first Asians to visit this small community, and one of the women I met gave me a pat on the head and said, "My, you speak English so beautifully." She had meant to compliment me, of course, but I still remember today how stunned and disappointed I was to be perceived as a foreigner.

If I felt intimidated and different in the "outside world," however, I felt safe and secure at home. There flowed from my parents not only love and warmth and caring for Keiko and me, but the richness of the Japanese culture, values, traditions and beliefs that were an integral part of their lives and which thus became a vital part of our own as well.

My mother, Iku Umegaki, the eldest daughter of a prefectural governor in Japan, came to the United States in 1916 to marry my father, Dwight Takashi Uchida, who had preceded her to America in 1906. Both were graduates of Doshisha University, one of the early Christian universities of Japan, and as was the custom of the day, their marriage was an arranged one. Seeing their long and happy marriage, however, I have always thought the professors who arranged the match must have taken great pride in the success of their endeavor.

After a few early years in Portland, Oregon, my parents lived in Oakland, California, and my father worked in the San Francisco offices of Mitsui and Company, a large Japanese business firm where he eventually became assistant manager. They moved later to Berkeley, the city which has always been and is now "home" for me.

My parents were early and active members of a

Family portrait with paternal grandmother, 1931

small Japanese church (now Sycamore Congregational Church), to which they devoted much of their time and energy. Every Sunday morning we piled into Papa's Buick, picked up three or four children on the way, and got to church in time for both my parents to teach Sunday school class. This meant that Keiko and I could never miss a Sunday either, and because my parents were giving and caring people, unable to be indifferent to the needs of others, we learned early the importance of being responsible for our fellow human beings.

The written word was always important in our family, and my mother often wrote poetry—the thirty-one-syllable Japanese *tanka*. Like most women of her day, however, she focused her attention on her family, and her creativity existed on the fringes of her life. She wrote her poems on scraps of paper and the backs of envelopes, and they were published by a friend in a small Japanese newsletter.

My mother also loved books, and our house was filled with them. Although she didn't find time to read much for herself, she often read Japanese stories to Keiko and me. Many of these were the Japanese folktales which I later included in my first published book, *The Dancing Kettle.*

Unlike my gentle dreamer mother, my father was a cheerful, practical, and energetic businessman who handled all the business matters of our house with great efficiency. He was also an avid letter writer, and influenced by my mother, he eventually tried his hand at writing *tanka* as well.

Between the two of them, my parents carried on a voluminous correspondence, mostly with friends and relatives in Japan. As a result, our mailbox was always bulging, and our home seemed constantly filled with visiting friends from Japan. Many were Doshisha alumni or professors and others were seminary students or long-winded ministers. The students usually spent at least two years in Berkeley, so were often invited to our home for Sunday and holiday dinners, and even worse for me, they often dropped by uninvited. Pressed and polished, with their squeaky shoes, their hair slicked down with camellia hair oil, they appeared for afternoon tea and stayed for supper, and I hated them with a passion for intruding on our family life.

But now these people who were so dull and annoying to me as a child, provide wonderful material for my writing, and I remember them not only with fascination, but with some guilt for the shabby way I treated them. I also remember the laughter, the wonderful smell of *sukiyaki* cooking at the table, and the after-dinner singing around our piano, and realize that in spite of ourselves, Keiko and I often had good times at these gatherings.

I believe our life's experiences are always with us, and I find that I draw constantly from the memories of the past. I also find bits and pieces of my child self turning up in my writing.

It seems to me I've been interested in books and writing for as long as I can remember. I was writing stories when I was ten, and being the child of frugal immigrant parents, I wrote them on brown wrapping paper which I cut up and bound into booklets, and because I am such a saver, I still have them. The first is titled, "Jimmy Chipmonk and His Friends: A Short Story for Small Children."

I not only wrote stories, I also kept a journal of important events which I began the day I graduated from elementary school. Of course my saver self kept that journal as well, and even today I can read of the special events of my young life, such as the times my parents took us to an opera or concert in San Francisco, or the day I got my first dog, or the sad day it died, when I drew a tombstone for him in my journal and decorated it with floral wreaths.

By putting these special happenings into words and writing them down, I was trying to hold on to and somehow preserve the magic as well as the joy and sadness of certain moments in my life, and I guess that's really what books and writing are all about.

Yoshiko and Keiko with their dog, about 1933

Junior high and high school were not very happy times, for those were the years when I felt more and more alienated and excluded, especially from the social activities of my white classmates. I couldn't wait to get out of high school. I increased my class load and graduated in two-and-a-half years, entering the University of California at Berkeley when I was only sixteen, immature and naive. There the exclusion of Japanese Americans from the social activities of white students was even greater than in high school, and my social life was confined to activities of the Japanese students clubs. We had our own dances, weenie roasts, picnics and parties, and I finally discovered the pleasures of dating.

All during my college years I never spoke first to a white student for fear of being rebuffed, and never went out socially with a white man until many years later. Although my closest friend now and for the past twenty-five years happens to be a white man, I probably would not have spoken to him nor gone out with him had we met during my college years.

It was during my senior year in college that the bombs fell on Pearl Harbor and my whole world fell apart. We were having Sunday dinner when we heard the unbelievable news on the radio. Assuming it was the act of a fanatic and certainly not even dreaming that it was the beginning of war with Japan, I went to the university to study for final exams.

When I returned home toward evening, my father was gone. The FBI had taken him for questioning, and we had no idea when he would return. We left the porch light on all night, hoping he would return shortly, but for three days and nights we had no word from him. Finally we learned that he as well as hundreds of other Japanese American community leaders had been seized on December 7th and were being held at the San Francisco Immigration Headquarters. Soon after, they were shipped to various prisoner-of-war camps, and my father was among those sent to Missoula, Montana.

Those were anxious days filled with false rumors of sabotage by the Japanese Americans in Hawaii (later completely refuted), growing campaigns of hatred and vilification by longtime anti-Asian pressure groups, and extremely troubling rumors about a "mass evacuation" of all the Japanese Americans from the West Coast. None of us believed our government would imprison its own citizens, but on February 19, 1942, President Franklin D. Roosevelt issued Executive Order 9066 which would uproot 120,000 Japanese Americans and imprison us behind barbed wire, without trial or hearing, simply because we looked like the enemy. Two-thirds of us were American citizens, and I was one of them.

Uchida (far left) with college classmates, 1941

Looking back on that tragic event today, I find it hard to believe that our government leaders could have violated our constitution so ruthlessly. I believe their betrayal was not only against the Japanese Americans, but against ALL Americans, for they damaged the very essence of our democratic beliefs.

By March a five-mile travel restriction and an 8:00 P.M. curfew were imposed on us, and for the next two months my mother, sister, and I tried to prepare for our forced removal by clearing out the house we had occupied for fifteen years. We worked frantically, selling things we should have kept and storing things we should have thrown out. Although friends came to help us, our task was made doubly difficult by the absence of my father. It was distressing to have to drop out from the university, but one of the saddest moments was having to part with our aging collie who died only a few months after he was separated from us.

On April 21, 1942, removal orders were issued for the Japanese of Berkeley, giving us exactly ten days to clear out of the area. On May 1, some fourteen hundred of us were shipped under armed guard to the Tanforan Racetrack which eventually housed eight thousand uprooted Japanese Americans in its stables and barracks.

By then we had become Family #13453, and when my father was released on parole to join us, the four of us lived for five months in a horse stall previously occupied by a single horse. Only thin wood partitions divided the families jammed into rows of horse stalls, and privacy became something we could only

remember with longing. I, of course, missed my graduation from the university, and my diploma was sent to me in a cardboard roll and presented to me in my horse stall by the camp mailman.

Schools, churches, and recreation centers were quickly organized, and with teachers in short supply, I signed up to teach a class of second graders. My sister, with a degree in child development from Mills College, organized the camp's two nursery schools.

By September, however, the entire camp was again uprooted. This time we were sent to a desolate concentration camp called Topaz, located in the middle of a vast and barren Utah desert. We discovered it to be a cluster of bleak tar-papered barracks, (none of which were complete when we arrived), surrounded by a barbed wire fence with guard towers at each corner. Each family was assigned to one of six rooms into which each barrack was divided, but there were no stoves for heat, and the lack of inner sheetrock walls allowed white powder-like dust to sift into the rooms from every crack in the siding as well as the hole in the roof where the stovepipe was to fit.

I again taught second grade, but the school barracks were as hopelessly inadequate as those in which we lived. The children and I often sat in our classroom bundled up in coats and scarves, shivering in morning temperatures of thirty degrees. On other days when the frequent raging dust storms swept through the desert and dust poured in from the roof, we feared for the children's safety and sent them home for the day.

In Topaz my sister again organized nursery

Topaz, Utah, 1942-43: "the concentration camp where I was interned. Hidden from view are the barbed wire fence and guard towers."

schools, my father chaired many of the committees needed to run the camp, and my mother, in her gentle nurturing way, tried to make a home in our bleak barrack room for our family and friends.

But life in a concentration camp, ringed by a barbed wire fence and guarded by armed sentries, grew increasingly intolerable, and with the help of the Student Relocation Committee (administered by the American Friends Service Committee), I obtained a fellowship enabling me to leave. In May 1943, Keiko and I left Topaz—she to work in the nursery school of Mt. Holyoke's Department of Education and I to do graduate work at Smith College, Northampton, Massachusetts. Not long after, my parents received permission to leave for Salt Lake City.

It had been a devastating and traumatic year which left a lasting impact on my life, but it was many years before I could write about the experience.

During my year at Smith College, I earned a Master's degree in education, and feeling at last like a full-fledged teacher, I accepted a job teaching a combined class of first and second graders in a small Quaker school on the outskirts of Philadelphia. But after my first year, I had the first of many bouts with mononucleosis and also realized that teaching was a twenty-four-hour job that left me no time nor energy

for writing. So I ended my brief teaching career and headed for New York City where my sister was teaching in a private school.

I spent the next few years working as a secretary at a job I could leave behind at the end of the day and was able to write in the evenings. I was writing short stories at the time, sending them to the *New Yorker,* *Atlantic Monthly* and *Harper's*—and routinely receiving printed rejection slips. After a time, however, the slips contained encouraging penciled notes and a *New Yorker* editor even met with me to suggest that I write about my concentration camp experiences.

I never made the *New Yorker,* but the article I wrote for them became the core of material which, after years of revisions, additions, submissions, and simply languishing in my files, eventually became my book for adults, *Desert Exile: The Uprooting of a Japanese American Family.* And many of the short stories I wrote during those days were published eventually in literature anthologies for young people.

Although I did place one short story at *Woman's Day,* I discovered soon thereafter that I could be more successful writing for children, and in 1952 a Ford Foundation Foreign Area Fellowship enabled me to escape my life as secretary/writer to spend two years in

Family portrait, 1943, "on the day my sister and I (far left) left Topaz for the outside world."

Japan. I had been there before as a child, but my memories of that visit were of such things as long boring afternoons when I'd counted the number of times my parents and their friends exchanged bows on first meeting (the most was thirteen!).

This time I loved everything about the country, and my years there were as restorative and enriching as the wartime experience had been devastating and depleting. I went primarily to collect more Japanese folktales (which were later included in *The Magic Listening Cap* and *The Sea of Gold*), but I grew increasingly interested in Japan's arts and crafts.

I learned about Japanese folk art from the three men who founded the Folk Art Movement of Japan: the eminent philosopher Soetsu Yanagi and two of Japan's leading potters, Shoji Hamada and Kanjiro Kawai. They opened my eyes to the honest, simple beauty of handcrafts made by rural villagers, taught me much about contemporary Japanese pottery and even about Zen which, for some fleeting moments, I thought I actually understood.

I translated such poems by Kanjiro Kawai as "I am you/ the you that only I can see," and many of them, along with a monograph about his life work, were published in a chapbook entitled, *We Do Not Work Alone*. I also wrote several articles dealing with Japanese crafts for the *Nippon Times*, and later for *Craft Horizons*, whose West Coast correspondent I was for a time.

On returning to California I was eager to try some handcrafts myself, and studied pottery, jewelry-making, and frame loom tapestry. I discovered, however, that none of it was as easy as it looked. My pots were often lopsided, my jewelry sometimes fell apart, and I could complete only one tapestry. I decided my talents lay not in creating handcraft, but in writing about it, and I soon discovered potters turning up in some of my children's books as well—*Takao and Grandfather's Sword, Rokubei and the Thousand Rice Bowls,* and *Makoto, The Smallest Boy.* And of course many of my subsequent books incorporated aspects of Japanese life that I had absorbed during my two years there—*The Forever Christmas Tree, Sumi's Prize, Sumi's Special Happening, Sumi and The Goat and The Tokyo Express, In-Between Miya,* and *Hisako's Mysteries.*

Most important, however, my years in Japan had made me aware of a new dimension to myself as a Japanese American and deepened my respect and admiration for the culture that had made my parents what they were. By then neither of them was in good health, and I remained in California to care for them and to give them what support and sustenance I could.

When my mother died in 1966, my father was already partially paralyzed from a stroke, and I felt moved to write a book especially for them and the other first-generation Japanese (the Issei), who had en-

Uchida in Paris, 1951

dured so much and been so strong.

The book I wrote was *Journey to Topaz*, the story of young Yuki Sakane and her family, based largely on my own journey to Topaz. Many years later, because so many children wanted to know what happened to Yuki and her family after the war, I wrote a sequel entitled *Journey Home*.

When I speak to children in schools today, they are full of questions about my two "Journey" books. I also tell them about my short story "The Bracelet," which deals with the uprooting, and show them the photographs in *Desert Exile*, which some of them have read.

I always ask them why they think I wrote these books about my wartime experiences, and they ask, "To tell about the camps? To tell how you felt?" But eventually, they come up with the right answer. "You wrote them so it won't happen again," they say. And I always make sure they understand that freedom is our most precious possession.

I also hope they get a sense of the strength and courage with which most Japanese Americans—especially the Issei—survived this devastating tragedy, for I believe their survival was truly a triumph of the human spirit.

Since *Journey to Topaz*, all of my books have been about the Japanese American experience in the United States, for by then the young third-generation Japanese Americans were seeking their identity and sense of self. I wanted not only to reinforce their self-knowledge and pride, but to give them and all young people a sense of continuity and kinship with the past.

In *Samurai of Gold Hill* I told the story of the first Japanese colonists who came to California shortly after the gold rush to establish their ill-fated tea and silk farm. About the same time I also wrote a novel for adults about a Japanese immigrant woman, but unfortunately, despite encouraging words from many editors and publishers, it has yet to find a home. The one thing I have learned as a writer, however, is to be patient; I still have hope that one day it will be published somewhere when the time is right.

My two picture books, *The Birthday Visitor* and *The Rooster Who Understood Japanese*, were attempts to fill the void about Japanese Americans in books for younger children. But most of my writing has been for the eight-to-twelve group, and my three recent books in this category have been about Rinko, a young Japanese American child growing up in Berkeley during the depression years: *A Jar of Dreams*, *The Best Bad Thing*, and *The Happiest Ending*.

These books are not based on my own life, for Rinko's family had more of a struggle to survive in those difficult times than we did. Still, there is much of

Uchida (second from left), with the British potter, Bernard Leach, and friends, Japan, 1953

Signing books after a school talk, Sacramento, 1975

me in Rinko; she has many of the same feelings and longings I had as a child. But she discovers pride in herself as a Japanese American much earlier than I did, and she has much more gumption as well. She dares to be bold and feisty when necessary, and she doesn't let her older brother push her around or tell her what to do.

Writing these three books was a real joy for me, for they brought back so many happy memories of the times and people I knew in my childhood. I felt again the spirit of hope and affirmation they expressed, which I hope I conveyed to my readers as well.

All my books have been about the Japanese or Japanese Americans, but while I cherish and take pride in my special heritage, I never want to lose my sense of connection with the community of man, for I feel the basic elements of humanity are present in all our strivings.

I am now happily settled again in Berkeley and feel very lucky to be a writer, doing what I love best. I love the freedom of being able to structure my own days—to work or play or to see my friends or to travel when I please. I think that kind of freedom is a luxury to be cherished.

I meet occasionally with a group of fellow writers in this area for sharing, support, and sometimes sympathy, and enjoy meeting other writers when I speak at conferences or meetings.

But I also enjoy the contact with college students when I speak about *Desert Exile,* and it is great fun to be with fourth, fifth, and sixth graders when I speak to them about my books. They often write me wonderful letters after my visits; I especially enjoyed one from a young man whose class I visited in Texas. "Thanks a lot for visiting our school," he wrote, "and getting us out of our afternoon classes." That kind of letter keeps me humble.

And perhaps the seven hundred folded-paper cranes given to me recently by some fifth graders will bring me the good fortune to continue writing many more books, and as one child wished for me, "the happiest life you will ever have!"

BIBLIOGRAPHY

FOR CHILDREN

Fiction:

The Dancing Kettle, and Other Japanese Folk Tales (illustrated by Richard C. Jones). New York: Harcourt, 1949.

Deborah Storms

Uchida at home in Berkeley, about 1980

New Friends for Susan (illustrated by Henry Sugimoto). New York: Scribner, 1951.

The Magic Listening Cap: More Folk Tales from Japan (illustrated by the author). New York: Harcourt, 1955.

The Full Circle (illustrated by the author). New York: Friendship, 1957.

Takao and Grandfather's Sword (illustrated by William M. Hutchinson). New York: Harcourt, 1958.

The Promised Year (illustrated by W. M. Hutchinson). New York: Harcourt, 1959.

Mik and the Prowler (illustrated by W. M. Hutchinson). New York: Harcourt, 1960.

Rokubei and the Thousand Rice Bowls (illustrated by Kazue Mizumura). New York: Scribner, 1962.

The Forever Christmas Tree (illustrated by K. Mizumura), New York: Scribner, 1963.

Sumi's Prize (illustrated by K. Mizumura). New York: Scribner, 1964.

The Sea of Gold, and Other Tales from Japan (illustrated by Marianne Yamaguchi). New York: Scribner, 1965.

Sumi's Special Happening (illustrated by K. Mizumura). New York: Scribner, 1966.

In-Between Miya (illustrated by Susan Bennett). New York: Scribner, 1967.

Hisako's Mysteries (illustrated by S. Bennett). New York: Scribner, 1969.

Sumi and the Goat and the Tokyo Express (illustrated by K. Mizumura). New York: Scribner, 1969.

Makoto, the Smallest Boy (illustrated by Akihito Shirakawa). New York: Crowell, 1970.

Journey to Topaz (illustrated by Donald Carrick). New York: Scribner, 1971; Berkeley, Calif.: Creative Arts, 1985.

Samurai of Gold Hill (illustrated by Ati Forberg). New York: Scribner, 1972; Berkeley, Calif.: Creative Arts, 1985.

The Birthday Visitor (illustrated by Charles Robinson). New York: Scribner, 1975.

The Rooster Who Understood Japanese (illustrated by C. Robinson). New York: Scribner, 1976.

Journey Home (sequel to *Journey to Topaz;* illustrated by C. Robinson). New York: Atheneum, 1978.

A Jar of Dreams. New York: Atheneum, 1981.

Tabi: Journey through Time, Stories of the Japanese in America. Nashville, Tenn.: United Methodist Publishing House, 1984.

The Best Bad Thing (sequel to *A Jar of Dreams*). New York: Atheneum, 1983.

The Happiest Ending (sequel to *The Best Bad Thing*). New York: Atheneum, 1985.

FOR ADULTS

Nonfiction:

We Do Not Work Alone: The Thoughts of Kanjiro Kawai. Kyoto, Japan: Folk Art Society, 1953.

The History of Sycamore Church. El Cerrito, Calif.: Sycamore Congregational Church, 1974.

Desert Exile: The Uprooting of a Japanese-American Family. Seattle, Wash.: University of Washington Press, 1982.

Rosemary Wells

1943-

A Swiss friend asked me not long ago, "What is the difference between *terrible, awful, dreadful,* and *horrible*?" I said that there were small differences too subtle and unstable to explain. I could not tell her when one word was used better than another. I showed her an entry in *Roget's Thesaurus* under *badness* and when Margrit let her eyes wander over the hundred or so entries there she declared mournfully that she'd never learn to speak English properly. That it had more words than Chinese. I said it did. She said that in her dialect of German there were two, maybe three commonly used words for badness. I could tell that Margrit didn't like the idea of a hundred-odd words for badness. Perhaps it struck her as wasteful, in much the same way as having a hundred bottles of milk in the icebox.

Another friend, who speaks Norwegian, assured me that there was only one real word in Norwegian for badness. The idea that a language may be "small" or "large" does not come up often, but I have to think about it because I must consider all of the English that I know every workday of my life. Is a language without a hundred words for badness like a piano with only twenty-two notes? If this is so, English is like a piano that would never fit in any room. It could never be gotten round a corner or hoisted through a window. English would be ten yards wide and ten keyboards deep.

I mention this when I speak to young writers about the art of writing. Like others in my profession, I use mostly the middle of the keyboard, knowing all the while that the other notes and stops and pedals are there.

Writing is always the last of the arts to show up as a talent in children. Writing has no Mozarts or Yehudi Menuhins. The closest thing to a prodigy in my lifetime has been Joyce Maynard, who as a Yale student turned out a superbly written book. Learning to write is like doing scales for fourteen years except you don't know you are doing them. Young writers hide. They have to. There are too many words and it takes years of reading many authors to know how to use words effectively. It also takes years before a young writer has the mental perspective to choose what to say and what not. There are exceptions. There are poems, for instance, written by very young children in abject circumstances

(ghettos for example). These poems ring very true and grab the heart immediately. They have the quality, though, of folk songs from a distant culture—remote, personal, disturbing and yet, not fully formed.

I "learned to write" in school. There was nothing wrong with that. However, there was as much chance of my really writing what was in my spirit as there is of a prisoner, whose mail is opened and inspected, writing that he has dug an escape tunnel.

In school we all knew about the ten-tiered, ten-yard-wide piano that is the English language. Most of the twelve years I spent there were devoted to deciphering it, learning how others used it, and practicing it. We wrote book reports, business letters, history papers, and occasionally, poetry. What I never learned about expressing ideas or feelings on paper is best explained in a chess metaphor.

I play chess once in a while. Anyone who plays knows about the utter concentration required to picture even three moves ahead. Champion chess players can project thirty moves and commit to memory countless openings and closings of famous games. Grand masters, however, actually become the game on the board in front of them. They play chess like tennis. They *are* the game. They obliterate everything else, all self, and become the sixteen men on the sixty-four squares. Writing is the same. You have to become the piece you are writing.

Very few young people who grow up to be writers know this lies in store for them, even if they write reams and reams. Young writers do odd things that they almost never acknowledge. They listen compulsively to other people's conversations (eavesdropping) and become so proficient at this (and at concealing it) that they are virtually human video tape recorders.

When writers are young they read for pleasure. When subjects are presented dryly, young writers tend to lose the thread and teachers often think they are blockheads or lazy.

Young writers very often have a quick memory for the lyrics of songs and recite them silently, over and over. Lyrics are poetry of a kind—words used powerfully in certain rhythms. This is very engaging and fascinating for young writers, but they consider it private business. They may listen to the words of popular music before they pay attention to the beat or the tune (whatever tunes may exist in current rock music). They become annoyed with indistinct meaning, sloppy rhyme, or lazy sentiments. But young writers seldom let on about the things they notice. During a science class, for instance, their attention may wander, not necessarily to a ball game after school or a boyfriend waiting down at a locker, but to the cut of a teacher's jacket, the color of a classmate's teeth, or the motives that lay behind a message carved into the desktop and studied many times before.

Young writers do not show off. To do so would be to stand naked among their fashionably dressed peers. Dancing or playing an instrument is at least tolerated by other children, if not sincerely admired, as an acceptable part of the culture. But writing is the most private of the arts. Young people hesitate to throw themselves into it, the way they might play the flute. Instead, they hide their talents. Writing would not only reveal their private selves (the private self can always be disguised in fiction). But writing would also reveal how keenly they observe others—how much they absorb of accents, gestures, and how they see into the soul under the clothes. To write the truth when one is young is to give away the fact that one knows others' secrets and has power over them (all writers have)—and that is the last thing a young writer wants to do.

This secret power of observation and deduction is usually the only thing a young writer knows about him or herself that has anything to do with the art of writing.

Drawing is quite different. Children who draw well early, like children who play music or hit a baseball three hundred feet, are noticed, complimented, and ascribed a future. They are called "talented." I was. I drew constantly. When I was a first grader, the eighth-grade teacher told me I could draw better than she or anyone in the eighth grade. This, of course, gave me a lot of confidence.

When the children in my first grade in 1949 were asked what they wanted to be when they grew up, the little boys all answered fireman, doctor, policeman, soldier. The girls, with unswerving sincerity, answered nurse, teacher, mother. Because I could say artist, I had a reprieve from what, even then, I considered to be a life-sentence of drudgery. When I became a teenager, the idea of being an artist was the only thing that stood between me and despair—I was gangly, underdeveloped, a social retard whose mother didn't like her watching "American Bandstand."

I drew curious subjects, at least they were considered curious by others. My mother tells me my first drawing was of an angry policeman (although at three I had never seen one). I drew cowboys, baseball players, medieval soldiers, and lots and lots of bloody fights. I never drew a woman or a girl until I was about fifteen. I don't know why. It must have seemed to me that males had all the fun in this world. Whatever was behind those piles of drawings, the drawings themselves were behind the writing; and now that I am over forty, I can say the writing is the better part of my skills. I try

Wells' parents, about 1950

Rosemary at her grandmother's house, about 1946

mightily to improve my illustrations but my heart is probably more in writing.

My father was a writer as well, a playwright, or at least he had been one by the time I came along when he was fifty. He stopped writing then. Earlier, he'd had a play produced on Broadway. It ran a good season in 1939. I remember being piggybacked around a television set of the play in about 1950, on Zachary Scott's shoulders. I was about six. It was a live production and Zachary Scott was the star.

One thing about the original play that my father loved to tell was that back in the thirties when he was casting it, he had a choice of two young actors for the lead. One was Roy Hargrave, the other an unknown—Humphrey Bogart. My father chose Hargrave.

My father had lived a very full life by the time I was born. He looked much younger than his fifty years, due to an outdoor existence, everyone said. He'd been a rancher in the Australian outback, fought in the trenches in World War I, and made his living as a Hollywood stunt rider in the days before talkies. He

knew Tom Mix. Just before my father died at the age of ninety—when he had total recall of events past and little memory of what had happened the hour before—I asked him if he'd known Ronald Reagan in Hollywood. He said, "Sure. He was all right. Never amounted to much, though."

Daddy never made a penny, really. But when I was little he was home during the day, and I am richer for having two full-time parents than if he had made a small fortune. In truth I had three full-time parents. They included my grandmother, who lived five miles away in a big house on the ocean. She called every day and I spent so much time in her enormous stucco house with its own beach that most of my sentimental and favorite memories, good and bad, come from that place and time on the New Jersey shore.

When my grandmother died, ten years ago, her house was bought by a man who didn't really explain his business. He paid for the house in cash from a suitcase. The trustees did not argue. The family were appalled and speculated for many weeks about the man's sources of income. The man made changes in the house.

I believe in ghosts the way I believe in vitamins or germs. I know my grandmother's ghost is in the house still because she loved that house like a second self. It was coral-colored stucco, with curved red tiles on the roof, built in the twenties after a fad for things "Spanish." Pigeons nested in the ivy that grew on the walls. There was a greenhouse, planted lushly with my grandmother's three favorite flowers—carnations, lilies, and snapdragons. Her house was always decorated with vases of these flowers, winter and summer. On Sundays, when we all gathered for dinner, a single snapdragon would be floating in our finger bowls. There was a fishpond with two granite fountains, one a cupid and the other a dolphin. My cousin and I tried to catch one of the huge old goldfish that lived under the lily pads with a small net that was kept along the garden wall. The fish were too fast for us. We never got one.

The man who bought my grandmother's house neglected the greenhouse, filled in the fishpond, and installed a jacuzzi. He ripped the ivy down and glazed over great portions of the walls. I wonder if, as he sleeps in her bedroom, her ghost has given him shingles, boils, or at least fallen arches for this. If my grandmother's ghost has remained true to her character she has given him all three by this time. On the other hand, if she has entered a paradise where passions of the moment and worldly insults to the flesh do not matter, then she has forgiven him. But she would also have had to forgive all the sins of Franklin Roosevelt, whom she called "that man" all the days of her life, and I doubt that even the beneficence of heaven could get her to forgive him.

My grandmother was small, only five feet two inches. She had been a great beauty in New York society long before I knew her. By her own admission she'd been a bad mother, an insensitive and materialistic woman. In mid-life she changed herself around and became tractable and understanding. She was a widow at thirty-eight (penicillin was still unknown when my grandfather died in 1931). She had become legally entangled with mediums who were trying to take her for every penny she owned. She married the lawyer who got her off the hook and sent the mediums packing. He was my Uncle Charlie, as fine a grandfather as anyone could have. She never went near a medium again.

The mediums were quite rapacious. Fakes, of course. When my mother was a little girl, she and her brother sneaked into the séances, hid behind the draperies and disrupted the proceedings, rapping away at the wrong moments. When my mother opted to go to Paris at the age of fourteen to dance (she later danced with Pavlova and in the Ballet Russe de Monte Carlo), my grandmother sent her there under the protection of a husband-and-wife team of mediums.

Uncle Charlie taught me to love the Dodgers. From the time I was a little girl and even into my teens, I wanted to be a baseball player much more than I wanted to be an artist. The love of the game has never left me. I still watch it on television and listen to it on the radio. I am an ardent Mets fan and anti-Yankee fan so there is much to root for and against here in New York. Uncle Charlie had played second base for Columbia University in his youth. To me this was almost the major leagues.

My grandmother got along with Uncle Charlie in a formal sort of way. She called him "Father" and slept in a separate room. Uncle Charlie wore silk paisley shirts from Sulka, only from Sulka. Even in the summer he buttoned them all the way to the top button and never rolled up the long sleeves. Garters held up his socks. I came across a pair of his garters one day and did not know what they were. One of the maids told me and I was astonished.

Uncle Charlie took me to Ebbet's Field. He encouraged me to whistle piercingly and yell loudly. I remember a game which the Dodgers won, coming from four runs behind with two out in the bottom of the ninth. Uncle Charlie and I were sitting behind a large Black family. They and we cheered until we were hoarse. Then they began to dance and jump and we joined them, throwing our arms around each other in wild joy. Uncle Charlie, the staid Jewish lawyer with the paisley Sulka shirts, who never touched a drop of liquor in his life, took a swig from the Black man's beer can. Uncle Charlie, who favored creamed spinach (which my mother called green mud) and who never kissed my grandmother in my presence except on the forehead, threw his arms around the Black man's wife. And because he was only five foot three inches and she was a good head taller, she lifted him off the ground, his feet nearly clearing the wooden stadium seats. He laughed and I laughed but when we went home we never told anyone.

One day I was told I would never see Uncle Charlie again because he and my grandmother had gotten a divorce. Another day, two years later, I was told I would really never see him again because he'd been in the club car of a train that went over the Raritan River, slipped its tracks, and fallen into the water, drowning everyone. My mother and father recalled him from time to time with humor and fondness. My grandmother only referred to him when absolutely necessary and then as "Mr. I-won't-say-who."

My grandmother resembled a bright little bird, all energy and quick blue eyes. She used to sit with me in the card room on nights I spent there and read aloud for long periods of time. The rhythm of her low modulated voice matched the sound of the breakers down at the beach, a hundred yards away. Living away from the ocean as I do now, I am aware of an incompleteness in the atmosphere. People who grow up in the mountains tend to feel that way too. Someday I'll move back. The waves, particularly at night, will always remind me of my grandmother's reading voice.

Her favorite poem was called *Evangeline.* I could not sit through much of it and begged her to read Kipling or Poe instead. Her favorite lotion, which was colorless, astringent-smelling, and came in a round flat bottle, was called also "Evangeline." She advised me to use it. In my unquestioning child's mind the poem and the lotion were logically related.

My parents were not really American. My father was English-Australian and my mother had spent half her life dancing in England and in France. Because of this I had a curious outlook on the 1950s world in the small New Jersey town where we lived. I was part of it because I had grown up there but I was also aware of another world, completely different, foreign and entirely romantic, a world mostly of my mother's and father's past that surrounded my life like an invisible aureole. Neither of my parents had gone very far in school. My mother had dropped out to dance when she was fourteen. My father had run away to a sheep ranch at the same age, where he stayed until he volunteered for the First World War. They did not really understand pep rallies, SAT scores, guidance counselors, or the jitterbug. They looked on these things as visitations from another planet.

I look back with some longing and wistfulness now and again on the simplicity of life in a seaside New Jersey town. My grandmother was rich, but my parents had little money. We took no vacations. We owned nothing in the way of fancy equipment because all there was to own, after all, were flickering black-and-white TVs that showed "I Love Lucy" and Edward R. Murrow, and inexpensive record players. No one had even heard of a speaker, come to think of it. Movies were most often musicals and Saturday afternoon Westerns at the Carlton theatre in Red Bank. Drugs were unknown; popular music appealed mostly to older teenagers; and I rode my bike everywhere. Safety was taken for granted.

My own children are much better educated than I was. They have been abroad; they have gone to Broadway plays and expensive restaurants—things that were absolutely unheard of in my childhood. But I wonder if when they grow up they will have memories as effulgent as many of mine.

The summers were stifling, five miles inland where we lived, and there was no air-conditioning. So we spent most summer evenings having supper at my grandmother's beach. Besides my parents and myself, my best friend Ginny was almost always included. Ginny and I were closer than any sisters could be. We shared every part of our lives from first grade through high school. The principal separated us in fourth grade for laughing and passing notes incessantly, but that didn't stop us from coming home after school together every day of the year.

Ginny was a Roman Catholic. Somehow the exigencies of her religion rubbed off on me although, as a nominal Episcopalian, I had no interest in religion per se. Because I spent much time in the O'Malley household where Ginny was a middle child of four, I became quite familiar with the Catholic Church's strictures. One Saturday when Ginny was in our parish house as a guest at my church's spring fair, she confided a tremendous desire to see pew three in the big church. Although she was allowed in the parish house, Ginny was forbidden, according to her priest, to set foot in a church of any other faith. Pew three was quite famous in our area. The church had been built before the Revolution. During the War for Independence it had been used as a hospital. A Hessian soldier was said to have bled to death on pew three. The black stains of the two hundred-year-old blood could still be seen in the dark oak of the pew, at least some sort of stain could be seen. Ginny just had to see it.

I sauntered into my own church, went down the aisle to the famous pew and lifted the cushion. Ginny stood for a moment in the door, framed by the May

sunlight, knowing she was about to commit a sin just by crossing the threshold. I remember the surprise on her face when she saw a normal brass cross up on the altar, as if she expected an exotic icon. She ran at top speed down the aisle. Skidding to a halt halfway, she decided she'd better genuflect, got up, took a quick look at the black stain, said "Wow!" and tore out of there as if the devil were on her very heels.

I accepted that superstition without much question. My parents would comment from time to time that Irish Catholics were more narrow-minded than other Catholics. For a reason I don't understand, all of the dogma and details of Ginny's religion stayed in my head. I have used Catholic protagonists in two novels, feeling very comfortable doing so. I have been asked many times if I am still a Catholic and what parochial school I went to. This is a great compliment. It means I got it right, because as a child I never once set foot in a Catholic church or a parochial school.

Every fine day and hot evening of the summers in my childhood were spent on the beach. My father loved to fish, and after he'd started a driftwood fire and my mother had put the corn and potatoes in the ashes to roast, Daddy would limp out to the end of the jetty, rod and tackle box in hand. The rocks that made up the jetty were large, black, and slimy with seaweed. My father had a bad leg from a war injury, but he never once slipped or fell. He fished for blues and stripers, casting every few minutes like Preacher Roe. And every few minutes my mother peered into the darkness and tried to see him at the end of the jetty. "Jim? Are you still there?" she called, and Daddy grunted so as not to disturb the fish.

Ginny and I danced around in the sand from the near end of the beach, where the fire was, to the far end where the posts of a long burned boardwalk were tall and the rocks huge, affording caves for us to crawl into at low tide. My mother hunted for mussels which lived in abundance on the rocks near the water. She cracked them open and ate the bright orange meat raw. I did not like mussels then but once in a while would eat one to please her.

If we were lucky the sea would turn blue phosphorous with hundreds of starlike creatures that were called St. Elmo's fire. If it was on, we went into the surf and let the brilliant shining wetness cover our bodies and hair, transforming us into living constellations. Jellyfish stung, sea crabs bit our toes, but we didn't care. Ginny's bathing suit was a yellow rubberized fabric which collected pockets of water on the back end that she was forever letting out, like a trumpet player emptying the spit valves.

Whenever we ate on the beach my grandmother would walk down from the house and stand on the

Daughter Marguerite, named after Wells' grandmother

wooden boardwalk, the wind blowing her grey curls and flapping her silk scarf. She always told us we were crazy to eat on the beach, that we would swallow sand and possibly step on rusty nails or broken glass. I never once saw my grandmother come down to the beach; she only stood along the railing above the stairs and looked out to sea.

Her house with its thick stucco walls and smooth stone floors was always cool, even in the worst heat of August. When I stayed there, I slept in the other bed in her room, an octagonal bedroom in a turret. At night before she turned out the light she drew the long yellow curtains over the windows, said her prayers and fell asleep, leaving me listening to the ocean. When I woke to the chirping of the birds that nested in the ivy outside, the room resembled an orange tent. The curtains hung in huge tapering vertical folds, the grain of the fabric running sideways. They looked to me like enormous carrots hanging on the windows. On the walls and tables were silver-framed photographs of ancestors and relations whose names I never kept straight. One picture showed an old man, hat in hand, entering a heaven filled with large stone angels. I stared at these pictures until Frank, the gardner, came up at seven o'clock to get the dogs and let them out. Then my grandmother rose, drew aside the curtains, flooding the room with morning light, and began to do her exercises.

My grandmother wore ten necklaces, five bracelets on each hand, and an everchanging selection of rings. She wore them to bed. As she did her deep knee-bends and flexed her arms over her head, her jewelry jangled like tiny sleigh bells. One at a time she would roll her feet on a Listerine bottle, claiming it prevented fallen arches.

The tiles and fixtures in her bathroom were black. My mother could never understand a black anything, particularly a black bathroom; but I liked it. I brushed my teeth over the black sink and took bubble baths in the black tub. Sometimes I slid aside the full-length mirror exposing the full-length medicine chest with its amazing contents.

There were rubber douches, the purpose of which I never dared ask. There was the ever-present bottle of Evangeline, a laxative in a box called Inner-Clean, many tonics and a linament used, the label said, by the Indians. And there were things for her nails.

My fingernails were a weekly source of distress for my grandmother. They also gave her an opportunity to admonish my mother in absentia with clucks of the tongue. She did my nails in her dressing room while I sat on a striped silk chaise lounge. Nearly everything in that room, from the furniture and the closet doors to the upholstery and the rug, was lime green. The windows were always opened and the room smelled of the sea. Glasses perched on her nose, grandmother cleaned under my nails, clipped them into ovals, filed them, pushed back the cuticles with an orange stick, oiled them, and then worked under each nail with a white pencil. "Now keep them that way," she would tell me when she finished, lighting a Lucky Strike and blowing the smoke out in a perfect blue stream. The next time I came back my nails once again looked as if I had been mining coal and once again she would attack them.

One day I found an iron jar on the shelf above her desk. It was covered with what I expected might be rubies and sapphires. It was Persian-looking and sealed shut. I opened it with one of her fingernail tools and before she could intervene I had puffed into the air a bit of the grey powder that lay on the cotton inside the jar. "Those were my mother's ashes!" she cried. I did not understand.

Every Sunday at noon and each holiday our small family would gather at the big house for dinner. When I was little my uncle would come with his wife and son and sometimes his stepson, a boy born of my aunt's first marriage. Billy was trouble. He said "ain't" and unimaginable swear words when the grown-ups were not around and, at times, within their earshot. He lived with his real father and stepmother in Baltimore which to me might as well have been Afghanistan. His father was a drunken lout, according to my family, his stepmother a dreamy no-account woman. Billy was always balling his little fists, shaking his jet black forelock out of his eyes. My grandmother tried to help him by speaking to him in loving, gentle moral platitudes, but they meant nothing at all to him. She had him sent to a succession of boys' private schools. He never lasted in any of them. I didn't hear about him again after I was twelve. It was whispered in the family that he had been arrested for dealing in drugs and sent to a reformatory. How this could be I didn't understand. To me drugs meant aspirins and Inner-Clean.

Quite suddenly, when I was about eight, my aunt, who was married to my mother's brother, went into a coma in a Baltimore hospital and never regained consciousness. She died of a brain tumor five days later. Again, I did not understand. I could only picture a coma as something like a toga. My parents did not go to Baltimore to see her; my uncle was so hurt by this slight that he did not talk to my mother for the next ten years although we saw him every Sunday, Easter, and Christmas. He took to drinking Southern Comfort in large amounts and told long bad jokes with scatological punch lines. Sometimes my father, trying to calm him down, took away the Southern Comfort. Other times my father let him have three or four stiff ones in the hope it would put him into a more cheerful oblivion. After she died, my uncle always spoke of my aunt as his "bride" or his "dead bride." I did not understand. I knew brides wore white and were brides for only a short time. Neither did I understand that the amber fluid in liquor bottles affected a person's nature, mind, speech. I thought it was just something grownups drank, the way they ate oysters or liver and other things children did not like.

There was usually an extra guest for dinner. On holidays, Thanksgiving and Christmas, my grandmother asked the chaplain at the local army fort to send over half-a-dozen soldiers who had no homes to go to. I loved those visitors, well-behaved cropped-haired young men, black and white, in their starched uniforms. Thanksgiving meant that even in the cold I could persuade them to play baseball out on the lawn.

Other than the soldiers, there was generally an aunt about my grandmother's age at dinner. How these women were related to me was too convoluted to understand.

Aunt Ethel reminded me of an ostrich. She was tall and gaunt and braided her hair in tight rings around the top of her head. She gave me hat pins with heads of pearl or other jewel-like materials and mints from her jet-beaded pocketbook. Aunt Ethel had pronounced bags under her eyes. I was sure she kept tears in them. I told my mother this and my mother laughed. She said when *she* was a little girl and Aunt Ethel was much younger, Ethel already had the baggy eyes and my mother, too, thought the bags were filled with tears.

On Aunt Ethel's birthday one June we celebrated with a lobster dinner. Aunt Ethel could not eat lobster, however, and had to make do with lamb chops. The cake was served. The cook had used a new recipe for the icing. It was so rubbery that the silver cake knife only stretched the icing unbroken from the top of the cake to the plate. A steak knife was brought in. Aunt Ethel looked sad about the lobster and the icing. My mother told my grandmother to fire the cook who, she was sure, stole a pound of butter every Thursday when she took her day off.

Aunt Beryl was quite different from Aunt Ethel. She was chunky, peppery, freckled, and redheaded. She smoked with a horn cigarette holder and drank manhattans with maraschino cherries floating among the ice cubes. Aunt Beryl was given to saying racy things and when my grandmother would put her finger to her lips and whisper, "Not in front of . . . !" Aunt Beryl always cackled and looked my way. "Time she grew up and knew about the world!" was Aunt Beryl's answer. Aunt Beryl was an interior decorator who had had a string of husbands and lived in New York City. She came down to the shore for frequent rests and when she did, she tried to reorganize and redecorate my grandmother's house, without any success. I can still see her, standing in the living room, one foot ahead of the other, manhattan tinkling in her hand, gazing calculatingly at some French tapestry that had been hung on the wrong wall.

All the rooms in the house were named, although the purposes and people they were named for were lost in the past even before I was born. There was a card room in which no one played cards. The telephone room had a telephone but so did other rooms. The hall took up a third of the house and was never used for any reason. Upstairs the bedrooms were named for people who had died or left the household long before. When my grandmother divorced Uncle Charlie, however, his room was renamed "the middle room."

When my grandmother and Uncle Charlie first moved into the house in the thirties, my mother had stuck several saucy decals of stripper girls on the tile walls inside his shower. The decals must have amused Uncle Charlie for he never removed them. After he departed the house, and this life, the decals were the only sign that he had ever been there.

Divorce was not common then. It was spoken of in whispers like the name of a dreadful illness. When my grandmother got her divorce she went off to Nevada and stayed at a ranch in the mountains for a month. According to my mother the ranch was populated by women getting divorces. Later, when I was sixteen, my grandmother took me there on a vacation. I rode Western in the Sierra Nevada mountains from sunup till evening for three weeks. My mother did not like my going. She did not want me to be around a lot of divorced women, but I never noticed any.

When my grandmother came back from Nevada with her divorce and had cleansed Uncle Charlie's existence from every surface of the house, she took to wearing Western-style clothes. She hung Indian calendars on the walls and placed a small totem pole next to the toaster in the kitchen. She bought many pairs of twill pants with slanted front pockets and mother-of-pearl snaps. These she wore with Western shirts and belts with large silver buckles inlaid with turquoise.

Out West she had met an artist, a "younger man," as my mother called him. Grandmother sent him some of my drawings and, when he replied admiringly, encouraged me to correspond with him. I did not mind writing the letters or sending my drawings. I did not understand why my grandmother took pleasure in this correspondence or why my mother faintly disapproved of it.

When I was thirteen and about to enter high school my parents suddenly decided, for reasons never explained, that I was to go to a first-class boarding school to get a real education.

I reacted badly. Boarding schools in the 1950s were very strict affairs. All daily life, even telephone calls and personal possessions, was subject to scrutiny, inspection, and constant supervision. I cried and did not eat for seven straight days. Then another seven days and another. I was allowed one weekend home per semester and took the very first one. The school was a jail to me although the other girls seemed to be having a grand time. I thought there was something wrong with me, deep down. So did the administration. There was no privacy, no time to draw. Constant noise, bells, mass camaraderie, uniforms that did not fit (mine bought secondhand from a graduate whose shape was very different from my own). I buckled under this regimen and came home to stay. I learned one thing there, though, that did frighten me deeply. I had always been at the top of my class in the public grammar school I had attended. I found that I was at the bottom of my class in this tough private school. I could not hope to match the scholarship of my mates; I was too ill-prepared. I only glimpsed this fact in the three weeks I was there, then I shut it away when I returned to the local public high school. Later I used that private school as the setting for a novel.

My grandmother told me, on my return home, that I had lost my first great battle with life. She was stuck with the tuition bill for the rest of the year.

It was right to come home though. Home was always filled with books, dogs, nineteenth-century music,

and other things my parents held in great esteem.

Acting was one of those things. Every week we saw the "Sid Caesar Show" and the "Honeymooners" on the small black-and-white TV. Those skits, or tiny plays—live comedy, written in a kind of innocence and endless silliness that is just not seen now—was the base for my picture book stories. I learned much more from Sid Caesar than from Shakespeare. Those playlets, presented every Saturday, contained the three most important ingredients for short stories (or picture-book plots): humor, recognizable characters and settings, and emotional content. They were theatre—and picture books are theatre, too.

My father was an extraordinary raconteur and amateur historian. He had been an actor in Hollywood and had kept his actor's good looks and charm all his life. He was a big man. He loved to cook. He loved good wine, good stories, good company. He read modern history endlessly and dinner-table discussion was often politics and the people in "the war," which meant either World War. I soaked it up and still love history better than any other subject. My father's knowledge was so extensive, and I retained so much of it, that I know more about history than if I had been formally educated in it.

My mother loved all of those things too (except for cooking). Whereas my father remained an Englishman at heart, mother was Pan-European and had an extraordinary ear for languages. I failed French, or nearly failed it, because I could not get the conjugations through my head; yet, like my mother, I speak it well and understand it because I have her ear.

The love of animals, books, good food, music and languages, theatre, were gifts to me in an extraordinarily close family. These gifts I have tried to pass to my own children. I cannot do so, however, with the aura of people and times past that so strongly surrounded my parents. In and out of their conversation flitted names with real characters attached, Noel Coward and Gertie Lawrence, people from the Russian Ballet, Melvyn Douglas and his wife, Helen Gahagan Douglas, whom my father had known well. Neither of my parents ever forgave Richard Nixon for his campaign against her. My parents were as rock-ribbed Democrats as my grandmother was a Republican. I remember shocking the whole fourth-grade class when I stood up and announced (as I had heard at home) that Joseph McCarthy was a stinko little rat.

I was brought up to think that FDR was nearly a saint, and I held that view despite my grandmother. She started a small barrel-shaped bank when the FDR dimes came out. She did her part to take those dimes out of circulation by dropping every one that crossed her palm into the slot of this little bank. She would only allow Liberty dimes into her change purse.

When I went to college I was determined to shed the high school stigma of "not being popular." At high school, where the girls around me grew into young women with enormous speed in freshman year, it took me a long time to catch up. College was a bit of a joke. I'd done badly in high school due to my own laziness and inability to take things like chemistry seriously. This was abetted by my parents' inability to take things like chemistry seriously. As a result of doing poorly and spending my all-important junior year larking around England with my mother and father, I could only get into the worst of colleges—and that's where I wound up.

It was a small private junior college in New York State (no longer in existence). I was the only girl there who had gone to public school and had no coming-out party in store. My roommate owned seventy-two pairs of shoes. The girl across the hall could not unpack half her trunks because the spacious closet allotted her was too small. My parents, innocent as usual, did not realize they'd gotten me into a finishing school for the daughters of immensely wealthy people. These daughters were the ones who did not go to Smith. Suddenly I went from ignominy (ranked 74th in my high school class), to the honor roll. As much as my grammar school had ill-prepared me for a good independent school education, my high school over-prepared me for this gorgeous, well-appointed junior college which appeared to gear its students exclusively for marriage and the social graces.

Still, it was great fun. The work was so easy I don't remember doing any part of it. The girls were pleasant and I made two life-long friends. Marriage was on everyone's mind, at least getting pinned or engaged was. I ought not to carp because, although I left those Halcyon Halls (as they were called in the handbook), I left for Boston because Boston had the closest art school to Dartmouth, and Dartmouth was where Tom Wells was, and after one blind date I was determined to marry Tom Wells.

I did. Before we tied the knot, however, we set up house for about a year in a tiny unheated apartment on Beacon Hill. We did not advise his parents that we were really living together. They were blue-blooded New Englanders and would have had (what my daughter calls) a spas attack had they known. My parents' reaction was different. Since the Boston strangler was still about, my mother was immensely relieved that I had moved in with Tom. They drove up from New Jersey and brought us a rotisserie as a congratulations present.

Rosemary and Tom Wells, 1965

Being married got me out of schools at last. Even art school was still school and not the real world. I had a succession of jobs, each lasting a few weeks, all culled from the classified pages of *The Boston Globe*. The last of these jobs was with a buyer of purses, shoes, and accessories in a large, cheap chain of women's clothing stores.

The offices, such as they were, were situated atop a huge truck depot in Alston, Massachusetts. My boss and I occupied a small pink cubicle about as big as a bathroom. The partitions were plywood. The heat was unbearable. It was my duty to sort the price tags that came to my desk in envelopes from all seven branches of the Lorraine shops every morning. The price tags were marked with multiple codes, and I had to enter each of six different codes into a ledger so that the store had an idea of what to reorder. There was a warehouse up there, filled with failed styles of shoes, bags, belts, and whatnots. These were the things that had not sold. They lay knee deep in an enormous jumble in a room as big as a baseball diamond. Sometimes I went in there to retrieve an item for my boss.

On a Friday afternoon, three weeks into the job, when my boss had left for the day and I had managed to organize seven hundred price tags into little piles according to codes and was about to enter them in the ledger, I decided that, since there was no air conditioning and no window, it wouldn't hurt to at least turn on the fan.

Monday morning I got Tom to call my boss, who must have been sitting, nearly in tears, among the scattered price tags that had been blown into every crevice, into the typewriters, behind the desk. He told her I had developed mononucleosis over the weekend. She was nice about it and never mentioned the carnage that greeted her that morning. I wanted to write her a letter of apology, even years later, but never had the courage.

At that point, when I was all of nineteen years old, I had my first lucky break and the only one I ever needed. I had hit the streets, seeking employment in every Boston publishing office I could find.

My portfolio was highly personal, filled with art school drawings and imagined book covers for my favorite novels. I hit upon one place, Allyn and Bacon, where they took me on for three weeks because one of the staff was going on vacation.

When the vacationing art editor came back they fired her. Apparently she'd exceeded her allowances for lateness on the time clock. I kept the job. And because it was a real job, in the real world, I never worked so hard in my life. All the laziness and reluctance to concentrate disappeared. I was assigned an American his-

From Stanley and Rhoda, *written and illustrated by Rosemary Wells. (Copyright © 1978 by Rosemary Wells. Reprinted by permission of The Dial Press.)*

tory book for Catholic high school seniors. It was thirteen hundred pages long and I had to send away for all the prints and photos that would illustrate it.

The book was wonderful. The Sisters of the Sacred Heart who were involved in the editorial end were splendid women. There was a party when it was published and I felt like a success at something for the first time in my life.

Tom applied to the Columbia School of Architecture two years later and we moved to New York. It was publishing again for me. I began to learn the art of book design. One day when I was on staff as a designer at Macmillan I presented a small illustrated dummy of a Gilbert and Sullivan song to the editor-in-chief. It was published and I was on my way.

The job I have now—writing and illustrating children's books, writing novels for teenagers—is pure delight. There are hard parts but no bad or boring parts, and that is more than can be said for any other line of work I know.

From A Lion for Lewis, *written and illustrated by Rosemary Wells. (Copyright © 1982 by Rosemary Wells. Reprinted by permission of The Dial Press.)*

Rosemary Wells holding daughter Victoria, 1973

I work at home, bankers' hours Monday through Friday, but I have been able for the last twelve years to be home as much as our two children need me.

The children and our home life have inspired, in part, many of my books. Our West Highland white terrier, Angus, had the shape and expressions to become Benjamin and Tulip, Timothy, and all the other animals I have made up for my stories. He also appears as himself in a couple of books.

The stories themselves, though, come from the air. I can't explain writing very well. My stories do not seem to come from any particularly creative instinct; rather, I "discover" them. They seem to have a life of their own somewhere in time, and it is my job to put them on paper.

I regret only that I cannot live other lives parallel to my own. Writing is a lonely profession and I am a gregarious sort of person. I would like someday to work for the FBI. Some part of me was never satisfied with years of tennis. I still yearn to play baseball.

I put into my books all of the things I remember (and I am still an accomplished eavesdropper—in restaurants, trains, and gatherings of any kind). Those remembrances are jumbled up and changed because fiction is always more palatable than truth. They become more true as they are honed and whittled into characters and stories.

There are many more people in my life—and heartbreaks and trouble and doubts. But it would take a whole book to tell them and even then, I would prefer to invent, change, and jumble because writing is better, and much more fun, that way.

Angus

Victoria Wells

BIBLIOGRAPHY

FOR CHILDREN

Books written and illustrated:

John and the Rarey. New York: Funk, 1969.

Michael and the Mitten Test. Englewood Cliffs, N.J.: Bradbury, 1969.

The First Child. New York: Hawthorn, 1970.

Martha's Birthday. Englewood Cliffs, N.J.: Bradbury, 1970.

Miranda's Pilgrims. New York: Bradbury, 1970.

The Fog Comes on Little Pig Feet. New York: Dial, 1972; London: Deutsch, 1976.

Unfortunately Harriet. New York: Dial, 1972.

Benjamin and Tulip. New York: Dial, 1973; Harmondsworth: Puffin Books, 1977.

Noisy Nora. New York: Dial, 1973; London: Collins, 1976.

None of the Above. New York: Dial, 1974.

Abdul. New York: Dial, 1975.

Morris's Disappearing Bag: A Christmas Story. New York: Dial, 1975; Harmondsworth: Kestrel Books, 1977.

Don't Spill It Again, James. New York: Dial, 1977.

Leave Well Enough Alone. New York: Dial, 1977

Stanley and Rhoda. New York: Dial, 1978; Harmondsworth: Kestrel Books, 1980.

Max's First Word. New York: Dial, 1979; London: Benn, 1980.

Max's New Suit. New York: Dial, 1979; London: Benn, 1980.

Max's Ride. New York: Dial, 1979; London: Benn, 1980.

Max's Toys: A Counting Book. New York: Dial, 1979; London: Benn, 1980.

When No One Was Looking. New York: Dial, 1980; London: Deutsch, 1984.

Good Night, Fred. New York: Dial, 1981: London: Macmillan, 1982.

Timothy Goes to School. New York: Dial, 1981; London: Kestrel Books, 1981.

A Lion for Lewis. New York: Dial, 1982; London: Macmillan, 1982.

Peabody. New York: Dial, 1983; London: Macmillan, 1984.

The Man in the Woods. New York: Dial, 1984.

Books illustrated:

A Song to Sing, O! by William S. Gilbert and Arthur Sullivan (from the *Yeomen of the Guard*). New York: Macmillan, 1968.

W.S. Gilbert's "The Duke of Plaza Toro," by W.S. Gilbert and A. Sullivan (from *The Gondoliers*). New York: Macmillan, 1969.

Hungry Fred, by Paula Fox. Englewood Cliffs, N.J.: Bradbury, 1969.

The Shooting of Dan McGrew [and] The Cremation of Sam McGee, by Robert W. Service. New York: Young Scott Books, 1969.

Why You Look Like You Whereas I Tend to Look Like Me, by Charlotte Pomerantz (with Susan Jeffers). New York: Young Scott Books, 1969.

The Cat That Walked by Himself, by Rudyard Kipling. New York: Hawthorn, 1970.

Marvin's Manhole, by Winifred Rosen Casey. New York: Dial, 1970.

A Hot Thirsty Day, by Marjorie Weinman Sharmat. New York: Macmillan, 1971; London: Collier-Macmillan, 1971.

Impossible Possum, by Ellen Conford. Boston: Little, Brown, 1971.

Two Sisters and Some Hornets, by Beryl Williams and Dorrit Davis. New York: Holiday House, 1972.

With a Deep-Sea Smile: Story Hour Stretches for Large or Small Groups, by Virginia A. Tashjian. Boston: Little, Brown, 1974.

Tell Me a Trudy, by Lore G. Segal. New York: Farrar, Straus, 1977.

Robb White

1909–

Robb White

My father was an Episcopalian missionary which is probably why I was born at Baguio on the Philippine island of Luzon.

As I recall, a few days after my birth they dumped me into a sort of hammock slung between two bamboo poles which were balanced on the shoulders of four

Filipino men and we all took off through the jungle for the high country of the Bontok tribe of Igorots. I think my ability on a trampoline stemmed from that journey because nobody seemed to care how high or in what direction I got bounced in that hammock.

When we finally got to Bontok we were surprised to see all the Igorots stalking around practically naked, the men armed with bolo knives, spears and arrows, because the U. S. Army in Baguio had assured us that they had tamed and civilized these people.

The "Rectory" we had been promised turned out to be an abandoned Igorot shack with a thatch roof and a floor raised a few feet off the ground to keep the wild animals out.

My father soon realized that the Igorots didn't need and didn't want any Episcopalian missionaries with only one small God because they already had about a thousand Gods of their own and if they wanted some heavenly advice they'd cook a dog and decipher the omens from the bones as they ate it. (I learned from them that grasshoppers are also tasty.)

This attitude suited my father who really didn't care much for preaching so he gave up trying to convert them and concentrated on the sublime blessings of iodine, castor oil, and baseball.

The Igorots loved baseball.

They are a handsome and fearsome people, famed for head-hunting and instant wars, with bronze-colored skin and straight black hair; a mixture of Malay, Indonesian, and Negroid peoples. It was rumored that they had been known to eat folks.

I was about three before I realized that I was the only kid around there with awful clammy white skin which, no matter how hard I scrubbed on it, would not come off.

And I was the only kid who couldn't run very fast nor climb a tree without falling out nor catch a fish with his bare hands. I even took a long time learning to talk Igorot (but not as long as it took me to learn to speak English).

I followed those Igorot kids around like a homeless puppy; a one-man minority group who could do nothing right.

As soon as I got out of sight of my house I'd strip off all my clothes and try to figure out how to make one of those sort of belts with a leaf in front that the Igorot kids wore. (One of the crystal days of my life was when they taught me how to weave some leaves together and twist some thin vines into a skinny rope which finally produced a G-string of my very own.)

I never cried in front of the Igorot kids even when they let me shoot one of their bows and arrows and, somehow, the arrow came backwards and hit me on the nose. And I didn't run like a coward when my first

attempt to hit something with one of their spears spiked a *big* kid in the leg and he said he wasn't even going to cook me before he ate me.

Those Igorot kids were absolutely superb people and I was a *mess*, a nobody from nowhere.

I couldn't even play baseball which, in addition to aggravating them, aggravated my father.

I tried. I even ate one of my mother's dogs to persuade them to let me be one of the boys. (Actually, *they* stole my mother's dog and cooked it up and ate it, only giving me a little piece of it. They liked my mother because as soon as they ate one of her dogs she'd get another one that tasted even better.)

My last two years in the Philippines we lived in Baguio, the summer capital, where my mother spent most of her time playing polo on the governor-general's team (going to China, Japan, and other lands) and my father spent most of his teaching at Bishop Brent's school.

He also took pity on a British lady named Miss Blue who had been sent for as a prospective bride by a British sailor who took one look at her and vanished entirely. She justified living with us for two years by tutoring me.

She taught me a rhyme which enabled me to reel off, in order, all the kings and queens of England, with dates. She also taught me that, when setting the table, the knife goes on the right (or is it the left?).

And, she taught me to speak *British* English, which seemed alright at the time because, although I could speak Igorot well, Tagalog fairly well, and Spanish enough to get by, the only English I had bothered to learn was how to get the necessities of life, such as food.

And that's all she taught me during those critical years when everybody else is learning about grammar and arithmetic (something *times* something produces something else).

I was glad to leave Baguio because the kids there showed no interest in spear-throwing, arrow-shooting, how to trap rats, make a G-string, or cook a dog.

As we sailed away for America I had high hopes and kind thoughts about American people my age.

America turned out to be Tarboro, North Carolina, which, I learned later, was practically owned by my grandfather who was a lawyer, judge, banker, cotton gin owner, Confederate colonel, and farmer who had his own eighteen-hole golf course.

All of which did me absolutely no good at all when, for the first time in my life, I was sent to a real school.

I can't blame anybody for what happened; after all, my parents didn't *invent* Black Marrow, Hawk

Mac Nair or *Rat* Boykin. They were just there when I got there.

But I still think my mother's theory that going to school barefooted was healthy didn't help me much when I trudged to school barefooted in the snow (stuff I had never even heard of) but otherwise dressed warmly in short pants, a bob-tailed coat and Eton collar, speaking with a British accent.

All I remember about going to school in Tarboro, North Carolina, is—*reee*-cess.

I had no time to spare learning anything because I had to concentrate totally on *reee*-cess and the invention of new and hopefully successful maneuvers to fit either the need to fight or flee.

Reee-cess meant coming out through some big wooden doors and down some bleak concrete steps and stepping down into the cold and muddy snow only to stand and wait.

Wait for *Black* Marrow, Hawk *Mac* Nair, and *Rat* Boykin to congeal out of the swirling, gray, cold mist and beat up on me until the bell rang, ending *reee*-cess.

Oh *God*, what I wouldn't have given to have had a few of my Igorot buddies with their spears and arrows and *long* bolo knives. We would've *killed* those sons of bitches and cooked them medium rare and served them to the people.

I didn't get any education in Tarboro, nor even in Virginia where mother and I spent the winter in a toolshed (nor during the time we lived in an abandoned insane asylum with a skeleton on a rope you could lower down the stairwell if you didn't like who was coming up).

In those days you were put into a grade at school only according to how old you were, without regard to what you knew.

You didn't have to produce any sort of records; if you were twelve years old you were put into the sixth grade. As my father drifted from one army base to another, then from one little parish to another, I managed to be promoted to the eighth grade without learning anything at all.

Until finally we settled down in Thomasville, Georgia, where an extremely rich man who wanted Sonny, his somewhat handicapped son, to have as normal a life as possible, set up a private school with six expensive professors and twenty-four boys handpicked by Sonny's father from what he called "all walks of life." I was the preacher's son "walk."

Sonny was a sweet kid who was smarter than most of us, with a fine sense of humor but whose problem was that his eyes wandered around separately and he had a hard time coordinating thought and speech and thought and movement, but nobody ever heard him complain about anything.

Because it took Sonny so long to say something, or write something, it was hard to tell whether he had learned what they were trying to teach us.

So the first rule at that school was that nobody went any faster than Sonny. Nobody was allowed to raise their hand and wave it around if they knew the answer—we waited for Sonny. And sometimes this could take all day.

The second rule was that *everybody* had to play in the band because that was the only thing the headmaster knew anything about and it didn't matter to him that maybe some of the students couldn't carry a tune in a wheelbarrow—they *played in the band.* So we spent most of the days in the Band Room um-pahing and tooting and tweet-tweeting while the headmaster stood on the podium yelling at us.

And since "everybody" included Sonny, he was permanently assigned to play the triangle. Every tune we played had at least one note for the triangle so we'd toot along until we got to that note then the whole band would screech to a halt and wait for Sonny to get it all together enough so he could hit the triangle with his little stick.

I went to that school for four years and left still not knowing any grammar (I thought a dangling participle was something that gave you a hernia) nor how to multiply, much less anything about fractions and all that good stuff.

At last I was sent to a school which intended to *teach* people things. The Episcopal High School at Alexandria, Virginia, which would have been the oldest prep school in the country if it had not been forced to close down during the War Between the States so the student body could go fight the Yankees.

I *liked* that school in spite of the fact that my father never got around to sending me any clothes so I had to make do with what I'd had on when I got there (when my corduroy pants started coming apart, I patched them with wide, yellow adhesive tape the football coach gave me). I had decided when I was thirteen that I was going to be a writer and the Episcopal High School introduced me to Latin and English literature, to history and geography. I think they tried to teach me other things such as math, chemistry, physics, but I couldn't see why a writer would need to know that sort of stuff, so I didn't pay much attention.

That was one of the few mistakes I've made in my life, but I didn't find it out until I got into the United States Naval Academy at Annapolis, Maryland.

Being a midshipman at the Naval Academy had no resemblance at all to being an undergraduate at UCLA or even Harvard. Our years were named, from the bottom, Plebe Year, then Youngster, Second Classman, First Classman. Everybody ate, slept, and were confined in an enormous gray stone building called Bancroft Hall. We were waked up at 6:00 A.M. *every* morning and immediately folded all the bedclothes over the foot of the bed and folded up the mattress (very thin) in the middle of the bed. Then we washed, shaved, got into full uniform, and "fell in."

We spent a hell of a lot of time falling in (which, for the one or two of you who don't know, means getting yourself into ranks and standing at attention). We then marched into the gigantic dining room for chow— breakfast at 7:00 A.M., gentlemen.

We marched to all meals, to all classes; we even had to march to church (which we also had to attend); and we did a lot of marching just for the hell of it, particularly on Saturday afternoons with rifles and in full dress uniforms with twenty-six brass buttons down the front, a white web belt, and a high stiff collar up to your ears.

Classes were held in various buildings around the place and you fell in with your books in your left hand and marched away, with a lonesome drummer (in the rain or snow or whatever) standing under a tree beating out the rhythm over and over.

You marched into the classroom and to your chair where you stood at attention until the professor said, "Seats."

You sat there in silence as he told you what your next topic in the book would be, or other matters, then he would say, "Class—draw slips and man the boards."

You would get up, march past his desk and draw a little slip of paper with a question printed on it, then go to your assigned space at the blackboard and, first, write your name and serial number in the right hand corner.

Then you would write the answer to the question on your slip and when you finished you would about-face and stand at parade rest until ordered to sit down.

When all were seated you would wait in silence as the professor went from answer to answer, writing the grades in a thick red notebook.

Then, as the bell rang, he would say, "Class— rise—march out." You would then fall in and march back to Bancroft Hall past the lonesome drummer and would be confined to your room to study until the bell rang for the next class.

At the end of this day of alternate hours of class and study, all hands except the Sick Squad were required to go out for some sort of sport and were not free until there was just time enough to shower and get back into uniform and march to supper.

After supper you could at last fool around—as long as you stayed inside Bancroft Hall. But, at exactly

10:00 P.M., you had to be in your room, and in your bed, with the lights out.

There was a high stone wall all the way around the campus which was guarded by some people called Jimmylegs and we were not allowed beyond those walls except for a few hours on the weekend (never, however, beyond 10:00 P.M.). Midshipmen were also not allowed to: drink, smoke, have a radio, ride in a car, much less *own* one, or have civilian clothes.

The school year at the Academy lasted eleven months, eight of them at the Academy and three aboard ship. The twelfth month— September—was vacation time when all the girls were back in school.

I discovered that not knowing the multiplication tables, nor exactly what fractions were and how to handle them, and even being pretty shakey with adding and subtracting, didn't help me much with the Academy's deluge of mathematical demands. Not only in ordinary classes about algebra and geometry, but there seemed to be a demand for numbers in chemistry, physics, steam and electrical engineering, drafting, astronomy, meteorology, and navigation.

Two-point-five was the edge of the abyss. To stay in the Academy you had to have a 2.5 average in all subjects.

During the first three years hanging by my fingernails to that 2.5 ledge didn't leave me much freedom to be a writer or do anything else. When a subject got into areas my lack of basic education (friends, I ain't preaching at you) couldn't handle, the only way to get that 2.5 was to memorize the book.

Finally, during my last year the hassle slacked off some but then a new problem began to take shape.

I really *liked* the Navy. It gave you all that stuff the recruiters promise you and a great deal more. Aside from the adventures it offered—the duty in ships on or under the sea, the aircraft squadrons, the shore maintenance and engineering—all that, plus the Navy gave you security—it fed you and housed and protected you, took care of your health, paid you well, rewarded you for good work and pensioned you.

I began to realize that the Navy is not a *job* that you report to at 8:00 A.M. and quit at 5:00 P.M. and have the weekends off and can get fired from no matter how good your work is. The Navy is something that you're *in.* For all the things the Navy gives you it asks in return that you *live* in the Navy. That you give it— your life.

After the years of the Academy's discipline and the six months serving as a crew member of a battleship and three-months duty at a naval air station, I had a pretty good idea of how much of a naval officer's life would belong to the Navy.

Which may be the reason why very few regular

Navy officers were also writers and none of them were prominent fiction writers.

All the above sounds as though my decision was reached only after careful and objective weighing of the pros and cons, but actually it could be called a stupid and quixotic choice by a fairly dumb individual—me.

For one reason, in 1931, the Great Depression had a stranglehold on the whole world. In the United States twenty million able-bodied people had not worked for two years, which meant that one out of every four people, including women and children, couldn't get a job. Banks were going broke all over the place and foreclosures were driving the people out of their homes, off their farms, ruining their businesses. Your bank account was not insured in those days so when your bank went broke it took your money with it.

The suicide rate was the highest in our history.

People were homeless, foodless, heatless, starving; and there was no welfare, no food stamps, no Social Security, no aid of any kind to anybody from any government.

Compared to the lives of the majority of young men, an officer in the Navy had it made in the shade.

In spite of all the reasons why I should not, on the 4th of June, 1931, I resigned my commission as Ensign, USN, and became an instant civilian with a bankroll of $485. Because I had no job, I had all the time in the world to become a writer.

That really shook my parents but I'm proud of them for behaving the way I hoped they would.

Being a preacher's son is a lot harder than being a preacher. Out on the street a preacher is a saint but when he comes home he can quit the saint business and then it's get-out-of-the-way time. But a preacher's son is expected to be a saint out on the street and keep on being a saint when he gets home.

So when I resigned (a thing that convinced a lot of my friends that I didn't have all my oars in the water) my father did what he'd always done. He ignored me. (And ignored me for the rest of his life. He never wrote me a letter nor even a postcard. Never helped me with money, advice, enthusiasm, nor compassion. We never talked on a level higher than baseball or the weather.)

Whether he had any concern for me out there in that cold Depression I don't know, because he never mentioned it.

My mother was a grand lady and, although she was inwardly terrified by what I had done and wanted to beat some common sense into my head with a club, she just wrote and said, "You've been talking about being a writer since you were thirteen years old, so now, with nothing else to do, I hope you'll get to be one. And, although you haven't got the brains God

gave a rock, I still admire you and even love you once in a while—but not much right now."

So I went to see my friend, Tex Wheeler, in Cleveland, Ohio.

Tex was a sculptor who had never been to Texas and wasn't named Tex. He came from Christmas, Florida, where his mother had wanted a girl to name Annette and his father wanted a boy to name Hugh so they compromised and named Tex Hughlette a name he didn't care for.

Tex could take a lump of clay and make it look exactly like a horse, and with all those horsey rich folks in Cleveland to buy his clay horses, he managed to eat well and live the way he wanted to which took me awhile to get used to after I moved in with him.

Tex's apartment was in a one-time mansion, now in the last stages of collapse. There was one big room, two little rooms, a bath, and a kitchen. Tex used the front room for his studio and slept in the room with a big noisy brass bed, while I slept in the other room on a couch with evil springs.

Tex set me a good example, because he worked hard all day, every day. He woke up at six and went through a routine so exact that I doubt if he was even aware of it. First, he would reach down beside his bed for the glass gallon jug of bootleg corn whiskey and get it balanced on his shoulder so he could gurgle down a good dose of it. Then he would reach up to the knob of the bed for his ten-gallon Stetson hat and set it on his head at an exact angle before taking another belt from the jug. Now, fortified, he would pull on his always shiny cowboy boots and, for the rest of the day, that was all he would put on.

It didn't matter to Tex who came to see him; whether it was one of his many girlfriends or a haughty matron from Bratnahl come to inspect the statue he was making of her horse, Tex wore only his hat and his boots, because, he said, putting on clothes in the daytime wore 'em out.

Tex was a good man. We could talk about what it was like to be an artist (which was a word we never used); how hard it was; not how hard the *work* was, but how hard it was to keep on going when nobody approved of what you did, nobody liked it enough to pay for it.

A good man.

As the ladies came in with pictures of their horses for him to sculpt, or to pay for the ones he had sculpted, it was impossible not to notice that the ladies looked a lot like their horses, and sometimes neighed.

However, one of them was still young enough not to look like her favorite horse, and when Tex was working and refused to talk to anybody, she'd sit around and talk with me. And, when she found out that I wanted to be a writer but needed a job to keep from starving before I got to be one, she said she might be able to do something about that.

That lady did a *lot* about that and within a week a friend of hers who was the president of the Cleveland subsidiary of DuPont hired me as a draftsman.

So I spent about a year on a high, spindly stool drawing blueprints of a Trail Space Ore Roaster, a contraption that would roast sulfur and the smoke would turn into sulfuric acid.

I didn't take advantage of that good luck to work very hard at learning to be a writer. But, I argued, after four Academy years of going to bed every night at 10:00 P.M. and getting up at 5:00 A.M., and being forbidden to smoke, drink, own a radio, or ride in a car, I deserved to play a little.

I played a *lot* and wrote a little.

Then, abruptly, the Good Times stopped rolling.

When we finished all the drawings for the Space Ore Roaster, the boss called me in and acted like he was doing me a big favor by sending me to New Castle, Pennsylvania, to be the construction engineer's assistant while the monster we'd been drawing got built.

No hurry, the boss said, the construction engineer, a Mr. George Washington Hill, would meet me at Du Pont's chemical plant in New Castle—*in the morning.*

1933–1937

As I approached in my Model-A Ford roadster with a rumble seat and isinglass side curtains, New Castle looked like the opening scenes of an outer space horror movie.

Ahead was a vast expanse of dead earth above which a mist, that seemed to contain thin threads of something's intestines, writhed slowly around. Through this I could see several huge blobs of glowing, pulsing light with the iridescent colors of dead fish. Snow fell in flakes already gray which swirled slowly and sadly around as though each flake was reluctant to land on that horrid earth.

At the chemical plant, a bleak place with a pall of the acrid smoke of burning sulfur like a roof over it, there was chaos but no George Washington Hill.

Nobody there to tell anybody what to do about anything as the freight trains and semis and self-propelleds kept coming and dumping miles of steel girders, I-beams, H-beams, T-beams, and just plain beams all over the place. They came with slabs of curved thick steel bigger than a four-bedroom house. They came with kegs and barrels and crates of rivets, bolts, and assorted hardware. Bundles of pipes of all sizes. Great

silent, shiny gray motors of all sorts. Backhoes, bulldozers, concrete mixers. A travelling crane whose neck stuck up into the gloomy sky stood motionless because no one was there to authorize anybody to do anything.

Frantic pleas to Cleveland just got me vague promises that G. Washington Hill would soon come galloping over the horizon but that didn't stop the crews standing around in the snow, without getting paid, from blaming *me* for this endless delay.

I wish I could tell you that I was a tower of strength as I led my troops to victory, but it didn't happen that way. I just called the foremen into the little shack I had at the plant and showed them the blueprints as I told them that I didn't know how to put the thing together, but thought that we needed to dig a big hole and pour a lot of concrete into it, so, gentlemen, how about we do that and then see what happens next?

For almost two years that little shack was where the plasterers and mechanics, machinists, electricians, plumbers, pipe fitters, riveters, big rig drivers, lead burners, chemists, glass cutters, and steel workers met to study the blueprints and figure out what we ought to do next.

I suspect now that George Washington Hill didn't exist and never had because nobody ever came from DuPont to interfere with what we were doing.

I lived in one room of an apartment above the book-store with a couple who were absolutely unsuited to each other but got along fine—most of the time.

Aunt Pearl (as she asked that I call her) was a *large* woman, large everywhere, and strong, and very sweet. Jack was a skinny little Irishman who was a roller in the tin mill, using long tongs eight hours a day to lift and throw hundred-pound white-hot steel ingots into a rolling mill.

I found out that the main friction between Aunt Pearl and Jack was that they didn't agree on how many drinks Jack deserved for throwing all that steel around.

I came home one night and found Aunt Pearl sitting in her favorite rocking chair with a thick layer of snow on her head, also layers of snow on her shoulders and a ski slope of snow down her ample bosom ending at a drift of snow in her lap and swirls of snow blowing in through the open window.

I politely asked if she'd like for me to close the window and she said it had gone with Jack.

I said, "What?"

And she said, "When I threw him out."

She was right; there were pieces of the window down on the sidewalk but no sign of Jack.

I finally found him snoozing under a blanket of snow on the awning of the book-store and it took the fire department twenty minutes to get him down.

Soon, with things staggering ahead at the chemical plant and Aunt Pearl mothering me (she provided me with a tube of toothpaste every Monday), my life became so automated that I didn't have to *think* about eating, washing, sleeping, waking up, going to and fro. I didn't even have to think about the laundry, making the bed, sweeping the floor....

In a restaurant across the street I ate the same things for breakfast and supper and they put the same kind of sandwiches in my lunch box every day. Breakfast cost 35¢, lunch 30¢, supper 50¢, rent $10 a month.

I ate breakfast at 6:00 A.M. then shaved and changed into dungarees at the plant. At 6:00 P.M. I showered and put on street clothes and drove home, stopping to eat supper at 6:30, then went across the street to chat with Aunt Pearl and Jack for a few minutes before retreating to my room where I read the paper, checked the mail, and at exactly 8:00 P.M. uncovered the typewriter and started trying to be a writer.

I would work until 2:00 A.M. and then go to bed.

I did this every night for more than a year. In New Castle I never had a date, never went to a movie, never had a drink in a saloon. All I did was try to be a writer.

Gradually the *way* I tried changed; changed from wasting a lot of time thinking about what it was like to *be* a writer; all that fame and glory and money; a mansion in Palm Beach but only a small villa on the French Riviera; a few Cadillacs and a yacht or two; gorgeous women by the yard....

I began to concentrate more on *how. How* to write; *how* to make it interesting. What to *do*? And it finally dawned on me that I was wasting time writing all these no good stories about people committing adultery in Paris because I'd never been to Paris or even committed adultery.

It wasn't necessary to experience everything I wrote about, but it was necessary to know enough about it to make it real.

Slowly, slowly I began to be a sterner judge and, at last, to admit into my private world an imaginary *Reader*. It wasn't good enough for what I wrote to entertain me, it had to entertain *Him*. He stood there, almost tangible enough to touch, and he was a *mean* scooter.

It took rewrite after rewrite after rewrite to make him *feel* it, to make him laugh, or cry, or get really excited. And if I got sloppy and wrote just to amuse myself that Reader went out to lunch and didn't promise to come back.

At the plant the Roaster took shape, the motors ran, the ball-mill rumbled, the huge rakes moved slowly around, the Cottrell precipitator precipitated and the conveyors conveyed raw sulfur into the thing and sulfur ash out of it.

Nobody bought anything I wrote. I had three books going around to the publishers, and dozens of stories flowing like the tide, out and back, endlessly.

Just before the final test run, the boss sent me out to East Chicago, Indiana, to see if that would be a good place to build another Space Roaster.

After two weeks there I had to admit in a report to the boss that East Chicago was probably better than New Castle—skilled labor more available, a better site, closer sources of supplies, etc.

I got home late one night and in two weeks Aunt Pearl had piled a lot of discouragement on my bed. The brown paper mailers, self-addressed and now containing rejection slips, were spread out on the bed like an open deck of cards. So were the newspapers. My two pay envelopes were in a separate pile, as were the bills, any first-class mail, and pleas for donations. My three novels were stacked in their boxes.

I was scraping this stuff off my bed when I saw the sign Aunt Pearl had printed in red ink and stood up on the pillow.

THE MAN WANTS YOU IN CLEVELAND TOMORROW NINE FOR CONFER WITH DUPONT PEOPLE.

Nine A.M. didn't leave me any time for sleep so I dumped the useless mail back on the bed and started gathering my uptown clothes and shiny shoes when I noticed one long, white envelope with a typed address.

Inside it was a check for $100 (a month's pay) for permission to publish "Night Watch," my story about standing the mid-watch on a battleship in heavy fog....

That was in July of 1934 and by September I was an unpaid member of a crew on a seventy-two-foot, thirty-year-old, gaff-rigged schooner drawing ten feet with a lead keel. The rest of the crew consisted of the skipper, who owned the boat, his wife, who hated the boat, and a sixteen-year-old, two hundred-pound, six-foot klepto- and homicidal-maniac, who hated everything.

Things are a little vague between the morning in Cleveland and now, in September, embarking in this boat in Boston. I was physically at the conference in Cleveland where I was told I would be the construction engineer in Indiana, at $500 a month, with total control of building another Space Roaster.

But when it came down to details—when would I have to leave and who were my bosses in Indiana and Illinois—I remember even now what that sudden thought felt like. It seemed to wipe out the men, the room, then Cleveland.

It was so simple. I had told a few people that I *wanted* to be a writer, or was *trying* to be a writer, and had told myself that I was *going* to be a writer, but I had never told anybody, even myself, that I *was* a writer.

I think I interrupted a man talking when I said that I didn't want to work for DuPont any more. The men made a lot of angry noise, mostly telling me I was crazy, but my boss just said, sort of sadly, "Robb....*why?*"

Now I could say it, and I said it. "Because, sir, now I am a writer."

The plan the skipper had for his boat was to turn it into a floating school with a dozen or so young boys who would cruise down to the West Indies while their parents paid handsomely for them to go to school aboard. (I was going to be the math and English lit professor.)

But when the mamas in the limos arrived at the Boston dock and saw our ancient wreck with sails so old you could poke a finger through them, they threw those kids back in the limos and vanished.

Only one couple said they'd pay double if we'd take their sixteen-year-old maniac and see if we could straighten him out. Keep him at sea, they said, as long as we wanted to.

In addition to the boy (who tried to kill me about once a week), we had the skipper's problem. The man did not believe in the benefits of sea room. In a storm he thought you couldn't get in trouble if you could see land, and I knew that it was land that got boats into trouble. So, although I had a sextant, chronometer, and Bowditch, the Skipper would not sail that boat out of sight of land.

Therefore when the full gale hit us and just about sank us, we were in plain sight of North Carolina's Cape Hatteras on the lee shore.

By the third night the schooner was helpless, the sails we needed having been blown out, the triatic stays yanked loose so the masts were lashing around like dangerous toothpicks, and all the anchors were dragging in the sandy bottom. The skipper decided somebody had to swim ashore and get the Coast Guard. He couldn't go because he was the skipper and his wife couldn't go because she'd been seasick in the main cabin bunk for three days and her dressing gown of pink feathers was soaked with oily bilge water, spilled food, and the diluted results of her illness. We didn't discuss it with the boy as he sat on the table with a .22 rifle.

So I was elected. On deck, in a pair of blue swim trunks and life preserver made of stiff slabs of cork, I secured one end of a thirty-foot-length of rope to my waist and then made fast the other end to a bitt on deck.

It was pitch dark and the blowing rain felt like millions of tiny icicles being driven in your skin. The roar of the surf sounded very close (actually it was two miles away).

I told the skipper that I'd get into the water, but if it was too wild or too cold I wasn't going to try it, so for him to stand by to pull me back if I hollered.

It was December 22nd and the water was not only cold as ice, but the wind was skimming the foam off the waves making it hard to breathe.

When I yelled for him to pull me back nothing happened.

So I began hauling in the rope and, somehow, was not surprised when the bitter end of it slid through my freezing hands.

Somebody wanted the Coast Guard so badly they had untied the rope so that I would have to go.

Trying to swim two miles in that wild, freezing, black water would be impossible wearing that stiff, heavy, soaked life preserver, so I shucked it off and began swimming in the general direction of the waves I could hear breaking on the beach.

All I remember about getting ashore was looking down the long, curving, oily blackness of the wave and then BLAM—and a detached knowledge that I was being pounded down and ground up in the cold harsh sand.

I had landed on Salter Path, one of the Outer Islands off the coast of North Carolina and didn't understand why, when I found some people, they looked at me in horror and ran screaming over the dunes.

Then one woman, opening her kitchen door to see what was causing all that disturbance, looked at me and said, "You are in pure distress."

I didn't realize that I was covered with blood and the wind had blown dry sand against me, coating me.

The Coast Guard saved the people, but did a lot of damage to the boat, so I said good-bye to the skipper and his wife and told the maniac in clear terms where he could go, then shipped out for the West Indies with a man named Mueller in his twenty-three-foot home-made sloop which capsized about 500 miles off the coast of the United States. After a very long day in the water we were picked up by a shrimp boat out of Florida.

After several more of such minor disasters, I finally landed on Dominica, in the British West Indies, and set up my typewriter in a flat above Barclay's Bank.

Dominica is one of the most beautiful, mysterious, and challenging islands in the Caribbean. It is wet and lush, with magnificent rain forests, threaded by rivers and waterfalls down its slopes, and pestilential poisonous lakes and beautiful people. I worked well there, selling enough short stories to keep me fed and happy while I wrote two more books, and my first book, *The Nub*, illustrated by Andrew Wyeth, was published.

It was in Dominica that I began thinking a lot about a girl in Thomasville, Georgia, I had met when I was a teenager. Her real name was Rosalie but everybody called her Rodie.

Rodie Mason was a girl who didn't *fit*. She didn't use any makeup, including lipstick, not because she was rebellious but because it was a waste of time. She never in her life went to a beauty parlor nor had her hair cut (she just let it grow and brushed it a lot). She was quiet and could say more in fewer but very exact words than anybody I know. And—she was *funny*, with a dry, wry wit. She didn't depend much on people nor demand anything from them and spent most of her free time in the woods or in the streams and lakes of the 8,000-acre plantation her family owned. There she had her horses and dogs and cats and squirrels and was a very competent amateur ornithologist.

And she had deep compassion and passion for the people she loved.

So I went back to Thomasville to see about Rodie.

Since I had last seen her she had put a slight but permanent bend in one of her legs by killing a mule with it. The way it happened was that, one dark night on the dirt road going home on her big Harley Davidson motorcycle, she ran into the back of an unlit wagon pulled by a mule and driven by an old black man.

The first thing the black man saw was this white girl sailing past him and hitting his mule in the back of its head with her knee. Then a big motorcycle split his wagon in two and ended up, still growling, right beside him.

Rodie killed the mule, broke her leg, and quit riding motorcycles.

It took me about a year to persuade Rodie to marry me and I never did convince her mother that I was a suitable husband for her darlin' daughter. But her mother came from Philadelphia so couldn't be expected to understand.

1937-1941

We were married in January 1937, and for the next six months lived a miserable life in a concrete shack in the British Virgin Islands infested with every bug known to man who bit or stung people. We lived most of the time in tents of mosquito netting and the only way I could get any writing done was to paddle our thirteen-foot sailboat out beyond the bugs' flight range, anchor it, and put the typewriter on the seat amidships. The trouble with that was the wind sometimes blew my best work out to sea, or rain soaked everything, or North Atlantic storms made the waves so erratic I couldn't find the keyboard.

In desperation we finally gave up trying to endure that place, even gave up trying to write anything and, by sunrise every morning we were sailing away from there in search of somewhere on one of the thirty-six uninhabited islands all around us that didn't have so many bugs.

In the weeks of searching we found many places where we would have been happy, only to find that each one had some reason why we couldn't live there. The place wasn't for sale, or belonged to the Crown, or the owner would only sell us all of a huge island for a huge price.

Finally there were only two islands left that we had not explored—Great Camanoe and Scrub Island which lay to the north of Tortola, the biggest and most important of the British Virgin Islands.

The only reason we sailed up there that day was because we didn't want to admit defeat before we had visited every place there was where we might live.

We anchored first in a small lagoon with a white beach and swam ashore to see if there were any bugs. When none attacked us, I wandered off along the beach in one direction and Rodie wandered away in the other direction, both of us depressed by the knowledge that this was a beautiful place for us, but there would be some damn reason why we couldn't live here.

In about fifteen minutes I saw Rodie wandering along the beach *toward* me and she saw me wandering *toward* her.

That was physically impossible because Scrub Island was at least five miles around and we certainly couldn't wander that far in fifteen minutes.

Too confused to think clearly, we started climbing up a little hill to find out how we had managed to meet each other in the middle of nowhere.

At the top of the hill there was a plumeria tree making the air smell sweet and, looking down, we saw the curving arm of a coral reef forming the lagoon of crystal clear water with our little boat floating peacefully at anchor.

We were standing on top of a tiny *island*.

I don't think we talked at all during the long sail back to Road Town, the capitol of the British Virgin Islands, because we both knew that this now was the time when our West Indian adventure was going to end or—begin.

In Road Town we found the island, that was too small to be on any chart we had, was a dot on the large scale chart and had a name—Marina Cay. We also found out that Marina Cay was for sale and at a price we could afford—*sixty dollars*.

Two days later everything we owned except the

bed was stacked on the beach at Marina Cay, with the coal pot (which is what the Tortolans call a barbecue grill) levelled on a pile of dead coral, kitchen utensils hanging from a branch of an enormous banyan tree, and the typewriter on one of the boat seats balanced on some rocks high enough for me to sit in the sand and write small masterpieces.

Marina Cay was a perfect little tropical island for two people. It lacked only a few civilized things. Although the hill was high enough to protect us from hurricanes or tidal waves there was nothing to protect us from the wind and rain or any wild animals who might live there. No shelter of any sort.

There were no neighbors, no phones, no radio, no doctors, no supermarkets (or even a mom'n'pop store), no cars or motors. No electricity, no gas (but plenty of kerosene for lamps and lanterns). No trains, planes, buses, or elevators; just the sailboat.

Also there was no fresh water on Marina Cay; no stream nor well nor basin.

But in a week or so our bed arrived on a native sloop which also brought us tools and lumber and an empty fifty-gallon oil drum.

The shed we built under the banyan tree was sixteen feet long by eight feet wide with the long, open side facing the lagoon, the other side and ends were closed against the trade wind. We installed a gutter along the low side of the sloping tar-papered roof which caught the rainwater and drained it into the oil drum which, after awhile, didn't taste so much like tar and oil.

Now we didn't have to sleep on the beach where the sand crabs thought we were an amusement park just for them to skateboard on.

We had been living in the shed for about six months when we got a cable saying my book, *The Smuggler's Sloop* (also illustrated by Andrew Wyeth), had won the prize for the Best Juvenile Book of the Year.

That news persuaded us to build a house on our island.

We sailed boatloads of sand over from the beaches on Beef Island and gravel from the beaches of Camanoe and built a thick-walled concrete house with a cistern that held 5,000 gallons of rainwater.

We could sit in our house and choose which lobsters walking around on the reef we wanted for lunch. We caught fish and crabs in traps, collected mangoes, coconuts, oranges, and limes from other islands and if we wanted some meat we'd trap a goat on Scrub Island, skin it out, and eat it.

The years on Marina Cay were good. A lot of books and stories got written and we found good friends among the Tortolans. We also found that life on

a desert island is about as fine as you can get.

Then three events coming in short order in 1941 put an abrupt end to that sweet life. First, Rodie got appendicitis and it took so long sailing her to the only doctor in St. Thomas she almost died. The second blow hit us in Thomasville, where Rodie was convalescing. The island government in Antigua wrote that something I had written had offended them, so my license to own land was withdrawn. (That government has never yet told me what they objected to.) Marina Cay was taken away from us with everything we owned there and we have never seen it since.

And then came my recall to active duty in the Navy.

1941-1984

I reported first to flight training at Pensacola, Florida, and then went with Air Group One to our aircraft carrier at San Diego, California, and between carrier duty served as Air Administration officer on Pacific islands like Majuro and Eniwetok. I finally ended up on the carrier *Natoma Bay* during the Battle of Leyte Gulf in the Philippines and thought for awhile as I survived a sinking ship that I was going to die where I had been born.

My tour of duty lasted seven years during which time I saw Rodie and my children only occasionally. There were lapses of years between the times I saw my son, also named Robb White; and my daughter, Barbara, was almost three years old before I saw her for the *first* time.

Those years in the Navy with only letters forming a fragile structure did not, in our case, support our marriage. When I at last came home, I was a stranger; and my family, my wife and children, were strangers to me. Rodie, forced to raise the children all by herself, had built a solid and complete world which, from necessity, no longer had a place, nor any great need, for me. And I, too, had spent too long in a world that was neither solid nor complete, but a world of sudden and unexpected upheavals; of empty, impersonal rooms ashore and crowded cabins at sea.

Another insidious thing threatened the marriage we had had at Marina Cay, and Rodie explained it exactly when she said, "We just are not interested in the same things any-more."

Rodie loved the loneliness of the forest and streams and lakes and paths and animals and birds and bugs of her plantation and so did her children.

After we separated, still good friends, I wandered, but while I did, I kept on writing. During the year I spent on the French Riviera I wrote two books and four serials. And then went on an anthropological expedition to the Near East, starting at Lebanon and going through Syria, Iraq, and Iran and then up into the mountains of Kurdistan, always digging in caves for traces of the Missing Link; (I drove the Jeep with a huge tank of formaldehyde in the back to preserve any specimens of birds, snakes, fish, or bugs for Harvard. I hauled this tank around for six months getting well preserved myself.)

I wrote *The Haunted Hound* in Beirut.

Then to England, France again, Ireland, Scotland, Italy......wandering......writing....

And then I got a letter from somebody in Hollywood asking if I'd like to write for a TV series called "Men of Annapolis." When I told him yes, I didn't tell him I'd never written for TV and didn't even know how it was done.

The way I got tangled up in TV writing was because Bill, the producer of "Men of Annapolis" couldn't persuade the Navy to accept any of the scripts his Hollywood writers were submitting, so, frantic about losing his series contract, he had searched the library and found that there was only one living fiction writer who had graduated from the Naval Academy— me.

I met Bill in an Annapolis hotel and he gave me a sample TV script to study, telling me that the Navy had given him only seven more days to come up with a story the Navy liked.

Writing a teleplay seemed to me so much easier than writing a story that I went ahead that night and had a complete script for him in the morning—which was the first script the Navy accepted. So I just kept on writing teleplays about my life in the Academy, which got the series on the screen and him off the hook.

Those stories not only made me a lot of money but, in the end, helped form a partnership with Bill to write and produce feature-length films.

When I moved out to Hollywood to write the first movie with Bill, I lived in the Roosevelt Hotel until a girl I'd met asked me one Sunday if I'd like to go to Malibu. I didn't know what or where Malibu was but I was willing to do anything to get out of the Roosevelt Hotel.

When I walked into the Malibu house of the people the girl had brought me to visit I couldn't say a word. A soft breeze was gently moving white cloud-like curtains at the ends of a solid glass wall beyond which was the *entire* blue, calm Pacific Ocean. It made me feel so close to being back on Marina Cay that I almost cried.

Before that day ended I had bought the house at 24334 Malibu Road. It was a thoroughly beat up, dog-gnawed little rectangular house set in a yard full of weeds and junk such as old refrigerators, gas stoves, and toilets. Inside the 900 square feet there were two tiny bedrooms, one tiny bathroom, one tiny kitchen, and one large living room with that magic glass wall looking out at the ocean.

The house was set on pilings and was about to fall into the sea.

Having never even *heard* the word escrow and not caring what it might mean, I paid the lady what she wanted for the house and moved in that same afternoon, sleeping uncomfortably on the slanting floor.

The next day I told Sears I had to have a bed, stove, and refrigerator in my house by nightfall. Then I got eight big hydraulic jacks and some timbers and got the jacks set on top of the pilings on which the house sat. Then I jacked it up level and made up my new bed.

That house was about the size of the one at Marina Cay but it was lonely there, with the only sound that of the moving sea.

The first film Bill and I made was called *Macabre.* (When I suggested that title Bill snorted, "What's that, something you threw up?" And I heard it pronounced everything from MAC-abree to Mah-CABE.)

I don't like horror pictures, but Bill had all sorts of gimmicks to lure people to pay money to see them. For *Macabre* we had a genuine Lloyd's insurance policy which would pay $10,000 to the heir of anybody who died of fright watching *Macabre.* Beside the ticket booth we had an actor dressed up as a doctor, with another one as a nurse with a gurney. Unfortunately, nobody ever died watching *Macabre.* In spite of that it made enough money for us to venture into a higher class of horror, with Vincent Price.

The gimmick for this one, *House on Haunted Hill,* was a skeleton which rose up out of a vat of fuming acid and floated out over the audience (actually it was pulled on a string run by a fishing reel in the projection booth). That skeleton turned out to be very expensive because the kids came with everything from bows and arrows to bazookas and shot down our skeletons.

For the next one, *The Tingler,* with Vincent, we screwed little motors under the theater seats with controls in the projection booth so, on cues in the film at the gasp spots, the projectionist could throw a switch which would violently vibrate the seats in waves. The first time this was tried was by accident in a San Fernando theater showing *The Nun's Story* on the night before our show was to open. Apparently the uninstructed projectionist with nothing else to do idly threw the switch at the time of the *Nun's* most sad and dramatic moment, suddenly shaking hell out of the people with their Kleenex at the ready.

These little motors turned out to be as expensive as our skeletons. The dear little kids came with screwdrivers, cold chisels, sledge hammers, and even miniature jackhammers and stole the motors. This theft, in 300 theaters a night, was costly.

It wasn't easy writing screenplays for a producer who would come bounding in saying things like, "I've got a GREAT idea. Fear is a worm that lives in your spinal column so write a story about that." Or about vats of acid or little motors or 3-D glasses or blood coming out of a faucet.

Somehow I managed to write five of those horror movies before finally beginning to feel like one of our shot-down skeletons so I moved up to writing for the "Perry Mason" show. I really enjoyed the four years I worked on that, because most of the the episodes were ingenious, intelligent, surprising, well written, and beautifully produced.

During all the years in Malibu I kept having this vague feeling of guilt; a sort of "What am I doing here? I don't belong here."

And the only way I could get rid of it was by writing books. In between the seven screenplays and dozens of TV scripts I wrote some pretty good books: *Surrender; Torpedo Run; Flight Deck; Silent Ship, Silent Sea; The Frogmen; The Survivor; Deathwatch.*

I am not joining the stream of writers who leave Hollywood with disdain, widely proclaiming that it is a cheap and tawdry place with all the artistic sensitivity of a rock. I left Hollywood simply because my house on the beach at Malibu kept trying to fall into the Pacific Ocean. I got tired of Sunday mornings down in the mud under the house cranking up those (now twenty-eight) hydraulic jacks. I even got a little weary of spending $50,000 to $75,000 every three or four years moving the house around and replacing the piles with longer piles that slid just as easily as short ones.

So I moved on up the coast to Montecito, a forested suburb of Santa Barbara, and bought a house resting on a solid concrete slab, surrounded by an acre of trees.

For about the first time in my life I cannot see an ocean from my window and I don't mind at all.

1985

About thirty years ago, on Broad Street in Thomasville, Georgia, I met a young girl with long black braids and golden skin covered with more freckles than a box of bran. She had startlingly blue eyes that *looked* at you and a sort of aura that spelled I DARE YOU TO.

She was Ann Crowther who was paying her tuition through Emory University with some grants and a lot of golf. Nobody could believe that such a sweet and innocent little girl, with those marvelous trusting eyes, would hustle you for large sums of money.

Being a married man all I could do that day was stand there in the sunshine and gasp.

I saw her once again, and then forever lost her when she went on to get her physical therapy degree at Columbia and I went to California.

But, one day when I was digging up bulbs in the Malibu garden some bare feet got in my way. Irritated, I looked up what the feet were connected to until I reached a vaguely familiar face but with a totally unfamiliar name because she had gotten married and even had two dissimilar children.

The boy was evidently going to become a six-and-a-half foot red-headed monster, and the girl, with those vivid Annie eyes was going to stop growing about barstool high.

I saw a good deal of that aggravation because Annie liked to bring her kids down to my house so they could go out on the beach and fill their cute little toy buckets with all manner of long-dead sea creatures which those adorable children would then hide in my house so cleverly that it would take days to follow the stench to the location.

I'm proud of the fact that Annie and I were honorable people when we were married to other people, but we did misbehave a little when both of us were single again, but only enough to make sure that we wanted to give marriage the best chance we could.

Annabelle's red-headed son, who lives about half a mile from us, looks like he ought to be embossed on a gold Greek coin. The little bitty girl is brilliant, gorgeous, and addicted to running twenty-five or thirty miles a week.

My children still live within twenty miles of their mother and all of them are truly remarkable, each in a different way.

And Rodie is still Rodie. When Tom, who works for her, shot a hole in her refrigerator, she listened to it for awhile and found that it was still running, so she patted it, apologized to it, and stuffed a towel in the hole; and the refrigerator is still running fine.

BIBLIOGRAPHY

Fiction:

The Nub (illustrated by Andrew Wyeth). Boston: Little, Brown, 1935.

Smuggler's Sloop (illustrated by A. Wyeth). Boston: Little, Brown, 1937.

Midshipman Lee (illustrated by Anton Otto Fischer). Boston: Little, Brown, 1938.

Run Masked. New York: Knopf, 1938; published as *Jungle Fury.* New York: Berkley Publishing, 1956.

In Privateer's Bay. New York: Harper, 1939.

Three against the Sea (illustrated by Aldren A. Watson). New York: Harper, 1940.

Sailor in the Sun (illustrated by Edward Shenton). New York: Harper, 1941.

The Lion's Paw (illustrated by Ralph Ray). Garden City, N.Y.: Doubleday, 1946.

Secret Sea (illustrated by Jay Hyde Barnum). Garden City, N.Y.: Doubleday, 1947.

Sail Away (illustrated by Dorothy Bayley Morse). Garden City, N.Y.: Doubleday, 1948.

Candy (illustrated by Gertrude Howe). Garden City, N.Y.: Doubleday, 1949.

The Haunted Hound (illustrated by Louis Glanzman). Garden City, N.Y.: Doubleday, 1950.

Deep Danger. Garden City, N.Y.: Doubleday, 1952.

Our Virgin Island. Garden City, N.Y.: Doubleday, 1953.

Midshipman Lee of the Naval Academy. New York: Random House, 1954.

Up Periscope. Garden City, N.Y.: Doubleday, 1956.

Flight Deck. Garden City, N.Y.: Doubleday, 1961.

Torpedo Run. Garden City, N.Y.: Doubleday, 1962.

The Survivor. Garden City, N.Y.: Doubleday, 1964.

Surrender. Garden City, N.Y.: Doubleday, 1966.

Silent Ship, Silent Sea. Garden City, N.Y.: Doubleday, 1967.

No Man's Land. Garden City, N.Y.: Doubleday, 1969.

Deathwatch. Garden City, N.Y.: Doubleday, 1972.

The Frogmen. Garden City, N.Y.: Doubleday, 1973.

The Long Way Down. Garden City, N.Y.: Doubleday, 1977.

Fire Storm. Garden City, N.Y.: Doubleday, 1979.

Two on the Isle: A Memory of Marina Cay. New York: W.W. Norton, 1985.

Screenplays:

House on Haunted Hill, Allied Artists Pictures Corporation, 1958.

Macabre, Allied Artists Pictures Corporation, 1958.

The Tingler, Columbia Pictures Corporation, 1959.

Up Periscope, Warner Brothers Pictures, 1959.

13 Ghosts, William Castle Productions, 1960.

Homicidal, William Castle Productions, 1961.

Author of television scripts for the series "Silent Service," "Men of Annapolis," and "Perry Mason."

Maia Wojciechowska

1927–

Maia Wojciechowska, 1974

Milton Ackoff

The past holds its own truths. They are private, not public truths.

When you go back to your past alone, you take a chance at excavating forgotten pain while looking for remembered happiness. And you may, if you are lucky, understand the present better and even learn about your future.

But going over your past publicly is somewhat like making a movie. You are its writer and its director and its star. But sooner or later you become its editor. From the patchwork of scenes you begin to discard, splice together sequences. The hardest decision is about what you leave out and what you retain, often at the risk of making yourself seem ridiculous. Is any of it true anymore? Is any of it false?

The past, like the movies, holds its own truths.

I wrote the above, some twelve years ago, as a preface to *Till the Break of Day: Memories 1939–1942.* I couldn't quarrel with any of it, but I learned something fascinating since the publication of that book. The past's truths are not sharable. My two brothers remembered those years very differently, were affected by other events and other people. It was our communal past only as far as geography went, but emotionally we each had our own past and it must be, like fingerprints, inexplicably different for each of us.

My father died in 1954. He died a Pole, never wishing to become an American citizen, urging his children and everyone else born in Poland to keep their Polish citizenship, and saying sad, desperate things like: "As long as we remain Poles we will have to fight for the return of our country. If we relinquish that citizenship we won't any longer demand the return, to us, of a free Poland. We will forfeit every right! Even the right of exile! We must never surrender ourselves to another country for we are Poles, robbed of our land. But we must return to a free Poland, either by fighting to free it or demanding an investigation into why Poland was sold." The year before he died this most private of men spoke at public meetings about the necessity not to compromise this "freeing of Poland." He wrote urgent letters trying to appeal to the conscience of those who "sold" Poland, who could "redress that treason" which happened at Yalta and was confirmed in Teheran. Until the last day of his life he considered himself "on forced leave" from the Polish Air Force, ready at a moment's notice to be called back to his job as a soldier. "We must expect to shed blood again," he said to his sons who would argue that Poles had shed enough blood.

A year before his death I promised my father that if he became terminally ill I would drive him up to a mountaintop and leave him there to die. "I want my body to rest in Poland," he said. "The Polish earth is light for us, the foreign soil too heavy." I did not know how sick he became after a routine operation. I didn't know until it was too late. My brother Chris swears he was murdered on orders from Moscow and there was a mysterious nurse who came from Washington and stayed until he was dead and then disappeared as suddenly as she had appeared. I didn't even go to his funeral for I knew I would only have to bury him

Warsaw, Poland, 1932: "In matching outfits which delighted Maia, age five, and totally humiliated Zbyszek, age seven."

again, in Poland, and my mother wished him there, in California, where she could tend his grave. Poles are as good at tending their dead as they are at dying.

By the time I was thirty-four I was most eager to grow up. I felt emotionally arrested by the war. I was still, emotionally, twelve-going-on-sixteen, rebellious and angry, seesawing between total happiness and utmost despair, naive and trusting, yet cynical, the way only children can be cynical. I was given to totally idiotic, often shocking, declarations which were made to impress, badly, those who heard them. I was outrageous and didn't know how to be anything else, or didn't want to try to be anything else, such as a grown-up. I had not begun to write children's books, except for one picture book of no particular merit. I knew that it was high time to grow up and the only way I was going to do that would be to go back to Poland to bury that kid who was giving me too much trouble at thirty-four.

It was 1961 and I did not expect to cry so much. Everything there made me cry.

Those were the bad days, when the spirit flagged, when despair was heard howling throughout the land. I cried when a conductor accused me of not putting all my pennies in the box, accused me of cheating. I cried when I could not buy any paper to write on, because I was a writer although not an author. I cried when I

managed to generate more garbage than a family of six. I cried when I talked to a doctor, a bone surgeon, and heard his story. He had been away from Poland for a year because he had devised some new technique of mending bones and had been invited to lecture in the West, in Belgium, France, Italy. When he came back to Poland, he was punished for having been away. He was given a desk and could not perform any operations. He got his pay but he saw no patients.

"Why and who is doing this to you?" I asked.

"The government. The bureaucrats. My hospital. And why? Because I got good at something and someone noticed. And that is not allowed. Everything must be kept on the level of mediocrity. If anyone shows talent it must be kept in the dark, it must not be used. They, the communists, dear lady, want us exterminated by mediocrity. That's how the communists kill. Not with guns, but by denying the possibility of greatness! Take that message back to your new country, to America. Stop arming yourselves with guns. Arm yourselves with excellence! Don't let shoddy movies be made, or once made, don't make them popular. You watch things on television that have no content, that say nothing new, show nothing of value and pretty soon you will become a communist. A communist is someone who, having no soul, supports anything that will kill the human spirit. Anything that diminishes godlike qualities in people is communism. That's why

Maia and Aunt Walcia, Cracow, Poland, 1937

a good communist does not allow God anywhere around. That's why there are so very few communists in Poland and so very many in a country like yours, in America. I was there for a short time. They don't call themselves communists. They are materialists. Same thing."

I asked the doctor if we could have dinner because I wanted to argue with him about American values and how it's not the same to be a communist and a capitalist.

"I'm sorry," he said. "I must attend to my planned suicide tonight."

He walked away and I cried because I knew that he had lived too long in a place where reasons for living were made fewer each day.

I also cried in the theatre. Over the years I've seen a dozen productions of Chekhov's *The Seagull,* in maybe half-a-dozen languages. The production I saw in Poland was so superior to anything I had seen that it left me limp with gratitude. I cried because it was so splendid and because the peasants, who were bussed in from the countryside, laughed in all the wrong places.

One day, to make me laugh, a cousin took me to

see what he did. He worked in the department of food supplies. He had a private office with a huge map of Warsaw. The map had multicolored pins on it. There were clusters of the same color all over the place, but each cluster was far away from the next. He explained his job. "I have to move different foods around so it will be very hard for people to find what they need." I did not understand.

He explained patiently, speaking slowly so that I would not miss the point: "What we have here, in communist Poland, is a government *against* the people. It's a government dedicating all its energies to making the citizens *continually* miserable. My job is to make sure people don't starve to death and yet hate themselves for being alive." He pointed to the cluster of blue pins. "Those pins are tomatoe paste cans. We have restriction on everything. You cannot buy more than one of anything, but right here, in this part of Warsaw, you can find all the tomatoe paste you'd wish to look at. You have to go there to purchase tomatoe paste. Now right here," he pointed to the yellow cluster of pins, "I've placed our supply of onions for this week. Of course the paste and the onions will be moved around, but in clusters, in a few days. That's my job, moving foodstuff around. But right here there is nothing but onions, and here," he pointed to another cluster of pins, this time brown ones, "we've got potatoes." He smiled. "Now let's say that you want to make potatoe soup tonight. You will have to travel all over Warsaw for your ingredients. Here," he pointed to green pins way up north, "for salt, and here," he pointed south, "for pepper, and you already know where you go for potatoes, onions, and tomatoe paste. Of course you're in my office looking at the map. If you were out on the street trying to buy stuff for soup tonight it would take you about six hours of scurrying around. How could a Polish housewife, after six hours spent in finding ingredients for soup, be expected to go to mass? Or lead some protesters? Or gossip about us governmental bureaucrats? You see the government, through vermin like me, keeps the citizens busy. They have to scurry for necessities. The Moscow party thinkers studied rats and decided it was the best way of keeping people placid—make them scurry around like so many rats in a maze, just to stay alive."

I began to shake my head thinking how lucky I was not having to live in Poland, but his next words made me less happy.

"You, in your new country, are not so very much different from us. It's not the government that makes you scurry around. It's the advertisers; it's free enterprise, capitalism. You want new cars and new clothes, new ice boxes and TV sets, and they are all there, not hidden in clusters, not even rationed, but available all over. Of course they do cost money, so you have to scurry after money. We don't have unemployment. Everyone here has to work. In America they want to work. We don't want to work to keep this monster alive, but we have to. You don't have to, but you want to. Scurrying around for things that only money can buy, you have no time to pray or protest or wonder what happened to happiness in life. Someone in your country must have been studying rats as well."

I was being educated all the time in Poland. I went to the studios of the Polski Film and saw short films that were unbelieveably great. "Why are they short?" I asked. "Because that's all the film they give us. Never enough for a feature." "But they are so great, can they be shown outside of Poland?" "No, they are too good. Poland exports only the mediocre, propaganda product. Nobody is going to see our good films. We have to knock off four awful films in order to be allowed to make one good one. And that is always a short one that nobody will see. But at least all of us working in film know what we can do if we were allowed. We're good!"

There was a whole new language in Poland in those days, having triple and quadruple meaning, a secret language which ridiculed the system, ridiculed life under the system, turned tears into laughter.

Aunt Walcia, just before World War II

My second week in Poland I went to see uncle Staś in Lodz. What was he doing in provincial Lodz? He was existing. He looked the same, almost, except older. He was still immaculately dressed, wore spats, carried a cane, had his shoes brilliantly shined. He looked like prewar uncle Staś. He told me that he could look like that in Lodz but wouldn't get away looking like that in Warsaw, so he stayed in Lodz because he valued the way he looked. He was obviously greatly admired and respected and had a coterie of friends gather around him for his ritual of tea drinking in a café. He had finally, after my grandmother died, married his mistress. And I finally found out from him what happened to my beloved aunts, Walcia and Andzia.

It seemed that all through the war they managed, somehow, to survive in Warsaw. But after the uprising, when ninety-nine percent of the city lay in ruins, the newly arrived communists ordered people to go to whatever relatives they might have outside of Warsaw. And my aunts were taken in by uncle Staś in Lodz. He

Uncle Stas, during Maia's only visit to Poland after World War II, Lodz, 1961

said that they were made "more strange" by the war. They still lived lives of "perfect cleanliness" but it must have been physically impossible. So their obsession with making everything sterile was now even more strongly wedged into their minds. He didn't say that they were madder than the hatter, but they must have been. He was very gentle telling me how it was impossible to lead the kind of life they led before the war. Even heating water was a luxury, and boiling it continuously to sterilize everything, as they wanted, was out of the question. And although he did not say it, I sensed that his wife and my beloved aunts must have waged a war as cruel as any.

Before the war my aunts, Andzia and Walcia, were allied with my grandmother against uncle Staś' mistress, referring to her as "that harlot," if they referred to her at all. What was it like for my aunts, with their great sense of loyalty, to exist under the roof of the woman they had thought despicable? And, more importantly, what was it like for Staś' wife? I didn't quite dare ask.

But my uncle sensed my curiosity and said: "Your aunts never talked to my wife. If they wished something they would communicate their needs to me and I would pass them on. My wife understood and forgave them, and your aunts kept their vows to my mother, your grandmother, never to speak to her. Anyway, life was not easy. They lived downstairs and we lived upstairs. They had one room with a small kitchen and the tragedy was, of course, that they never had enough hot, boiling water. But they managed and we saw them each day. But one day the door remained locked when I knocked and Walcia said that Andzia was not feeling well. I asked if they needed anything and she said no. It went on like that for a week. Usually my wife would go to the market and try to get some food for all of us, and she too began to worry. At the end of the week I broke the door down."

He looked down, as if terribly ashamed and I held my breath knowing that something awful, tragic, had happened beyond the closed door.

"Walcia was combing Andzia's hair. She had your aunt Andzia dressed in a nightgown, seated on the chair, and Walcia was talking to her. There was this terrible smell in the room . . . Andzia had been dead for over a week by then."

I saw it all as if I were there, as if I, too, had combed her hair, not wishing her to leave yet, not wanting to be left alone in this world without her. They had always talked about it, ever since I could remember anything at all, I remembered my aunts saying that they could never live one without the other. They had always planned to die together, and yet they would play those games of theirs—Andzia, the angelic

Aunt Andzia, not long before her death

one, saying that she would die first because God was merciful. And Walcia, the strong, domineering one, saying that no such thing was going to happen. They would die together, at the same hour, the same moment. And as a small child I would listen to them and I believed, without knowing, that they had died together. And now, knowing how it happened, I said my thanks to God. Andzia had to go first. It was only fair.

"The most cruel, the most ironic thing happened," uncle Staś went on. "Walcia died the next day. She seemed perfectly healthy, except her mind was with her sister, refusing to accept her death. I had an autopsy performed and do you know what Walcia died of? Filth! Dirt!" He tried to find the piece of paper to show me the medical word. But in his agitation could not find it. "Can you imagine! It was Walcia, all along, all her life, who was such a nut about cleanliness. And she dies of filth!" He must have loved them, I decided then, because I had never seen him angry or shouting before. "I just don't know. Taking care of the dead body must have caused it. She had no immunity at all. She was the cleanest person in the world and they had water and the gas to boil it. Of course she did not die of filth! She died because she couldn't go on without Andzia. They were like twins."

"Trying to lay the past to rest," Warsaw, Poland, 1961

I went alone to their grave. They were buried in one grave, actually in one coffin. "They would have wanted it that way," as uncle Staś explained. He had already mentioned that it had cost him a pretty penny to get the gravedigger to put them in the same box. I agreed. They would have wanted it that way. I brought some flowers and cleaned the grave of weeds. They had a very cheap, rusty little sign, just their names and dates of birth and death on a tin cross. I polished the cross as best as I could. I was there for a few hours, and in that short space of time I remembered all the thousands of hours we had spent together. And when I got off my knees to go home I could not find my sunglasses. It was the strangest thing. I simply knew that they wanted something of mine with them and took the sunglasses. There was no other, no more logical explanation. They didn't ask, they took. And it was only right. I never gave anything to them that I could remember.

I came back from the cemetery determined to transport them to the family grave in Warsaw. I didn't care what it would take; this I had to do for them. My maternal grandmother had what always seemed to me the very best family gravesite in all of Warsaw. It was located on the main avenue, just beyond the iron gate, the easiest of all graves to find.

My fondest memories had to do with All Souls' Day (Halloween in America) when the family gathered to pay their respects to their dead. The great cemetery would be transformed by millions of flickering candles, by an ocean of flowers. People bundled up would move by the light of those candles, in the shadows of those flowers, tending to the cleaning of their graves. Families had family graves, and the oldest seemed the best. Ours was one of the oldest and one of the biggest. The names of all the departed were etched into the marble, with plenty of marble left for new names and dates. Before the war everyone in the family knew there was enough space for twelve more coffins. Once the spaces were all filled the crypt would be sealed forever. As it was, the big stone would be moved aside by a forklift whenever anyone was buried in that family grave.

Before going to Lodz to see uncle Staś I had visited the grave and the only new name on it was my grandmother, *Stefania Rudakowska, 1866-1944*. Andzia and Walcia always expected to be buried next to her, their sister. I always figured that I would end up there as well, and certainly my mother and father would be brought to rest there too. I was pretty sure that in spite of social and other differences not only Staś but his wife as well would end up there.

On my way back to Staś' apartment I decided to move my aunts immediately to Warsaw, to that marvellous family grave. When I told him, he looked very dubious.

"It will be very difficult," my uncle Staś said. "Maybe even impossible."

"Listen," I said, "in a bureaucracy such as this I know I'd need a permit. I am ready to grease some palms. I will transport them by train and I will travel with the coffin in the baggage car. I wish you'd come with me because I won't know how to arrange things on the other end, getting them in the family grave . . ."

"It will be impossible," uncle Staś finally said, "because there is no more space left in our family grave."

"You're crazy," I said. "I was there only three days ago and grandmother, your mother, is the only one who got buried there since the war. That would leave eleven spaces for eleven more coffins. Everybody knows that!"

"There is just one space left," he said.

"Come again?"

"Just one space left and I thought I could have it," he said.

Grandfather Rudakowski

It was my turn to get angry. I shouted at him that I would be bringing my mother and my father from America soon and tomorrow I was taking my aunts to that grave, and that if he gave some spaces to his friends all he had to do was throw the stiffs out of there.

"You don't understand," he said after my anger was exhausted. "Things were very tough during the war. I was running the racetrack in Warsaw. My assignment from the underground was to financially ruin as many of the biggies in the Gestapo as I could . . ."

"How did we get into horses from the grave?" I asked, feeling that he was going to pull some con on me. After all, my uncle Staś was known before the war as the family con man.

"I was going to come to that, how that grave saved my life, but if you don't want to hear about it . . ."

"Sure," I said. He wouldn't lie to me, I decided. Not to his own niece. Not at his age.

We went out to his favorite café and a small crowd gathered around us as he told me the story of the great race. He must have told it many times before, or was a better actor than I thought. He told it so well that I remember it as if it had been a movie. As a matter of fact it would make a great movie.

Stefania Rudakowska

It seems that very shortly after the Germans invaded Poland in September of 1939, an order went out to reopen the racetrack and my uncle was put in some position at the top, having had connections there. (Actually the only connection I think he had was as a gambler. It was he, single-handedly who lost a family fortune with his gambling. He rarely won. And my mother always said that it was he, her brother, who introduced my father to gambling. The two used to gamble together a lot.)

"By spring of 1940 I had gained the confidence of the top Gestapo men in Warsaw," my uncle was saying, and I began to concentrate on the story. "I had given them many tips on the right horses and they trusted me as their official handicapper. I began to figure out the way to totally ruin the top Gestapo dog in one single race." The crowd at the café drew nearer. "Everyone, from jockeys to the grooms, and of course the top echelons of the Polish Underground, were in on the scam. Its secret name was NAG. I had promised the Gestapo man that if I ever found one single horse, preferably a long-shot that could make him rich, I'd let him know. I finally spotted the horse I wanted him to be ruined by, a filly with absolutely no chance of becoming a racing horse, not even if someone implanted wings on her back. She was brought to me by a peasant boy and offered to me for ten zlotys. 'She's as swift as the wind,' the kid said. That very day I went to see the Gestapo dog and told him there would be a filly, a 100-to-1 long-shot running next Saturday and if he could manage to divest himself of a lot of his treasures he would bankrupt even the Swiss bankers with his winnings.

"The following day he sold both his cars for one-tenth their worth to a man who said he would get back his cars if he won. The man was one of ours. The Gestapo man let go of his great collection of paintings to a man who made him a loan and promised to give them back if he won the race. The man was also ours. He let go of his silver and his jewels to another of our men for a measly sum, but also with a promise that he could redeem the stuff. Altogether he was able to raise over a million zlotys for things worth one hundred times as much. But he was happy. After all he had a horse that could not lose and he would have, after the race, one hundred million zlotys, and would redeem all his treasures. He was a very happy man when he gave a party the night before the race. I was there, drinking champagne, eating caviar, and so were our men who had bought his things at low prices. Already those things were distributed where they could not be found, and the men themselves were ready to leave for parts unknown at the party's end. I, however, had decided to stick it out to the very end of the great race.

"You see it was all planned like a bank robbery, with a lot of bright people involved, with great precision in timing. We were so certain of our great success, of going down in history as the neatest con ever, that during the party I suggested our host call the Führer himself and get him to place a bet on this sure thing that would have odds of 100-to-1. The Führer told our host to put 100 zlotys on the horse. We raised our glasses and our host laughed after he had drunk the toast to the horse that would make him rich. He said that if something was to happen to that horse he would be totally destroyed. I laughed right along with him."

Uncle Staś obviously enjoyed telling the story and took great pains that those who came to hear it heard it well. His voice was pretty loud in that café and I caught myself thinking that maybe his great con was part of a con he was pulling on me.

"Everything had to go like clockwork for everyone to be safe after the race. This was to be the very last time Polish horses were racing for the Germans, that was the underground's decision. The ticket takers, the bet collectors, the barmen, and even the cleaning staff was to leave at the start of that race. The jockeys, of course, would have to take their chances but the Germans had great respect for them . . . and we knew they'd be safe—except, perhaps, for the jockey on that nag that would come in last. I myself had arranged for a plane to taxi up on the other side of the stands. The plane was as close to me as the starting gate, a mere hundred yards.

"She broke out well. She was wearing gold and a number eight. She was third and furthest from the rails when suddenly, before the first turn, I see her, the horse of history, our 100-to-1 nag, turn! She was making directly toward me, where I was standing and I began to run toward the plane. She was a faster horse than I took her for. We reached the plane at the same time and the jockey jumped out of the saddle right at the plane's door, the filly was still running as we taxied off."

The small crowd broke into applause as the story came to the end.

"So what happened to eleven spaces in the family grave?" I asked him as he was waving to the waiter to refill his cup of tea.

He looked shocked, as if I had breached some rule of etiquette. I waited patiently.

"You did not guess how my life was saved?" he asked. "It was the owner of the plane, of course. I traded my escape for the ten spaces in the grave. You see," he lowered his head piously, "the pilot's family, all ten of them, were wiped out by a rare disease and he had no place to put them." His head remained lowered and after a while he began to snore. He was getting on in years and I felt sorry for him. But I still didn't believe him and when I got back to Warsaw I checked out the race story. It seemed to be true. A relative told me that Staś had something to do with it all, but didn't know exactly what.

"You might not remember," she told me, "but when you and your brother Zbyszek were small kids you always asked for money for your name-days and Christmas. For years nobody knew what you ever did with all that money but one day we found out that your uncle Staś was making bets with you kids. And he always won," she added.

"What happened to the family grave?" I wanted to know.

"During the war whenever uncle Staś needed money he'd sell a space in the family grave," she told me. "To tell you the truth I think he had someone ferret horizontally from your family grave into others because it seems to me he sold about a hundred spaces during the war and you couldn't have had more than a dozen in yours."

Before leaving Poland I called uncle Staś and told him that I was putting $100 in an envelope. It was to take care of the expense of removing all those strange stiffs from our grave and putting my aunts there. I reminded him that I'd be coming back with the bodies of my mother and father and I expected to find a lot of space there.

"I bet you," he said, "I'll die before my sister, your mother."

"How much?" I caught myself saying. And he answered, "A hundred dollars?"

A few years later my younger brother Chris went to Poland and found him in need of more care. He ordered the best wheelchair around and uncle Staś travelled around Lodz in that as if it were his Cadillac. Chris wanted him to come to America, but uncle Staś thought it was too late for him.

"If I were in my prime," he told Chris, "I would take on America."

"I'd like to see you in Las Vegas."

"You should have seen me in Monte Carlo."

Before he left Poland, my brother Chris made arrangements for a nurse and other amenities for my uncle, and the last two years of his life he lived in the manner he had been accustomed to, except more so. For over twenty years it was my other brother, Zbyszek, who had been sending him, regularly, enough money to live on and keep up that front that was so important to him. After all, uncle Staś was the only male member of our family who had always lived like a true aristocrat, having never had a job of any kind.

Hyères, France, 1941: Maia (right), with her mother and brothers.

I did not get rid of that young Maia while in Poland, and a year later I went back to Europe to retrace my past in France to perhaps lose her there. In *Till the Break of Day* I had written about that colony of Poles in the town of Hyères. I had one photograph of the four of us, my two brothers, Chris and Zbyszek and my mother, in front of the hotel, and I used to stare at it and wonder. How come I looked so starved and they didn't? How come I looked so ugly and they didn't? How come the three of us kids looked so guilty? Or was it my imagination? And mother, she looked so strong and stern just the opposite of what she was. I wanted to remember more of it, revisit what I felt were the places where my most formative years were spent.

It was strange—in all those places there was only one ghost, that of my father. He had not been with us, not in Sables-d'Olonne, not in Bordeaux, not in Vichy, or Grenoble, or Hyères, yet it was he, and he alone, I kept thinking of. I retraced nothing of my own past, found no clues to anything except the fact that I loved him dearly and he died without ever knowing how I had felt about him. I don't think I ever told him that I loved him.

Someone had once asked me what a growing kid needs most, and I had said: "A hero the kid can love, admire, forget his or her ego in front of, that's what a kid needs most."

My father had consistently been my hero. We had almost two years of "normal" life as a family and those two years were in Washington, D.C., where he was the Air Attaché at the Polish Embassy.

I didn't get to know him well. He was still shrouded, as always, in great mystery. What did he really think? About everything—the war, us being in America, the kind of life we led? What did he feel about being with us, around us, for so long this time? What did he want out of life, out of me? I don't know if those questions were so precise in my mind, or whether I was quite that curious then. Like all hero-worshippers that came before me, I was not about to demystify my hero. We played tennis together; I always lost to him. He would remind me that my mother wanted me to concentrate on my homework. (Didn't *he* care about my homework?) He thought my mother was right in wanting my lights out at eleven on weekdays. (Did *he* know that sometimes I was still reading when daylight came?) He took us for drives, to New York City one weekend (where I took pictures of the animals in the Museum of Natural History and lied in school that I had been to Africa for the weekend). And to Monticello where he spoke about the miracle of the American Declaration of Independence to us as if, suddenly, he wished to teach us something. It was so rare, him assuming the role of someone who wanted us to

Lt. Col. Zygmunt Wojciechowski, Washington, D.C., 1944

know something specific. He was, my hero, my father, just like mercury. I had once broken a thermometer and tried to get hold of the mercury and couldn't. So I knew he was like that.

I was not in love with my father during those years, fifteen to seventeen. I was in love with Lord Byron. In my wallet I carried his picture, one I took with my camera from an engraving in a book. We went to Fort Leavenworth, Kansas, for the fall of 1944, and I showed his picture to a girl who showed me the picture of her boyfriend.

"He looks strange, like a man or something," she said squinting, not understanding this was just a photograph of an engraving. "How old is he?"

I did some very fast calculation in my head.

"One hundred and fifty-six . . ."

It was the first time I heard anyone scream with a definite "EEEK" sound. The news of my having a boyfriend age 156 spread very fast. I couldn't even explain to anyone that he had died when he was only thirty-six because whenever I tried to bring him up the kids would laugh too hard to care what I was trying to say.

But in Kansas Lord Byron almost encountered some competition. He was tall and dark and handsome and had blue eyes. And he told me that his was the most important job on the football field. I used to go to every game and watch him intently but never could figure out what football was all about. He would mostly sit on the bench, or if others were seated on the bench, he'd sit on the ground. And he had a bucket of water. Most of the time he held it, but sometimes he'd put it down and I would try to figure out if his putting down the bucket had anything to do with the screams of the crowd and the change in score. Sometimes it seemed like it did, sometimes it seemed like it didn't. At least five times each quarter this boy I was having a crush on, would race to someone in the field and that player would take a drink from the bucket, and then he would race back to the sidelines. I'd always break into wild applause and cheers of "yeah!" whenever he'd race on the field and whenever he'd come back, but I was the only one applauding and yelling.

Years later, when I went to a Yale-Princeton game with my husband, Selden Rodman, I tried to explain to him what I knew about football and he thought I was crazy. By then they didn't have water boys on the fields. I still feel that boy was not really lying to me about his importance. He must have seen the game from his particular vantage point, and aren't we all just like him?

Poland was taken away from us by a senile President Roosevelt and what I considered the two archvillains of my time, Stalin and Churchill. After

they met at Yalta my father flew to London, certain that the Polish armed forces would mobilize and invade their homeland and free it from the new oppressors. After all, didn't we fight the war first; didn't we lose more men in uniform than any other country; didn't we, the Poles, suffer more; weren't we more determined to defeat the Germans, and the Russians?

I was playing basketball at the Sacred Heart High School in Los Angeles when a weeping nun announced that President Roosevelt was dead. I applauded and shouted: "Thank God the bastard is dead!" and was immediately sent home and told not to show my face around for at least a week. What would happen to Poland now, I wondered.

What happened to Poland only Poles who were there know. The Russians looked around and picked the most Semitic-looking, Polish-speaking Jew as the chief of the secret police for Poland. His photograph along with his infamous deeds of cruelty and terror were in the papers everyday, reviving once again anti-Semitic feelings among the Poles, feelings killed by the Nazi persecution. Outside of Poland the communist propaganda machines used the Jews themselves to fan the flames of anti-Semitism. The Poles found themselves robbed of their dead. "Six million Jews were murdered in concentration camps," became a new fact and was accepted as the truth, while the factual truth was that three million Poles, who were not Jews, perished in those camps along with an equal number of Polish Jews. The communist rulers in Poland knew that as long as Poles *appeared* to be anti-Semitic nobody would give much of a damn about the country and what agony it was going through. And they succeeded. Until Solidarity in 1980 Poland was far away on the back burners of world consciousness. And with the advent of Solidarity, the world heard but did not understand what happened there. (And what happened was a total discreditation of communism by the workers, the very people communism was invented for. It was done by a worker called Lech Walesa, not by a philosopher or a politician.)

It became totally hopeless for my father to stay on in London, waiting for his president (there was, and still is, a Polish government-in-exile. It was, and still is, totally ignored) to give him and the rest of the Polish soldiers their marching orders. He returned to us in 1947, totally defeated in spirit. He had been away for more than two years and I could not bear to see him so sad. I fled to New York, to become a writer.

I had written a number of short stories, all on the theme of Poles in exile, and had given those stories to someone who knew Rupert Hughes, an American writer. One night Mr. Hughes called me up. It was after midnight. He was crying. He said he was *that* moved by my stories. I was on a New York-bound bus that same morning with thoughts of fame dancing in my head. Getting off the bus in Santa Fe I was so taken by the place I missed that bus, and a couple of others, while walking around promising myself to live there one day. (It took me almost twenty-five years to keep the promise. And when I went there to live I only stayed ten years.) A few days later I managed to recover the manuscript and my suitcase from the terminal in New York City and went straight to what I considered the best publisher, Harper Brothers. I considered them the best because I liked the building they were in. It seemed to me to be as classy as my stories. I took the elevator to the "editorial" floor and handed my manuscript to the receptionist with the words: "I shall be back tomorrow."

Unfortunately I did not ask her to give it to someone to read. I imagined all that night, which I spent walking the New York streets, that someone was burning the midnight oil reading my words, crying perhaps, as Mr. Hughes had cried. I could not wait for the Harper offices to open the next day. I was there before the receptionist. When she finally assumed her chair I stood in front of her. I had come back for the contract but also I expected to make changes. Wordlessly she handed me back my manuscript. I took it to the nearest rest room, opened it. There was not even a rejection slip. Nothing. I was totally appalled and decided right there and then not to have anything to do with writing. I was finished with that career. I would resume my tennis career.

I spent the second night in New York City at the apartment of a friend of my mother's near Columbia University. I had exactly one dime to my name. Before I set off with it I used their phone to make an appointment to see a Mr. Elwood Cooke. I told him that I would be willing to teach tennis at his courts in Tudor City if he was willing to give me a job. He said to come and see him that very afternoon.

I walked all the way from Broadway and 111th Street to the Brooklyn Bridge. I considered it the most beautiful bridge in the world. I threw my last dime into the East river from that bridge and then walked another sixty blocks to my appointment. I was free of worldly goods, I thought, free as a bird. I just wished I had wings because my feet hurt so much.

"You have the worst damn swing I've ever seen in my life," said Elwood Cooke as I demonstrated to him the swing taught to me by Henri Cochet and improved on by René Lacoste before the war. I told him that he didn't have to give me a job but he could not insult me. After all I was the Polish junior champion and had, back in 1936, in Cannes at the age of eleven taken the King of Sweden to 5-0, my favor. And would have beaten him at love but for my father who came by and ordered me to drop the set without offending the king. I did an artful job of losing.

"O.K. You get $15 a week and a place to live."

I became a full-time tennis teacher and a part-time baby-sitter for his kid, Diana. I got a room in their apartment and started a long friendship with his wife, Sarah Palrey Cooke (later Danzig). The fifteen dollars didn't go far. Elwood was cheap in those days, Sarah was busy, and I had to feed myself. "I said a place to live, not room and board," my tough master would inform me whenever I asked for either a raise or some food.

There were all kinds of fringe benefits in spite of the fact that I did more rolling, brushing, and painting of the lines than I did teaching. I kept over-hearing all sorts of marvellous things said about me. "She's either got the longest legs or the shortest shorts I've ever seen," was my favorite. I could go to Forest Hills and sit among the players and I met them all; they were Elwood's and Sarah's friends, of course. And my employers were champion players themselves.

When it rained I didn't work, instead I hussled pool. There was a terrific pool place on Forty-second and Third in those days. I would rush to it at the first sign of rain and bet whatever seemed decent that I could beat anyone in the place. I made all my shots behind my back in those days and used to upset the players with my constant chatter. They used to yell a lot at me to shut up but I made more money there than I did slaving away from five to midnight for Elwood Cooke.

But the best thing of all was meeting Selden Rodman. He was a poet, married, and lived right above the tennis courts. He could see me whenever he wanted to, but I could not see him because there was a tree growing by his windows that cast dark shadows. Was he watching me or wasn't he, I used to wonder. We fell in love, maybe at the same time. It must have been great love, for I used to run all the way from Sixty-seventh Street and Third to Forty-second and First at eleven each night just to get a glimpse of him buying the *New York Times*. We married in 1950. Had our daughter in 1951. Divorced in 1957. And remained friends ever since. (The nicest thing ever written about me can be found in the book of Newbery/Caldecott acceptance speeches. It was written by Selden.)

Before I got married to Selden I went to Monterey, California, to visit my family. My older brother was on his own by then, living in Los Angeles, working for NBC, about to get married. We had a picture taken together, the three of us, and we looked handsome indeed. I thought my father at peace. He had a good job teaching at the military language school. Chris for the

Selden Rodman, 1950

new traitors, in front of the Polish-American Congress. He wore his Polish uniform and spoke "for the dead soldiers who are not here to see Polish honor on the block of expediency." Polish-Americans did not understand him; there was not a trace of America in him. He spoke to them as a lover of Poland and they simply thought that he wanted them "to do something." I am sure he wanted them to die for Poland, just as he was willing to do. The most passionate of his speeches was interrupted by cries of "Enough!" by those who wanted to make accommodations now, not seek a new war. He went back to California totally defeated. He stopped to see me and Selden and tried to make us understand that he had witnessed "the second selling of Poland" but we did not understand his pain.

The autopsy report said nothing about my father having died of a broken heart caused by being away from the country without which he could not exist. All along, from the beginning, when I was a small child, I knew he loved someone better than any of us. I remember once shouting at my mother: "Why aren't you unfaithful to him? He cheats on you all the time. With Poland!"

first time seemed happy. After all, he had the full attention of both of his parents now, he was alone with them, did not need to share anything. They looked like a normal family.

"American foreign policy," my father declared during that visit, "is run by imbeciles for idiots. They simply don't understand the nature of communism, which is not economic or social but spiritual. It is the destruction of the human spirit, that is what communism is!"

Whether he quit or was fired I don't know. All I know is that he had become a different sort of a fighter now. He wrote to everyone, appealing to the conscience of the world to reach out to Poland that was plunged into darkness behind the iron curtain. When my family came to visit us—Selden, our baby Oriana, and me—I was too busy being a housewife, a wife, and mother to wonder what happened to his eyes. They were clouded now by despair as much as cataract. Later, when we visited my parents in California he was a tragic figure. He spent his days in the garage doing carpentry, painting remembered buildings in Warsaw, writing letters on his typewriter. Once a year he would deliver telephone books. His solitude was interrupted only to play bridge, which he did the same way as he used to duel, and to argue Polish politics. There were now those who accepted the fate of Poland and were ready to return, or at least visit. There were factions urging "collaboration," "resumption of normal relationships." He went to Washington to denounce those

My mother was a better wife than she was a mother, I felt, and I was going to concentrate on being a good mother since I didn't have all it took to be a good wife. I was far too independent. I used to take off and ski-bum when I grew restless, and I grew restless a lot. But how could an independent, restless woman be a good mother? Wasn't I happy when Oriana, age three, packed up a little bag and said she was running away from home? I told her to write once in a while and waved good-bye. She kept walking up the driveway dressed in a coat far too warm for the day and I kept sneaking from one bush to another, watch-

Zbyszek, age twenty-four, Maia, twenty-two, and Chris, sixteen, Monterey, California, 1949

Oakland, New Jersey, 1951: clockwise, Maia holding daughter Oriana, her parents, brothers Chris and Zbyszek, and husband Selden Rodman

Mexico, 1957: "The year I trained to be a bullfighter— with a brave cow who had been fought before."

ing her hesitant progress. I was letting go of my child, like a bird mother. That was good mothering. The kid didn't make it all the way to the road. She turned back and went into her room to unpack.

"I decided not to run away," she told me later.

"I think that was a terrific decision," I told her.

She was being brought up by me not to feel guilty, which I considered the greatest sin of parenting. Still by the time we got divorced, when she was seven, I thought it was Selden, not I, who would make a better parent. After all, I was still not out of my adolescence. I had gone to Europe on my Harley Davidson, trained to be a bullfighter in Mexico. I was still not grown up enough to be a full-time mother. What I would be good at, I thought, would be a weekend mother. But if Selden ever remarried I would grow up in a hurry. The kid was ours, but she would become my responsibility, not his new wife's.

I went to Spain for six months in an attempt to grow up. I wrote a god-awful self-pitying novel and slept a lot, a coward's easy escape from life. I felt guilty as hell over that "wise" decision I had made, leaving Oriana with her father.

Becoming a full-time writer "for a living" was my way, I think, of growing up. That I began to write children's books was perhaps my way of not cutting

myself away from the childhood too drastically. After I developed a short story into the novel *Shadow of a Bull,* I resigned my job as a publicity director for a publishing firm and went to Los Angeles to tell my mother and brothers that I had decided to become a writer. So far I was out ten dollars, which I paid Oriana for the use of the title. I couldn't come up with one; she came up with a handful and our choice was *Shadow of a Bull.*

My family was not impressed. "You made a horrible mistake divorcing Selden," they all said to me. I went to see the children's librarian at the main branch of the L.A. Library. I heard that she was the "greatest living authority" on children's books. Not having read any but having written one, I was most anxious to know what she would think.

"I gave up my last job to become a children's book writer," I announced to this perfect stranger. "I would like your opinion about the book I just wrote." She looked relieved that I didn't have the manuscript with me.

"What is it about?" she asked.

"It's about a boy who is being forced to become a bullfighter."

"It's about bullfighting?" she asked in an incredulous voice.

"It has bullfighting for background."

"What I would advise you to do is to get your job back. No librarian will buy a book about bullfighting and children's books are bought by librarians."

I was totally defeated as I walked to her door to go out into the world deprived of my chosen profession.

"Of course," she said to my back before I had a chance to close her door, "I could be wrong. If it's very well written it won't matter that it's about bullfighting."

"It is!" I shouted and danced out of her office.

The first publisher who saw it, Atheneum, bought

Maia on the Harley Davidson she rode through Europe, 1958

the book. To me it was not so much a children's book as a very artful conversion of a short story into a short novel. I had written it in two weeks, using the short story as an outline. They made me change the ending and the editor inserted a word, "companionable" on the last page which drastically altered an already phony ending. By the time I learned that I won the Newbery Award I hated the book. But during the award dinner in Detroit I spotted the librarian from Los Angeles, rushed off the podium and reminded her how we met. She didn't remember me. So much for fame and glory.

I spent a lot of time that year, 1965, autographing and taking out that damn word "companionable" from the last page. (Atheneum, threatened by me with a lawsuit, finally managed, in the sixth edition, to eliminate that word that was never mine, that I objected to in manuscript, in galleys, in page proofs, and in the first edition. The time it took me to erase it from every copy I ever came across I estimate was greater than the time it took me to write the book. Irony!)

By the time *Shadow* came out I was living with Oriana, during the summer in a tower in New Jersey, and during the winter in Selden's guest house. I bought her a horse and, when she didn't like to ride her, I rode her and wrote a love book to the creature (*A Kingdom in a Horse*). Later I would buy Oriana a Morgan and myself a pony and we would race each other, me hating each moment, she adoring it all.

My kid had grown up splendidly. I don't know when exactly I decided that she was far superior to her parents, as a human being, but I certainly knew it the day she wrote on my back, with a magic marker: "This is my mother in whom I am well pleased."

She had explained that in case the plane crashed (I was flying somewhere), when my body was found they would know that I was loved by a daughter. And she didn't paraphrase some writer! She paraphrased God, the Father!

I was having a marvellous time, with her, with my writing, with life, and out of the blue I learned I had cancer. Strange! I had wanted to die five years before and the cancer was five years old. I was sure that at least in my case, the disease made a sort of suicidal sense. But not now, not for me. I almost died of curious and self-induced complications but recovered from a death bed when I had to chase away some kids who broke into the house. But that's too long a story for here.

I always had to have a very valid reason for writing another book, since each book, I figured, would kill at least five trees. I use a lot of paper, writing and re-writing, and of course my books are printed on paper. If I thought that the bindings take glue and it takes horses to make glue I don't think I would write at all.

I wrote *Hollywood Kid* because I wanted to know desperately how life would be for a boy if his mother was Marilyn Monroe. I wrote *A Single Light* to find out how good a writer I was. I said to myself what if I took for my major character someone who did not speak, who could not hear, and who did not really think all that much? I'd be up against a brick wall or in the rapids without a paddle. But if I pulled it off I'd know that I was a good writer. To get rid of some guilts about not marrying a man with three boys I wrote *Hey, What's Wrong with This One?* and dedicated the book to the kids. By the time the book came out they were not speaking to me.

That book was too easy so I challenged myself with the next. What if I'd write a monologue? As I was working on *Don't Play Dead before You Have To,* a book was published, a novel by Philip Roth, which also used that form. I didn't read *Portnoy's Complaint* until I finished mine and decided that he was better out of the starting gate but I won the race making it all the way to the finish line.

I was surprised to discover that many people, maybe even Lewis Carroll himself, confused *Alice in Wonderland* with *Through the Looking Glass,* which I thought a far better book. Walking through Harlem I saw a girl who looked as if she might be losing touch with reality and I wrote *Through the Broken Mirror with Alice.* When I handed the book to my editor she said: "Blacks don't play chess." I said bullshit. I saw a whole slew of old black guys playing chess. "Black children don't understand chess." So I drove to Harlem and picked up a kid and asked him if black kids know about chess. He told me he played all the time. I put a dime in the pay phone and had him talk to my editor. He told her that most kids were like him and chess was not only for honkeys.

I felt like writing my personal requiem for bullfighting because in Spain a hungry young man without a sense of honor was a sensation. His name was El Cordobés and he was cheapening everything Manolete stood, and died, for. And that's how *Life and Death of a Brave Bull* came about. I finally had to re-write the very first book I ever wrote. I did it from memory because it was about how I was growing up during the war and I called that one *Till the Break of Day*. There was also *Winter Tales from Poland*, a shoddy publishing job.

I was being difficult with editors. Too critical of the stuff that was coming out and finding favor with the critics as well as the readers, so I stopped writing. When I went back to it, after five years of not practicing my craft, it was because I could not find the truth about Hemingway's end. I found these words of his, written to his brother:

> Nothing is worth a damn but the truth as you know it, and create it in fiction.

And I wrote about a man like him and guessed at what might have happened to bring him to such a sad end. I wrote it as a novel for adults and its title is *The People in His Life*.

Maia and Richard Larkin, Oakland, New Jersey, 1972

Daughters Leonora (front) and Oriana, with Hugh MacRae, Santa Fe, New Mexico, 1979

And then, last year, I went back to a book I wrote for kids ten years ago when I thought I could publish my own stuff. *How God Got Christian into Trouble* didn't seem to have aged badly while lying in a drawer. I had liked it all along and made it shorter and simpler for younger kids. I think younger kids tend to be nicer nowadays. My own kid, Leonora (twelve going on ten), doesn't want to grow up and I don't blame her. After all, it took me a few dozen years to make the move myself.

I figure that there are three stages in everyone's life. Childhood and youth which shape us although we're far too dumb to know that. Adulthood which is sort of like gathering chips and looking for a good poker game to get into. And old age, the wise age. Which can turn into Lent or Advent. It ought to be either a great wait for redemption or being a witness to it. But it's certainly that stage of life where things have to begin to make sense or else we've been doing nothing but wasting time.

My third stage of life began when Leonora came into my life one day in early 1973. I had married for the second time and knew the marriage to have been a dreadful mistake, not only because Richard Larkin was twenty years younger than I, but also because he was in some ways much too old for me. Leonora was just perfect. She was a baby and it would be years, I felt, before she would object to my loving her too much. She never left me for the first two years. I carried her first across my chest, then on my back. And at two I sent her off to school, just so she could be free of my hugs and kisses for a while each day.

Laina with grandmother Maia, and great-grandmother Madame Wojciechowska,
Los Angeles, California, 1983

She must have been born an entertainer, or at least must have decided to have an entertainer's soul before she was even one year old. If she doesn't sing, she dresses up; if she doesn't dress up, she dances; if she doesn't dance she is performing a play she has created. She lives in a multiplicity of worlds she creates, and the only cruel world she inhabits is that of the school. She has always been mocked, made fun of, and it keeps hurting more rather than less. It doesn't matter that I keep telling her that of course the kids will have to be mean, how could they help themselves? After all, she is the greatest, the sweetest, the most wonderful kid in the world. They're jealous and that's why they are mean. She is special and they are not.

"You don't understand," she tells me. "You never needed friends when you were a kid. But I do. I want friends."

We keep thinking that it will change. She is only ten, having already been eleven and twelve, and she wants to go back to two and stop there. Of course they are not all mean and nasty and cruel in her school. There are some very nice kids who stand out just like Leonora does. Their eyes, like hers, are kind and bright instead of dull and nasty. (I've just written a story about a very special kid and a bunch that aren't, inspired, of course, by Leonora's life.)

And Leonora, like Oriana, has Haiti. She had gone there several times and will go this year again, to get away from the familiar, from TV and the cruelty of kids and the necessity to conform. She will go to that special country where people instinctively know that it is important to laugh, on a daily basis, and not to take such things as politicians seriously.

It's hard to be writing for kids and know that the fullness of life doesn't happen until you're fifty. Maybe it's not like that with others, but I finally came of age at fifty. It happened the day I got kicked out of school in Socorro, New Mexico. I was on a Federal grant, the only time I ever took a penny of taxpayers' money, and for a good reason, I had to ask the principal what made him such an asshole and got kicked out of his school.

It was the most wonderful time of my life, a time of daily beatitudes for a whole month. Everything began to make sense, suddenly, beautifully. The past, the present, the future—mine and the world's—became splendidly, horrendously right! I had a whole month of perfect happiness. I don't know why it didn't last but maybe, it will happen again in heaven, this state of total integration. It was a marvellously spiritual experience and I am sure I could never have it before getting to that ripe age of fifty.

"The three of us, thirty-five years later." Chris, Maia, Zbyszek, Los Angeles, California, 1984

I had it all, in a different sense from Helen Gurley Brown. I had all that I ever wanted to have, which did not include money or power. I saw people change. Most especially my mother, after she was eighty and suddenly, beautifully let go of so much junk that she treasured.

I saw her two weeks before she died and was astounded at the sudden peace that seemed to radiate from her. We talked, that last time, about death and she told me how, all through her life she never feared it, and how now she was looking forward to it as if to a friend's visit. That last time, when I saw her, she said that if she had anything to say about her departure from this life, she'd ask God to take her on a Friday in May, at 3:00 p.m. "But," she added smiling, "that would be too frivolous a request to pray for." She died on Friday, May 24th, at 3:00 p.m. as a companion was helping her to lie down for a rest. I, who envied her all my life, her grace, her beauty and her relationship with her husband, give thanks to my Lord for having seen my mother work towards the salvation of her immortal soul even after her body betrayed her.

I saw my older daughter become a marvellous human being, her very own person, and a great artist. And I saw her marry a splendid young man who not only makes her happy but who seems to grow wise ahead of time. And I finally had talks with my brothers. And I am beginning to see the terrific adult that Leonora will become. And I helped some kids understand certain things, kids like Keesha, our Fresh Air friend. And most of all I lived long enough to become a grandmother.

It must be the best-kept secret in the world. Nobody had told me, nobody's telling anyone, what a sheer, splendid, uncontaminated joy it is to be a grandparent! It would be hard for a kid to understand that it's worth growing old simply for that. For grandparenthood. Laina is her name and happiness is her game. And it's no secret that we love each other.

If someone would ask me, "What would you change if you had a chance to change something?" I would say everything. Because I had it all. The width and the depth of it. And I would grab for something new.

BIBLIOGRAPHY

FOR CHILDREN

Fiction:

Market Day for 'Ti André, as Maia Rodman (illustrated by Wilson Bigaud). New York: Viking, 1952.

Shadow of a Bull (illustrated by Alvin Smith). New York: Atheneum, 1964.

A Kingdom in a Horse. New York: Harper, 1965.

The Hollywood Kid. New York: Harper, 1966.

A Single Light. New York: Harper, 1968.

Tuned Out. New York: Harper, 1968.

Hey, What's Wrong with This One? (illustrated by Joan Sandin). New York: Harper, 1969.

Don't Play Dead before You Have To. New York: Harper, 1970.

The Life and Death of a Brave Bull (illustrated by John Groth). New York: Harcourt, 1972.

Through the Broken Mirror with Alice (includes parts of *Through the Looking Glass* by Lewis Carroll). New York: Harcourt, 1972.

Winter Tales from Poland (illustrated by Laszlo Kubinyi). Garden City, N.Y.: Doubleday, 1973.

How God Got Christian into Trouble. Philadelphia: Westminster, 1984.

Nonfiction:

Till the Break of Day: Memories 1939–1942 (autobiography). New York: Harcourt, 1972.

Odyssey of Courage: The Story of Alvar Núñez Cabeza de Vaca (illustrated by Alvin Smith). New York: Atheneum, 1965.

FOR ADULTS

Fiction:

The People in His Life, as Maia Rodman. New York: Stein and Day, 1980.

Nonfiction:

The Loved Look: International Hairstyling Guide, as Maia Rodman. New York: American Hairdresser, 1960.

The Rotten Years. Garden City, N.Y.: Doubleday, 1971.

Translator of:

The Bridge to the Other Side, by Monika Kotowska. Garden City, N.Y.: Doubleday, 1970.

Jane Yolen

1939–

SOMETHING ABOUT THE AUTHOR . . .

All the lives of the great fantasy writers are chock-a-block full of wild and improbable childhoods, adventures in mysterious lands, amazing and fortuitous coincidences, and strange, wasting illnesses. It used to bother me that I had lived such an ordinary life: born in New York City, public school education, an uneventful childhood with no major traumas, college that was smooth but unexciting, marriage (no divorce) to the same man for over twenty years, and three children. How could I possibly be a fantasy writer, a *good* fantasy writer, even (my secret hope) a *great* writer of memorable books?

The only things out of the ordinary that ever happened to me have been: losing my fencing foil in Grand Central Station during a date with a college boyfriend; learning to ride on the great white Lipizzaner horses from an instructor who spoke only loud and unintelligible German; taking a ballet class from the famous ballerina Maria Tallchief who, afterwards, hung her practice tutu on my locker; chasing after my father, the International Kite Flying Champion, when his twelve-by-twelve-foot kite had dragged him into Long Island Sound; hiking up Mount Pelion in Greece while my husband drove our van because a recent earthquake had made riding in it uncomfortable for me since I was seven-and-one-half months pregnant; swapping songs with Yemenite pickers as we worked side by side in an orange grove in Israel; falling into the swollen Colorado River after a wave had knocked me off our raft into a serpentine rapids filled with forty-two-degree water; mushing in a dogsled in Alaska in the middle of March; saving my eight-and-a-half-year-old son from a three-and-a-half-foot black-tailed rattler; having my seventy-fifth book published before my forty-sixth birthday; and . . . .

I guess any life has its strange adventures and wild accomplishments. What seems to the one who lives it a very ordinary life might sound fairly improbable, wonderful, even fantastic to somebody else. Have I told you about the Melasian merman I saw in Greenwich, England? I have a photo of it. How about learning to do the twist in a bar filled with New York City's finest garbagemen? Well, at least I haven't yet had a wasting illness.

In Which I Recount Events Before My Birth— and What Followed

Two different kinds of immigrant experience informed my life. My father's family were merchants and storytellers (some called them well-off liars!). My mother's family were intellectuals. I seem to have gotten a bit of both, though not enough of either.

My father's grandfather had been an innkeeper and a teller of tales in the small Finno-Russian village where he lived. He had gone to a *gymnasium*, a high school to which young Jewish boys were rarely allowed

The Yolens in America; Jane's grandparents, Mina and Sampson, surrounded by their children and grandchildren. "Only Will, my father, is missing!"

to go. (They mostly went to religious schools.) He had come home with his head stuffed with stories he passed off as his own. "Romeo and Juliet" in Yiddish was a favorite at the inn. His daughter Mina, a vivacious redhead, married Sampson Yolen, after whom I am named. Sampson's family had a bottling company. My father liked to say that his family was "in oil," but it was cooking oil and paraffin, not the kind that comes shooting up from the ground and makes fortunes. Mina and Sampson had eight living children and my father, Will, was the next to the last. There were twenty years between oldest and youngest, a spread that was to leave my father with the feeling that he had been unnoticed and unappreciated. He left home early and, though I knew all my aunts and uncles and tens of cousins and second cousins, I never really had a good sense of what my father's early life had been like. In fact I was thirty-five before I found out that he had not been born in Waterbury, Connecticut, but had come to this country as a four-year-old and is a naturalized citizen.

In a sense my father invented himself. He came from a family that had little regard for formal education but a lot for making a living and telling tall tales. He became a newspaperman, a foreign correspondent, then a publicity man for Warner Brothers films, the head of midway publicity for the 1939 World's Fair, and a promotion man for WNEW radio. He owned his own publicity firm for a while and his own film company, and ended up as a vice-president in charge of books and magazine articles for the largest public relations firm in the world. He created the job that he had and, in a large part, created a certain kind of public relations. And he re-created kite flying in America. In the 1950s he declared himself Western Hemisphere Kite Flying Champion and then proceeded to defend his title and publicize the sport to such an extent that he forced a renaissance in kiting that is still going on. He was pictured in *Life* magazine flying kites, is in the *Guinness Book of World Records* for kiting, and was also in *Ripley's Believe It or Not.*

When he was still a newspaperman, my father met a beautiful young social worker in New York, Isabelle Berlin. Third oldest of six children, she was a brilliant Phi Beta Kappa graduate of Randolph Macon College in Virginia. Her parents, Fanny and Daniel Berlin, had owned a clothing store in Newport News, Virginia, and raised their children in a brick house in Hampton Roads, near the Chesapeake Bay. Education was always emphasized in the Berlin family. One of the relatives of the Berlins had been a rabbi instrumental in reestablishing Hebrew as a living language.

Isabelle's two younger brothers became a doctor and a lawyer; her sisters all were psychiatric social workers. Master's degrees, doctorates, Phi Beta Kappas were the norm in her family; they were all brilliant, handsome, and quirky. My mother, though, had no idea that she was beautiful and she adored my father for choosing her. When they were married—first secretly at city hall and then, months later, in a religious ceremony—she could not believe her luck. Her husband was a blue-eyed, pint-sized charmer, a newspaperman with energy, great dreams, and a future that no one doubted would be wonderful.

For five years they led a busy New York City life. My father moved out of newspaper work into the life of a publicity flack. In fact, when I was born, February 11, 1939, he was doing publicity for the MacAlpine Hotel and they were living in an apartment right in the hotel. My birth was announced in the gossip columns, next to the pictures of bathing beauties.

My mother quit her social work job in order to raise me (and later my brother Steven, born November 4, 1942) and she never had a paying job again. Years later, when we were teens, she did volunteer work, heading a family service organization and reading to the blind. In her free time she wrote, mostly short stories that did not sell, and made up crossword puzzles and double acrostics that did.

I remember practically nothing about my early childhood. Some of it was spent in New York City; about a year and a half was in California when my

Will and Isabelle Yolen, 1935

Jane with her mother, 1939

father was doing publicity for Warner's. We lived in a beautiful ranch house next door to Walter Brennan, the grizzled Western star. I have no memory of it. What I do remember, however, is the two years we lived with my Grandma Fanny and Grandpa Dan when my father was stationed in England during World War II. My father was head of the secret radio broadcasting to Europe, called ABSIE. So mother and Steve (who was only a baby) and I moved into the Hampton Roads house. The reason I recall that time so vividly was that my grandfather, whom I adored, died of a sudden and unexpected heart attack while we were there.

One morning I woke up and heard a strange sound. It was my grandmother sobbing and sobbing. She cried for months—at least it seems so in my memory—and I was afraid ever to go back into her bedroom, that place of death, even though it was connected by a long closet to the bedroom I shared with Steve. We had loved to play in that closet, running through it with the fresh-smelling clothes brushing over our heads, hour by hour. After my grandfather died, the house seemed haunted and cold. I began to be afraid to go up the long stairs alone because the first door on the left at the top of the stairs was my grandparents' bedroom. Every night after Grandpa's death I closed the closet door and shoved a chair up under the handle. Years later, when my middle child, Adam, had

the same kind of fears because of our house's long, dark hallway, I remembered that time in Virginia.

My Berlin cousins lived close by and for those two years we were inseparable. My cousin Michael Garrick, about a year older than I, used to lead me into trouble, which is not to say that I was an unwilling participant. We would go down to the Bay and wade in it though we had been warned again and again not to. And we were always found out because the Bay was fouled with fuel oil from the great tankers and destroyers that docked there before crossing the ocean to England to aid in the Allied war effort. Michael's and my legs were always coated with the oil when we had been sneaking around. Once we even dared to swim in the Bay, and were both royally spanked for that trick and forced to soak in my grandmother's big tub for an hour, then spanked again. When I was a teenager and spent a summer vacation in Virginia, I fell in love briefly with my cousin Michael. He was not interested in me but in biology, chemistry, and tennis. I was a failure at all three.

I was a failure as a Southerner, too, because all the other girls on the block had names like "Frances Bird" and "Mary Alice." I was just plain Jane.

Years later I would put our neighbors, Frances Bird, Willard A., and Bubba into a mystery novel

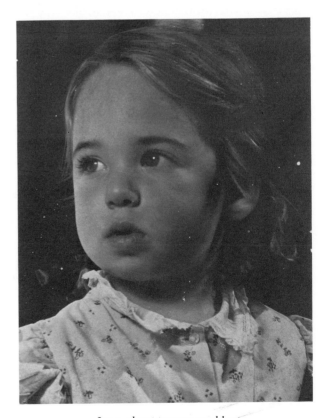

Jane, about two years old

Jane, left, at family summer camp in Bar Harbor, Maine, about 1946

called *The Inway Investigators,* but I set the story in the small New England town of Conway—which I called Inway—where we then lived. The grandmother in my picture book *No Bath Tonight* has the same sense of humor and love of life that my Grandmother Fanny had. And the line in *Commander Toad in Space,* about not being brave unless you are first very much afraid, comes from something I used to tell my son Adam, something my mother used to tell me, when confronted with those stairs. So the little bits and pieces of my childhood informed my stories, disguised by both memory and time.

In Which My Early School Days Are Detailed

I was in half a dozen schools by second grade, both public and private, as my mother looked for the best school for me. We lived on Central Park West, which was elegant, but on Ninety-seventh Street, which was not. The public school I was supposed to attend was dark, dirty, and to my mother's mind, totally inappropriate for me, so I was shifted from place to place. One time we even lied about where we lived to get into a better school, but I was too young to remember the pretend address, and so was found out. And kicked out.

But I was also an early reader. When I read our semester's reading book overnight, the teacher had no

alternative but to skip me into second grade. I spent the remainder of my elementary school days at PS 93 which is now only a parking lot on Ninety-third Street and Columbus Avenue. I walked to and from school with my best friend Diane Sheffield who lived in the apartment across the hall. She was skinny and blonde, I was plump and dark, but the boys seemed to pull my pigtails as often as hers. We were both tomboys, and we played rough-and-tumble games in the grass and rocks of Central Park.

At PS 93 the teachers encouraged my reading and writing. I won gold stars and gold stars and more gold stars. I was the gold star star. And I was also pretty impossibly full of myself. In first or second grade I wrote the school musical, lyrics *and* music, in which everyone was some kind of vegetable. I played the lead carrot. Our finale was a salad. Another gold star.

The next year I wrote a song, a story, and drew an elaborate map of something called "Candy Cane Island." The lyrics went something like:

> Where is that Candy Cane Island,
> Where in the world can it be?
> Right over dreamland, across the canal,
> Just come and follow me.

When I was in my forties, a boy from that class whom I hadn't seen or heard from in over twenty years wrote to me. He remembered the entire song! All I really remembered from PS 93, besides my first kiss in the school yard, were the names of all the boys and girls, in alphabetical order. I had been class secretary for three years in a row and had to read out the roll call every morning. Even today, as a party trick, I can call them out. "Alan, Arthur, Barry, Bruce, Carl, Claude . . ." the boys begin. "Barbara, Breena, Carol, Diane, Dolores, Ellen, Gail C., Gail S., Jane, Judy, June . . ." the girls.

Gold stars, roll calls, my first (and second) kiss and the slap I dished out for it, are all I really recall. And marching around Fire Island with my friend Susan Hodes, singing songs and passing a hat. Some days we collected enough for several sodas *and* an ice cream. Our harmonies, especially on "Dona Nobis Pacem," were terrific.

In sixth grade I took a test for one of the New York special schools and was accepted by Hunter, an all girls' school for "intelligently gifted" students. With my gold stars and my writing ability, I expected to be a superior gift to Hunter. To my surprise—and horror—I was barely in the middle of the class and managed to stay there only by studying extremely hard. Once again, though, I was elected to class secretary, two years in a row. I can still say the names (in alphabetical order of *last* names): "Adele, Berliner, Brenner, Cutney, Damoshek, Deutsch . . ." I was to use many of those names—and the names of two men I almost married—in a short story called "Names" that I wrote years later.

Since it was clear that I was not nearly as smart as I had thought, I turned my attention to those gifts I did have. Music became a mainstay in my life. I starred as Hansel in our class rendition of Humperdinck's *Hansel and Gretel,* though I was about a head shorter than the girl who played Gretel. She had a pure lyric soprano voice while I had a low alto. I also played piano, with more vigor than talent, and liked to write little songs. I also was one of the leading dancers in my class at Balanchine's American School of Ballet, again a question more of vigor than ability, plus a genius for remembering the complicated succession of steps. My writing continued to bring me approval, though Hunter did not give gold stars. I wrote my eighth-grade social studies essay in rhyme. It was all about New York State's manufacturing, with a great rhyme for Otis Elevators which I have, quite thankfully, forgotten. I also wrote my first two books: a nonfiction book on pirates, which I bound with a linen-over-cardboard cover, and a novel. The novel was seventeen pages long and included a trip by covered wagon across the West, death by snake bite, a plague of locusts, the birth of an infant on the road, a prairie fire, slaughter by Indians, and marriage to a schoolmarm. It was a masterpiece of economy.

This reflected later in my appreciation for the short form. Short stories and poetry have remained my first loves. I have come to writing full-scale novels almost reluctantly, and it is always a struggle for me to make them long enough. Somehow seventeen pages still seems about right! Music, too, has remained an important part of my writing. Many of my books have been inspired by songs: *Dream Weaver* by a bad rock song; *Bird of Time* by a rock song mis-heard; *Greyling* and "The White Seal Maid" by a folk song; the solution of "Princess Heart O' Stone" by an Irish ditty. There are often lyrics in the stories that I write, and I have also written three song books (*The Fireside Song Book of Birds and Beasts, Rounds about Rounds,* and *The Lullaby Songbook*), two musical plays, and half an opera. I write songs and song lyrics for folksingers, some of which have been recorded. A number of my stories have been about musicians: *The Magic Three of Solatia, The Minstrel and the Mountain,* and "The Boy Who Sang for Death" among them. And songs that I composed are in at least two of my books: *Spider Jane* and *All in the Woodland Early.*

In Which I Really Get Educated (Sort Of)

My parents sent me off to summer camp two years in a row, when I was twelve and thirteen. It was a wonderful Quaker camp in Vermont called Indianbrook (now Farm and Wilderness), where I learned about pacifism, swimming, storytelling, mucking out horse stalls, planting a garden, and kissing, not necessarily in that order. At the end of the second summer, my Aunt Isabelle and Uncle Harry came to take Steve and me home because our parents had suddenly and without warning bought a house in Westport, Connecticut. We were not even allowed to go back to New York to say good-by. It was quite a blow to me for two reasons. My camp boyfriend, my first, was a second cousin once removed who lived in New York. And I had just been accepted into the High School of Music and Art, and I was desperate to go.

So I did not get to say farewells or exchange addresses with any of my school or ballet friends and the worst loss was Ann Rosenwasser who was my best friend at both places. Ann, who was much brighter than I and a better dancer, with a great arch (I was flat-footed and cared about such things), had been my partner for over two years in a strange little game of imagination in which we pretended she was the prima ballerina of The Company (the New York City Ballet Company, which was Balanchine's) and I was the top young choreographer. We each included in the game a kind of soap opera schedule of events having to do with boyfriends (mine was supposedly Jacques D'Amboise, the youngest man in the company who was destined in real life to become the *premier danseur* of the company). We spent hours at "The Game," as we called it, play-acting the parts and devising intricate plots for both the ballets and our lives. After finishing Hunter High School, Ann actually became a member of the corps de ballet of the New York City Ballet Company. But while I continued to dance in Connecticut, it became increasingly clear that my body type harkened back to the Yolens—short, squat, and while athletic and grace-ful, not sylphlike and anorexic like a Balanchine dancer. One day I plan to write a novel about "The Game," but meanwhile such characters as Plain Jane in *Sleeping Ugly* and Borne in *The Lady and the Merman* reflect a lot of my ideas about physical beauty. And the attention to plots, both the romance of young love and the romance of storybook ballets which Ann and I worked on, has stayed with me for all of my writing life.

In Westport I started school at Bedford Junior High School, and went on to Staples High School where I was involved with the singing groups, the liter-ary groups, and was captain of the girls' basketball team. (Even though I was the shortest one on the team, I could jump just like a dancer. Training will out!) I took piano lessons, ballet lessons, and horseback riding lessons. I wrote a lot of poetry, including one poem, "Death, You Do Not Frighten Me," which won a Scholastic Writing Award. And when our senior class voted for "The Perfect Senior," it was my voice they chose. That is probably why many of my heroines have lovely, low voices—and can sing.

My first best friend in Westport was Stella Colan-drea who was Catholic. I had never really been close to anyone but Jews and Quakers before. But I began going to church—and Christmas Midnight Mass—with Stella who sang in the choir with the loveliest soprano voice I had ever heard. She had a wicked sense of humor, too. We used to do our homework on the roof of her porch, right outside her bedroom window, on warm evenings. We'd also make up naughty limer-icks about the boys in our class, being terrible flirts the both of us. It was because of Stella's influence that I became enamored of different religions. My own Juda-ism and camp-discovered Quakerism were the most morally appealing, but the panoply of Catholic rites seem to have taken hold of my imagination and wind in and out of many of the elaborate religious rituals I write about in my fantasy tales. And, since I am an Arthurian buff and a lover of things medieval, knowing a bit about the church helps. In *The Magic Three of Solatia*, the ceremony of Thrittem is a kind of bar mitz-vah crossed with a silent Quaker meeting. In *Cards of*

Jane as captain of the Staples High School girls' basketball team, 1956

Grief, I worked in storytelling, seders, and the Mass, along with Communion, Confession, and the Viaticum, if you read it with care.

Later on in high school my two closest girlfriends were LeeAnn Walker and Mariette Hartley, the one an artist, the other an actress—the two careers I would have loved if I had not been a writer. Mariette and I especially have kept in touch over the years. I had her in mind to play the part of Sister Agatha in *The Gift of Sarah Barker*, writing the description to fit her. Unfortu-nately it has not been made into a movie.

I was only marginally popular in high school, running around with two very different crowds: the intellectuals and the fast social crowd. I was a non-drinker and too slow for the latter, too fast and flirty and insubstantial for the former. I developed a wise-cracking, cynical patter and an ability to tell funny stories which was, I think, why I was kept around in each. In college I dropped that veneer and let my natural poetic and romantic side show.

The greatest influence on me in high school was neither parents nor friends but my cousin-in-law

Honey Knopp. A pacifist, a peace activist, who held hootenannies (music fests) at her home, Honey gave me my first copy of George Fox's *Journal.* (Fox was the founder of Quakerism and I wrote a biography of him, *Friend: The Story of George Fox and the Quakers.*) This secret, alien, meditative, poetic side I kept well hidden throughout much of high school except from Honey and some of the people I met at her house. This was in the mid-1950s, when to be interested in such things branded one an outsider, a beatnik, a left-winger. I adored Honey and her husband Burt, and their home became my haven. Oh, I still went to basketball games and dances and parties, wisecracking with my friends and being outrageous. But Honey called out another side of me. Her influence can be seen in many of my books: *The Minstrel and the Mountain, The Boy Who Sang for Death, The Transfigured Hart, The Hundredth Dove, The Gift of Sarah Barker* among them. My poetry, much of which I shared only with Honey and my mother, was filled with the imagery of life/death, light/dark, and cadences of the folk songs I learned at the hoots.

From Staples I went on to Smith College, an all-women's college in western Massachusetts, one of the famous Ivy League's Seven Sisters. It was a choice that would, all unknowingly, change my life. It made me aware of friendships possible—and impossible—with women. It created in me a longing for a particular countryside, that of New England. It charged me with a sense of leftsidedness, of an alien or changeling awareness. And it taught me, really, about poetry and literature and the written word.

Smith had not been my first choice. I had wanted to go to Radcliffe (partially because a boyfriend was in Boston) or to Swarthmore, a coed Quaker school. But though I was accepted by Smith, Wellesley and Oberlin, my two top choices did not want me. I had been high—but not top—of my class, ranked seventh in a class of over two hundred. I had had good—but not spectacular—test scores. I had been captain of the basketball team, news editor of the paper, head of the Jewish Youth Group, vice-president of the Spanish, Latin and jazz clubs, in the top singing group, winner of the "I Speak for Democracy" contest, winner of the school's English prize, and contributor to the literary magazine. But still I did not stand out enough. So I chose Smith because Smith emphasized that everyone at Smith sang. I loved singing.

Actually I only sang for a year in the choirs at Smith before turning my attention elsewhere. I didn't find it easy making good friends at Smith. I just didn't like women that much. Except for LeeAnn and Mariette, most of my friends in high school had been boys. In fact I ran around with a gang of boys who lived nearby, one more boy amongst them. So I made some

Jane at a bridge game at Wesleyan College, 1959

Eliot Glassheim

of my earliest friends among the faculty.

The five greatest influences on me while I was at Smith were: a teacher of seventeenth-century poetry, Joel Dorius, who showed me just how beautiful language could be; my first advisor and critic of my poetry, Marie Boroff, who showed me that one might be critical of the writing without tearing down the writer; Dudley Harmon, the head of the Smith News Bureau, who believed in my future with the written word; Edna Williams, a gracious teacher of Chaucer who made me realize that women could be scholars and live the life of the mind without giving up gentleness and beauty; and Bill Van Voris, my senior advisor and an anarchic soul, who gave me the greatest gift—that of self-recognition. He made me believe that being a writer was a wonderful thing to be for itself, not because it was easy and familiar and meant gold stars.

At Smith I wrote vast amounts of poetry and studied English and Russian literature, minored in religion, and took a smattering of history, sociology, and geology. I also discovered I had a flair for both politics and poetry and a minor talent for the musical stage. I ran many of the campus organizations, wrote and performed in the class musicals, and penned my final exam in American Intellectual History in verse, thereby receiving an A⁺ for a C⁻ worth of knowledge. But it was poetry—and folksinging, which I did with a boy friend, Mike Lieber, from Trinity College—that became the real constants in my life. My early poetic efforts were published in Smith's *Grecourt Review, Poetry Digest,* and other small magazines. I won all of the poetry prizes given out my senior year. The folk songs I had first begun learning at Honey's and then with Mike (who went on to become an anthropologist and studio musician) became part of both my writing and my later great interest in oral storytelling.

In Which I Join the Work Force

I had earned spending money by babysitting in high school and working one summer as a "page" in the local library. (I was almost fired from the library because I wore a strapless sundress one impossibly hot afternoon, and it was considered "unsuitable.")

My summer between high school and college I went to an American Friends (Quaker) Service Committee work camp in Yellow Springs, Ohio, where I worked harder than I had ever worked before—for no pay. We built an outdoor education center for migrant laborers' children, ran a day-care program for them, and traveled by bus through the South learning about race relations and singing peace songs.

The summer of my freshman/sophomore year, I worked as a cub reporter for the *Bridgeport Sunday Herald.* It was there I wrote my first signed pieces for a newspaper. My very first byline read "by Joan Yolen." I did not take it as a sign. But I quickly learned that I was not a tough reporter when the editor assigned me to write an article on welfare recipients. I came back after the interviews and cried at my desk. I wanted to help those people, not write about them.

The next summer I was a camp counselor. I had wanted to go with the AFSC to Alaska to help move a village of tubercular Eskimo. But my parents would not let me go, so I spent two months being a junior counselor in New Jersey. The following summer I lived in New York City with another Smith student and worked for *Newsweek* magazine as a summer intern. Mostly I delivered mail, went for coffee, sorted photos, and helped in the research and checking departments. It was not glamorous.

My real life work began when I graduated, broke up with my fiancé because—as I told him—"I have to find out if I can be a writer," and moved to New York City for good. Or so I thought. I got another summer internship, this time with *This Week* magazine, on the

strength of my scrapbook of bylined magazine and newspaper articles from such diverse places as the *Bridgeport Sunday Herald,* the *New Haven Register* (about Smith College activities), and *Popular Mechanics* (about kites). I stayed there until halfway through the fall, in the research department, mail room, and facts-checking department, and then all the editors returned from vacation and there was no room for me. Knowing that would probably happen, I had already lined up another job, with the *Saturday Review.*

At *SR,* I was in the production department, a job which meant I had to help lay out the magazine, as well as choose the cartoons and let the poetry editor know how much room we had for a poem. To my horror, poetry was seen as "filler" material. We would need a three-inch poem, or a seven-inch poem. However, the production manager and I did not get along, and a few days before Christmas I was fired. In fact, I was the seventh person she had fired within two years, and I had already been warned by friends at *This Week* that life for the underlings at *SR* was usually short and not so sweet.

I spent the first few months of 1961 trying to make a living as a free-lance writer. I researched and helped write a book for my father who had been asked to do *The Young Sportsman's Guide to Kite Flying.* Since he loved signing contracts, signing autographs, and countersigning checks, but not writing books, he hired me to put it together. And I loved—and still love—the writing part best of all. It was no hardship, but the pay was very low! With the help of my father's best friend, Will Oursler (author of *The Greatest Story Ever Told*), I also got a number of small free-lance assignments, including writing short, pithy bios for Cleveland Amory's *Celebrity Register.* My best line was about the then-Senator from Connecticut, Thomas Dodd, a silver-toned orator of the old school. I wrote that he "had one of the finest voices to ever vox the populi." That was my first in-print pun. Later such things were to show up regularly in books like *The Witch Who Wasn't,* in short stories like "The Five Points of Roguery" and "Inn of the Demon Camel," and in my "Commander Toad" series.

But the life of a free-lancer is long on searching and short on payment. I was literally living in a garret, a skylit studio apartment in the attic of a three-story house on Commerce Street in Greenwich Village, next to the Cherry Lane Theater. And I was beginning to write books.

The Commerce Street garret was actually my second venture in living in the city. The first, a ground-floor "shotgun" or "railroad" apartment, where the rooms are laid out all in a row and connected by sliding doors, had not been as successful. I lived there with two roommates, young women I had met that summer when I had been commuting from my parents' home in New Rochelle. One woman was to remain my roommate for another six months, the other (who was a friend of the singing group called The Clancy Brothers and Tommy Makem) lasted only two. The problem was partly the Clancys who used to spend a lot of time at our apartment with their friends and hangers-on (who were legion in those days), and partly the layout of the apartment. But that place was special for a different reason.

Between the three roommates, we knew about half of the young artists, writers, musicians, and radical politicians in the Village the summer of 1960. We invited everyone we could think of to our housewarming party, and the Clancys brought even more. There were so many people coming in the front door of our ground-floor apartment, that one handsome moustached young man decided not to wait any longer and climbed through the window. He saw me standing in the crowd, my long dark braid over one shoulder, and came over, kissed me on the nape of the neck, and introduced himself.

"I'm David Stemple," he said, with a slow smile. "I'm a friend of one of the girls who lives here."

"I'm Jane Yolen," was my icy reply. "And I'm one of those girls. You're not *my* friend!"

It was not a great beginning.

Two mornings later (it was a *wild* party!), the

Jane and David, just before their wedding, September 2, 1962

Jane beside a painting of David, at the time of their engagement, 1961

landlord threw the three of us out, relenting only when we began to weep simultaneously in a flood tide that threatened to drown him. We lasted in the apartment only two more months.

David Stemple and I were married in 1962, after a slow-starting friendship and a long courtship, in the garden of my parents' New Rochelle house. By that time he had a beard as well. All my cousins showed up at the wedding with fake beards in his honor, and my brother and other folk musicians played such songs as "I Wish I Were Single Again," which I performed with great gusto. My father, who had warned me that David "was not the marrying kind," professed admiration at my choice. We are married to this day. Years after our marriage, while recounting this story to some school children who wanted to know if my "real" life was in my stories, I realized that my fairy tale *The Girl Who Loved the Wind,* which is dedicated to David, is about our meeting. In it a Persian girl is kept in a walled-in palace by her overprotective father until the day the wind leaps over the garden wall and sweeps her away into the wide, everchanging world.

About the time I was being married in New York something else happened that would set the pattern of my life for good. I received a letter from an editor at A.A. Knopf. She wrote that she had been traveling around the colleges asking about recent graduates who might be working on book manuscripts. At Smith she talked to Dudley Harmon at the News Bureau. Now, if she had approached the English department, this story might have a different ending. I was thought of as a poet and a journalist by the department, not a novelist. But Dudley, my journalism mentor, believed in me. She told Judith Jones, the editor, that there was only one recent graduate with talent—me. It wasn't true, of course. There were many better writers who graduated at the same time. But Dudley was faithful to her young protégée, which is why I—and not any other recent Smith grad—received a letter from Ms. Jones. She asked if I had a book-length manuscript she might see.

Well, there is no getting around it. I lied. I wrote to her and said that of course I had several book ideas, what budding young author does not. In fact I had none, only a group of poems in less-than-final stages and my magazine articles. I would have thought little more about it, just filed it away for future reference, except that Ms. Jones wrote back and asked to see me and my books.

Caught in the web of this deceit I, who always prided myself on my honesty, realized there was nothing to do but sit down at my typewriter and get something done quickly. Children's books! I thought. They'd be the easiest and quickest. (I was to discover painfully and thoroughly over the next twenty or so writing years that, in fact, children's books are among the most difficult things to write—well. They have the compression of a poem where every single word must count. As the great stage director Stanislavsky once remarked to a young actor who was going to perform in front of an audience of children for the first time: "Act as you always do—only better." Words for would-be children's books writers as well.) However, I knew very little about children's books; I had been reading adult books since ninth grade (this was before the advent of young adult books, which arrived on the book scene after I was past being a young adult). What I remembered was—*pictures.* The problem was that I could not draw. Luckily, or so I thought, a high school friend with whom I had shared a boyfriend on and off for eight years had moved to New York; and she was an artist. So Susan Purdy and I put together several quick little picture books without regard to the nature of the beast. One was an alphabet book of names (sounding remarkably like the roll call from elementary school), one was a kite flying book (thanks Dad!), one was about a whale who wanted to be a minnow (which David laconically remarked was awfully autobiographical). I also set down ideas for two longer

books. One was to be about kite flying, putting in all the romance and lore I had not been able to shoehorn into *The Young Sportsman's Guide,* and a one-page idea about a book on lady pirates cribbed from the report I had done in eighth grade.

Armed with these "book-length manuscripts" I went to see Judith Jones. I still wonder what she must have thought of me. Though she was ever gracious and spent several hours talking to me, she did not (needless to say) buy anything. However she did introduce me to Virginie Fowler, the children's book editor, who was, I must honestly report, equally appalled at my lack of knowledge and the temerity I showed in bringing such feeble material to their attention.

Of course I was crushed. Rejection, in person or by rejection letter, is never easy to take. But it is one of the constants in the world of publishing and anyone too shaken in confidence by a first refusal (or a second or a twenty-second) will never make it in the writing world. Susan Purdy was crushed as well. But we still had those books to sell, so we gamely began sending them around in the more traditional way, from editor to editor. They all came back. I could paper a wall with those rejection letters if I had them still.

Then my father remarked that he had a friend, who was a vice-president of David McKay Publishing Company, that he would be happy to introduce me to. I hesitated about half a minute, embarrassed to use any influence, until I realized that Judith Jones had been "influence" and it hadn't gotten me published—but it had gotten me a personalized course in writing and literature. "Introduce me," I said at last.

Eleanor Rawson at McKay was as polite and as generous as Judith Jones had been, and she also introduced me to her children's book editor, a muffin-shaped woman named Rose Dobbs. Rose greeted me with the words, "I never buy from unknown writers."

Eleanor Rawson left me in the care of this dragon and I slumped down in my chair, fearful of what would happen next.

She dismissed the alphabet book quickly, and only glanced and grimaced at the whale. She paused a little longer over the kite picture book, and longer still over the history of kites, explaining in a matter-of-fact voice, "It doesn't know if it wants to be an adult book or a children's book." Then she studied the one-page synopsis of *Pirates in Petticoats,* and tapped it with her finger.

"This interests me," she said.

I sat up in my chair.

"But I never buy from unknowns."

I slipped back down.

"Still . . ."

Up I shot.

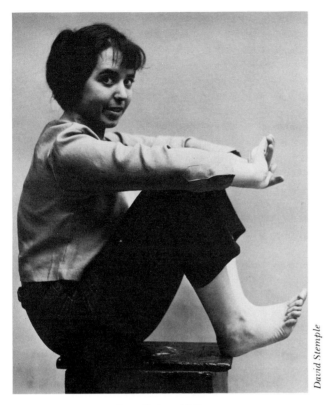

Jane Yolen, 1962

". . . this interests me. Leave it with me for a few weeks. I want to think about it."

I was dismissed. I couldn't leave her office fast enough.

It wasn't two weeks—it was several months—and I still had to pay rent and eat, so I found a job. I worked as first reader, manuscript clerk, and assistant editor at Gold Medal Books, a paperback house known for its western novels and spy thrillers, what we called in the trade "bang-bang-shoot'em-ups." Eventually I even got to write cut-lines, those one-liners on the covers that explain pithily what a book is about. I was famous for about a moment in publishing as the one who coined "She was all things to two men" for some Gothic novel.

And then, on my birthday, February 11, 1961, the phone rang at work. It was Rose Dobbs, summoning me to her office. She did not say why.

It was snowing lightly as I walked the several blocks to get there at lunchtime. Once more in the dragon's lair, I huddled down in my chair again.

Ms. Dobbs looked up at me. I remember she had a hair net on, with those little colored beads that seemed to be winking and blinking at me.

Preemptively she said, "I never buy from unknowns."

I nodded.

"But . . . ," and she hesitated, putting one plump finger atop the paper on her desk. I could read upside down. It was my synopsis, slightly wrinkled and coffee-stained.

"But . . . ," I prompted.

"But this interests me and I know you have written magazine articles and worked on your father's book. So you are not *entirely* unknown. Do you think you could write a full-length manuscript?"

I took a deep breath, then didn't trust my voice, and nodded instead.

"Then I shall give you a contract," she said. "And you will deliver a 150-page manuscript to me in one year."

I nodded again.

"But I won't give you any money in advance," she said. "Because you are an unknown and I don't take such chances."

I said in a very small voice, "If you give me a *little* bit of money, then I couldn't back out of it. I'd have to finish." I shut my mouth quickly, amazed at my own boldness.

"Well . . . all right," she said, well-placed pauses apparently the coin of her trade. "All right. But remember, you must not tell anyone about this. It would get around. And I would be flooded with unknowns."

We shook hands and I escaped once more from the dragon and ran out into the street. There was suddenly a different kind of light in the air. Dazed, I walked the two blocks to the Overseas Press Club where my father usually had lunch. He was secretary of the club, and later would become president. Sure enough, he was sitting at the bar with a variety of cronies.

"Dad!" I shouted as I ran in, "I've sold a book!"

Everyone's head turned. This, after all, was a club dedicated to writing.

"My daughter's *first* book," said my father, gesturing expansively. "Drinks are on me."

The bar was suddenly mobbed, but my father looked meaningfully first at me and then at the bartender. "And a Coke for my little girl."

Not every author's story of a first book goes like that. It is rare, indeed, that an editor buys a synopsis from an unknown. But Rose Dobbs took a chance that *Pirates in Petticoats* would turn into a solid book. And though the book is out of print now and Rose may be dead, it was her willingness to sit down with a young writer a year later and go over the completed manuscript, word by word by word, that started me on the path of publication.

Rose bought a second book from me, a picture book called *See This Little Line,* but I hated the orange and purple illustrations and the sans serif type she chose for it. We didn't see eye-to-eye on the visual look of the book, and she never bought anything more from me. She never bought anything from my friend, Susan Purdy, either. And though Susan is now a well-known illustrator (and author, too), she and I have never worked together on a published book. We went our separate ways professionally, but at the beginning we were there helping one another.

In Which I Keep Writing, Writing, Writing—and Working

My desk at Gold Medal Books became a repository for soon-to-be-famous derrieres. Since my office was right next to the editor-in-chief's, young authors waiting to talk to him often sat on the edge of my desk and chatted till they were summoned. Kurt Vonnegut and Harlan Ellison were the ones I remember best, Vonnegut because he was nervous and Ellison because he could barely sit still. I came to understand that as talented as a writer might be (and they are certainly two of the best), publishing is a buyer's market. The writer trying to sell his or her work is in the inferior or beggar's position. And even today, with more than seventy published books, I often feel this way.

Working at Gold Medal was always fun—and funny—but as I had sold two children's books I wanted to find out more about my newly-chosen field. (It had chosen me, not I it.) So I changed jobs and became an associate editor with Rutledge Press, a small packaging house.

Rutledge (and the adult division, Ridge Press) created books, hiring writers and illustrators and then selling the entire "package" to a larger publishing company for distribution. Since a number of the books were created "in house," that is to say, the editors wrote the stuff, I actually authored a number of published books that do not carry my name. There was a counting rhyme book for Doubleday with pictures by Gail Haley (who later won the Caldecott medal for *A Story, a Story*) called *One, Two, Buckle My Shoe*. Any nontraditional rhymes in the book, I wrote. I also created games, puzzles, and activities for a variety of Activity books that Rutledge put together, my ability to write instant verse (harkening back to the days of Candy Cane Island, Otis Elevators, and my final exam) serving me well.

While I was at Rutledge, my first two books were finally published, making me a very minor minor sort of celebrity. But under the terms of my contract with Rutledge, I had to submit all my new book ideas to the company first. That was a major annoyance, though

they never actually bought anything from me. I learned a lot working there, mostly about book production and how art and text have to mesh. I also learned how to do a book index. But I learned a lot of bad habits, too, especially a facileness which I have worked hard to lose over the years. And I have been left with a kind of sneering attitude towards book packagers.

One of the Rutledge Press editors was a charming, multitalented, slightly scatty woman named Frances Keene. When she left Rutledge to become editor-in-chief of the children's book department at Macmillan, she called me up and asked to see a story I had submitted to Rutledge, *The Witch Who Wasn't*. It was the beginning of an editorial relationship that I *really* count as the start of my writing career. Keene (as she preferred to be called) was a great teacher as well as a fine editor. She taught me to trust my storytelling ability and to work against being too quick. She once said, in her gentle, chiding manner, always delivered with a kind of wise-woman smile, "Don't let your facility betray you." She was right. She also pushed me into delving deeply into folklore while at the same time recognizing my comedic talents. Eventually at Macmillan—and later on at Funk and Wagnalls—she published five of my books. If she had remained in publishing, instead of becoming a college professor, we would have worked together a great deal more.

Through Keene's influence, I was beginning to prefer a more literary approach to children's books, and if there was one thing Rutledge Press was not, it was literary. So I looked around for a new job and found one, surprisingly, with Virginie Fowler, the editor at Knopf who had so kindly but permanently turned down my feeble stories three years earlier. She remembered me with affection, evidently, and offered me the job at once. I became her assistant editor and spent almost three years working happily and learning about the literature of childhood. Along the way I got to meet some of the finest authors and illustrators in the business: Roger Duvoisin (courtly and generous), Beni Montresor (elegant and aloof), Roald Dahl (very tall, mysterious, funny) among them. I also got to write jacket copy for Knopf books, my two most famous being for Dahl's *Charlie and the Chocolate Factory* and Ian Fleming's *Chitty-Chitty-Bang-Bang*.

And of course I was writing, writing, writing. At this point I had practically stopped writing serious poetry, but my poetic instinct was finding its way into my stories in other ways—as chants, as euphonious names, as songs.

David and I were living on the third floor of a renovated East Village brownstone. He was working at IBM, doing mysterious things with computers, none of which I understood. I had started a weekly writer's workshop with several other aspiring young writers and editors of children's books. Included were Jean Van Leeuwen, Alice Bach, Jim Giblin, Richard Curtis, Anne Huston. We took turns meeting at one another's apartments to read our work aloud and critique it. It was my first such group, but over the years I have been involved in many continuing workshops and find them indispensable. They make me want to have something to read, if not every week, at least several times a month. They also help sharpen the critical faculties. (And there are other benefits. Anne Huston and I wrote a book together, *Trust a City Kid,* which Jim Giblin edited for his company. Publishing children's books is a very inbred business.) I also found I have a good eye and ear for criticism. Over the years I have run many ongoing groups and taught at seminars and conferences on writing children's books across the country. Many of my students have become published authors, and I love to help them fine-tune their work and find an interested publisher. I truly believe that no one gets to the top without a leg up along the way. I certainly did not. I think it is imperative, therefore, to turn around and help others. As I wrote in my book *Touch Magic,* "one must touch magic—and pass it on."

In Which We Live Off the Land etc. for Nine Months

After five years in New York David and I were getting restless. He had been working on an early Fortran compiler at IBM as well as being a free-lance photographer. I was working as an editor and writing at the office by getting there an hour earlier than everyone, staying an hour later, and rarely going out for lunch. I wrote on weekends, I wrote in the evenings, and I loved the writing. But we were both ready for some radical change. So we decided to save my entire salary and live on his for the year, buy a VW camper bus in Europe, and travel until our money ran out.

A year and almost $10,000 later, we were ready.

We gave my mother power of attorney over our checking account, sold most of our furniture, stored the rest with friends, put a down payment on a blue van which we planned to pick up in Cologne, Germany, and quit our jobs.

Then in August 1965 we set sail.

I have to explain that in most ways David is more adventurous than I. One of four sons of two West Virginia teachers (his father was also superintendent of schools for a number of years), David was born and grew up in the small mountain town of Webster Springs. He lived one life in their brick two-story home on the main street where his mother also taught piano, and another life in the woods, hunting, fishing, and

trapping. So he developed a kind of *other* sight for things in nature, a peripheral vision that I, a city girl transplanted to the suburbs for my adolescence, had never known. He has taught me some of this over the years. At the very least he has made me aware of birds (he has become an avid birder the past five years), trees, flowers, weeds, the subtle interlacing of the seasons and the world of growing things. He was also the perfect partner for a yearlong camping trip. Slow to anger, with a wicked sense of the absurd, a fine memory for history, and the ability to speak German and workaday French, he charted our course through the cities, towns, and forests with ease. Only the London roundabouts gave him any trouble. I, on the other hand, am a quick igniter with only a passable sense of direction. The only language I had studied in school was Spanish. I could read García Lorca and Cervantes in the original but I could not order lunch.

And so we set sail on the *Castel Felice,* a small ocean liner filled with what seemed to be an overflow from Greenwich Village. It was, without a doubt, the hippest ship afloat. A strange, sweet smell hung in the air. And the passengers were always engaged in singing, putting on plays, poetry readings, etc. (We had a madrigal group formed aboard ship and led by Joel Cohen, now director of the Boston Camerata but then a student going to Paris to study with the famous Nadia Boulanger.) I had my typewriter with me and tried to sit on deck and write something every day.

David and I really only had two things planned for the trip. He had a commission to mount a photographic show for his alma mater, West Virginia University, with the pictures he would take in Greece. And we wanted to see the International Sheepdog Trials in Cardiff, Wales—because it sounded like fun. Other than that, we had no firm plans. We planned only to drift through the countryside of Europe and the midEast for as long as our money lasted.

We spent nine glorious months that way. We camped in the Paris park, the Bois de Boulogne; traveled down the Rhine; stayed in a bed-and-breakfast hotel in Mumbles, Wales; wandered around museums in Spain, France, Italy, and England; picked wildflowers atop mountains and swam in the Mediterranean Sea. The month in Italy I seemed to be sick a lot. We thought it was bronchitis picked up in England, possibly a slight flu.

Actually I was pregnant.

We found that out in Rome, in between visits to the Colosseum and a museum, from a doctor who—luckily—spoke English. My Italian sounded a lot like Spanish and David's Italian sounded a lot like French, and neither of us would have made total sense of the news the doctor gave us if he had told us in Italian.

Jane and David, Naples, Italy

book of our travels, bits and pieces of our wanderings have already found their way into my stories. In Greece, for example, we spent one night in an olive grove, which became the setting for *The Girl Who Cried Flowers*. We stayed another night in a different Greek forest, the backdrop for "The Sleep of Trees." In Thessaly, the tableland inspired the opening of *The Boy Who Had Wings*. The mountains sheering off into the sea in Wales were the background for *Greyling*. And so it went: places and people we met were stored away in my memory and months, even years, later were transformed into the magical landscapes of my tales.

In Which I Become a Country Gal

We returned home in May aboard a large ocean liner. As the boat sailed through the tail end of a great storm, everyone on board seemed to be sick, except for the five obviously pregnant ladies who carried with them their own ballast. We were the only ones who ate and enjoyed ourselves throughout the trip.

David and I moved in with my parents who were now living in a lovely apartment in New York. Or at least I moved in with them. David spent much of his time out interviewing for jobs. We wanted to be in an

We were delighted because we wanted a family, but we decided not to cut our camping trip short. We would continue traveling until the very end of my pregnancy and then come home. I really wanted to have the baby in America, not in a strange country where I knew no one. It turned out to be a wonderful decision. After a month of only slight indisposition, I felt terrific. We sailed from Italy to Israel where we spent three months. For five weeks we worked at a small kibbutz, Kivutzat Shiller. I picked oranges and swapped songs with the Yemenite hired help. David worked in the chicken farm and also out in the fields picking bananas. We went snorkeling in the Red Sea, collected pottery shards at archeological digs, and lived for awhile on the beach at Eilat. At last we sailed for Greece so that David could spend a month taking pictures for his show.

About twice a week I sent a journal/letter home to my mother. She saved all the letters and so we have a complete account of our months on the road. But even if I never use that material directly in a detailed

Isabelle and Will Yolen, 1967

academic area in either Pennsylvania or Massachusetts/Connecticut. The best offer came from the University of Massachusetts Computer Center in Amherst. David took the job, we bought a seven-room house in Conway in mid-June, and began trying to fill it with furniture from auctions. On July 1, two weeks earlier than expected, I gave birth to a baby girl we named Heidi Elisabet.

Heidi was not my only production, however. Before leaving for Europe I had gotten an agent, the best in the business, a tall, dark-haired, mothering woman named Marilyn Marlow. But the entire time we had been in Europe, Marilyn had been unable to sell anything for me. She was distraught about it, conferring often with my mother. Knowing I was about to return, she put on an extra push, and nudged a few editors into early decisions. So it was that two days after I returned, I got a phone call at my parents' house. Marilyn wanted me to come to her office. When I arrived, Marilyn was smiling her wonderful sly I've-got-something-special smile. She had just sold three books for me—on the same day!

One of the books—*It All Depends,* which I had written at the kibbutz—was sold to my old editor, Frances Keene, now at Funk and Wagnalls. The other two books were the ones that Keene had purchased for Macmillan before she left and the new editor had turned back to me, on my birthday in 1965, with the admonition "You do not know how to write. Perhaps if you have a child, when it is six months old, you will begin to understand how to write for children." Those two books, *The Minstrel and the Mountain* and *The Emperor and the Kite,* were sold to an editor who would become another seminal influence in my writing life: Ann K. Beneduce of World Publishing Company. I met her that first week I was home, waddling into her office, eight months pregnant. Ann—an elegant, quiet, persuasive woman with an ageless face and an artist's eye for detail—became my friend from that first meeting. She *loved* fairy tales and, for the next fifteen years or so, she was to be my major editor, publishing my first fairy tale collections and pushing me to try my wings in other genres as well. She announced to the world that I was the "American Hans Christian Andersen," and while I have always felt that claim quite a bit wide of the mark, she produced book after book in the handsomest way possible, including *The Girl Who Cried Flowers, The Hundredth Dove, Dream Weaver, Neptune Rising, The Girl Who Loved the Wind, The Seeing Stick . . .* the list goes on and on. We worked on almost thirty books together.

And so I became a born-again New Englander with a small child, a true free-lance writer, with several publishers vying for my stories and an agent who was always looking out for my best interests. With only small variations, it was to be my life from then on.

By living in western Massachusetts in the Connecticut (or Pioneer) Valley, we were near five great colleges—Smith, Amherst, Mt. Holyoke, Hampshire, and the University of Massachusetts. That meant we were close to a wide assortment of cultural activities, yet surrounded by trees. Every day there were lectures, symphonies, art exhibits. In the nearby towns were artists, artisans, academics, writers. At the same time, we were right where birds sang cheerily in the mornings, our neighbors grew mammoth tomatoes, and maple sugar buckets hung on our own trees. It was certainly a wonderful setting for an author.

I also found that having a new baby stimulated my imagination. This was true with Heidi, and later on, with each of my sons. A new baby meant that I was often sitting quietly for long periods of time nursing the child in the quiet darkness. There was nothing else to do but think—and dream. And what I thought and dreamt were stories. They just flowed out of me.

Of course having an infant also meant that I had to readjust my time and make every little bit of freedom work for me. One cannot type out a story if a baby is crying, or needs feeding, or changing. So another pattern began to emerge, a way of using those little patch pieces of time and quilting them together to make a larger story.

And then there was David. With a fine critical eye and an appreciative nature, he had always been my greatest supporter, the first one who read everything I wrote. He took more than a father's usual share of time with Heidi. Long before the concept of being a *house husband,* or *augmented fathering,* became popular, he was putting it into action. He would cart Heidi off for long rides or walks in the woods, partly so that I could have time to write, partly so he could have more time with his daughter.

When Heidi was three months old, we noticed something wrong with her legs. The bones below the knees were bent at a strange angle, like a cowboy's bowed legs. The specialist put her in casts for four months, then into a contraption called a "Denny Brown splint." "Don't be surprised," he warned us, "if she has trouble walking." Never daunted, she began *running* at ten and a half months and ended up as a medal-winning gymnast and captain of the high school cheerleading squad which won trophies in every tournament in Massachusetts. She has grown into a very headstrong, determined young woman, articulate, individual, empathic. She is the prototype for Sarah Barker in *The Gift of Sarah Barker* and, except for the red hair, looks like her as well. She posed for a number of book jackets drawn by a local artist, so the picture of

Jane and her children, Heidi, Jason (foreground), and Adam, 1975

Melissa on the jacket of *The Stone Silenus* is really Heidi. Some of the lines are hers, too.

A year after Heidi's birth I had an early miscarriage, then got pregnant again and gave birth in 1968 to a lusty eight-pounder, Adam Douglas. Towheaded, an early walker, early talker, a reader at age two and a half, left-handed Adam was always a handful. He used to rock himself to sleep at night in his crib and was always drumming on chairs and stairs. He is extremely musical, plays piano and guitar (and used to play cello), formed his own rock band, and at fifteen did the musical arrangements for *The Lullaby Songbook,* which I edited. His photograph (as well as his sister's and brother's) can be seen in *Milkweed Days,* and he is the accident-prone part of Jeremy in *No Bath Tonight.*

We moved to the Boston area for two years while David and some of his friends began a computer company, and the house we had there was one of those wonderful four-chimney Georgian brick houses. It was so elegant and we were so—*not* elegant—that I always felt that the house was slumming to have us living there. Our third child, Jason Frederic, was born while we lived in Bolton, another big baby, he was almost nine pounds. Jason had a placid disposition and a ready smile. He rarely cried. From the beginning he was interested in animals, animals, animals—and trucks. Now as a teenager, he is still interested in those same things. He is easygoing, sweet-tempered, and shy.

He is also the dirty part of Jeremy in *No Bath Tonight* and the male counterpart of Melissa's younger sister Melanie in *The Stone Silenus.*

Just nine days after Jason was born, my mother died. A smoker, she had developed lung cancer that traveled quickly into the lymph glands. The doctor told us she had six months to live. She lived eight. She died never having seen Jason, only a photograph of him I had sent special delivery from the hospital. Her death affected me in ways I am still discovering.

For years I have mourned her in my tales. *The Bird of Time* was begun the day I heard she had cancer, my way of wanting to slow time down or stop time altogether. I dedicated that story to her memory. "The Boy Who Sang for Death" carries in it a line that I realized only later was meant for her. The boy Karl says "Any gift I have I would give to get my mother back." In *Cards of Grief* I invented a culture in which grieving is the highest art, and the story comes straight from my heart.

In Which We Slide Back into the Valley Again

There is a joke in western Massachusetts that the Connecticut Valley is greased. There's no escaping it. You may try to leave, but you always come sliding back down into it again. And so, when Jason

Jane Yolen, Hatfield, Connecticut, 1981

Bill Burkhart

was about a year old, we left the Boston area, and returned to the Valley. David went back to work at the computer center at the University and we found a fourteen-room farmhouse in the small Polish farm community of Hatfield, population 3,000.

Of course we were (and still are) a bit of an anomaly in the town. The bulk of our neighbors are older, Catholic, Polish, farmers and blue-collar workers. At first we were thought of as hippies, then we began to put down roots. I planted a garden and in one of the large barns on the property we started a crafts center. Over seven years we gave space to craftspersons of all sorts—potters, leather workers, silversmiths, and the like. Because of the barn, stories came. "The Pot Child" was one that came directly, "Man of Rock, Man of Stone" indirectly.

In the early 1970s I became very involved with the newly-formed Society of Children's Book Writers. On the board of directors since its beginning, I have also run SCBW conferences for ten years in western Massachusetts, and a monthly writers/illustrators workshop. I am once again involved in a weekly critique group, with local authors Patricia MacLachlan, Ann Turner, Shulamith Oppenheim, and Zane Kotker. And I helped start the weekly "Bay State Writers Guild," so named because we meet at the Bay State Bar and swap publishing stories in-between drinks.

My writing day begins at eight in the morning, after the children are off to school, and sometimes does not end until four or five in the afternoon. I believe in something William Faulkner said: "I only write when I am inspired. Fortunately I am inspired every day at nine o'clock." For me writing is work *and* pleasure, and I am very focused.

For most of my writing life I wrote books for young readers, but as my own children grew and their interests changed, mine did, too. I took more and more lecturing and teaching jobs, which meant that I became involved in the history of children's literature as well. For about five years I stopped writing for younger children and concentrated on older boys and girls and fiction for adults. Only in 1984 did I turn again to picture books.

I think one of the reasons I went through this change was my children—and the other my father. In 1982, extremely ill with Parkinson's disease, my father moved in with us. After one death-defying hospital stay (the doctors had given him up but he did not die), we brought him home to be taken care of by nurses. For over three years my house always had at least one RN in residence at all times. Such a change, of course, found its way into my stories. *The Stone Silenus* is very much about my father and me, and *Cards of Grief* is a death-centered fantasy novel. "Old Herald," a rather brutal science fiction story, is about tending an old, ill, and crotchety artist. Some of the power in those stories has been fed intravenously with my father's blood.

It was in the 1980s that I was discovered! Adults as well as children were suddenly reading my tales. Or perhaps it was just that the boys and girls who had loved my stories were growing up and remembering them. My stories started appearing regularly in adult magazines like *Fantasy and Science Fiction* and *Isaac Asimov's SF Magazine.* I became a much-anthologized short story writer, in such collections as *The Year's Best Fantasy Stories, The Hundred Greatest Fantasy Short Shorts* (in which I had *three* tales), *Heroic Visions, Hecate's Cauldron,* and many, many textbooks. Storytellers had begun a renaissance in America and they were coming upon my work. I now receive about one letter a month from storytellers requesting permission to tell one or more of my stories. And there is no guessing what things they will tell. One told "Dawn Strider" at a wedding, another told "The Pot Child" at nursing homes, another told "The White Seal Maid" at feminist gatherings.

Gabriel Cooney

The family gathered at Jane and David's house for brother Steve's wedding: front row, Jane, her father Will, newlyweds Maria and Steve; second row, Jason, Steve's son Greg, and Adam; standing, Heidi and David

One teller even told a shortened hand-signed/spoken version of my novel *The Mermaid's Three Wisdoms,* which is about a hearing-impaired child.

So my life, like anyone else's, is a patchwork of past and present. By writing this long autobiographical essay, I see that clearly for the first time. And I also can see a pattern that might tell me my future—as long as I remain consistent.

I consider myself a poet and a storyteller. Being "America's Hans Christian Andersen" means trying to walk in much-too-large seven-league boots. I just want to go on writing and discovering my stories for the rest of my life because I know that in my tales I make public what is private, transforming my own joy and sadness into tales for the people. The folk.

But the wonderful thing about stories is that other folk can turn them around and make private what is public; that is, they take into themselves the story they

read or hear and make it their own. Stories do not exist on the page or in the mouth, they exist *between.* Between writer and reader, between teller and listener. I wrote *The Girl Who Loved the Wind* for myself, out of my own history. But recently I received a letter from a nurse who told me that she had read the story to a dying child, and the story had eased the little girl through her final pain. The *story* did that—not me. But if I can continue to write with as much honesty and love as I can muster, I will truly have touched magic— and passed it on.

BIBLIOGRAPHY

FOR CHILDREN

Fiction:

See This Little Line? (picture book; illustrated by Kathleen Elgin). New York: McKay, 1963.

The Witch Who Wasn't (illustrated by Arnold Roth). New York: Macmillan, 1964.

Gwinellen, the Princess Who Could Not Sleep (illustrated by Ed Renfro). New York: Macmillan, 1965.

Trust a City Kid, with Anne Huston (illustrated by J. C. Kocsis). New York: Lothrop, 1966.

The Emperor and the Kite (illustrated by Ed Young). Cleveland, Ohio: World Publishing, 1967.

Isabel's Noel (illustrated by A. Roth). New York: Funk, 1967.

The Minstrel and the Mountain (illustrated by Anne Rockwell). Cleveland, Ohio: World Publishing, 1967.

Greyling: A Picture Story from the Islands of Shetland (illustrated by William Stobbs). Cleveland, Ohio: World Publishing, 1968.

The Longest Name on the Block (illustrated by Peter Madden). New York: Funk, 1968.

The Inway Investigators; or, The Mystery at McCracken's Place (illustrated by Allan Eitzen). New York: Seabury, 1969.

The Wizard of Washington Square (illustrated by Ray Cruz). New York: World Publishing, 1969.

Hobo Toad and the Motorcycle Gang (illustrated by Emily McCully). New York: World Publishing, 1970.

The Seventh Mandarin (illustrated by Ed Young). New York: Seabury, 1970.

The Bird of Time (illustrated by Mercer Mayer). New York: Crowell, 1971.

The Girl Who Loved the Wind (illustrated by Ed Young). New York: Crowell, 1972.

The Adventures of Eeka Mouse (illustrated by Myra Gibson McKee). Middletown, Conn.: Xerox Education Publications, 1974.

The Boy Who Had Wings (illustrated by Helga Aichinger). New York: Crowell, 1974.

The Girl Who Cried Flowers, and Other Tales (includes "Dawn Strider"; illustrated by David Palladini). New York: Crowell, 1974.

The Magic Three of Solatia (illustrated by Julia Noonan). New York: Crowell, 1974.

The Rainbow Rider (illustrated by Michael Foreman). New York: Crowell, 1974.

The Little Spotted Fish (picture book; illustrated by Friso Henstra). New York: Seabury, 1975.

The Transfigured Hart (illustrated by Donna Diamond). New York: Crowell, 1975.

Milkweed Days (photographs by Gabriel Amadeus Cooney). New York: Crowell, 1976.

The Moon Ribbon, and Other Tales (illustrated by D. Palladini). New York: Crowell, 1976.

The Giants' Farm (illustrated by Tomie de Paola). New York: Seabury, 1977.

Hanna Dreaming (photographs by Alan R. Epstein). Springfield, Mass.: Museum of Fine Arts, 1977.

The Hundredth Dove, and Other Tales (includes "The White Seal Maid" and "The Lady and the Merman"; illustrated by D. Palladini). New York: Crowell, 1977.

The Seeing Stick (illustrated by Remy Charlip and Demetra Maraslis). New York: Crowell, 1977.

The Sultan's Perfect Tree (illustrated by Barbara Garrison). New York: Parents Magazine Press, 1977.

No Bath Tonight (picture book; illustrated by Nancy Winslow Parker). New York: Crowell, 1978.

The Mermaid's Three Wisdoms (illustrated by Laura Rader). New York: Collins and World, 1978.

The Simple Prince (illustrated by Jack Kent). New York: Parents Magazine Press, 1978.

Spider Jane (illustrated by Stefan Bernath). New York: Coward, 1978.

Dream Weaver, and Other Tales (includes "Princess Heart O' Stone"; illustrated by Michael Hague). New York: Collins and World, 1979.

The Giants Go Camping (illustrated by T. de Paola). New York: Seabury, 1979.

Commander Toad in Space (illustrated by Bruce Degen). New York: Coward, 1980.

Mice on Ice (illustrated by Lawrence Di Fiori). New York: Dutton, 1980.

The Robot and Rebecca: The Mystery of the Code-Carrying Kids (illustrated by Jurg Obrist). New York: Knopf, 1980.

Spider Jane on the Move (illustrated by S. Bernath). New York: Coward, 1980.

The Acorn Quest (illustrated by Susanna Natti). New York: Crowell, 1981.

The Boy Who Spoke Chimp (illustrated by David Wiesner). New York: Knopf, 1981.

Brothers of the Wind (illustrated by Barbara Berger). New York: Philomel, 1981.

The Robot and Rebecca: The Missing Owser (illustrated by Lady McCrady). New York: Knopf, 1981.

Shirlick Holmes and the Case of the Wandering Wardrobe (illustrated by Anthony Rao). New York: Coward, 1981.

Sleeping Ugly (illustrated by Diane Stanley). New York: Coward, 1981.

Uncle Lemon's Spring (illustrated by Glen Rounds). New York: Unicorn/Dutton, 1981.

Commander Toad and the Planet of the Grapes (illustrated by B. Degen). New York: Coward, 1982.

Neptune Rising: Songs and Tales of the Undersea Folk (illustrated by D. Wiesner). New York: Philomel, 1982.

Commander Toad and the Big Black Hole (illustrated by B. Degen). New York: Coward, 1983.

Tales of Wonder. New York: Schocken Books, 1983.

Children of the Wolf. New York: Viking, 1984.

Commander Toad and the Dis-Asteroid (illustrated by B. Degen). New York: Coward, 1985.

Poetry:

It All Depends (picture book; illustrated by Don Bolognese). New York: Funk, 1969.

An Invitation to the Butterfly Ball (picture book; illustrated by Jane Breskin Zalben). New York: Parents Magazine Press, 1976.

All in the Woodland Early: An ABC Book (picture book; illustrated by J.B. Zalben). Cleveland, Ohio: Collins and World, 1979.

Dragon Night, and Other Lullabies (illustrated by Demi). New York: Methuen, 1980.

How Beastly! A Menagerie of Nonsense Poems (illustrated by James Marshall). New York: Collins and World, 1980.

Nonfiction:.

Pirates in Petticoats (illustrated by Leonard Vosburgh). New York: McKay, 1963.

World on a String: The Story of Kites. Cleveland, Ohio: World Publishing, 1969.

Friend: The Story of George Fox and the Quakers. New York: Seabury, 1972.

The Wizard Islands (illustrated by Robert Quackenbush). New York: Crowell, 1973.

Ring Out! A Book of Bells (illustrated by Richard Cuffari). New York: Seabury, 1974.

Simple Gifts: The Story of the Shakers (illustrated by Betty Fraser). New York: Viking, 1976.

Plays:

Robin Hood, music by Barbara Green, first produced in Boston, 1967.

The Bird of Time, music by Karen Simon, first produced in Northampton, Mass., 1982.

Editor of:

Zoo 2000: Twelve Stories of Science Fiction and Fantasy Beasts. New York: Seabury, 1973.

The Fireside Song Book of Birds and Beasts (illustrated by Peter Parnall; music by B. Green). New York: Simon and Schuster, 1972.

Rounds about Rounds (illustrated by Gail Gibbons; music by B. Green). New York: F. Watts, 1977.

Shape Shifters: Fantasy and Science Fiction Tales about Humans Who Can Change Their Shapes. New York: Seabury, 1978.

The Lullaby Songbook (illustrated by Charles Mikolaycak; music by Adam Stemple). New York: Harcourt, 1986.

Dragons and Dreams, with Martin H. Greenburg and Charles G. Waugh. New York: Harper & Row, 1986.

FOR YOUNG ADULTS

Fiction:

The Gift of Sarah Barker. New York: Viking, 1981.

Dragon's Blood. New York: Delacorte, 1982.

Heart's Blood. New York: Delacorte, 1984.

The Stone Silenus. New York: Philomel, 1984.

FOR ADULTS

Fiction:

Cards of Grief. New York: Ace, 1984.

Dragonfield, and Other Stories. New York: Ace, 1985.

Merlin's Booke. New York: Ace, 1986.

Nonfiction:

Writing Books for Children. Boston: The Writer, 1973.

Touch Magic: Fantasy, Faerie, and Folklore in the Literature of Childhood. New York: Philomel, 1981.

Index

INDEX